Italian Renaissance Studies

ITALIAN
RENAISSANCE
STUDIES

EDITED BY E. F. JACOB

FABER AND FABER

24 Russell Square

London

First published in mcmlx
by Faber and Faber Limited
24 Russell Square London WC1
Second impression mcmlxvi
Printed in Great Britain by
Latimer Trend & Co Ltd Whitstable
All rights reserved

© *Faber and Faber Limited*
1960

CONTENTS

CONTENTS

ILLUSTRATIONS
after page 304

ACKNOWLEDGEMENTS

The Editor would express his grateful thanks to Professor John Hale for the biographical note and for much help and advice; to Professor Wind for reading part of the proofs and for assistance with the illustrations; and to Mrs. Rosamond Leys (R. J. Mitchell) for the index to the volume.

E. F. Jacob

INTRODUCTION

An approach to the Renaissance

This book, written by an English circle of scholars, is dedicated to the memory of a historian who devoted her life to the study of the Renaissance in Italy. Dr. Ady's main interest lay in the signorial families and their influence upon the structure of the Italian city-state and upon Italian society during the fifteenth century. Two sentences from her British Academy Lecture 'Morals and Manners of the Quattrocento' summarize her interest in the period:

'There are moments in history when events combine to give to the members of a certain class and nation the opportunity to fashion the mode of their existence after the ideal of the good life as they see it.'

'Few men and women have enjoyed so unrestricted an opportunity for self-expression as the ruling families of Quattrocento Italy.'[1]

Whether in depicting the Sforza, the Medici or the Bentivoglio, or the ascent of a Piccolomini to the papacy, she wrote as one primarily concerned with the influence of persons upon government and public life, with civic institutions and diplomacy more than with philosophy and literature. As a political biographer and analyst, working from the authorities with exemplary technique, she maintained a firm control over her material, unaffected by fashion in Renaissance study. But the concreteness marking all she did implied no lack of response to the art and the scholarship of this astonishing period, interest in which she consistently

[1] *Proc. British Academy*, xxviii (1942), 179.

encouraged through years of teaching and example. That the studies which follow should comprise archival scholarship and artistic interpretation is a testimony to the breadth of her historical outlook.

A word may be said about their character. Though in a composite work one cannot expect unity of method and treatment nor strict co-ordination of subject-matter, the themes selected none the less group themselves in their own way. After some general reflections upon the concept of the Renaissance and upon the political background and historiography of the Italian Renaissance in particular, the writers consider the position of Italy against the background of medieval Europe and the realization by the Italians of their own special place in Renaissance development; the contribution of Italian humanism to Europe; and the hard discipline of war and invasion and need for stronger morale which so powerfully impressed the mind of Machiavelli. Four central essays then deal with the technique of signorial government and administration, and with the circumstances under which great families or interests dominated (or ceased to dominate) Italian society. The financial stake which the citizens of Florence had in the Medici *stato* becomes clear. But more general questions are raised. To what extent were signorial institutions revolutionary? How far did they utilize the existing councils and governmental bodies of the Italian city-state? The answers given vary with the states themselves: thus at Milan the feudal relationship between the lord and his vassals may be said to have continued in a modified form; at Florence under Lorenzo de' Medici there are fundamental changes in the organs controlling the election of citizens to the Councils; at Rimini, and in the Romagna generally, the old communal bodies are retained under the Malatesta domination.

The six papers that follow are concerned with various aspects of art, letters and scholarship; patronage finds illustration in a study of Cosimo de' Medici's relation with artists; the reactions between biblical literature and painting are considered in an analysis of the Maccabean histories on the Sistine ceiling. Thence one passes to the *Canzone a ballo* in the hands of Poliziano and Lorenzo de' Medici; to an examination of the nature and appeal of the latin verse written by the humanists; and to studies of the formation of an Italian literary language; the beginnings of Italian antiquarianism and the learning of archaeologists; the influence in English Court circles of Italian astrology. A *corolla*, perhaps rather than a *catena*, yet representative of English work now in progress within the Italian field.

I

As with all major historical periods, the study of the Renais-sance has undergone notable changes in these fifty years.[1] The era is no longer regarded as one of powerful and uninhibited individualism. The criticisms of medievalists directed against the so-called originality of Renaissance men and Renaissance ideas have gone far to demonstrate the enduring nature of medieval concepts and institutions. A new periodization has emerged, partly because scholars are no longer restricting their field of vision to Italy, partly owing to the growth of interest in medieval humanism. Students of religion have for some time engaged in de-paganizing the Renaissance, explaining, for instance, that a Christian Renaissance existed long before Colet, More and Erasmus, whether in the devotional movement in the Nether-lands or in the beginnings of cultivated French piety; or pointing to the importance, particularly for the history of art, of the pagan mystery cults when interpreted by the Christian Platonists of the Medicean circle.[2] The significance the Renaissance attached to classical mythology and to the classical gods is shown to be not necessarily un-Christian but rather a development of medieval

[1] For transformations in the concept of the Renaissance see Federico Chabod, *Machiavelli and the Renaissance* (London, 1958). The more recent views on period-ization are discussed in the essays of Delio Cantimori and E. F. Jacob, 'La Periodizzazione dell' Età del Rinascimento nella Storia d'Italia e in quella d' Europa', *Relazioni del X Congresso Internazionale di Scienze Storiche* (Roma 4-11 Sett. 1955), iv (Florence, 1955).

[2] Cf. Edgar Wind, *Pagan Mysteries in the Renaissance* (London, 1958), for the treatment of paganism by an historian of art.

moralization, which concentrated upon types and examples of the vices and virtues. In literature as in iconography the Renaissance has been firmly set within the framework of a tradition running more or less continuously from classical times.

To the nineteenth century, and indeed to a good deal of the early twentieth, the term *medieval humanism* would have appeared self-contradictory. The humanism which stood for a critical appreciation of art and letters and an understanding of their relation to life was firmly associated in people's minds with the Italian Renaissance, and the Renaissance was considered to be the period in Italian history in which the study of classical art and the discovery or rediscovery of classical literature led to new activities of the human spirit, long held under by asceticism and intolerant authority. A famous passage in Jakob Burckhardt's *Civilization of the Renaissance* will come to mind (it was later taken up by the late R. G. Collingwood in his *Speculum Mentis*):

'In the Middle Ages both ideas of human consciousness—that which turned outward towards the world and that which turned inward towards man himself—lay dreaming or half-dreaming beneath a common veil. The veil was woven of faith, illusion and childish prepossession through which the world and history had been clad in strange lives. Man was conscious of himself only as a member of a race, people, party, family or corporation—only through some general category. In Italy this veil first melted into air: . . . man became a spiritual individual and recognized himself as such. In the same way the Greek had once distinguished himself from the barbarian.'

Around this discovered individualism the later nineteenth-century concept of the Renaissance was built. It lingers still in many of the textbooks; it is especially attractive in an age of ministries and planning and egalitarian doctrines, and it has sufficient truth to make it still worth reading and examining. A great deal of modern Renaissance scholarship, when it is not occupied with the graphic and plastic arts, has been concerned with the scrutiny and criticism of Burckhardt's celebrated thesis that the Renaissance was the discovery of the world and of man himself.

The reaction of the medievalists has certainly had the effect of seriously questioning Burckhardt's notion of the 'veil' of faith, illusion and childish prepossession, and his predominantly Italian view of Renaissance inspiration and the Renaissance individual; but to take Burckhardt to task for ignorance of the Middle Ages is hardly fair. As Sir Kenneth Clark has pointed out, he started as a writer on medieval history and gothic architecture:

> . . . but on his first visit to Italy he recognized immediately a new stylistic and cultural society which corresponded with a harmony in his own nature. He called it the Renaissance—then a term of rare and doubtful usage—and from this intuitive recognition, based on the enjoyment of art, he proceeded to an intellectual justification in every branch of human life which on the whole has resisted a century of criticism.[1]

Clark makes the important point that Burckhardt's great gift lay in relating individual works to their background: in fact he once called himself the painter of backgrounds. This background is now seen in clearer perspective than in Burckhardt's day; for an important factor, entirely basic, in the changed view of the Renaissance is the advance of archival and administrative study. The progress made in the exploration of local, municipal or family records among private archives, as well as of chancery, fiscal or tabellionate records among public, have led researchers to bring to bear upon the history of art the same exacting methods and standards as are employed in political and economic history; so that, although a higher degree of sensibility is unquestionably required, the history of painting or sculpture or other arts is not regarded as a subject above or outside the ordinary canons of historical criticism. A new reciprocity between the art historian and the general historian exists, based on the conviction that to understand a work of art (and, by understanding, to look at it as the painter or sculptor imagined it) aids from without, the aids of history, theology and literature, must be invoked. If there was

[1] 'The Study of Art History', *The Universities Quarterly*, vol. x, no. 3 (May 1956). The young Burckhardt's interests are clearly seen in his *Briefe* (ed. Max Burckhardt), particularly those to Heinrich Schneider in Bd. 1.

any tendency to regard the Renaissance as a 'pure' cultural move-ment having its own technique and exempt from the ordinary rules of historical study, that has now disappeared. Archival investigation has added richly to every part of the subject. Only one example need be given. The story of Florentine families, particularly of banking firms, told from their archives and their diaries by scholars like Sapori,[1] Castellani,[2] Davidsohn[3] and de Roover,[4] and amongst contributors to this book, Philip Jones,[5] has revealed the high degree of initiative and technique prevalent among the sophisticated merchant class of the later Middle Ages.[6] Such writers have driven home the commonsense point that the development of any art depends, as Fichtenau pointed out in the case of the Carolingian Renaissance, both on intelligent patron-age and financial inducement: they have provided much of the background against which civic and signorial initiative can be evaluated.

Another great factor in the changed outlook upon the Renais-sance is the realization that it is no longer possible to regard the medieval period from the twelfth century onwards as static or even slow-moving in the realm of politics or ideas. This is so familiar that one hesitates to restate it. Our view of later medieval scholasti-cism has been revolutionized by appreciation of the struggle that was in progress from the middle of the fourteenth century onwards

[1] Especially *Una campagnia di Calimala* (1932); *Le crisi delle campagnie mercantile dei Bardi e dei Peruzzi* (1932); *Studi di storia economica medievale* (1940). chs. iv and v; cf. R. S. Lopez, 'Italian Leadership in the Medieval Business World', *Journal of Economic History*, viii, 63–8, reviewing the second and enlarged edition of Sapori (1947).

[2] *Nuove Testi fiorentini del Dugento* (1952).

[3] *Geschichte von Florenz*, esp. vol. iii.

[4] 'A Florentine firm of cloth manufacturers: Management and Organisation of a sixteenth-century business', *Speculum*, xvi (1941), 3, 33; *The Medici Bank* (1948); *Money, Credit and Banking in Medieval Bruges* (1948).

[5] 'Florentine Families and Florentine Diaries', *Studies in Italian Medieval History presented to Miss E. M. Jamison* (1956), pp. 183–206.

[6] Cf. Y. Renouard, *Les Hommes d'affaires Italiens et l'avènement de la Renaissance* (1949), especially pp. 10–12: The Marchesa Iris Origo, *The Merchant of Prato* (1957).

between Ockhamist scepticism and the Platonistic Augustinian tradition, which, stemming from the Victorines, found its highest expression in the intuitionist theories of Cusanus and the German School. That *docta ignorantia* should have attempted to unite the new logic and the old mysticism in a synthesis based upon mathematical principles was a notable advance in the history of thought. In political theory there is the momentous contest between an absolutism propounded to justify the papal plenitude of power and the doctrine of the Conciliar thinkers and churchmen. Jurists have thrown new light upon political and constructional ideologies by tracing theories of absolute and undivided sovereignty back to the age of the Decretalists, and of doctrines opposed to them, to a steadily accumulating body of canonist speculation about the corporate nature of the Church. In the borderland of theology, logic and metaphysics, as Anneliese Maier has shown, new theories of scientific method were gradually coming to birth; while in the realm of technology new devices were aiding the soldier, the engineer and the printer. Most of all, students of humanism itself, writers like P. O. Kristeller, B. L. Ullman, Myron Gilmore, Ernst Curtius and Roberto Weiss have notably widened the conception of the Renaissance both as a period and as a movement in the history of literary and artistic achievement, not least by presenting it through its medieval derivations: its theology, for example, or its Aristotelianism. As a period, these students of humanism have pointed to the long overlapping of what, for want of better terms, we may call 'medieval' and 'Renaissance' elements in the movement; they have demonstrated with the help of iconography the continuance of the classical and, almost as important, the patristic tradition throughout the course of the Middle Ages: they have indicated the strongly medieval content of much Renaissance philosophy and literature. In so doing they have not diminished, but have on the contrary enlarged our notion of the Italian contribution to the Renaissance as a general European phenomenon, while they have pointed to its great debt to other countries, particularly Burgundy and northern Europe.

Yet if belief in the continuous flow of culture has undermined the older periodization, it has sometimes led to a neglect of what the more progressive minds in the fourteenth and fifteenth centuries regarded as happening within their own age and their own experience. To the idea of the sudden awakening of the human spirit, the magic flowering of personality at a distinct period of European civilization, there has now succeeded the concept of a developing consciousness, the roots of which are found to be deep in the Latin past. This was not the way in which the early pioneers of the Renaissance were regarded by their contemporaries: they were considered to be creative artists, the poets in particular. As B. L. Ullman has pointed out, it was their achievement in poetry that indicated that something new was stirring and that the thousand years of torpor had ended. It was the poets more than the pictorial artists to whom the fourteenth-century humanists attributed the greatest importance. Coluccio Salutati asserted that poetry presupposed *totium trivium, quadrivium, philosophiam omnem, humana divinaque et omnes prorsus scientias*:[1] that all the arts were handmaids to poetry. The idea of an awakening from slumber was used by the humanists to suggest a return to the life of ancient Rome, and the reading of the Latin classics was associated with literary creation from the very beginning. The return to the Muses, banished from Italy, was, according to Boccaccio, realized in the poetry of Dante, though Petrarch was not to agree about a writer to whom the objection was that he wrote in the vernacular. Some twenty years later Filippo Villani in his book on famous citizens of Florence puts Dante between Claudian and Petrarch as one of the five great poets of Florence, and in particular the one who brought Florence back to light *ex abysso tenebrarum*. Between 1433 and 1437 Sicco Polenton finished a history of Latin literature, in which, after deploring the fact that poetical talent and real eloquence went to sleep after Juvenal, he observed that with Dante the muses were waking from the sleep of a thousand years: *quasi longissimo e somno excitabantur Musae*. In fact, as Ullman has pointed out, Boccaccio, Salutati, Villani,

[1] *Studies in the Italian Renaissance* (1955), pp. 12 f.

Polenton, all mention Dante as the first to awaken the muses. Boccaccio too, as early as 1348–53 when commenting on the figures in Giotto's paintings, so lifelike that people thought them human beings, held that the artist had, in the same way, revived the art of poetry buried for centuries; and an even more excitatory effect was attributed to Cimabue. Consciousness that something of creative importance was happening in Italy can be observed, as will be seen, in contemporary historiography. Gregorio Dati's *Istoria di Firenze* shows his understanding of the need for a balance of power transcending the boundaries of single regions. It is perhaps more in Leonardo Bruni's work, the *Laudatio Florentinae Urbis*, that the classical appeal to the days of the Roman Republic can best be heard, for his theory of the founding of Florence at that time is the pivot of his claim that Florence was heir to a great tradition of Liberty.[1] The new Italian historiography, going back to ancient history, was conscious both of the Roman past and of the claims of civic duty upon the ordinary citizen. And it was written in the language and idiom of ancient civility, represented by Cicero, because this was the medium in which the civic virtues seemed for good and all portrayed.

In any social or artistic movement there are leading personalities and a host of other competent executives or craftsmen who form its penumbra and reproduce, with a high degree of success, the manner and spirit of their masters: but here in the Italian Renaissance one is struck by the numbers of genuinely creative persons, people who carry their response to the problems confronting them much further and with greater success than the average technician: and do so while keeping within the idiom, and aided by the ordinary media, of their profession without mannerism or extravagance. There was more challenge and response and a greater concentration of gifted personalities in Italy during the period 1390–1550 than any time elsewhere since the beginning of the twelfth century, perhaps even since the fifth and fourth centuries in

[1] Emphasized by Hans Baron, *Humanistic and Political Literature in Florence and Venice at the beginning of the Quattrocento* (Harvard, 1955), pp. 5–11. On Bruni's *Laudatio*, cf. ch. iv.

Attica. For genius to be realized in action, for people of high talent not to be mute and conventional, it above all matters at what time and into what circumstances they are born. In his *Aesthetics and History* (1950) Mr. Berenson drew attention to the epitaph of Pope Hadrian VI in Santa Maria dell' Anima: *Quantum refert in quae tempora vel optimi cujusque virtus incidet*: how much the ability of even the most gifted depends upon the time at which it is likely to appear. The *virtus* of a Hitler or a Stalin in 1875, for example, would have been as guiltless of their country's blood as the village Cromwell in Gray's *Elegy*. In art it is the same. 'Can we imagine that Raphael could have arisen in our twelfth century or a Michelangelo in the Trecento, any more than a Picasso or a Joyce in the audacious but still rational eigh-teen-nineties?'[1] The men of the early *Quattrocento* were heirs to a particular type of inheritance. They either watched, or their parents watched, the transformation of a feudal society into a society governed by capital and by diplomacy allied to military ability. From the end of the thirteenth century—the turning-point in the history of Europe—Italy, prompted by a precocious com-mercial development, began to shake off medieval formulae and to adopt an economic rather than a theocentric concept of life.[2]

The Italians chose the political path of local independence and piecemeal development. Their new rulers were merchants and industrialists, or despots who generally enjoyed the support, and guarded the interests of, the economic oligarchies. The back-ground was right for such initiative, for there was no unity in Italy, no political law, no accepted juridical criterion by which to measure the validity of government. The criteria of accomplish-ment and enterprise and vitality which are the constituents of *virtù* held the field unchallenged.

In other words, by the beginning of the fourteenth century Italy had broken with the political tradition of medieval Europe, even though her jurists might still argue about the sovereignty of the

[1] p. 176.
[2] D. M. Bueno de Mesquita, 'Some condottiere of the Trecento', *Proc. British Academy*, xxxii (1946), 221.

emperor or the superiority of the pope. To the Florentine of the period the pope was the lord of a territorial state with which his own might enter into competition or enmity. Centuries before Boniface VIII the Church had invaded the political arena: 'The temporal power emerged in the eighth century and from that time onwards it was continuously one of the most important factors of papal authority.'[1] Years before the return of Gregory XI from Avignon the Holy See had been fighting to preserve the integrity of its own territories, and had been trying, with the encouragement of Charles IV, to incorporate the central Italian cities in an enlarged papal state, had been employing the best-trained captains and using its spiritual resources (especially the Crusading Tenth) for the struggle against its opponents. The contest of John XXIII against Ladislas of Naples, the papacy against the new Hungaro-Neapolitan state, marks the climax of this policy. Is it not remarkable that even in the 1320's Marsilius of Padua has to devote a section of his *Defensor Pacis* to an explana-tion of the word 'spiritual', trying to reduce it to its original meaning instead of its merely business connotation? The economic mechanism of the Avignonese papacy shows the Lucca, Sienese or Florentine merchant making to the papal treasury the advances it needed to pay for its campaigns and the papal collectors trans-ferring to the merchant the product of their labours. The supreme spiritual power, having defeated the Hohenstaufen, was now taking its part in the rough and tumble of Italian politics, calling in cadets of the French royal house to aid its territorial designs in central Italy and using its spiritual weapons of indulgence and ex-communication for more than self-defence.

By the end of Clement V's pontificate it had become clear that neither external force nor internal agreement would change the twofold pattern of Italian political life. With the failure of Henry VII's expedition and the ruin of Dante's hopes for a general pacification, it was evident that in northern Italy the *signoria* (the rule of a noble or *arriviste* local dynasty), and in central Italy

[1] P. D. Partner, *The Papal State under Martin V* (British School at Rome, 1958), p. v.

the mercantile and industrial commune, had come to stay. In the north there was to be fierce competition between the *signori*, the absorption of the smaller by the greater until the Visconti state of Milan had eaten up almost all the Lombard lordships— the Gonzaga of Mantua, the Carrara of Padua, the Scaligeri of Verona and Vicenza—and the former exclusively maritime City of Venice had carved out of the mainland a principality to act as a counterpoise to Milanese predominance. Politically, therefore, the Italian Renaissance was born in a struggle of ideo, logies: which was the better, to be brought up in a civic princi, pality, firmly ruled by an adherent of Milan, peaceful and disci, plined, with no democratic nonsense, but no chance of expressing one's will politically or taking responsibility for power; or in a commune where the tradition of civic freedom was maintained by the large *Arti*, the guilds, a city run by the Ottimati, the leaders of its great textile and banking interests? Here the citizen was a member of a group and self,expression lay through tactful manipulation. Both gave opportunities of a different type. It is worth remembering, when making the contrast, that in the com, mune the leading citizens did not live in expensive suburbs or drive to meetings of a *balia* or to their offices or shops. They did not live in country houses like the London merchants of the fifteenth century; at Florence, Fiesole or Settignano was roughly the radius. The commune was a highly organized industrial society, dominated by interests and factions, but able to persuade all living in it that the government and its decisions were theirs exclusively. The former type, the signorial type, was heavily taxed, but free from internal commotion, saving always the dagger at the top; maintaining a public state, a tasteful order, the lord seldom seen, but living, as Filippo Maria Visconti did, in a sort of artistic Kremlin, with agents watching everybody; a place conducive to poets and panegyrists, close to which might be a not, able university like Padua, frequented by artists like Mantegna and Giovanni Bellini: a centre of enlightened patronage.

By the beginning of 1380 northern and central Italy had reached a degree of differentiation in their political structure and attitude such as had never been known there in medieval times. Between the Po and the Alps brooded the peace of the new lordship and the destruction of republican freedom had, for the time being, reached its consummation on those beautiful and hopeless plains. Tuscany, on the other hand, had become the home of a provincial coalition of city republics, and a large burden of responsible leadership fell on Florentine shoulders. Venice, neighbour of Padua which had in 1386 been absorbed by Milan, stood aside. In 1389 Florentine envoys warned the Doge of the danger approaching. They were charged to explain that the Visconti was endeavouring to obtain the rule of the whole of Italy 'by taking possession of the Florentine state and then of the states of the Venetian and the Genoese; for the other is one of no account, once he has subjugated these'.

The Venetian government replied that they could see no reason for alarm. Venice felt herself secure in her lagoons and would not throw herself into the decisive encounter between the unifying monarchy of the north and the tradition of communal independence.[1] Florence was left to wage armed war against Giangaleazzo in 1390-2. The dangers implied in the struggle with the Visconti monarchy had by then become so clear that Florence could enter the struggle with manifestoes proclaiming that the goal of the 'tyrant of Lombardy' was now to be discerned: he wanted to become king. He had been telling Italy that he was the champion of peace at the very time when he was destroying the liberty of Verona and Padua. 'These are the labours for peace by which, as he contends, he has struggled for the *Pace Italica*.' The louder therefore became Florence's proclamations of her liberal aims. Giovanni da Prato calls Florence 'a fountainhead of freedom' and Domenico Bandini terms her as *Italicae libertatis mater*— mother of Italian liberty. In his short description of the Florentine constitution, probably written in the 1430's, Leonardo Bruni says:

'One of the democratic characteristics of our constitution is that

[1] Hans Baron, 'A Struggle for Liberty in the Renaissance', *American Historical Review*, lviii (1953), 275.

we worship freedom more than anything else, as the end and goal of our commonwealth.'[1]

Was Florence the mother of Italian liberty? If the peace of Italy at which Giangaleazzo was professedly aiming was his own despotic peace, so Florence, while professing hatred of tyrants and addressing them in official correspondence as *dominus, dominator,* etc., was not always too careful to define what she meant by liberty or the defence of liberty. The Florentines might tell Robert of Naples that they disliked despots in their immediate vicinity: but the weakest point in their claim to defend the liberty of the Tuscan towns was their own territorial policy. It afforded opportunities for intervention outside Tuscany and must sometimes have made Florentine declarations appear hypocritical, particularly in the case of towns over which Florence had gained control. For what purposes, it may be asked, did they pour money into the pocket of the condottiere Fortebraccio? A frequent Florentine argument was that such towns had been 'liberated' or 'protected' from tyranny.[2] In 1361 Florence had intervened in Volterra and put an end to the *signoria* of the Belforti and had obtained custody of the frontiers. Again, in the case of Lucca, she arranged in a treaty with Venice that it was to become a Florentine possession, 'at her governance, ownership and rule', i.e. to do as she liked with, but later she returned to her original position and stated that if Lucca was acquired, she would restore to her 'the ancient commune' after 'the dire tyranny to which she has been subjected'. There is a mixture of motive: preservation of the Tuscan communes from despotism may be involved to justify Florentine intervention; clearly it was Florence's policy and interest during the fourteenth century to safeguard and when necessary to restore the communal régime in the Tuscan towns which had come under her control. Ideology and self-restraint coincided, and ancient history was adduced by the humanists to strengthen the claim. When Florence professed concern for the liberty of a town,

---

[1] Cited by N. Rubinstein, 'Florence and the Despots in the Fourteenth Century', *Trans. Roy. Hist. Soc.*, 5th Ser., no. 2 (1952), 22.

[2] Ibid., p. 33.

her opponents were not slow to see the chink in her armour. 'They reduce the liberty of their neighbours to serfdom whenever they can', wrote Pope Gregory XI in 1375.[1]

A certain amount of disingenuousness is inevitable in the conduct of all diplomacy. The best face must be put upon aggression; and any defence offered for it must be inspired by the highest motives. These observations upon Milan and Florence may serve to emphasize the fact that the fathers and mothers of the great Renaissance generation of the *Quattrocento* were brought up in a varied and challenging political atmosphere, where the city and the interests of the community were everything. Both within and without the city-state there were the tensions and clashes which Italians have always relished, however much they may complain about them. The ideal of the men of the *Quattrocento* was a versatile activity in the interests of the republic. The best illustration of this is the splendid narrative pictures of Venetian fifteenth-century art in which the themes are set against a city-state background. Carpaccio's 'St. Ursula'; Gentile Bellini's study of the Piazza in the 'Preaching of St. Mark', or his Corpus Christi picture; and others which will be familiar. A further example of this ideal is provided in the revival, by the humanists, of the study of Cicero. The new Cicero is not the solitary of the Middle Ages, but the active citizen-humanist who used the leisure of his country house to work for Rome. If it were the solitude and contemplation upon which monastic Europe fixed for approval in Cicero's work, in the later fourteenth and fifteenth centuries it was his learned activity, and the connection he established between the active and the practical life, in the service of the State. In the *De Legibus* Cicero has already looked upon it as his task 'to bring learning out of the gloomy depths of the study, and scholarly leisure not merely into the sunlight and the dust, but also into the fighting line and the centre of the conflict'.[2] In his *De Oratore* he has shown in the figures of the great Romans of the past what

[1] Ibid., p. 35.
[2] Hans Baron, 'Cicero and the Roman Civic Spirit', *Bull. John Rylands Lib.*, xxii (1938), 35, quoting *De Officiis*, i, 1-4.

culture could mean to a citizen in the needs of his daily life. Cato Censorius is here described as the kind of a citizen who knew how to unite theory and practice, private and public interests; his studies in the law did not prevent him from being a busy lawyer; from his duties as an orator in the Forum or as a member of the Senate he was never debarred by private business. Marcus Crassus, the leading speaker in the dialogue, had never discontinued his activity in the law courts for theoretical pursuits, and yet had at tained an exceptional degree of intellectual development. Cicero points, as a model, to the citizen 'who does not impress others as pursuing philosophical studies and yet is studying'. This indeed was and remained Cicero's highest ideal of civic culture. When, in later years, he defended himself against those who questioned his ability for philosophic work after a life-long political career, he boasted that he too 'had been studying philosophy most earnestly at the very time when he seemed to be doing so least'.[1]

It was this aspect of Cicero that had specially appealed to Coluccio Salutati, the Florentine Secretary of State who in 1392 had discovered the *Epistolae familiares*. Petrarch's discovery had been the *Epistolae ad Atticum*; but whereas Petrarch's pleasure at finding them had been turned to disappointment that Cicero's civic spirit had led him to forsake a philosophical retreat, Salutati the Florentine honoured and admired those very characteristics of Cicero which Petrarch deprecated in a philosopher. Hoping to justify Cicero for taking part in the civil war, Salutati declared that, according to the *Noctes Atticae* of Aulus Gellius, Solon had already discovered that a citizen who in time of civic unrest con tinued leading his private life was to be considered unfaithful to the city and expelled. Cicero therefore had not forgotten the duties of a 'sapiens' when he took part in the struggle for the liberty of the Republic. About 1415 Leonardo Bruni built on these foundations his biography of Cicero—*Cicero novus*. The title was significant. In opposition to the old Cicero of the Middle Ages and of Petrarch, the 'new' Cicero of the Florentine Renais sance no longer appeared as a figure in whom a political career

[1] Baron, ibid., p. 76.

and a more intellectually productive life of philosophy were at variance; in Cicero was realized the ideal union of political action and literary creation; for literary and political activities were, in the words of Dr. Baron, two parts of one and the same task: the work of a Roman citizen for his *patria* and the Latin Empire of Rome. Cicero became capable, Bruni says:

'In spite of the great claims made on him by a state which ruled the world, of writing more than philosophers whose lives are spent in leisure and study; and on the other hand, in spite of intense preoccupation with his studies, and his literary work, he was capable of accomplishing more practical work than people unburdened with interest in literary matters.'[1]

II

This is the spirit that animates Renaissance historiography. In his notable book, *The Renaissance in Historical Thought* (1948), Professor Wallace K. Ferguson speaks of the humanist historians as making certain definite contributions to the modern organization and periodization of history. 'They broke', he says, 'with the theological world history of the medieval chronicles, abandoned the idea of perpetual doctrines and established a new periodization on secular grounds, thereby setting up one of the two boundaries of the Middle Ages.' It is true that they did these things; it need not be assumed that they were the first to do them.

The work of the humanists had been anticipated by the popular chronicles of the fourteenth and fifteenth centuries. 'By the end of the fourteenth there was a general demand for historical works in the vernacular, more akin in spirit than the monastic chronicle to the rhymed epics which had been favoured so long and which in any case were being adapted as prose romances to cater for an increasingly sophisticated audience. These tendencies, by no means confined to England, are illustrated by the two most significant changes in English historiography during the fourteenth century: the multiplications, continuations and translations of the two great works, the *Brut* (of Anglo-French origin) and the *Polychronicon*.'[2]

t [1] Ibid., p. 90.

[2] D. Hay, *Polydore Vergil, Renaissance Historian and Man of Letters*, Oxford, 1952.

The *Brut* and the *Polychronicon* are admittedly compilations; but they are highly indicative of public demand. As many as one hundred and sixty copies of the *Brut* in the original French, in English and in Latin have been identified, in what are called the 'Long' and 'Short' versions and the various continuations.[1] Caxton, by printing the *Brut* and by both printing and continuing Higden (in Trevisa's English rendering) to 1461 bears witness to the place which the two works held among contemporaries. By the end of the fifteenth century the *Brut* had appeared in six printed editions, and the *Polychronicon* in two.

The city chronicle is the other great popular development.[2] The narratives have, like London chronicles of Arnold Fitz Thed-mar, their origin in lists of urban office-holders. Soon local patriotism and antiquarian interest turned them into more ambitious forms. At least twenty-five annalists were at work in London during the fifteenth century and the type developed into the Tudor Chronicle proper, found on a greater scale in Fabyan, Hall and so forth. Fabyan's *Newe Chronycles of England and of Fraunce* is in its later part a city chronicle, but the work is more than this and is justifiably termed by its author 'the concordance of histories'. It is divided into seven parts; the first from Brute to Molmutius, the second to the Roman invasion, the third to the death of Lucius; the fourth to the end of Roman rule, the fifth to Cadwallader, the sixth to Harold, and the last from 1066–1485. In its patristic mythology it is typical of the reawakened interest in the classical foundations of the English past. In his preface Fabyan discusses the chronological problems involved in relating the creation, the fall of Troy and the foundation of Rome to early

---

[1] F. W. Brie, *Geschichte und Quellen der Mittelenglischen Prosachronik: the Brut of England oder The Chronicles of England* (Marburg, 1905). Cf. John Taylor, 'The French Brut and the Reign of Edward II', *Eng. Hist. Rev.*, lxxii (July 1957), 425 f.

[2] On this cf. Starke, *Populäre Englische Chroniken des 15 Jahrhunderts* (Berlin, 1935); also *The Great Chronicle of London*, ed. A. H. Thomas and I. D. Thornley, esp. pp. xxxiii–xliv, which discusses the influence of the archetypes upon contemporary examples.

English history. He provides a perfect example of a trait alluded to above; insistence upon the continuous progress of civilization from its classical origins; for Fabyan's argument is that Brute took possession of Albion in 1136 B.C.: the latest age, the seventh period, comes at the end of the pageant of history.

What then is history for the intelligent burgess or the local schoolmaster or the chantry priest who taught many young people in town and country parishes—for the connection of the cantarists with education in the fifteenth century is a subject which is only beginning to be appreciated?[1] Fortunately there is evidence of what history meant for the Vicars Choral of York Minster and, through their plays and pageants, for the citizens of York.[2] Among the rules governing life in the Bedern, the residence of the York vicars, is the following:

'Every vicar shall repeat his histories, and any vicar who shall not fulfil this requirement shall be accused before the chapter, and, if found guilty, be expelled.'[3]

At the end of his first year of office, a vicar was expected to know by heart not only the psalms in Latin, but also his history tables. These were evidently the contents of two large triptychs covered with skins on which a hand of the later fourteenth century has written what the vicars were supposed to commit to heart. The first triptych begins with the opening words of the Bible, *In principio creavit Deus coelum et terram*: the narrative then follows the course of the old testament with additions often found in medieval histories, e.g. the defeat of Lucifer by St. Michael; the creation of Adam and Eve, the garden of Eden; the fall, the murder of Abel, the tower of Babel and so forth, via the Exodus and the Kings, to the birth of Christ 4278 years after the flood. Then came the exploits of Alexander the Great, after which a sudden move is made to England, the dates 870, 880 and 898 being predominant, especially in connection with St. Oswald,

---

[1] Emphasized by A. Hamilton Thompson, *The English Clergy and their Organization in the later Middle Ages* (1947), pp. 155-7.

[2] *York Civic Records,* ed. Anglo Raine (Yorks. Arch. Soc.), I, *passim.*

[3] F. Harrison, *Life in a Medieval College* (1952), pp. 65-7.

the Northumbrian King and Martyr. The story then proceeds via Bede, Dunstan, Edgar and Athelstan, to the defeat of Harold at Hastings, the Norman Conquest, the struggle between Edward I and John Balliol, and the battle of Bannockburn 'at which 20,000 Englishmen were slain': there is a mention of the Hundred Years War and the Black Death, and the first triptych ends with the building of the four eastern bays of the choir of York Minster under Archbishop John Thoresby (1352–73). The work of Thoresby is referred to as *novum opus ecclesie Eboracensis*. The second triptych is entirely ecclesiastical, and gives various Papal and royal grants to the Church of York and mentions the foundation of a Church there by Edwin and Paulinus and the building of suc⁄cessive churches on the site, especially the church built by Thomas of Bayeux. Then comes a very brief summary of the work of some of the medieval historians, Henry of Huntingdon, William of Malmesbury, Alfred of Beverley and a mention of the bulls granted to the Minster by Gregory V, Honorius and Coelestine.

This is selective local history of a highly northern kind. In this and the next century there are the remarkably interesting Shrews⁄bury annals, which, beginning (1377) simply with lists of town officials in the orthodox fashion, broaden into an extended narrative of local happenings drawn from the administrative records of the town and obviously written up year by year. One feature which the reader will notice is the number of suicides carefully recorded. Such perhaps was what history meant to the upper ranks of the burgesses and townsfolk; but if a university student of the fifteenth century had been asked what history was, he would undoubtedly have mentioned the names of Orosius, Bede, William of Malmesbury and either Henry of Huntingdon or Geoffrey of Monmouth, and a more learned one might have started with Eusebius, the Historia Tripartita of Cassiodorus and ended with Matthew Paris and Higden. This is orthodox history for clerks. Now from the popular and theological schemes the humanist historians differed in a way which shows them to be neither wholly modern nor entirely medieval.

If an Italian humanist like Tito Livio, biographer of Henry

V, had been required to justify his writing of history, he might have replied that it is a form of literature highly regarded by the ancients, and presenting admirable opportunities for the exercise of style: that it has great practical value for its inculcation of moral and political lessons, and finally that in the historian history celebrated the past and present glories of his native land and the state to which it was dedicated. But the historian had also a responsibility, particularly in judging individuals. Sicco of Polenton claimed, with Cicero, that history was the 'witness of time and the light of truth', and that the historian had the responsi-bility of a sworn witness. Historians differed from the poets because 'the latter are free and wander at times as they are allowed to do', while historians always go along the path of truth and think it wicked and a crime to depart from what is true. 'For to one writing history it is prescribed that he shall say no false thing and shall hide no true one, but follow and acquit his task that the praise shall not be withdrawn from any man, nor false and fictitious commendation added to any. For this is the head and foundation of history always so to follow and remember the truth that the charge of mendacity can never be brought or any suspicion of grudge or favour had.'[1]

The gests of kings were in the epic tradition: they were a part of *solatium*, the sort of intelligent mental recreation that William of Wykeham's scholars in Oxford were allowed by the statutes on Saturday evenings. The literary aim was conscious and important. History was to divert and edify. The later Middle Ages laid stress on ethical and moral problems rather than on examples of divine intervention in human affairs, although, as Mr. Hay has recently shown, a no less poetic acceptance of ἀτή, or even the idea of destiny borrowed from the classics, had a strong place in the work of some writers like Polydor Vergil: but it also had, as the work of Vergil makes clear,[2] the task of rectification, of sweeping away error and in guiding men to a right attitude towards legend as well as towards the miraculous.

[1] *Sicconis Polentoni scriptorum illustrium Latinae Linguae Libri* xviii, ed. B. L. Ullman, v, 43.
[2] *Polydore Vergil, Renaissance Historian and Man of Letters* (1952), pp. 106 f.

Above all, in a number of early humanists, there can be seen a clear perception that the state or the nation is the unit of historical development. The new political point of view and a patriotic aim led to a new organization and periodization of history. The standpoint of the humanist historian was secular and, if one may coin the word, Marsilian. The Italian writers set out to write the political history of the Italian states, and since these arose only after the collapse of the Roman Empire, these historians, as Ferguson has pointed out,[1] who did not confine themselves to contemporary events naturally began their story with the decline of the Empire and carried it through the period in which com-munes arose and grew into powerful territorial states. They often began by the whole Italian scene and narrowed it down to the state, though still discussing the others in relation to it. The history of Italy thus came to be separated from world history, and history as a whole to be divided into two great periods, antiquity and the period that followed the decline of the Roman Empire.

The Florentine Chronicle of Giovanni Villani is an admirable example, too well known to demand exposition here, of the transi-tion from the orthodox medieval to the humanist stage. It was, however, Petrarch who gave the division between ancient and later history a new significance based on admiration for pagan Roman literature and the ideal of the virtuous republican city of Rome; the period prior to the adoption of Christianity by the Roman Emperors he called *ancient*, the period from that event down to the modern age *modern* (*nova*); and the modern age he characterized as one of barbarism and darkness. For it he had little but contempt; for him history was exclusively Roman: *Quid est enim aliud omnis historia quam Romana laus?* His own major histori-cal work he devoted to the lives of illustrious Romans: the *De viris illustribus* is exclusively so conceived. There had been there-fore no *translatio imperii*. The Roman *imperium* was inalienable, hav-ing sprung from the virtue of the Roman people. If the Roman *imperium* is not in Rome, where, he asked, is it? The remarkable thing is that if Petrarch did not have the medieval faith in the

[1] Op. cit., p. 6.

continuation of the Roman Empire, he had believed just as strongly in the mystical continuation of the *virtus romana* among the Roman populace of his own day and in the possible rebirth of ancient republic Rome. It was in keeping with this that he should approve Cola di Rienzi's revolution.

It has been pertinently remarked[1] that this identification of virtuous republican Rome with the papal city as it was in the fourteenth century, bore such little relation to reality that it made no great impression on the later Italian humanists. True enough, they were influenced by Petrarch's admiration for Roman anti-quity; but they did not hope for a rebirth of the Roman state. The post-glossators who extolled the *Imperium Romanum* were not advocating a localization of the Emperor. The Emperor stood for *iura imperialia*, but he was not *de facto* lord of the Eternal City. In the same way the humanists developed a different sort of patriotism; one focused upon particular states, cities and even families and concentrated upon the second of the periods of world history, the modern age, the age since the collapse of the Empire. It is not surprising that a pupil of Coluccio Salutati, to whom I have already alluded, has been acclaimed by scholars as 'the first true humanist historian': *The History of the Florentine People*[2] by Leonardo Bruni the Aretine, Chancellor of Florence, reveals many of the traits of the literary school of classically trained historians: his book was encouraged by the state government, and reveals an appreciable civic patriotism and is distinguished by its purely secular attitude. It also set, as a critic has observed, 'a high standard for style and coherence, for the critical use of and rejec-tion of legend, and for the interpretation of political history in the light of human motives and natural causes. It is a book which derives much from Aristotelian politics with its emphasis on the connection between civic virtue and the life of the City State.' It is not concerned here with the affinities between the Politics and Cicero's treatises, notably the *De Officiis* and the *De republica*: it need only be said that the one seemed to confirm and reinforce

---

[1] By Ferguson, op. cit., p. 9.
[2] Muratori, *Scriptores Rerum Italicarum* xix, ed. Santini, 909 f.

the words of the other, and this strain of what Gierke called 'antique-modern' thought had upon the later Middle Ages a powerful influence which it is impossible to ignore.

Like Petrarch, it is republican Rome for which Bruni displays admiration. Rome, he thinks, reached the height of her power in that period: the decline began with the loss of political freedom under the despotism of the Emperors. As he says, 'the Roman *imperium* began to go to ruin when first the name of Caesar fell like a disaster upon the City'. Freedom ceased when the imperial title appeared, and, 'following after liberty, virtue departed'. For Bruni, the Roman Empire in the West ended when the barbarian invasions began; the revival by Charlemagne was the act of a usurper. Now the interesting thing about Bruni is his refusal to regard the modern post-Roman period as a decline. Indeed, the absence of the Emperors in Germany and the fact that only very few resided there for any length of time led the cities of Italy to remember their freedom and 'begin to grow and flourish and return to their original power'. As soon as the Italian cities had recovered political freedom, they began to revive: the darkest period was then past; history thenceforth reveals the growth of the communes with their struggle for independence, leading to the collapse of the Hohenstaufen Empire and the eventual rise of the Florentine republic. This comparative optimism is found in the very much more laboured and richly documented works of Flavio Biondo of Forli; the two principal are the *Historiarum ab inclinatione Romanorum imperii decades* which aimed at restoring to public notice the thousand and thirty years following the sack of Rome by the Goths in '412' (410); and the *Italia Illustrata* (printed at Basel, 1531).

Biondo challenges attention for his refusal to be mesmerized into style. Herein he resembles the great Swiss historian who, nearly a hundred years later, wrote the story of the Confederation that had successfully defied both the Hapsburgs and the centrifugal forces at work: Gilg Tschudi is to many only a name: but the Berne patriot is probably the most careful and scientific user of documents and charters throughout the whole century, a historian who gives chapter and verse for all the major facts he narrates and yet is more than a compiler or a constitutional textbook. Biondo is not Tschudi: but he had learned from Guarino of Verona both relevance and extreme attention to accuracy, and if he did not follow Guarino's advice to the historian (about 1446) about the need for beauty of form, he practises the detachment advocated by that teacher, to the extent of being charged with writing in a pedestrian way; in so much that Bruni, who is the leader of the rhetorical school, refused to admit him as an acquaintance. In a way Biondo was a lonely figure.

It is of great significance that in both France and England the first humanist histories of these countries were written by Italians who approached their subject more or less in the manner of Biondi. Both Paolo Emili and Polydore Vergil in writing the history of countries not their own were able to apply detachment and objectivity more easily than native writers in Italy or else-where. That they were employed at all may have been due to a desire to present French and English history in a form acceptable to the new humanism. The result is very interesting for its union of elegance and detachment. Professor Hay has put the aim of these writers succinctly: 'the sanction of international humanism was precisely what the French and English dynasties wished to invoke. To secure this, they were willing to jettison portions of the historical myth which (for other reasons) they encouraged among native authors.'[1] Brutus and Arthur—to the indignation of the English antiquaries (especially Leland) and English poets—had to disappear. But if the origin of some popular legends were for Vergil to be found in the gullibility of the vulgar, when he came to the miraculous and the prodigious, Vergil is entirely medieval, and his *Anglica historia* contains 'an astonishing number of por-tents and miracles—astonishing because the sceptical treatment of the supernatural is so regularly taken as a yardstick for the measurement of humanism in historians'.[2] Yet in point of fact the Renaissance saw a quickened interest in prodigies and the

[1] Hay, *Polydore Vergil*, p. 151.
[2] Ibid., p. 111.

supernatural in all its forms, and there is no need to mention the fact that astrologers reigned in many European courts. In the *Discorsi* Machiavelli notes that important events in states are regularly preceded by prognostications, revelations or prodigies; the thunderbolt which struck the Duomo at Florence presaged the death of Lorenzo de' Medici.

> *When beggars die there are no comets seen;*
> *The heavens themselves blaze forth the death of princes.*

It has been well observed that the patronage of historiography by Italian city-states was closely related to diplomacy, and called for apologetics rather than objectivity; accordingly it stressed, even more than Guarino had done, the need in such partisan works for a brilliance of execution which would sweep away any doubts about the matter by the admiration it provoked of the manner in which the story was told. Yet the manner, the shapely idiom, the inevitability of the story were not everything: behind lay the aim of emphasizing a single principle.

More than the duty of upholding the *princeps*, it is the duty of participating in the life of the State that is incumbent upon the Renaissance man: and the highest form of participation lies precisely in those institutions that gather up, as it were, and express the supreme power of the *respublica*.

First men must be educated up to that participation. A northern example, taken from this country, may suffice. It was written by Thomas Chaundler, the Oxford Chancellor who also held, from 1452 to 1467, the Chancellorship of Wells. Chaundler was the devoted adherent of Bishop Bekynton of Bath and Wells, a loyal Wykehamist, to whom he addressed three of his main works, the *Libellus de laudibus duarum civitatum*, a panegyric of the two places: the *Collocuciones de laudibus nobilis Antistitis Wilhelmi de Wykeham*, *and the Allocuciones*, both panegyrics on Wykeham. Together with the *Liber Apologeticus* these texts are termed by Dr. M. R. James 'the Chaundler Manuscripts', part of which he printed for the Roxburghe Club; the full text of the *Collocuciones* and part of the *Allocuciones* have been transcribed and translated by Shirley

Bridges (Mrs. Corke).[1] The *Libellus* and the *Collocuciones* are written in the form of a dispute between two persons who then appeal to the judgement of a third. The *Collocuciones* in its first draft was meant, Chaundler says, for reading aloud *coram rege solacii*, before the King of Solace, at Christmas and presumably at Wells (we know that dramatic performances took place in New College at Christmas in the sixteenth century).[2] The *Libellus* says that the work would be introduced *coram tua paternitate*, i.e. before Bekynton himself. Our only interest in the first is that a great part of the material is lifted from Leonardo Bruni's *Laudatio Florentinae Urbis* and the *De Laudibus Mediolanensium Urbis Panegyricus* of Pier Candido Decembrio. The two speakers in it, Andrew and Peter, are made to adapt to their own northern context sentences from the description of Florence: e.g. 'Lying to the north are the mountains of Fiesole' becomes 'lying to the north and east are mountains', and so forth.[3]

The *Collocuciones* or conversations take place at Wells on six days, not necessarily all consecutive, in the house of Thomas Chaundler, Chancellor of the Cathedral and Warden of New College. The disputants are Pannescius 'who is said to know all' and Ferrandus 'of a slower and less penetrating intellect'. Arriving in Wells, these two begin to discuss William of Wykeham, taking as their point of departure the motto adopted by his college at Winchester, *Mores componunt hominem*, 'Manners makyth man'. In the second *collocucio* they decide to prove the truth of their dictum by considering the opinions of Cicero and Aristotle, and find Wykeham to be wise according to the definitions of these philosophers.[4] In the third they consider various definitions of courage, quoting the *Rhetorica ad Herennium* to demonstrate what

---

[1] In her Oxford B. Litt. thesis on Thomas Chaundler, Chapter ix, to which she has kindly permitted me to refer and to which I am indebted for the matter which follows.

[2] F. S. Boas, *University Drama in the Tudor Age,* pp. 6–7.

[3] Bridges, *Thomas Chaundler,* i, 139; text in ii, 119–28.

[4] Part of the *Libellus* is printed by T. Klette, *Beiträge Zur Geschichte und Litteratur der Italienischen Gelehrtenrenaissance,* ii (Greifswald, 1889), 84–105.

Cicero thinks. In the sixth *collocucio* by means of question and answer the two speakers and the Chancellor prove Wykeham to be just, using as evidence, besides Cicero's opinions, the existence of Wykeham's foundations.

Chaundler says that his treatise is based on the extract made by a friend and pupil to whom he taught philosophy: the scholar, who was fond of him, gave the undigested collections to his friend and preceptor while Warden of Winchester. Dr. James, rightly we think, maintained that it was a New College scholar who offered his collections to Chaundler to edit and transform: the matter for consideration is what the young man collected. The extract made for the *Collocuciones* came from the works of Cicero, Aristotle, St. Augustine and Lactantius. In the Dialogue Ferrand favours the views of Aristotle, but Pannescius, who does most of the talking, inclines to Cicero, and there are many examples from the *De Officiis*, a few from the Tusculan *Disputatione* and one from the *De Oratore*. 'Some skill is shown in putting these into the framework of the discussion (which proves that since manners make man Wykeham excelled in all the cardinal virtues), and at the same time keeping the argument in its pre-ordained course. It is, however, a very tedious work, its sterile wastes only enlivened by a few details such as the description of the pale faces of the students of Oxford and by the characters of pompous prosy Pannescius, and the impatient and cheeky Ferrandus.'[1] The strongly didactic nature of the *Collocuciones* distinguishes them from most of the conversations between friends represented in humanist dialogue. None the less, Mrs. Corke thinks, they are in form made more like a classical dialogue than the *Libellus* and the work is apparently modelled on the Tusculan Disputations.[2] This entitles it to be classed with humanist work, and other common features can be found. Like Bruni's dialogue *Ad Petrum Paulum Istrum,* it deals with a subject of interest to a small circle; like Lorenzo Valla's *De voluptate ac vero bono,* it tries to find the ultimate good. And its form is not quite without

[1] Bridges, op. cit., i, 143.
[2] Ibid.

parallel. Humanist dialogues are of many different types, and nearest to Chaundler's work is Tito Livio Frulovisi, *De republica*, given to Oxford University in 1444.[1]

The two *Collocuciones* that form the complement to Chaundler's *Allocuciones* make the purpose of his writing clear. The Chancellor must prove that Wykeham is worthy, not only according to the standards of gentile philosophers, but by those of the holy fathers. The work that follows is in the main a collection of long extracts from St. Augustine, Lactantius, Ambrose and Gregory. With all their shortcomings, the dialogues justify examination since the praise of Wykeham is based upon an educational ideal wholly characteristic of humanist thought: Wykeham is portrayed as a man who living in the world is able, through his scholarship and devotion to study, to set his mind on ultimate things: to effect a mixture of learning, religion and public life, to blend *grammatica* and *res publica*: a characteristic exemplified by Chaundler and by Bekynton himself, and justified in the list of able clerks whom Chaundler in his writings called *dilectissimi*. It is the characteristic beloved of English humanists: the gentle, religious and on the whole rather unadventurous humanism of these islands, free from the asperities evinced by the more ruthless and thorough-going Italian minds: a humanism loth to break entirely with the Middle Ages. How different it is from the outlook of those brought face to face with actual institutions and with the government of city-states! It was not the maxims of Cicero, but the hard course of Roman history depicted by Livy that inspired Machiavelli to apply the lessons of the past. For him, in the *Discorsi*, it is possible to govern by following their teaching; they serve to show the great difference that exists between the government of republics of modern times and of antiquity. It is, he says, to the actual government of states that one must attribute the reverses and the remarkable successes that still strike this age; for there, when men are slack and feeble, Fortune delights to let her power break forth; and because she is inconstant, one sees and will continually see republics and kingdoms become the playthings of revolution, until

[1] Bridges, op. cit., i, 144.

there rises a man sufficiently versed in the fair institutions of antiquity to apply them vigorously and so prevent Fortune from de-
ploying, at each return of the sun, all the extent of her power. The
statesman is continually engaged in a struggle with Fortune:
things happen half by the operation of Fortune, half through the
human will, and Fortune is continually encroaching unless kept
in check by the strong individual, educated in the events and
institutions of past history. By learning of these, he is able at any
time to co-operate with her. The essential art of the Prince, he says
in the *Principe*, is to maintain his state in equilibrium. It is not a
question of being just, great or magnanimous, but of conserving
his governmental authority. Let the people fear authority and be
satisfied with its lot; and the statesman's actions must be judged
by whether they have the expected effect upon the popular conscience. This is as far as we can reconcile the Florentine Secretary's
political writings: one monarchical, the other popular in tendency:
different as the *Discorsi* and the *Principe* may be, they do at any
rate meet on the common ground of the need for the study of
history and institutions; and the states of antiquity, just as much
as the history of Tuscany and of Florence, provide the training.

History then, for the Florentine, provides the instruction and the
experience, though in part of his work it is the Borgia general
who stands as the example before his eyes. It is not medieval
examples of justice, fortitude, virtue or vice which history is now
expected to afford: but instances where strong men have controlled
fate and prevailed through virtuosity and sagacity. The humanist
historian is therefore now a realist, convinced of the utilitarian value
of his study, patriotic and proof against all policies of concession
and co-operation, save for limited ends. He is the logical counterpart of the Marsilian *homo politicus*, who will only justify institutions by reference to the unity and peace of the *civitas*. Constitu-
tionally, as the essays below make plain, the Principate was not
revolutionary. The leader who has come by arms or intrigue or
heredity to dominate the city may indeed understand the technique of war; but he is also a master of councils and assemblies,
working out his policy through, and not against, the complicated

constitution of the State, keeping it solvent (if he can), his finger always on the public pulse. In the chapters below examples are given of this statecraft, from the rule of the Medici in the Florentine oligarchy, of the Sforza at Milan and of the Malatesta at Rimini: as also from the shrewd financial direction of the Papal State, much assisted towards its Renaissance prosperity by the sale of offices.

If the Principate knew how to use existing forms of govern, ment for its own ends, it knew also how to beautify and make more interesting life within the City: both in the arts and in litera, ture. In the rich and varied field, questions of the greatest moment arise. How do we account for the strongly individuated local schools and artistic traditions in so comparatively small an area and in so restricted a period? The contrast between the diversities of Italy and the more unified culture of the Burgundian dominions at once springs to mind. The art of the Flemish urban centres reflects the activities of the ducal court. Both the duke and his great administrators are patrons of art and the central tradition is reflected in the localities. In Italy it is different. Is therefore the great differentiation in style and method in any way connected with the structure of local society? Do university humanist circles in the mercantile aristocracies produce characteristic forms of art? To what extent are the differences of the schools and workshops due in any degree to the tastes and the rivalries of contemporary patrons? Then, in the choice of themes and subjects there is a great deal still to be found out purely on the intellectual and literary influences that were brought to bear upon the artists: parti, cularly in the direction of theology and its allegorical manifesta, tions. The Sistine Chapel itself provides, as Professor Wind points out below,[1] no inconsiderable a commentary on contemporary philosophical and religious literature. And why, when there are such strong local traditions among the artists, is there a far greater measure of uniformity and centralization in literature? Along the two parallel lines of Latin and vernacular, the beginnings of a unified language in poetry were already becoming apparent by

[1] *Infra*, pp. 312–27.

the end of the fourteenth century, and in the best Tuscan tradition. In Latin, the humanism of the *Quattrocento* has often been condemned for producing an artificial language: but the Latin of the humanists is not just the aping of classical forms: it exists, at its best, as a noble means of expression in its own right.[1] In the vernacular, if there was chivalrous epic, there were also the *Canti di ballo* written by men like Lorenzo de' Medici and Politian which concentrate, as one writer here says, 'on a radiant life-giving joy, which they find in love'.[2] The Principate was a great, but not by any means the sole, employer of humanists, artists and craftsmen: the Strozzi could vie with the Medici, and within a leading family different members would specialize in different branches of art: Cosimo de' Medici would befriend the 'royal art of architecture' as well as the bronze foundry, while painting was left to his sons Piero and Giovanni:[3] to be a universal arbiter of taste was not claimed by many—Lorenzo is one of the exceptions —though artistic versatility in execution was widespread. The 'great and learned in Italy' (to describe them as such), people like Leonello d'Este, Cosimo, Cyriac of Ancona's patron Eugenius IV, Pietro Donato bishop of Padua, Leonardo Bruni, had a range of taste that proclaimed not only the connoisseur but also the antiquarian. The true antiquarians, perhaps, belong to the sixteenth rather than to the fifteenth century: bishop Antonio Agustin, the Spanish Auditor of the Rota, or Cyriac of Ancona whom one of our contributors calls the 'archetype of the peripatetic early Renaissance antiquary'.[4] Interestingly enough, it was rather the Italian academies of the *Quattrocento* that led outside Italy to the growth of foundations which had as one of their results the study of the national past as much as of the philosophy of the day. If debates on the active and the contemplative life and the dignity of men aroused enthusiasm, so also did Italian studies of classical archaeology, especially among German humanists, who believed that their own past could be rescued from oblivion thanks to Italian methods. The learned academy

[1] *Infra*, pp. 357–63.
[2] *Infra*, p. 334.
[3] *Infra*, p. 297.
[4] *Infra*, p. 468.

may be one of the more important contributions of Italian humanists.

A great civilization is not built upon magnificence alone. Self-
denial, forethought and forbearing are needed, qualities which
historians are not always ready to concede to the makers of the
Italian Renaissance.

'Patience serves as a protection against wrong as clothes do
against the cold. For if you put on more clothes as the cold increases it will have no power to hurt you. So in like manner you
must grow in patience when you meet with great wrongs and
they will be powerless to vex your mind.'

'Intellectual passion drives out sensuality.'

'You can have neither a greater nor a less dominion than that
over yourself.'

'Thou, O God, dost sell unto us all good things at the price of
labour.'

These passages, as all will recognize, are found in the notebooks of Leonardo da Vinci.

Denys Hay

ITALY AND BARBARIAN EUROPE

The French attack of 1494 was regarded by many Italians at the time and shortly after as a 'barbarian' invasion—the first of a fresh series. The purpose of the following pages is to ask with what justification the Italians regarded the situation in this light, to examine briefly the political and cultural relations of the peninsula and the rest of Europe, and to survey some of the evidence for the use and significance of the term 'barbarian' in the Renaissance period.

The catalogue of the invasions of Italy is a long one. In histori⁄ cal times it starts with the Gauls, whose sack of Rome in 390 B.C. was often remembered by the French and Italians of the fifteenth and sixteenth centuries. The third century B.C. saw the Punic wars, culminating in Hannibal's descent on north Italy. There then ensued some centuries when Italy was free from outside attack, at the enormous price of devoting most of her energy to containing the turbulent migratory peoples of the north.

The collapse of the Empire under the pressure of attack from German and Slav tribes was, of course, the barbarian invasion *par excellence*. In the fourth and fifth centuries the peninsula suc⁄ cumbed to the invading Goths and Vandals. Italy was for a time divided between German masters and Greek governors, respon⁄ sible to the emperor at Constantinople. And then, after the Lombard influx of the sixth century and the failure of the Greeks to make good their reconquest, the peninsula finally entered on its career as a group of distinct territories, bound only by history to the universal state which had once been centred on Rome.

The Italian Middle Ages are remarkable for the repeated invasions of the peninsula by outside princes and peoples—

remarkable, that is to say, by comparison with other regions of the Continent. The Moslems, it is true, conquered much of Spain and invaded France; Hungarian horsemen ravaged Germany and occasionally terrorized more distant areas; the Danes conquered half of England and the Normans all of it. But when all is said and done the subsequent history of Spain, Germany, France and England is remarkably self-contained. Spain admittedly had her *Reconquista*: but this was mainly an internal affair. Germany spread slowly east and north; and subsequently some German areas were lost in the later Middle Ages—but they were lost spontaneously and not by foreign attack. France and England may seem exceptional, for a French prince led French forces on English soil in the early thirteenth century and in the later Middle Ages Edward III and Henry V successfully invaded France. Yet the French attack on England was negligible and the Hundred Years War in the event was to give the English only a fugitive superiority in France: only for some thirty years in the fourteenth century and for about as long in the fifteenth century was France seriously debilitated by invasion: civil war was another matter in both France and England, and, indeed, explains in each country the foreign invasions to which we have referred.

Very different was the experience of the principalities which emerged from the Dark Ages in Italy. Carolingian intervention culminated in the assumption of the imperial title by Charle-magne in 800: thereafter the Franks and later the Germans had a constitutional interest in the politics of the peninsula. Italy was the *regnum Italicum*, her crown the diadem on the head of an emperor who was king of Germany. The eleventh and twelfth centuries witnessed the repeated attempts of German monarchs to make good their claims south of the Alps, and of popes to frustrate the effective power of rulers whom they rightly considered to be their principal rivals: in the process the south of Italy and Sicily were conquered by Norman knights. From this competition between pope and emperor for the political control of Italy other princes acquired an interest in intervention. The Hohenstaufen, rulers of south Italy in the early thirteenth century, were so great a threat to the papacy that the Angevins were encouraged to undertake the destruction of Frederick II and his descendants. In their turn the Aragonese ousted the Angevins from Sicily and aimed intermittently at securing Naples as well. By the end of the thirteenth century Germans, French and Spaniards all had ambitions, fortified by what they considered to be legal rights, in the divided and subdivided peninsula.

To this tale of invasions the fourteenth and fifteenth centuries were to add others. Imperial pretensions were, it is true, of less moment than they had been: the Italian expeditions of Henry VII (1310–13) and Lewis IV (1327–30) cannot be regarded as con-stituting a threat comparable to the interventions of Barbarossa; and the later appearances of emperors south of the Alps were even less pretentious. But north of Rome republics and tyrants still looked to the emperor as a source of *de jure* authority, south of Rome the Aragonese dynasty strove to extend its control from Sicily to Naples and a fresh generation of Angevins was prepared to pledge its resources, and at times the resources of the French king, in an effort to oust the Spaniards from the *Regno*. The popes continued their policy of enlisting foreign support to resist all native attempts at a general superiority in Italy. Established as they were at Avignon during most of the fourteenth century, and then weakened by two generations of bitter schism, the popes were, indeed, more prone than ever they had been to sacrifice Italy to the conquests of non-Italian princes. The French pope, Clement VII, in 1379 constituted the bulk of the Papal States into the 'kingdom of Adria' and granted it to Louis of Anjou. Earlier popes had been willing to bribe non-Italian princes to protect the lands and power of the Church in Italy by grants and privileges elsewhere in the peninsula: the dismemberment of these very lands was a much more radical step.

Clement VII was a Frenchman, whose only hope of obtaining control in Italy was by force of French arms; his 'kingdom of Adria' proved a chimaera. But the Italian popes who opposed him, and their successors after the schism ended in 1417, main-tained the old policy of dividing in order to rule, and of alliance with foreign kings. What was different about the fifteenth century was that a number of powerful Italian princes were now on the scene—bigger figures than their fourteenth-century prototypes, with the prospect of longer tenure of power, with larger resources and a correspondingly advanced sense of political opportunity and even of political responsibility. Cosimo and Lorenzo de' Medici, Filippo Maria Visconti and Lodovico Sforza, Alfonso V and Ferrante may not have disposed of the same wealth as Venice, but for decades at a time they enjoyed a stability of power not unlike that of the Republic of St. Mark.

Yet the existence of principalities on this scale of course carried with it the association of Italian rulers with contemporary princes outside Italy. The Aragonese were in any event tied to Sicily and later to Naples; Florence had her traditional association with France; the Visconti and the Sforza looked at both Aragon and France with apprehension, and were even concerned to keep when possible on good terms with the Empire. In view of all this the events of 1494 are something of an anticlimax, for the up-heaval had nearly occurred more than once already. In 1447, when Filippo Maria Visconti died, the Milanese inheritance lay open to attack: and attack came. Alfonso V moved north, Charles VII east and Frederick III, though in no state to move anywhere, asserted his claim as overlord: that Sforza was vic-torious in 1450 in large part because he deflected French activity towards Naples is a further anticipation of 1494. Alfonso's death in 1458 was productive of further moves similar to those that occurred when Ferrante died, for Alfonso was followed in Naples only by Ferrante; Sicily was linked to Aragon and the Spaniards were once more an outside power so far as the south of the penin-sula was concerned. From this point onwards French and Spanish intrigue in Italy mounted in intensity and effectiveness: at any moment general war might have resulted; 'only deliberate avoid-ance of armed intervention on the part of Louis XI and Anne of Beaujeu had prevented any one of the quarrels of the last twenty years from culminating in a French invasion'.[1]

[1] C. M. Ady, 'Florence and North Italy', *Cambridge Medieval History*, viii, 218.

The invasion of 1494 and the ensuing wars in Italy were admittedly a formidable change from the intermittent support given earlier by the French crown to the Italian claims of Orleans and Anjou. But this should not blind us to the constant activity of foreign troops in fifteenth-century Italy. The soldiers of France, Spain and Germany were no strangers to Italy long before 1494. The predatory actions of the Swiss in the Milanese date from 1412 and were regularly renewed: it was no accident that after Lodi the Swiss were included in the Italian League of 1455. As for France the catalogue of Angevin expeditions is long and only broken in the 1480's when the claims of René passed to the French crown: the political revolutions at Genoa are a measure of this French participation in Italian warfare. Alfonso V's control in Naples had been backed by military forces which were predominantly Catalan.

War had thus involved Italy deeply with her neighbours, and over the centuries had united the fortunes of the states of the peninsula with the fortunes of the rest of Europe. Italy's indebtedness to her neighbours in a more general sense are no less striking, although the convention that Italy in the Renaissance was the benefactress of mankind tends to make them seem less important.

Socially, the structure of the Italian commune was undoubtedly an original creation. But the bulk of the land was, even in the later Middle Ages, organized on a predominantly rural plane, revolving round, not cities, but lords of land. In all that pertained to feudalism and monarchy Italians were pupils of the Franks and not their masters. Gothic and Lombard invaders doubtless laid the foundations of the Italian feudal world, but the bonds thus created were renewed and extended by the activities of the German emperors in the north and in the south by the Normans and Angevins. A confused memory of these influences lingers on in Machiavelli:

'E la Italia, poi che la fu in mano de' Franciosi, mutò in parte forma e ordine, per avere preso il papa nel temporale piú autorità, e avendo quegli condotto in essa il nome de' conti e de' marchesi, come prima da Longino, esarco di Ravenna, vi erano stati posti i nomi de' duchi.'[1]

This exotic terminology, indeed, gained ground as time went on: however bourgeois they sometimes were by origin, the counts and marquises of Renaissance Italy pay unconscious tribute to the unity of Italy and the rest of medieval Christendom.

Italy was even more indebted in the cultural field. For the two centuries running from Abelard to Ockham, France was the mother of scholarship and letters. From France radiated out that interest in literature which has been called the twelfth-century Renaissance. In France developed philosophical and theological studies which culminated in the thirteenth-century enthronement of rational speculation as the highest form of university activity. To this Italy contributed little but Italians much. Save for Bologna, the story of the Italian universities in the central Middle Ages is not of much moment and it is hard to see how Aquinas, or Bonaventure, or Marsilio of Padua, could have displayed their talents in their homeland as well as they did in Paris. And Bologna, where civil law was the one great achievement of higher education in Italy, was a centre from which northern Europe learned, at the least, as much as Italy.

In no field was northern influence more marked in Italy than in vernacular literature. Italy could boast no native Italian literature as old as French, German or Spanish. The court of the German Frederick II was the first centre of Italian poetry, the poetry of the 'Sicilian School'; the great fructifier of Italian genius was French, and more particularly Provençal. In a very real sense Italian literature was provoked by the more mature linguistic development of the north. The debt was not merely linguistic but extended to style and subject-matter. A great range of Italian literature, from lyrics to *novelle*, bears the imprint of French inspiration; Boiardo, Ariosto, Folengo, Tasso were all poets of stories which had been born and developed in France, in the period when France could claim to be the medium of the *gesta*

[1] *Istorie Fiorentine,* i, xi (ed. Carli, i, 29).

Dei, when her kings, dukes and counts were the ideal types of Christian secular society.[1]

In the field of the fine arts Italy was also extraordinarily indebted to her neighbours. Sixteenth-century Italians readily conceded both the superior religious sentiment and the technical innovations of Flemish painters. This, however, is only a small part of northern influences which, in and after the thirteenth century, began power-fully to affect peninsular art and architecture, hitherto dominated by Byzantium. From this bondage Italian genius was released by the Gothic. The road which was to lead, through Giotto and Masaccio, to Leonardo and Michelangelo, begins in France.

In war and in peace the peoples of Italy had thus been, more perhaps than other countries of Europe, moulded by contact with their neighbours.[2] Yet these neighbouring peoples were described as 'barbarians' by many Italians at the end of the fifteenth century. What is the history of the term 'barbarian'? What did it imply for an Italian at this time?

Barbarian to a Greek signified one whose culture and language were not Greek. As taken over by the Romans the exclusive term was given a somewhat wider meaning: it was applied to those who dwelt beyond the bounds of Roman society, beyond the frontiers of the Empire; in a narrower sense it was applied to grammatical error.

These concepts had an extraordinarily prolonged career. In the Eastern Empire the contempt for all that was non-Greek sur-vived the barbarian invasions, the loss of the Greek provinces in the west, and the shrinkage of Byzantine power in the Balkans and Asia Minor. Anna Commena in the eleventh century still treats the Franks contemptuously as barbarians[3] and so describes on one occasion the spiritual leader of the west, the pope.[4] This

---

[1] Cf. P. O. Kristeller's remarks in *Studies in Renaissance Thought and Letters* (Rome, 1956), pp. 553–83, and especially pp. 555–6, 575–6.

[2] Cf. G. Volpe, *Momenti di Storia Italiana* (Florence, 1925), pp. 303 ff.

[3] See G. Buckler, *Anna Commena* (London, 1929), pp. 440–1.

[4] Ibid., p. 308, n. 2.

arrogant superiority was one of the minor symptoms of the tensions which divided the Christian world into two.

In the west the influence of Christianity made inroads on the simple antithesis, Roman or Italian and Barbarian.[1] The pressure of the German and Slav tribes in the third, fourth and fifth centuries was at first capable of being viewed in these terms, for it was the Roman world which was Christian: the barbarians were pretty much the same as non-Christians at this stage. But it was a stage which did not last. Soon the barbarians of the north were converted and, conscious of their own barbarism, tended to weaken or extend the expression to mean, not only non-Italian, but also non-Christian. By the tenth century the chancery of the German kings was regularly issuing charters which referred to the *Christian* and *Barbarian* parts of the kingdom; thus Otto III made a grant to the merchants of Magdeburg allowing them to traffic *ubique in nostro regno, non solummodo Christianis, sed etiam barbaricis regionibus*.[2] William of Malmesbury can even make the pope at the Council of Clermont deny Christianity to the barbarous peoples of Europe: 'Who could term Christian those barbarians who in their distant islands dwell in the frozen ocean, living like beasts?'[3] And Roger Bacon goes even further and makes barbarian and rational the poles of opposition—a

[1] See the article 'Barbari' in *Enciclopedia Italiana*, vi, 123-4.

[2] See article cit. for reference. The thesis of this article is disputed by Rodolfo de Mattei, 'Sul concetto di barbaro e barbarie nel medio evo', *Studi de Storia e Diritto in onore di Enrico Besta*, iv (Milan, 1939), 483-501, who tries to prove that for all practical purposes the Roman distinction between Italian and barbarian survived and was current throughout the medieval period. He shows, indeed, that all the citations of the *Enciclopedia* author are equivocal save those referring to the German kings; but he shows that in Germany, where the distinction mattered, it was almost common form (p. 497), a point which goes against him. But the *Enciclopedia* writer and his critic have by no means surveyed all the evidence—and it cannot be presented here in any detail. A point to be remembered is the existence of Barbary—a geographical reminder of ethnical barbarism. Another development of significance is the word 'brave', *bravus, bravo*. It seems likely that this derives ultimately from *barbarus*. See W. Meyer-Lübke, *Romanisches etymologisches Wörterbuch*, 3rd ed. (Heidelberg, 1935), p. 78.

[3] Malmesbury, Rolls Ser. ii, 395.

reasonable extension of meaning to be made in the thirteenth century when rationalism and Christianity were more closely bound together than ever before or since.[1] The Italian Balbi in his dictionary (1286) defines *barbarus* as *crudelis, incultus, austerus, stolidus, et est nomen crudelitatis et austeritatis.* 'Formerly,' he goes on, 'all races were termed barbarous save the Greeks and Latins.'[2]

Admittedly an equation of Christianity with civilization or rationality on the one hand and an assumption that it is opposed to barbarism on the other, brings the use of the term barbarian very close in spirit to the original sense which it had for the classical world. And that sense was far from being neglected in the Middle Ages. In the patristic period the concept was naturally kept alive, and it is also found in many Dark Age writers.[3] Among the texts of the schoolmasters Roman literary values were remembered, and many a clerk must have re-echoed Einhard's modest self-description: *homo barbarus, et in Romana locutione perparum exercitatus.*[4] The grammarians, indeed, developed still further the ancient literary usage of 'barbarism'. For the Roman a literary barbarism was essentially a spoken error; *barbarolexis* an error in the form of a word. Very early in the Middle Ages these meanings shift and Isidore of Seville can explain that 'barbarism is the wrong spelling or pronunciation of a word', *barbarolexis* 'when a word of a barbarian language is introduced into Latin'.[5] These terms become firmly embedded in medieval grammatical theory and are repeated down the centuries by educationists:[6] Balbi naturally devotes far more space in the *Catholicon* to *barbarismus* and derivative critical words than he does to *barbarus*. *Latinitas* remained the opposite of literary barbarism, as it had been for the Romans.[7]

---

[1] *Opus Majus*, ed. Bridges, 1, 301.
[2] *Catholicon* Johannis Januensis (Lyons, 1489), s.v.
[3] See R. de Mattei's very useful survey, quoted above.
[4] *Vita Karoli*, proem.
[5] *Etymologiarum*, ed. W. M. Lindsay (Oxford, 1911), lib. i, xxxii, 1, 2.
[6] John of Salisbury, *Metalogicon*, trans. D. D. McGarry (Berkeley, 1955), p. 52.
[7] C. S. Baldwin, *Medieval Rhetoric and Poetic* (New York, 1928), p. 216.

By the fourteenth century barbarian had thus come to mean someone who was non-Christian (with an associated lack of civilization and rationality), at another level, a writer of bad Latin, and, also an ancient sense, one who was outside the cultural world of Rome. In the Italy of the fourteenth century this last meaning, the original sense of the word, was to be given again its full weight. The Italian patriot of the period was taught by Petrarch to view his northern neighbours under a rubric to which the worst associations were conveyed. For Petrarch in poetry, and briefly and uncomfortably in practice for Cola di Rienzo, *Italia* emerged as the ultimate terrestrial loyalty. The peninsula, cut off by God from the *rabies barbarica* of the north by the *Alpes aerias, barbarico oppositas furori*, was the home of all that made life kind, the heart of a Church which was literally Roman.[1] This attitude was not only displayed by Petrarch in his Latin writings: it was also Petrarch in glowing vernacular indignation—a more potent and influential matter altogether. The famous canzone 'Italia mia' is a hymn to the concept of an Italy which needs only domestic peace for the release of ancient valour, the expulsion of foreign barbarians. Written in the mid-1340's,[2] these verses expressed a position which only strengthened as time went on and as the scholarly discipline of the humanists was diffused through Italy.

In the next generation we find Guelf Florence at war with a papacy still absent from Italy. According to the Florentines, the French pope was now flooding the peninsula with foreign mercenary soldiers as well as with brutal and grasping French priests. The war of the 'Otto Santi' went far to precipitating a general use of barbarian for the foreigner in current Florentine political jargon and the pages of the official letters written in 1376 by Coluccio Salutati, who had just become chancellor, are full of a spirit which identified Florence with Italy, Italy with

[1] To Urban V, 1366, *Sen.* vii, 1; *Epistolae Selectae*, ed. A. F. Johnson (Oxford, 1923), pp. 165–6.

[2] For the date of 'Italia mia' see *Rime*, ed. G. Carducci and S. Ferrari (Florence, 1924), pp. 202–3.

Latinitas and barbarism with the French and the English mer
cenaries.[1]

'Italy', Florence informed the Romans, 'by the efforts of your
ancestors was mistress of the world: we shall not tolerate her being
subdued by foreigners and barbarians.'[2] The Italian company of
St. George was thanked by the *signoria* a little later: 'God made
the barbarians cowardly and you bold and strong . . . you deserve
to be called the liberators of Italy.'[3] Despite a very different view
point, much the same attitude is displayed by Pier Paolo Vergerio:
'There is no room in Italy for barbarians'—'Italy which in reputa
tion and in fact stands out above all other nations.'[4]

This view of the Italian past was confirmed by the sober scholar
ship of Flavio Biondo, whose *Roma instaurata* and *Roma triumphans*
were supplemented by his *Italia illustrata* of 1453 and who viewed
the whole of Christendom from an Italian standpoint in his
history of the Middle Ages, the *Decades* (1440–52, first edition
1483). From these works later Italian historians drew the material
for a view of the past which constantly harked back to the golden
days of Rome. This is what lies behind the analysis by Machiavelli
of Italy's disunity—both in early times when popes caused the
attacks of barbarians[5] and in the fifteenth century when the hordes
again devastate the land;[6] it was for a redeemer, *un suo redentore,*
who would liberate Italy from *questo barbaro dominio*, that Machia
velli wrote his *Prince*.[7] This is what lies behind the sad description

---

[1] Cf. E. Duprè Theseider, *I papi di Avignone e la questione Romana* (Florence,
1939), pp. 178–9.

[2] M. Gherardi, 'La guerra dei Fiorentini con Papa Gregorio XI, detta la Guerra
degli Otto Santi', *Archivio Storico Italiano,* 3rd series, V, pt. ii (Florence, 1867),
35–131; appendix of documents, no. 140, in VII, pt. i (1868), 223.

[3] 11 May 1379. Printed in the appendix to F. T. Perrens, *Histoire de Florence,*
v, 473–4.

[4] 22 January 1391. P. P. Vergerio, *Epistolario*, ed. L. Smith, Fonti per la storia
d'Italia (Rome, 1934), pp. 46, 53: 'Quanto enim et nomine et re ceteris nationibus
clarior extat Italia, tanto magis, etc. . . . .' 'Indignetur et obstrepat quantumlibet
despecta barbaries: illi in Italia nullus locus est.'

[5] *Istorie Fiorentine,* ed. cit., i, 26.   [6] Ibid., ii, 4.

[7] Ed. L. A. Burd, p. 371; cf. F. Ercole, *Da Carlo VIII a Carlo V. La crisi della
libertà Italiana*, especially pp. 217–22.

by Guicciardini of the year 1494—*anno infelicissimo all' Italia, e in verità anno primo degli anni miserabili, perchè aperse la porta a innumerabili e oribili calamità.*[1] And this is why Guicciardini listed the expulsion from Italy of all the barbarians as one of the (probably unattain‚ able) desires of his life—

'Tre cose desidero vedere innanzi alla mia morte; ma dubito, ancora che io vivessi molto, non ne vedere alcuna: uno vivere di republica bene ordinato nella città nostra, Italia liberata da tutti e Barbari, e liberato il mondo dalla tirannide di questi scelerati preti.'[2]

The resulting picture, idealizing not only the place of Roman antiquity but the balance of power in Italy after the Peace of Lodi, entered the canon of Italian historical mythology. Over a century later Muratori practically repeats Guicciardini;[3] modern writers mostly follow the same pattern.

It is important to remember, on the other hand, that the Italian contemporaries of Biondo and Guicciardini did not all view Italy as a haven of culture threatened by a barbarous trans‚Alpine world. If they had done so no French king, however powerful, could have made headway for a moment. On the contrary, Italian politics were and remained essentially centred on local issues, and Italian political speculation thus remained, for all its penetration, curiously divorced from the 'Italia' to which so much lip service was paid. Of all the powers in the peninsula only the papacy could have been expected to take a broad view. And it would have been strange if the papal curia, traditionally bound to the service of Christendom, not of Italy, staffed as it still was with a fair number of 'barbarian' officials, had taken a consistently anti‚ barbarian line. This was, of course, changing and by the time of Leo X the curia was more homogeneously Italian: Paris de Grassis *does* use the term barbarian,[4] for example, while his

---

[1] *Storia d'Italia* (Paris, 1837), i, 127.

[2] *Ricordi*, no. 236: *Opere inedite*, ed. G. Canestrini (Florence, 1857), p. 154.

[3] *Annali d'Italia*, IX, 570: 'Cominciarono in quest' Anno i guai dell' Italia, guai di lunga durata', etc.

[4] Quoted Pastor, *History of the Popes*, trans. and ed. Antrobus, vi, 345.

predecessor as master of ceremonies, the Strassburger John Bur,
chard, does not—though violently hostile to the French.[1] And the
pope who bore the brunt of the first French attack was himself a
barbarian, the Borgia Alexander VI. Some small use does seem
to have been made of the concept of barbarian,Italian antithesis in
practical politics. Giovanni Bentivoglio in March 1494 urged
Ludovico Sforza's envoy to tell his master that 'we Italians should
not allow barbarian peoples to come between us especially as their
claws and teeth are long'.[2] Another occasion when practical men
put their thoughts and policies forward in this way was in the
debate at Venice in 1498 when Guicciardini reports Trevisan as
foreshadowing a possible alliance between the *casa di Austria*
and the French, 'a union of barbarians, eternal enemies of Italy'.[3]
Above all, for Julius II the notion of barbarian hostility seems to
have been a genuine inspiration. His 'Fuori i Barbari' was pro,
bably never spoken in so many words.[4] But he undoubtedly said
as much on more than one occasion[5] and when Guicciardini
analysed Julius's aims he made the same point: the pope's desire
di cacciare il re di Francia di tutto quello possedeva in Italia derived, he
wrote, either from the pope's harbouring an ancient grudge
against them, or because over the years his suspicions grew into
hate, or because he desired 'the glory of being the man who
liberated Italy from the barbarians'—*la cupidità della gloria di
essere stato, come diceva poi, liberatore d'Italia dai barbari.*[6] The same
desire (according to the same authority) inspired Leo X.[7]

But these examples are not impressive when set beside the
general indifference not only of Italian princes and governments,

[1] RR. II. SS., ed. Celani, p. 541: the Cardinal of Gurk has a lily carved in
his heart. Latin continued to be the language used within the Curia till 1480,
Pastor, i, 242 n.

[2] Quoted C. M. Ady, *The Bentivoglio of Bologna* (London, 1937), p. 114.

[3] *Storia d'Italia*, ed. cit., ii, 48; the basis of the hostility is 'la diversità degli
animi tra i Barbari e gl'Italiani', p. 49.

[4] Pastor, vi, 322 n.

[5] Pastor, loc. cit.; Creighton, *History of the Papacy*, v, 76–7.

[6] *Storia d'Italia*, iii, 159; note the qualification of 'poi'.

[7] Ibid., iv, 354.

but of many of the humanists themselves. Bernardo Rucellai's *De bello italico*, completed between 1506 and 1509,[1] does occasionally make play with Italy's *barbarus hostis*,[2] but this is not in any sense important for his frigid and efficient analysis of Charles VIII's relations with Italy. It is also salutary to remember that older usages of 'barbarian' were not entirely swept out in Renaissance Italy. Giovanni Rucellai, the father of Bernardo, used the word in a sense essentially opposed, not to Italian values, but to nonChristian values: he thanks God that he has made him 'a rational creature, a Christian, and not a Turk, a Moor or a barbarian'.[3] Marsilio Ficino's *exhortatio ad bellum contra barbaros* was intended to stir up resistance to the Turks.[4] The defence of Christendom was, in fact, in the hands of Balkan 'barbarians'.

In Italy, too, the technical, literary meaning of 'barbarous', noticed as a feature of medieval rhetorical teaching, was positively encouraged by the humanists. For them there was, it is true, a close association between the notion of linguistic propriety and general civility: the Romans' greatest achievement, said Valla, was their language.[5] As time went on there was an evercloser connection between *Latinitas* in its grammatical sense and Italian culture. Politian could urge a lively and living attitude to Latin composition: only slavish copying of a model author saved some little men from barbarism.[6] But within a generation Ciceronianism was all but triumphant in Italy, and the papacy encouraged this in its efforts to use scholarship as a prop for the Church.[7]

Fierce indeed were the diatribes launched against the defenders

---

[1] F. Gilbert, 'Bernardo Rucellai and the Orti Oricellari', *Journ. Warb. and Court. Institutes*, xii (1949), 111–12, note.

[2] B. Oricellarii, *De Bello Italico* (London, 1724), p. 3; cf. p. 100, 'barbari externique principes, quorum finibus Gallia continenter cingitur'.

[3] Zibaldone (1466), quoted W. H. Woodward, *Studies in Education during the age of the Renaissance* (Cambridge, 1906), p. 78.

[4] Kristeller, op. cit., p. 112 and n.

[5] Preface to the *Elegantiae, Prosatori Latini del Quattrocento*, ed. E. Garin (MilanNaples, 1952), pp. 594–601.

[6] Ibid., p. 902.

[7] G. Toffanin, *Storia Letteraria d'Italia: Il Cinquecento* (Milan, 1945), p. 16.

of the vernacular by those, like Lazzaro Bonamico, who regarded it as a barbarous corruption of Latin. Violent were the recrimina' tions against Longolius (Christophe Longueuil), the stranger from Malines who humbly sought Ciceronian perfection in Rome.[1] The papal plan to grant him official Roman citizenship provoked a storm against him which in 1519 drove him from the city in shame and despair: he was accused of having dared to compare Italy with France in an early work; of having praised Erasmus and Budé, who were barbarians; of having been bribed into visiting Italy in order to acquire the best books to take back to the barbarians, so that they could dispute Italian primacy; above all he was regarded in Rome of being guilty of being a barbarian himself. But the chief indignation of the poetasters and literary politicians was reserved for Erasmus, whose *Ciceronianus*, poking fun at the whole idea of an absolute Latin in the current Roman manner, was published in 1528. Erasmus's views were no secret before this: he had meditated his position from at least 1516,[2] and his argument that exaggerated Ciceronian diction was pagan and irreligious gave the ensuing debate added bitterness; for Italians it tended to put the author even more clearly in the Lutheran camp.[3]

The Italian *questione della lingua* in fact soon abandoned the sterile problem of whether Latin should be the sole vehicle of literature. Ciceronianism won, inside and outside Italy, but was confined to the limited field of Latin: Petrarchism played a similar role in the vernacular. This changed the conventional picture of Latin's unique place in the linguistic hierarchy. One finds, as early as the *Ercolano* of Benedetto Varchi (1560), an analysis of the term barbarian which is entirely devoid of the emotional over' tones to which the events of 1494 and later might have been supposed to contribute. In the dialogue Varchi divides all languages into certain basic categories and his interlocutor asks

[1] Ibid., pp. 22-5; R. Sabbadini, *Storia del Ciceronianismo* (Turin, 1885), pp. 52-7.

[2] Angiolo Gambaro, *Il Ciceronianus di Erasmo* (Turin, 1950), pp. 2-6.

[3] Ibid., pp. 41-7; Sabbadini, pp. 59-66.

why one of these divisions is not between barbarous tongues and the rest. Varchi replies:

'This word *barbaro* is equivocal and can signify more than one thing. Thus, when it refers to the spirit, a "barbarous man" means a "cruel man", a "brute of a man", with savage habits. When it refers to variations between regions, or their remoteness, *barbaro* means any one who is not of your own country, and is practically equivalent to "strange", or "foreign". But when it refers to speech, which was its first and proper meaning, *barbaro* is applied to all those who do not speak one of the "noble" languages, or who, though using one of them, do not obey the rules and instructions of the grammarians.'[1]

And Varchi adds that he could not exclude Hebrew, French, Spanish, German, *e molte altre* from the list of languages in which style was possible.

With all of this the barbarians could agree. Were they not being told by Italians, who presumably should know, that as a result of the wars 'good literature, both Latin and Greek, was emptied out of Italy, and poured across the Alps into Germany, France, England and Scotland'?[2] Had they not embarked on their own campaign against barbarism? Erasmus had printed his *Antibarbarorum Libri* in 1520: but this, like the *Ciceronianus*, was an old story, going back to 1495.[3] In it Erasmus defended good literature as a worthy human purpose; the rest of his life was a

[1] *L'Ercolano* (ed. Milan, n.d.), pp. 111–12: 'Questo nome *barbaro* è voce equi-voca, cioè significa più cose, perciocchè, quando si riferisce all' animo, un uomo barbaro vuol dire un uomo crudele, un uomo bestiale e di costumi efferati; quando si riferisce alla diversità, o lontananza delle regioni, barbaro si chiama chiunque non è del tuo paese, ed è quasi quel medesimo che strano, o straniero; ma quando si riferisce al favellare, che fu il suo primo e proprio significato, barbaro si dice di tutti coloro, i quali non favellano in alcuna delle lingue nobili, o se pure favellano in alcuna d'esse, non favellano correttamente, non osservando le regole e gli ammaestramenti de' grammatici.'

[2] P. Vergil, *Anglica Historia*, ed. Hay (Camden Series, 1950), p. 145: 'Iisdem temporibus perfectae literae similiter latinae atque graecae ex Italia bellis nefariis exclusae, exterminatae, expulsáe, sese trans Alpes per omnem Germaniam, Galliam, Angliam, Scotiamque effuderunt.'

[3] *Opus epistolarum*, ed. Allen, i, 121 note.

commentary on the thesis that scholarship should be pure and compatible with a devout Christianity; barbarism for Erasmus was thus opposed to reason and Christianity, as we have met it already.[1]

In every northern country a campaign to secure a new curriculum, an attitude to letters comparable with that of the Italian humanist, was being waged in the sixteenth century.

'Emulate, noble men, the ancient nobility of Rome, which after taking over the empire of the Greeks, assimilated all their wisdom and eloquence, so much so that it is hard to decide whether it has equalled all the Greek discoveries and equipment of learning or surpassed them. In the same way you who have taken over the empire of the Italians should cast off repulsive barbarism and seek to acquire Roman culture.'[2]

Thus Conrad Celtis (Pickel) at Ingolstadt in 1492, speaking, as he said himself, as a 'manikin born as some say in the midst of barbarians and drunkards'[3] to an audience whose leaders the Italians would describe 'merely as the barbarians'. National sentiment doubtless helps to explain the vehemence with which the new programme was adovcated in the north.[4] But it spread because it answered other needs than a petty desire to score off the Italians. Its success was remarkable. In every northern country the victory of the humanist schoolmaster was complete, and, though there were few Guarinos or Vittorinos, Italy had no scholar of the stature of Erasmus. Even more significant, the main counter-attack to Erasmus's *Ciceronianus* was conducted by a Frenchman, Etienne Dolet, and a Frenchman by adoption, Julius Caesar Scaliger.[5]

.   .   .

[1] Above, p. 56.

[2] Conrad Celtis, *Selections*, ed. and trans. L. Forster (Cambridge, 1948), p. 43.

[3] Ibid., p. 37.

[4] See P. S. Allen, *The Age of Erasmus* (Oxford, 1914), pp. 264–8, and the collection of references to German-Italian hostility in the correspondence of Erasmus, *Opus Epist.*, iv, 280, line 67 note.

[5] Sabbadini, pp. 68–71.

For an honest Frenchman or Englishman the superiority of the Italian was far from evident, but Italian consciousness of superiority was not the only unpleasant feature of peninsular society. Lemaire de Belges (for example) found much to admire in Italian literature while thinking French literature just as good in different ways:[1] but he could not find Italian republicanism palatable, and hated the 'tyrants' at Venice.[2] No right-thinking barbarian in the north could find himself fond of the papacy, at all events until it had been crushed politically and rent by the Reformation, and the Leonine identification of civilization with papal Rome undoubtedly exacerbated an already tender situation. Yet the fact remains that, despite such antagonisms, we witness in the sixteenth century the adoption in the north, not only of an educational reform of Italian origin, but also an acceptance of those deeper changes in moral outlook which are coincident with humanism—the new attitude to the active life and to wealth which were hammered out in *Quattrocento* Italy.

The diffusion of the cultural achievements of Renaissance Italy thus proceeded in two ways: on the one hand the new pedantry spread among schoolmasters and scholars; on the other hand a new view of social obligations and rewards spread among the ruling classes.

As for the first, it needs little elaboration, save to point out that the process (somewhat as in Italy) moved from a Latin basis to a basis in both Latin and the vernaculars. The poets and dramatists learned humanity (or Latin) at school: they wrote in French or English. From the *rinascita del vero testo classico* the French movement, for instance, proceeded to the *culto del volgare*.[3] Joachim du Bellay argued in his *Deffence et illustration de la Langue Francoyse*, 'that the French language should not be called barbarous.'[4] There were contemporaries of du Bellay who went so

---

[1] *Concorde des deux Languages*, ed. Frappier, pp. 4–5; *Illustrations de Gaule*, ed. Stecher, i, 11.   [2] *Illustrations*, i, 7.

[3] See the admirable chapter in Franco Simone, *La Conscienza della rinascita negli humanisti Francesi* (Rome, 1949), pp. 91–157.

[4] Edited H. Chamard (1948), pp. 15–21.

far as to describe as 'barbarians' ink-horn terms', some of the neologisms involved in the latinized vernaculars. Montaigne, the best possible example of the effects of the new humanist education, brings us back to the sound moral division between civilized people and all the rest when in his *Essais* he reflects on cannibals.[1]

Montaigne was a burgess turned gentleman: it was through this mixture, and rather through the gentleman part of it than through the burgess part of it, that the essential changes in moral values referred to above were passed from Italy to the north. The most important single contribution to a diffusion of Italian values was Castiglione's *Courtier*. This is seen not merely in the translations which appeared (for example the French versions of 1537 and 1538, Hoby's English of 1561), or the printing outside Italy of the Italian text, or the turning of it into Latin for pedagogical purposes, but above all by the way in which it stimulated other countries to produce similar studies. Claude Chappuys and Philibert de Vienne in France, Sir Thomas Elyot and Roger Ascham in England (to name only a few) vulgarized and made local application of Castiglione and other Italian writers on education and manners.[2] Renaissance Italy, destroyed by the Barbarians politically and economically, was the victor in letters, social values, and, though it has not seen touched on here, the fine arts.

Yet the paradoxical truth is that what made possible in the first place the elaboration of the new Italian attitudes, just as what made possible later the transmission of these attitudes across the Alps, was precisely the divisions of Italian society which had provoked in the peninsula the use of the concept of *Italia* and the related idea of barbarism. The Tuscan and Lombard communities which produced a self-conscious bourgeois society, the small courts where Vittorino and Guarino taught, the Urbino of Castiglione are all peculiar to the Italian scene, and cannot be exactly paralleled elsewhere. Had Italian unity been accomplished in the fourteenth century as Dante and Petrarch hoped and had

[1] Ed. M. Rat, i, 234.
[2] Cf. A. Tilley, *Literature of the French Renaissance*, i, 48–9; W. H. Woodward, *Education during the Renaissance*, pp. 269–322.

the peninsula then embarked on the centralizing path of France, Spain and England, it is hard to see how the crystallization of the new moral and political values could have happened. The crisis of liberty so well analysed by Dr. Hans Baron[1] derived from a situation in which Florence was pitted against Milan, where what was viewed as politically and culturally essential reposed in a multiplicity of governments. It is equally evident that, had a congeries of genuine republics survived in fifteenth-century Italy, the Italian message would have penetrated much slower than it did among the French, the English and the rest. The Italian prince as patron of fine art and literature, as the centre of political and social activity, as the fount of a courtesy which could be readily adapted to chivalric traditions, was himself in every sense a product of the bourgeois environment: but he acted as a bridge over which ideas and attitudes could pass to the kings and gentry of the north. The price of the victory of the Italian Renaissance in European civilization was the existence in Italy of a variety of states: in helping to maintain such a situation by intervention and intrigue the 'barbarians' thus contributed directly to their ultimate absorption of new ways of thought and action.

As far as the antithesis between Italy and barbarism was concerned, the sixteenth century saw its end. It lingered on as an irritation to foreigners; but the foreigner was too firmly established in the peninsula, the political nullity of the country too self-evident, for Italian superiority to have genuine meaning. The 'Italianate' Englishman or Frenchman might be an object of fun or exasperation to his compatriots, but already in the pages of the *Courtier* Castiglione has to castigate Italians who ape the ways of France and Spain.[2] By a fresh *translatio litterarum* the home of literature and art was again to be France. And there Montesquieu calmly summarized the matters touched on in the preceding pages. Of the barbarians who had engulfed the Roman empire

[1] Hans Baron, *The Crisis of the Early Italian Renaissance*, 2 vols. (Princeton, 1955).

[2] *Il Cortegiano*, ed. Cian (1947), pp. 69–70, 174–5, 193.

he states: *ces peuples n'étaient point proprement barbares, puisqu'ils étaient libres.* Italy he describes as *une nation autrefois maîtresse du Monde, aujourd'hui esclave de toutes les autres.*[1] French *civilisation* is to replace Italian *civiltà.*[2] Barbarism is to become a necessary stage in the evolution of all mankind.

[1] *Lettres persanes,* no. cxxxvi.

[2] E. Benveniste, 'Civilisation: Contribution à l'histoire du mot', *Éventail de l'histoire vivante. Offert . . . à Lucien Febvre,* i, 47–54.

Roberto Weiss

ITALIAN HUMANISM IN WESTERN EUROPE: 1460–1520

Humanism started to assert itself in Italy in the age of Petrarch. During the last quarter of the fourteenth century its position was considerably consolidated, thanks mainly to the efforts of Coluccio Salutati, and to such an extent that the generation which followed that of Salutati included such great humanists as Poggio and Leonardo Bruni. During the first half of the fifteenth century humanism conditioned the intellectual climate of Italy. During the second half of this century Italian humanism reached its highest peaks and was able to show to a fascinated Europe not only new vistas in the interpretation of the classical world, but also the ways in which this interpretation could be brought to bear upon contemporary circumstances. Humanism was not to remain an Italian monopoly for very long. Contacts with other European countries soon made its achievement known across the Alps. It is therefore not surprising to find how already by the second half of the fifteenth century humanism had been able to secure more than one enthusiastic imitator outside Italy. What one might call the exportation of Italian humanism was made possible by a variety of causes. There were of course the many exchanges between Italy and the other countries of Europe. There was the fact that Rome was the headquarters of the papacy, which meant that crowds of ecclesiastics and laymen, many of whom were highly literate, resorted there to worship at the shrines of the apostles or transact business at the Curia, where the papal chancery had been entirely in humanist hands since the times of the Great Schism. Another factor that contributed to the spreading of humanism in foreign lands was that a large number of papal officials, many of whom had marked leanings towards humanist studies, when they were not humanists themselves, were con-tinually being sent abroad on missions, which often meant a stay of several years in a foreign country.[1] And besides all this there were also the many foreign students who came in considerable number to read for degrees at Italian universities and particularly at Padua and Bologna,[2] thus coming into contact with humanist teaching and humanist texts. Copies of such texts sent or brought over from Italy played also a considerable role in the spreading of humanist ideas. Finally several Italian humanists went to seek their fortune abroad or were sent there in some official capacity, and once outside Italy were often able to arouse an interest for their new brand of learning in some of those scholars with whom they came into contact.

Already during the second half of the fifteenth century a con-siderable number of Italian humanists were teaching in foreign countries. Invariably they taught rhetoric or lectured on such authors as Vergil or Terence. Only exceptionally they taught Greek, this being generally the monopoly of Byzantine refugees. The clearly superior elegance of their Latin made these humanists also sought by princes as secretaries or court poets, thus enabling them to exert often an influence scarcely inferior to that of their teaching colleagues. It is true that with the exception of the elder Beroaldo and Girolamo Aleandro, no first-rate humanist went to teach outside Italy or served at a foreign court. But what was second rate in a humanist-inflated Italy was definitely exceptional across the Alps, which certainly explains their success away from home and the influence of their teaching.

Visitors to Italy and Italian humanists outside Italy made the expansion of Italian humanism abroad a reality during the latter half of the fifteenth century. It would, however, be a mistake to

[1] For a picture of the humanist activity of a papal official abroad see for instance J. Haller, *Piero da Monte: ein gelehrter und päpstlicher Beamter des 15 Jahrhunderts* (Rome, 1941).

[2] See for instance R. J. Mitchell, 'English Student Life in Early Renaissance Italy', *Italian Studies*, vii (1952), pp. 62–81.

assume that Italian humanism once accepted was developed in an identical way in the various European countries. This was certainly not the case. Just as the new Italian attitude towards the humanities and what they implied was not taken over simultaneously throughout western Europe, so local circumstances in European countries were also very much instrumental in moulding the local exploitation of humanism. One feature of Italian humanism might be received enthusiastically in one country but not necessarily in another, where some different feature might instead prove more attractive. The aspects of Italian humanism which appealed in France or England were not necessarily the same which secured devotees in Germany or Spain.

An account of Italian humanism would hardly be possible within the limits of this paper.[1] It may nevertheless not be out of place to emphasize some of its more salient features. Not so much because they happened to be some of its salient features as because they assist us in perceiving what appealed and what was rejected across the Alps. Now if we view Italian humanism in its best period, that is to say during the second half of the fifteenth century, we cannot help being struck by its grip upon what was best in the intellectual life of the country. It is true that even in Italy a good deal of university teaching continued on traditional lines. But it is also true that even in the most conservative universities humanist teaching was welcomed and that humanists could be found lecturing side by side with old-fashioned Aristotelians. Rather than the universities, the real strongholds of humanism were generally the academies. But only generally, for at Ferrara the university was a humanist base and remained so even after the death of Guarino, and Politian and Pomponio Leto were university teachers. Still during the second half of the fifteenth century humanism in Rome means the Accademia Romana just as humanism in Florence means Ficino's Accademia Platonica and humanism in Naples the Accademia Pontaniana. Here one particular word should be said about Venice, whose 'Latin

---

[1] Here I may draw attention to an admirable account of Italian humanism recently published: C. Dionisotti, *Discorso sull' umanesimo italiano* (Verona, 1956).

Quarter' was some twenty-five miles away at Padua. In Venice the situation was different. Until the last decades of the fifteenth century, Venetian humanism was dominated by amateurs drawn from the ruling class. The history of Venetian humanism shows a striking series of amateurs, with figures of the calibre of Leonardo Giustinian, Gregorio Correr and Francesco and Ermolao Barbaro. The humanist activity of school teachers in Venice became insignificant after Guarino's departure in 1419, while the school of Rialto remained rigidly confined to philosophical learning of the traditional kind.[1] Towards the end of the century there was however a change. The publishing activity of Aldus led to the establishment of an academy, where professionals and amateurs found themselves on a similar footing and where Greek literature was what Platonism was to the Florentine and archaeology to the Roman academy.

The second half of the fifteenth century witnessed the final conquest of Greek and the discovery of Greek poetry, hitherto hardly studied at all. Similarly efforts were also made then in Italy towards the mastery of Hebrew and some oriental languages, and such a mastery found its humanist culmination not in biblical studies, where Giannozzo Manetti had already indicated new ways, but in the esoteric encyclopaedism of Pico. By then humanism had chosen not one but both the ways open to it, that of philology (and by this is meant 'philologia', not linguistics) and that of philosophy. This did not mean that the choice of one was a bar to the other. Cristoforo Landino wrote for instance the *Disputationes Camaldulenses*, but was also the author of commentaries on Vergil and Dante. Philological humanism reached its highest peak with Politian and Ermolao Barbaro. The *Miscellanea* of Politian and the *Castigationes Plinianae* of Ermolao Barbaro were, however, also the swan-songs of philological humanism in Italy. For Parrasio did not fulfil his early promise, while Crinito's *De honesta disciplina* has everything that there is in

[1] For this important school, completely unknown until recently, see B. Nardi, 'Letteratura e cultura veneziana nel Quattrocento' in the collective volume *Civiltà veneziana del Quattrocento* (Firenze, 1957), pp. 101-45.

Politian's *Miscellanea* except Politian's genius. It was after a series of swift strokes of doom had deprived Italy of Politian, Pico, and Ermolao Barbaro within less than two years that the *trans-latio studii* started. Already in the early sixteenth century humanist supremacy had crossed the Alps. The true and worthy successor of Politian's *Miscellanea* was not a treatise by an Italian but the *De asse* by Budé. It was, however, Politian and Barbaro that gave a programme to European humanism, just as Valla had imposed his stylistics upon it a generation earlier. In Italy the fate of philological humanism was instead to turn into the flam-boyant rhetoric of a Tomeo or an Amaseo or in the narrow antiquarianism of the pupils of Pomponio Leto. In a way these two aspects, rhetoric and antiquarianism, were also those which had made philological humanism possible. For the real masters of Politian and Ermolao Barbaro were Valla and Biondo, that is to say the highest exponents of the new grammar and the new archaeology.

Philosophical humanism shows a direct linear descent from Petrarch via Salutati and Bruni, both of whom left treatises on moral philosophy which became immediately very popular throughout Europe. Its horizons were narrow at first. Valla en-larged them and gave them new strength, until the new mastery of Greek set upon satisfying the pressing demands for a complete Plato and a better Aristotle for those who had no Greek. The quarrel between the devotees of Plato and those of Aristotle which raged in the fourteen-sixties was ultimately a quarrel between two gifted Byzantine refugees. Still the quarrel nearly split the humanist world of Italy, where Plato found an inferior Aquinas in Ficino. But humanist thought could not remain fully satisfied with what was ultimately an antiquarian approach to philosophy. New issues had arisen and the need of discussing them was clearly imperative. Little wonder, then, that debates on the active and contemplative life and the dignity of man aroused as much enthusiasm in humanist circles as the appreciation of the subtler shades in the speculation of Plato and Aristotle. After Ficino the christianiza-tion of Plato was carried further by Egidio da Viterbo, the great

Augustinian theologian. On the other hand the true followers of Ermolao Barbaro's Aristotelianism were to be found across the Alps and were called Ximenes and Lefèvre d'Etaples, while in Italy Vernia, Pomponazzi and Achillini represented instead a traditional Aristotelianism with a new look and quite independent of humanist tradition. And if from philosophy we turn to politics, one might well ask what was humanist influence there. The answer here is that we are forced to distinguish. Apart from the fact that the political treatises by humanists are medieval in out-look and only humanistic in presentation and that the true humanists in this field chose to write in the everyday language and begin with Machiavelli, it is possible to see that the stylistic and rhetorical preoccupations of humanism soon eliminated the *dictamen* and what it stood for from chancery practice. Style was power or at any rate it was thought to be power. Hence from the days of Petrarch onwards very few were the Italian chanceries free from humanist domination. The series of Florentine chan-cellors from Salutati down to Marcello Adriani shows some among the best names in Florentine humanism, such as Bruni, Marsuppini, Poggio, Scala and so on. The same applies to Visconti-Sforza Milan or Aragonese Naples, where King Ferrante's secretary, that is to say chief minister, was first Antonello Petrucci, who had learnt his letters from Valla, and then no one less than Pontano. Humanism as translated into chancery practice was used to uphold the established powers. The inspira-tion of classical antiquity, on the other hand, would often lead to a yearning for a freedom hardly known and even less under-stood. Already the Caesar-Scipio controversy between Guarino and Poggio,[1] where Guarino meant Leonello d'Este and where the issue was really monarchy versus republic, had shown that the humanist camp had not given up altogether what were believed to be the freedom ideals of the ancients. While the un-doubted fact that all the great political conspiracies of the Renais-sance, from that of Stefano Porcari down to that of Pier Paolo Boscoli, were inspired by a humanist ideology, shows quite

[1] E. Walser, *Poggius Florentinus* (Leipzig-Berlin, 1914), pp. 164-80.

clearly the readiness to translate such an ideology into action. But on the whole revolutionary activity was an exception in Italian humanism, whose typical representative was rather the court poet, whose productions, whether in Latin or in Italian, swamped literary production during the last decades of the fifteenth and the first decades of the sixteenth century.

Geographical and other reasons made it inevitable for France to succumb to humanism at a comparatively early date. Humanist influence was already evident in France during the late fourteenth century, when the traditions of Petrarch were continued by such scholars as Gontier and Pierre Col, Jean de Montreuil and Nicholas de Clemanges.[1] But this humanist activity, which had started so promisingly, did not reach a second generation, being instead submerged in the desolation brought about by the last phases of the Hundred Years War: and although French churchmen with a taste for the humanities were certainly not lacking in the court of Rome (Cardinal Jean Jouffroy was not the only case), it would be rash to talk again of humanist activity in France before the fourteen/sixties. The change in the situation was brought about then by mainly two things. On one side by an appetite for new intellectual horizons, which was certainly felt in the more enlightened circles of Paris University, and secondly by the more normal conditions following the end of the Hundred Years War. Accordingly the teaching of Gregorio Tifernate in Paris could scarcely have started at a more opportune moment, and it is certainly not exaggerated to say that it and it alone was responsible for the new wave of interest in Italian humanism. It is true that Gregorio's teaching in Paris only lasted from 1456-8.[2] These two years were nevertheless quite sufficient to arouse interest not only in Greek, then utterly for/gotten despite the existence of an unbroken tradition of Greek scholarship dating from Carolingian times at the monastery of

---

[1] On this see A. Coville, *Gontier et Pierre Col et l'humanisme en France au temps de Charles VI* (Paris, 1934).

[2] L. Delaruelle, 'Une vie d'humaniste du XVe siècle: Gregoire Tifernas', *Mélanges d'archéologie et d'histoire*, xix (1899), 9–33.

St. Denis,[1] but also in the humanist rhetoric of the Italians. It is therefore not surprising to find that two Parisian masters who had sat at Gregorio's feet, Robert Gaguin and Guillaume Fichet, were responsible for the acceptance of the new values from Italy in Paris. What really attracted them most was not so much Greek or the new approach to the classics, as the new humanist rhetoric, which mainly differed from the traditional one in being directly based on classical sources. Humanist rhetoric was accordingly what they aimed to master and divulge, while their main pre-occupation was the conquest of a more polished Latin style and a less barbarous versification in that language. Within a university divided by the struggle between Nominalists and Realists, Fichet and Gaguin stood as the upholders of a new formal elegance, of this but of nothing else, and it seems doubtful that their example and enthusiasm would have been sufficient had no fresh in-fluences arrived from Italy. Fichet and Gaguin together with Angelo Cato, the Italian-born archbishop of Vienne, had succeeded in establishing a climate not unfavourable to humanism in France, which in turn made the employment of other Italian humanists as lecturers a possibility. Some twenty years after Gregorio Tifernate a humanist far abler, the elder Beroaldo, was teaching in Paris.[2] Here Beroaldo's successors, Fausto Andrelini, Girolamo Balbo, and Cornelio Vitelli, secured a quick notoriety with their unseemly quarrels.[3] Balbo and Vitelli soon vanished from Paris. Andrelini instead clung to his post and through his office of poet laureate was able to introduce new standards of taste in court circles, which also made possible the appreciation of the new humanist historiography which Paolo Emilio of Verona was able to introduce into France.

Italian rhetoric and its by-products alone would not have

[1] See R. Weiss, 'Lo studio del greco all' abbazia di San Dionigi durante il medio evo', *Rivista di Storia della Chiesa in Italia*, vi (1952), 426–38.

[2] J. B. Wadsworth, 'Filippo Beroaldo the Elder and the Early Renaissance in Lyons', *Medievalia et Humanistica*, Fasc. 11 (1957), pp. 78–89.

[3] The best account of these quarrels is P. S. Allen, 'Hieronymus Balbus in Paris', *English Historical Review*, xvii (1902), 417–28.

succeeded in inserting the humanist approach into the cultural structure of France. Here the indifferent teaching of the third-rate Greek George Hermonymos proved nevertheless not quite valueless. Not so much because of his very few accomplishments, as because he was able to open a little wider those gates of Greek learning which Gregorio Tifernate had unfastened. His greatest merit was to have made Budé Greek-conscious, though the amount which Budé secured from Hermonymos was negligible. Who really turned Budé into an accomplished Greek scholar were instead the italianized Greek John Lascaris, who went to Paris after graduating through the Florence of Lorenzo de' Medici and the Venice of Aldus, and Girolamo Aleandro, whose popularity in Paris was soon immense, although his inaugural lecture alone lasted for two hours and a half![1] With such masters what was best in Italian humanism was certainly available in early sixteenth-century France. It would, however, be mistaken to assume that the humanism of the Italians had been solely brought into France by humanist teachers. Even before the Italian wars Frenchmen went to Italy to study with considerable results. Politian was certainly not an unknown name in France; nor indeed was Ermolao Barbaro, whose approach to Aristotle secured quickly more than one French devotee. As for Pico della Mirandola, apart from everything else, his sojourn in France from 1485-8[2] had alone been sufficient to make more than one culti-vated Frenchman aware of his achievement. To say that by 1520 Italian humanist values had become naturalized in France is not exaggerated. What was issued by the printing presses, and not only by those of Paris, would be sufficient to prove this. But besides this, the achievement of a scholar like Budé is enough to show the legacy of Politian at its best. Budé was exceptional. It would therefore be rash to take him as a typical example of early sixteenth-century humanist culture in France, just as it would be

[1] And would have lasted four hours had Aleandro not read it quickly; cf. P. S. Allen, *The Age of Erasmus* (Oxford, 1914), pp. 112-13.

[2] L. Dorez and L. Thuasne, *Pic de la Mirandole en France (1485-1488)* (Paris, 1897).

dangerous to consider as such Lefèvre d'Etaples, whose interests of a humanist nature were linked to an attraction for mysticism and an encyclopaedic approach on the Pico type. If Budé was the French Politian, Lefèvre d'Etaples was the Pico of France, but a Pico who lived close to ninety years, to end as a living ana-chronism in a Europe torn by the new divisions of Christendom. The typical exponents of French humanism before Robert Estienne inaugurated a new age were really closer to Gaguin and Fichet than to Budé and Lefèvre. In a way they still clung to the traditional values, though at the same time they were ready to enrich them by the acceptance of what they thought was the best that Italy could offer, and in their case the best could range from Valla's *Elegantiae* and Politian's *Miscellanea* to the second-rate poetry of Battista Mantovano. On the whole it was a choice seldom sup-ported by real discrimination, yet it was this choice that deter-mined the development of humanism in France.

England also had started to feel the impact of Italian human-ism at an early stage. This had been mainly, if not solely, possible through the enlightened patronage of Humfrey, Duke of Glou-cester. It was mostly through his donations of humanist texts to Oxford in 1439 and 1444, his exchanges with Italian scholars like Bruni and Decembrio, and the employment of humanists like Tito Livio Frulovisi and Antonio Beccaria in his own house-hold, that Humfrey was able to turn the attention of his country-men upon the humanism of Italy. One of the results of this was that more than one Englishman went to Ferrara to read under Guarino da Verona. Now if Humfrey's household was the cradle of English humanism, the school of Guarino was certainly its preparatory school. So much so that already in the fourteen-fifties William Grey, Bishop of Ely, and John Tiptoft, Earl of Worcester, could be found indulging in a patronage of scholars definitely on Italian lines, John Free was able to display a grasp of Latin and a knowledge of Greek not inferior to that of his best Italian contemporaries, while John Gunthorpe and Robert Flemmyng could be seen alternating their ecclesiastical and diplo-matic duties with the pursuit of humanist activities on typically

Italian lines. Little wonder, then, that even at a conservative centre like Oxford the prevailing attitude was quite definitely not hostile to the new studies. Rather than a threat to the established learning, humanism, or more exactly humanist rhetoric, was considered instead desirable enough to justify the employment of the Milanese Stefano Surigone, whose teaching in Oxford must have taken place at some period between 1464 and 1471.[1] This Oxford teaching of Surigone was not without influence. Let it suffice to remember that one of his pupils was none other than William Sellyng, that is to say a man who became one of the foremost English humanists of his time. Apart from this, it also paved the way for the teaching of other scholars from Italy at a later date. Thus in the late fourteen-seventies humanist rhetoric was being taught at Cambridge by another Italian, the Franciscan Lorenzo da Savona, whose lectures proved successful enough to be printed in England twice in full and once in abridged form in 1479–80. After Lorenzo returned home his tradition was continued in Cambridge for many years by Caio Auberino. But next to Surigone the most influential Italian teacher in 15th-century England was Cornelio Vitelli. Surigone had started the ball of humanist teaching rolling: it was Vitelli that consolidated the grip of the new traditions upon Oxford. What was his part in the introduction of Greek in Oxford is uncertain. We know, on the other hand, that Greek was already studied in England in the fourteen-sixties in the household of George Neville, Archbishop of York. The introduction of Greek in England, where the legacy of Robert Grosseteste and Roger Bacon in this field had run dry by the early fourteenth century,[2] had been at first the result of Byzantine refugee rather than Italian activity. Some of those Englishmen who had acquired the rudiments of Greek in England were, however, able to consolidate their knowledge in Italy. There is no doubt that most of Sellyng's Greek was acquired at

[1] R. Weiss, *Humanism in England during the Fifteenth Century*, 2nd ed. (Oxford, 1957), p. 138, n. 6.
[2] On this see R. Weiss, 'The Study of Greek in England during the Fourteenth Century', *Rinascimento*, ii (1951), 209–39.

Padua or Bologna, just as Grocin's was mostly learnt in the Florence of Politian. Florence was in more than one way the successor of Ferrara as far as English humanism was concerned. For the class-room of Politian and the academy of Ficino exerted the most powerful influence on English humanism until the very last years of the fifteenth century, when it was replaced by Padua. It is quite true that in the field of Latin grammar Italian influence exerted itself upon England through Valla's *Elegantiae*, the role of which is comparable to that of Fowler's *Modern English Usage* nowadays, and the manuals of Perotti and Sulpizio Verulano. Yet for the other aspects of humanism Florence was certainly England's main source. Admittedly Rome's role had not been indifferent either. But after the fourteen-seventies Rome was left practically without Greek, so much so that in 1487 Alessandro Farnese, the future Pope Paul III, had to move from Rome to Florence in order to find satisfactory tuition in that language.[1] It was therefore to Florence that Grocin went and no doubt that experience made him, just as it was there that Linacre developed his latent humanist leanings.[2] What Politian was to Grocin and Linacre, Marsilio Ficino was to John Colet, with whom he is now known to have been in contact;[3] and whether or not Colet actually met Pico, it is certain that he owed also very much to him and that he was impressed by Pico's hero Savonarola. Pico and Ficino were also able to exert some remote control upon English humanist thought. Here such a control was shown at its best in Sir Thomas More, who never went to Italy. His outlook was nevertheless moulded to some extent by what was best in Italian humanist doctrine, so that his own approach to the classics is not much different from that followed at Politian's school.

[1] *Carteggio umanistico di Alessandro Farnese*, ed. A. Frugoni (Firenze, 1950), p. 32.

[2] For Linacre in Florence see R. Weiss, 'Un allievo inglese del Poliziano: Thomas Linacre', in *Il Poliziano e il suo tempo: Atti del IV convegno internazionale di studi sul Rinascimento* (Firenze, 1957), pp. 231-6.

[3] R. Marcel, 'Les "decouvertes" d'Erasme en Angleterre', *Bibliothèque d'humanisme et Renaissance*, xiv (1952), 122.

More's debt to Ficino and Pico is clear. Yet in his hands such a debt did not weigh upon him, but acted instead rather as a stimu-lus to original speculation.

Italian humanist influence went well beyond university circles. From the days of Edward IV onwards the court itself became affected by it. Humanist courtly poetry in Latin, of the kind so fashionable then in the Italian princely courts, found also some patronage there. Now this kind of poetry had already been practised in England in the days of Duke Humfrey, for whom Tito Livio Frulovisi had written the *Humfroidos*, an epic panegyric in Latin hexameters celebrating the Duke's deeds in Flanders.[1] The *Humfroidos* came too early to inaugurate a tradition of human-ist court poetry. It is indeed necessary to reach the later years of Edward IV to find this kind of poetry, or perhaps more correctly versification, established in England. From then onwards its development was swift, so swift that when in 1489 Robert Gaguin, then on a visit to England, was indiscreet enough to issue an epigram of dubious taste on Henry VII, he was promptly smothered under a deluge of biting poems by the humanists hanging around the court.[2] Such a humanist climate at court was made possible thanks mainly to the activity of two Italians, the papal collector Giovanni Gigli and the wandering scholar Pietro Carmeliano, who once in England ceased his wanderings and found instead a lucrative niche for himself in the royal house-hold. In view of the favourable atmosphere prevalent in court circles it is not surprising that humanist historiography should have also grown within their shadow with Polydore Vergil, after whom the writing of history on the old lines was rapidly abandoned in England.

Italian humanism had been able to change in a few decades the complexion of intellectual life in England. This change was

[1] On the *Humfroidos* see R. Weiss, 'Humphrey, Duke of Gloucester, and Tito Livio Frulovisi', *Fritz Saxl 1890–1948 : A Volume of Memorial Essays from His Friends in England* (London, 1957), pp. 218–27.

[2] R. Weiss, 'Cornelio Vitelli in France and England', *Journal of the Warburg Institute*, ii (1939), 223–4.

brought about smoothly and without any real hostilities between the humanists and the old-fashioned schoolmen. Even the fracas between the self-styled Greeks and Trojans at Oxford was only directed against Greek, and included no suggestion that Alexander of Villedieu should replace the usurper Valla and Perotti. The new criticism based on Valla and practised by Grocin and Colet does not seem to have aroused many protests in Oxford, where humanist ideals found their culmination in the programme of the new Corpus Christi College. In this field of humanism, Cambridge, which had been so much outdistanced by Oxford during the fifteenth century, found in the early sixteenth century its Duke Humfrey in John Fisher, who meant for Cambridge not only a trilingual college, but also the teaching of Erasmus.

By the end of the first quarter of the sixteenth century the influence of Italian humanism had not reached either Ireland or Wales. And even Scotland, despite its universities and Hector Boece's friendship with Erasmus, showed no real outside humanist influence during the early decades of the century. This was not surprising in such peripheric countries, just as it is not surprising that similar conditions prevailed in Scandinavia. Such conditions were not prevailing instead in the Low Countries, which showed during the second half of the fifteenth century a tripartite cultural picture. There was the intellectual activity prevailing at the court of the Burgundian dukes, with its emphasis on vernacular literature and a taste for classical mythology, which found its pictorial expression in tapestry and book illumination rather than in painting. Its approach to Antiquity was, however, that of medieval romanticism, which conceived Hercules as a Sarrasin baron and visualized Alexander or Priamus as feudal kings surrounded by their peers. Jean Mielot admittedly composed occasionally some Latin verse,[1] but this far from confirms that humanist values had really penetrated this last stronghold of medieval ideals of chivalry. Humanism exerted instead some appeal on the followers of the *Devotio Moderna* and on the theologians of

[1] C. A. J. Armstrong, 'Verses by Jean Mielot on Edward IV and Richard Earl of Warwick', *Medium Aevum*, xiii (1939), 193-7.

Louvain. It is, however, undeniable that in both these cases what proved attractive was the grammatical and rhetorical element and this above all for utilitarian reasons. Humanist textbooks were read in the schools of the Brethren of the Common Life not because of the new conceptions behind them, but because they provided better and clearer expositions of grammar and a polished and elegant Latin. The greatest of their teachers, the Deventer headmaster Alexander Hegius, was by no means insensitive to the allure of humanist rhetoric. Yet his teaching alone would not have been able to form a scholar like Rudolf Agricola, whose achievement was very much the result of the impact of Renaissance Italy upon the foundations laid at the school of the Brethren of the Common Life. Such an impact would not prevail always. The educational background of Wessel Gansfort was not much different from Agricola's. Yet the Florence of Ficino and the Rome of Pomponio Leto failed to impress him and to the end he never wavered in his Occamist loyalties. Italy did in fact, if anything, increase his enthusiasm for Church reform and biblical studies, in which he found his knowledge of Greek and Hebrew quite invaluable. Gansfort was certainly more of a typical representative of the Low Countries' approach to the humanities than Agricola. The more brilliant Agricola was ready to assume the garb of an Italian humanist. Gansfort preferred instead to play the role of an enlightened theologian, who was not prepared to repudiate his cultural heritage, though he was certainly ready to revise and enrich it.

The background of Agricola and Gansfort was also the early background of Erasmus. Yet Erasmus belonged to European humanism rather than to that of any particular country. In him we find the meeting of many streams, of the *Devotio Moderna* and of pre-Reformation Paris, of the critical approach of Valla and the speculative approach of Colet, of the hellenism of Aldus and the biblical philology of the early Reformers. All these many currents were admirably co-ordinated by a striking common sense and by an innate dislike for any extremes, be they Catholic or Protestant. What Erasmus would have liked above all was a Reformation within the Church. It was instead his lot to remain in a Church without Reformation and to be abused by both Protestants and Catholics.

With Erasmus we can see that the *translatio studii*, the depar﹣ture of humanist supremacy from Italy, had already taken place. The ideals of the Brethren of the Common Life were merged into the complex cosmopolitanism of Erasmus and the biblical humanism of the Reformers. Louvain showed instead how Italian humanism could also appeal to the most rigid theologians. Had it not been so it would be scarcely conceivable that humanist teachers like Stefano Surigone[1] and Cornelio Vitelli[2] would have found employment there. What made the teaching of these Italians acceptable in Louvain was not, however, their outlook but what was the commonest reason for the acceptance of human﹣ist teaching outside Italy, namely that their rhetoric was more up to date than what was available locally.

It is at least doubtful that such sporadic humanist teaching had a great influence in the moulding of taste. It is nevertheless per﹣missible to wonder whether the definite attraction towards Greek, which made printing in that language at Louvain start in 1515 and find its culmination in Busleiden's foundation of a trilingual college in 1517, may not have had its origins in the teaching of Vitelli and Surigone. Such a taste of Greek may have been humanist in origin, but it was certainly not any preoccupation of a humanist character that gave it increase. For Greek was really studied in early sixteenth﹣century Louvain on account of its importance in biblical studies. This was also why the study of it was so strongly opposed there by the more conservative theologians, such as Dorpius and Latomus.

The humanism of the Low Countries showed on the whole a readiness to accept Greek and the rhetoric of the Italians. It would, however, be exaggerated to say that it went very deep in its accep﹣tance of Italian humanism. If we compare its approach to it with

[1] H. de Vocht, *History of the Foundation and the Rise of the Collegium Trilingue Lovaniense 1517–1550*, pt. I (Louvain, 1951), p. 159.

[2] Ibid., pt. I, pp. 166–72.

that of the German world, and by that is meant not only Germany but also Austria and German-speaking Switzerland, we shall find that here the approach was both broader and deeper. It is in fact possible to say that in more than one way the German world was the one which came closest to that of Renaissance Italy as far as humanism was concerned. While in other parts of western Europe the tendency was for humanism to be absorbed into the existing cultural structure and often used at first to further what had been the aims of scholasticism, in the German world it showed instead greater variety than elsewhere in its manifestations alongside with a greater readiness to pursue humanist studies for their own sake. The influence of Italian humanism was undoubtedly strong in the German lands. But then many German students had been attending Italian universities during the later Middle Ages. Moreover, some of the finest minds of the fifteenth century, such as Nicholas of Cusa, Gregory Heimburg and Albert von Eyb had studied in Italy, where they had not been indifferent to humanist studies. And to this may be added that more than one Italian humanist was teaching in German universities during the second half of the fifteenth century. The Florentine Jacopo Publicio lectured at Erfurt, Leipzig and Basle[1] in 1467–70, Stefano Surigone taught at Cologne and Strassburg,[2] Cinzio da Borgo Sansepolcro at Vienna.[3] Their teaching had, however, been the usual rhetorical one, just as rhetorical was that of those Germans, such as Peter Luder,[4] who tried to teach the humanities on the Italian pattern in German universities. This demand for rhetoric alongside with an appetite for philosophical speculation, explains why the writings of Valla, Ficino and Pico proved so popular, and it also explains the powerful appeal exerted later

---

[1] E. P. Goldschmidt, *Hieronymus Münzer und seine Bibliothek* (London, 1938), p. 16.

[2] British Museum, MS. Arundel 249, fos. 94v, 96r, 98r, 103v, 112v, 116r.

[3] G. Bauch, *Die Reception des Humanismus in Wien* (Bresslau, 1923), pp. 25–7.

[4] For Luder see W. Wattenbach, *Peter Luder der erste humanistische Lehrer in Heidelberg, Erfurt, Leipzig, Basel* (Karlsruhe, 1869); G. Ritter, *Die heidelberger Universität*, i (Heidelberg, 1936), 457–63.

by Lefèvre d'Etaples. But the unique development achieved by German humanism must be sought ultimately in the wide first-hand knowledge of Italy, which was in turn instrumental in creating an urge to emulate the Italians and show that the Germans could be as good as them and even better. So the academies of Ficino and Pomponio Leto furnished a pattern, which was followed in the *sodalitates* founded by Conrad Celtis on the banks of the Rhine and the Danube, where the emphasis was, however, not on Platonist philosophy or classical archaeology, but on Latin versification. This was certainly a field which achieved here its greatest popularity outside Italy, although no German came near the heights reached by Politian or Pontano.

Needless to say, early German humanism did not remain insensitive to Greek. Here also Greek had been sought at first on account of the help it afforded in theological studies. Such was on the whole the approach to it of Reuchlin, who turned a homily of Proclus into Latin as early as 1488, and of Beatus Rhenanus, whose literary remains include a Latin text of two sermons by Gregory of Nazianzum. This does not mean that a humanist approach to Greek was not also to be found. Agricola's teaching of this language at Heidelberg was certainly not inspired by theological preoccupations and rather on Italian lines. Admittedly a utilitarian conception of Greek had been unavoidable in the intellectual climate of late fifteenth-century Germany. But by the beginning of the next century a humanist approach seemed to prevail here, this being shown for instance by the lectures of Richard Croke and his successor Mosellanus at Leipzig.

The theological and philological interests which made possible the rise of Greek studies stimulated also the study of Hebrew outside Jewish circles. Hebrew was certainly noticed and studied by Celtis, Peutinger, Trithemius, and many others. It was Reuchlin's lot to become the best German humanist scholar in this field and to show its potentialities. And it is interesting to note here that whereas in other countries it was Greek that brought a split between schoolmen and humanists, it was Hebrew that caused such a split in Germany. The feud between Reuchlin and the Cologne Dominicans on the Hebrew books issue became the struggle between the old-fashioned ideas and the new ones, that very struggle which was to merge into the broader issues of the Reformation.

By the time of the Reformation, most German humanists had definitely chosen what might be called the *via moderna*. But until then they had continued to draw inspiration from Italy. Peutinger could express his indignation at Pomponio Leto's attempt to deprive Germany of the glory of the invention of printing,[1] while Ulrich von Hutten exalted in his *Arminius* German resistance to Rome through the ages. Yet the philological pattern remained on Italian lines. Editions of classical writers such as Regiomontanus' Manilius or Celtis' text of the *Germania* of Tacitus down to Beatus Rhenanus' Velleius Paterculus are not dissimilar to those by Italian humanists. Here, in the editorial field, the Germans struck, however, a new note by editing also some Latin medieval writers. Thus Hrotswitha's comedies found an editor in Conrad Celtis, who was also responsible for preparing for the press a text of the *Ligurinus* by Gunther the Cistercian. This extension of editorial activity to medieval texts was not due to the fact that they were medieval, but because they illustrated the German past. This the German humanists meant to emphasize in contrast to the Roman past, even before Rome came to represent everything that was against the Reformation, and such a devotion for it was also instrumental in stimulating antiquarian and archaeological as well as historical research. It is true that it was the school of Pomponio Leto that introduced Peutinger to archaeology. But once back home Peutinger remained chiefly interested in Roman antiquities, provided they were connected with Germany. In these antiquarian studies other Italian humanists besides Leto also supplied useful examples to be followed. Thus Biondo's *Italia illustrata* led Celtis to conceive a *Germania illustrata*, humanist commentaries on classical texts

---

[1] *Sermones conviviales conradi Peutingeri de mirandis Germaniae antiquitatibus* (Argentinae, 1506), fo. cir.

of the type of those by Perotti and Calderini inspired Beatus Rhenanus to compose one on Tacitus' *Germania*, while the new humanist historiography was also taken over to illustrate the German past.

The German past, they believed, could be rescued from oblivion, thanks to the new scholarship revealed by Italian humanism. This should not, however, be taken to mean that antiquarian research was not also pursued in Germany for its own sake. John von Dalberg[1] and Leto's pupil Jacob Questemberg[2] had no axes to grind in their studies on ancient numismatics, and similarly devoid of ulterior motives were the antiquarian activities of the two Schedel, who alternated the study of classical literature with that of epigraphy and other archaeological pursuits, modelled in part upon those of Ciriaco d'Ancona and Giovanni Marcanova.

On the whole the horizons of German humanism proved wider than those of any other country in western Europe with the exception of Italy. Early German humanism did not produce a scholar of the calibre of Erasmus, Budé or More. Still seen as a whole the German-speaking world was the only one where humanism did not remain for long the handmaid of scholasticism, and it was actually the first on this side of the Alps to assert its independence from the conservative theologians, striking at the same time an original note by making it an instrument of German patriotism. A comparison between the impact of Italian humanism on German and on Castilian intellectual life brings home at once the fundamental difference between the two. Contacts between the Castilian kingdom and Italian humanism may already be detected in the days of King John II, who was the recipient of translations from the Greek by Pier Candido Decembrio.[3] It was the period when Alfonso de Santa Maria, Bishop

---

[1] G. Mercati, *Opere minori*, iv (Rome, 1937), 443.

[2] Vatican Library, MS. Vat. lat. 3906, fos. 1–23. For this treatise see Mercati, *Opere minori*, iv, 437–46, 453–9.

[3] V. Zaccaria, 'Sulle opere di Pier Candido Decembrio', *Rinascimento*, vii (1956), 23–4.

of Burgos,[1] was in close relation with the humanist world of Italy during his stay at the Council of Basle. Such contacts led to his advertising at home the achievements of the Italians, with the result that several Spaniards went to study in Italy during the second half of the fifteenth century. Several of those scholars who eventually became the leading lights of Spanish humanism, such as Alonso Hernandez de Palencia, Antonio de Nebrija, and others, finished their education in Italy and once home they tried to introduce the new values and spread the knowledge of Greek secured there. It was thus typical that Nebrija should have taken steps about improving the dubious Latin prevailing in his country as soon as he returned from Italy in 1473. Such activity and the fact that the teaching of grammar and rhetoric on tradi/ tional lines was no longer deemed satisfactory, led to the employ/ ment of Italian humanists at such a conservative stronghold as Salamanca, where Pomponio Mantovano was already active about 1473.[2] From 1484 Lucio Marineo Siculo was also on the Salamanca lecturing staff, where he was joined by Pietro Martire d'Anghiera three years later. These humanists prepared to some extent a favourable ground for humanism at Salamanca, with the result that even Greek was taught there in the late fifteenth century, when courses on this language were given by Arias Barbosa, a Portuguese who had been privileged to be taught by Politian. Also Nebrija taught at Salamanca for several years and Nebrija was doubtless the greatest exponent of early humanism in Spain. In him that tendency towards applying the humanities to biblical studies is already evident. Nebrija's pursuits ranged from grammar to history, from lexicography to the pronuncia/ tion of Greek; yet his real passion was the study of the Bible. It was in fact his activity in this field that angered the narrow divines of Salamanca and forced him to leave his chair and repair to the more favourable atmosphere of Alcalá.

[1] On him see L. Serrano, *Los conversos Don Pablo de Santa Maria y don Alfonso de Cartagena obispos de Burgos* (Madrid, 1942).

[2] C. Lynn, *A College Professor of the Renaissance—Lucio Marineo Siculo among the Spanish Humanists* (Chicago, 1937), p. 103.

If Nebrija was the Spanish Politian, Fernando de Cordoba[1] was obviously its Pico as well as its Ficino. For in him a marked tendency towards the more esoteric sides of philosophy was linked to the pursuit of an impossibly ambitious programme, this being nothing less than the conciliation between the philosophy of Plato and that of Aristotle.

Parallel to the rise of humanist activity at Salamanca was a similar rise at court, where, however, it seldom strayed at first beyond the rhetorical boundaries. At court the appreciation of polished Latin for political purposes was already evident under Henry IV, when the post of Latin secretary was held by Alonso Hernandez de Palencia. Such an appreciation for humanist Latin at court is confirmed further more by the fact that Alonso was succeeded in the secretaryship by Pietro Martire of Anghiera. While Martire held this office, the education of the eldest princess was entrusted to another humanist of Italy, Antonio Geraldini, whose Latin poetry had not lacked admirers at home.[2] It was within this courtly atmosphere that Pietro Martire became also the historiographer of the New World, while Nebrija followed the new conceptions of history in his activity as historiographer royal.

By the beginning of the sixteenth century Castilian humanism had two centres: the court of the Catholic kings and the University of Salamanca. It would, however, have been scarcely possible for this humanism to develop had it remained confined within such boundaries. It is, however, clear that in Castile humanism had shown also a bend towards biblical studies, this being particularly evident in the activity of Nebrija. Now such a tendency was definitely not encouraged at Salamanca. Its development was made instead possible by the foundation of a new university at Alcalá in 1508. It is quite clear that the founder of this university, Cardinal Ximenes, had not been prompted in his action by

---

[1] On his exchanges with Italian humanists see A. Morel Fatio, 'Maître Fernande de Cordoue et les humanistes italiens du XVe siècle', *Recueil de travaux d'erudition dediés à la mémoire de J. Havet* (Paris, 1895), pp. 521-33.

[2] *The Sacred Eclogues of Antonio Geraldini,* ed. W. P. Mustard (Baltimore, 1924), p. 13.

humanist considerations. What he really had in mind was an institution dedicated to ecclesiastical learning and the theology of Duns Scotus. But Ximenes also believed that no one could be a good theologian without Greek. It was therefore inevitable for Alcalà to become the leading centre of Greek studies in the country. Nor did humanist activity at Alcalà stop here. For the Christian interests present in Castilian humanism found also a favourable ground for development at Alcalà. Besides Greek also the other languages of the Bible were deeply studied there. The Complutensian Bible, on which were engaged for several years the best Greek and Oriental scholars available, was the greatest monument of early Spanish humanism. It was also at Alcalà that Greek texts were printed for the first time in Spain and where the chair of that language displayed an impressive series of teachers, starting with the Greek Demetrius Dukas, who taught there from 1512–18.

The Complutensian Bible was only one of Ximenes' ambitious schemes. Another one, which was never completed owing to his death, was the publication of the whole of Aristotle both in the original and in a new Latin translation. He also tried in vain to attract Erasmus over to Spain. Erasmus never crossed the Pyrenees. All the same he exerted a deep influence in Spain, where opposition to the new ideas found its expression in the polemic writings of Lopez de Zuniga, who proved equally hostile to Erasmus and Lefèvre d'Etaples.

On the whole early Castilian humanism was a Christian humanism. What was offered by Italy was taken over to improve rhetoric, develop humanist philology, and inaugurate a knowledge of Greek. But this new knowledge was mainly directed towards the furtherance of theological and biblical learning. This was an approach which found much less of a response in Aragon. During the fifteenth century, Aragon gave two popes to the Church, Calixtus III and his nephew Alexander VI. Moreover, with King Alfonso V Naples had become the seat of the Aragonese monarchy, and the resort of humanists like Panormita and Valla. Yet for all its links with Italy, Aragon remained a humanist backwater. It is true that humanist historiography and the study of Spanish antiquities were among the pursuits of Cardinal Joan Margarit i Pau[1] and that a sound knowledge of Greek was achieved by his nephew Gironi i Pau.[2] But neither this nor the foundation of a university at Valencia in 1500 with the express aim of stimulating the humanities, was able to arouse the interest in this subject which took place in Castile. Humanist influence in Aragon hardly strayed beyond the grammatical sphere, the *Synonima* and the *Isagogicon* of Jeronimo Amiguet showing clearly the shallow hold of humanism on his country.

Humanism did not make at first a great impression in Portugal, though Jacopo Publicio had taught there some time between 1465 and 1480[3] and Cataldo Parisio had been active at Coimbra until 1495, when he moved to the king's court.[4] What, however, made a great difference and more than anything else stimulated the rise of humanism in Portugal was the teaching of Politian in far-away Florence. For the fame of his teaching was great enough to induce several Portuguese to go over to Italy to be taught by him. Henrique Cayado, a pupil of Parisio, arrived in Florence too late, Politian having died soon after his arrival, so that he had to read first under Marcello Adriani and then at Bologna, where he was befriended by Beroaldo and Codro Urceo and was able to publish his Latin poems.[5] Arias Barbosa had been instead more fortunate and had been able to profit from Politian's teaching, and so had been the three sons of the Great Chancellor Texeira.[6] Barbosa became the first professor of Greek at Salamanca.

[1] R. B. Tate, 'Italian Humanism and Spanish Historiography of the Fifteenth Century', *Bulletin of the John Rylands Library*, xxxiv (1951), 137–65; Id., 'Joan Margarit i Pau, Bishop of Gerona', *Speculum*, xxvii (1952), 28–42; Id., *Joan Margarit i Pau, Cardinal-Bishop of Gerona* (Manchester, 1955).

[2] E. Müntz and P. Fabre, *La Bibliothèque du Vatican au XVe siècle* (Paris, 1887), p. 311.

[3] Bibliothèque Nationale, Paris, MS. Lat. 7809, fo. 2v.

[4] Lynn, op. cit., pp. 106–7.

[5] *The Eclogues of Henrique Cayado*, ed. W. P. Mustard (Baltimore, 1931), pp. 10–18.

[6] Ibid., pp. 95–6.

Nor did Texeira's sons once back home give up humanist studies, as is shown for instance by the Latin oration addressed to King John II by Ludovico Texeira. This king had also corresponded with Politian[1] and encouraged humanist activity. Indeed by the beginning of the sixteenth century Latin oratory and grammar on humanist lines were certainly to be found in Portugal. Handbooks like those by Estevan Cavaillero and Pastraña show this to have been the case. But to assume from this that humanism prevailed in Portugal by 1520 would certainly be rash.

By 1520 European humanism was entering into a new phase. Supremacy in the field had by then shifted across the Alps and it was not long before Renaissance humanism was replaced by the new classical scholarship of the Estiennes, the Scaligers, Vettori and Muretus. Italian influence continued in sixteenth-century Europe. But now the role played by humanism was taken over by vernacular literature, and the place of Valla and Politian was assumed by the writings of Petrarch, Castiglione and Ariosto. Petrarchism was in fact to flood Europe, just as humanism had done a couple of generations earlier.

[1] G. Battelli, 'La corrispondenza del Poliziano col re Don Giovanni II di Portogallo', *La Rinascita,* ii (1939), 280–98.

J. R. Hale

WAR AND PUBLIC OPINION
IN RENAISSANCE ITALY

Quatro nouanta quatro cento e mille
De l'anno che dio prese carne, essendo
Tutte le parte del mondo tranquille,
Le creature in gran pace viuendo,
Marte con turbulente suo fauille
Poner le volse insanguinoso mendo,
Mettendo in cuore a vn tramontan signore
De l'uniuerso farsi Imperatore.[1]

Contemporaries would not have been surprised by the significance with which the year 1494 was invested by later historians.
Within a generation it was seen as marking the end of one period
and the beginning of another. Before it lay a time of quiet prosperity, after it came an age of battle and disaster. As it became
increasingly clear that the barbarians had come to stay, the contrast
was painted in heightened colours; rueful self-criticism darkening
the present, while nostalgia lightened the past. Before: a time of
splendour and renown; after: an age in which Italian claims to
prolong the glories of the Roman past had become a mockery.
Of all these contrasts the most obvious was between a period of
peace and one of war or, at least, between a period of mild wars
that did little more than trace patterns on the surface of the waters
of Italian civilization, and one of savage wars that raised great
waves and littered the shores with wreckage. The fact that this

[1] *Guerre horrende d'Italia* . . . (Venice), 1535, canto I, verse 2, punctuated,
abbreviations resolved.

contrast did not involve the arts, which continued to flourish, was no consolation: the historians, the political theorists and the moralists who recorded this sad division took little interest in them. The fame of Italy, for them, was bound up with her independence: a freedom from foreign meddling that allowed the states of the peninsula to pursue private advantage to the common good. The arts, it is true, gilded the links binding New Rome to Old Rome, but the links themselves were independence and reputation, and the defeats that followed 1494 came near to breaking them.

In contrasting the periods that preceded 1494 and followed it there was much exaggeration. For Guicciardini, the youthful historian of Florence, Lorenzo de' Medici was a tricksy tyrant; the same historian, writing about Italy as a whole a generation of disappointments later, hailed him as the genius who had presided over the peninsula's golden age. Machiavelli deepened the contrast between the bloody wars of the *Cinquecento* and those which preceded it by making the latter seem such holiday flourishes that the blood he staunched in the military history of the *Quattrocento* has only been set flowing again in the present century.[1] The change that came over the nature of warfare after 1494 was overstressed by Machiavelli in the interest of proving a thesis about the relative merits of militiamen to *condottieri*, as it was by Guicciardini in the interest of turning the knife in the wound to Italy's self-esteem, but a change there certainly was, and it was greeted with widespread horror. This horror, however, was not directed against large-scale war as such, as opposed to earlier small-scale wars, nor even against a long period of such wars; nor was it directed to any important extent against the changed nature of war—more bloody, more total, more expensive. It was caused by the evidence provided by these wars of a failure of morale, a failure of the Italian character to meet their challenge.

Why were Italian armies beaten by barbarian ones? When every excuse on the score of technical inferiority, lack of training and divided command had been made the conclusion still remained:

[1] Notably by W. Block in his *Die Condottieri* (Berlin, 1913).

the Italian soldier was inferior to his rival. What had made him inferior, and what could be done to improve him? These questions could not be answered in straightforward military terms. A good soldier is the product of his whole environment, not just of a military academy. The failure of the Italian soldiers in war was due, it was felt, to their corrupt condition in peace. Faulty constitutions had not provided the setting needed for the development of responsible citizens capable of defending themselves. The practical problems—how to provide good native troops—intensified concern with constitutional reform. Interest in the individual's behaviour not only at the polls but on the battlefield led to a new and urgent preoccupation with all the forces that could condition him to do his best there: political, economic and religious.

The extent to which an interest in military affairs influenced political thought is best exemplified by Machiavelli. His political ideas were dominated by a scorn of modern armies and an admiration for the constitutional framework that had supported the finest army of all, that of the Roman republic, and his main concern—the transformation of the bad citizen into the good soldier—directed every aspect of his thought about the state and the individual's place in it, just as his overriding interest in war and war-like crisis directed his thinking about international relations.

Before showing, however, that the horror which followed 1494 —or, more properly, Fornovo, in 1495, the first full battle of the Italian Wars—was due to a revelation of the poor state of Italian morale, it must be stressed, and in some detail, that this horror was not a reaction against war as such, nor, primarily, against the nature of the warfare waged by the French and Spanish and their Swiss and German allies.

Despite nostalgic regrets for the 'peaceful' *Quattrocento*,[1] it was

[1] For an extreme example see Paolo Giovio, *Historie del suo tempo*, trans. Lodovico Domenichi (Venice, 1555), p. 21: 'Questo anno, che fu dal parto della Vergine mccccxciiii, apportò a tutto il mondo una lietissima pace, quale doppo Augusto non si ricordava alcuna età de gli antichi. Ma questa pace, che nel primo aspetto sicura, e fiorita, havea empiuto gli huomini di buona speranza di

accepted that wars were inevitable. The cyclical theories of Machiavelli (valour brings peace, peace idleness, idleness dis' order, disorder ruin, ruin good order, good order valour, etc.) and of Luigi da Porto (peace brings riches, riches pride, pride wrath, wrath war, war poverty, poverty mildness, mildness peace, peace riches, etc.) took war as a matter of course, as a red splash on Fortune's turning wheel.[1] Some Italian rulers were profession' ally bound to accept the inevitability of wars, for their prosperity depended on an ability to supplement tax and toll with the fees of war. The gift of Pollaiuolo's helmet from the city of Florence to Federigo of Urbino was entirely suitable: the duke's arms were as necessary to him as they might be on occasion to some less military neighbour state.[2] Nor did the practice of the papacy imply that war was undesirable in itself. It was, again, appropriate that the Duke of Modena should celebrate the news of Pius II's elec' tion by holding military manœuvres.[3] The 'bloody armour' for the wearing of which Julius II was so roundly swinged by Eras' mus was only one of the more sensational symbols of the popes' dependence on war to hold their own in the hurly'burly of inter' national rivalries.[4] Pasquino was robed as Mars for his festival in

tranquilità al mondo, subito sparse per tutte le provincie una molto crudele e lunghissima guerra.'

And Giovio sounds, too, the note of humiliation. He writes of Fornovo: 'Questo è quel notabil fatto d'arme del Taro, dove con alquanto maggior temerità, che dapocaggine noi perdemmo l'antica riputatione della militia Italiana: e con nostra inescusabil vergogna incomminciammo à essere in disprezzo alle nationi straniere....' Ibid., p. 101v.

For Ammirato, writing a generation later, the 'peaceful quattrocento' had been worn down to the status of a cliché. The 26th book of his *Dell' Istorie Fiorentine* refers to the years that preceded 1494: 'Questa è quella pace tanto celebrata per le memorie de' nostri scrittori. . . .' Guicciardini had written as early as 1509, in the *Storie Fiorentine*, of 'quegli tempi lieti che erano innanzi al 94'. 1859, p. 255.

[1] *Lettere Storiche di Luigi da Porto*, ed. Bressan (Firenze, 1857), pp. 26 and 46. Machiavelli, *Istorie Fiorentine*, beginning of fifth book.

[2] Millard Meiss, *Andrea Mantegna as Illuminator* (Hamburg, 1957), p. 1.

[3] *Commentaries*, trans. F. A. Gragg, *Smith College Studies in History*, xxii, nos. 1-2, p. 106 (book 1).

[4] In the *Julius Exclusus*.

May 1512 by the Bishop of Camerino, and bellicose and jingoistic verses were attached to him, calling all faithful Italians to help the pope expel the French with fire and sword.[1]

The ideal of princely state-craft—a nice knowledge of when to achieve restraint and when to apply force—expressed, too, an unquestioning acceptance of war. The bombshell *impresa* of Duke Alfonso of Ferrara with its motto *Loco et Tempore* implied that the Duke was prepared at the right juncture to allow restraint to explode into violence.[2] Leonardo's mechanical lion with its breast full of lilies was a graceful acknowledgement that Louis XII also possessed this necessary combination of restraint and potential violence.[3] Similarly Federigo da Montefeltro chose an *impresa* which balanced a sword against an olive branch,[4] and Machiavelli impressed upon rulers the need for combining the lion's qualities with those of the fox.

And all these antitheses were but extensions into the realm of politics of special aspects of the many-sidedness expected of the good man, a many-sidedness which expected the same hand to be able to wield both the pen and the sword. For Cicero and Quintilian, the ideal orator—conversant with all subjects, fired by all causes, understanding the feelings of men of all ranks and all occupations—needed to be *homo universalis*. This ideal of many-sidedness appealed to the Renaissance partly because authors could still exploit an otherwise outmoded encyclopaedism and canalize reflections on every human quality into a portrait of an ideal type whether cardinal, soldier or courtier; partly because

---

[1] D. Gnoli, in 'Storia di Pasquino', *Nuova Antologia* (1890), pp. 280–3, gives some extracts. My attention was drawn to the relevant pasquinades in the Vittorio Emanuele Library in Rome by Mr. David Chambers.

[2] Illustrated in Paolo Giovio, *Imprese* . . . (Lyone, 1574), p. 80, who says that he wore the *impresa* at the battle of Ravenna, 1512. A medal of -1505 with a bust of Alfonso shows him wearing a cuirass with a flaming bomb on the breast. It is illustrated (plate 60) in Edgar Wind, *Pagan Mysteries of the Renaissance*, 1958, where there is a general discussion of this concept.

[3] This point is made by Professor E. Wind in the *Journal of the Warburg and Courtauld Institutes* (1943), p. 222.

[4] Hill, op. cit., no. 304.

it dignified dilettantism; partly because it solved—or shelved—the dilemma of how to harmonize the active with the contem plative life. The most striking conjunction was that which showed the same man as successful both on the battlefield and in the study,[1] and as, outside the Republics, the patron class was also the warrior class, it was stressed by soldiers and intellectuals alike.

Castiglione lauded the conjunction and was praised for it him self. Da Porto required it of his heroes and was possibly the most appealing of all its exemplifiers. Pius II recorded with pride that his forebears were not only among the oldest and noblest families in Siena but also were illustrious both in arms and in letters. Each state described in his *Commentaries* is given due praise for its prowess in war, and in the lists of prominent citizens, soldiers are given a conspicuous place among the rest. The question, which is preferable: arms or letters? with the invariable answer: both must be combined, was, of course, one of those weary clichés which, like the mock battle staged for Lucrezia d'Este's marriage to Annibale Bentivoglio between Wisdom and Fortune, was bound to end in a draw.[2] In the princely states, where the profession of arms was taken for granted, it was commonly up to Letters to prove a place beside Arms.

> *Nè mi par che convenga a gentilezza* [said
>   Boiardo's Agricane]
> *Star tutto il giorno ne' libri a pensare;*
> *Ma la forza del corpo e la destrezza*
> *Conviense al cavalliero esercitare.*
> *Dottrina al prete ed al dottor sta bene:*
> *Io tanto saccio quanto mi conviene.*

---

[1] Federigo of Urbino was shown in the famous portrait by Justus of Ghent as reading in his study while clad in full armour, and his successor, Guid' Ubaldo, was described by Polydore Vergil as 'principi saeculo nostro latinae linguae simul et graecae, ac militaris disciplinae peritissimo'. *Anglica Historia*, ed. Denys Hay, Camden Series (1950), p. 140.

[2] C. M. Ady, *Morals and Manners of the Quattrocento*, Annual Italian Lecture of the British Academy, 1942, p. 17.

Rispose Orlando:—Io tiro teco a un segno,
Che l'arme son de l'omo il primo onore;
Ma non già che il saper faccia men degno,
Anzi lo adorna come un prato il fiore.[1]

In republics, on the other hand, especially in Florence (for in Venice young noblemen often served on galleys as 'bowmen of the quarterdeck') it took special crisis and special spleading to persuade the citizens out of their conviction that though arms were all very well in their place, that place was in the hands of others. When the Florentine militia was instituted in 1506, special provision was made for church parades in the course of which the citizen troops were to be harangued on the importance of combining arms with trade or study. In the greatest crisis of all, the siege of the Last Republic, the theme was stated and restated with the greatest urgency. The political need for self-defence was obvious: what was needed was to persuade the citizen to stop despising the trade of arms. *Questa è la virtù della disciplina militare,* said Pandolfini in the course of his harangue to the militia in 1528, *la quale supera tutte le altre scienzie et virtù.*[2] Luigi Alamanni spoke to them of the *glorioso et salutevole campo delle armi.*[3] Bartolommeo Cavalcanti, in the most stirring of these harangues, charged his audience of amateur soldiers to remember the feats of the citizen-soldier of Athens, of Sparta and of Rome, and to compensate for generations of debilitating refinement by reacquiring a military frame of mind. *Scacciamo da noi ogni molle pensiero, spogliamoci d'ogni effeminato habito; non le donnesche delicatezze, ma piu tosto la militare antica rozzezza a noi giudichiamo convenirsi.* And lest this picture should be too dismaying to the more fastidious of his auditors, he brought in the cult of many-sidedness by loading his picture of the ideal soldier with so many qualities— firmness, temperance, obedience, devoutness, and so on—that he became hardly distinguishable from the ideal man.[4]

---

[1] *Orlando Innamorato* lib. i, canto 18, 43-4.
[2] *Archivio Storico Italiano,* ser. i, vol. xv, 351.   [3] Ibid., p. 346.
[4] His harangue is printed in F. Sansovino, *Diverse Orationi . . .* (Venetia, 1561).

The difficulty of persuading civilians to become soldiers had no connection with their views about war as such. Broadly speaking, the rulers of states like Rimini, Urbino, Mantua and Ferrara favoured wars because they made money out of them, while republics were dubious because of the cost involved in hiring mercenaries. But it would be quite wrong to push this into a contrast between militarism and pacifism. Florence indulged in loud sabre-rattling by proxy whenever her trading interests were threatened, and her citizens, no less than the inhabitants of other Italian states, were familiar with ideas and sights and sounds that helped them take war for granted and did much, indeed, to glorify it.

Just as the martial scene was thought to be the most fitting theme for the epic,[1] so it was for the pageant. For the stage-managers of processions and spectacles military life had much to offer. Jousts and mock battles for the piazza, parades of horsemen, magnificently accoutred, for the streets. Piero de' Medici diverted his fellow-citizens' attention from failure in real war by staging a mock battle and a mock siege so splendid that it would be difficult, Machiavelli remarked, to imagine anything finer.[2] For the designer of carnival costume and floats nothing was better suited than the military triumph, with its swaggering conquerors, its cowering prisoners, passing under arches modelled on those of Severus and Constantine. To amuse his people in peacetime, Lorenzo, hero of the golden age, staged such triumphs, and in jousts and mock battles encouraged them to play at war.

The legitimacy of settling differences by resorting to arms, even if only to allow divine justice to operate more swiftly than it could by diplomatic and legal means, was emphasized by the very altars where men prayed for peace. Saints in armour suggested a divine sanction of arms, and if the warlike character of St. Michael and St. George was allegorized away by their being pitted against evil beasts, warrior saints like St. Maurice (made protector of an order of chivalry—René of Anjou's Order of the

---

[1] See R. C. Williams, 'The purpose of poetry and particularly the Epic as discussed by critical writers of the sixteenth century in Italy', *Romanic Review* (1921), pp. 1–20. [2] *Istorie Fiorentine* ed. Mazzoni and Casella, p. 579.

Crescent—as recently as 1448), St. Victor, St. Eustace and St. Proculus appeared as straightforward warriors with whom any soldier might identify himself—St. Proculus, indeed, being associated with specific acts of violence, for the head he is some, times made to hold is, unconventionally for a martyr, not his own. The pacific aspect of the incarnation itself created no uneasy ten, sions in the soldier's conscience. On the breastplate of an Italian armour of the period of the Italian wars was etched a frieze show, ing the Virgin and Child between St. Paul and St. George. Below them was the inscription: CHRISTUS RES [REX] VENIT IN PACE ET DEUS HOMO FACTUS ES[T].[1]

The Church was quick to associate itself with artillery as well and thus to veil to some extent the increasing horrors involved in the use of gunpowder. Representations of St. Barbara, formerly rare, increased with the use of guns, for on account of the thunder and lightning that destroyed her treacherous father, she was con, nected with explosions, whether they were brought about harm, lessly by firework makers or lethally by gunners. Her image was represented on cannon, and according to the rules issued by Charles V to the artillery school in Sicily, each gunner, as he put the ball into his piece, was to make the sign of the cross over its muzzle and call on the Saint's aid.[2] Palma Vecchio's altar, piece in S. Maria Formosa in Venice, which shows the saint standing among cannon, was painted for the Association of *Bombardieri*. And it appears that not only was she invoked by gunners to protect them from being blown up by their own pieces (an invocation which doubtless merged with a desire that their aim might be straight), but also by those who feared being shot at. A mid, *Quattrocento* broadsheet shows a man interceding with the saint on behalf of a figure at whose breast a cannon has just discharged its ball.[3]

---

[1] Sir James Mann, 'Notes on the armour of the Maximilian period and the Italian wars', *Archaeologia* (1929), p. 225.

[2] S. Peine, *St. Barbara die Schutzheilige der Bergleute und der Artillerie* (Freiberg, 1896), p. 10.

[3] Reproduced in P. Heitz, *Italienische Einblattdrucke*, Strassburg, 1933, pt. 1, no. 18.

The horrific nature of guns was veiled, too, in other ways. The festive value of detonations was quickly appreciated, and guns took their place with music and dancing on occasions of special rejoicing. After the capture of Francis I at Pavia in 1525 the allied ambassadors in Venice were supplied with gunpowder from the arsenal to use at their celebrations.[1] The arts, by prettify-ing and glamourizing guns, did much to make them seem less terrifying. The golden cannon made for Charles V was only one of the innumerable attempts to put guns into court dress.[2] Cannon appear in Agostino Busti's monument to Gaston de Foix among the corselets, the piled arms and the drums of heroic triumphs à l'antique. Intricately carved, on ornate carriages, appearing as they do in the company of putti, satyrs and Roman standards, Busti's guns are robbed of any unpleasant associations: they blend dis-creetly with the calmly triumphant mood of the monument as a whole. And when naked *amori* play at shooting one another with pistols, as they were made to do on a *Cinquecento* powder flask,[3] then crafts and arts can be said to have done their utmost to tint the lenses through which the Renaissance looked at war. Illumin-ated manuscripts and printed books, too, had done much to domesticate the gun, regardless of theme. Biblical scenes might contain guns; military books were on occasion supplied with woodcuts of religious subjects, and in an age which was beginning to take archaeology seriously, illustrations of Roman battles could show guns battering at city walls, and bullets filling the air as rival galleys came together on the ocean.[4]

There was, indeed, some notion that the ancients had used gun-

---

[1] *Calendar of State Papers, Venetian 1520–1526*, nos. 736 and 942.

[2] Ibid., no. 1021.

[3] Plate XV of H. J. Jackson and C. E. Whitelaw, *European Hand Firearms* (London, 1923).

[4] As in the Venetian edition, 1493, of Livy's *Decades*, and the subsequent editions of 1495 (Latin) and 1506 (Italian). The German edition (Mentz, 1505) had different illustrations, including some unusually clear and detailed drawings of firearms. These illustrations were taken over for the Spanish edition of 1520 (Çaragoça). Firearms occur, too, in the separately illustrated Paris edition of 1514.

powder, for descriptions of their sieges and battles involved the use of propellant engines and combustibles (like Greek fire) which could be used to give a noble ancestry to modern explosives. An important aspect of the lively interest in ancient history was a fascination with the wars of antiquity. Classical military writers like Vegetius, Frontinus, Onosander and Aelian were printed and reprinted. Contemporary authors like Valturio in his *De Re Militari*, printed at Verona in 1472, reflected this fascination, and larded their observations on modern war with lessons of dubious relevance taken from antiquity, and yielded, in their descriptions of weapons and gadgets, to the armchair warrior's delight in ingenuity at the expense, sometimes, of practicability. Certainly the complex grappling devices recommended by Valturio for siege-work could never have been mounted, nor could his telescopic or revolving gun-turrets have been brought to bear. His device for enabling men to swim under water for long periods is not dissimilar to Leonardo's, but that Valturio's device appealed to the ingenuity rather than the common sense of his readers is made clear when his submarine trooper is shown in full armour.

The more complex war becomes, the more veins of interest it taps.[1] Many of these are concerned more with technology than directly with killing. It is possible to study fortification and artillery without really being concerned with human beings at all. The latent mathematician, the vestigial engineer in many a man of letters, responds to these orderly and calculable elements in war. The Italian wars saw the beginnings of fortification as a science, and the reduction of ballistic observations to rule. A beautiful arquebus appealed not only to a craftsman like Cellini but to a

---

[1] Jacob Burckhardt, *Civilisation of the Renaissance in Italy* (Phaidon ed., 1944), p. 63: 'The Italian literature of the day is rich in descriptions of wars and strategic devices, written for the use of educated men in general as well as of specialists, while the contemporary narratives of northerns, such as the "Burgundian War" by Diebold Schilling, still retain the shapelessness and matter-of-fact dryness of a mere chronicle.' According to Joseph Schnitzer (*Savonarola*, Munich, 1924, i, 392 and 480) *Schlachtenbücher* were among the demoralizing influences sought out for burning by the friar.

princely collector, like Alessandro de' Medici.[1] The special features of modern war, the example of its serious and orderly treatment by the historians of antiquity, and the worship paid to men
who had achieved greatness in arms as well as in letters, made it
appropriate that a Renaissance bishop should write, as Paolo
Giovo did, biographies of famous soldiers.

The *Quattrocento*, then, had been a time when wars were restricted in scope, when casualties had been moderate and the impact of war on civilians had been slight, and at the same time it
had been a time when the appeal of war as something glamorous
and intriguing had been made on a more complex and penetrating
level than ever before. Italy, if less warlike at Lorenzo's death than
she had been a hundred years before, was certainly not less war-
minded. War may have receded from the public imagination to
the extent to which its sombre association had dimmed, but this
retreat was more than compensated for by the advance made in
its heroic and decorative aspect.

Symbolic of these developments were changes in the person of
Mars himself. The once terrifying god of war became tamed and
dandyfied. To the Middle Ages, which looked on war as something which, though capable of being turned to good account,
was potentially evil, the war god was a bloodthirsty warrior,
tinged with the demoniacal. His aspect was rough and forbidding,
his progress through the skies inspired terror and dismay.[2] His
Planetenkinder were not only soldiers but robbers and murderers,
and his chariot stormed impartially over pitched battles and
lonely scenes of assassination and rape. Unless there were special
circumstances, as at Florence and Rome, where ancient statues
identified with Mars became something like secular patron saints,[3]

[1] See Cellini's account of his dealings with Alessandro in 1535. Vasari's
portrait shows him seated in armour, holding a small culverin.

[2] See, for example, F. Saxl, *Der Islam* (1912), plate 12 and the accompanying
description of Mars from the *Liber Introductorius* of Michael Scotus. For many references to the medieval Mars, see Jean Seznec, *La Survivance des Dieux Antiques*
(London, 1940, Eng. trans. New York, 1953), *passim*.

[3] F. von Bezold, *Das Fortleben der antiken Götter im mittelalterlichen Humanismus*
(Leipzig, 1922), p. 32.

Mars represented war at its most brutal. Then, in the late four-teenth and early fifteenth centuries, he began to change. He came increasingly to typify the chivalrous ideal of knighthood, and he was seen less as the warrior than as the lover of Venus. If he still rules the sky over battlefields, it was as the perfect knight looking down approvingly on an ordered combat in which no blood was seen to flow. In Cossa's decorations for the Palazzo Schifanoia he kneels in chains before his mistress, and a generation later Botticelli showed him naked and defenceless in the company of Venus. The theme was eagerly followed up by the painters of every school, and when they turned, as did Perugino, Schiavone, and Sodom, to portraying the surprising of the lovers by Vulcan, Mars appeared in not only an unmartial but a downright ridicu-lous light. The appeal of the Mars and Venus theme was, of course, a strong one. It enabled the artist to contrast the metallic and the soft, armour with flesh. It played with the familiar anti-thesis of force and tenderness, the fashionable image of beauty taming cruelty, mildness subduing ferocity. It was as suitable for a political allegory as for a marriage picture.[1]

In his paintings for the Palazzo Rucellai in Rome, Giacomo Zucchi, dismayed by the bloodshed of his own epoch, deliberately portrayed Mars once more as the bloodthirsty warrior, the personi-fication of anger, dissension and violence.[2] This was a breach with the *Cinquecento* tradition whereby Mars, when he was portrayed as a personification of war—a tradition maintained alongside that of the victim of Venus and sport of Vulcan—appeared as a personi-fication of the glorious, triumphant, heroic side of war. If a ruler was given the attributes of Mars it was not to indicate that he was bloodthirsty but valorous. Cellini designed a piece of sculpture for Francis I in which the god of war, some fifty-four feet high, was accompanied by four other figures, not wolves and furies, but the arts and sciences, Learning, Design, Music and Liberality. 'The

[1] This is suggested of Botticelli's painting by E. Gombrich in *Journal of the War-burg and Courtauld Institutes* (1945), pp. 49-50.

[2] As he explains in his *Discorso sopra li dei de' Gentili, e loro imprese* (Rome, 1602), reprinted by F. Saxl, *Antike Götter in der Spätrenaissance* (Leipzig, 1927). See p. 49.

great statue in the centre', Cellini explained to his patron, 'represents your Majesty himself, the god Mars, unique in valour: and
you employ your valour justly and devoutly, in the defence of your
glory.'[1] In fact as war became more depraved, the god of war
became more respectable. It was only in illustrations designed for
bourgeois consumption—for the classes, that is, who saw war in
terms less of glory than of death and taxes—that Mars retained his
seamier aspects. It was as the feral bringer of destruction that he
drive his chariot in Florentine astrological broadsheets over scenes
of carnage, abduction and looting.

This transformation of Mars meant that he was no longer
appropriate as a personification of war as something brutal,
something to be deplored. The artist or writer seeking for an
image that would convey disapproval or horror or grief had to
turn elsewhere. To associate Mars with gunpowder, for instance,
would have been unthinkable. The need for a pejorative image
led to the disinterment of Bellona. As the companion of Mars,
sometimes his charioteer or harbinger, she had made tentative
appearances before the *Cinquecento*, but it was the Italian wars
that saw her reinstated as a war goddess in her own right. In
1523 and 1528 the same woodcut title-page was used for two
books printed in Venice, the *Duello* of Paris de Puteo and the
Libro continente appertenentie ad Capitanii of Battista della Valle. On
either side of the page was a triumphal pile of arms. On one side a
pile of *armes blanches*: swords and maces, bows and axes. Over
this presided the figure of Mars. On the other side was a pile of
firearms and explosives, bombs, mortars, arquebuses, cannon
and kegs of powder. Presiding over this new-fangled arsenal was
an image of Bellona. The cult of the Roman war goddess was
well known at least since Boccaccio's *Genealogia Deorum*, and it
was dwelt on in detail by Giraldi in 1548. In Cartari's account

---

[1] *Life*, translated by George Bull (Penguin Books, 1956), p. 271. The conceit
was not new. When Louis XII had entered Milan in May 1507, he was met by a
procession which included the chariot of Mars who sat on a throne surrounded by
the cardinal virtues. J. Chartrou, *Les Entrées Solonnelles et Triomphales à la Renaissance* (Paris, 1928), p. 76.

of the gods of the ancients he dwelt on her bloodthirsty and ruinous nature.[1]

In the history of popular attitudes of war the gentling of Mars must take, of course, a very marginal place. The shot from a gilt and exquisitely chased cannon was as lethal as a shot from a plain iron one. No one believed that battles were as ordered and pageant-like as Uccello made them look, and no one was misled by the dearth of casualties in a carnival siege into thinking that real cities were taken without loss of life. But the arts played a part in keeping the idea of war familiar. With their power to prettify and dignify, they prevented the more appalling aspects of war from leading either to a conspiracy of silence or to a sense of dread. Wherever the glare of battle became too great for the eye to bear, the arts interposed a gauze which softened its intensity.

Because the *Quattrocento*—and especially the period following the convention of Lodi in 1454—had been dubbed a peaceful age, it must not be looked upon as an age when statesmen did not think about war, or whose population was not constantly kept in mind of it. When the French blow came, Italy was not psychologically unprepared for war, even if some of her inhabitants were reluctant to do any fighting themselves. There had been enough military activity[2] to make sure that as far as military technique was concerned, her armies contained units that were

---

[1] Like Mars, Bellona came to have a heroic aspect, but she continued to be associated with gunpowder, and not only in Italy. Miss Frances Yates drew my attention to François Billon, *Le Fort Inexpugnable de l'Honneur du Sexe Feminin* (Paris, 1555), where the woodcut borders at the beginning of each book show a female figure in the act of applying a match to cannon. Cf. Milton's description in *Paradise Lost*, ii, lines 920-4, of the Fiend looking back on the pit:

> . . . Nor was his eare less peal'd
> With noises loud and ruinous (to compare
> Great things with small) than when Bellona storms,
> With all her battering Engines bent to rase
> Som Capital City.

[2] See Piero Pieri, *Il Rinascimento e la Crisi Militare Italiana* (1952), part two, especially ch. iii. See also E. W. Nelson, 'The origins of modern balance-of-power diplomacy' in *Medievalia et Humanistica* (1942), pp. 124-42.

not inferior to the French and their allies. Nothing was considered deplorable about war, or even the long continuance of
war, apart from the losses it entailed. Even the comparatively un-
militaristic Florentine republic decorated its holy of holies, the
Sala del Gran Consiglio, where the God-given constitution
expressed itself most fully, with battle scenes, and Venice, in the
peaceful year 1490, took great pains to obtain expert tuition for
young men both in the city and on the mainland, in the use of a
weapon which the government saw would become increasingly
important in future wars—the arquebus.

Italy, like France, had recruitment problems. Men were reluctant to leave a certain livelihood for an uncertain and increasingly
hazardous one. There must have been many like the unheroic
hero of *Ruzzante Returns from the Wars*, who limps back home
without leave, to lick his wounds and cure his pox in Venice:
'Canchero ai campi, alla guerra, ai soldati. Dico non mi accalap-
pieranno piú in guerra. Ora non sentirò piú, come sentiva, quei
rumori tamburini. E trombe e allarmi. Ormài non avrò piú paura.
Quando sentivo l'allarme, sembravo un tordo che avesse ricevuto
una botta. E schioppi, artiglieria. Ora so che non mi raggiunger-
anno. Semmai mi prenderanno in culo.'[1]

But there were others like da Porto for whom war was still a
glamorous opportunity to show how the *cortegiano* should behave
in action; brave, courteous, love-smitten, able to dash off a sonnet
when there was a lull in the fighting and, with an eye cocked
shrewdly at present promotion and future fame, indulging in self-
advertisement. For his class, warfare presented a series of splendid
and legitimate opportunities for the individual to shine and show
his worth. Such men preferred small actions where their deeds
could be noted to sprawling operations which would absorb
and conceal them. Da Porto wrote that it was more praiseworthy
to fight a hundred against a hundred than a thousand against
a thousand, 'because in a small number everybody's *virtù* can be

---

[1] This is from the Italian version of Beolco's Venetian dialect given in *Teatro
Italiano*, i, ed. Silvio d'Amico (Milan, 1955), p. 453. I owe this reference to
Mrs. C. Roaf.

seen'. And he goes on to say, even more revealingly, that this cannot happen in a great battle, and so people simply do not take the trouble and risk to display *virtù*. This is the temperament of men who thought of the military life more in terms of the combat of Barletta in 1503 between thirteen Italian and thirteen French knights, than of campaigns and mêlées like that of the Garigliano in the same year, the temperament for which the printing presses catered with a flood of chivalrous romances full of single combats and deeds of individual derring do. It is a temperament whose ideal of fighting conflicted with the actual nature of war.

The Italian war effort was hampered in many ways: by political disunity, by the reluctance of governments to trust the troops they employed, by the tendency of some *condottiere* leaders to think of themselves rather than the cause they were paid to support, especially when their *condotta* was nearing the end of its term. But important, too, was this courtier-knight feeling among the officer class. The larger the scale on which wars were carried out, the more important it was that the individual should allow himself to serve the interests of an overall plan. How difficult he found it is made disturbingly clear by Castiglione. It must be understood, says Federico Fregoso in *Il Cortegiano*, 'that where the Courtier is at skirmish, or assault, or battaile upon the land, or in such other places of enterprise, he ought to worke the matter wisely in separ- ating him selfe from the multitude, and undertake notable and bolde feates which hee hath to doe, with as litle company as he can, and in the sight of noble men that be of most estimation in the campe, and especially in the presence and (if it were possible) before the very eyes of his king or great personage he is in service withall: for in deede it is meete to set forth to the shew things wel done.'[1] Elsewhere in the book Castiglione's audience is reminded that 'in great matters and adventures in wars the true provocation is glory'—but it was the glory of the individual, not of the cause for which he was fighting.

Da Porto, with his affection for *bellissime scaramucce* and his romantic enthusiasm for individuals like the mysterious Hungarian

[1] Book 2, ch. 8, Hoby's trans.

knight who turned up in Gradisca 'like a true knight-errant', was dismayed to a quite unmilitary degree when he himself was wounded. From the way in which he described the episode to Bembo it might almost seem that there was a tacit agreement between the fates and the courtier-knight that if he obeyed the rules of chivalry he would not be cut off in the flower of his youth and in an unspectacular manner. He described his wound— 'which out-does all other wounds and even death itself'—with aggrieved self-pity and concluded the letter, which pathetically he had to dictate *dalla mia debolissima voce*, by complaining of the chance that had struck him down when these *belle guerre* were at their peak.[1]

The Italian wars were not, alas, *belle guerre*, they were wars for survival. They involved unglamorous defensive campaigns and inconclusive battles, they required the subordination of the individual, they saw unprecedented loss of life. The courtier-knight, intent on his own glory, or anxious to shine in the eyes of a prince who, very probably, was accustomed to turning his coat to suit his own convenience and not that of Italy as a whole, was a less effective instrument than his French equivalent. But this dwelling on one of the weaknesses of Italian arms is simply a means of demonstrating how prepared Italy was for warfare—of a kind, and to prevent the complaints of authors such as Machiavelli that men have lost their military virtues and interests from being applied to Italy as a whole.[2] The sense of shock, the cries of dismay that singled out 1494 as *anno infelicissimo*, these were not caused by the bringing of war to a country set in the ways of peace.

Nor were they caused by the fact that war took a turn for the worse. There is no doubt that the hazards of war became abruptly more drastic with the arrival of the French. The alarm caused by their sack of Fivizzano on their advance into Tuscany was sustained by their behaviour on entering the kingdom of Naples,

---

[1] The letter describing his wound is no. 59. See also pp. 191 and 194.

[2] For some other reactions see V. Cian, 'La coscienza politica nazionale nel Rinascimento' in his *Scritti Minori*, ii, Torino, 1936, especially p. 155, a reference I owe to Professor Grayson.

where after taking Monte di San Giovanni they murdered the populace and set fire to the town. 'This way of making war, not having been practised in Italy for many centuries,' noted Guicciardini, 'filled the whole kingdom with the greatest terror.'[1] As in sieges so in battles. Of Fornovo, fought in the next year on the French withdrawal from the peninsula, he wrote that the effete Italians were amazed how much blood could be shed in the course of an hour's fighting. To the atrocities of the French and their Swiss allies[2] after 1494 and the Spaniards after 1503 were added those of the Germans after 1509, who behaved, in the opinion of the sober Venetian Priuli, worse than infidels, looting churches, violating women and assassinating the very children.[3] On the surrender of Vicenza, in spite of terms which guaranteed the safety of the inhabitants, the behaviour of the Germans was so violent that large numbers of men, and more women and children, took refuge in a system of caverns nearby. The Germans thereupon lit fires in the entrances until they were all dead.[4] And so it went on. The sack of Brescia by the French and Germans and the sack of Prato by the Spaniards in 1512 were the occasions for more lamentation at the unheard-of cruelty and callousness with which war was being waged.[5]

Most shocking was its spreading to non-combatants. With long lines of communications, which at times broke down entirely, the French were forced to live off the country. Erratic pay forced the Germans and Swiss to do the same. The Spaniards, isolated in

---

[1] *Storia d'Italia*, ed. C. Panigada, i (Bari, 1929), 106.

[2] Ibid., p. 171. Cf. Commines, *Mémoires*, ed. B. de Mandrot, ii (Paris, 1903), 251.

[3] Muratori, *Rerum Italicarum Scriptores*, 1928, xxiv, fasc. ii, parte iii, p. 184.

[4] Da Porto, op. cit., p. 203, Guicciardini, op. cit., iii, 15.

[5] See, for instance, *Il miserando sacco di Prato cantato in terza rima da Stefano Guizzalotti* in *Archivio Storico Italiano*, ser. i, vol. i, pp. 263–71, where the poet declares (p. 265):

> Non tanta crudeltà Turchi infedeli
> Usaron mai cotanto alli Cristiani,
> Quanto ch'a Prato gli Spagnoi crudeli,

and goes on to particularize them.

Naples in 1504, were forced to supply themselves as best they could, a situation all the more deplorable, Guicciardini recorded, in that it was a novel one. 'For ever since the times of antiquity in which military discipline was severely exercised, the soldiery had been always licentious and burdensome to the people, yet they never gave themselves a loose to all manner of disorders, but lived for the most part on their pay, and their licentiousness was restrained within tolerable bounds. But the Spaniards in Italy were the first that presumed to maintain themselves wholly on the substance of the people.' And he dourly adds, 'This was the beginning of a corruption which soon spread.'[1]

When his narrative approaches the bloody consequences of the League of Cambrai, he again sounds the same note:

'Though many wars and revolutions had happened in Italy during the last fourteen years, yet the disputes being often terminated without blood, or mostly at the expense of the lives of the barbarians engaged in them, the people suffered less than their princes. But now a door being opened to new contentions, there followed a train of mischievous and cruel events which overspread the face of Italy, and affected the Italians themselves, who saw nothing but scenes of infinite slaughter, plunder and the destruction of multitudes of town and cities, attended with military licentiousness, no less destructive to friends than foes.'[2]

Even after making some allowance for Guicciardini's masochistic bias, it is clear that he is expressing generally what local records and popular printed laments and prophecies say in detail. Yet alongside complaints of the ruthlessness of the barbarians went positive admiration for it. If war were to be waged at all it should be waged whole-heartedly. Guicciardini praised the dash and the uncompromising will-to-win of the French soldier; Machiavelli did not swerve from his admiration for the Swiss after their devastation of Pontremoli, nor because of their reluctance to be burdened with prisoners. As the wars proceeded, the Turks themselves, the very symbols of ruthlessness, were increasingly held up to admiration at the expense of the ill-disciplined and

[1] Ibid., ii, 138. [2] Ibid., ii, 245.

irresolute Italian soldiery.[1] If war were to be waged effectively, it must be waged *à l'outrance*, and the grief of the afflicted populace was deepened by the fact that their troops did not seem capable of replying in kind.

This, then, was the greatest shock provided by 1494 and the years that followed: the realization that the Italians, though prepared for war and equipped to wage it, were to become the abject prey of barbarian nations which had once bowed the knee at the name of Rome. Where were Caesar, Fabius and Scipio? Where was the *élan* that had made the legionaries so terrible? What had become of the military virtues, the morale without which the best-prepared, the best-equipped army is useless? Under conventional queries as to what had become of the glory, the fair name of Italy, lay a more searching concern with what had happened to the Italian character; among conventional explanations given in terms of the complainant's *bête noire*—luxury, it might be, or irreligion, or immorality—were others which depended on a scrutiny of recent history and a reassessment of the individual of the social and political organization in which he grows up. From technical books of military instruction to works of political theory, a novel concern with morale made itself felt, caused not by abstract twinges of millenarianism or reform but the humiliation of actual defeats.

The lines on which this heart-searching was to be conducted had been anticipated in Florence during the struggle against the Visconti in the early *Quattrocento*,[2] and traced again by Alberti in the *Della Famiglia*. The preservation and reputation of States, he wrote in the *proemio*, do not depend on providence but on *le buone e sancte discipline del vivere*. Looking back into the past in a way which must have seemed balefully prophetic to his readers after 1494, he pointed out that as long as *da noi furono le optime e sanctissime nostre vetustissime discipline observate*, the greatness of

---

[1] By Paolo Giovio, for instance, in his *Turcicarum Rerum Commentarius* (Paris, 1539), p. 83.

[2] Hans Baron, *The Crisis of the Early Italian Renaissance*, 2 vols. (Princeton, 1955).

Rome endured, and every nation, however barbarous and fero-
cious, feared and obeyed her. Among the qualities that made
Rome great was *la iustitia di Torquato, qual per osservare la militare
disciplina non perdonò al figliuolo*, and it was *colle quali virtù non meno
che col ferro et colla forza* that her rule was buttressed. But once the
good laws and *sanctissime consuete discipline* are lost, Italy is lost.
*E le barbare nationi . . . quali soleano al tuo venerando nome, Italia,
rimettere ogni suberbia, ogni ira, e tremare, subito queste tutte presoro
audacia d'inrumpere in mezzo al tuo sanctissimo seno, Italia, sino ad
incendere el nido e lla propria antica sedia dello imperio di tutti gli imperii.*[1]

1494 was to show how far *sancte discipline* had lapsed. In comparing the forces ranged on either side in that year, Guicciardini
was not content to give names and numbers; he compared their
morale. The French: intrepid and valorous; the Swiss, who by
stern training and practice had *rinnovata la fama antica della ferocia*;
and the Italians who *non aveano, nè per natura nè per accidente,
stimolo estraordinario al bene servire*; poor material, and often poorly
led. Speaking of Virginio Orsini's decision to let his sons serve
on the French side while he himself fought for Naples, Guicciardini comments that this decision amazed the French, *non assueti
a queste sottili distinzioni de' soldati d'Italia*. He speaks sarcastically of
the *cautela italiana* with which the Duke of Ferrara, while himself
professing neutrality on the formation of the League of 1495,
allowed his son to fight for Milan against the French. And sum-
ming up the Italian resistance to the French conquest of Naples
he concluded that it displayed *nè virtù nè animo nè consiglio, non
cupidità d'onore non potenza non fede*, and that the whole sorry business
ended *con sommo vituperio e derisione della milizia italiana e con gravis-
simo pericolo e ignominia di tutti.*[2] And this concern with morale was
not felt only by Florentine writers with their tradition of concern
for social ethics. Castiglione, referring in *The Courtier* to the fact
that the Italians had not displayed of late much valour in arms,
sought *la vera causa delle nostre ruine e della virtù prostrata, se non
morta, negli animi nostri*, that moral failure as a result of which

---

[1] Ed. R. Spongano, Florence, 1946, pp. 7–8.
[2] The passages quoted are from op. cit., i, 73, 99, 140, 106 and 113.

il nome italiano è ridotto in obrobrio, nè si ritrovano se non pochi che osino non dirò morire, ma pur entrare in uno pericolo.[1]

For Castiglione these reflections did not lead to the consideration of any constitutional changes. Not that he was unconcerned with political theory: the fourth book is largely concerned with proving—to the great convenience of the courtier—that the best government is that of a prince. Urbino was already organized for war. What was needed was an improvement in morale through the private self-education of the courtier. But in Florence, where the state was not organized for war, concern with morale was firmly linked with concern for the constitution. What was wrong with a political organization that had left the state reliant on the arms of mercenaries, and the citizens devoid of military feeling? What measures should be taken to secure a civic militia, and, once having obtained it, what measures should be taken to make sure that it was used only against the enemies of the state, and not against the state itself? The experience of war, then, led to consideration of the formal structure of government: the sort of constitution that worked best in an emergency when crucial decisions had to be made quickly and definitely; and it led, too, to a consideration of the personal element: the way constitutional changes could improve the civic temper of the populace as a whole.[2]

No political thinker was more influenced by the spectacle of Italy's military defeats than Machiavelli. It is worth recalling the sheer bulk of references to specifically military matters in his work. About one-sixth of the *Prince*, about one-fifth of the *Discourses*, the whole of the *Art of War*. Of the rather few generalizations in the *Florentine History* a large number are concerned with military affairs, and Books 1 and 2 end, and Books 3, 5 and 6 begin, with discussions about war and valour. War, after all, was Machiavelli's hobby-horse. From his first months of office in 1498 he had showed an interest in the technicalities of war. On diplomatic

---

[1] Ed. Cian, 4th ed., Florence, 1947, pp. 109 and 411.

[2] For these points, see the political discourses of Guicciardini, especially the *Del Modo di Ordinare il Governo Popolare* and the *Dialogo del Reggimento di Firenze*, ed. Palmarocchi (Bari, 1932), pp. 65–7 and 90–2.

missions abroad he had seen armies in the process of formation and in the field. He had been made responsible for the organiza-tion of his darling project, the Florentine militia in 1506, and though dismayed, he was not daunted by its poor showing against the Spaniards at Prato in 1512. By temperament a keen armchair soldier, his diplomatic career had shown him that Florence would be despised until she had a strong army of her own, his knowledge of his city's history showed him why she had none, his study of Roman history showed him how one could be built up. As a student of the international scene he thought of the armies which foreign powers could put into the field. As a student of the Florentine constitution—as who could not be, in a period of experiment and crisis?—he thought of the citizen as a potential soldier. From the time he devoted to military matters—first the militia, then the city's fortifications—the space he gave them in his works, and the enthusiasm with which he wrote of them, it is probable that Machiavelli would have wished to be remembered, first and foremost, as a great writer on war. Certainly it is the topic on which he speaks to us with least reservation. Hobby-horses can be ridden over ground impracticable for real ones, and thus we learn more about the character of their riders. Any aspect of Machiavelli's work—his use of ancient history, his disturbing blend of sober observation and almost trancelike conjecture—can be studied best when Machiavelli has entered his *scrittoro* at San Cascino and, having passed into *le antique corti delli antiqui uomini*, talks to the great soldiers there.

He started from the contention that the Italian armies of his own day were despicable. He speaks of them as a 'blind chance rabble', 'the scorn of the world', the result of fighting having been 'reduced to a trade so vile that any peddling captain, in whom the mere ghost of ancient valour had reappeared, would have laughed them to scorn'.[1] The best armies, like those of Rome, were those that combined ardour with discipline. Next are those which had ardour without discipline, like the Gauls'. Last came those who

[1] In ed. Mazzoni and Casella: *Discorsi*, iii, c. 36, p. 251: *Arte della Guerra*, vii, 366; *Istorie Fiorentine*, i, 407.

'have neither natural courage nor discipline. Of this kind are the Italian armies of our time, which are of no use at all.'[1]

Machiavelli looked back on two ages with special nostalgia. One was that of the Roman Republic, the other was the Florentine *Trecento*. Both were periods when fresh territories and glory had been gained by citizens fighting for their own countries.[2] Since then Florence, like all Italy, had come to rely on mercenary troops, dangerous in peace, fickle in war, eating up the profits of victory and doubling the hazards of defeat. And the employment of mercenaries and auxiliaries was not the only way in which the citizen had burked the responsibility of taking arms himself. He put device after device between himself and each threat. He trusted first to diplomacy to win him allies, then he attempted to stop an opposing army with subsidies and treaties.[3] If these failed, he tried to turn it back at the borders of the state, and if their defence failed, to rely on fortresses, and on artillery as a last resort to prevent his having to come to blows himself. All mistaken, and all vain; 'it is the heart and vital parts of the body that should be protected', he wrote in the *Discourses*,[4] 'and not the extremities, for without the latter life is possible, but without the former death is certain.' The citizen must learn to fight. For hired troops must be substituted a militia. I venture to affirm that the first state in Italy that shall take up this suggestion, he concluded, 'fia . . . signore di questa provincia'.[5]

But the quality of a militia, as Machiavelli saw, depended on the quality of the citizens, and they had become corrupted by peace

---

[1] *Discorsi*, iii, c. 36.

[2] For a criticism of Machiavelli's interpretation, see P. Pieri, *Guerra e Politica negli Scrittori Italiani* (Milan, 1955), ch. 1.

[3] Luca Landucci comments sardonically when taxes were raised on one such occasion, in 1480, 'We Florentines have the wise custom of giving money in payment to everyone who does us an injury, and who destroys and pillages our territory . . . it will always be the same; anyone who wants money from the Florentines has only to do them an injury.' *A Florentine Diary*, ed. I. del Badia, Eng. ed. 1927, p. 30.

[4] iii, c. 30.

[5] *Arte della Guerra*, Mazzoni and Casella, p. 367.

and luxury. To pursue their own affairs the better, they had left the business of fighting to others, and had come to think, as Rome in her greatness had never thought, that the civilian and military aspects of life were quite discordant. Things had gone so far that if a young man elected to go to the wars, his reputation would actually suffer for it.[1] Machiavelli begins his *Art of War* by introducing into the city garden of Cosimo Rucellai a soldier, Fabrizio Colonna, who has come to Florence from the wars in Lombardy. Invited to admire it, he says bluntly that Cosimo's grandfather, who founded the garden, would have done better if he had lived actively and hardily like the ancients, rather than providing for leisure and luxurious ease. His host agrees, but adds that his grandfather, in fact, had 'found it impossible either for himself or his sons to practise what he most approved: for such was the corruption of the age he lived in, that if anyone had spirit enough to deviate ever so little from the common customs and manner of living of those times, he would have been universally ridiculed'. But Machiavelli was convinced that affairs could change, and declared in the preface 'that it is not even yet impossible to revive the discipline of our ancestors, and in some measure to retrieve the reputation of our soldiery'.

What was needed, he suggested, was the re-education of the citizen, and this could be achieved by means of a good military organization. Without such a training, riches, pride, dominion itself is empty. This was obvious simply from the example of Florence. And he pointed to the situation of the Venetians when they had lost their first battle against the French in 1509. 'Their miserable baseness of spirit, caused by a wretched military organization, made them lose at a single blow their courage and their state.' With a sound organization, morale can be improved, valour return and great deeds once more be possible.

More than this: in securing a good militia, a corrupt state will be made healthy. Just as poor military institutions or—in Florence's case—only vestigial ones can sap civic spirit, so good military institutions can restore it. Once get rid of the false notion that there

[1] Guicciardini, *Dialogo del Reggimento di Firenze*, ed. cit., p. 91.

is a fundamental split between the soldier and the citizen, and it will then be clear that as the ideal soldier is also the perfect citizen, to improve him in one capacity is to improve him in the other. The corrupt citizen, through the influence of good military institution, becomes a good soldier, and, at the same time, a better citizen. From a sound military organization follow good laws, and these too help in the re/education of the citizen. A corrupt state, in fact, can be reformed by the right military organization.

It follows from this that the political theorist who wants good laws should also be a military theorist intent on producing good soldiers. Army reform will produce the right citizen material for the best possible state, whereas 'without good military organiza/tion there can neither be good laws nor anything else good.' It follows too that the military theorist who wants good soldiers is planning something with necessary political consequences. A state's constitution is affected by the martial temper of the populace and the specific nature of the way in which they are organized for war.

He recognized that the bad citizen could only be made into a good soldier by strong persuasion. The Soderini republic could put men into uniform but it could not make real soldiers of them. One of the main tragedies of Italy was that her rulers had been too weak to introduce good military institutions. These can only be put into effect 'through the method I have described and with the co/operation of some powerful princes'.[1] Bad soldiers must, then, be made into good ones by a prince. This will involve their becoming reformed citizens, capable of governing themselves once more. The finest political type the world had seen was, for Machiavelli, the citizen of the Roman republic. The best way of rescuing a corrupt Florence was, by introducing Roman military institutions, to reanimate the citizens of Florence. But this was a time of crisis, and the process had to be carried out quickly, before it was too late.

At this point, however, the argument blurs. The neat solution would have been: let a prince, then, compel military reforms in

[1] Ed. cit., *Arte della Guerra*, p. 366.

Florence in the interest of an improved civic temper. Machiavelli advised the Medici, it is true, to foster the sense of political responsibility among the Florentines in preparation for a return to more broadly based republican institutions on the death of Cardinal Giulio and Leo X, but this was to be done through reviving the *Consiglio Grande*. Just as Machiavelli's plans for a militia were flawed by his distrust of armed city-dwellers as opposed to men from the contado, so his conviction that a prince could best produce (as Cesare Borgia had done) a resolute native soldiery failed at the point of applying the conclusion to Florence. His attitude both to the citizen and to the state was affected by his preoccupation with war, but his prejudice against the armed townsman and his inherited republican bias prevented him from thinking in terms even of a temporary military autocracy for his native city.

War, too, affected his attitude towards political morality, adding an infection from its own drama to his conviction that for a public figure in a time of crisis to luxuriate in a private conscience was irresponsible, for 'although deceit is detestable in all other things, yet in the conduct of war it is laudable and honourable', and he stresses the importance of 'those feints and stratagems which you employ against an enemy that distrusts you, and in the employment of which properly consists the art of war'.[1] What he has in mind are the tricks reported of Roman and Greek generals by ancient military writers, but it is difficult not to feel that the ruthlessness and deviousness necessary on the eve of battle, and sanctified by classical example, was considered appropriate by Machiavelli to any time of crisis and emergency in the intervals of battles, in the intervals even of wars, when peace itself was but an uneasy pause from combat. In the chapter from the *Discourses* quoted above, he makes it clear that he does not confuse these military stratagems 'with perfidy, which breaks pledged faith and treaties'. He distinguishes between placid peace which must not be broken by deceit, and a state of uneasy peace, continually on the verge of war, and which must therefore borrow the manners of war. And Machiavelli's whole active life was passed in a period of crisis, of war or warlike peace, when politicians and generals alike could plead necessity, and when political thinkers who were also students of war could find it easy to grant that plea.

If these wars affected political and constitutional ideas—and Machiavelli was exceptional only in the depth of his interest— they also affected historical thought. From time to time it was admitted that the Italians were more skilled or more resourceful than their adversaries, that individual Italians might be braver, but the dominant judgement was cynical and contributed to that note of disillusioned analysis which has been seen as a salient factor in the 'modern' tone of Renaissance historiography. The later Renaissance cannot be understood without taking into account the pessimism induced by defeats inflicted on a society which had no quarrel with war as an activity in itself. 'Misera Italia,' mourned an anonymous poet after the sack of Rome in 1527,

> *Misera Italia, a che condotta sei*
> *suggetta al nome che più fiate hai vinto;*
> *la gloria, el pregio e quel vigore è estinto,*
> *che già dato ti fu da' sommi Dei.*[1]

[1] *La Presa di Roma* (Sonetto), ed. F. Mango in *Scelta di Curiosità Letterarie*, Bologna, 1886. Punctuated.

L. F. Marks

THE FINANCIAL OLIGARCHY IN FLORENCE UNDER LORENZO

The Lorentian political system was born out of the turbulent years of the Pazzi conspiracy and the following wars. The foundations had been well laid many years before. In 1458 the newly formed Council of the Hundred had usurped many of the powers previously vested solely in the ancient Councils of the People and the Commune. The *balìa*, or extraordinary commission, had already become a regular expedient of government in times of crisis or sudden change. But it was not till 1480, after the papal threat had been successfully parried, that the copingstone was placed in position—the Council of Seventy with its two permanent committees, the twelve *Procuratori* and the *Otto di Pratica*. The pattern of oligarchical rule was complete; whatever powers the old communal councils had exercised in the past they now became mere ciphers. Political power rested with the Seventy and the Hundred in whose hands it remained until the revolution of 1494.

Of the constitutional role of the Council of the Hundred before and after these changes we know a great deal. The registers of its deliberations from 1459 till 1494 have survived. From its inception it was clearly intended to have legislative precedence over the other councils in all matters of vital state importance. Under this heading were included elections, contracts with mercenary troops, and, perhaps most important of all, taxation.[1] On all such

---

[1] *Consiglio del Cento. Deliberazioni.* Reg. 1, fo. 11v. '. . . quando tales provisiones et proposte essent de materiis negotiis seu rebus pertinentibus ad STATUM seu BURSAS aut SCRUCTINEA aut ad onera vel Conductas gentium armigerum . . . quod novum consilium del Cento debeat esse primum. . . .' All references in this article are to sources in the Archivio di Stato, Florence.

matters the vote was to be taken first in the Hundred and only after it had spoken in the People and the Commune. At first the Hundred was not empowered to sanction laws by its own authority. But this restriction did not last long. The *balia* of 1471 vested authority over financial measures solely in the Hundred.[1] In 1475 for the last time the ancient councils of the city were allowed to vote on a *riforma* of the *Monte Comune*, the major financial legislation in the Florentine calendar.[2] By 1477 the Hundred was deciding policy regarding the precious *Monte di dote*, or dowry bank for Florentine maidens.[3] Henceforth the official financial history of the republic is recorded in the *Deliberazioni* of the Hundred and no longer in the *Provvisioni* of the Commune.

Less is known about the activities of the Council of Seventy. None of its registers survive and its votes are not recorded in the *Libri Fabarum*.[4] It was always consulted on new legislation before the Hundred but it always seems to have retained a consultative and *ad hoc* rather than a permanent and legislative character. But what essentially was its role in the system of government in Florence? What motives lay behind its formation? In what ways did it bolster the powers of the oligarchy after 1480?

Records of some decisions taken independently by the Council of Seventy do survive. These belong to the months immediately after its formation and are in fact to be found among the last pages of the volume containing the deliberations of the thirty-man *balia* of 1480—the body which in an enlarged form was reconstituted as the Seventy.[5] In June 1480 the *balia* had granted special

---

[1] Cf. V. Ricchioni, *La Costituzione politica di Firenze ai tempi di Lorenzo il Magnifico* (Siena, 1913), p. 46.

[2] A 'reform' of the *Monte Comune* consisted of a reordering of interest rates, etc., in line with the general financial situation. Their provisions would normally remain in force for about five years but as the overall situation deteriorated after 1470 they became more regular. After 1494 the *Monte* was reformed annually.

[3] Cento, reg. 2, fos. 2–4. Libri Fabarum 70, fos. 60–1.

[4] The Libri Fabarum, which record all proposals made in the legislative councils with votes, do not survive for the years 1481–92. Cf. D. Marzi, *La cancelleria della repubblica fiorentina* (Rocca S. Casciano, 1910), p. 515.

[5] Balie, 31, fos. 115v–19.

authority to the Council of Seventy, together with the *signoria* and the Colleges concerning appointments of officials of the *Monte Comune*, exaction of certain taxes and arrangements for securing state loans.[1] The decisions which we find at the end of the volume relate solely to these matters. The early days of the Council of Seventy, as of the *balia* which preceded it, were dominated by matters of finance.

The details of the decisions are somewhat complex, but they centre around a single theme. Florence was being called on to provide sizeable sums of money for diplomatic purposes at a time when the scars left by the immense exertions of the Pazzi war were still far from healed. The practice was for money to be advanced to the government through the *Monte Comune*, or state bank, against the security of current or future taxes. Responsibility for raising these loans and seeing to their repayment rested with the Officials of the *Monte*, themselves usually leading financiers who were elected annually, and who often subscribed loans from their own private resources. During their period of office they adminis‐tered all the revenues of the *Monte* which included all the receipts of the indirect taxes as well as whatever direct taxes had been assigned by legislation to it. In the last months of 1480 the finan‐cial situation, although by no means as grave as it had been during the fighting, was still serious. The conclusion of peace had saddled Florence with large debts—to the King of Naples, to his son Alfonso, Duke of Calabria, and to the Pope—for which a total of 46,000 florins was needed. Loans had to be raised, security guaranteed.

A mere ten years previously similar matters had been voted on by the ancient communal councils. What this had meant in terms of real popular control would be difficult to determine. But by 1480 even the pretence had been abandoned. The decisions taken by the Seventy were not in themselves startling or innova‐tory. A previous loan of 40,000 florins voted in May 1480 had resulted in serious loss due to the delay in recovering the capital debt from tax receipts. Tax revenues up to the following May

---

[1] Ibid., fo. 115v.

were pledged to the *Monte* Officials. These Officials were then ordered to loan a further 20,000 florins against the following year's revenue which would be repaid to them by the Officials for 1481. At first the Officials demurred but finally accepted with the proviso that greater security would be arranged. The Seventy responded sympathetically to this request and fixed a date, April 30 next, by which all repayment must be made. Severe penalties were ordered for any default. But the Officials for 1481, four of whom were actually members of the Seventy,[1] were commissioned to raise further loans up to a total of 46,000 florins against special taxes previously voted by the Hundred. This sum was to be further guaranteed by a body of citizens 'including some leading persons', all of whom therefore had a direct interest in seeing that the taxes were paid promptly and in full.

Clearly the Council of Seventy in the first few months of its existence had played a vital part in keeping the credit machinery of the Florentine republic running smoothly. This in itself pro-vokes the question of how far its formation in 1480 was prompted by motives arising from the sphere of public finance. Other evi-dence strengthens this impression, most of all the composition of the membership of the Council. A glance of the original members of the *balia* shows that they were preponderantly men who as Officials of the *Monte Comune* over the previous ten years had been intimately concerned with the financial affairs of the republic, especially in their credit aspect. When additional members were co-opted to form the Council of Seventy the pro-portion of *Monte* Officials dropped slightly but not significantly especially if account is taken of family affiliations.[2]

The evidence can be interpreted variously. It could be argued that the urge for tighter control over public funds and financial policy on the part of a close-knit oligarchy was the determining

[1] Giovanni Bonsi, Lapo Niccolini, Pierfilippo Pandolfini and Tommaso Davanzati, Tratte, 82, fo. 105.

[2] For the members of the *balia* and the Council of Seventy see Ricchioni, op. cit., pp. 57 and 62. These can be compared with the names of *Monte* Officials in Tratte, 82, fos. 104-5.

factor in the constitutional changes of 1480. On the other hand, what is true of public finance could also be held to be true for other fields in the political and economic life of the city, and it could be said that what needs explanation is the broader phenomenon of the rise of the oligarchy. The sources from which a thorough-going analysis of the Medician government in Florence could be constructed still remain largely unexplored. This essay is an attempt to fill in one part of the picture, a part which cannot yet be placed correctly into the general framework, but which needs to be properly understood before the picture itself can be drawn.

The heart of the financial problem lay in the state of credit. By the middle years of the fifteenth century the *Monte Comune* had developed from being the financial device—the funded debt—it had been at its foundation in 1345 and had become the central financial institution of the republic.[1] A law of 1470 spoke of it in glowing, if ponderous, metaphor: 'The *Monte* is the heart of this body which we call city . . . every limb, large and small, must contribute to preserving this heart as the guardian fortress, immovable rock and enduring certainty of the salvation of the whole body and government of your State.'[2]

In principle the *Monte* was the consolidated public debt, paying interest to all those who had holdings in respect of past loans. But it is the nature of all credit institutions to grow. This was especially the case in fifteenth-century Florence where the increased cost of warfare, constant wars, and energetic diplomatic activity led to endless demands for fresh loans, and hence to a constant inflation of the debt. Not since the time of the Ciompi had any voice been raised for cancellation of the debt and the history of the *Monte* in the first half of the fifteenth century was one of ever more complex expedients to maintain credit. Wider in-roads were made into the revenues of the republic and greater powers were granted to the *Monte* officials in their administration. At the same time more areas of public expenditure were made the

[1] B. Barbadoro, *Le finanze della repubblica fiorentina; imposta diretta e debito pubblico fino all'instituzione del Monte* (Florence, 1929).

[2] Registri delle provvisioni, 161, fo. 168.

responsibility of the Officials, so that by about 1470 the details of a *Monte* 'reform' came to resemble a budget for the entire republic. The old *camera* or treasury fell almost into disuse, its staff axed, as every item of public and military spending passed over to the *Monte*.

Thus at about the period when St. Antonino was formulating his compromises on the delicate question of usury, the credit system was seeping quickly into every vein of Florentine financial life. The *catasto* returns of 1427 show that almost all citizens had some *Monte* holdings in respect of past loans, forced or otherwise. Two years earlier, in 1425, the credit area had been greatly enlarged by the opening of a new *Monte*,[1] that for dowries for the daughters of Florentine citizens. This form of popular investment was widely exploited. Founded at the time of the war against Filippo Maria Visconti as a means of alleviating pressure on the public debt it rapidly began to dominate the whole machinery of the *Monte Comune*. By 1470 the interests owing to dowry credits in the *Monte delle doti* totalled 198,000 florins—well over half the annual revenues of the city—as compared with 148,000 florins owing to all other ordinary Monte credits together.[2]

A Florentine father could obtain a holding in the *Monte delle doti* in his baby daughter's name in either of two ways—by investing cash, or by converting his existing *Monte Comune* stock at rates declarable by the *Monte* Officials. In both cases the result was the same. *The Monte delle doti* acquired ordinary *Monte Comune* stock on which interest would continue to be paid. Each year the accrued interest would be used to purchase fresh stock and thus the rate of interest on the holding would increase. At the end of fifteen years, when the daughter was of marriageable age, the total amount of stock accumulated would be redeemed for cash by the *Monte delle doti*, and it was this cash payment which constituted the dowry. If the daughter died or entered a convent before the dowry had matured her father would have to forfeit a half of the endowment.

[1] S. Ammirato, *Istoria Fiorentina* (Florence, 1647), part 2, Book xix, p. 1020.
[2] Reg. provv. 161, fo. 170.

The advantages of the system to the government lay in the gradual extinction of ordinary *Monte* stock and also in the fact that the mortality rate among Florentine children must have been high enough to make the scheme a workable economic proposition. Another factor which contributed to the profitability of the scheme was the steady drop in the market price of ordinary *Monte* stock due to the inexorable inflation of the public debt.[1] Once the *Monte delle doti* had become established the Officials seem to have pursued a policy of depressing this price still further. As the dowry payment was made in cash this fall was bound to operate in favour of the *Monte*.

But the scheme was not without its hazards. The provision of a suitable dowry for one's daughter was not merely a financial luxury. It was a social necessity, especially at a time when social convention was tending to ossify. Without a generous endowment the average Florentine maiden could not hope to win a husband. The early success of the *Monte delle doti* surely derived most of its original impetus from this fact. But to make such a social institution dependent on the financial well-being of the state could have serious repercussions. What if the state at some future date would find itself unable to meet even a part of its commitments to the young ladies?

The state, for its part, recognized the gravity of its responsibility. Severe penalties were decreed for Officials of the *Monte* who failed to make the necessary annual payments to the dowry fund, Attempts were made to limit the total sums invested, at first by setting maxima according to social status and later by fixing a total limitation. But as early as 1467 it had been shown that under serious financial stress the dowry fund would have to make its contribution to the city exchequer. This was at the time of the war against Venice, Ferrara and the Papacy. To meet military expenditure the Officials of the *Monte* had been freed from making the usual repurchases of stock, with disastrous results for the

[1] In 1470 the market price of ordinary *Monte* stock stood at 35 (Reg. provv. 161, fo. 173) and it tended to drop gradually thereafter.

Monte delle doti.[1] In view of the well-known charges often levelled against Lorenzo de Medici of having tampered with the dowry fund, it is useful to note that the practice had been begun before he came to power. But it would be incorrect to imply that the state was already taking its responsibilities lightly. On the contrary, great effort was exerted to safeguard the solvency of the *Doti*, as for instance in the *Monte* reform of 1470.[2]

In that year the *Monte Comune* was still suffering from a deficit due to continued military expenditure. But in allocating revenues the *Monte delle doti* was given clear precedence over all other ordinary investments. Terms for payments of these other interests were left vague, the Officials being instructed to pay them 'from time to time, as conveniently as they can from the revenues of the *Monte*'. Further, the rate of interest was lowered from $3\frac{3}{8}$ per cent to $3\frac{1}{4}$ per cent. This was in line with the general trend. At the beginning of the century *Monte* interest had stood at 5 per cent.

The arrangements to meet the serious situation in the dowry bank were much more specific. 165,000 florins were allocated to the repayment of accrued dowries. Even so it was admitted that a further 50,000 florins would still be owing at the end of the year. As the sums allocated could not be substantially increased the prospect held out was one of ever-multiplying debt and ever-longer delays between the consummation of marriage and the receipt of the dowry. We learn that this situation had arisen several times in the past. When it had happened the practice followed had been to close the subscription list at the *Monte delle doti*, thus consolidating the debt, and open a fresh list. This had been done in 1465 and it was this list, the fourth since the foundation of the fund, which had suffered from the failure of the *Monte*

[1] Reg. provv. 161, fo. 171: '. . . pel quarto Monte delle doti delle fanciulle che s'ordino 1465 . . . non si sono facte le debite ricompere, anzi quasi niente s'è ricomperato per essersi levato le pene agli uficiali del Monte, perche e' potessino servire di danari il vostro comune . . .'

[2] Reg. provv. 161, fos. 167-74v. Certain figures in this reform have been reprinted in Ricchioni, op. cit., p. 35, and H. Sieveking, *Studio sulle finanze genovesi nel medioevo e in particolare sulla Casa di S. Giorgio*. In *Atti della Societa Ligure di Storia Patria*, xxxv (Genoa, 1905), 149.

Officials to make the necessary repurchases of stock. In the words of the reform: '. . . when the time comes to repay the dowries of this *Monte* there will be a big shortage, and it will not be possible to repay the creditors at the time due, with great loss to the citizens and their daughters'. In order to defer the threatened failure the old device of closing the list was ordered again and a new, fifth, *Monte* opened for fresh subscriptions.

The details of the financial operation of the *Monte delle doti* are complex and ingenious, but the general picture is simple. High public expenditure, especially on warfare, had drained the re-sources of the state to the point where the solvency of the dowry fund had become seriously endangered. But as by this time the *Monte Comune* as a whole had spread its net over all the revenues of the republic it was not at all easy to see where fresh funds could be found to meet the increasing deficit. It is understandable how in this situation any unjustified expenditure by the *Monte Comune* would be looked on as a threat to the dowries. But Lorenzo him-self did not create the difficulties. He inherited them and it became his task, and that of the oligarchy with which he was associated, to devise means of easing the situation within the framework of his general financial policy.

It seems unlikely that Lorenzo embarked upon any clearly thought-out policy of diminishing the resources of the *Monte delle doti*. The crisis was rather an endemic one stemming from the gradual decline in ordinary revenues which resulted from the shrinking economic activity of Florence throughout the fifteenth century. A strictly curtailed military and diplomatic policy might have saved the situation, but this was not a part of the Lorentian vision. The war against the rebellious Volterra in 1472 cost the *Monte Comune* upwards of 200,000 florins,[1] and in the following year the Monte was called on to foot the bill for the lavish enter-tainment offered to the Duchess of Ferrara during her stay in Florence.[2] Inevitably the *Monte delle doti* suffered.

Those who stood to suffer from a crisis in the dowry fund were the main body of Florentine citizens. A crisis in the whole *Monte*

[1] Cento, reg. 2, fo. 2.   [2] Ibid.

Comune, however, threatened a narrower but more powerful group—those who advanced short-term war loans at high interest rates. Without these loans the state could not function. For those who advanced them the rewards were attractive. Interest never dropped below 12 per cent and often rose far higher. At the lowest rate, the profit on loans of 200,000 florins would be 24,000 florins, a considerable sum which somehow had to be met from *Monte* revenues. Provided these revenues were secure, war itself could be a source of profit to the moneylenders. But only the state could guarantee the security, and its weapon in doing this would naturally be the *Monte* itself. Within the body of *Monte* creditors a serious conflict of interests therefore arose: those who held dowry credits found their interests increasingly sacrificed to those of the large-scale lenders. The conflict would tend to intensify at times of war when the strain on the *Monte* increased and when extraordinary taxation gave added cause for resentment to the majority of citizens. But in one form or another the conflict remained a permanent feature of Florentine financial life for the next forty years.

A first aim of the oligarchy was to free the *Monte Comune* as far as possible from legislative restrictions. This was not achieved without a struggle. The *Monte* reform of 1470, which undoubtedly had been received with dismay by the main body of citizens, ran into heavy opposition in the councils. It was only passed 'after great effort and almost with violence', says Rinuccini.[1] Early in 1471 an attempt was made to grant the Officials of the *Monte* wide powers to increase customs yields, but the proposal was rejected.[2] In the winter of 1474–5 it took nearly three months for a proposal to be forced through the councils freeing the Officials from the usual penalties for not having made the necessary allocations to the diminution of the public debt.[3] A similar proposal made in 1479 at the height of the financial difficulties of the Pazzi war was

[1] *Ricordi storici di Francesco di Cino Rinuccini dal 1282 al 1460, colla continuazione di Alemanno e Neri suoi figli fino al 1506* (Florence, 1840), p. cxiv.

[2] Libri fabarum, 69, fos. 68–70.

[3] Lib. fab. 70, fos. 11–15v.

rejected three times in the Council of the People before finally being passed by one vote.[1] In 1474 special powers were confirmed to the *Monte* Officials for confiscation of the property of tax debtors. Many of these debtors took their cases to the court of the *Podesta* where the confiscations were annulled but finally the superior authority of the *Monte* was established.[2]

Considerable difficulty was also aroused by the new *Monte* reform of 1475.[3] A feature of this measure was the wide area of discretion left to the *Monte* Officials over the allocation of funds. No detailed accounts were rendered as in 1470 and what figures were given of expenditure raise as many queries as they answer. For example, it was decreed that the sum devoted to paying accrued dowries should be raised from 150,000 to 175,000 florins, but nowhere was it indicated how this higher figure would be met. The whole measure—the last of its kind to be placed before the ancient councils of the Commune—creates an impression of holding out illusory hopes which cannot be supported by facts. It is admitted, for example, that even with the increased allocation it may not be possible to give full payment of accrued dowries. The Officials are therefore only obliged to pay a fifth of the amount due. For the rest the newly wedded wife must wait 'until her turn comes up'.

The 1475 reform was intended to remain in force for six years but by 1477 the crisis had deepened so dangerously as to demand desperate measures. A special law was passed placing the management of the *Monte Comune* for one year entirely in the hands of the Council of the Hundred which proceeded immediately to enact its own reform.[4]

Within the Hundred language could be frank. The *Monte* is described realistically as the institution which 'safeguards the income of the Commune and makes men ready to make all the payments they have to make to it, because they see that all its income is transformed either into an increase in the purses of the citizens and of the whole people with regard to dowries and

---

[1] Lib. fab. 70, fos. 146v-7.
[3] Lib. fab. 70, fo. 11v.
[2] Reg. provv. 166, fos. 4v-5.
[4] Cento, reg. 2, fos. 2-4.

interests, or into a saving for them', because the *Monte* has taken over a large number of public expenses which previously were met from other sources.[1] These included the costs of provisioning fortresses in the dominions at Pisa and Leghorn and a large annual grant to the universities of Florence and Pisa, as well as the expenses of the Volterra war. The result had been a great inflation of the public debt. Interest payments on the debt were in such disorder that for over two years they had lagged behind to the extent of about 60,000 florins. In the dowry fund the strain was severe: '175,000 florins cash are devoted to the dowries and nevertheless they are over sixteen months behind. Poor men are selling their investments and not realizing their capital whose proceeds ought to support the burdens of marriage. They suffer loss, and not only them but others who are more powerful. There is a great deal of outcry and infamy in the city. If no remedy is found this institution, which is so useful to the citizens, will be ruined. . . .' We then learn that the amount owing to accrued dowries has reached the enormous total of 468,000 florins, of which more than 240,000 had already been demanded by people who had consummated their marriages and paid the necessary stamp duty.

The measures taken to meet the situation were half-hearted. Certain governmental economies were ordered including the abolition of the ancient office of *Capitano del Popolo*, 'because he no longer has anything to do'. One-thirteenth of all ordinary interest payments was in future to be retained by the *Monte*, thus effectively lowering the rate to 3 per cent. To boost revenues an increase of the duty on wine by three *soldi* per barrel was decreed, an increase which must have been extremely unpopular.[2]

---

[1] The expenses of the *Signoria*, fire-guards and salaries of foreign rectors, in all about 18,000 florins, had been borne by the taxes until 1461 when special *monti* were created to meet them.

[2] Cento, reg. 2, fo. 3; Rinuccini, op. cit., p. cxxvi; L. Landucci, *Diario Fiorentino*, ed. I. del Badia (Florence, 1883), p. 16. It is interesting that while Rinuccini mentions all three measures Landucci, the shopkeeper, is only concerned to record the increased cost of wine.

This was in June 1477. The following year saw the Pazzi conspiracy and the outbreak of fresh conflicts. In May 1478 Paulantonio Solderini put before the Council of the People a proposal that, as an emergency measure, the amount payable to the *Monte delle doti* should be reduced from 200,000 to 100,000 florins, the difference to be devoted to 'the defence of the republic'. The proposal was carried by overwhelming majorities in all three councils.[1] Six months later it was officially recognized that the *Monte delle doti* would no longer be able to consider repayment of dowries in full. The character of the institution was to change profoundly. Henceforth the *Monte* was to pay out only a fraction of the sum due as a cash payment. At first this stood at one-fifth. The remaining unpaid part of the dowry was to be removed from the ordinary books of creditors and inscribed in a new list where it would become eligible to receive an annual interest of 7 per cent until such time as the *Monte* would be able to repay the capital. Not all creditors would be entitled to enjoy this benefit immediately, for the amount of capital to be transferred to the new list was limited by the financial state of the *Monte*. In 1478 this figure was fixed generously at 200,000 florins but in future years it was to be reduced far below this.[2]

Once again the ingenuity of the Florentine financial experts had come to the rescue. The result of the change was to be far-reaching on the general pattern of public finances, and the change itself was a masterpiece of compromise which must have made it reasonably acceptable to the mass of dowry creditors. What was envisaged in effect was a further inflation of the total capital debt borne by the *Monte Comune*, But a debt is a double-edged weapon. The investor might resent the delay in recovering his capital, but in return he is offered a new source of earning power for his money. A bond which bore interest at the rate of 7 per cent was worth at least as much as its paper value in ready cash. It could be sold in the stock market, used as security in business transactions or pledged for a mortgage. Its value depended ultimately on the state

---

[1] Reg. provv. 169, fos. 22-4v; Lib. fab. 70, fo. 124.

[2] Reg. provv. 169, fo. 84v.

of public credit, but the inauguration of the new fund provided the government with a better chance of meeting its commitments than would have been the case if the practice of attempting to repay dowries in full had been maintained. The new measure, in the event, proved a powerful stimulus to public confidence. During 1479, despite continued financial strain on the whole city, the amount invested in the *Monte delle doti* rose threefold and forced the government to take steps once again to limit investment.[1]

The Florentine citizen had been long accustomed to look on the state as a source of profit. It took the courage of a Savonarola to exhort him to lend money gratis and even he had little success in altering the attitude.[2] We have seen how the financial strains of the Pazzi war affected the dowry fund. What were their effects on the other major source of profit, the war loans?

The costs of the war were met almost entirely by large-scale loans by the Officials of the *Monte Comune* and others, against the security of extremely high direct taxes. These taxes were supplemented by other measures such as levies on the Church and arbitrary forced imposts on the citizens and others. The law of May 1478 which freed the *Monte* from some of its commitments to the dowries had authorized the Officials to raise up to 200,000 florins.[3] In August special 'Officials of the Bank' were elected to loan 30,000 florins, and at the same time special incentives were offered to encourage speedy payment of the taxes.[4] But only three months later the serious defeat at Monte San Savino led to fresh difficulties. Extremely high taxes were ordered for 1479 (367,450 florins) and against this security it was decided to elect twice the usual number of *Monte* officials with obligations to raise 100,000 florins in cash for the wars.[5] By the summer of 1479, on the eve

---

[1] Balie, 31, fo. 104, in the *Monte* reform for 1480.

[2] Sermon of 28 October 1496, in *Prediche italiane ai Fiorentini*, ed. Cognasso, Palmarocchi (Perugia and Venice, 1930, etc.).

[3] Reg. provv. 169, fos. 22-4v.   [4] Reg. provv. 169, fos. 52-3v.

[5] Reg. provv. 169, fos. 87-8. Tratte, 82, fo. 104v. This tax total represented the highest figure for any year in the fifteenth century. See G. Canestrini, *La scienza e l'arte di stato* (Florence, 1862), p. 254.

of fresh fighting in the Val di Chiana, ten more officials were chosen to provide immediately an extra 70,000 florins.[1] It is not surprising that once again the officials were freed from their normal obligations to the various *monti* though this was not agreed to without much difficulty.[2] In September 1479 special commissioners were appointed with powers to exact tax debts accrued since May 1478 when the war began, but this was supplementary to further measures calling for fresh loans and levying new taxes.[3]

It was at this point, after nearly two years of warfare and continuous demands for money, that serious signs of strain began to appear. We have already described the results of this on the dowry fund. In December 1479 an *accatto*, or forced loan, previously decreed was abandoned.[4] At the same time the greatest difficulty was encountered in raising new loans. An attempt to raise 36,000 florins for the Ten of War had to be drastically curtailed.[5] In the following February tough opposition almost blocked a proposal that the Ten of War should be allowed a free hand to raise loans on their own account against the security of the current taxes.[6] What would have been the consequences had the war continued much longer it is difficult to tell, but it is clear that the credit of the *Monte Comune* had been stretched almost to breaking-point. It was at this point that Lorenzo returned to Florence from Naples having concluded the treaty by which the war was to end.

[1] Reg. provv. 170, fos. 46v-7.
[2] It took six days for this to be forced through the councils. Lib. fab. 70, fos. 146v–147v.
[3] Cento, 2, fo. 42.
[4] Cento, 2, fo. 46. It is stated in the preamble that it had caused great unrest and economic dislocation. Rinuccini, however, suggests that the real reason for its repeal was that certain leading persons in Florence, including the Gonfaloniere Tommaso Soderini (*vecchio rapace, iniquo e tiranico*) were informed secretly of how much they would be called on to pay; op. cit., p. cxxxi.
[5] Reg. provv. 170, fos. 80v-1v.
[6] Reg. provv. 170, fos. 105v-6v. The measure was rejected four times in the People and twice in the Council of the Commune. Lib. fab. 70, fos. 163-4.

The war which had saved the Lorentian state had placed it in great debt to the oligarchs, the men who as Officials of the *Monte* or 'Officials of the Bank' had had to provide the finances for waging the war. Now the price had to be paid. This is the context in which the constitutional reform of 1480 has to be set. The effect of the changes was to remove the credit institutions of the republic once and for all out of the influence of the old communal councils. At first these were placed in the hands of the *balìa*. Then, as we saw earlier, they were made over to the Council of Seventy. Finally, by a provision of 24 July 1481, control over the *Monte Comune* and all the indirect taxes—the customs and other items of ordinary revenue which formed the mainstay of the securities of the *Monte*—was made over to the Council of the Hundred.[1] This, it is true, was intended as a temporary measure lasting one year, but for the purposes of the government this was enough, for the Hundred proceeded immediately to delegate its powers to a commission of seventeen leading citizens, including the five Officials of the *Monte*, who embarked directly on a complete reform of all aspects of the financial administration with the purpose of strengthening the resources of the *Monte*.[2] Thus the oligarchy was in a position to carry out its policy while maintaining at least an outward respect for constitutional forms. Nine years later, when the finances of the city again called for drastic measures, exactly the same expedient was revived, when the second Commission of Seventeen Reformers carried out further changes in the operation of the *Monte delle doti* and the currency.

The constitutional changes of 1480–1 placed the financial resources of the Florentine state firmly in the hands of a narrow oligarchy. This control was exercised through the Council of Seventy, from whose members were drawn almost exclusively the Officials of the *Monte*.[3] Its deliberations were placed for en

[1] Reg. provv. 172, fos. 81v–4. Provision of 24 July 1481.

[2] Cento, 2, fo. 56v. Law of 4 August 1481.

[3] Tratte, 82, fo. 105. Often, as in 1482, 1483, 1485, 1487 and 1492, these Officials were reappointed for a further year, a practice which had hardly ever been operated before 1480.

dorsement before the Hundred which retained its legislative powers over new tax laws.

After 1480 investment in the war loans could therefore be looked on as a relatively safe and highly lucrative speculation. Between 1482 and 1487, in order to meet the demands of the Ferrara war and the campaign against Pietrasanta the Officials of the *Monte* provided the vast total of 818,000 florins, often subscribing several thousand florins over the sums actually voted. The rate of interest on these loans rose to as high as 16 per cent, a return of about 130,000 florins or nearly one half of the entire annual income from indirect taxes.[1] In January 1484 they were asked to provide 160,000 florins against security from all the resources of the *Monte*.[2] Some months later it was stated that they had actually loaned 174,000 florins on which the interest charged amounted to almost 30,000 florins or more than the receipts from a complete levy of the *decima scalata*, the direct tax inaugurated by the *balia* of 1480.[3]

The loan system was relatively straightforward. After consultations among the Seventy and the *Signoria* a measure would be passed through the Hundred calling on the Officials of the *Monte* to provide the sums required and at the same time imposing the taxes which would guarantee repayment of the capital and interest. If in the meantime fresh demands arose and the Officials had raised more than originally requested additional security would be arranged at the earliest date. The degree of mutual understanding among the persons concerned must have been considerable. Often we have the impression that the official act merely sets the seal on some less publicly made agreements. In September 1483, for example, an act of the Hundred states that

[1] Cento, 2, fos. 62 v, 70, 75, 79v, 83, 92v, 96, 98 and 103v for details of these loans.

[2] fo. 92v.

[3] Canestrini, op. cit., pp. 228–38. This tax represented a step forward towards the *decima* of 1495, a tax based solely on revenues from fixed property. It replaced the previous basis of assessment, the *catasto* of 1427, which had been past revised in 1469.

the *Monte* Officials have provided 50,000 florins more than the 100,000 florins requested the previous January. For this extra sum no security had been granted. At the same time the Ten of War, elected for the war of Ferrara, had raised privately 'several thousands of florins' on their own account. This money must surely have been subscribed in anticipation of a measure guarantee, ing repayment from the *Monte*, and this is what actually happens. New Officials are ordered to be chosen by the *Signoria* and the Colleges 'without any formality or approval' to pay out immedi, ately 20,000 florins to the Ten of War which will cover their present needs as well as the repayment of the money already borrowed by them. As security they are granted the entire income of the *Monte* and the receipts of the taxes present and future. In addition they are vested with powers to enforce payment of all outstanding tax debts from the citizens 'who for a little while past have been rebelling against paying not through inability but through laziness'.[1]

This provision is typical of many during this period. Every new loan was accompanied by fresh direct taxes. But it is impor, tant to note that the Officials were given a comparatively free hand in allocating their securities. The reforms of the *Monte Comune* prior to 1480 were usually specific in their instructions to the Officials. During these years however the loans are raised against the *whole* income of the *Monte*. Since the Officials themselves were men most intimately connected with the operation of the war loans it can be reasonably assumed that these credits received first claim on the resources of the *Monte*. It is not surprising, there, fore, that the exercise of this vital office was kept closely under the control of the oligarchy itself. Between 1482 and 1494 only twenty,six families shared in the office. And the names are those of the ruling groups themselves: Salviati, Albizzi, Tornabuoni, Davanzati, Gianfigliazzi, Pandolfini, Guicciardini. Throughout this period the office of overseer at the *Monte* was exercised with, out interruption by Lorenzo's creature, Antonio di Bernardo di Miniato Dini, one of the first to incur the popular wrath in 1494.

[1] Cento, 2, fo. 79v.

Lorenzo himself did not become an Official of the *Monte* until 1488, and held office for only two years. But this in itself was unimportant. It would have been unthinkable for a difference of interests to have arisen between the *Monte Comune* and the holders of political power. In men like Tommaso Soderini, Jacopo Guicciardini, Donato Acciaiuoli, Bongianno Gianfigliazzi and Antonio Pucci politics and finance coincided.[1]

The claims of the war loans in these years were given precedence in the affairs of the *Monte*. In second place stood the dowry fund. Between them these two forms of speculation divided the revenues of the state. After 1480 all other forms of investment were slashed almost to nothing. The *balia* of 1480 had begun the process when it declared that only 25,000 florins should be made available for paying ordinary *Monte* interests.[2] In subsequent years the practice of retaining a proportion of the interest payments was resorted to frequently. In January 1483 the Hundred ordered that all outstanding interest payments should be consolidated into a single debt and then cut by 25 per cent.[3] It was by methods like these that the older *monti* were whittled away. The final blow came in 1489 when a further consolidation of the debt was ordered and this time cut by one half. By 1490 interest had fallen to 1 per cent.[4]

These attacks on the credit of the older *monti* must have been looked on as essential if the *Monte Comune* were to find sufficient funds to maintain the well-being of the dowry fund. We saw how in 1478 the *Monte delle doti* with its new 7 per cent holdings had emerged as a new form of gilt-edged security. All the financial measures in the 1480's paid special attention to the claims of the new credits and only in one year, 1484, were the *Monte* officials freed from their obligations to the dowry fund.[5] Nevertheless, the success of the new system inaugurated in 1480 proved to be short-lived and by 1488 it was admitted that a large number of creditors for endowments which had matured six years earlier had still

---

[1] Tratte, 82, fo. 105.
[2] Balie, 31, fos. 102–5.
[3] Cento, 2, fo. 76v: . . . *et delle decte paghe cosi accozate . . . se ne cancelli la quarta parte in utilità del monte . . . .*
[4] Cento, 3, fo. 19v.
[5] Cento, 2, fo. 93.

received no benefits other than the original payment of one-quarter of the sum owing to them.[1] On the other hand the attractiveness of the *Monte delle doti* does not seem greatly to have diminished, for in 1485, as a means of quickly raising cash, it was decided to offer favourable terms to those who were ready to invest gold in the dowry fund.[2]

What further inroads into the solvency of the *Doti* might have been committed had the wars continued another decade it is diffi-cult to say. But after 1488 the financial state of Florence settled down on a peacetime footing which was to last until 1494. Direct taxation was allowed to fall considerably; there were no extraordinary demands for money which could not be met from a normal annual levy of the *decima scalata*.[3] The government could finally face up to a full-scale review of the workings of the financial machine. These were the motives which led in 1490 to the setting up of the second Commission of Seventeen Reformers, the com-mission which has gained so much unwarranted notoriety from Guicciardini's erroneous description.[4]

The declared purpose of the new commission was to preserve the revenues of the *Monte*, principally by attacking corruption in the administration of the customs, and at the same time to take

[1] Ibid., fo. 122.

[2] Ibid., fo. 98v. The preamble to this measure gives a stark picture of the financial hardships borne by the mass of citizens in these years. The loan system itself seems to have caused heart-searching even in governmental circles as reference is made to the impossibility of raising further sums immediately in this way because of the *quasi insopportabili interessi*.

[3] The figure of direct taxes for 1487 was 160,000 florins. By 1490 it had dropped to 105,000 florins. In 1487 the total levy expected from the *decima scalata* was cut by 3,000 florins. The situation was further eased by the fact that larger instalments of the direct taxes were allowed to be paid out of *Monte* interests instead of cash.

[4] Guicciardini confused the two commissions of 1481 and 1490 and was apparently unaware of the precedent set by the earlier body. Also he exaggerated its powers by implying that they were to extend over political and constitutional matters. *Opere*, ed. Palmarocchi, vi (Bari, 1931), 70. Cf. N. Rubinstein, 'Le Storie Fiorentine and the Memorie di Famiglia by Francesco Guicciardini', *Rinascimento*, 4, pp. 222-5; also Dr. C. M. Ady's *Lorenzo dei Medici and Renaissance Italy* (London, 1955), p. 87.

steps 'in some way to help the dowry fund' so that everyone may derive some advantage from it.[1] During the year of its office the Seventeen carried out an exhaustive survey of all aspects of the administration and passed numerous decrees aimed at eliminating every possibility of fraud. It also dealt with weightier matters: fiscal reforms designed to encourage trade, especially silk exports; the problems raised by the introduction of a new copper currency in 1490; reform of the financial and economic administration of the *contado* where a newly ordered direct tax in 1489 had revealed widespread anomalies and disaffection; and finally in June 1491 the Seventeen were given special powers to legislate in order to arrest economic decline at Pisa.[2]

The most unpopular measure passed by the Seventeen was that affecting the new currency. Its purpose was to bolster the revenues of the *Monte* which since 1472 had been suffering from a de- valuation of the copper *quattrino*. It had been ordered in April 1490 that the silver content in this coin should be restored to what it had been before 1472. But the new coin was to keep its money value of 4 *denari* whereas the old currency was to be worth only 3 *denari*. In other words those citizens who possessed old *quattrini* were to find its value cut by 25 per cent. As this currency was widely used in payment of taxes, especially customs duties, the result was a sudden increase in the real rates. The Seventeen, in working out the new system, made some reductions in rates in certain cases of special hardship but did nothing to alleviate the main burden and it was not until 1494 that this was done. The introduction of the *moneta biancha*, as it was called, was certainly one of the most unpopular acts of the Medici government in its last years.[3]

[1] Cento, 3, fo. 1.

[2] The full deliberations of the Seventeen are recorded in the last volume (3) of the deliberations of the Hundred.

[3] Cf. Landucci, op. cit., p. 61, who confuses the different stages of the cur- rency reform but clearly sees that their result was *che si paga piu el quarto*. The increases were the first object of attack after the revolution of 1494 but only appar- ently as a sop to popular feeling for the old rates were restored in 1496 and were to remain. See P. Parenti, *La Istoria Fiorentina*, MS in Biblioteca Nazionale di Firenze,

The new arrangements introduced by the Seventeen into the *Monte delle doti* were announced as compensation for the new burdens which the citizens were being asked to shoulder. They admit that feeling is running high and say that the best way to counter this is to provide some relief for those with accrued dowries. The new plans envisaged a further extension of the system introduced in 1478. It was ordered that all dowries matured since 1483 which had so far received no capital repayment should be grouped into two lists, the older credits to be made eligible for receiving an annual interest of 4 per cent and the newer list 3 per cent. These new interests were to enjoy all the privileges and security granted previously to the 7 per cent fund. It was envisaged that each year as it became possible to pay off a proportion of the capital of the 7 per cent interests an equivalent sum should be moved up from the 4 per cent list, thus leaving room for promotion from the 3 per cent list, which in turn would be refilled with those who had so far had no benefits from their dowry investment.[1]

With this measure the evolution of the *Monte delle doti* was complete. In this form it continued throughout the vicissitudes of the next forty years and was still virtually unchanged when the Florentine republic was replaced by the Grand Duchy of Tuscany after 1530. The original purpose of the dowry fund had been forgotten but in its place there was now a new form of investment which was profitable and more secure than any other widely enjoyed holdings in the *Monte Comune*. The *Monte delle doti* continued to be the principal method by which the large body of Florentine citizens was able to exploit the revenues of the state, and in this form had taken over most of the old functions of the *Monte Comune*. After 1494 when forced loans were levied to finance the wars the only acceptable guarantee was that these loans should be inscribed in the books of interest of the 7 per cent dowry fund.[2]

Carte Magliabecchiane Cod. 11 IV fo. (a)196. Reg. Provv. 185, fo. 4v (Provision of 2 December 1494) and 187 fo. 52v (Provision of 12 August 1496); cf. Landucci, op. cit., p. 136.

[1] *Deliberazioni dei XVII Riformatori*, in Cento, reg. 3, fo. 24.

[2] Reg. provv. 187, fo. 2.

When these wars began to make serious demands on the financial resources of the republic the greatest popular ire was aroused when the dowry interests were threatened by the claims of the large-interest war loans and this conflict was considered fundamental to the political divisions which rent the Savonarolist republic. Piero Parenti did not exaggerate when he referred to the 3 per cent, 4 per cent and 7 per cent interests as *il sussidio dello universale*.[1]

The Seventeen Reformers of 1490 worked to strengthen and streamline the financial structure of the state which had been evolving over the past half-century. Apart from the inflation of customs rates and the methods of assessment of direct taxation this structure was accepted in its entirety by the new government after 1494.[2] Constitutional changes made it possible for the popular voice to make itself heard in defending its own interests, but no concerted attempt was made to alter the system itself.

It would be easy to dwell on the numerous abuses of the system as operated under Lorenzo. These fill the pages of Rinuccini and Cambi. There is much evidence from official sources to back up the charges of partiality in tax assessments, arbitrariness in alloca-tion of interests and widespread hardship due to the constant high level of taxation during the 1480's.[3] What is perhaps surprising is that these complaints were echoed in official organs of the state, such as the Council of the Hundred whose deliberations often deal with attempts to make the impact of the direct taxes more equitable.[4] Scandals must have been frequent, as, for example, in 1484 when the officials of the *Monte* were given a free hand in enforcing payments of tax arrears. Many debtors were sent to

[1] Op. cit., Codice II, ii, 132, fo. 14. March 1500: '. . . romore grandissimo ne fussi in popolo il quale si vedea privato de 7, 4, et 3 per cento ch'erano il subsidio loro, d'onde se pasceano . . .'

[2] Essentially the *decima* of 1495 represented the culmination of a process of evolu-tion in the principles of assessment for direct taxation which can been traced throughout the fifteenth century. No contemporary evidence can be adduced to present it in any way as a revolutionary change and it was accepted in its entirety by the restored Medicean government after 1512.

[3] Cento, 2, fos. 105v and 113v.

[4] Ibid.

prison, in breach of normal practice.[1] Clearly the Officials of the
Monte were coming to be regarded as the most powerful magistracy in the city. After 1494, when certain steps were taken to
limit their powers, it became increasingly difficult to find citizens
willing to serve as Officials.[2]

But it would be wrong to overemphasize the abuses, important
as they were in nourishing political feeling against the Medici.
It was the basic financial structure which proved decisive in the
long-term development of the city. The subordination of all
financial arrangements to the dictates of the credit mechanism
was the major factor. It meant that the state itself had come to be
looked on as a source of profit, an outlook which contributed
greatly to the emergence of a *rentier* mentality among the wealthier
Florentine families. Political power meant a say in the affairs of
the *Monte*. Even military policy became subordinate to the
demands of credit. Given the high level of expenditure created
by the mercenary system a vicious circle was created in which the
city became more and more dependent on its rich men. Since war
loans involved high interests a point was soon reached where
fresh taxes would be eaten up paying interest on past loans. Under
the Medici the popular opposition which this provoked had no
means of expression. After 1494 it broke out in full force, but was
powerless to alter the system.

There were other, subtler, effects. On economic life the result
must have been a continual draining of capital from the lower
orders of citizens and a rapid accumulation in the higher ranks.
What this meant in terms of arrested industrial expansion still
needs further investigation and it could possibly be shown that
the financial structure of the state in the fifteenth century effectively
prevented capital accumulation among those classes who were
most directly interested in increasing production. Guicciardini

[1] Here the government were attacking a well-established custom by which tax
debtors would make a *composizione* for their arrears with the *Monte* officials.
Rinuccini attacks the government for a breach of faith: op. cit., p. cxxxvii.

[2] Cf. L. Marks, 'La crisi finanziaria a Firenze dal 1494 al 1502', *Archivio
Storico Italiano* (1945), Disp. 1.

mentions these people as being the main victim of Lorenzo's fiscal policy.[1] Again, financial considerations played a vital part in determining relations between Florence and her neighbouring countryside. Through the *Monte* the Florentine citizen was an exploiter of the *contado* and the *distretto* for it was from these areas that a part of the *Monte* revenues was derived. This applied to the dowry fund as well to the large-interest loans.

The political system under Lorenzo was more adjusted to suit the requirements of the financial régime than any other form of government devised over the last half-century of the commune's existence. As such it possessed a stability and resistance which gave it distinct advantages over the republican experiments of the Savonarolist era. On the other hand, the failure of the post-1494 governments to tackle the public finances in a fundamental way was perhaps not the least of the factors making for their ultimate collapse.

[1] Cf. 'Del modo di assicurare lo stato ai Medici', *Opere*, ed. Palmarocchi, vii (Bari, 1932), 277.

Nicolai Rubinstein

POLITICS AND CONSTITUTION
IN FLORENCE AT THE END
OF THE FIFTEENTH CENTURY

On 9 November 1494 a revolution took place in Florence the result of which was the flight of Piero di Lorenzo de' Medici and the collapse of the régime which Piero's father, grandfather and great-grandfather had built up since the day in 1434 when Cosimo returned from his exile in Venice. The principal cause of this débâcle was Piero's diplomacy in connection with the French expedition to Italy. After having given the King of Naples his unlimited support against Charles VIII, Piero capitulated after Charles's entry into Tuscany and surrendered to him the most important Florentine fortresses on the way from Western Lombardy to Rome, including that of Pisa. The result of this agreement, which was made on Piero's own initiative without the consent of the Florentine *Signoria*,[1] was a reaction against Piero in Florence which led first to the decision to send official embassies to Charles on November 2 and 5, and then, on November 9, after the return of Piero to the city, to government action and a popular rising against him, and to the flight of Piero and of his brothers Giuliano and Giovanni.

Although Piero's disastrous diplomacy was the main cause of these events, the ground had been prepared for some time by the increasing unpopularity of Piero among the group of citizens who supported the Medici and who, on the death of Lorenzo the

---

[1] Cf. Agnolo e Francesco Gaddi, *Priorista*, extracts in *Arch. Stor. Ital.*, IV, ii (1853), p. 43: 'non havendo alcun mandato o commissione dal publico, di sua propria authorità . . .'.

Magnificent in 1492, had transferred their loyalty to his son. The change in the foundation of Medici rule can perhaps be illustrated by a comparison between Piero's journey to the French camp and that which, in somewhat similar circumstances, his father under- took fifteen years earlier to Naples, to negotiate peace with King Ferrante and thus to put an end to a military crisis in which Florence found herself as a result of the Pazzi War, which in its turn had been caused by Lorenzo's ascendancy in that city.[1] Piero's action was clearly modelled on that of his father, to the extent that even the letter he wrote back to Florence when on the way to the French camp imitates in style and content the letter of justification which Lorenzo wrote to the Florentine *Signoria* before embarking for Naples.[2] But while Lorenzo could rightly hope to preserve his position in Florence during his absence through the loyalty of the Medici party, Piero's reliance on it proved to be over-optimistic. One might press the comparison even further: Lorenzo's absence in Naples provided an oppor- tunity for oppositional elements within the Medicean régime (*stato*) which, according to Guicciardini, might have become dangerous had it not been for the loyalists holding the fort until Lorenzo's return in the wake of a great diplomatic success; in November 1494 a split among Piero's followers led to his fall after he had returned to Florence empty-handed.[3] The ascendancy of the Medici depended primarily on the support of their party. Despite the strengthening of Lorenzo's position after the Pazzi

[1] On the Pazzi War see C. M. Ady, *Lorenzo dei Medici and Renaissance Italy* (London, 1955), ch. 8.

[2] Lorenzo's letter is ed. in G. Ruscelli, *Lettere di Principi*, ii (Venice, 1575), fo. 11-v, and is quoted in full in English trans. by Dr. Ady, pp. 75-6. Piero's letter is in A. Desjardins-G. Canestrini, *Négociations diplomatiques de la France avec la Toscane*, i (Paris, 1859), 587-8 (26 October 1494).

[3] On opposition to Lorenzo in 1479-80 see F. Guicciardini, 'Memorie di famiglia', in *Scritti autobiografici e rari*, ed. R. Palmarocchi (Bari, 1936), p. 37, and *Storie fiorentine*, ed. R. Palmarocchi (Bari, 1931), p. 52. On the value of these works as historical evidence see N. Rubinstein, 'The *Storie Fiorentine* and the *Memorie di Famiglia* by Francesco Guicciardini', *Rinascimento*, iv (1953), 171 ff., esp. pp. 187 and 220.

War and the creation of the Council of Seventy, the foundation of Medici power in the *cittadini dello stato* remained substantially the same and continued so after his death. Piero, however, does not seem to have fully appreciated this. His cavalier treatment of leading aristocrats or *ottimati* and his increasing reliance on Medici clients[1] may have sprung from a mistaken belief that the Medici régime was sufficiently on the way to institutional permanency to allow him to pay less attention to the feelings of the *ottimati* among his supporters. The social rise of his family—Piero, a son and husband of an Orsini, his brother Giovanni, a cardinal—as well as the smooth transfer of power after his father's death may have confirmed him in this belief. In fact, Piero required the full support of the Medicean party in a crisis just as much as, and indeed, owing to his lesser personal qualities, more than Lorenzo. Having alienated some of its most influential members helped to tip the scales in November 1494. It was because a number of his leading followers deserted him during this supreme crisis that Piero fell from power; without this, the popular rising on November 9 would probably never have taken place.

One of the cornerstones of Medici ascendancy was control of elections to the government. The events of November 9 showed that such control was inadequate if the party was split and if the opposition inside it was able to carry the day. The new *Signoria* which began its two months' term of office on November 1, had been, as usual, chosen from among the staunch supporters of the régime.[2] However, it soon emerged that two of the *Signori* were opposed to Piero, and a similar situation prevailed among the important office of the Sixteen *gonfalonieri*; and a meeting of leading citizens of the Medici régime, which was summoned by the *Signoria* to advise it on the dangerous situation in which

[1] See, e.g., Guicciardini, *Storie*, pp. 84–6.
[2] B. Cerretani, *Storia fiorentina*, MS. Florence. Biblioteca Nazionale, II, III, 74, fo. 180v: 'Piero diceva avere facto una signoria più a suo propoxito che mai per alchuno tempo.' Guicciardini, p. 96: 'uomini tutti stati scelti per amici grandi ed affezionati del reggimento'.

Florence found itself, proved to be highly critical of Piero.[1] Although the opponents to Piero were at first a small minority, they rapidly gained the upper hand. This, rather than the popular rising, proved the decisive element in the revolution of November 9.[2] The *Signoria*, having ordered Piero to appear before it within an hour, refused him entry together with his armed retinue and summoned the people to the Piazza by ringing the great bell of the palace. It was only after these events, which telescoped the collapse of the Medici control of the government, that the people began to riot, the *Signoria* fanning the flame by forbidding anyone to come to Piero's aid.[3]

The political developments which followed on Piero's expulsion

[1] P. Parenti, *Storia fiorentina,* partly ed. by J. Schnitzer, *Quellen und Forschungen zur Geschichte Savonarolas,* iv (Leipzig, 1910), 9. Parenti adds, however, that many citizens refused to attend the meeting, which advised the *Signoria* to send a second embassy to Charles VIII. The embassy, which included Savonarola, left Florence on 5 November. Cerretani, op. cit., fo. 180v, states that the meeting was one of the Council of Seventy, which since 1480 had been the central organ of control of the Medici régime, with the addition of citizens whose names had, at one time or the other, been drawn for the office of *Gonfaloniere di Giustizia.*

[2] There are a number of contemporary or near-contemporary accounts of the revolution of 9 November 1494; the most important ones are Parenti, op. cit., MS, Florence, Bibl. Naz., II, IV, 169, fos. 191r ff. (not ed. by Schnitzer); L. Landucci, *A Florentine Diary from 1450 to 1516,* ed. I. Del Badia (English trans. London, 1927), pp. 60 ff.; Filippo e Alamanno Rinuccini, *Ricordi storici,* ed. G. Aiazzi (Florence, 1840), pp. clii–cliii; Agnolo e Francesco Gaddi, op. cit., pp. 44–5; Cerretani, op. cit., fos. 191v ff. (ed. by L. v. Ranke, 'Savonarola und die florentinische Republik . . .', *Historisch-biografische Schriften* (Leipzig, 1877), pp. 338–340); Guicciardini, op. cit., pp. 97 ff. Cf. also J. Nardi, *Istorie della città di Firenze,* ed. L. Arbib, i (Florence, 1838–41), 36 ff.

[3] Florence, Archivio di Stato, Deliberazioni dei Signori, ordinaria autorità, 96, fo. 86v. Parenti, Landucci and Rinuccini state that the *Signoria* placed a price on Piero's head, while Gaddi reports that Piero received from them notice that he had been made a rebel. But there is no entry to this effect in the register of Deliberazioni until 20 November, on which day the *Signoria* declared Piero a rebel and offered 2,000 florins to anyone who delivered him alive to them (ibid., fo. 96r–t). According to Cerretani, fo. 194v, one of Piero's enemies, who was in the Palazzo on the 9th, was responsible for the proclamation being made on that day that the *Signori* had made Piero a rebel and had placed a price on his head, although they had not yet come to a final decision.

fall into two periods, from November 9 to December 2 and from December 3 to December 23. The first period was marked by an attempt to reorganize the government with a minimum of constitutional change by restoring, for all intents and purposes, the situation which had existed before the establishment of Medici ascendancy. During the second period, this conservative and traditionalist approach was gradually replaced by a programme of radical constitutional reform, which finally resulted in the new republican constitution which was passed by the councils on December 22 and 23. During both periods, the *ottimati*, many of whom had belonged to the Medici *stato* while others had only now recovered political rights, tried to preserve their ascendancy and indeed to strengthen their position; but while at first they hoped to be able to do so without substantially broadening the basis of government, the conviction soon spread among them that far-reaching concessions and changes might be advisable, partly in order to counter popular dissatisfaction and partly to prevent a few of the most powerful citizens from using this opportunity to establish a narrow oligarchy. The question remained whether a broadening of the basis of government would still leave the *ottimati* in a position of ascendancy.

Parenti writes that on November 30, that is two days after the French army had left Florence, the *Signoria* summoned a special meeting of citizens (*pratica*) to advise them 'on what the people's wishes were concerning the future constitution of the city'.[1] The answer was to seek popular sanction through a general assembly (*parlamento*), i.e. by resorting to the traditional plebiscitarian method which was used in Florence on exceptional occasions to sanction special legislation. The law of the *parlamento* of December 2 confirmed the abolition of the councils established under the Medici, which had already taken place on November 11 by

---

[1] Parenti, MS cit., fo. 208v: 'come pareva [si] desiderasse del popolo della forma in cui la città a reggere per l'advenire s'avessi'. On the institution of the *pratiche* see now F. Gilbert, 'Florentine political assumptions in the period of Savonarola and Soderini', *Journal of the Warburg and Courtauld Institutes*, xx (1957), 187 ff.

order of the *Signoria*,[1] and provided for the return to the situation which had existed before 1434. The election of the *Signoria* was temporarily entrusted to a committee of twenty *accoppiatori*, until the purged electoral lists were ready; when this was the case, election by lot was to be restored.[2] Rinuccini says that these reforms were 'all in favour of the people' and therefore 'unanimously approved by the people';[3] another contemporary diarist, Parenti, states more shrewdly that a large section of the population was not satisfied but that the law was nevertheless passed by the assembly: 'we know how things are done on such occasions: some people shouted yea, and this was considered to be enough'.[4] In fact, the restoration of the constitutional machinery which had been in force before the rise of the Medici might well mean also the restoration of the 'oligarchy' which had ruled Florence until 1434. One of the leading architects of the revolution, Piero Capponi, who had been elected a member of the twenty *accoppiatori* on December 3,[5] expressed a few months later what was doubtless in the minds of many *ottimati* at the time, although not all of them would have put it in so idealistic a vein. 'I am convinced', he writes in July 1495 to Francesco Valori, 'that in Florence government is possible only if 25 or 30 aristocrats [*uomini da bene*] look after the interests of this poor city, without regard to any selfish interest or ambition, and with the tacit consent of the people, though not by law.'[6]

---

[1] Deliberazioni, cit., fo. 88v.

[2] Cf. N. Rubinstein, 'I primi anni del Consiglio Maggiore di Firenze (1494–1499)', *Arch. Stor. Ital.*, cxii (1954), 151–2.

[3] Op. cit., pp. clv–clvi.

[4] Ed. Schnitzer, p. 22. Henceforth all page references to Parenti's *Storia fiorentina* will be to Schnitzer's edition and all folio references to the MSS in the Biblioteca Nazionale.

[5] Parenti, p. 20.

[6] 'Io mi persuado, che in Firenze non si possi governare se di consenso del popolo, non per legge, ma per sua tacita concessione, XXV o XXX uomini da bene, postposta ogni loro privata passione, ambizione e avarizia, non pigliono la cura d'attendere a quella povera città . . .'; ed. in *Arch. Stor. Ital.*, IV, ii (1853), 59–60 (28 July 1495).

As far as the social structure of government went, this restoration implied a large measure of continuity. Indeed, the reform of
December 2, while confirming the abolition of Medici institutions and making it possible to deprive adherents of Piero of
political rights or influence, was at the same time meant to preserve and strengthen the political power of the leading Florentine
families, including many who had belonged to the old régime.
It was characteristic of this attempt to secure continuity in government that the all-important committee of *accoppiatori*, as well as
the new Ten of War[1] and the new *Otto di Guardia e Balia*,[2] were
to be elected by the *Signoria* of November–December with the
help of the *Sedici Gonfalonieri* and the *Dodici Buoni Uomini*[3]—that
is by the same *Signoria* which had been elected under Piero de'
Medici and which had played so decisive a part in his fall. What
was even more characteristic was the fact that no fewer than fifteen
of the Twenty can be found among the citizens who during the
electoral 'scrutiny' of 1472 were included in the electoral lists for
the highest office of the state, the *Gonfaloniere di Giustizia*, and who
were consequently considered at that time both prominent and
trustworthy supporters of the Medici régime.[4]

According to Parenti's *History*, there was much dissatisfaction
among the 'good citizens' about this settlement. They complained that having fought for liberty, they now saw that they
had done so 'not for the liberty of the people, but for preserving
in power the same men who had been ruling before'.[5] At the
same time, the fall of the Medici had brought into the open many
political and personal feuds between their followers and enemies,
which after the removal of the external danger from Charles VIII's
army, were liable to lead to civil war. It was at this critical juncture

[1] Or *Dieci di Libertà e Pace*, as this office was now called.

[2] In charge of administration of justice.

[3] The *accoppiatori* and the Ten were to take part in the election of the Eight.

[4] The lists are in Florence, Archivio di Stato, Med. av. Pr., 86, fos. 321v–
328r. On the reform of 2 December, see also A. Anzilotti, *La crisi costituzionale
della Repubblica fiorentina* (Florence, 1912), pp. 39–41.

[5] Op. cit., p. 21.

that Savonarola intervened with a plea for a more radical constitutional reform. His authority in Florence had been vastly
enhanced by the apparent fulfilment of his prophecies regarding
the coming of the French, by his role during their presence, and
by his attempt, according to many decisive, to induce Charles
VIII to a speedy departure. His intervention in the internal
politics of Florence, which culminated in his great political sermon of December 14, was undoubtedly one of the principal
factors in bringing about the reforms passed by the Councils of
the People and of the Commune on December 22 and 23, which
transformed the foundations of the Florentine constitution by
establishing a Great Council on the Venetian model. Did the
initiative for establishing the new 'popular government' come from
Savonarola, and to what extent was his intervention decisive?

Savonarola himself constantly claimed, later on, that the new
régime was his own achievement, and as such the work of God,[1]
and his followers naturally followed suit. Uncommitted writers
of the sixteenth century were more cautious;[2] but modern
historians of this period, as a rule primarily concerned with
Savonarola, tend to stress his decisive influence. The complexity
of the political situation in Florence and the available contemporary evidence may give rise to some scepticism about so simple
an explanation of the origins of the constitutional reform of
December 22–23. Above all else, it is difficult to understand,
against the background of Florentine political traditions, why the

---

[1] Cf., e.g., his letter of 1495 or 1496 in *Le Lettere di Girolamo Savonarola*, ed. R.
Ridolfi (Florence, 1933), p. 95: this 'governo da me introdocto'; *Prediche di
F. Girolamo Savonarola*, ed. G. Baccini (Florence, 1889), p. 423 (20 August 1496):
'Io ho persuaso il Consiglio grande. . . . Questo governo adunque è da Dio . . .';
p. 313 (26 June 1496): 'Io ti dico che il Salvatore ha fatto questo governo lui';
cf. also Savonarola, *Trattato circa il reggimento e governo della città di Firenze*, ii, 2,
ed. A. de Rians (Florence, 1847), p. 43. This claim is also emphasized in the anti-
Savonarolian pamphlet *Epistola responsiva a frate Hieronnymo da Ferrara dell ordine de
frati dal amico suo*, n.p., n.d. (Florence, 1497?): 'vi forzate mostrare questo governo
esser stato introdocto da voi come instrumento dell' altissimo . . .'.

[2] Cf., e.g., Guicciardini, p. 107 (but cf. pp. 158–9); Donato Giannotti, 'Della
repubblica fiorentina', *Opere*, ed. F.-L. Polidori, i(Florence, 1850), 87.

ottimati who had just succeeded in restoring the political régime which had existed before the rise of the Medici, should now suddenly undo their work and accept a popular constitution proposed by the Prior of San Marco. The followers of Savonarola were quite alive to this dilemma; the anonymous *Vita latina* of Savonarola[1] and its Italian version, the so-called Burlamacchi *Vita*,[2] tried to solve it by explaining Savonarola's success in supernatural terms. In doing so, they expressed *Piagnoni* tradition which ultimately went back to Savonarola himself. 'The serf of God', writes the author of the *Vita latina*,[3] 'said . . . that they must create a popular régime, that is a Great Council, and that this was the will of God; but all the citizens began to contradict it. . . .' Of the citizens who were nevertheless appointed to pre-pare schemes for a reform, three-fourths were against a democratic Council. Savonarola, however, preached that they would create it even against their wish, and that 'the white beans would be turned into black ones',[4] i.e., that the nays would be turned into yeas. Finally, these citizens decided, under popular pressure, to propose the establishment of the Great Council, since they were convinced that this proposal would not be passed by the *Signoria* and its small council (the *Collegi*); but God, 'in order to fulfil the words of the man of God', made the law pass by changing the colour of the white (nay) beans into black.[5] Let us briefly

---

[1] MS Florence, Bibl. Naz., Conv. soppr., I, VII, 28, fos. 17v-18r.

[2] *La vita del Beato Ieronimo Savonarola, scritta da un anonimo del sec. XVI e già attri-buita a Fra Pacifico Burlamacchi*, ed. R. Ridolfi (Florence, 1937), pp. 77-8. On the relationship between the two Lives see Ridolfi, *Le Lettere di Girolamo Savonarola. Nuovi contributi* . . . (Florence, 1936), pp. 19-34.

[3] Fo. 17v. Pseudo-Burlamacchi, p. 77. Pseudo-Burlamacchi's account diverges from its Latin source only in minor details.

[4] Pseudo-Burlamacchi corrects here an evident slip in the *Vita latina*, which has 'fabe nigre in albas'; I follow the Italian version.

[5] In his sermon of 1 April 1495 (P. Villari-E. Casanova, *Scelta di prediche e scritti di fra Girolamo Savonarola* (Florence, 1898) p. 149) and, in identical terms, in his *Compendio di revelatione* (Florence, 18 August 1495), fo. b iiii, Savonarola himself gives a similar but more natural explanation of the passage of the reform law: 'Et dixi che niuno potrebbe resistere a questa sua volunta: perche lui farebbe le fave bianche diventar nere, cioe che muterebbe gli cuori di coloro che

examine the course of events which led up to the decision to establish the Great Council.

On December 7, that is only five days after the *parlamento*, Savonarola mentioned in a sermon the necessity for further re/ form,[1] and on the 14th exhorted the Florentines to imitate the Venetian constitution, with the exception of the Doge; in other words, to establish a Great Council on the Venetian pattern.[2] In the same sermon, he suggested that drafts for the reform law were to be prepared by the sixteen *gonfalonieri* after popular con/ sultation, from which they were finally to select one. According to Landucci, 'many schemes of government were taken to the *Palazzo*' on December 19.[3] On the following day, according to the Ferrarese ambassador, the controversies on the policy to be adopted reached a climax; throughout the day, discussions took place at their palace between the *Signoria* and the magistracies; and the orator adds that if no immediate solution could be found there was danger of 'great and dangerous disorder'. Fortunately, these forebodings did not come true, for on the 21st he writes that the conflicts of opinion regarding the form of the government had been completely settled.[4] The day after, the Council of the People in fact passed the reform bill, and on the 23rd it was passed by the Council of the Commune and thus became law.[5] Man/ fredi states that it was passed unanimously—in fact it was passed with a large majority—and that this showed the unity which Florence had now recovered.[6]

contradicevano, et haveano deliberato di dare ne partiti le fave bianche, et farebbele loro dare nere. Et cosi fu, come manifestamente si sa . . .' (*Compendio*, loc. cit.).

[1] *Prediche italiane ai Fiorentini*, i, ed. F. Cognasso (Perugia/Venice, 1930), 117.

[2] Ibid., p. 195. He had already hinted at this on the 7th.

[3] Landucci, p. 77.

[4] Extracts from Manfredo de' Manfredi's dispatches in A. Cappelli, 'Fra Girolamo Savonarola e notizie intorno il suo tempo', *Atti e Mem. d. Deput. di storia patria per le prov. Modenesi e Parmensi*, iv (1868), 337.

[5] Florence, Archivio di Stato, Provvisioni, 185, fos. 9r-13v.

[6] Cappelli, p. 338. The law was passed by the Council of the People with 229 votes against 35, and by the Council of the Commune with 195 against 16: Provvisioni, cit., fo. 13r.

What happened behind the scenes during these fateful days? The decision on the new form of government did not lie, in the first place, with Savonarola or the councils, but with the government and the highest magistracies, that is with the men of the conservative reform of 2 December. Savonarola, in his sermons, does not mention the discussions in the ruling circle, Landucci, of humble social station, has evidently no knowledge of them, while the Ferrarese envoy has only some general secondhand information. The most circumstantial account can be found in Parenti's *History*; some firsthand evidence exists in fragments of the reform schemes which are preserved in the Florentine State Archives.[1]

Parenti's account is important enough to be quoted fully.[2] 'When the principal citizens noticed the anger of the people, they were afraid that it might in time turn against them and wondered how they could strengthen or consolidate their position, which they found to be subject to sudden change . . ., and finally some of them came to favour a constitution closely akin to that of Venice. . . . But since there was opposition to this scheme among them, those who were in favour of it came to an agreement with Fra Ieronimo'; and Savonarola, whose authority was already very great, put their case from the pulpit, and preached that Florence could not survive unless she accepted this reform.[3] But once Savonarola had begun to intervene on the political scene, there were increasing doubts among the *ottimati* about the wisdom of using him as a mouthpiece: they began to complain that they had come under the power of the Friar, and that to rule a convent and to rule a city were two different things.[4]

According to Parenti there were, then, two motives for the desire of a number of *ottimati* to change the constitution of Florence: the wish to counter popular dissatisfaction with the

[1] Carte Strozziane, seconda serie, 95. They will be edited by Professor F. Gilbert. [2] Parenti, pp. 26–7.

[3] Cf. also Guicciardini, loc. cit., who however oversimplifies the situation by ascribing the initiative to Paolantonio Soderini alone.

[4] Parenti, pp. 28–9.

conservative reform of December 2 and thus to prevent another revolution, and the determination to strengthen and consolidate their predominance within the framework of a new constitution.

Another motive for the reform is supplied by Bernardo Rucellai, one of the *ottimati* who had played a leading part in the revolution and had been elected to the Twenty *accoppiatori*, in the introduction to his description of Rome. He states that when the future constitution was being discussed after the departure of Charles VIII, some citizens wanted to establish an oligarchy, and that in order to prevent them from achieving their aim, other citizens preferred to make a radical change and adopt a broader and practically popular form of government.[1] In fact, such apprehensions received, after the creation of the Great Council, some substantiation from the behaviour of the Twenty.[2] There seems, then, to have been, from the beginning, a certain ambiguity about the significance of the proposed new constitution. Savonarola and his followers viewed the Great Council as the foundation of a popular régime; but it was also possible, and even more natural, to consider it as the social as well as constitutional counterpart of the Venetian *Gran Consiglio*, the bulwark of the Venetian nobility. This constitutional ambivalence goes far towards explaining the conflicting contemporary interpretations of the role and functions of the Great Council. In the end, everything depended on whether the emphasis was placed on the aristocratic or the democratic aspects of the new constitution.

A somewhat similar contrast seems to have existed between the political philosophy of Savonarola and the approach of the Florentine *ottimati* to the new reform. The latter were politicians brought up in the realistic traditions of Florentine politics;

[1] '. . . quum de ordinanda civitate constituendoque imperio cives inter se dissiderent, quod alii paucorum potentiam sectarentur, pars conturbari miscerique omnia, quo minus valerent ipsi, mallent, tum demum ambitione paucorum factum est, ut civitas distracta seditionibus laxiorem Reipublicae formam, ne dicam popularem, amplecteretur.' *De Urbe Roma*, ed. D. M. Becucci (Florence, 1770), introduction, col. 19. The passage is quoted by F. Gilbert (see below, p. 173, n. 4), p. 109, n. 1.

[2] See Parenti, pp. 58, 60, 64; Guicciardini, pp. 115–16.

Savonarola was a foreigner and a friar educated in the traditions of the Dominican schools. The fragments of the reform schemes which have come down to us show how the reform of the con‑stitution was discussed in strictly practical terms, with a wealth of technical details—much as any constitutional reform would have been discussed in fifteenth‑century Florence; Savonarola's political sermon of December 14, on the other hand, presents us with a piece of Dominican political philosophy adapted to Florentine conditions.

Savonarola elaborated his political theory in his *Trattato circa il reggimento di Firenze*, written at the beginning of 1498; but his interpretation of the new Florentine constitution had remained substantially unchanged. It was, according to him, a *governo civile*, and as such natural to Florence.[1] *Governo civile* is the Italian translation of *regimen politicum*; the concept is Aristotelian, but Savonarola derived it evidently from the continuation of St. Thomas's *De regimine principum* by Ptolemy of Lucca, which was then generally ascribed to Aquinas.[2] *Regimen politicum*, for Ptolemy of Lucca, was the republican form of government, as it had existed in Athens and Rome and as it then existed in Italy. Its existence in Italian cities was a mark of the superiority of their national character over that of other regions which were fit only for despotic rule, and was natural to them.[3] Savonarola simply adapts the same argument to Florence: although theoretically monarchy is the best form of government, a republic is that natural to the Florentines, owing to their intelligence and spirited‑ness;[4] and long custom of free institutions has strengthened this

---

[1] i, 3; iii, 1; ed. de Rians, pp. 12–16, 40.

[2] On the rendering of πολιτεία by *civilitas* in medieval Latin translations of the *Politics* and in works referring to it, see L. Minio‑Paluello, 'Tre note alla "Mon‑archia"', in *Medioevo e Rinascimento. Studi in onore di Bruno Nardi*, ii (Florence, 1955), 513–22 (on Ptolemy of Lucca, p. 519).

[3] *De regimine principum*, iv, 1 and 8.

[4] *Trattato*, i, 3, pp. 13–14; he had used the same argument before in his sermons; cf. *Prediche italiane*, i, 183–4 (14 December 1494), ii, ed. Cognasso (Perugia‑Venice, 1930), 409 (11 October 1495); *Prediche*, ed. Baccini, p. 332 (29 June 1496).

natural inclination to republican liberty. It is clear then that Savonarola tries to fit Florentine realities into a pre-existing philosophical pattern; his political philosophy does not spring from these realities but is superimposed on them. In this philo-sophical pattern the concept of a Great Council on the Venetian model constitutes a somewhat extraneous element; there was no reason why the ancient Florentine constitution could not have continued to provide an adequate basis for a *reggimento civile*. In the sermon of December 14, when he proposed the Great Council for the first time, he thus introduces an institutional element which seems to jar somewhat with the theoretical moral preaching on good government which had gone before. Is this due to the fact that while the political philosophy of the *governo civile* reflects Savonarola's own views, the original responsibility for the scheme of a great Council belonged to Florentine citizens?

The controversies over the political significance of the Great Council begin with the preparation of the reform schemes. The *Signoria* gave this preparation already a less democratic turn than Savonarola had suggested. Instead of the schemes being prepared by the Sixteen after popular consultation, practically all the highest magistracies, including the Twenty *accoppiatori*, were put in charge of it. The membership of some of these magistracies still dated back to the Medici period; the others had been elected after the conservative reform of December 2. To entrust the preparation of the new constitution to these magistracies more-over followed the time-honoured Florentine practice to discuss important reforms in special committees and councils, as against the revolutionary suggestion by Savonarola of a kind of popular referendum, which was entirely out of keeping with Florentine tradition.

As far as we can see, the discussions on the reform schemes turned largely on the membership of the Great Council and on the method of election to offices. In the surviving documents, there is no opposition to the Great Council as such; but there was wide scope for a more aristocratic or democratic interpreta-tion of it. The observations on one of the schemes by Piero

Capponi, who represented the conservative wing of the *ottimati*, are of special interest to us. While he does not attack the idea of the Great Council, he tries to limit its functions and powers. Moreover, he wants to put at its side a senate, in its turn based on the Venetian model of the *Pregadi*.[1] He furthermore suggests that the final decision on the method of electing the *Signoria* should be postponed for the time being—'for in the course of one or two years some flaws in the new constitution might emerge, which would not matter so much elsewhere, but which would matter a great deal when it comes to the election of the highest magistracy'.[2]

Was the new electoral system, as finally adopted in the reform law, of filling vacancies to all the higher magistracies by election in the Council instead of by lot, more in the interest of the *ottimati* or of the people? This question remained, as we shall see, one of the crucial problems of the new republican régime. As to Capponi's plea for a senate, it was partly met by the creation, on December 22–23, of the Council of Eighty, which was to be elected every six months by the Great Council. The Eighty proved to wield far less power than the *Pregadi*; yet they could be taken to represent, potentially, an aristocratic feature of the new constitution.

Closely connected with the constitutional problem was that of the treatment of members of the defeated régime, and especially of those who were responsible for the ill-treatment of political opponents. It might in fact have been expected that the expulsion of the Medici would be followed not only by a rehabilitation and return of their enemies, but also by the prosecution of their followers and collaborators, and particularly of those who had clung to Piero to the very end. There were many precedents for

---

[1] 'Come a Vinegia', loc. cit., no. 19, fo. 241r.

[2] Ibid., fo. 241r: 'che in questo tempo d'uno anno o di dua che si vedrebbe qualche errore nelle cose facte, le quali nell' altre cose non importerebbono molto, ma nel primo magistrato importerebbono assai'. On the other hand, another reform scheme, probably that of the *Dieci*, which clearly reflects the impact of Savonarola, comes out in favour of election, from the beginning, of the *Signoria* as of the other high magistracies by the Great Council. Ibid., no. 12, fo. 70.

this in Florentine history, the most relevant being the banishments and persecutions that had followed on Cosimo de' Medici's return to Florence in 1434. Moreover, political persecution would be liable to produce personal or family feuds; and the past victims of the Medici régime who had returned to Florence after the revolution and had recovered political rights,[1] might well ask themselves why the fate of their adversaries should now be better than their own had been. That no such persecution took place was due largely, though not exclusively, to the intervention of Savonarola. There was apparently little hesitation to proceed against men who owed everything to the Medici and who had been their political agents, especially where unpopularity with the masses coincided with the dislike of the *ottimati* for parvenus; thus Antonio di Bernardo Miniati, *provveditore* of the *Monte*, was hanged and Ser Giovanni di Bartolomeo Guidi, one of the leading officials of the chancery, was sent to prison.[2] Other members of the chancery were dismissed from their posts, among them the First Chancellor, Bartolomeo Scala, who had been an outstanding personality of the Medicean régime; but some of them, including Scala, were shortly afterwards reinstated, doubtless because of their professional qualifications.[3] Compared with these measures, the prosecution of Medicean *ottimati* came into an altogether different category. While it could be defended by historical precedent, desire of revenge and considerations of internal security, there were also weighty arguments against it, such as the need for internal unity at a time when Florence was isolated in Italy and at war with Pisa; moreover, the *ottimati* of the new régime might wish to protect relatives and perhaps even themselves from being prosecuted for past collaboration with the Medici.

---

[1] Cerretani, fos. 197v-8r: 'tornò fra pochi giorni Lorenzo e Giovanni [di Pierfrancesco] de' Medici e tutti e Pazzi, alquanti de' Peruzzi, Barbadori, Neroni, Acciaiuoli, Ghuaschoni, Strozzi et molti altri . . .' Cf. Landucci, p. 65. The relevant ordinances of the *Signoria* are in Deliberazioni, ord. aut., 96, fos. 87r (9 November), 92v (13 November), 99r-v (28 November), etc.

[2] Landucci, pp. 75, 79. D. Marzi, *La cancelleria della repubblica fiorentina* (Rocca S. Casciano, 1910), pp. 261-2.

[3] Marzi, pp. 267-8, 270-1.

As to Savonarola, it was perhaps not surprising that, as a priest, and with his high sense of his mission, he should have used his enormous influence in Florence to persuade the citizens to forgive past offences; as he said himself, priests had done the same in Florence at all periods of her history;[1] and his great rival as a preacher at the beginning of 1495, the Franciscan Domenico da Ponzo, in his turn admonished the Florentines to peace and unity.[2] Savonarola also seems to have felt that internal pacification was an indispensable accessory of constitutional reform; in his first great political sermon, of December 14, he also pleaded for the *pace universale* between the citizens of the old and the new régime and for an amnesty.[3]

In the discussions preceding the creation of the Great Council, the question of a political amnesty played a prominent role; according to the Ferrarese ambassador, the final acceptance by the government and other high magistracies of the former went hand in hand with that of the latter.[4] But while the new constitutional reform was passed by the councils on the following day, the amnesty did not become law until March 19, after long discussions and controveries, in which Savonarola once more took a leading and perhaps decisive part.[5] The same law also curtailed the powers of the *Signoria* to punish political offences with a two-third majority by allowing an appeal to the Great Council, which had equally been demanded by Savonarola.[6]

[1] *Prediche italiane*, ii, 91-2 (20 January 1495).

[2] Parenti, p. 45. Ever since his return from Pisa Savonarola had, in his sermons, admonished the citizens to *misericordia*: *Prediche italiane*, i, 53-4, 64-5.

[3] Ibid., p. 196.

[4] Cappelli, pp. 337-8.

[5] The minutes of the discussions in the *pratiche* of 6, 8, 9 and 15 March are extant in Florence, Arch. di St., Consulte e Pratiche, 61, fos. 3r-6v (another copy on fos. 9r-12v). The amnesty covered 'qualunche fusse suto fautore dello stato che reggieva e resse da dì VIIII di novembre proxime passato indietro', etc.; see following note.

[6] The so-called law of the six beans, from the votes of six members of the *Signoria* of nine. It actually forms part of the same *provvisione* as the amnesty: Provvisioni, 185, fos. 90v-2v. Cf. Savonarola's sermon of 6 January 1495 in *Prediche italiane*, ii, 10 ff.

However much Savonarola's influence contributed to bringing about the passage of these laws, there were also other factors
responsible for it. The *Signoria* of March–April was, in contrast
to its predecessor of January–February, favourable to this legislation, according to Parenti less so because of their sympathies for
Savonarola than owing to some of its members being close relatives of enemies of the new régime.[1] The citizens who had belonged
to Piero's *stato* were naturally in favour of an amnesty and of a
curtailment of the government's criminal jurisdiction, and those
of them who were in the Great Council could vote for these
measures, together with *ottimati* who supported the new constitution but who might have misgivings about wholesale measures
against Mediceans.[2]

One of the results of the amnesty of 19 March 1495 was in
fact to strengthen the position of the *ottimati* in the new republic,
by preventing the outlawing of many members of their class;
another was to draw the adherents of the Medici together with
Savonarola and his followers, who had supported the amnesty
so successfully. This opportunist 'alliance' between *Bigi* and
Frateschi was one of the major aspects of the complex pattern of
Florentine politics which developed after the introduction of the
new constitution.

Had it not been for Savonarola and the extraordinary position
he had acquired in the political life of the city, that pattern would
have doubtless been much simpler. Immediately after the fall of
the Medici, there were principally two political groups facing
each other, the adherents of the old and those of the new régime,
which might well have remained, for the time being, the only
two major parties: Piero's determination to return to Florence and
recover his lost position, for once, would have kept the Medici
party in being as the declared enemy of the new régime and of its
supporters. It was the split of the citizens into adherents and
opponents of Savonarola which introduced a new element and
complicated the political situation. This new party division,

[1] pp. 39, 44.
[2] See Parenti, p. 41; cf. also p. 101. Guicciardini, pp. 107-8.

which began to take shape shortly after the establishment of the Great Council,[1] soon deepened and widened to the extent of over-shadowing the existing factions without, however, eliminating them.

We can do no more, in this context, than give a few general observations on the character and activities of these *parti*, or *sette*, which dominated the political scene until 1498 and beyond. They were political groups held together by common interests and aims rather than organization and, with the important exception of the *Frateschi* party, without much direct leadership; and yet, owing to the personal character of Florentine politics, coherent enough for common political action. Undoubtedly the most compact as well as numerous was the *Frateschi* party. If this was due to the personal influence of Savonarola, his relations with his followers were nevertheless not without ambiguities. Quite apart from the fact that many of them were on the fringe of his party, the nature of Savonarola's office as Prior of San Marco, as well as his views on his spiritual mission, made it difficult, if not impossible, for him to become a party leader in the traditional Florentine sense. There does not seem to be any reason to doubt the essential genuineness of the picture Savonarola himself drew of his relations with the *Frateschi* in his confession during his trial; he appears as the power behind the scenes, laying down general principles of action, but leaving everyday political deci-sions to the leading citizens among his followers.[2] As he puts it, common political action was largely secured by personal know-

---

[1] See R. Ridolfi, *Vita di Girolamo Savonarola* (Rome, 1952), pp. 160 ff.

[2] Cf. 'Processi', in P. Villari, *La storia di Girolamo Savonarola*, ii (new ed., Florence, 1888), p. clvii: 'erano il proposito fermo di non mimpaciare mai de particulari: sappendo maxime che i ciptadini mi seguitavano lo facevano meglio et meglio lo sapevano fare che io non intendevo et a me bastava che mantenesseno il governo che io desideravo . . .' There follows a list of leading *Frateschi*. Cf. also *Prediche*, ed. Baccini, p. 424 (20 August 1496): 'Delle particularità della legge non me ne curo . . . dello stato tuo tu sai che io non me ne impaccio'; *Prediche sopra l'Esodo*, ed. P. G. Ricci, ii (Rome, 1956), 195 (sermon of 14 March 1498): 'Io mi sto nella mia cella, e non cerco li tuoi particulari delle cose dello stato tuo', etc.; 'Processi', Villari, ii, pp. clxxix, clxxx. On the question of the reliability of the *Processi* see R. Ridolfi, 'I processi del Savonarola', *Bibliofilia*, xlv (1943), 3-41.

ledge among the *Frateschi*, who would meet at his sermons and know each other at least by sight.[1] This picture seems to be substantially accurate, although it is doubtless underdrawn: Savonarola appears to have exercised his influence through his principal followers, although in his sermons he tried from time to time to influence legislation in the Great Council directly.[2] Thus when Francesco Valori finally decided to give the *Frateschi* his unlimited support, he emerged as the head of that party; a position which he appears to have assumed from the beginning of 1497[3] and which was greatly strengthened by his role in the condemnation, in the summer of that year, of five prominent citizens for their part in a Medicean conspiracy. According to Parenti,[4] this appeared to have made him into the first citizen of Florence and practically into her ruler. However, there seem to have been misgivings, among the principal *Frateschi*, about the authority he had acquired.[5]

The *Frateschi*, as the other parties, naturally aimed at filling

Although the depositions of Savonarola were extracted under torture and subsequently 'edited', they constitute, if used with due caution, a historical source of first importance. Cf. also E. Armstrong, in *Cambr. Mod. Hist.*, i (Cambridge, 1902), 182–3.

[1] Ibid., p. clvi: 'chi andava alla predicha . . . si cognoscevano tutti in viso et io li cognoscevo et questo era la forza principale di questa cosa'.

[2] As for instance in the case of the law of six beans, see above, pp. 164–5.

[3] Parenti, p. 155 (January 1497): 'El Valori . . . si scoperse finalmente partigiano del frate et d'essersi fatto capo di quella setta . . .' Guicciardini, p. 130, on Valori's *gonfalonierato* of January–February 1497: 'Fucci tirato con favore della parte del frate, della quale fu assolutamente fatto capo.'

[4] p. 213; similarly Guicciardini, p. 145. According to the deposition of Andrea Cambini, one of Valori's closest friends and supporters, Valori strenuously denied that he wished to make himself *capo*; but Cambini's defence cannot be accepted at its face value; 'Processi', Villari, ii, p. cclxxvi.

[5] Cf. especially the confession of Fra Silvestro, ibid., p. ccxxvii. Savonarola, however, although he was not without suspicions (pp. clv, clviii, clxxx), seems to have accepted him as the most powerful citizen of his party and as something like his chief lieutenant. If we are to believe his deposition before the Papal commissioners, he had 'disegnato che Francesco Valori fussi il primo e il capo di tutti' (p. clxxxi) and thought of himself as 'un Signore che ha uno capitano nel quale si riposa, et il mio capitano era Francesco Valori'; but this reads like a crude summary of what Savonarola doubtless considered a more subtle relationship.

the highest magistracies, and especially the *Signoria*, with their followers, and the new electoral system of the Great Council pro-vided ample scope for this. How important control of the *Signoria* was is shown by the events of April and May 1498, when the fall and execution of Savonarola was largely due to a *Signoria* with an *Arrabbiati* majority—just as in 1494, when the expulsion of Piero had been primarily the work of a *Signoria* in which his enemies had assumed preponderance. The mutual knowledge of the *Frateschi*, which Savonarola called the *forza principale della cosa*, may have been by and large sufficient to make them vote for each other, and the same applied undoubtedly also to the other political groups. But whether so loose a system was really adequate to secure permanent control was doubtful, as was shown for instance by the fact that even before 1498 the *Frateschi* did not always succeed in securing a *Signoria* which was entirely to their liking.[1] It was, therefore, clearly tempting to supplement the loose party formations with more strictly organized groups, with more or less clearly defined membership and obligations. There had been legislation against *compagnie* and *intelligenze* through-out the fifteenth century in order to prevent organized opposi-tion.[2] They were once more prohibited by the reform law of 2 December 1494, 'for the preservation of the liberty and the peace' of Florence;[3] and the prohibition was re-enacted on 13 August 1495, this time with specific reference to the Great Council.[4] It could now also be argued that they interfered with the free exercise of the vote.

One of the principal heads of the accusation against Savonarola

---

[1] *Signoria* of March–April 1497: Parenti, p. 166: 'le parti ristrettesi, ciascuna a favorire e suoi si messe. Finalmente si fece mixta, el capo cioe il gonfaloniere della justitia fu Bernardo del Nero, avversario al frate'; May–June 1497, Guicciardini, p. 133: 'quattro fave, benchè con grande difficultà, in suo (scil. Savonarola's) favore'; July–August 1497: Parenti, p. 201: 'non in tutto a propositi de frateschi riusci' (the Milanese orator, however, states that the *Frateschi* were in the majority: Villari, ii, p. xxix).

[2] In 1419, 1444, 1455 and 1458: Arch. di St., Provvisioni, 109, fos. 160v–162v; 134, fos. 208v-9r; 146, fos. 147r-8r; Balie, 29, fos. 4v-5r.

[3] Provvisioni, 185, fo. 6v. [4] Provvisioni, 186, fos. 91v-2r.

in April 1498 was that he had organized an *intelligenza*, which he strenuously denied: at the utmost, he is stated to have said, there existed at San Marco a *mezza intelligenza*.[1] It was not the first time that such an accusation was levelled against him;[2] thus the signing of the petition to Alexander VI in Savonarola's favour in June 1497 was interpreted by the anti-*Frateschi* to be '*aperta intelligenza* and hence against the law and to be punished'.[3] But apart from this one instance, when over 350 citizens signed the petition, there was nothing concrete the enemies of Savonarola could put their finger on. Parenti, anxious to define a party which despite its cohesion was not an *intelligenza* in the technical sense, calls it an *intelligenza in spirito*.[4]

While it might appear at times as if the division of the citizens into *Frateschi* and their enemies had taken the place of all other conflicts, with both parties including adherents of Piero as well as his enemies, *ottimati* as well as *popolani*, such an impression would be misleading. *Bianchi*, *Bigi* and *ottimati*, whatever their individual relations to the two great parties, had a political identity of their own and were capable of some form of common action; while the *popolo* by its very numbers represented a much more amorphous section of the population.

[1] 'Processi', Villari, ii, p. clvii: 'Et benche molti venisseno a san Marco per divotione: credo molti anchora per beneficiarsi et vedersi et fare una meza intelligentia.' In his sermons, he more than once denied that there existed an *intelligenza* at San Marco: see *Prediche*, ed. Baccini, pp. 32 (8 May 1496), 429 (20 August 1496), 440 (21 August 1496); Villari-Casanova, *Scelta di prediche*, p. 279 (4 May 1497), cf. Parenti, p. 184.

[2] See Parenti, p. 126 (June 1946): attempts by Savonarola's enemies, 'per... farlo venire in sospetto di tenere intelligenza con parte de cittadini', and preceding note.

[3] Parenti, p. 202. In his deposition, Fra Silvestro is stated to have admitted that it was an *intelligenza*, although the only one ever formed by the *Frateschi*: 'Processi', Villari, ii, p. ccxxii (cf. Parenti, pp. 274-5), and Savonarola himself implies that he thought the *subscriptione* would have its effect in the Great Council by binding his followers more closely together (pp. clxix–clxx), which practically amounted to an *intelligenza*.

[4] He explains that 'intelligenze in spirito chiamo le non per scrittura ne per giuramento fatte, ma per similitudine di pareri et medesimo consenso et volonta' (p. 137; cf. p. 136).

It is more difficult to give a satisfactory picture of the structure and activities of these groups than of the *Frateschi*, on whom our evidence is relatively plentiful. Florentine historians like Parenti, Cerretani and Guicciardini, who were inclined to write con-temporary history in terms of social and party conflicts, provide us with much valuable material; but their observations on politi-cal groups sometimes over-simplify the situation and often repre-sent already historical interpretations, especially if they were written at some distance from the event. Generally used at random by modern scholars, these observations have not always received the critical analysis they deserve. The following remarks, which are, in part, based on such an analysis, do not claim to constitute more than a contribution to a better understanding of political facts and developments whose complex character sometimes seems to defy precise definition and which still provides ample opportunity for detailed research. The question hinges largely on the continuity of political power as exercised by social or political groups. If the Medicean *stato* fell primarily because it became divided, the conservative reform of 2 December 1494 constituted an attempt to secure the continued ascendancy of the *ottimati* who had been prominent in government and administra-tion under the Medici, although in a different constitutional setting and with the exclusion of some citizens and the addition of others. The second reform of December 22–23 had created a new situation, and it remained to be seen to what extent the hopes of those who, according to Parenti, believed that it would help to secure such a continuity, were justified.

The Florentines, with their predilection for new political terms to describe new political facts, coined names not only for the adherents and enemies of Savonarola, but also for other political groups. These terms have one thing in common: they go, as it were, in pairs, because the Florentines liked to have for each term a pejorative alternative. Thus the most popular term of abuse corresponding to *Frateschi* was *Piagnoni*,[1] that corresponding

---

[1] Other names were *Collitorti*, *Stropiccioni*, *Masticapaternostri*; see Villari, i, 363. They all reflect the somewhat crude but realistic Florentine sense of humour.

to *Disperati*, as the enemies of Savonarola are sometimes called, *Arrabbiati*.[1] As for the *Bianchi* and *Bigi*, they were, in a sense, com﹍ plementary, the 'grey ones' being those citizens who did not manage to be 'white ones'.[2] The difference between them could be defined, in moral terms, as one between good and bad citizens,[3] but what mattered most was the political contrast between them. The *Bianchi* were the citizens who supported the new republic, although they may have belonged to the old régime; the *Bigi* were the citizens of the Medici régime who had continued to back Piero to the end and would have welcomed his return. One might say, in other words, that the *Bigi* would have been *Bianchi* if they had chosen the right political course and sided with the new régime; but they did not manage to 'clear' themselves as their more republican, or more opportunistic, companions had done.

To what extent the members of the old régime were to be admitted to government and administration under the new régime soon became a pressing and highly controversial political question. Already in May 1495 we find complaints that 'the *Bigi* were again called to the *pratiche*, and that under the pretext of the great external danger, they were asked for their opinions as highly experienced men, so that they once more began to acquire political power'.[4] A year later, things were said to have come to such a point that the adherents of Piero, with the support of Savonarola whose preaching for peace and unity coincided with their interests, were almost more successful in elections to offices than their opponents,[5] and leading *Bianchi* lamented that they had

---

[1] These terms appear fairly late: for *Disperati*, see Somenzi, letter of 29 June 1497, ibid., ii, p. xxx; Parenti, p. 220 (December 1497); for *Arrabbiati*, cf. 'Processi', Villari, ii, p. ccxxix *et passim*; *Lettere di Savonarola*, p. 95.

[2] For the earliest use of these terms see Savonarola, *Prediche italiane*, i, 366 (27 December 1494), ii, 92 (20 January 1495); Parenti, pp. 39 (January 1495), 41 (March 1495).

[3] Cf. Savonarola, *Prediche italiane*, ii, 92; Parenti, p. 41: 'male vixuti ne tempi passati cittadini, e quali per comune vocabolo Bigi si chiamavano'.

[4] Parenti, p. 61.

[5] Ibid., p. 101 (February 1496).

been removed from government.[1] In fact, from an early date members of the old régime seem to have assisted each other in the Great Council; and if they lacked the leadership and enthu‑ siasm of the *Frateschi*, they had in common misfortunes and fear of persecution and were bound together by past collaboration and present loyalties as well as personal and family connections. In Parenti's words, the 'citizens who had been used to govern under the old régime' formed an *intelligenza in spirito*, just like the *Frateschi*.[2] If it could be argued in favour of these men that their experience in government made them indispensable in times of crisis, it might also be said that it was only possible to win them over to the new régime by giving them political office. Such con‑ fidence had, however, its limits; thus when, in April 1497, Piero de' Medici made his unsuccessful attempt to return to Florence, old loyalties assumed new strength: leading *Bigi* were placed under arrest,[3] while Piero, according to the confession of Lamberto dell' Antella, had planned to crush the principal *Bianchi* families once he had returned to Florence.[4] The execution, in August, of five leading citizens who had been involved in this Medicean conspiracy, after an appeal to the Great Council according to the 'law of the six beans' had not been allowed, throws a vivid light on the passions and hatred which the Medicean question could still stir up in Florence.

Cerretani, in describing, in his *Florentine History*, the politically significant groups after the fall of Piero, distinguishes the citizens who had 'lately ruled the town with Piero de' Medici' from those who 'took part in the government of Lorenzo' and after his death began to turn against his son, as well as from those whose families had not occupied any place in government or administration under either Piero or Lorenzo and who wished to do so now. While Cerretani mentions that some of the Mediceans were men

[1] Ibid., p. 98 (February 1496).

[2] p. 136; see also above, pp. 165, 168.

[3] Parenti, p. 181; Cerretani in Schnitzer, op. cit., iii (Munich, 1904), 42-3; Guicciardini, p. 133.

[4] Villari, ii, p. xxi: 'fa pensiero spianare queste case'.

of lower social standing, he emphasizes that the rest were *nobili* and *ricchi*.[1] There were *ottimati* in all parties;[2] but over and above the division into *Bianchi* and *Bigi*, *Frateschi* and *Arrabbiati*, there was a broad community of interests and traditions among them, which was, for instance, reflected during the dramatic events following on Savonarola's arrest, when anti-Savonarolian aristo- crats tried to shield leading *Frateschi* from popular fury.[3] However much the conflicts between *Frateschi* and *Arriabbiati* dominated the forefront of the political scene until Savonarola's execution, the desire of the aristocrats to preserve and strengthen their political influence remained a basic factor in Florentine politics. After the fall of Piero and the first conservative reform, some of them had hoped that this could be achieved within the framework of a new republican constitution. They had clearly not anticipated the impact of the popular element on the Great Council and the powerful influence of Savonarola in favour of popular govern- ment. Characteristic of the disappointments which were the result of the creation of the Great Council was the attitude of Bernardo Rucellai, who had belonged to Lorenzo's inner circle but had become estranged from Piero and had in the end played a leading role in the revolution; he had been elected one of the Twenty *accoppiatori*. The decision to adopt what he considered a quasi-popular constitution was distasteful to him and soon made him withdraw from public life and finally choose voluntary exile.[4] Only few *ottimati*, however, took such an extreme and fastidious course. Many of them evidently continued to hope, after the establishment of the Great Council, that the new con- stitution would in the end work out in their favour. The realization

[1] Op. cit., pp. 39–40.

[2] For the *Frateschi*, see the list of the citizens who in 1497 signed the petition to Alexander VI, in Villari-Casanova, pp. 514–18; 'Processi', Villari, ii, p. clvii; Cerretani, p. 40; Guicciardini, pp. 123–4.

[3] Parenti, p. 268: 'E primati ogni diligentia missono in salvare e capi frateschi, sichome equali et simili a loro.'

[4] See the fundamental article by F. Gilbert, 'Bernardo Rucellai and the Orti Oricellari . . . ', *Journal of the Warburg and Courtauld Institutes*, xii (1949), 101 ff., esp. pp. 107–10.

of such hopes depended, however, largely on their ability to take advantage of the new electoral system. If influence, prestige and experience would stand them in good stead in the elections by vote in the Great Council, other factors, such as Savonarola's preaching for popular government, might work against them. It was therefore not surprising that attempts should be made by *ottimati* to influence elections in their favour through concerted action in the Great Council. Parenti writes that in October 1495, 'it became known that the leading citizens had formed an *intelligenza* to support only each other and their followers'.[1] A few months later, on 26 April 1496, the day on which the new *Signoria* of May–June was to be elected, it was discovered that a list of about forty-five candidates had been secretly circulated in the Great Council.[2] The list had been drawn up by an *intelligenza* which had already acted on previous occasions, and the successful candidates were in their turn to support its members in elections to offices. In fact, the 'conspirators' did not wish to overthrow the régime but to secure offices, *valersi dell' offitii*. They appeared to be opposed both to the *Frateschi* and the *Bigi* and their machinations in the Council; one of the leaders of the *intelligenza*, Filippo Corbizzi, asserted in his evidence before the *Signoria* and the Eight that their aim had been 'to impede the other *intelligenza* which had been created at San Marco' and in this way to secure an equal distribution of offices among the citizens.[3] More than 200 citizens took part in the *intelligenza*, and

[1] Parenti, p. 84: 'si conoscea, che e primati facto haveano intelligentia di non altri che loro sequaci favorire'.

[2] The following account is based on Parenti's detailed narrative, MS, Bibl. Naz., II. II. 130, fos. 5v ff.; only a few passages are ed. by Schnitzer, iv, 115-16, 117. Some other passages are quoted by Ranke, op. cit., pp. 267-8, who is the only modern historian briefly to discuss this incident. Cf. also Cerretani, fos. 224v-5r; Rinuccini, p. clx; M. Sanuto, *I Diarii*, i (Venice, 1879), col. 121; Manfredi, in Cappelli, op. cit., p. 368. According to Guicciardini, pp. 125-6, the *intelligenza* was of 'inimici del frate ed inimici del consiglio', but this statement is only partly supported by Parenti's more circumstantial and reliable account.

[3] Parenti, fo. 8v: 'per ostare all' altra intelligenza creatasi a San Marco, a cagione ciascuno cittadino per rata participassi dell' utile, et honori della sua città'.

all the men whose names had been circulated belonged to the greatest families;[1] some of these, however, were, according to Parenti, ignorant of the secret counsels of the leaders.[2] The dis-covery of the plot resulted in life sentences for the three ringleaders; of the others, only twenty-four were deprived of political rights for one or two years[3]—a comparatively mild punishment, which was probably due to the conviction that the *intelligenza* had not been directed against the constitution, and to the desire to avoid, in Parenti's words, 'greater scandal' by not making public the names of all those who were implicated.[4]

This incident, which has been all but overlooked by modern historians,[5] throws a vivid light on some of the social cross-currents of Florentine politics during those years and on the attempts to influence elections by concerted action. It was unfor-tunate for the *ottimati* that the gradual alteration, from 1497 on-wards, of the new electoral system in favour of election by lot deprived them increasingly of such opportunities, besides being bound to lessen the efficacy of their personal prestige and social

---

[1] Fo. 7r: 'tutti di principali case, et consueti al reggimento'. According to Cerretani, fos. 224v-5r, the *intelligenza* consisted of 'homini di buone case, ma di qualità per altro debolissime, e non usi a havere nè loro nè loro patri molta condi-tione nel regimento'—a judgement which may have been based on the names of the twenty-four citizens who were subsequently *ammoniti*; cf. the—not entirely accurate—list in Sanuto, loc. cit. According to Parenti, more than two hundred citizens were involved in the *intelligenza*.

[2] '. . . che inscienti erano alcuni dell' intrinseco di chi l'intelligenza guidava' (fo. 7v).

[3] The former, Filippo Corbizzi, Giovanni Benizzi and Giovanni da Tignano, as well as a number of citizens who had been *ammoniti*, appealed to the Great Council on 8 and 9 May, but their appeal failed (Deliberazioni, 98, fos. 45r, 45v, 46r).

[4] A law increasing the penalties for *intelligenze* was passed by the Great Council on 25 January 1497 (Provvisioni, cit., 187, fo. 110r-v), after having been rejected on 22 June and on 14 and 27 August 1496 (Florence, Archivio di Stato, Libri fabarum, 71, fos. 67r, 71r, 72v). Cf. Parenti, MS II. II. 130, fo. 45r. The proem of the law criticizes, implicitly, the relatively mild treatment of the citizens who had been found guilty in April 1496.

[5] Ranke discusses it briefly in 'Savonarola . . .', op. cit., pp. 267-8.

standing; and it was inevitable that this development should affect their attitude to the republican régime.

The reform between 1497 and 1499 of the electoral system re-presents perhaps the most important change in the new constitu-tion before the creation of the office of *Gonfaloniere* for life. It was due partly to technical and partly to political causes.

The process of creating the new Florentine constitution had, in fact, not come to an end with the reform law of 22–23 December 1494.[1] Some aspects of the new constitution had been left to be decided on at a later date, such as the precise number of offices which were to be filled by voting in the Great Council, and new problems emerged after the Great Council had come into existence. Certain of these problems were prevalently techni-cal; others were predominantly political, although a hard and fast distinction is not always possible. Of the former, the most important was that of making the new council a viable organ of government and legislation. The Florentines had realized from the beginning that a council which was meant to include a con-siderable proportion of the citizens was liable to be unmanageable; hence it had been laid down that in case the citizens admitted to it exceeded the figure of 1,500, the Council should be divided into three sections which were to sit for six months in rotation. But the number of qualified citizens appears to have by far surpassed general expectations: when the registers of the *beneficiati* were complete it emerged that they were well over 3,000. Consequently the regulation concerning the division into sections came into force. But once the first *consiglio terzato* had begun its six months' session at the end of January 1495, considerable difficulties were experienced in achiev-ing the two-thirds quorum necessary for elections and legislation.

This was primarily due to the fact that the new constitution laid down that otherwise qualified members of the Council were not allowed to attend meetings if they had not paid up their taxes. In view of the heavy burden of taxation, which was to grow considerably in the following years owing to the war against

[1] In the following section, I summarize some of the results of my article on the *Consiglio Maggiore*, loc. cit.

Pisa,[1] it was not surprising that a large proportion of the members of the Council were in that position. Another cause of the difficulties in reaching the quorum was voluntary non-attendance. The manifold functions of the Great Council, and especially the innumerable elections it had to carry out (including, after the early resignation of the Twenty *accoppiatori* in June 1495, also that of the *Signoria*), necessitated frequent and long meetings, which were bound to interfere with the business and private life of its members.

After some cautious attempts to modify the regulations governing the quorum, it was decided, in July 1495, to cut the Gordian knot by abandoning altogether the system of *consigli terzati* and instituting instead meetings of the entire Great Council, with a quorum of 1,000. This decision came into force once the new hall of the Great Council in the Palace of the *Signoria* was ready, and regular meetings began in May 1496. This reorganization did not solve the problem which had been its primary cause, but in some ways intensified it, since from now on the Great Council was in continuous session, instead of three sections of it meeting for six-monthly sessions only; and the *Signoria* continued to experience frequent difficulties in securing the necessary quorum. Heavy fines for non-attendance seem to have had relatively scant effect; and while the regulations concerning tax arrears were slightly alleviated, their elimination would have struck at a fundamental principle of Florentine constitutional practice, by which the acceptance of state offices was made dependent upon the discharge of what was then considered one of the foremost public duties of the citizen. This principle, which incidentally had also the practical effect of encouraging citizens to pay their taxes, formed an essential element of the constitution of the Great Council, and despite the great difficulties it created, the Florentines obstinately refused to abolish it.[2] Another way out would

---

[1] See L. F. Marks, 'La crisi finanziaria a Firenze dal 1494 al 1502', *Arch. Stor. Ital.*, cxii (1954), 42 ff.

[2] Only on a few exceptional occasions, when a particularly large attendance was desired, was an exemption from it granted, e.g. for the two first solemn meetings in the new hall of the Council.

have been to lower the quorum; but this too would have run counter to one of the basic concepts of the new republican con' stitution, that of a large council which could truly be considered *signore della città*.[1] There remained the possibility of reducing the work of the Council and with it the number and duration of its meetings, and thus to lighten the burden of attendance for the Florentine merchants and artisans. This could be done by modifying the electoral machinery of the Great Council and by extending the number of the offices which were filled by lot at the expense of those which were filled by voting: a policy which was in fact adopted between 1497 and 1499. In a series of laws from 12 May 1497 to 31 May 1499, the electoral system of the new republican constitution was progressively remodelled by giving an ever greater place to election by sortition. When this reform was completed in May 1499, all the highest offices, in' cluding the *Signoria*, were filled by an ingenious system combining election by voting and by lot, while the other offices were to be filled by lot only.

Considerations of a practical and technical nature were one of the main causes of these reforms of the electoral system, but they were not the only one. We have seen that from the very beginning, a certain ambiguity attached to the constitutional and social significance of the Great Council. This ambiguity is perhaps easiest to grasp in the new electoral system. Was this system, as embodied in the law of December 23, aristocratic or democratic; was it more in favour of the *ottimati* or of the *popolani*? While Savonarola considered election by voting an integral part of the new popular constitution,[2] a number of *ottimati* seem from the outset to have expected that it would turn out in their favour, and

---

[1] Cf. Savonarola, *Trattato*, iii, 1, p. 40: 'perchè il piccolo numero poterìa essere corrotto con amicizie e parentadi, e danari, bisogna costituire uno grande numero di cittadini. . . . Fatto dunque questo numero di cittadini . . . non è dubbio che questo è il signore della città.'

[2] In December 1496 he strongly opposed attempts to extend sortition at the expense of election by voting: cf. *Prediche sopra Ezechiele*, ed. R. Ridolfi, i (Rome, 1955), 96–7 (13 December).

Parenti goes as far as to say that *il modo dell' electione non ad altro fine trovato era, che per rendere lo stato alla nobiltà*—in other words, to give the aristocrats greater power than they had possessed under the Medici.[1] Indeed, although numbers were against them, it might well be hoped that their social standing and their experience in government would make it easy for them to defeat other citizens in election to offices, and especially to the highest offices of the state. Others doubtless remained in favour of the traditional sortition, which had been the programme of the conservative reform of December 2.

If in December 1494 there could still be doubts about the social implications of the new electoral system, a clarification soon took place after the Great Council had come into existence. In the first popular enthusiasm for the Great Council *gente nuova*, in the words of the Ferrarese orator, were elected to high office;[2] towards the end of 1495 he reports, with some exaggeration, that the *ottimati* 'are not too happy, as they are not held in as great esteem by the *popolani* as they would like and believe they deserve; none or few of them are ever elected to magistracies . . . by this council of the people . . .'.[3] But the novelty gradually wore off and the prestige and influence of the *ottimati* came increasingly into their own again. Moreover, just as the *Frateschi* helped each other in elections, so also, as we have seen, did the *ottimati*.[4] Thus we find once more a considerable proportion of the highest offices going to the families which had been used to hold them under the Medici and before.[5] The result of this was that the *popolani* in the

[1] p. 30.

[2] See Manfredi in Cappelli, p. 346 (16 May 1495), on the election of the new *Dieci*: they are 'homini che pocho ne cognosco io, essendo gente nova tutti che hanno pocha experientia de stato . . .', and p. 366, on the election of the *Signoria* of November–December 1495.

[3] Ibid.

[4] See above, pp. 172 ff.

[5] Guicciardini says in 1508 or 1509, in his *Storie* (p. 137): 'girando la elezione degli ufici in pochi e strignendosi a un numero di dugento cittadini o pochi più'. If this is exaggerated, it nevertheless probably reflects fairly accurately *ottimati* views on this subject.

Great Council came to regard election by lot to be in their favour, while the aristocrats were increasingly satisfied with the new system of elections by an absolute and relative majority; the lot came to stand for *governo largo*, elections by voting for *governo stretto*.[1] The reforms of the electoral system partly fulfilled technical requirements; but they were also meant to satisfy popular de‑ mands.[2] When they were completed in May 1499, ordinary citizens doubtless stood a better chance of being elected than before, since many offices were now filled by lot, while in others the candidates had only to secure an absolute majority to have their names placed in the voting bags for the final sortition. Guicciardini later dated from this change in the electoral system the decline of the predominance of the *ottimati* and consequently their growing opposition to the republic; but according to Parenti, the reform did not affect them quite as unfavourably; although the *popolani* were now satisfied, he says, the *uomini di più qualità* always received more votes than the others.[3] Guicciardini, who belonged to one of those *ottimati* families which collaborated with the new régime without committing themselves too much to it, is probably a better authority on the reaction of many members of his class to the reform than Parenti. It doubtless contributed, in the long run, to their opposition to the republican régime and to their desire to reform it along oligarchical lines. In 1502 an attempt to create a senate with life membership was unsuccessful; instead it was decided to establish the office of *Gonfaloniere* for life on the Venetian model. When Savonarola had urged the Floren‑ tines, on 14 December 1494, to imitate the Venetian constitu‑ tion, he had expressly excepted the office of the Doge,[4] and it was precisely this office which the Florentines now undertook to

---

[1] Guicciardini, *Storie*, pp. 136–7, and also 'Dialogo del reggimento di Firenze', *Dialogo e discorsi del reggimento di Firenze*, ed. R. Palmarocchi (Bari, 1932), pp. 47, 80.

[2] See Rubinstein, 'I primi anni', p. 336.

[3] MS II, IV, 170, fo. 79 (May 1499).

[4] *Prediche italiane*, i, 195: 'pigliate exemplo da loro resecando però qualche cosa di quelle che non sono a proposito . . . come è quella del duce'.

imitate. If in 1494 there was, as we have seen, some equivocation about the constitutional character of the new régime,[1] in 1502 the *ottimati* made a supreme effort, after all their previous disappointments, to give it an aristocratic turn. A senate would have served their aim best, and indeed remained an *ottimati* ideal for a long period;[2] the *Gonfalonierato* for life might at least appear as a first step in this direction.[3] That many aristocrats were once more disappointed was primarily due to the personality of the *Gonfaloniere* Piero Soderini, who had no desire to promote an oligarchical programme. The strengthening of the Medici party among the *ottimati*, for which the death of Piero de' Medici in 1503 created favourable conditions, Giovanni and Giuliano being both more tactful and less compromised, was almost inevitable and prepared the way for the restoration of the Medici in September 1512.

No account of the political development of Florence at the end of the fifteenth century could be complete without at least some words on the foreign policy of that city, for foreign and internal politics were so closely entwined during those years as to make the one often appear a symptom of the other. That this was so was, in the first place, due to Savonarola's championship of the alliance with France after the conclusion, on 25 November 1494, of the treaty of alliance between Florence and Charles VIII; for the question of whether to remain loyal to France, despite her failure to restore Pisa or to join the League of Venice which had been concluded on 31 March 1495, became now part of the conflict between *Frateschi* and *Arrabbiati*. The isolation of Florence in Italy after she had refused to join the league and her inability to recover Pisa despite Charles's promises gave this question a special urgency. In Florence as well as abroad, it was argued that it was Savonarola

---

[1] See above, pp. 159 ff.

[2] See, e.g., Guicciardini, 'Dialogo', pp. 118 ff. A reform project of probably 1527 suggests the creation of a senate with life membership: Florence, Archivio di Stato, Carte Strozz., ser. 2a, 95, no. 14, fo. 821.

[3] See R. v. Albertini, *Das Florentinische Staatsbewusstsein im Übergang von der Republik zum Prinzipat* (Berne, 1955), pp. 29–30.

and his party who prevented the Florentines from joining.[1] This in turn was bound to affect the political conflicts in Florence, as the opponents of the *Frateschi* could hope to get assistance from Milan or from the pope. Thus, in 1496, there were rumours in Florence during the Tuscan expedition of the king of the Romans, Maximilian, who was a member of the league, that the principal citizens wanted Florence to join the league in order to overthrow the popular constitution,[2] while at the beginning of the following year, Francesco Valori's internal policy was believed to be aimed largely at the pro-league party.[3] True, Savonarola himself seems to have had some doubts, early in 1497, about the value of the French alliance; but this was only a temporary wavering.[4]

When on 13 May 1497 Alexander VI excommunicated Savonarola, one of his principal motives was doubtless to induce Florence to join the league by acting against the man who was the main obstacle to it.[5] Thus Savonarola's support of the French alliance helped to bring about his ultimate downfall, just as opposition to France had been one of the causes of the fall of Piero de' Medici. Nothing could illustrate more vividly the inter-play of foreign and internal politics in Florence.

At the same time, while the *Frateschi* were in favour of the French alliance, not all those who were in its favour were *Frateschi*. The controversies over foreign policy resulted, indeed, in a further party division, so that one could now speak in Florence of a French party and a league party. There were strong arguments in favour of the French alliance independently from Savonarola's preaching, such as a diplomatic tradition of long standing, Floren-tine commercial interests in France and the hope to recover Pisa with French help.[6] The conflicts of opinion between pro-French

[1] Cf., e.g., Parenti, p. 191; Gentile Becchi to the *Dieci* from Rome, 19 March 1497, in A. Gherardi, *Nuovi documenti e studi intorno a Girolamo Savonarola* (Florence, 1887), p. 155.

[2] Parenti, p. 144; cf. p. 149.   [3] Ibid., p. 155.

[4] *Prediche sopra Ezechiele*, i, 289; cf. Parenti, pp. 162-3 (February 1497); Sanuto, i, cols. 533-4 (March).

[5] See Villari, ii, 30; Ridolfi, i, 297.

[6] See, e.g., Parenti, pp. 68, 89; Guicciardini, *Storie*, p. 121.

and anti-French survived the death of Savonarola, and flared up again in 1507, as a result of Maximilian's Italian expedition; and again, they were connected with internal factions, this time over the policy of Piero Soderini.[1] Finally in 1512, when the French alliance led to military intervention against Florence by the new League of Venice, the surrender of the city was followed by the restoration of the Medici.

However powerful the impact of Savonarola on the internal and foreign policy of Florence between 1494 and 1498, he did not succeed in altering substantially the social structure of Florentine politics, and was only partly responsible for what changes did take place; the French alliance, so vigorously supported by him, reflected also a long Florentine tradition; and his fall made only little difference in such matters as the reforms of the Great Council and the loyalty to France, or in the major problem of Florentine politics, the position of the *ottimati* in the state. Florentine history of the end of the fifteenth century has too often been written in terms of 'Savonarola and his time'. What mattered most, in the end, were the political traditions and problems of a city which, as Guicciardini said later on, was already old and set in her ways,[2] and which Savonarola, who was not a native of Florence, perhaps never fully understood, as he himself seems to have admitted in so many words.[3] It was natural enough that he should have become, in more than one sense, an *insegna et instrumento*, a symbol and instrument,[4] of conflicting forces— at a time when he believed that he was well on the way to transforming Florence into a model state on the Thomistic pattern.

[1] Ibid., pp. 297 ff.

[2] 'Dialogo', pp. 81-2.

[3] See, e.g., 'Processi', Villari, ii, p. clvii (cit. p. 166, n. 2). Francesco Altoviti criticizes the 'foreigner' Savonarola on account of his having introduced new laws into Florence: 'non bisogna che Fra Girolamo forestiero porti le sue nuove leggi a Fiorentini, nè che lui porti la sapientia in Athene . . .' (*Defensione contro all' archa di Fra Girolamo*, n.p., n.d. (Florence, 1497?)).

[4] 'Processi', Villari, ii, p. clvi: for my followers 'bastava havermi per insegna et instrumento coprendosi sotto il mio mantello'.

D. M. Bueno de Mesquita

LUDOVICO SFORZA AND
HIS VASSALS[1]

A. Feudatories of the Piacentino

On an evening at the beginning of March in the year 1484, the Podestà of Piacenza witnessed a strange and alarming scene in the streets of the city. 'In this past night,' he wrote to the Duke of Milan, 'I have seen with my own eyes, around the palace and in the piazza of Piacenza, some 300 people carrying weapons of attack; and what is more, men fully armed on horseback with banners, and even with their lances; so that it seemed the whole of Piacenza went in fear. However, nothing further happened.' He was sure, he added, that the Commissarius, the Ducal Commissioner, would send a full account, but he thought it his duty to make his own report as he had been an eye witness.[2]

The throng crowding the streets on a late winter's night, the arms they carried in flagrant defiance of the law, were unwelcome apparitions to those responsible for maintaining order in the city. At Milan, in the Ducal Chancery, the Podestà's letter sounded ominous enough to be marked for the attention of Ludovico Sforza, the young Duke's uncle, guardian and Lieutenant-General.[3] Two days later the Commissioner, who had written

---

[1] All the documents quoted are in the Archivio di Stato, Milan: Sforzesco, series Cart[eggio] Int[erno], Miss[ive], and Reg[istri] Duc[ali]. I would like to thank the Director and officials of the Archives for their courtesy and help, and the Board of the Faculty of Modern History in the University of Oxford for their help in facilitating a visit to Milan.

[2] Cart. Int. 875, 3 March 1484, letter of the Podestà Filippo Petrasancta.

[3] On the back, 'M. d. Lud'. This was subsequently crossed out, and the letter marked for filing ('in filza').

direct to Ludovico but whose letter had apparently not reached
the Chancery, was ordered to explain what had happened.[1]
Meanwhile the City Council of Piacenza, the Prior and Anziani,
in a prudent attempt to mollify its rulers, prepared a statement
designed to show the episode in a less sinister light. 'On the night
of Tuesday last, which was our Carnival, some young men . . .
some on foot, and a few on horseback' had been out in the streets,
'seeking amusement, and some to dance as they are wont to do
on such days'. There had been no harm or damage or misconduct. The Podestà and Commissioner, both recently appointed,
and unfamiliar with the customs of the city, had misunderstood
what was going on.[2]

The government, preoccupied at the time with the War of
Ferrara, could not in any case have dealt easily with so general a
breach of the law forbidding the carrying of weapons during
night-time. It soon transpired, however, that the Carnival celebrations were not quite so innocent and customary as the City
Council professed to believe. The Podestà wrote again, at the end
of the following week, that 'Count Bartolomeo Scotto and Count
Daniele Todesco, who had been at their castles, came to the city
and held a meeting, in particular with Counts Bartolomeo and
Gianfrancesco Anguissola; and they so arranged peace, quiet and
settlement among the clans[3] of their followers, and especially of
their young men who were the cause of the affair, that they are
brought to good behaviour. And indeed I know by my own
understanding that these gentlemen are wholly devoted to your
Excellency's will, and to the good government of the State.'[4]

These public festivities, when the bands of rival noble families
roamed the streets, had been a likely source of disturbance in the
Italian cities during the Middle Ages. The rivalries and the habits
survived into the age of the Sforza, and on this occasion, although

---

[1] Ibid., 7 March 1484, letter of the Commissioner Matteo Corte. I have found
nothing about this episode in the relevant register of Missive, vol. 163.

[2] Cart. Int. 875, 6 March 1484, 'Prior et Antiani' to the Duke.

[3] 'Casine.'

[4] Cart. Int. 875, 13 March 1484, letter of Filippo Petrasancta.

conflict was avoided, it is clear that the danger had been there. Some of the rivalries made sufficient impact to find a place in the chronicles of the times. The feud between Rossi and Pallavicini held the city of Parma in terror for years, and culminated, under the pressure of Ludovico Sforza's friendship for the Pallavicini, in the rebellion of Piermaria Rosso with the backing of Venice in 1482.[1] The Scotti and Anguissola of Piacenza were not quite on the same footing as these two families in terms of power, but their conduct and their relations with the government are none the less indicative of the problems of the Sforza in the administra-tion of their dominions, and it is in this light that I propose to examine them, during the twenty years when Ludovico Sforza controlled the affairs of the state.

The four families of Scotti and Anguissola, Landi and Fon-tana, virtually controlled the Commune of Piacenza in the thir-teenth century. Two hundred years later they were vassals of the Sforza, and divided their time between their castles, sited for the most part in and above the valleys which led from the Apennine passes to the Lombard Plain,[2] and their houses in the city, where they still enjoyed great influence and power. Even in the sixteenth century they dominated the City Council and the General Assembly.[3] Certain officials directly represented the four *squadre* or *domus*,[4] and a letter of Bartolomeo Scotto shows him exercis-ing his family's right of nomination to these posts.[5] When the Marquis Ludovico Sforza di Fogliano complained to the Duke that Count Manfredo Lando had trespassed on his jurisdiction in the *contado*, he ascribed the Count's insolence to the fact that

---

[1] A. Pezzana, *Storia della Città di Parma*, iv (1852), *passim*.

[2] Cf. the comments of E. Nasalli Rocca in *Boll[ettino] St[orico] Piac[entino]*, xxiv (1929), 104–5, on the siting of these castles.

[3] Cf. the incident recorded by C. Poggiali, *Memorie Storiche di Piacenza*, viii (1760), 336–7, and commented on by W. Cesarini-Sforza in *Boll. St. Piac.*, v (1910), 74.

[4] C. Santoro, *Gli Uffici del Dominio Sforzesco, 1450–1500* (Milan, Fondazione Treccani degli Alfieri, 1948), pp. 497–9.

[5] Cart. Int. 877, 24 July 1498: 'Io per la squadra Scotta ho facto ellectione di m. Nicolao Ricio per advocato, e Francisco Gandino per sindico.'

'the Count is *capo di parte* in Piacenza, and feels that he has authority and favour here and elsewhere'.[1]

However divided these families might be among themselves over the distribution of their properties, they still retained in their dealings with outsiders something of the solidarity which had marked the feudal *consorterie* of the Lombard countryside. The *nobiles de Anguissolis* wrote to the government to support the claims of the widow of one of their number.[2] *Fidelissimi servitores nobiles Domus de Fontana* wrote on two occasions to the Duke on behalf of the Arcelli, who were a branch of the same clan.[3] A petition subscribed by forty-seven men bearing the name of either Fontana or Arcelli[4] indicates one of the reasons why these old families were still a force of which the Sforza had to take account. But the records of the central government are naturally more con- cerned with their quarrels and transgressions than with this sense of unity, and the career of Count Bartolomeo Scotto will serve to show the time and attention which the government devoted to the affairs of the Duke's vassals.

On the death of his father in 1461, Bartolomeo became the senior member of the Scotti Counts of Vigoleno, on whom the genial fancy of that least parochial of rulers the Emperor Sigis- mund had bestowed the right to call themselves Douglas Scotti in memory of their reputed origins. Bartolomeo's dispute with his nephews Jacopo, Cristoforo, Giovanni and Piero over the possession of Vigoleno[5] had already led to acts of violence by 1465, and dragged on for thirty years. After Ludovico Sforza's return to Milan in September 1479 the castle was awarded to the nephews, who had attached themselves to his cause during his exile.[6] But this was by no means the end of the matter. In the first

---

[1] Cart. Int. 873, 17 September 1480.

[2] Cart. Int. 875, 9 April 1485.

[3] Cart. Int. 873, 19 December 1479 and 25 April 1480.

[4] Cart. Int. 874, 6 December 1482.

[5] Between the Apennine streams Ongina and Stirone, some 18 miles S.E. of Piacenza.

[6] G. Bonazzi, 'Cronica', *Rerum Italicarum Scriptores*, nuova serie, xxii, pt. 3, 38 and 60; P. del Giudice, 'I Consigli Ducali', *Rendiconti dell' Istituto Lombardo*,

place, Bartolomeo showed no inclination to accept the verdict, and had to be left to cool his indignation in custody for a while before he submitted. Duchess Bona, the Duke's mother, personally laid down the terms for his release: the surrender of Vigoleno and bail of 8,000 ducats that he would not leave Milan without permission.[1] Vigoleno was in the hands of the government by the end of February 1480,[2] and three weeks later Bartolomeo was free to go where he pleased.[3] But these measures seem merely to have enforced a preliminary judgement on seisin, for the case was again before the Privy Council in April and May.[4]

The nephews were in trouble early in 1481, summoned to Milan and fined for an offence against the Visdomini.[5] Vigoleno was again in the hands of the government in March, pending the settlement of a dispute between Bartolomeo and Giovanni Scotto.[6] There was danger of a conflict between Scotti and Pallavicini at the beginning of 1483.[7] Two of the nephews, Cristoforo and Piero, came to blows at the end of the year over the castle of Carpaneto,[8] and Piero proposed that he should be allowed to use force in defence of his rights, but the idea of condoning selfhelp proved too much even for the harassed Commissioner of

2, xxxii (1899), 338; G. Manfredi, 'I Conti Scotti e Vigoleno', Boll. St. Piac., xlix (1954), 16-21. I have been unable to see L. Naldi (1859) and L. Balduzzi (1883) on the genealogy of the Scotti.

[1] Miss. 146, fo. 164 and t., 24 February 1480, to Ambrosino Longhinana (Capitaneus custodie ducalis). On fulfilment of the terms, 'lo debiate relaxare de presone et metterlo in sua libertà'. Below the secretary's initial, 'Bonna Duchesa de Milano manu propria.'

[2] Cart. Int. 873, 9 March 1480, letter of the Commissioner's Vicar.

[3] Miss. 146, fo. 229 and t., 22 March 1480, to Ambrosino Longhinana.

[4] Cart. Int. 873, 11 and 23 April, 12 and 15 May 1480; a letter of Bartolomeo, 8 April, quoted by Manfredi in Boll. St. Piac., xlix, 21.

[5] Cart. Int. 874, 11 January and 1 March 1481, letter of the Commissioner Gianantonio Cotta, and of the Maestri delle Entrate at Milan.

[6] Ibid., 17 March, 15, 26, 30 April, 26 June 1481, letters of Gianjacopo Cotta; 22 May and 6 June, letters of the government.

[7] Ibid., 15 January 1483, letter of Cesare Porro from Castell' Arquato.

[8] Another fief of the Scotti, between the streams Chero and Vezzano, about twelve miles S.E. of Piacenza.

Piacenza.[1] Negotiations broke down in the middle of January 1484, both parties stood armed, and further breaches of the peace seemed likely.[2] The government then intervened and took over Carpaneto,[3] but disorders brewing in the Val di Nure early in February were thought to be connected with this dispute.[4] The case seems by then to have been evoked to the Ducal Council in Milan,[5] but whatever verdict was reached did not end the quarrel. Cristoforo, apparently backed now by his uncle Bartolomeo, made a raid on the castle, probably in August 1485,[6] and was complaining to the government shortly afterwards about Piero's misconduct.[7] In the intervening period he had launched an attack on the castle of Zena held by Cesare Alfonso da Parma,[8] and this case too was promptly evoked to Milan in the Duke's name.[9]

At the end of 1490[10] Bartolomeo Scotto appealed to the government in a dispute with a neighbour over a salt-mine.[11] The quarrel with his nephews cropped up again at the beginning of 1493.

[1] Cart. Int. 874, 29 December 1483, letter of Matteo Corte: 'Prefato Conte Petro me ha scripto che lassa andare fora che luy se diffenderà de facto, el che non ho voluto asentire, dubitando che vostra Excellentia gli farà tuta provisione gli piaccia.' There is another letter of Corte on the next day about this dispute.

[2] Cart. Int. 875, 16 January 1484, letter of Matteo Corte.

[3] Ibid., 26 January 1484, the same.

[4] Ibid., 3 February 1484, the same.

[5] Miss. 163, fo. 31 t., 9 February 1484, reply to Corte's letter of 3 February on the state of the Val di Nure: 'sono qui l'una parte et l'altra, et noy deliberamo intendere questa cosa'.

[6] Letter of Piero to Bartolomeo Scotto published by G. Manfredi in Boll. St. Piac., xlix, 21–3. A notarial record showing Cristoforo and Giovanni in possession of Carpaneto and defying Ducal orders is referred to in Boll. St. Piac., xi (1916,) 106, with the date 9 September 1448—possibly a misprint for 1484.

[7] Cart. Int. 875, 29 October 1485, letters of Cristoforo Scotto.

[8] Ibid., 17, 19 and 24 April 1484, letter of Matteo Corte. Zena lies about two miles N.E. of Carpaneto.

[9] Miss. 163, fo. 88 and t., 20 April 1484, reply to Corte's of 17 April.

[10] My main source for this narrative, the Carteggio Interno for Piacenza, contains very few letters for the years 1486 to 1489.

[11] Cart. Int. 875, 16 December 1490, a long letter of the Commissioner Gianfrancesco Visconti.

The government called for the record of the previous settlement,[1] and this time Ludovico Sforza personally ordered two members of the family to negotiate an accord.[2] It is unlikely that they succeeded. Bartolomeo was summoned to Milan in August,[3] probably in connection with this case, for he wrote to Ludovico early in 1494, 'recording to your Excellency how many burdens and expenses I have suffered through having done my lord's will', and grumbling about the powerful connections his rivals had in Milan and among the local officials.[4] Eighteen months later he was again engaged in a controversy with his nephew Jacopo, and the Bishop of Piacenza was now called on to try his hand as a peacemaker.[5]

Bartolomeo had meanwhile run into difficulties of another kind. In 1492 he bought some lands in the Val di Nure,[6] borrowing 3,000 ducats for the purpose from Gaspare Stanga. By the end of 1494 he still owed 1,000 ducats, and the creditor had arranged for troops to be billeted in Piacenza at the Count's expense as a means of encouraging prompt payment. Bartolomeo appealed to the Duke for help in collecting his rents and securing a moratorium on his debt.[7] The government wrote to the Captain of the Val di Nure to help the Count on the first point, but professed not to be able to interfere with the rights of the creditor. 'You will do well therefore, over the postponement of payment, to get in touch with Gaspare Stanga, whose concern it is whether to do it or not. We are sure that, since he is a gentleman,[8] he will not fail to meet your request if he can do so without loss to himself.'[9] The Stanga were well entrenched at court, where Gaspare's

---

[1] Ibid., 14 January 1493, letter of the Commissioner Gianfrancesco Marliano.

[2] Ibid., 8 March 1493, Giovanni Scotto to Ludovico Sforza.

[3] Ibid., 7 August 1493, letter of Gianfrancesco Marliano.

[4] Cart. Int. 876, 26 February 1494, Bartolomeo Scotto to Ludovico Sforza.

[5] Ibid., 18 September 1495, letter of the Commissioner Ambrogio del Maino.

[6] A 'prorogatio feudalis investiture' was granted on 31 May 1493 (and renewed on 28 August 1494); Reg. Duc. 48, fo. 232.

[7] Cart. Int. 876, 1 January 1495, letter of Bartolomeo Scotto.

[8] 'Essendo zentilhomo.'

[9] Miss. 193, fo. 143, 7 January 1495, 'Comiti Bartholommeo Scotto'.

brother Marchesino was among the closest associates of Ludovico Sforza, and any reprieve that Bartolomeo secured was of short duration, for in June the Commissioner of Piacenza, on orders from the government, was again 'placing many soldiers at the expense of Count Bartolomeo Scotto, for Gaspare Stanga's debt'.[1] Bartolomeo had had recourse to the moneylenders, but this only brought him a severe rap over the knuckles, and a threat of more drastic action if he did not pay his debts. 'The more honourable your place in society, the greater shame upon you for allowing a complaint of you to reach us of the kind that is contained in the enclosed petition of Albertino de' Medici. There is no need to tell you how greatly honour demands that you give satisfaction to those who are entitled to it, and especially when you have had the service of a loan of money.'[2] He must behave like a gentleman, even if his creditors did not.

These troubles may have kept Bartolomeo quiet for a time, but he was active again by 1498. In March the government intervened in a case between him and Franceschina Borromea, guardian of the heir of Count Sforza Secondo.[3] In May it was concerned with a fresh controversy between him and Cristoforo.[4] In December he was summoned to Milan in person or by proxy to answer a complaint laid by Alfonso Visconti, and the summons was renewed a month later,[5] but by that time his health was probably beginning to fail.

This catalogue of spasmodic violence and protracted litigation may not be complete. It is certainly not exceptional. The Anguissola have a similar record. Their dossier includes an accusation of homicide,[6] an attack on Rivergaro in the Val di

---

[1] Cart. Int. 876, 12 June 1495, letter of Ambrogio del Maino.

[2] Miss. 193, fo. 197 and t., 'Comiti Bartholommeo Scotto consiliario'.

[3] Miss. 209, fo. 44, 28 April 1498, cancelling an order of 25 March to suspend local hearing of the case. A new order to suspend issued on 15 June: ibid., fo. 77 and t.

[4] Ibid., fo. 66, 25 May 1498, to the Bishop of Piacenza's Vicar.

[5] Ibid., fos. 194 and 212 and t. (numbered 124 and 142), 20 December 1498 and 22 January 1499, 'Commissario Placentie'.

[6] Cart. Int. 874, 20 March 1481, letter of the Commissioner Gianantonio Cotta.

Trebbia,[1] the seizure of the castle of Zena,[2] suspicion of instigat-
ing an assault on a tax-collector,[3] and the violent expulsion of
the tenant of a mill.[4] These incidents in the life of the Contado
were liable to have repercussions within the city, and on two
occasions at least, besides the Carnival of 1484, the Anguissola
had a hand in the series of criminal outbreaks which afflicted
Piacenza between 1483 and 1486.[5] On the first of these occasions,
the Commissioner described two hostile companies loose in the
city, carrying arms regardless of all decrees, one led by a man
whom he describes as 'the favourite of the Anguissola', the other
backed by a group of Count Sforza Secondo's lieutenants.[6] In
the second case, two years later, the Commissioner wrote: 'In the
past few days, after the beginning of the quarrel between the
Anguissola and the men of Roncovero over the death of Giancarlo Anguissola's attendant,[7] bad characters have multiplied so
much in this city, and boldness in carrying arms by day and night,
that I fear one day they will produce some serious disorder.'[8]

Yet however much trouble the Anguissola or the Scotti gave
to the government, and they obviously gave a good deal, the
Sforza recognized and were prepared to rely on the influence of
these families. As soon as the court heard that Bartolomeo Scotto
was seriously ill, the Commissioner of Piacenza was told to take
measures, in the event of his death, to secure the smooth succession
to their inheritance of the sons of this lord 'devoted to our State
and among the leading men of the city'.[9] Ludovico Sforza
placed particular trust in the loyalty of the Anguissola. When the

[1] Cart. Int. 875, 5 January 1485 (second side), copy of the government's letter
to Counts Bartolomeo and Annibale Anguissola.

[2] Ibid., 15 October 1485, letter of the Podestà Filippo Petrasancta.

[3] Ibid., 7 July 1493, letter of the Podestà Ilario Gentile to Ludovico Sforza.

[4] Cart. Int. 877, 26 October 1497, letter of the Commissioner Ambrogio Zancha.

[5] I hope to discuss these outbreaks in more detail elsewhere, in relation to the
problems and methods of Sforza government.

[6] Cart. Int. 874, 15 August 1483, letter of Gianbattista Castiglione.

[7] 'Staffero.'

[8] Cart. Int. 875, 25 August 1485, letter of Antonio Crivelli.

[9] Miss. 209, fo. 237 and t. (numbered 177 and t.), 26 February 1499.

security of Piacenza became an important political consideration at the beginning of 1482, the government instructed the Com' missioner to use without any reservation the help and advice of Count Gianfrancesco Anguissola and his family, 'because you will always find them most ready and reliable in all good pur' poses, and more vigilant in our affairs than in their own'.[1] The Commissioner, reporting the Count's arrival in the city, added: 'I am most grateful for his coming; for in view of his loyalty to your Excellency's State, and also his knowledge and the credit he has in this city, especially among men of worth, I am sure his activities will be a great support to me.'[2] And indeed he did on several occasions seek the advice of the Count and of his brother Bartolomeo.[3]

When Rivergaro was enfeoffed in 1484 to Antonio Carac' ciolo,[4] a Neapolitan who had followed the fortunes of the Sforza, married an Anguissola and settled in Lombardy, the Anguissola had cause to consider themselves shabbily treated. They had a claim to the fief, and at one point mustered their forces to assert it.[5] But the decision came from Ludovico Sforza, as Gian' francesco Anguissola wrote later to the first Secretary, Bartolomeo Calco, 'and we have made no resistance'.[6] And in another critical moment for the state, ten years later, it was again to the Anguissola that Ludovico Sforza turned, this time in the person of Bartolomeo's son Annibale. Five days after the battle of For' novo, the Commissioner reported that Annibale had arrived in Piacenza with Ludovico's letter of credence, and that his coming was very welcome to all and exactly what was needed.[7]

---

[1] Cart. Int. 874, 7 January 1482, copy of a letter to the Commissioner Gian' antonio Cotta.   [2] Ibid., 10 January 1482, letter of Gianantonio Cotta.

[3] Ibid., 3 February 1482, the same: 'Havendone più volte participato cum li conti Bartolomeo et Johanne Francesco Anguissola.'

[4] C. Poggiali, *Memorie storiche di Piacenza*, viii (1760), 89-90; G. V. Boselli, *Delle Storie Piacentine*, ii (1804), 265.

[5] 'Intendemo che havete conducte alcuni armati al loco de Revergario, qual cosa c'è molestissima.' The letter cit. *supra*, p. 192, n. 1.

[6] Cart. Int. 875, 4 October 1485.

[7] Cart. Int. 876, 11 July 1495, letter of Ambrogio del Maino.

These old families, whose continuing status and influence in the affairs of the cities made their place in the state a special prob-lem for the Dukes, formed only one element among the vassals of the Sforza. The curious case of the daughters of Giovanni Albertazzi illustrates the diversity of the conditions of fiefs and of their holders. In June 1494 the Duke granted the succession to the feudal rights held in the villages of Ronco and Zenevetero by the late Giovanni Albertazzi, known as de Compiano, to his daughters of marriageable age.[1] Albertazzi had bought the fief of the *dazi*, or excise duties, on victuals in the two villages in 1466 for £400[2] which would give an annual income of £24 at the normal purchase value in Lombardy during the fifteenth century.[3] This gives us little guide to Albertazzi's status, but he had in fact acquired the office of Treasurer of Piacenza in 1461, and was wealthy enough to lend £3,000 to the city;[4] and he knew how to profit by his office, if an accusation that he extorted £60 and more from a man who owed 18s. to the Ducal *Camera* be true, though he denied the charge[5]. A long letter of the Commissioner of Pia-cenza, however, reveals that his daughters petitioned for succession to his fief, which lawfully escheated to the Duke after his death without male issue, on the ground that they had no other dowry with which to find suitable husbands. The petition went to the Commissioner, in accordance with normal routine, for a full report on the circumstances. He replied that there were three daughters, the eldest of whom had been *matura viro* for some years; before and after their father's death, they had maintained them-selves *ex quottidiano* by weaving and other woman's work, and by seeking alms.[6]

[1] Reg. Duc. 48, fos. 249–51, 7 June 1494.

[2] A record of the enfeoffment may exist, but I have taken these facts from the letter quoted *infra*, n. 6.

[3] To give 6 per cent rent, according to C. Cipolla, *Money Prices and Civilization* (Princeton University Press, 1956), p. 65.   [4] Santoro, op. cit., pp. 492–3.

[5] This is revealed in a letter published by F. Fossati in *Arch[ivio] St[orico] Lomb[ardo]*, 8, v (1954–5), 420.

[6] 'Ex erogatione elemosinarum.' Cart. Int. 875, 6 December 1493, letter of Gianfrancesco Marliano.

At the other extreme, the two most powerful feudatories of the Piacentino were men of different antecedents again. They belonged to the newer nobility of soldiers and descendants of soldiers, the men who had led the armies of Visconti and Sforza and were endowed in return with fiefs and jurisdictions *jure feudi honorifici nobilis et gentilis*.

Sforza Secondo, Count of Borgonovo, has already appeared in these pages. The outlines of the career of this natural and legitimated son of Duke Francesco Sforza are known.[1] He got into very serious trouble in 1461, and again in 1467, for activities regarded as treasonable. By the 1470's he had accepted his place as a commander in the armies of the Sforza,[2] in which capacity he was signally defeated by Roberto San Severino in 1478, but had better success in the less testing assignment against the Rossi of Parma in 1483. Meanwhile he settled down to the life of a feudal lord at Borgonovo, a stronghold commanding the outlet of the Val Tidone into the Plain, twelve miles west of Piacenza.

The outlook of Sforza Secondo seems to have differed from that of the older feudal families only in being bolder and more confident. When the brother of his doctor was murdered by a peasant 'without any reason, and solely for jealousy of a woman', he did execution himself, and thereafter informed the Duke's officials of his action. 'His lordship had the assassin arrested in the territory of Bilegno,'[3] the Commissioner and Podestà reported to the Duke, 'and then had him put to death. . . . We have written back to the lord Sforza that it would have been more suitable to send the criminal here to us and allow us to perform a sentence of that kind, and we have encouraged him to be ready in future to leave such punishments to be made by those whose business it is.'[4] The government promptly asked for more information—

[1] A. Giulini, 'Di alcuni figli di Francesco I Sforza', *Arch. St. Lomb.*, xliii (1916), 34-8; L. Cerri, 'I Conti Sforza-Visconti e il Feudo di Borgonovo', *Archivio Storico per le Provincie Parmensi*, nuova serie, xv (1915), 125-30.

[2] *Arch. St. Lomb.*, iii (1876), 453, 505, 507, 511.

[3] Two miles S.E. of Borgonovo.

[4] Cart. Int. 873, 26 April 1480, letter of Guidantonio Arcimboldi and Teodoro Madregnano.

was the criminal caught within the Count's jurisdiction, was he entitled to exercise *merum et mixtum Imperium* there?[1] I do not know what the outcome was, but a tone of notably mild remonstrance seems normally to have been adopted towards Sforza Secondo's transgressions. When Gianfrancesco Arcelli complained that the Count had sent troops into his 'jurisdiction' to seize one of his drovers[2] and carry him off to Borgonovo, committing many acts of insolence on the way, a not unfriendly admonition went off to 'our very dear uncle', urging him to fulfil his duties and keep his men in control. 'Above all else we hold it contrary to justice and honour that you should send to arrest anyone in another's jurisdiction. Our Commissioner of Piacenza is there at hand, our other officials are there, who will not fail to do you right at your request, without doing it on your own account in another's jurisdiction.' The prisoner was to be released. 'If you claim that you are entitled to anything from him, you should apply to our Commissioner of Piacenza, who will administer good right.' But if the Count would not release the man, he was to send to Milan to explain his action.[3]

This last proviso gives away all the rest of the letter. Commissioners and other officials carried no weight at Borgonovo. Two years later, when the Commissioner proposed to serve a summons there, again on a plaint of the Arcelli, the Count sent his chancellor 'to give me to understand that if I interfere in any way against the lord Sforza and his men, ill will come to me. . . . And so, since the lord Sforza is of great condition and uncle of your Excellency, it has seemed best to me to leave the matter and do no more, but to give you a report of the whole business, and make it clear to you that, if the summons cannot be served, the case cannot proceed, and all that has been done will be of no avail.'[4]

[1] Miss. 146, fo. 302 t., 28 April 1480, 'Commissario et Potestati Placentie'.

[2] 'Suo Bergamino', a proprietor or leader of transhumant herds: F. Cherubini, *Vocabolario Milanese-Italiano*, i (1839), 92.

[3] Cart. Int. 874, 2 September 1481, letter of the Duke to Sforza Secondo.

[4] Cart. Int. 875, 31 January 1484, letter of Matteo Corte.

It will be recalled that Sforza's lieutenants contributed to the disorders in Piacenza during the summer of 1483. When the Commissioner arrested one of the ringleaders 'on information received', Sforza Secondo claimed the man as one of his followers, 'and on this pretext wished me to release him, promising that he would behave better in the future',[1] and the Commissioner's letter leaves the impression that he had no option but to accept this unconvincing assurance. An epidemic of plague added to the troubles of the local authorities in the following winter, and Sforza Secondo's men took it on themselves to engage in a series of skirmishes with the men employed by the health department in Piacenza to collect and bury the bodies of the dead at night. Two weeks after reporting the message brought by Sforza's chancellor, the Commissioner again appealed to the Duke, forwarding a letter in which the Count asserted the right of his men to carry arms in the city, and asking for instructions how to deal with them.[2] When the government answered in general terms that its orders were to be enforced and severe punishment meted out to scoundrels who disobeyed,[3] the Commissioner wrote once more. 'Your Excellency knows well enough what it is in my power to do against the lord Sforza's men, in view of the authority that he has.'[4] This time the government wrote to the Count to tell him not to interfere with the pursuit of criminals in his franchise, without commenting on the fact that the criminals were his men.[5]

Barely two months later the Duke appointed Sforza Secondo Governor of Piacenza, in view of his great merits, with the special task of putting an end to the serious disorders in the city which were causing 'no small inconvenience and loss to our state'.[6]

[1] Cart. Int. 874, 15 August 1483, letter of Gianbattista Castiglione.

[2] Cart. Int. 875, 13 February 1484, letter of Matteo Corte.

[3] Miss. 163, fo. 50 t., 24 February 1484, to the Commissioner and the Commissioner of Taxes, in answer to a letter of the latter.

[4] Cart. Int. 875, 27 February 1484, letter of Matteo Corte.

[5] Miss. 163, fo. 57, 5 March 1484, to Sforza Secondo.

[6] Annales Placentini, in *Rerum Italicarum Scriptores*, xx, 975 D. The letter of appointment, 14 May 1484, in Poggiali, op. cit., viii, 81–2.

This ingenious appointment, suggested by the Bishop of Pia-cenza,[1] who had common interests with Sforza against the Arcelli, had no effect; after three weeks in the city, the Count fled from the plague back to Borgonovo,[2] and he was causing trouble to the Commissioner again in the following year.[3] He remained in high favour at court, however, and the marriage of his son Francesco to Franceschina Borromea in 1486 was celebrated with great pomp in Milan. Thereafter, until his death in December 1491, I have found no evidence of his activities. Francesco, his eldest legitimated son, had died early in the same year, and while the government took an interest in the fate of Sforza's other natural children,[4] the fief of Borgonovo passed to Francesco's small son, in the wardship of his mother and of her father Count Giovanni Borromeo.[5] Sforza Secondo's affairs took some time to wind up. His creditors had recourse to the government in 1494 to secure payment of £720,[6] and his tailor—how enduring social habits are—was still pressing for settlement of his account in 1498.[7] His books on alchemy and astrology attracted the attention of Ludovico Sforza, an expert in these matters.[8] Indeed, but for an unusual concatenation of temperament, upbringing and opportunity, this was the sort of life that Ludovico himself might well have led.

The other great military vassal of the Piacentino was Sforza Secondo's brother-in-law, Count Piero dal Verme. Piero was

[1] In a letter of 16 October 1483, published by L. Ambiveri in *Archivio Storico per le Provincie Parmensi*, nuova serie, vi (1906), 238-9.

[2] *Annales Placentini*, loc. cit., 975 E.

[3] Cart. Int. 875, 12 and 16 April 1485, letters of Antonio Crivelli.

[4] Ibid., 29 February and 12 March 1492, letter of Count Borella de Sichis, the Commissioner, and a letter of the Duke to him.

[5] Reg. Duc. 48, fos. 227 t.-8 and 231 t.-2, 1 February and 19 May 1493, relate to the enfeoffment of the boy's guardians.

[6] Miss. 193, fo. 131 and t., 29 October 1494, 'Domine Franceschine Vicecomiti Borromee'.

[7] Miss. 209, fo. 171 and t., 17 November 1498, to the same on behalf of Tommaso de Fontana 'pro sua mercede de manifature de robe facte al quondam signore Sforza', which suggests to me the narrower meaning of 'robe'.

[8] L. Fumi, 'L'Inquisizione Romana', *Arch. St. Lomb.*, 4, xiii (1910), 87.

involved in the same disgrace as Sforza Secondo in 1467, and it is indicative of his strength that one of the terms of his pardon was a limit set to the military forces he was allowed to maintain.[1] He inherited the great estates accumulated by his grandfather, the loyal Captain-General of three generations of the Visconti, and by his father who had fought in the service of Filippo Visconti. These fiefs lay in many parts of the Dominion, but one large block of them, south of the Po, was solid enough to earn the title of *regione Vermasca*,[2] and included in the Piacentino the franchise of Bobbio in the Val di Trebbia, and Castel San Giovanni in the Plain on the old Via Postumia, not far north of Borgonovo.

Even in the greatest franchises, the government normally retained for itself the profits of the salt monopoly, regulating the details by conventions with the lords of fiefs.[3] When the state accounts of 1479 were being prepared for audit, it was found that Piero dal Verme still owed £2,324 12s. on this score, as well as an unspecified sum outstanding from 1478. The government called for prompt and integral settlement, 'so that we do not have to remind you again, and we are certain you will do this, for the obligation and duty you have. Otherwise we shall find ourselves displeased with you. We expect you to reply in acknowledgement of this letter and to report what arrangements you have made.'[4] The Count's answer took the form of an offer of payment in kind by a consignment of woad, which was still grown in the region of Tortona for the Lombard cloth industry.[5] The government rejected this proposal, pointing out, in terms of some vigour which deserve to be recorded in full,[6] that it was not the Duke's business to sell woad, that he needed hard cash and expected to get it without any more frivolous evasions.

[1] Boselli, op. cit., ii, 281-2, n. 34. For his *condotta* in 1475, *Arch. St. Lomb.*, iii (1876), 511.

[2] E. Nasalli Rocca, 'Problemi Storici di Bobbio', *Arch. St. Lomb.*, 8, iv (1953), 255-9.

[3] C. Morbio, *Codice Visconteo-Sforzesco* (Milan, 1846), pp. 411-12, Doc. 199.

[4] Miss. 146, fo. 145 t., 14 February 1480, 'Comiti Petro de Verme'.

[5] G. Barbieri, *Economia e Politica nel Ducato di Milano* (Milan, 1938), pp. 198-200.

[6] Doc. 1 at the end of this paper.

Another incident of a similar kind occurred at about the same time. The government appointed an official to deal with grain frauds at Bobbio, and instructed the Count to provide lodging for him. Verme countered with a request that the office should be bestowed on his Podestà of his city of Bobbio, but the official was already nominated, and the government sent a special courier to command compliance with its orders.[1] The Deputies for grain at Milan were not over-confident, for they wrote again twelve days later to say that the official was on his way, and required the Count to see that the officers and men of his franchise gave credence and obedience 'as they would do to you yourself'.[2]

It was while government departments were chivvying him in this way that Verme decided to draw closer to the personal circle of the Sforza. A fortnight after this last letter his chancellor was in Milan, assuring the Duke of his 'very good will and faithful and most devoted disposition towards us and our State', and making an offer 'that has been most gratifying and most highly acceptable to us'.[3] The Count was summoned to Milan to make final arrangements, and wasted no time, for barely a fortnight later he celebrated his wedding there with Chiara Sforza, a natural daughter of Galeazzo Maria and half-sister of the Duke.[4]

This step did not secure immunity from the attentions of the government, but it may have increased Verme's confidence in dealing with them. The local officials in any case regularly turned to the Duke when action was needed. When a campaign was being prepared against recalcitrant debtors of the *Camera* in the Val di Nure, the Commissioner asked the Duke to write to the Count's officers, instructing them to support the enterprise and not to help or receive the men of the valley.[5] The official in charge

---

[1] Miss. 146, fo. 206 and t., 11 March 1480, 'Comiti Petro de Verme': 'el vostro Potestate nella vostra cità de Bobio'.

[2] Ibid., fo. 230, 23 March 1480, to the same, 'per Deputatos super ordinibus bladorum'.

[3] Ibid., fo. 260 and t., 8 April 1480, to Verme.

[4] Bonazzi, 'Cronica', loc. cit., p. 69.

[5] Cart. Int. 873, 21 December 1480, letter of Gianantonio Cotta.

of the salt monopoly complained, as the government wrote to Verme, that debtors were to be found in the Count's territories, especially on market days, whom 'he cannot arrest in your lands, nor find any support for that purpose'.[1] When it was decided to form a local defence force in Monte di Brianza against the Venetian army, Verme was asked to tell 'your Podestà of Pieve d'Incino' to organize a similar force.[2] When Verme ordered his Podestà to intervene in the affairs of a village in derogation of rights claimed by the Cardinal Archbishop of Milan, who was a loyal supporter of Ludovico Sforza, the most tactful terms were used in urging him to withdraw. 'We do not doubt that you have done it all for a good purpose and with reasonable cause', but he must not run the risk of incurring ecclesiastical censures.[3]

The government did not consider itself debarred from issuing orders directly to the officers of Verme's franchise, but the lord of the franchise was informed at the same time and asked to command his men to execute the Duke's commission.[4] This was perhaps an act of courtesy, but it was also a necessary measure to secure compliance. We have seen how Sforza Secondo spoke to the representatives of the Duke, and franchisal officials were apt to follow the lead of their lords. Verme's town of Castel San Giovanni closed its gates on one occasion to the citizens of Piacenza, for fear of the plague. The ViceCommissioner of Piacenza, acting on instructions from Milan, sent a messenger to secure the withdrawal of this embargo, but he was not allowed to enter the town. The ViceCommissioner sent a formal letter of command addressed to the lieutenant of Verme's Podestà. The lieutenant replied that he did not propose to allow the messenger or anyone

---

[1] Ibid., copy of a letter to Verme (and 'in simili modo domino Antonio Carazo') in the folder for December 1480.

[2] Miss. 159, fo. 97, 2 July 1483. For the district of Brianza in the Milanese Contado, and its relations with Pieve d'Incino, R. Beretta in *Arch. St. Lomb.*, xxxviii (1911), pt. 2, 365–78.

[3] Miss. 159, fo. 82 t., 7 June 1483, to Verme.

[4] Miss. 163, fo. 26 t., 4 February 1484, to Verme: 'Havemo scripto al Potestà vostra de Bobio. . . . Il perchè vogliati scriverli ch'el eseguisca quanto li havemo commisso.'

else from Piacenza to enter the town, 'and that he did not have to obey Ducal letters, but only the letters of Count Piero'. The Vice-Commissioner, whose letters are those of an active and efficient administrator, concluded that only a direct order from the Duke to the Count would gain the day.[1]

When Piero dal Verme died in 1485, Ludovico Sforza excluded his brothers from the succession to his fiefs. One of the chief beneficiaries was the much-favoured Galeazzo San Severino, but the main franchise in the Piacentino, Bobbio and Castel San Giovanni, remained in the hands of the Ducal *Camera*. The decision ran counter to Lombard feudal custom, and the devious but successful method by which it was enforced reflects both the limitations and the reserves of strength in Sforza government.[2] Ludovico's motives have generally been called in question, but it may be that policy as well as greed prompted him to this course. When a second-grade franchisal official categorically declares that he does not have to obey the letters of the prince, we may wonder into what land or what century we have strayed. If this, the major Italian despotic principality of the Renaissance, was in any sense the crucible of the modern state, it burned with a slow fire and much of the old metal remained unconsumed.

B. *The Government and the Feudatories*

The verdicts passed on the government of the Sforza in the fifty years since the publication of Miss Ady's *History of Milan under the Sforza* have not been entirely unanimous. Malaguzzi Valeri, supporting himself largely by reference to the Ducal decrees, drew an affectionate portrait of Ludovico Sforza as a benevolent and impartial despot, determined to subdue the insolence of feudal lords and protect his subjects from their rapacity.[3]

[1] Cart. Int. 874, 7 November 1483, letter of Bartolomeo Vistarino. His acknowledgement of the patent of his appointment as Vice-Commissioner, sent from Milan on 23 October: ibid., 25 October 1483.

[2] For the disinheritance of the Verme, Poggiali, op. cit., viii, 94–5.

[3] F. Malaguzzi Valeri, *La Corte di Lodovico il Moro*, especially i (Milan, 1913), 44–5, 107–63, 365–76.

Professor Barbieri, using the notarial records to supplement the decrees, reached provisional conclusions favourable to the good sense of the economic policy of the Milanese dukes within the limited economic conceptions of their time.[1] The most recent re-appraisal of Milanese history in this period, on the other hand, suggests in general terms that Ludovico Sforza fell because he failed to cope with the problem of an over-powerful feudal class. 'It was, in substance, the crisis of Italian feudal society, which had not known how to or had not been able to open the breach to the new forces of the bourgeoisie, which had asserted or were in pro-cess of asserting themselves in other countries of Europe.'[2]

A few episodes, gleaned from a minute fraction of the Archivio Sforzesco and most of them incomplete, cannot lead to any very firm conclusion on these problems. But the study of the administra-tion of the Sforza, governed by the great mass of still uncalendared material in the Archivio Sforzesco, is perhaps hardly ripe for a fresh reappraisal at this stage. Some forty years ago Felice Fossati introduced an important essay on the nature of the authority exercised by the Dukes of Milan as 'a part of the analytical studies needed to prepare a synthesis'.[3] In spite of the progress made, notably through the work of Professor Caterina Santoro,[4] there is still much to be done in the way of analytical studies, supported by the records of the government, before we can be sure that we understand exactly how it worked and why—on what sort of service it relied, to what sorts of pressure it was susceptible, how it affected the lives of the Duke's subjects and what kind of response it evoked from them. Much of the interest of the anecdotes I have related lies in the evidence of their language, of the terms in which

---

[1] G. Barbieri, *Economia e Politica nel Ducato di Milano* (Milan, 1938).

[2] F. Catalano, in *Storia di Milano*, ed. Fondazione Treccani degli Alfieri, vii (1956), 508. Similarly N. Valeri, ibid., 518-19.

[3] F. Fossati, 'Rapporti fra una "terra" e i suoi signori', *Arch St. Lomb.*, xli (1914), 109-20.

[4] C. Santoro, *Gli Uffici del Dominio Sforzesco*, cit. *Vide* also Professor Santoro's chapter on the formal structure of the government, in the *Treccani degli Alfieri Storia di Milano*, vii, 520-38.

the government and the feudatories of the Duke conducted their relations with one another, but they may also help to define some of the questions on the answers to which a general verdict on the rule of the Sforza must depend.[1]

I am not concerned here with the juridical character of these neo-feudal relations, adapted by the Visconti and the Sforza to their needs, nor with the internal organization of fiefs and the exercise of seigneurial rights by their lords.[2] The cohesion and independence of the greatest franchises may be gauged by the fact that it was possible for them to issue their own statutes, as did the Pallavicini;[3] and even the Landi received an oath of fealty from all the heads of families dwelling within their fiefs.[4] But the rights of feudal lords varied according to the condition of the fief, and obviously all enfeoffments did not have the same political significance.[5] When Gussola and Martignana in the district of Cremona were granted to the military commander Gianpiero Bergamino with the title and dignity of a county, he received them with all the trappings of rights and immunities, headed by *merum et mixtum Imperium*, appropriate to his new comi-tal status.[6] This grant, earned by his military attainments, placed him in the top rank of feudal society, alongside the sort of men whose relations with the Duke I have described. Can the same be said of the numerous enfeoffments made to faithful curial officials? The chancellor Lorenzo Mozzanica received *merum et mixtum*

---

[1] The emergence of an embryonic civil service under the Sforza, discussed by Professor Chabod in *Actes du Colloque sur la Renaissance 1956* (published in 1958), p. 67, is not in itself incompatible with the conditions I have portrayed above; but the subject awaits more detailed investigation.

[2] These problems were discussed by G. Barni, *L'Organizzazione di un Feudo della Val di Parma* (Milan, 1939); and C. Magni, *Il Tramonto del Feudo Lombardo* (Milan, 1937).

[3] E. Nasalli Rocca, 'Gli Statuti dello Stato Pallavicino', *Boll. St. Piac.*, xxi (1926), 145-56, and xxii (1927), 17-26, 67-76.

[4] *Boll. St. Piac.*, xxi (1926), 64.

[5] Barni, 'La formazione interna dello Stato Visconteo', *Arch. St. Lomb.*, nuova serie, vi (1941), 24-6, rightly stressed the distinction.

[6] Reg. Duc. 29, fo. 129, 25 January 1486.

Imperium over four villages granted to him in the district of Lodi.[1]
But this may have been exceptional, and certainly a number of
grants to these men conferred a lesser jurisdiction or merely the
enjoyment of specified revenues. The sale of fiefs had a different
motive again, though it might lead to the same results. When the
Marquis Pallavicino Pallavicino bought the fief of the excise
duties on a number of commodities at Vianino and its territory,
with the *jus cogendi* and the fines arising from it, for $16\frac{2}{3}$ times the
estimated annual value, he was probably reinforcing his territorial
power as well as investing his capital; the Duke was capitalizing
a regular source of income because 'at present he is in need of
money to provide for the occasions of his state'.[2]

It would be an arduous task, but one not without value, to
compile a feudal map of the Dominion which would show, as
far as the records allow, the extent, distribution, character and
date of enfeoffments. An immense chasm separates Giovanni
Albertazzi from Piero dal Verme, as far as their political potentialities are concerned. It has long been accepted that there was a
steady multiplication of enfeoffments in Lombardy during the
fifteenth century, culminating in the time of Ludovico Sforza;[3]
but an analysis on a qualitative as well as a quantitative basis is
needed in order to gain a reliable picture of the application of the
fief to the practical needs and policies of the dukes. If it is true
that Ludovico Sforza was particularly generous in granting fiefs,
it would be useful to know more precisely what kind of men the
beneficiaries were, and what sort of benefits they received.

When all reservations have been made, however, there can be
no doubt that the major vassals of the Sforza, the men with
franchise and following and influence in *contado* or city or both,
composed a formidable element in the society of the state. And
the government, while it demanded that they should respect the
rights of others, professed its intention to respect their rights.
When Giancarlo Anguissola complained that orders given to

[1] Reg. Duc. 48, fo. 6 and t., 22 April 1486.
[2] Reg. Duc. 29, fo. 35-42 t., 27 April 1481.
[3] P. Verri, *Storia di Milano*, ii (Milan, 1798), 121, n. 1.

the Podestà of Piacenza to investigate and punish a crime con-
travened the terms of his feudal investiture, the government called
for a full report, declaring that 'it is not our will that any injury
should be done to anyone in the jurisdictions granted to them'.[1]
But the Sforza certainly did not regard franchise as inviolable,
and they seem to have used their Vicars-General a good deal in
their dealings with franchise-holders because the regional officials,
as we have seen, did not always command enough respect. The
Vicars-General, who presided over the investigation of the conduct of officials at the end of their term of office, carried a special
authority as representatives of the prince, and received many *ad
hoc* commissions in the course of their journeys.[2] When Francesco
Guasconi was travelling round the western part of the Duchy
early in 1480, he was ordered to interrupt his itinerary and go to
Chignolo, the centre of Gianstefano Todeschino's jurisdiction,[3]
in pursuit of criminals who had fled into the franchise. He was to
explain his instructions to the lord of the fief, and then 'proceed
against the outlaws and those guilty of manslaughter, and punish
them according to the nature of their fault, with the participation
of Gianstefano, to whom you will make it clear that this is not
done to the detriment of his jurisdiction, but to cleanse the country
of criminals. And alike there as in the other lands of feudatories,
where they themselves do not provide against breaches of the
peace, you will fulfil your instructions.'[4] On the following day, a
complaint having arrived at Milan of the conduct of 'the Commissioner of Arona and other men of the Counts Giovanni and
Vitaliano Borromei', he was told to speed up his work and, as
soon as he had finished at Chignolo, to go on to the Novarese,
investigate these charges and punish those who had failed in their
duty.[5] His report on his activities at Chignolo brought a warm

---

[1] Cart. Int. 874, 11 December 1481, copy of a Ducal letter to the Podestà of
Piacenza.

[2] Santoro, Uffici, cit., xxix.   [3] Ibid., 345 and n. 2.

[4] Miss. 146, fo. 121 and t., 31 January 1480, 'Francischo de Guasconibus Vicario
Generali'.

[5] Ibid., fo. 123 t., 1 February 1480, to the same.

commendation and, in answer to a query, the order that 'the sentences you impose yourself within the jurisdictions of feudal lords you are to attach to our *Camera*'.[1] When the government had to intervene to enforce the law within the franchises, it naturally expected to take the resultant fines and confiscations, which were normally attached to the jurisdiction of the lord of the fief.[2]

What service did the Sforza expect from their vassals, in return for the undoubted trouble they caused? The records of enfeoff-ments express their obligations by a general reference to feudal law, in such terms as 'to do and perform all those things which feudatories are obliged towards their lords to do and perform according to the condition of their fiefs'.[3] When Ludovico Sforza mobilized his army in July 1499, the feudatories with all their forces were summoned as well as the Communal levies,[4] but it is not clear that those who were not soldiers with a *condotta* had a specific military commitment. They were certainly respon-sible for the maintenance of their own castles in a good state of defence and equipped with military stores. When the government ran short of saltpetre during the War of Ferrara, it appealed to Count Manfredo Lando who was reported to have a good supply.[5] At the time of the Neapolitan attack on Rapallo in September 1494, Federico Lando assured Ludovico Sforza of the pre-cautions he had taken in the always unstable Val di Nure.[6] In the following year, a few days before the battle of Fornovo, Count Giovanni Anguissola wrote from Riva, in answer to a letter of the Duke, to say that he would see to it that 'these places of mine are well guarded'.[7] When his cousins at Vigolzone heard of this, piqued that they had been neglected, they promptly declared that

[1] Ibid., fo. 128, 5 February 1480, to the same.

[2] This procedure follows the lines laid down in the account of secretarial duties published by C. Santoro in *Arch. St. Lomb.*, nuova serie, iv (1939), 43.

[3] From the enfeoffment of Mozzanica, cit. *supra*, p. 205 and n.1.

[4] Boselli, op. cit., iii, 2.

[5] Miss. 159, fo. 78 t., 3 June 1483.

[6] Cart. Int. 876, 9 September 1494, letter of Count Federico Lando.

[7] Ibid., 1 July 1495, from 'Johannes Anguissola Comes et eques'.

they were no less devoted and ready to serve the Duke.[2] In 1499, when the forces of Louis XII of France were already on the move, an appeal was made for guns for the Milanese army. Count Pompeo Lando replied that he had no fortress in the Plain, and that at Compiano he had only his third share of the family's artillery, 'which is very little' and quite unsuitable, 'for it is very light artillery, old and in poor condition . . . and even so it is needed in the castle, in view of its situation'.[2] Written in good faith or no, the letter indicates the obligations of lords of castles, as well as some negligence in fulfilling them.

The bonds of service and devotion created by the fealty of vassals to the Duke in fact enhanced their liability to sudden calls of a miscellaneous kind. They were summoned to attend the Duke on special occasions,[3] and Galeazzo Maria Sforza held a feudal court at Christmas,[4] though I have found no evidence that the practice continued after his death. Their financial relations with the Duke, which cannot be fully treated here, were of a similar character. Although they enjoyed certain exemptions, a contemporary writer noted that the feudatories of the Piacentino were assessed at 10,000 ducats for the subsidy of 1499 to meet the final crisis of Ludovico's reign, compared with the 12,000 ducats imposed on the rest of the *communitas* of Piacenza.[5] On the occasion of Duke Giangaleazzo's marriage, they received particularly barefaced demands for costly gifts to the bride.[6] In addition they might be called on to make loans at short notice, with

---

[1] Ibid., 5 July 1495, 'nobiles domini Anguissola, . . . ex Vigulzono'.

[2] Cart. Int. 877, 24 July 1499.

[3] Bartolomeo Scotto and Manfredo Lando were among the feudatories summoned at short notice to do honour to the visting King of Denmark in 1476: 'Diarii di Cicco Simonetta', ed. A. R. Natale, in *Arch. St. Lomb.*, 8, vi (1956), 75-6.

[4] Originally intended to meet three times a year, according to G. Ghilini, *Annali d'Alessandria* (Milan, 1666), p. 104 b. A reference will be found in *Arch. St. Lomb.*, iii, 460 n. 4. Only the Christmas assemblies are mentioned in 'Diarii di Cicco', cit., ibid., 8, i (1948-9), 80 (1472), to vi (1956), 61 (1475).

[5] Poggiali, op. cit., viii, 142; cf. Boselli, op. cit., iii, 2.

[6] Pezzana, op. cit., v, Doc. 19 (to Gianantonio di San Vitale, 15 November 1488); *Arch. St. Lomb.*, lii (1925), 208 (to Antonio Trivulzio, 17 November).

such sanctions as those imposed on Battista Anguissola who was forbidden to leave Milan until he had paid, and if he failed to pay 'we will use other measures'.[1] 'God is my witness,' Count Matteo Scotto replied in 1494 to a request for a loan of 500 ducats to be paid within two days, 'I have not got it at the moment. But as I have never been obdurate to any wish or pleasure of your Excellency, and am the less willing to be so now in view of the heavy expenses you have to meet, I offer you with good spirit 800 *staia* of corn, by the measure of Piacenza, gratis at your dis⁄ posal. I pray you to deign to accept it in that good spirit in which I offer it to you.'[2] Feudatories were often short of cash, and corn was probably a more acceptable commodity to the government than woad.

Taken by itself, all this may do less than justice to the Sforza, for theirs was not in any strict sense a feudal state, but one in which this kind of feudal society played a prominent and by no means always beneficial part. The first Sforza Duke inherited an already strong fabric of feudal tenure and immunities in Lombardy, and probably enlarged it to provide for the leaders of his army. The peculiar circumstances of Ludovico Sforza's position in the Duchy and of his accession in 1494 cannot have encouraged him to promote any general upheaval in the social structure of the state. It is not likely that he could have envisaged more than a change of emphasis in that society. We know, however, that able rulers elsewhere and at other times had used feudal relations as a transitional means of harnessing and controlling the actual distribution of political force to their own benefit, and it is abundantly clear that the Sforza had constant provocation to reflect on the need to integrate their vassals into a political system adapted to their ideas of government and to the needs of their state.

The feudal rights of the old nobility of Lombardy antedated the authority of the Visconti and the Sforza. It has been suggested

---

[1] Poggiali, op. cit., viii, 101-2.

[2] Cart. Int. 876, 19 October 1494, 'Matheus Scottus Comes' to Ludovico Sforza. A similar demand to the Counts Todescho is mentioned in a letter of the 'Referendarius' Luigi Carugo: ibid., 3 October 1494.

that they felt no obligations towards or respect for the new dynasty, which accordingly created a 'new feudalism' to help in the struggle against the old—a new class of vassals utterly bound to the Duke because they were liable to forfeiture at his will, and for whom 'it was indispensable to hold high the power and prestige of the lord of Milan, because it was beyond doubt that, if he fell, they too would lose all their privileges and possessions'.[1] Traces of a difference in status between the new *feudatari forensi* and the old Communal families have been found in Pia-cenza even in the sixteenth century.[2] But however valid the dis-tinction may be for the political conditions of the fourteenth century, and even though a juridical distinction survived, I doubt whether it will help greatly to explain the attitude of Ludovico Sforza towards his vassals. Ludovico showed how effectively he could deal with individual vassals when he wished, and those who suffered included some of the leading feudatories of the state. But some of the new families were by now as great and as dangerous as the old, and the list of Ludovico's victims does not fit readily into one or other of these categories—the Rossi of Parma, the heirs of Piero dal Verme, Filippo Eustachi and Luigi Terzago, the Caccia and Tornielli of Novara, and the Borromei, 'lords of all the fortresses of Lake Maggiore',[3] whose great franchise built up in the fifteenth century to confront the Swiss of the Valais might well have been broken in the end by Ludovico's patient hostility.[4] On the other hand great clans like the Vis-conti, and the oldest and noblest of them all, the Pallavicini with their marchional title dating from the middle of the tenth century, seem to have continued to enjoy his favour, and the professions of loyalty and devotion that I have quoted, for what they are worth, came from the oldest families of Piacenza.

---

[1] Barni, art. cit. in *Arch. St. Lomb.*, nuova serie, vi (1941), 39–40.

[2] E. Nasalli Rocca in *Boll. St. Piac.*, xxiv (1929), 106–7.

[3] B. Corio, *Storio di Milano*, ed. E. de Magri, iii (Milan, 1857), 80.

[4] A. Giulini in *Arch. St. Lomb.*, 4, xiii (1910), 262, n. 3, 263, n. 6, 264, n. 1; ibid., xlii (1915), 243–4. Cf. C. Magenta, *Visconti e Sforza nel Castello di Pavia*, i (Milan, 1883), 558.

What determined the distribution of Ludovico Sforza's favours and enmity among his vassals? Indiscriminate greed? Personal differences? A choice between that alignment of family and social interests for which contemporaries still used the terms Guelf and Ghibelline, confidently expecting their readers to know what they meant? The slow execution of a broadly conceived policy designed to secure a better adjustment of authority within the state? The phasing of Ludovico's dealings with the feudatories might repay closer attention than it has yet received.

In 1483 Ludovico Sforza decided to buy back the rights in the village of San Damiano which his brother had sold in fief with a power of redemption, in other words as pledge for a loan. Ludovico pressed the matter in spite of opposition from the feoffees, a branch of the Anguissola family, who showed great reluctance to attend at Milan and collect their redemption money.[1] Ludovico's decision may well have been prompted by purely contingent reasons, but it would be interesting to know whether any other examples can be found of the recovery of alienated rights by these means.

There still remains the problem of a genuine alternative to the policy of the Sforza. The verdict I have quoted on their failure to open the way for the bourgeoisie of their dominions makes a striking commentary on the changing conditions of European economy. The merchants of Lombardy had made their own way, in the great days of Italian economic expansion, without calling on princes to do the work for them. But the answer to this prob' lem is not likely to be found in the provincial cities. The letters of the City Council of Piacenza harp on the poverty of city and district, and reports, admittedly no less partial, from other cities gives a similar picture of the once flourishing centres of Lombardy now vegetating in decay.[2] Rightly or wrongly, the Visconti and

---

[1] Miss. 159, fos. 95 and t., 111, 143, 28 June, 2 July, 25 August 1483; Cart. Int. 874, 28 July 1483, letter of Gianbattista Castiglione. For San Damiano, G. C. Medici in *Arch. St. Lomb.*, lvii (1930), 298, n. 2.

[2] G. Rovelli, *Storia di Como*, parte III, tomo i (Como, 1802), 348-9 (1481); Pezzana, op. cit., v, 353, n. 3 (1497). The rising economic prosperity of Lombardy

the Sforza had largely identified the economic interests of their dominions with the commercial and industrial prosperity of Milan. Botero could still write, a century later, in support of those mercantilist principles of which anticipations have been found in the economic policy of the Sforza,[1] that 'the duties from the merchandise of Milan are worth more to the Catholic King than the mines of Zacatecas or Jalisco'.[2] Until the movements and potentialities of Italian economy in the fifteenth century are more fully elucidated, we are not likely to be able to judge fairly what more the Sforza could have done for the commercial and indus-trial interests of their cities, but it seems clear that Milan enjoyed special favour in this as in other respects. Ludovico Sforza could certainly give vigorous expression to the principle that trade and industry played a vital part in the well-being of the state.[3] On the other hand, the merchant guild of Piacenza complained in 1485 that the quarrels of feudal lords in the *contado* threatened to produce conditions more disastrous for trade than those which had prevailed in the previous year during the War of Ferrara.[4] But this was a bad time in the Piacentino, and again there is a possibility of phases and fluctuations in the power of the Sforza to impose a determined policy. The margin of force at the disposal of the government to keep a generally unruly population in order seems at times to have been a dangerously narrow one, but that is a subject which lies outside the scope of this essay.[5]

in this period, and the redistribution of wealth which accompanied it, have received fresh emphasis since these pages were written; see now Professor Cipolla's chapter in volume viii of the Treccani degli Alfieri *Storia di Milano*. Did they apply to the whole Dominion? And what part, if any, did the Sforza themselves play in these processes? They are themes which are notably absent from the correspondence of the government and its agents in Piacenza in the time of Ludovico Sforza.

[1] Barbieri, op. cit., p. 236.

[2] G. Botero, *Della Ragion di Stato*, ed. L. Firpo (Turin, 1948), p. 249. English translation by P. J. and D. P. Waley (London, 1956), p. 152.

[3] E.g. the letter quoted by F. Fossati, in *Arch. St. Lomb.*, xli (1914), 151.

[4] Cart. Int. 875, 16 April 1485, petition subscribed by twelve merchants of Piacenza.

[5] I hope to be able to publish some of the evidence elsewhere.

In any case policy was not and could hardly be determined only by reference to the internal economy of the state. The Sforza inherited on the one hand political preoccupations which required priority to be given to a dangerous and expensive foreign policy and the military needs it created, and on the other a structure of society at least partly adapted to meet those needs. In the complex interaction of domestic and external affairs on one another, it is not obvious that the Sforza would have increased their chance of survival if they had rejected these priorities. And they might at least claim some credit, in the stage of military organization which prevailed in Italy in the fifteenth century, for the attempt to use feudal relations as a means of maintaining a substantial nucleus of their army within the Dominion. But Ludovico Sforza, who lacked military talent and would not tolerate rivals in the state, seems to have fallen between two stools in this respect; both Roberto San Severino and Gianjacopo Trivulzio, the only two soldiers of real distinction who served in his armies, eventually fled from his dominions and fought for his enemies.

The extent to which the feudal character of Lombard society contributed to the military bankruptcy of the Sforza, however, needs to be considered with circumspection. I have little doubt that constant and heavy demands for money did more than anything else to increase Ludovico Sforza's unpopularity during the last lustre of his rule. An experienced observer commented on the fact before the end of 1494.[1] Ludovico himself admitted at the beginning of 1497 that 'his subjects have little love for him',[2] but he was probably not thinking of his feudal vassals in general. Those of the Piacentino had certainly given him little cause for anxiety during the passage of a hostile French army through his dominions in the summer of 1495. Their assurances may be compared with a notice he received at the same time of unrest and incipient rebellion in the *contado*. I publish this very brief letter in

---

[1] The Ferrarese ambassador at Milan, quoted by A. Segre in *Arch. St. Lomb.*, xxix (1902), pt. 2, 284 (I suggest 'subditi' for 'soldati').

[2] M. Sanuto, *Diarii*, i (Venice, 1879), 493.

full[1] because it illustrates the astonishing legend, which apparently survived the experience of Naples a few months earlier, that the subjects of the King of France were free, and that their freedom consisted in not paying taxes unless they wanted to. If the armies of Louis XII in 1499 had needed a secret weapon, they could hardly have devised a more insidious one. The legend in fact reappeared within the city of Piacenza at the end of 1499. At the time of Ludovico Sforza's flight from Lombardy, the city government had rescinded the excise duties in the name of its new lord, the French king. When Gianjacopo Trivulzio in the same king's name called for payment of the duties, the General Council of the city replied that they would not pay, 'because they are under the royal Majesty of France, by reason of which they ought all to be free'.[2]

The vassals of the Sforza had felt the weight of their demands, especially in the last years of Ludovico's rule. They had less excuse than the *contadini* for believing the legend, but they may have had some hope of making use of it. Some of them (but how many?) proved lukewarm in the defence of their Duke in 1499 and 1500. Very few of them felt that their allegiance need outlast the presence of the ruler in his dominions. It was an attitude common enough among all classes in Italian society at the time. When the City Council of Piacenza, in March 1500, envisaged the surrender of the city 'to whomsoever victory in battle shall have destined it',[3] they voiced a widespread sentiment of political fatalism, in words almost identical with those in which Luigi da Porto was to report the decision of Vicenza in similar circumstances a decade later.[4]

The Lombard nobility, like the Lombard population as a whole, made no ado about accepting the sovereignty of the King

---

[1] Doc. 2 at the end of this paper.

[2] Boselli, op. cit., iii, 8, from the register of Provisions of the Commune, 16 December 1499.

[3] Ibid., iii, 13, 7 March 1500, from the same source.

[4] L. da Porto, *Lettere Storiche*, ed. B. Bressan (Florence, 1857), p. 145: 'essa obbedirebbe a quello che vincesse'.

of France in recognition of the verdict of battle, because they hoped to relieve the burdens upon themselves and because no deep-seated loyalty to the fallen dynasty stood in their way. The Sforza had not known how to create a widespread loyalty of that kind. The political momentum of five centuries of Italian history was surely against them in their efforts to do so. The evidence of these pages lends comfort to the opinion that they ruled over an ill-balanced state, in which a feudal society held too great a place, and had too disruptive an effect. The attitude of the dukes to their vassals, in its mixture of indulgence and pressure, is certainly open to criticism; and it did not save the dynasty in the end. Could a more profound political insight on the part of the rulers have achieved a more effective organization of the social structure of the state, resilient enough to save them from disaster? I think it is worth reflecting on the magnitude of the task, and questioning the records as exhaustively as they allow about the means at the disposal of the Sforza, and the manner in which they used them.

Document I (*vide* page 199 and note 4)

Missive, Reg. 146, fo. 164 t.

COMITI PETRO DE VERME

Non aspectavamo da voy in questi nostri bisogni n'havesti scripto che per satisfare alla Camera nostra per el vostro sale sì de l'anno proxime passato quanto del 1478 daresti tanti gualdi. Perchè sapete asay che non è nostro officio de vendere gualdi, ma ad voy, che incombe el caricho, non seria inconveniente ad con-vertirli in denari. Como se sia, nostra intentione è de volere dinari contanti et non gualdi. Et non specta anchora noy ad intendere che quelli dal piano nè da montagna habiano pagato, per essere vostro caricho. Sed sollum voy seti obligato. Per il che ve carichamo che postposte queste frivole oppositione non dagasti demora ad saldare integramente da qui indreto. Mediolani xxiiij Februarii 1480.

Document 2 (*vide* page 214)

Carteggio Interno 876, 13 June 1495

Illustrissimo Signore mio. Doppo che heri scripsi a la Excellentia vostra, havendo el Commissario de le tasse mandato fori in
alcuni loci ad scodere dinari de tasse, gli è stato resposto che non
è più tempo de pagare tasse nè angarie, et che el venerà el Re de
Franza che li farà exempti. M'è parso notificarlo a la Excellentia
vostra, a la quale me recomando. Placentie 13 Junii 1495.

E. Ill. v. servitor Ambrosinus de Maiyno.

(Tergo) Illustrissimo principi et excellentissimo domino domino
Ludovico Marie Sfortie domino Duci Mediolani, domino
meo singularissimo.

Per postas.   Cito   Cito
                    Cito.

P. J. Jones

THE END OF MALATESTA RULE
IN RIMINI

I

When Pope Alexander VI in 1498 prepared to dispossess the despots ruling as nominal vicars of the papacy in Romagna and and March of Ancona, and plant his son Cesare Borgia in their place, there was nothing new in either purpose.[1] What was new was his total success. For centuries popes and their legates had fought to establish some fragile authority over feudatories, communes, and finally despots, and papal sovereignty everywhere was based upon local compact or checked by local franchise. Since the Schism certainly several popes had recovered territory from despotic rule, but often only to give it again to members of their family or to squander the spoils of reconquest among interested friends and allies.[2] For this reason the papacy in 1498 was not inherently much stronger nor were the despotisms inherently much weaker than in the past, but this traditional balance of strength had dramatically ceased, like every other familiar relationship in Italian politics, with the new era of foreign conquest. Although the Borgia pursued their policy with unusual resolution and lack of scruple and drew unprecedented sums from the Camera Apostolica, the first and decisive reason for their success

[1] Cf. P. J. Jones, 'The vicariate of the Malatesta of Rimini', *English Historical Review*, lxvii (1952), to which this study of Malatesta government is a sequel.

[2] This was very clear in 1463, after Pius II's long and vindictive war against the Malatesta, when the pope's miscellaneous allies and hangers-on had all to be rewarded with territory. The main beneficiaries were his nephew, Antonio Piccolomini, and his general, Federigo d'Urbino; but scraps of land and privilege were thrown to most others as well, including a second nephew, Giacopo.

was their military alliance with the King of France. It was with foreign troops that Cesare Borgia in three brief campaigns between October 1499 and 1502 won his papal principality, indiscriminately displacing the old despotic families and the new, Riarii, Sforza and Malatesta, Manfredi, Montefeltro, Della Rovere and Varani. Only good luck and a hasty convention guaranteed by France, Florence and Ferrara saved Giovanni Bentivoglio in Bologna.[1]

One town alone, Faenza under Astorre Manfredi, offered serious resistance.[2]

> *Tuto el mondo è spaventato*
> *Come senten cridar franza.*[3]

Urbino was ready to fight, but the duke, Guidobaldo, decided to withdraw in the hope of better times, sparing his subjects useless bloodshed.[4] Elsewhere there was little spirit for war. At Imola and Forlì Caterina Sforza prepared her castles for a long defence; but the towns of Imola and Forlì surrendered without a blow. When asked to declare their feelings the Forlivesi quoted the case of Alfonso of Aragon and Ludovico il Moro who had both renounced resistance for the sake of their peoples; a new pope, they said, would certainly restore Caterina and her sons to power. Among themselves they spoke more plainly. Luffo Numai, representing one of the noblest and oldest families of Forlì, openly condemned the 'tyrannous' government of Ordelaffi and Riarii,

[1] In 1506 he in turn fell before an alliance of French and papal arms.

[2] The siege of Faenza (November 1500–April 1501) was observed with astonished applause by contemporaries. Even so the Val di Lamone, always hostile to the city, surrendered at once to Cesare Borgia. G. C. Tonduzzi, *Historie di Faenza* (1675), pp. 554–60. A. Messeri, A. Calzi, *Faenza nella storia e nell' arte* (1909), pp. 216–17. G. Donati, *La fine della signoria dei Manfredi in Faenza* (Turin, 1938), pp. 154 seq.

[3] 'Lamento di Caterina Sforza Riario', in P. D. Pasolini, *Caterina Sforza*, iii (Rome, 1893), 811.

[4] Later in 1502 the Urbinati rose against the Borgia, but again Guidobaldo, back in Urbino, advised submission and withdrew: F. Madiai, 'Diari delle cose di Urbino', *Archivio Storico per le Marche e l'Umbria*, iii (1886), 432, 435. F. Ugolini, *Storia dei conti e duchi d'Urbino*, ii (Florence, 1859), 90, 97.

praising the greater freedom of papal rule, and persuaded the citizens to let Caterina fight her own wars with her mercenary troops. In these towns political disaffection compromised resis-tance.[1] At Pesaro, Rimini and Camerino, where hostility to the reigning lords were also present, the conclusion was the same: the citizen nobility opposed resistance, denounced the evils of despotic rule, and opened negotiations with the enemy.[2] Aided by the *parte contrarie in le citade* Cesare Borgia conquered his state *cum picola faticha et fastidio*.[3]

When threatened in the past the despots of Romagna had always been able to claim support from powerful neighbouring states, Florence, Milan or Venice. Since the Visconti wars of the fourteenth century they had come increasingly to accept their client status as *accomandati* and mercenary captains of these greater powers, whose interest it was to keep the papacy weak and whose habit it became to consider Romagna a proper field of competing influence and territorial encroachment. All the despots held military *condotte*, short-term contracts of hire which needed con-stant and careful renewal. Some *condotte* made allowance for the despot's own territorial interests;[4] but in the later fifteenth century financial weakness combined with political calculation to make *condotte* a necessity for some of these *signori*, and by 1498 the anxious correspondence with their richer neighbours shows how dependent

[1] Pasolini, loc. cit., ii, 135–62. Cf. A[rchivio di] S[tato,] F[irenze], Signori, Lega-zioni, 24, fo. 96v.

[2] B. Feliciangeli, *Sull' acquisto di Pesaro fatto da Cesare Borgia* (Camerino, 1900), pp. 41–5. C. Lilii, *Dell' historia di Camerino*, ii (Camerino s.d.), 252–9. For Rimini *vide infra*.

[3] Priuli, in L. A. Muratori, *Rerum italicarum scriptores*, new ed., xxiv, pt. 3, ii, 70. Cesare Borgia's professed purpose was not 'tirannegiare, ma . . . spegnere i tiranni': E. Alvisi, *Cesare Borgia duca di Romagna* (Imola, 1878), p. 293. To confirm this impression tax and other concessions were made to most towns on surrender.

[4] Canestrini in *Archivio storico italiano*, vx, pp. lxxx seq. Cf. Sigismondo Malatesta's *condotta* with Alfonso of Naples in 1447 (L. Osio, *Documenti diplomatici tratti dagli archivi milanesi* (Milan, 1864–77), iii, no. ccccxxiii); yet it was partly because he put his territorial interests first that Sigismondo repudiated this *condotta* and so committed the first in a series of impolitic actions which resulted twenty years later in the near destruction of his principality.

they were becoming on what Caterina Sforza called a *sub-sidio*.[1] Caterina's son Ottaviano held a Florentine *condotta*,[2] Pandolfo Malatesta and the Duke of Urbino were in Venetian service,[3] and so was Astorre Manfredi, after an earlier period of hire by Florence, which threatened to become a military protectorate, and then by Milan. Due to reckless tax concessions in 1488 Astorre needed a *condotta* to avoid bankruptcy.[4] Giovanni Bentivoglio, though rich, was in the pay of Ludovico Sforza, with whose family he was long and intimately bound,[5] and it was in hope of hire and protection by Ludovico that Giovanni Sforza of Pesaro renounced a Venetian *condotta* at this time.[6] Pensioner princes like these had no independent policies; at Rimini and Faenza they could scarcely claim to rule over independent states.[7] Bound by *condotte* they stood or fell with the powers that paid them, less secure even than families of the feudal class from which most of them were descended.

[1] Pasolini, loc. cit., iii, doc. 525; cf. doc. 410. Idem, 'Nuovi documenti su Caterina Sforza', *Atti e Memorie della R. Deputazione di Storia Patria per la provincia di Romagna* (1897), p. 167.

[2] Pasolini, loc. cit., ii, 23 seq. L. G. Pélissier, *Louis XII et Ludovic Sforza* (Paris, 1896), i, 216 seq.

[3] M. Sanuto, *Diarii*, ed. F. Stefani (Venice, 1879 seq.), ii, 992, 1140, 1185; and *infra*.

[4] Pasolini, loc. cit., iii, doc. 797. Donati, loc. cit., *passim*. A. Missiroli, *Astorgio III Manfredi, signore di Faenza (1488–1501). Parte prima* (Bologna, 1912), *passim*. Ottaviano Manfredi, pretender to Faenza against Astorre, was now favoured, now restrained (even to the point of imprisonment) by the neighbouring and competing powers, according as their influence in Faenza rose and fell: A. Virgili, 'L'assassinio di Ott. Manfredi (13 aprile 1499)', *Arch. Stor. Ital.*, 5th series, xxvii (1901). Missiroli, loc. cit. Idem, 'Faenza e il pretendente Ott. Manfredi nel 1488', *La Romagna*, v (1908).

[5] G. Gozzadini, *Memorie per la vita di Giovanni II Bentivoglio* (Bologna, 1839). C. M. Ady, *The Bentivoglio of Bologna* (Oxford, 1937). R. Patrizi Sacchetti, 'La caduta dei Bentivoglio e il ritorno di Bologna al dominio della Chiesa', *Atti e Memorie Romagna* cit., new series, ii (1950–1).

[6] Feliciangeli, loc. cit., pp. 13, 16, etc.

[7] Sigismondo dei Conti remarked that Rimini, Pesaro and Faenza were governed more by Venice, Florence and Milan than by the papacy: *Le storie dei suoi tempi dal 1475 al 1510*, ii (Florence, 1883), 227–8.

The foreign invasions also broke up these relations of patronage and dependence. The greater states either lost their diplomatic freedom, like Florence, or succumbed like Naples and Milan to the conqueror. Only Venice remained independent enough to intercede unsuccessfully on behalf of Malatesta and Manfredi.[1] The Florentines, preoccupied with the Pisan war and fearful for their own domains, abandoned Caterina Sforza (not without some hope of securing Forlì themselves), and assured the Borgia they never dreamed *ne sotto acqua ne sopra acqua* of disturbing the enterprise in Romagna. Giovanni Sforza obtained neither help nor *condotta* from Milan and after the fall of Ludovico was left defenceless like the Bentivoglio before the Borgia. All the states sought the friendship of the French king, who was Cesare Borgia's principal support, and deserted their clients. Still in 1502 the Duke of Urbino lost his dominion after appealing without reply to all the *potentati* of Italy.[2]

On all sides therefore the established position of the smaller despots was suddenly undermined. Their papal overlord was at last not only minded but able to dispossess them, their patrons and protectors were disarmed, and the discontents at home, which few despots were ever able to satisfy, dangerously liberated. At Rimini, where the Malatesta family had been governing for more than two hundred years, the conjunction of all these weaknesses is particularly clear.

II

The Malatesta despotism in both its rise and its development was typical of Italian despotism generally. The first Malatesta appear as 'feudal' lords established in the Apennine hinterland and *contado* of Rimini, who about 1200 were forced into formal

---

[1] A. Bonardi, 'Venezia e Cesare Borgia', *Atti della R. Deputazione Veneta di Storia Patria* (1909–10), and *infra*. For a compromise design of Ludovico Sforza to save the vicars in Romagna (February 1499) *vide* Pélissier in *Archivio della Società Romana di Storia Patria*, xviii (1895), 112–13, 117–18.

[2] *ASF., Signori, Legazioni*, 24, fos. 90v, 92v–3r, 96r; 26, fos. 9r seq., 43v, 44r, 45r. Pasolini, loc. cit., ii, 90 seq., 108–9, 132 seq. Pélissier, *Louis XII*, i, 64–5 and *passim*. Feliciangeli, loc. cit., pp. 20 seq. Madiai, loc. cit., pp. 435.

submission to the commune. Since they kept their seigneurial rights and property—property to which they steadily added, especially by marriage and emphyteutic grants from churches— they simply carried their power and influence with them into the town, where by 1250 they had captured the leadership of one great urban faction, the Guelf, and by 1295 of Rimini itself. In that year by force and duplicity they finally overcame their Ghibelline opponents, the Parcitadi, an urban family as rich and noble as themselves, who with their followers were killed or exiled, banned by the Church and deprived of their lands, and never regained political importance.

The chronicler of Rimini says that Malatesta da Verucchio, head of the family, was now created *signore dela città*,[1] and this he was in substance but not yet in title. For some time the Mala- testa were content to be *maggiori e come capi della terra, ma non signori a bachetta*[2] and the despotism remained undefined and anonymous until 1334, when Malatesta 'Guastafamiglia' and his brother Galeotto were granted *plenitudo potestatis* in a series of acts by the general council of Rimini. They and their heirs were then perpetually absolved from obedience to all statutes and em- powered to proceed against anyone *ad sui comodum pro libito volun- tatis*; treachery to the Malatesta was declared treason. For counsel in government they could gather what friends they liked in a *consilium credentie* and its decisions would be law. Finally election of the *podestà* was surrendered to Malatesta, chosen *defen- sor* of Rimini for life with 'free and perpetual lordship', *Baylia* and *arbitrium* extending over all revenue and jurisdiction. When it came abdication by the commune was formally complete.[3]

---

[1] *Cronache malatestiane dei secoli xiv e xv*, Muratori, loc. cit., new ed., xv, pt. 2, 7. Cf. *Marcha di Marco Battagli da Rimini*, ibid., xvi, pt. 3, 30: 'tunc inceperunt dominationem liberam possidere'.

[2] *Cronaca malatestiana di ser Baldo Branchi*, Muratori, loc. cit., new ed., xv, pt. 2, 159.

[3] *Statuto di Rimini*, Roma, Biblioteca del Senato, fos. 198, 215v–18r, 224v–5r, 253r. F. G. Battaglini, *Memorie istoriche di Rimino*, etc. (Bologna, 1789), pp. 183–6. L. Tonini, *Storia civile e sacra riminese* (Rimini, 1848 seq.), iv, pt. 2, 134–5, 137–8. G. Salvioli, *Gli statuti inediti di Rimini* (Ancona, 1880), p. 26. Up to 1334 the chroniclers describe each successive Malatesta indiscriminately as head of the Parte

During the same first half of the fourteenth century and by similar stages the Malatesta obtained power in nearby Pesaro, Fano and Fossombrone, which from 1355, together with Rimini and still other towns and villages, they governed both as lords and as papal vicars *in temporalibus*. Rimini was the first and last city ruled by the Malatesta, but for more than a century formed only part of the Malatesta state.

This state, like every *signoria*, was a union of communes and their territories, each subjected to one family but surviving with its councils and officials in dependent partnership with the lord.[1] It was not merely that the word 'commune' itself continued in official use—that officials were still officials of the 'commune', rights ascribed to 'lord and commune', or exiles declared enemies of 'lord and commune'; the structure of communal government was never radically changed. At Rimini both councils, great and small, were retained and even the office of the *Quattro Ufficiali*, inherited from the most 'popular' phase of government in the thirteenth century. At Pesaro the corresponding office of the four *capitani del popolo* was eventually suppressed, but the councils went on, just like the *Anziani* and council of Cesena and the councils of Fano and Fossombrone. Even rural communes—places like Montalboddo and Santarcangelo, Pergola, Savignano and many more—kept their various assemblies and some jealousy for their ancient rights.[2]

Guelfa and lord of the city, which expresses their position clearly enough; but a phrase in the statutes of Rimini refers back to Malatestino, Pandolfo and Ferrantino Malatesta (who dominated between 1312 and 1331) as 'olim potestates *et deffensores* civitatis arimini', though no contemporary act confirms this title, and in 1327 Ferrantino is called in a letter of Charles of Calabria 'capitaneus civitatis Arimini': *MGH. Leges*, sect. iv, vol. vi, 176–7. The reality of their power was undisguised, but its only formal expression was the office of *podestà*, frequently though not consistently held by the Malatesta from 1301: P. J. Jones, *The Malatesta of Rimini* (D. Phil. thesis, 1949, Bodleian Library, Oxford), pp. 155–8.

[1] For what follows, *vide* Jones, *Malatesta*, pp. 727, 741–53.

[2] In 1424 the commune of Savignano complained to Carlo Malatesta that it was not allowed by Gaspare di Galeotto Malatesta to exercise its proper jurisdiction in S. Mauro: A. Battaglini, *Saggio di rime volgari di Gio. Bruni de' Parcitadi* (Rimini, 1783), p. 40.

The meetings of the greater council (*consiglio generale*), if irregular, were never merely formal, nor were its powers, though they varied from commune to commune, simply negligible. It still chose some officials, in most cases subordinate officials of the kind with whom citizens had day-to-day dealings, but at Pesaro this privilege was unusually wide, including the right to nominate the *ufficiali di danno dato* and the captains of the *contado*. Occasion-ally communes were allowed to choose the principal officials as well. Elective offices are attested everywhere and however slight they may seem in status and pay, were clearly valued by the sub-ject: Fano in 1405 and Rimini in 1461 both petitioned the Mala-testa to 'remit' certain offices which by custom *se solevano cavare pro brevi*. The general council also kept a modest part in public finance and legislation. Statutes were normally draughted or collected by commissions of the council; decrees were not only addressed to the council or read, published and approved in the council, but also proposed and prepared by the council;[1] taxes were imposed as well as voted by the council. In short the General Council was intermittently involved in most government business —dispatching envoys, granting troops and organizing defence, presenting and hearing petitions, raising loans, farming taxes, and even at Fano electing new councillors.[2]

The sum of these activities may not have been much, but this was partly because the routine work of the general councils had passed in every urban commune to a smaller body—at Rimini comprising only twelve members, at Fano thirty-three or twenty-four,[3] but conceived all the same as fully representing the city.

---

[1] There is also evidence that in Rimini, Pesaro and Fano the communal seals and stamps continued in regular use, though the Malatesta also issued decrees under their own seals, while in Fano during the fourteenth century, Galeotto's initial found its way on to the public seals: Jones, *Malatesta*, pp. 747, n. 3, 769, n. 1.

[2] In Sansepolcro (1390) the commune was allowed to determine the member-ship of the public council—fifteen lists of twenty each: L. Coleschi, *Storia della città di Sansepolcro* (Città di Castello, 1886), p. 62. A. Battaglini, *Saggio* cit., p. 54, n. 31, etc.

[3] In Fano the number seems to have been fixed after a petition to Pandolfo Malatesta in 1405 asking him to determine 'certo numero de Consigleri Citadinj

This smaller council was the point of articulation between com‚ mune and *signoria*: it stood for the commune beside the officials sent by the lord and took a regular part in government, at Fano meeting almost monthly. Like the General Council but with greater freedom, it chose officials,[1] issued decrees and *reforma‚ tiones*, and shared in taxation.[2] At times it had every appearance of independence, writing to other cities, petitioning the pope, and governing in the absence of the lord.

The survival of the councils already shows that the Malatesta like most Italian despots long remained satisfied with the exercise of power, disinclined to institutional change. The creative era of government lay behind in the period of communal independence, and what the commune had created was now used, as local opportunity suggested, but not replaced by the despot.

This indifference to forms marked especially the financial relations of lord and commune. In Rimini the Malatesta had been given control of all revenue,[3] but in the early days of their rule special payments may have been made by the commune to main‚ tain their court.[4] At Pesaro certainly, despite the authority con‚ ferred by the papal vicariate, they continued to the end salaried

I quali sopra ifacti del comuno e bisognj che tucto eldi occurreno haybano a prove‚ dere con lioffitialj Vostrj': A[rchivio comunale di] F[ano], Cancelleria, Consigli, i, fo. 34r.

[1] In the neighbouring state of Urbino also most offices were still elective: G. Luzzatto, 'Comune e principato in Urbino nei sec. xv e xvi', *Le Marche*, v.

[2] At Fano it raised taxes to pay the doctors and masters of grammar it had appointed, and for other purposes, taxes collected by specially elected *depositarii*. In 1442 Sigismondo Malatesta assigned Fano the duty on exported oil: *AF. Cod. Mal.*, 3, fo. 23. *Statuta Civitatis Fani* (1568), *Tractatus Gabellarum*. Rimini also had its limited *intrada* and *spexa*, and after the fall of the Malatesta sought some increase of its share of taxation from the Venetian and then the papal government: Sanuto, *Diarii*, v, 496, 559, 644. Tonini, loc. cit., vi, pt. 2, 805–6, 842. In smaller places, like Santarcangelo, there were still some revenues 'che expecta al comuno': G. Castellani, *I Malatesta a Santarcangelo* (Venice, 1906), pp. 33–4.

[3] *Supra*, p. 222. This was probably true at Cervia also: *Statuta Civitatis Cerviae* (Ravenna, 1558), pp. 23–5.

[4] Tonini, loc. cit., iv, pt. 1, 100 seq.

lords of the city with a monthly *provisio*.[1] *Provedigioni* were paid also in the early fifteenth century by S. Sepolcro, Pergola, Mondavio and other small places, and down to 1389 by Fano as well.[2] Many communes continued to pay the *podestà* and other chief officials. At Pesaro all salaries were paid by the commune and only at Rimini, Fano and possibly Cesena were most paid by the lord.[3] Yet whatever the conventions in use final control of all revenue belonged to the Malatesta. If they had a 'provision', no custom forbade their use of other revenue.[4] If councils of the commune took decisions touching finance, it was only by leave of the Malatesta. Where before the General Council had imposed all taxes, most were now imposed by the lord. While special *colte* were raised to satisfy an active and importunate government, the older revenues, *dazii* and *estimi*, were closely regulated from above.[5] Tax immunities, already common before Malatesta rule, were now the lord's concern; in course of time they spread far beyond the members of the despot's family and became the

---

[1] The system remained under the Sforza, who replaced the Malatesta in 1445, but Cesare Borgia took charge of all revenue, as did Gio. Sforza on his return in 1503: L. Tonini, *Le imposte pagate in Rimini nel sec. xiv* (Bologna, 1872, printed from *Atti Memorie, Romagna*), pp. 37–9. A. degli Abati-Olivieri-Giordani, *Memorie del porto di Pesaro* (1774), pp. 17–19. Idem, *Della zecca di Pesaro* (in G. A. Zanetti, *Nuova raccolta delle monete d'Italia*, i, 1775), pp. 217–18. Alvisi, loc. cit., p. 248. Feliciangeli, 'Delle relazioni' cit.; p. 405, n. 3. G. Vaccai, *La vita municipale sotto i Malatesta, gli Sforza, e i della Rovere, signori di Pesaro* (Pesaro, 1928), pp. 119, 176, n. 1.

[2] Jones, *Malatesta*, pp. 755–6. The monthly payment in Fano is last recorded in 1389 (*AF. Depositeria, Entrata ed uscita*, 69); the Malatesta may then have taken formal control of all revenue such as they already had in Rimini, but occasional 'provisions' to individual Malatesta do occur later (ibid., *Cod. Mal.*, 76, 79, fos.51r, 52v, 53v, etc., 95), as well as payments to the Malatesta court (ibid., 74, 76, 87, fo. 91r). Cf. a letter of Pandolfo Malatesta, April 1415: 'Io ho sentido che de presente se domanda oltra la rata usata per quelli magnifici mei fradelli a fano ducati mille e perche io ho magior bisogno che io havesse mai Vecomando che guardiate che delemei intrate voi non ne tochate niente', etc. (ibid., 5, fo. 40v).

[3] Jones, *Malatesta*, p. 758, n. 2.

[4] Not even at Pesaro: ibid., p. 759, n. 1.

[5] Ibid., pp. 738, n. 2, 759, n. 4, 760, n. 1.

subject of petition and complaint.[1] The lord decided how much income should be spent, and the communal accounts, though basically unchanged, listed endless payments *di chomandamento del signore*, to the lord's *depositario*, or to the factor who managed his estates.[2]

All officials of importance in government as well as revenue were appointed by the Malatesta: *podestà*, vicars, castellans, chancellors, *officiales custodie* and *dampnorum datorum*, *referendarii*, *depositarii* and so on. At Rimini the list was especially long.[3] Of all these offices the *podesteria* was by tradition pre-eminent: at Pesaro and Fossombrone, where they had not been elected *domini* or *defensores*, it was for many years held by the Malatesta themselves, until well established as papal vicars.[4] The *podestà* therefore was normally nominated or recommended by the lord, though not without regard for local feeling, and if efficient or in favour might remain for years beyond the statutory limit of six or twelve months.[5] This was the easier because the *podestà* had lost all political importance and was now more than anything charged with judicial business. For this reason the Malatesta often sent a vicar to govern in their absence beside or above the *podestà* of the principal towns, who had authority to issue laws and statutes and was in every way the vicegerent of the lord.[6]

---

[1] To the traditional immunities of justices, doctors, students, etc., the Malatesta soon added others granted their 'familiares, domestici, aulici, etc.'; at Rimini already by 1349 there were exempt 'ex gratia domini' as well as 'ex beneficio statuti comutiis'. Their numbers so grew that the Malatesta themselves had to restrict exemption to certain classes and check the sale of property to exempt. Even so Fano in 1413, Rimini in 1461, Ripa and other places in 1460, all desired the number of immunities to be reduced: ibid., p. 761, n. 1.

[2] Ibid., p. 762.

[3] Ibid., pp. 762-3.

[4] A. degli Abati-Olivieri-Giordani, *Orazioni in morte di alcuni signori di Pesaro, della casa Malatesta* (1784), pp. xiii seq. Tonini, loc. cit., iv, pt. 1, 328. A. Vernarecci, *Fossombrone dai tempi antichissimi*, i (Fossombrone, 1903, 1914), 306. At Rimini after 1342 and Fano after 1336, where Malatesta Guastafamiglia and Galeotto were *defensores*, no Malatesta was ever *podestà*.

[5] Jones, loc. cit., pp. 727-8.

[6] Sigismondo Malatesta used his sons to represent him: ibid., pp. 728-30.

However represented, by vicar or *podestà*, the Malatesta always reserved some jurisdiction to themselves. Routine justice cer‑ tainly was never their concern, but they often intervened to pardon offences and remit fines, decide what crimes could be compounded for, suspend statutory penalties or grant immunity from particular laws.[1] Interference with statute was no abuse of power since both as lords and as papal vicars the Malatesta were fully invested with control of legislation. In practice this ex‑ pressed a political not a legal revolution, touching constitutional rather than civil or criminal law. The greater part of Malatesta legislation consisted of decrees published by the town crier on all kinds of occasional business. Often they simply reaffirmed exist‑ ing statutes, and the formulas used—*volumus et mandamus, fanno bandire et comandare*, etc.—lacked the solemnity of permanent law. But the distinction between statute and decree was not sharp. Decrees are interspersed among the statutes and many modified the statutes even permanently, or were given statu‑ tory force.[2] In this way a confusion of supplementary *reformationes* arose round the older laws, inviting new editions of the statutes. Rimini, Pesaro, Fano, Bertinoro and many more places all received new statutes from the Malatesta. A few of these editions —as at Rimini (1334) and Pesaro (1343, 1412, 1423)—obviously record phases in the rise or consolidation of the Malatesta *signoria*; but most have no political reference at all.[3]

Changes of substance in the law were few, but all law like all government now rested on the sanction of the despot. So the councils of the commune, whatever their initiative in administra‑ tion, were compliant and subordinate assemblies. The General Council especially, at one time the focus of municipal government,

---

[1] For some offences (e.g. usury) the penalty was wholly at the lord's discretion. *Stat. Rimini*, fos. 264r, 351v. R. Mariotti, *Bandi malatestiani nel comune di Fano* (Fano, 1892), p. 35. G. Bagli, 'Bandi malatestiani', *Atti Memorie Romagna* cit. (1885), pp. 84‑5. L. Maraschini, *Lettere malatestiane* (Osimo, 1902), no. 16.

[2] In 1478, after the expulsion of the Malatesta, Fano decided to remove their decrees from the statutes: P. M. Amiani, *Memorie istoriche della città di Fano*, ii (1751), 45.

[3] Jones, *Malatesta*, pp. 731‑4.

had little power left, and although its sessions as already said were not merely formal, it met infrequently, was convened and led by the lord's *podestà* or vicar, and much of its business was confined to presenting petitions. Numbers and attendance were fixed by the Malatesta, who at Rimini at least themselves remained members of the council.[1] At Fano, Pesaro and Fossombrone the number of councillors was reduced.[2] The smaller council, while more active, was also more closely connected with the rise and progress of the *signoria*.[3] It was usually nominated by the lord and like the General Council met and transacted all business at the word and in the presence of the lord's official. Like the General Council again it was often occupied with framing peti⁄ tions or seeking licence to act.[4]

Combined in common dependence on one ruling family it might be supposed that the several communes of the Malatesta state, however little altered in their local institutions, would have slowly undergone some rudimentary unification. In fact the union remained purely personal. The Malatesta usually divided their dominions and Rimini was never a 'capital' or even head of a feudal honour. At times certainly laws were published for more than one city,[5] and the statutes of one commune adopted from those of another. A higher appellate jurisdiction was introduced,[6] and during the fifteenth century the control of revenue centralized.[7] This was all, and such unity as developed did not extend outside

[1] When Carlo Malatesta in 1398, with the help of seventeen electors, chose the councillors of Rimini (197 in all), they included Carlo himself, Malatesta of Pesaro, and nine other members of the Malatesta family, as well as many dependents and adherents: Tonini, loc. cit., iv, pt. 2, doc. ccvii. Cf. Jones, *Malatesta*, pp. 771-2.

[2] Jones, *Malatesta*, pp. 770-4.

[3] For example *supra*, p. 225, n. 2. For other details and analogies at Fano, Cesena, etc., *vide* Jones, *Malatesta*, p. 774.

[4] Ibid., pp. 774-7.

[5] Ibid., p. 779. On the other hand laws could just as often be confined to one city and its *contado*.

[6] Probably by Galeotto Malatesta: ibid., p. 779, n. 3.

[7] By Pandolfo III Malatesta and his son Sigismondo, though only within the portions of the Malatesta state they governed: ibid., pp. 763-4.

the territory assigned by partition to each member of the family. Communal loyalties still remained lively enough to discourage unification. Old jealousies between cities survived and squabbles over boundaries could still exasperate the feelings of neighbouring towns.[1] As at Urbino there was more centralization of authority than unity of administration.[2] The Malatesta state was conserva/ tive, and uniformity from town to town it was neither in the power nor within the ambition of the Malatesta to impose. In some places they administered the revenues themselves, in others they used indirect control. In some the officials were paid by them, in others by the commune. But everywhere the communal constitution survived to resume independent life should despotism fail in power or popularity.

III

Among the despotisms of Romagna the Malatesta *signoria* was for long the most settled and secure.[3] If described as 'tyrants' as they sometimes were, especially in the fourteenth century, this only meant in contemporary language that the Malatesta had obtained despotic power, superseding the commune. And what/ ever their reputation abroad might be, at home they retained popularity. Sigismondo Malatesta, *fex Italie*, denounced as a monster by his enemy Pius II, was popular with his subjects

---

[1] Under the Malatesta, as under other *signori*, this local feeling, by threatening the integrity of the older city/state, could, however, promote the new unity of the *signoria*. For example Santarcangelo, which had always resisted government by Rimini, when recovered from the pope in 1358 became *directly* subject to the Mala/ esta and not to Rimini. Again in 1460 Ripa was granted independence of Senigallia by Sigismondo Malatesta, with its own official under the lord: ibid., p.t 780, n. 2.

[2] Luzzatto, loc. cit., pp. 195–6.

[3] Tonini, loc. cit., iv, pt. 1, 385. Cf. Sacchetti, writing of the Malatesta in the last decade of the fourteenth century.

> Giusto governo in questi sempre giace
> e di lor terre poca guardia fanno
> perché a' terrieri tal signoria piace.

(*Il Libro delle Rime*, ed. A. Chiari, 1936, p. 332, ll. 12–14)

almost to the last. With time 'a native and genuine reverence' gathered round the Malatesta,[1] so that in 1446 for instance the Venetians thought it wise to warn Francesco Sforza that their lands would be difficult of attack: *sonno terre forti et molto affec- tionati ad li Signori loro.*[2] This was later confirmed during Sigis- mondo's war with the pope when Rimini, Fano and the smaller places round stood firm as long as possible despite inadequate defences. So the question arises why the Malatesta in the later fifteenth century came to forfeit the loyalty of generations?

Grievances had always abounded, of a kind common to all medieval governments. They derived in part from the low level of public morality which more than once united the Malatesta with their subjects in complaint of misgovernment by officials. All leading officials were examined ('syndicated') before retiring by representatives either of the Malatesta or of the commune,[3] but such inquests were neither reliable nor a certain restraint on mis- conduct. During the hundred years from Galeotto to Sigismondo Malatesta legislation was continuous forbidding delays in justice, checking bribery and the irresponsible use of torture, and rebuk- ing financial officials quick to pay themselves once or twice over but slow to collect the revenue.[4]

A still more irritating cause of discontent, for which the Mala- testa were themselves responsible, was government control of trade, the details of indirect taxation, and the sale and movement of all commodities. Not that the Malatesta neglected the interests of trade or industry,[5] and whenever possible they did reduce customs' duties and *dazi*. At Rimini under Carlo Malatesta (+ 1429) the sale of bread and wine was said to have been free.[6] At Fano in

---

[1] *Vide* the interesting letter of the Bishop of Rimini, June 1522: C. Clementini, *Raccolto storica della fondatione di Rimino*, ii (Rimini, 1617), 682–6.

[2] Osio, loc. cit., iii, doc. 358, pp. 428 seq.

[3] Jones, *Malatesta*, p. 785, n. 1. The Malatesta kept a close watch on their servants and the 'reviews' (*mostre*) they ordered periodically record the smallest details of officials, even their personal appearance.

[4] Ibid., pp. 785–6.   [5] Ibid., pp. 782, n. 4, 787, n. 1.

[6] Battaglini, *Memorie*, pp. 226–7. Carlo also lifted duties in times of scarcity, prohibiting export and controlling prices. By contrast Pandolfaccio, last of the

1417 Pandolfo Malatesta halved the duties on incoming mer/
chandise owing to the distressed state of the city and in 1439 his
son Sigismondo, on petition, limited the *passagium* to what it had
been in Pandolfo's day, because it was keeping away merchants
trading between Tuscany and the Marches. Two years before
Sigismondo had also suppressed at one stroke fourteen separate
dazi imposed at Rimini, and in 1454 local freedom of traffic was
an article in the peace between Sigismondo and his brother Mala/
testa Novello. Finally in 1468, no doubt to curry favour, Isotta,
Roberto and Malatesta de' Malatesta granted a general liberty to
anyone native or 'foreign' wishing to import *panni pignolati*, spices,
shoes and other merchandise, *et questo perchè per molte rasone et
experientie se intende esser grande benificatione de questa terra*. These
concessions if upheld were doubtless well received, but indirect
taxes were too rich a source of revenue to be lightly surrendered
and the Malatesta could never long relax and were even reluc/
tant to delegate their control of trade. The only resource of the
discontented was to petition at least for freedom of traffic inside
the Malatesta state or with friendly powers outside.[1]

It was not in practice possible for the Malatesta to grant any
considerable freedom of trade or relief from taxation. Economic
sanctions were a normal consequence of war and the Malatesta
were constantly at war. For this and their schemes of territorial
expansion they needed all the money they could raise and there is
no doubt that the demands of war finance were oppressive. Nor
did taxes for war imply any general immunity from military
service. Apart from certain police duties—service in the watch,
the hue and cry—the subjects of the Malatesta were liable in

Malatesta, to meet the cost of personal extravagance granted the *tratta* of corn in
1487, though there was dearth in the city; but he had to withdraw his permission,
fearing popular unrest. In 1493 many died of hunger in Rimini, but there is no
evidence that the government acted. Four years later Pandolfo did allow corn to be
fetched from Venice to relieve famine: Clementini, loc. cit., ii, 231–2, 568. Sanuto,
loc. cit., i, 558–9, 614. A. Cappelli, 'Di Pandolfo Malatesta ultimo signore di
Rimini, *Atti Memorie Dep. SP. prov. Modenesi e Parmensi*, i (1863), 423.

[1] Jones, *Malatesta*, pp. 787–9.

emergency to conscription for defence. This service they owed the Malatesta both as successors of the commune and as vicars of the pope. It fell mainly though not exclusively on the country districts and more than once the Malatesta had to call out *uno homo per casa* and use *fanterie paesane*.[1] They were not therefore depen‚ dent only on mercenary troops or afraid to see their subjects armed; but the levy of peasants and townsmen remained exceptional and the permanent forces of the Malatesta were always paid. At Rimini the Malatesta were granted the right to hire mercenaries and from the time of Malatesta Guastafamiglia always kept a body of *stipendiarii* who were alone allowed to carry arms.[2] In time of war this force was expanded and the main duty of the subject was then less to serve himself than to pay the service of others. The taxes raised for troops were frequent and heavy and when not collected for troops were used to pay the expenses of purvey‚ ance. Purveyance was a general practice and no less a source of grievance in Romagna under the Malatesta than elsewhere in Italy and Europe, and the country people were especially vexed with demands to furnish arms and supplies or billet mercenary soldiers. It was the country people also who bore the burden of 'corvées' (*factiones*)—digging ditches, repairing roads, building fortifications; the townsmen met their obligation in money.[3]

If taxes did not yield enough or were slow of payment the

[1] Ibid., p. 736. Some importance the Malatesta must have attached to this un‚ trained force, since *cavalcate generali* were the one duty from which Galeotto Mala‚ testa Belfiore in 1386 did not exempt immigrants to Cervia; but the militia was not always reliable, and one cause of annoyance under Pandolfaccio was his survey in 1497 of men fit for arms in Rimini: *Stat. Cerviae*, ed. cit., iii. Clementini, loc. cit., ii, 576.

[2] *Stat. Rimini*, fos. 262v–3r, 339r. Cf. Jones, *Malatesta*, p. 737.

[3] Jones, ibid., pp. 737–40, 790. War and troops were not the only occasion of extraordinary taxes. When the Malatesta bought Sansepolcro in 1370 for 10,000 florins, their cities had to pay; likewise when Bertinoro was pledged to the Mala‚ testa in 1394. The taxes asked in 1417 to ransom Carlo Malatesta from Braccio were so untimely that they caused open unrest in Sansepolcro and the *contado* of Fano. The communes also paid the papal *census* and other subsidies to Rome, and were expected to pay gifts when Malatesta were born, married or buried: ibid., pp. 790–1.

Malatesta borrowed money, either locally or from abroad,[1] and when the loans were large the subject communes had to guarantee repayment. Loans were taken also from the Jews, who though generally detested as 'bloodsucking' usurers,[2] never lost the interested favour of the Malatesta. A further and final source of income, on which the Malatesta became increasingly dependent, was the profession of arms and the uncertain pay of *condottiere*.[3] But whatever expedients were tried—extraordinary taxes, loans or *condotte*—and however heavy taxation may have been, there is every sign that during the fifteenth century the financial state of the Malatesta steadily deteriorated.

This financial weakness first overtook the Malatesta of Pesaro, who formed a separate branch of the family after 1385. Pandolfo II Malatesta, lord of Pesaro and Fossombrone, died in 1373 *signore de molto moneta e altri grandi texori*, but his son Malatesta died heavily in debt. He was reduced in 1413 to having church property secularized in order to limit exemptions from taxa-tion, and he seems never to have been able to pay the dowry of his daughter Paola Agnesi, wife of Gianfrancesco Gonzaga. Galeazzo who succeeded him and finally sold Pesaro and Fossom-brone in 1445, lacked the competence or the power to repair his finances. He was perpetually harassed by creditors and for a time had to commit part of his territory to foreign hands.[4]

The Malatesta of Rimini suffered a similar if slower impover-ishment. Early in the fifteenth century Fano still provided Pan-dolfo III Malatesta with a considerable revenue, exceeding his expenditure, but this favourable balance was soon unsettled by his

---

[1] For loans raised in Fano and other communes *vide AF. Cod. Mal.*, 21, fos. 133–138, 142v (for the cost of acquiring Bergamo and Iesi), 147r–9v, etc.; *Cod. Mal.*, 99 (1442). Loans abroad were made for example in the fourteenth century from the Della Scala and the Gozzadini of Bologna: Jones, loc. cit., p. 792, n. 1.

[2] The phrase is used in a petition from Rimini, 1461: *Stat. Rimini*, fo. 375r. For details *vide* Jones, loc. cit., p. 792.   [3] *Vide infra.*

[4] Jones, *Malatesta*, pp. 664, n. 4, 794. Idem, 'Vicariate' cit., p. 349, n. 3. For debts of the Malatesta of Pesaro to the Certosa of Florence (1405) and to Niccolò da Uzzano, Andrea de' Bardi and Vieri Guadagni (1409) *vide ASF., Diplomatico, Certosa*, 22.1.1404/5; *Urbino, Div. B.*, filza viii.

costly conquests in Lombardy.[1] Rimini also yielded an ample income at this time, estimated in 1371 at about £80,000 *(lib. Rav.)* or over 47,000 ducats;[2] by the end of the fifteenth century this income had fallen to less than 10,000 ducats.[3] Petty economies were tried at various times. The pardon of fines was forbidden for the loss it caused to revenue, salaries were cut and tax immunities reduced. At the same time the *census* to Rome fell into arrears.[4] But nothing availed to remedy a weakness from which the whole Malatesta state seems to have suffered, lord and subject alike. In 1524 Balacco Balacchi of Rimini complained that whereas in the time of Carlo Malatesta one suburb alone numbered 10,000 people, the entire city of Rimini could not now muster so many, and that while in Carlo's day the city had boasted sixty ships it now had none.[5] His complaint seems justified. In 1371, despite the heavy mortality caused by the Black Death twenty years before, Rimini had 2,240 hearths, which the *contado* made up to 5,505, and this agrees well with the sixteenth-century estimate of the population at this time as between 20,000 and 30,000 souls. By 1511 the number of 'mouths' in Rimini was said to be 4,933, and shortly after in 1524 the population of the city over five years of age was calculated to be 5,500 and of the *contado* 6,500.[6]

Balacchi ascribed the slow decay of Rimini to misgovernment

[1] Jones, *Malatesta*, pp. 688, 794–5.

[2] A. Theiner, *Codex diplomaticus dominii temporalis sanctae sedis*, ii (1862), 525. Tonini, *Imposte* cit., p. 19. In 1368 the ducat was worth 33s. 6d. (Theiner, loc. cit., p. 461), so that £80,000 represented about 47,760 ducats or roughly the sum (40,000 ducats) that Carlo Malatesta was held a century after his death to have received each year from Rimini: Clementini, loc. cit., ii, 224. Tonini, *Storia*, vi, pt. 1, 191–2.

[3] 9,224 ducats, Lib. 3 14s., of which 1,190 ducats were patrimonial income: Sanuto, loc. cit., v, 489. In 1524 the revenue of Rimini was said to have fallen still more, to 4,000 ducats: Tonini, *Storia*, vi, pt. 1, 192.

[4] Jones, *Malatesta*, pp. 795–6. 'Vicariate', pp. 348–9.

[5] Tonini, *Storia*, vi., pt. 1, 192.

[6] Theiner, loc. cit., ii, 525. Clementini, loc. cit., ii, 224. Tonini, loc. cit., vi, pt. 1, 85, 191–2. ASF., *Carte Strozziane*, 1a Serie, 238, fo. 140. The population of Fano, town and territory, in the mid-fourteenth century was computed at 4,500 hearths; in 1480 the urban population is thought to have been 3,000–3,500 souls:

and harsh taxation, but although some *contadini* may have been caused to emigrate by forced works and requisitions,[1] those contemporaries were probably nearer the truth who blamed pestilence and war.[2] In 1417 the Malatesta were already granting financial concessions to Fano, exhausted by their continuous warfare in the March of Ancona. Later on the wars waged locally by Sigismondo, which he did much himself to provoke, brought suffering and hardship throughout his territory. The final struggle with Piccinino and Pius II made irreparable the damage of earlier years, undoing any good effects to be expected from the liberal fiscal policy announced in 1437. By the end of 1461 Rimini was crippled. Complaints came in as well from the March of Ancona, and Sigismondo had to renounce all hope of keeping the *literati* he had attracted to his court or of paying his artists with money. After 1463, with most of his territory gone, he was more than ever bound to his pay of *condottiere*. When he came to make his will he had little to bestow and the inventory of his goods in 1468 does not reveal a man of wealth or ostentation. His son Roberto attempted greater display and was said to have spent 35,000 ducats on his wedding with Isabetta da Montefeltro; but he too had to live as a mercenary captain and found a papal *census* of 1,000 ducats burdensome. Pandolfo who succeeded him also sought

---

Theiner, loc. cit., ii, 343. F. Bonasera, *Fano. Studio di geografia urbana* (*Studia Picena*, xx, 1951), p. 86.　　　　　　　　　　[1] *Stat. Rimini*, fo. 374v (1461).

[2] 'Quoniam civitas haec Ariminea bellorum turbinibus et epidemiarum infortuniis, quibus saepe perturbata retroactis temporibus ac vexata fuit, non solum divitiis verum etiam Civibus et personis eam incolentibus exhausta et fere denudata reperitur': Tonini, loc. cit., vi, pt. 2, 835 (a. 1508). Sigismondo had introduced his relief of taxation in 1437 (*supra*, p. 232) because of what he called the 'danni, detrimenti, et diminutioni' suffered by Rimini 'già longo tempo fo . . . per morie, per guerre, et per altre male condictione de tempi'. What little is known, however, of Italian population figures 1350–1500 suggests deeper causes may have been at work. At Rimini and Fano a local expression of decline was the progressive silting up of their seaports which neither the Malatesta nor later rulers were successful in arresting. Guicciardini in 1525 said the port of Rimini could be reclaimed but only at an expense which Rimini alone could never meet: *Opere inedite*, ed. Canestrini, viii, 406. L. Tonini, *Il porto di Rimini* (printed from *Atti Memorie Romagna*, iii, 1864), p. 106. Idem, *Storia*, vi, pt. 2, 843, cl. xii. Bonasera, loc. cit., p. 73.

the pay of *condottiere*. His revenues were slight and from either poverty or meanness he failed to pay the handsome dowry due by her father's will to his sister Giovanna. Against the richly sub-sidized Borgia he was powerless.[1]

All classes suffered by the wars and exactions of the Malatesta, but it may be doubted whether all suffered equally and whether the Malatesta disturbed even mildly the prejudices and privileges of communal society. It is sometimes claimed that the despots were kinder to the peasantry than the communes before them. The history of Malatesta rule only suggests that the peasantry had less incentive to rebel than the wealthier urban families who might expect by successful revolution to assume control themselves. The Malatesta certainly granted occasional favours to the *contadini* and sometimes freed a country place from dependence on the town, but no permanent relief of *corvées* or purveyance was offered and no attempt made to redress the unequal distribution of taxes between country and town which continued under the Malatesta to cause periodic unrest and perpetual discontent. It was innova-tion enough if the Malatesta now appointed most officials in the *contado*. At best they may have moderated urban domination of the country, and when they fell from power it was mostly *con-tadini* who desired their return.[2]

No deliberate policy to change the relations of town and terri-tory, urban landlord and rustic tenant, could be expected of the Malatesta who like all despots were themselves great landowners and came originally of that class. Their patrimonial properties, which grew with every accession of territory and each fresh city won, lay thickly everywhere and lasted as a source of income and influence as long as the *signoria*.[3] They were of every kind, com-prising agricultural land, houses, shops and palaces, woods,

[1] Jones, *Malatesta*, pp. 797–9 and *infra*.

[2] As at Cesena in 1469 and Rimini after 1500. On the Malatesta and the *contado* vide Jones, loc. cit., pp. 801–4. *Supra*, p. 233, and *infra*, pp. 251, n. 1, 254, n. 2, 226.

[3] Even after their fall the Malatesta retained their private lands: *Cronache For-livesi di A. Bernardi*, ed. G. Mazzatinti (Bologna, 1895–7), i, pt. 2, 315. Sanuto, loc. cit., v, 560. They began and finished as landowners.

water-courses and mills. Mills were especially profitable and almost became in time a monopoly of the Malatesta. In Pesaro and
Fano at least, and probably elsewhere, even the mills of the commune passed to the lord.[2] Some land the Malatesta held emphy-
teutically of the Church, but most they acquired by purchase or
exchange, testamentary bequest or gift—though not all gifts may
have been voluntary. The property of rebels, traitors and offenders
against the law also fell to the Malatesta as *signori* and papal vicars.

This private 'demesne' was usually administered apart by
factors and yielded a valuable return. In 1409 the income of
Pandolfo Malatesta's factor at Fano amounted to nearly £11,000,
not counting large quantities of wine, oil and other produce, and
still in the last years of Malatesta rule Pandolfaccio drew one-
ninth of his revenue *di le sue possessione*.[2] Most of this money
was spent locally in paying 'manorial' officials and wage labour,
buying beasts and crops, repairing buildings and providing
hospitality.[3] Though sums might be assigned the factor from
public revenue, the income he administered came normally from
rents, including food rents, and the sale of animals and produce,
especially grain. The mills controlled by the Malatesta, even if
sometimes farmed, probably increased their grain income and in
1409 money from the sale of corn was the largest single item in the
factor's table of receipts.[4] The March of Ancona was an agricultural region subject to less restrictions on the export of corn
than other parts of Italy. Rimini also was said to produce a grain
surplus.[5] So the Malatesta disposed of their corn not only locally,

---

[1] At Pesaro they included fulling mills: Vaccai, loc. cit., pp. 200–2. A. degli
Abati-Olivieri-Giordani, *Memorie di Alessandro Sforza* (1785), pp. xxvi–xxvii.

[2] *AF. Cod. Mal.*, 19. Sanuto, loc. cit., v, 489.

[3] *AF. Cod. Mal.*, 10, 19, 39, 72, 80–3, 88–91, 111–12. The factor's accounts ot
1436–8 show hundreds of wage-labourers being employed: ibid., p. 80.

[4] £3,209 7s. 7d.: *AF. Cod. Mal.*, 19. In 1372 Malatesta Ungaro left by will
10,000 *star. Arim.* of corn: Tonini, *Storia*, iv, pt. 2, 316, 318.

[5] In 1524 it was calculated that the territory of Rimini normally produced 24,000
stara of wheat of which 'the city' took at least 12,000 'per il manzare', leaving 4,000
for seed and a surplus of 8,000: *ASF., Carte Strozziane.* 1a Serie. 238, fo. 141.
But cf. *supra*, p. 231, n. 6.

though this was usually the case, but also abroad. On one occasion Pandolfo III Malatesta received nearly £22,000 from selling corn to Venice.[1]

As a source of income trade in corn was of less account than the distribution and sale of salt, which brought in more than any other category of Malatesta revenue, public or private. There had been a salt tax already under the commune, and even before they acquired Cervia (1383) the Malatesta had their salt deposits (*canipae salis*), just as later, when Cervia was in their hands, they continued to obtain salt from other places. But once possessed of Cervia, which they governed for nearly a century, their profits rose enormously. It was now that they established a salt monopoly under a special administration, supplying not only their own domains but Tuscany and other parts of Romagna and the March as well. Its value to the Malatesta is disclosed by the care with which they shared the salt supplies of Cervia when dividing up their state. Even when Cervia had passed to Venice their salt monopoly continued. It yielded Pandolfaccio about one-fifth of his income and one concession made by Cesare Borgia in 1500 was to reduce the price at which the Malatesta had been selling salt in Rimini and its *contado*.[2]

Both the salt monopoly and the sale of corn show how despotic power improved the opportunities of the Malatesta for private gain. But despotism like feudalism earlier obscured the distinction of public and private rights. Before ever they rose to power in Rimini the Malatesta combined rights over property with rights over men and their patrimony as despots cannot be sharply separated from the villages and castles of which they were hereditary lords or were later created *signori* and papal vicars. To their original thirteenth-century lordships, like Verucchio, Roncofreddo and Gradara, they made continual additions, permanent

---

[1] *AF. Cod. Mal.*, 21, fo. 238r. In 1406 on the other hand Pandolfo Malatesta formed a company to buy corn and import it tax free, taking half the profits himself: ibid., 4, fos. 4v-5r.

[2] For details *vide* Jones, *Malatesta*, pp. 701-4; and generally on the Malatesta estates, ibid., pp. 695-701.

or temporary, often by conquest or commendation, sometimes by grant from the emperor, the pope, or the Church of Ravenna. The ancient territorial power of the archbishops of Ravenna persisted in the background of Romagnol politics after the rise of the communes and *signorie*, and in 1356 Malatesta Guasta-famiglia was invested with a series of castles which in violation of the archbishop's rights had long been subject to Rimini and Pesaro. In effect they were now transferred from the commune to the lord, but long before this the commune had itself surrendered parts of the *contado* to the Malatesta. Even Verucchio and Gradara, two of their oldest possessions, may have been granted the Mala-testa, the first by Rimini and the second by Pesaro. In 1332 Rimini added Montefiore, Castelnuovo, Scorticata and Sogliano. Accompanied by full powers of *merum et mixtum imperium* these places passed from the general jurisdiction of the commune into dependence on the Malatesta and in that relation they remained until the war with Pius II. Gradara, Verucchio and Montefiore were *signorie* in miniature enclosed within the larger lordship over Rimini and Pesaro.[1] But as the power of the Malatesta grew these small hereditary lordships must have lost much of their original distinctness, tending once more to become part of the *contado* from which they had been separated. They did not, like the private estates, escape the general forfeiture to the papacy.[2]

At no time did the Malatesta keep their demesne estates and castles to themselves. If communes had sometimes granted land by fief, the rise of the *signorie* involved an immediate return to the habits of feudal lordship and monarchy. So land and juris-diction—and not only demesne land and jurisdiction—were used

[1] Verucchio is usually described as a *castrum* with a commune, statutes, a general council and two smaller councils of 12 and 36, presided over by a *capitano* nominated by the Malatesta. In 1336 and 1341 Ferrantino Malatesta was *dominus* and *defensor* of Verucchio: F. Antonini, *Supplemento della chronica di Verucchio* (1621). G. Pecci, 'Il governo di Verucchio e gli statuti della metà del sec. xv', *Atti Memorie Emilia Romagna*, iii (1938). Montefiore and Gradara were similar: Jones, *Malatesta*, p. 707, n. 4.

[2] For details on these lordships *vide* Jones, *Malatesta*, pp. 704–8.

to maintain a wife or mistress,[1] make up a marriage portion,[2] or most of all to reward clients and officials and hold together in dependence on the lord the many branches, inconspicuous but important, of the Malatesta *consorteria*. The Malatesta family was prolific and although the record of its many members is often reticent or still concealed in notarial deeds, it is enough to indicate beside the person of the despot others *de ipsa progenie* who, barely noticed by the chroniclers, often gave steady service to the *signoria*. Such was Giuliozzo Malatesta who in 1339 and 1343 was Malatesta vicar in Fossombrone and whose sons were possessed of lands and castles both there and in Rimini. Another was Gio. di Tino di Gianciotto, who served the Malatesta from 1334 to his death in 1375. Eight of his sons were adherents of Carlo Malatesta in 1389 and five were members of the Riminese General Council in 1398. All had property in Rimini and elsewhere and held the privileges—immunity from taxes, the right to carry arms and so on—accorded the Malatesta by the commune, until in 1431 Gio. di Ramberto tried to seize power for himself and was exiled. The descendants of Gaspare, an illegitimate son of Galeotto Malatesta, had a similar history. They too were generously endowed with land in Rimini and Cesena until after a century of unpretentious service they were tempted during Pandolfaccio's minority to make their authority as regents permanent.[3] Even the Malatesta counts of Ghiaggiolo and Sogliano, whose independent lordship went back to the thirteenth century,

---

[1] From 1454 for example the revenues of Montemarciano were being administered on behalf of 'Dompna Ysopta de limalatesti': *AF. Cod. Mal.*, 111. For other examples *vide* Jones, *Malatesta*, p. 708, n. 1.

[2] Thus the Torre di Gualdo which was assigned in dower to Parisina Malatesta in 1419 and then returned eight years after as the dower of Margherita d' Este, the betrothed of Galeotto Roberto, was not only a source of rent. Galeotto, Margherita and their factors were to have civil and criminal jurisdiction, and their *homines* and *coloni* exemption 'ab omni gravamine reali et personali seu misto'. It was to be a small dependent *signoria* apart: M. Fantuzzi, *Monumenti ravennati dei secoli di mezzo*, v (Venice, 1801), 423–6. La Stacciola and Le Fratte were other cases: Zonghi, loc. cit., pp. 64–5. T. Zampetti, *Giulio Cesare Varano* (1900), pp. 31–2, 104–5.

[3] *Infra*, p. 246.

sometimes took office and held land of their greater cousins in Rimini. But these two families, like the counts of Cusercole and Carpegna, who were related to the Malatesta stock, never belonged to the class of paid dependants of the Malatesta. They were rather political clients with a place beside the Malatesta themselves in the territorial baronage of Romagna, Montefeltro and the March of Ancona. The Malatesta of Rimini attracted many clients and *raccomandati* from this class and they illustrate the means of influence by which the *signoria* was developed and maintained.[1]

How this influence was exercised is best shown by the record of the citizen families, noble or bureaucratic, who helped the Malatesta to govern their state. Every commune had its class of nobles, of *cittadini* in the fullest sense. By tradition they were the leaders of municipal life and as such continued to command a natural place in the councils of the commune. But they also expected employment in the armies and administration of the lord. Some were old-established urban families like the Benci and Belmonti, Castracani, Adimari, Perleoni, Degli Atti or Roelli; others, like the Andarelli, Maschi or Valturi, came from small places in the Malatesta state, Gradara, Sant' Agata, Macerata Feltria, while a few had migrated from the Malatesta castles of Montefiore and Verucchio.[2] Their services were used both at home and abroad by the Malatesta, who also followed the general practice of seeking offices for their subjects in other states.[3] Even so it was a grievance that local office was not reserved to local men,[4] and in 1431 what encouraged Gio. di Ramberto Malatesta to attempt his *coup d'état* was discontent among the twelve councillors of Rimini—such men as Ludovico Belmonte and Leonardo

---

[1] Jones, *Malatesta*, pp. 709–14, based principally on the works of Clementini, the Battaglini, and Tonini.

[2] Ibid., p. 715.

[3] Ibid., pp. 715, 805. *ASF., Mediceo avanti il principato*, filza xxvi, n. 299, filza C ins. n. 167, filza Guid. nn. 157, 159. G. Franceschini, 'Su la signoria di Galeotto Malatesta a Borgo S. Sepolcro', *Studi Romagnoli*, ii (1951), 42.

[4] Petition from Rimini, 1461: *Stat. Rimini.*, fo. 374v.

Roello—whom Galeotto Roberto Malatesta had replaced by
'foreigners' from Ferrara. In fact the Malatesta drew able and
ambitious men to their dominions from all over Italy. The servants
of Pandolfo III Malatesta in the March of Ancona came from
Brescia, Pavia, Cremona, Bologna, Florence, Vigevano, Trento
and other cities. At Cesena the families most employed by the
Malatesta had all been first established there by Galeotto Malatesta and his successors. Some of these immigrants were exiles or
dispossessed families of neighbouring states. The Migliorati of
Fermo and the Brancaleoni of Castel Durante were of this class.
One of the Florentine Alberti entered Malatesta service and a
Benedetto de' Gambacorti of Pisa was a counsellor and *racco-
mandatus* of Sigismondo.[1]

Whether of foreign or local origin men who served the Malatesta well could expect some recompense in land or some immunity from taxes, and when land was not directly given it might
come by way of marriage. The Malatesta, especially the lesser
members of the family, never disdained alliances with the local
nobility and so in time became connected with the urban aristocracy of nearly all their cities.[2] In one sense therefore the *signoria*
might be represented as simply a system of family and property
relationships in which the Malatesta occupied the centre of a
wide class of vassals, feudatories and urban *ottimati*. A Malatesta
'interest' was slowly formed, which was neither Guelf nor Ghibelline. At Cesena and S. Sepolcro it is true Malatesta rule remained
Guelf and partisan;[3] but in Rimini the Parcitadi or some of them
were allowed to return, at Fano the Malatesta ultimately made
peace with the exiled Carignani, and in Fossombrone they

[1] Jones, *Malatesta*, pp. 423 seq., 716–17. A. Sapori, *Libri degli Alberti del Giudice*
(Milan, 1952), p. xc.

[2] As at Rimini, Fano, Cesena, Pesaro, Sansepolcro, Fossombrone, and Santarcangelo: Jones, loc. cit., pp. 718–19.

[3] At Cesena at least until 1400, at Sansepolcro even longer: Theiner, loc. cit., iii,
61. S. Chiaramonte, *Historiae Caesenae libri xvi* (in J. G. Graevius, *Thesaurus
Antiq. et Hist. Italiae*, Lugduni Batavorum, 1723–5), pp. 382, 395–6, 404, 406–7.
R. Zazzeri, *Storia di Cesena* (1889), pp. 248, 252. Coleschi, loc. cit., pp. 65, 201.
Franceschini, loc. cit., p. 46.

mediated between hostile families.[1] In every town a class existed, proud and jealous of its status, which if lifted into power would form a natural oligarchy. There is nothing to suggest that this class was deeply discontented throughout the two hundred years of Malatesta rule, held down by repressive measures. Rather does the whole history of such families as the Riminese Belmonti reveal the intimate interdependence of *signoria* and aristocracy.[2] It was when the Malatesta began to alienate members of this class in the time of Isotta, Roberto and Pandolfaccio that their strength was undermined.

IV

The first signs of possible disaffection appeared in Rimini dur, ing the closing years of Sigismondo Malatesta.[3] It seems at least that when Sigismondo left for the Morea as Venetian commander in 1464 he had to take hostages with him from many Riminese families.[4] The very terms of peace with the pope in 1463 un, settled traditional loyalties. They granted the Malatesta Bertinoro, Cesena and Rimini only for life, and by promising the return after many generations of direct lordship by the Church created a papal following in the Malatesta state. In Cesena the papal party predominated and when Malatesta Novello died in 1465 an attempt by his nephew Roberto Malatesta to become *signore*

[1] A. Battaglini, *Saggio*, p. 54, n. 31 and *passim*. Amiani, loc. cit., pp. 324–5. Vernarecci, loc. cit., i, 319.

[2] P. Belmonti, *Genealogia della famiglia Belmonti* (Rimini, 1671), *passim*.

[3] The rising started by Gio. di Ramberto in 1431, despite repercussions in Fano and Cesena, had no popular support and was only directed in any case to sub, stituting one Malatesta for others. By contrast a popular riot had broken out a year before when Martin V attempted to recover the Malatesta state for the Church, and in 1431 the Malatesta of Pesaro were driven out by a popular revolt against taxa, tion, strengthened by foreign intrigue: Jones, *Malatesta*, pp. 418–28. In 1418(?) the Ghibellines of Sansepolcro had raised the cry of *libertà* and attempted a revolt against taxation: Coleschi, loc. cit.

[4] G. Soranzo, 'Sigismondo Pandolfo Malatesta in Morea e le vicende del suo dominio', *Atti Memorie Romagna* (1917–18), pp. 227, 277–8. However, his return in 1466 was received with joy, not only in Rimini but in other former Malatesta places round.

in defiance of the pope failed of popular support. He was given the vicariate of Meldola, Polenta and other small lordships once governed by the Malatesta, but Cesena and Bertinoro escheated to the Church.[1]

The papacy had partisans in Rimini as well as was shown in 1465 when Sigismondo, absent in Morea, was rumoured dead and a number of Riminesi declared at once for the Church. Down to the end Sigismondo hoped so far to modify the treaty of 1463 as to secure Rimini once again for his family, and on his death in October 1468 he bequeathed the state to his wife Isotta and their son Sallustio. Isotta degli Atti, a vindictive and ambi- tious woman, who planned to govern through her own son, was disliked in Rimini, but Roberto Malatesta, a bastard son of Sigismondo, had a stronger following and this permitted him to defy the papacy with greater success than at Cesena three years before and take possession of Rimini himself. On the news of Sigismondo's death Roberto, then in papal service, went to the pope, Paul II, and deceitfully agreed to recover Rimini for the Church in return for a promise of Senigallia and Mondavio. At the same time a group of Riminese citizens, among them Matteo Belmonti, Matteo Lazzarini, Pietro Genari and Raimondo Mala- testa, all once devoted servants of Sigismondo, conspired together in favour of Roberto who with their connivance entered Rimini unchallenged. There for a brief period he ruled in common with Isotta and Sallustio, but the accord did not last. Undivided power soon passed to Roberto who during the summer of 1470 had Sallustio quietly murdered and Isotta thrust into unprotesting obscurity. It was to Roberto alone that the papacy in 1473 after prolonged war and negotiation at last renewed the grant of Rimini in hereditary vicariate.[2]

---

[1] For detailed references *vide* Jones, *Malatesta*, pp. 589–90. G. Franceschini, 'Violante Montefeltro Malatesti signora di Cesena', *Studi Romagnoli*, i (1950), 161.

[2] Clementini, loc. cit., ii, 458, 469. F. G. Battaglini, *Della vita* cit., pp. 540–1, 670–3. Tonini, *Storia*, v, pt. 2, 247–51. Jones, *Malatesta*, pp. 588, 597–603. Late in 1470 Valerio Malatesta was also murdered, while Isotta, who died after, was said to have been poisoned by Roberto. For the murder of Sallustio the

Roberto Malatesta, known as the 'Magnificent' and highly esteemed all over Italy, died prematurely in 1482 and once again Rimini had to face the government of a doting woman ambitious for herself and her son. The woman was Elisabetta Aldovrandini, Roberto's mistress, and her son Pandolfo, a minor of seven years and the last Malatesta to rule. Before his death Roberto had provided for a regency, appointing beside Elisabetta Galeotto and Raimondo Malatesta, the descendants of Gaspare di Galeotto. For ten years under Galeotto Malatesta *gubernator* the regents administered affairs without serious unquiet,[1] and dissension when it came was limited at first to members of the government. Galeotto and Raimondo fell out among themselves and in 1492 Raimondo was murdered. The crime was bitterly resented by Elisabetta whose special favour to Raimondo seems to have caused his death, and in self-defence Galeotto conspired the further step of putting Pandolfo to death and seizing power himself. But the plot became known and the leaders were taken and executed. None of these events caused any disturbance in Rimini and though Gio. Bentivoglio sent help from Bologna, it was not required.[2]

Pandolfo Malatesta should now have held sole authority in Rimini. His period of tutelage seemed over and he could at last feel free *dove era servo*.[3] In reality the greater share of power was claimed by Elisabetta and the members of her family, the Aldovrandini, whom she brought into office and influence. The government led by Galeotto Malatesta may have had some merits. It was at least the government of a man and a Malatesta. But no good is spoken of the régime which supplanted it. From all accounts Pandolfo Malatesta, *homo de mala natura, dissoluto in*

Riminese family of the Marchiselli were made the innocent scapegoats: Clementini, loc. cit., ii, 509–11.

[1] Only the grant of permission to export corn in 1487 caused disturbances: *supra*, p. 231, n. 6.

[2] *Diario Ferrarese*, in Mutarori, loc. cit., new ed., xxiv, pt. 7, 127. C. Ghirardacci, *Della Historia di Bologna*, ibid., xxxiii, pt. 1, 265, 267. Clementini, loc. cit., ii, 566–7. F. G. Battaglini, *Memorie*, p. 283. Cappelli, loc. cit., pp. 426–9. Tonini, *Storia*, v, pt. 1, 413–19, 491–2.

[3] As he wrote in a letter to the Duke of Ferrara: Cappelli, loc. cit., p. 427.

ogni vizio,[1] grew up detestably vicious and violent and according to Clementini he owed his vices to the training of his mother. This was evidently the belief of Ercole d'Este, Duke of Ferrara, who even before the death of Raimondo and Galeotto Malatesta had sent one of his closest counsellors, Bartolomeo Cavalieri, to the court of Rimini in 1491 to see that Pandolfo received the education proper to a prince and detach him if possible from the profligate idlers with whom Elisabetta, ambitious for power, had surrounded him. The next year Ercole himself visited Rimini and took Carlo Malatesta, Pandolfo's brother, away with him to be trained in arms with his own sons at Ferrara. Cavalieri stayed on, despite opposition from Elisabetta, but in the summer of 1493 she at last got rid of him and he was as glad to leave as she was to see him go.[2]

If Pandolfo was in fact raised in vice by his mother he may have repaid the kindness by having her poisoned. Early in 1496 she already complained to the Venetian government that Pandolfo was plotting to kill his brother and herself, and when she died unexpectedly in the following year during a visit to her daughter in Tuscany, Pandolfo was said to have had her poisoned.[3] In a letter to the Duke of Ferrara, however, Pandolfo professed himself inconsolable and he certainly had reason to grieve. This time he was indeed left in sole command of Rimini. Such freedom was fatal to his rule and to the Malatesta despotism and within two months of his mother's death he had provoked the only serious conspiracy ever formed against the Malatesta in Rimini.

The plot was prepared by members of the upper class, of families like the Adimari and Belmonti, who had prospered

---

[1] D. Malipiero, *Annali veneti*, ed. F. Longo, in *Arch. Stor. Ital.*, vii, pt. 2, 499, who continues: 'l'ha venenà so pare, e ha fatto morire un so fratel menore'.

[2] Cappelli, loc. cit., pp. 423 seq., 431 seq. Tonini, *Storia*, v, pt. 1, 410–13.

[3] M. Brosch, *Papst Julius II u. die Gründung d. Kirchenstaates* (Gotha, 1878), p. 325, n. 18. Cappelli, loc. cit., p. 436. Marin Sanuto gives a favourable opinion of Elisabetta: 'dona bellissima, giovene et molto saputa, la qual con il suo ingegno governava il stato di Rimano et il fiol signor Pandolfo, reprendendolo che non si portava a modo il padre' (loc. cit., i, 752–3); but as a Venetian he was partisan: cf. *infra*, p. 253.

under Malatesta government and served it often, but who were most exposed to the licence and caprice of tyranny.[1] They rose, in Caterina Sforza's words, because offended 'in their property, their honour and their persons'.[2] Marin Sanuto blamed particularly Pandolfo's desire to exercise *questa tirania di voler haver quelle done li piaceva et con quelle usar*.[3] They resented also Pandolfo's over-generous affection for the courtier Borso da Ferrara. Pandolfo himself either ignored or did not suspect their animosity, but the Venetians were awake to it and sent a representative to try and keep the peace. The plan was to murder every member of the Malatesta family when gathered in the church of S. Giovanni Evangelista on Sunday, 28 January 1498, and then to raise the crowd with cries of *libertà*. Like the Pazzi conspiracy in Florence twenty years before the attempt miscarried and like Lorenzo il Magnifico Pandolfo was able to escape, after an ignominious climb over the organ and high altar. He took refuge in the *rocca* and owed his safety, says Clementini, to the *plebe* by whom he was 'much loved'; but Caterina Sforza—who was certainly no friend of Pandolfo—wrote that after this attack he was 'hated universally' in Rimini. The conspirators who did not get away were punished with death or exile, but plotting went on both in Rimini and among the exiles outside, and when Cesare Borgia invaded Romagna he was joined by the fugitives from Malatesta misrule. The end came quickly. Unrest in Rimini deprived the Malatesta of any effective power, and when faced with the threat of siege by the Borgia army in October 1500, Pandolfo could only transfer authority to the council. It was the council which came to terms with Cesare Borgia and negotiated the final abdication by the Malatesta of all

[1] Even so not all families were driven into opposition. The Tignosi for example and the Battagli remained partisans of the Malatesta: Belmonti, loc. cit., pp. 155, 244–5.

[2] Pasolini, loc. cit., iii, 286.

[3] Loc. cit., i, 861. Few, however, of the Malatesta were above the morals of their age. Roberto had taken Elisabetta Aldovrandini from her husband and another Elisabetta, wife of Adimari degli Adimari, in both cases, it was later said, by force: Cappelli, loc. cit., p. 454.

claims to rule in Rimini. Resistance was never contemplated even by Pandolfo and whatever remained of the 'native and genuine reverence' once felt for their lords by the citizens of Rimini shrank from useless conflict.[1]

This was not the first time in recent years that Rimini had obeyed foreign influence or responded to foreign power, and the surrender to Cesare Borgia, however much a capitulation to force, only confirmed a tendency long present. More perhaps than any other lordship in Romagna were Rimini and the Malatesta state controlled during the later fifteenth century by greater powers out-side. When Sigismondo Malatesta was reported dead in 1465 there were already some Riminesi who urged in preference to papal rule the protectorate of a foreign state like Florence or Milan. At Rimini no doubt, just as at Forlì, it was recognized that the day of the small independent commune was over.[2] But the same was true of the small independent *signoria*, and if the Malatesta sur-vived their war with Pius II it was due more than anything to foreign support.

The object of the war had been to destroy the Malatesta utterly. As it was they lost Fano, Senigallia, Gradara and much of the Riminese *contado*, and their state was saved from total dismem-berment only by the resolute intercession of the Venetians, followed by other Italian rulers, especially Sforza, who feared that Venice and not the pope would replace the Malatesta.[3] Relations with

[1] *Cron. Forl. di A. Bernardi* cit., i/1, pp. 159–60, i/2, p. 315. Sanuto, loc. cit., i, 861–3, iii, 266, 296, 375, 400, 404, 653, 782, 911, 938. *Diario Ferrarese* cit., pp. 278, 301. Priuli, loc. cit., i, 80, ii, 63. Malipiero, loc. cit., pp. 498–9. Sigismondo de' Conti, loc. cit., ii, 228. Ghirardacci, loc. cit., p. 300. Clementini, loc. cit., ii, 577–84. F. G. Battaglini, *Memorie*, p. 291. Tonini, *Storia*, v, pt. 2, 321–35. Alvisi, loc. cit., pp. 129–30 and doc. 20. Pasolini, loc. cit., iii, docs. 781, 788. Feliciangeli, *Sull' acquisto*, docs. viii, x. Ady, loc. cit., p. 123.

[2] In a debate in the council of Forlì, following the murder of Girolamo Riario in 1488, it was argued that the city was too weak and small to live independently (as had been possible, that is, in the thirteenth century), so Forlì was surrendered to a papal envoy: Pasolini, loc. cit., i, 213.

[3] Even so Venice obtained Cervia by purchase from Domenico Malatesta Novello. On the war in general *vide* G. Soranzo, *Pio II e la politica ital. nella lotta contro i Malatesta* (Padua, 1911). For further references *vide* Jones, loc. cit., pp. 570–83.

Venice had always been close, but Venetian friendship was no longer disinterested or merely politic, and from this time a con-nection was formed between Rimini and Venice which matured years later when Rimini passed for a period under Venetian rule. In 1464 Sigismondo took service with Venice in the Morea and while he was away Venetian troops were garrisoned in Rimini at his desire to keep the peace and protect his state and family. Further help was sent by Venice to Isotta and Sallustio in 1465 when Sigismondo was believed dead, and the steady penetration of Venetian influence began to rouse hostility in both Rimini and Rome.[1] Venetian influence was active in Cesena also and on the death of Malatesta Novello (November 1465) a party headed by the *podestà* offered the city to Venice. It was mainly from fear of Venice that Paul II granted Meldola and the other places in vicariate to Roberto Malatesta, and in February 1466 he warned the Venetians that Rimini was papal territory and must in due course fell to the Church *pleno jure*. Sigismondo chose unwisely when precisely at this time he chose Venice to support a request to the pope for restitution of his former lands. Paul II only wanted to separate the Malatesta from Venice and he did in fact secure Sigismondo for papal service as *condottiere*; but when Sigismondo died in 1468 there were still Venetian troops in Rimini.[2]

Roberto Malatesta had meantime formed other and wider friendships in Italy, especially with the Sforza, and relying on these had already tried to keep Cesena for the Malatesta in 1465, ap-pealing for help indifferently to Florence, Venice, Milan and the pope; but no one heeded him and he had to let the city go. It[3] was otherwise at Rimini in 1468–9. Jealous of Ventian encroach-ments in Romagna, the Italian League of Naples, Florence and Milan this time gave Roberto all support. As a result Venetian influence in Rimini was for the moment broken. Isotta and Sallustio, whom Venetian help alone had kept in power, were

---

[1] For hostility in Rimini *vide* Zippel, in Muratori, loc. cit., new ed., iii, pt. 16, 166, n. 3. Soranzo, 'Sigismondo Pandolfo Malatesta' cit., pp. 243–7, Massèra, in *N. Arch. Veneto* (1919), pp. 232–3.

[2] Jones, loc. cit., pp. 590–6.   [3] *Supra*, pp. 244–5.

deposed by Roberto and the Venetian garrison sent home. Most governments, it is true, refused to go to war about Rimini, but Ferrante of Naples sent troops to Romagna, which enabled Roberto to defeat the papal army (30 August 1469), recover the Riminese *contado*, and go on to occupy much of Fanese territory as well.[1] Only Venice checked his advance, encouraged to active intervention by substantial hopes of getting Rimini herself.[2] Slowly the combined diplomacy of the Malatesta's allies induced the pope to negotiate. Roberto was granted Rimini, both city and *contado*, but his other conquests reverted to the Church. So much at the end of ten years were the Malatesta able to save from the wreck of 1463.[3]

Nothing shows more clearly than Roberto's failure at Cesena and subsequent success at Rimini the unqualified dependence of the Malatesta now on foreign favour and support. There was certainly no foreign garrison in Rimini while Roberto Malatesta ruled, but it was to foreign powers that he owed his state and in command of foreign armies that he spent his life. He was an accomplished soldier and his reign is mostly a record of contracts of hire, differences over pay, changes of political allegiance and war. *Io non naqui de casa che sia usa d'andare mendicando*, he protested to the pope when his pay was in arrears, but 'mendicant' his family had to be if dependent on mercenary contracts. They needed pay and they continued to need protection. Late in 1479 the Venetian government, which had recently taken Roberto into service, opposed a plan by Sixtus IV and Girolamo Riario to expel the Malatesta from Rimini.[4]

The territorial ambitions of Riario in Romagna were notorious

---

[1] Sigismondo, Roberto and even Pandolfo Malatesta continued to have supporters in Fano, Cesena and other lost territories, not least among the peasantry: Jones, loc. cit., pp. 585, 600.

[2] At first the Venetians were backward in helping the pope but Paul got the consistory to agree to ceding Rimini to Venice if it should be necessary.

[3] Jones, loc. cit., pp. 599–603. Cf. T. Mathis, *Il problema di Rimini nell' anno 1469* (Tesi di Laurea. Univ. di Firenze, Facoltà di Lettere e Filosofia, 1955–6).

[4] Jones, loc. cit., pp. 604–9. E. Piva, *La guerra di Ferrara del 1482. Periodo primo* (Padua, 1893), pp. 29–30.

and when Roberto Malatesta died in September 1482 fighting for the papacy and Venice, it was generally suspected that Sixtus IV intended to occupy Rimini for one of his family.[1] The occasion seemed opportune. Pandolfo Malatesta was a minor, born out of wedlock, and Rimini was reported by a Florentine envoy to be *ghovernato et recto in modo e da Tali homini che ha bisogno della gratia didio et piu che ordinario*. In the event Pandolfo's succession was undisturbed. Any papal plan to dispossess the Malatesta was quietly withdrawn and Sixtus lost no time in declaring Roberto's sons legitimate and investing them with Rimini.[2]

The pope may simply have deferred his designs on Rimini, or he may, as Fabronio suggests, have accepted advice from Lorenzo de' Medici;[3] but it is no less possible that he acted from suspicion of Venice. Venetian influence in Rimini was reviving and at just this time a plot was discovered to surrender the city to Venice. In April of the next year the Venetians were rumoured to have made another attempt on Rimini and word spread that Pandolfo, a son of Sigismondo Malatesta, *con le spalle e genti de' Veneziani hanno corso la terra di Rimini, e che la terra gridava Marco, Marco, la rocca autem Chiesa, Chiesa*. The principal forces contending for power in Rimini, Venice and the papacy, 'Marco' and 'Chiesa', were here suddenly revealed. Two years later Pope Innocent VIII desired the Malatesta to admit a papal garrison to Rimini as a defence against the Venetians.[4]

[1] *Vide* letter of G. C. da Varano, September 1482: Lilii, loc. cit., ii, 236. It was also rumoured without foundation that Girolamo Riario had poisoned Roberto.

[2] *ASF., Mediceo avanti il principato*, filza xxxviii, n. 504 (12.10.1482). Jones, loc. cit., pp. 609–11.

[3] A. Cappelli, *Lettere di Lorenzo il Magnifico*, in *Atti Memorie Mod. Parm.* cit., i (1863), 267–8. A. Fabronius, *Laurentii Medicis magnifici vita* (Pisa, 1784), i, 124. Florence certainly sent an envoy to report on Rimini (October 1482) and if possible bring the Malatesta over to the League: *ASF., Signoria, Legazioni, Commissioni*, etc., 77, fos. 153r–4v. *Dieci di Balìa, Missive*, 14, fos. 62v, 75r; *Legazioni e Commissarie*, 5, fo. 182r.

[4] *ASF., Dieci di Balìa, Carteggio Responsive*, 27, fos. 258–61, 270. Jones, *Malatesta*, p. 612. In the summer of 1482 Venice had resisted the proposal of Sixtus IV and Gir. Riario to take Faenza from the Manfredi, desiring Faenza for herself if anyone: Piva, loc. cit., p. 104.

In the contest for influence in Romagna which increasingly engaged the Italian powers in the late fifteenth century, the highest ambition of the Malatesta, as of their neighbours at Faenza and Forlì, was to obtain a regular *condotta*, annual pay for themselves and a small body of troops, from any state ready to grant it. Pandolfo Malatesta, though only a boy, was first hired by Florence, Naples and Milan, then by the pope. In 1489, when his papal *condotta* was due to elapse, he offered his services to Venice, sought money for troops from Florence, and besought Lorenzo de' Medici to persuade the pope to renew his contract. Venice for the moment had no money to spare, Florence would offer only a verbal promise of protection and goodwill, and finally the pope alone consented to retain Pandolfo in his service. The surviving letters plainly express the 'mendicant' condition of the smaller *signori*.[1]

The search for *condotte* went on, but Pandolfo Malatesta was no soldier. In his case at least the *condotta* was a political instrument, a form of commendation. This became clear in 1493 when Pandolfo entered Venetian service and his mother placed Rimini under Venetian protection—*essendo questo stato debole e povero di aderenti*. The *condotta* was a subsidy, the price not of military service (which was scarcely rendered) but of political control, and Venetian 'protection' soon tightened into Venetian supremacy. When Pandolfo intrigued in Cesena his followers raised the cry of 'Marco' as well as 'Pandolfo' (1495). When he disobeyed a Venetian command to go to Naples he received a letter of imperious rebuke, as if a peccant officer of Venetian provincial government (1496). And after the conspiracy of 1498 it was the Venetian representative who prevailed in Rimini and maintained Pandolfo in power. This was why the rumour spread that Pandolfo intended to give up Rimini to Venice for land in Friuli, and this was why Venice alone tried to prevent the Borgia from taking Rimini in 1500. As late as the summer of 1500 the Venetians continued to negotiate with the pope, Pandolfo an

[1] Jones, loc. cit., pp. 613–14. *ASF.*, *Mediceo avanti il princ.*, filza xli, nn. 396, 421; li, n. 572.

inactive spectator, and only the Turkish offensive in the Near East compelled them to give way. In September Pandolfo was told he must fend for himself and his *condotta* was not renewed. A desperate last visit to Venice by Carlo Malatesta achieved nothing and in October Pandolfo was in flight from Rimini.[1]

V

When the storm was over and the Borgia pope had died (August 1503), the disinherited despots returned, with foreign help, to Romagna and the March, and where they could count on papal favour and a strong enough party among the citizens, they recovered power. The conditions of survival had not changed, but papal favour was now especially needed, if the work of Cesare Borgia was to be even partially undone. Kinship with Pope Julius II enabled the Della Rovere, Montefeltro and Da Varano to keep Senigallia, Urbino and Camerino, and Gio. Sforza at Pesaro obtained papal support. Elsewhere the papal party—as at Imola, Forlì and Forlimpopoli—or papal policy in alliance with foreign arms—as at Perugia, Bologna, Rimini, Faenza, Ravenna—sooner or later prevailed during the ten years' pontificate of Julius II. At Rimini the Malatesta had neither papal nor popular support. Only the *contadini* rose in their favour;[2] in the city most men wanted Venice or the Church. For a month (22 October–24 November 1503) Pandolfo did recover Rimini, but only once again as helpless retainer of Venice,[3] and when the Venetians decided to take Rimini themselves, he could only submit. Six years later the Venetians also lost Rimini, to the Church. Twice more the Malatesta tried to reimpose their rule, but

[1] Jones, loc. cit., pp. 616–18, 622, 630–2.

[2] Sanuto, loc. cit., v, 70, 72; cf. p. 751. Ghirardacci, loc cit., p. 324. Already under Cesare Borgia certain castles had risen for Pandolfo Malatesta provoked by taxation and the greater burdens placed on the *contado* than on the town: Sanuto, loc. cit., iv, 378. Clementini, loc. cit., ii, 589–90. Tonini, *Storia*, vi, pt. 2, 786–7.

[3] The Venetian Giustinian commented: 'lo potemo reputar nostro senza nostra spexa': *Dispacci*, ed. P. Villari, ii (Florence, 1876), 224.

opposition was too strong. Under Venetian and then papal government the nobility had been granted far more autonomy than the Malatesta ever allowed, and oligarchical privilege secured by statute without special favour to any family. Even so the Malatesta still had followers, 'Pandolfeschi' or 'Guelfs', with whose help they were briefly restored to Rimini in 1522 and 1527–8; but Pandolfo and his son Sigismondo II had learned nothing from thirty years of conspiracy and exile. Their only policy was partisan violence and vendetta, which turned every class against them, *si cittadinj, artifficj, plebei e contadinj, commo altrj*. By different methods they might have won Rimini back. Pope Clement VII, it seems, was disposed in extremity to revive the papal vicariate, but the citizens besought him to set them free, and in June 1528 a papal army once again expelled the Malatesta from Rimini, this time for good.[1]

[1] Jones, loc. cit., pp. 809–20.

Peter Partner

THE 'BUDGET' OF THE ROMAN CHURCH IN THE RENAISSANCE PERIOD

It is well known that the income of the popes was hard hit by the Great Schism and the Council of Constance. In 1429 it was said by a commission of cardinals which sat to discuss Church reform that papal income had fallen to a third of its level before the Schism.[1] But it is difficult to gain a coherent picture of papal finance in the Renaissance period, since in the fifteenth century the centralized system of book-keeping practised by the Avignonese popes had broken down, and instead of referring to a single *Exitus et Introitus* series the scholar has to do the best he can with a number of untidily kept accounts under different heads of income and expenditure—accounts which in many cases have failed to survive.[2] As the fifteenth century goes on this lack of system becomes even more marked, and it becomes necessary to consult, besides the *Introitus et Exitus* volumes, the accounts of provincial treasurers, of the farmers of the salt monopoly and of the income from transhumance dues (*dogana dei pascoli*) and grain export licences (*tratte*). In the Roman Court proper, separate accounts are kept for particular kinds of expenditure, such as the Crusade which had assigned to it the revenues from the new papal

[1] J. Haller, *Concilium Basiliense*, i (1896), 173-4.

[2] For the Avignonese system see *Vatikanische Quellen zur Geschichte der päpstlichen Hof- und Finanzverwaltung*, i-vi (1910-37), particularly Goeller's introduction to the first volume. For the fifteenth century the best guide is still A. Gottlob, *Aus der Camera apostolica des XV. Jahrhunderts* (1889), supplemented by E. Goeller, 'Untersuchungen über das Inventar des Finanzarchivs der Renaissancepäpste', in *Miscellanea Fr. Ehrle*, v (1924), 227-72.

alum mines. Some of these special accounts, particularly the 'secret' account of the pope and the virtually new income from compositions, venal offices, and dispensations which was con, solidated late in the century under the office of the Datary, have most of them long since disappeared.[1] To estimate papal income in detail for this period is therefore a laborious affair, which even after much work in the Roman Archives must still involve a considerable element of conjecture. But it is also a matter of interest to the historian, of importance in some of the more debat, able questions which concern the papacy of the Renaissance and Reformation period.

It is clear that the drying up of many revenues which had formerly been collected for the popes by apostolic collectors sent to the various provinces and transmitted by them direct to the Apostolic Chamber, forced the popes to compensate for these lost taxes by imposing new dues on the transactions of persons doing business of one kind or another at the Roman Court itself. These new dues thus differed in one important respect from the old ones. Whereas the tenths and first-fruits and so on had in the fourteenth century gone almost straight from the clergy taxed to the pope, the new taxes were most of them imposed through the bureaucracy of the Roman Court, and in some cases (particularly that of the Datary) a new bureaucracy was created to collect them. The pope thus hung round his own neck an intolerable weight of officials whom he could not well dislodge; all the proposals for the 'reformation' of the Roman Court in the fifteenth and early sixteenth centuries are directed not to abolishing or even to pruning the curial bureaucracy, but merely to ensure its smooth running and to ironing out the more obvious anomalies of its operation.[2] Even had they been put into practice (which they were not) they were reforms of detail and not of principle. And the intractability

[1] See Goeller's article cited above, and my article, 'Camera Papae: problems of Papal Finance in the later Middle Ages', *Journal of Ecclesiastical History*, iv (1953), 55–68.

[2] W. von Hofmann, *Forschungen zur Geschichte der kurialen Behörden vom Schisma bis zur Reformation*, i (1914), 304–29.

of the system was hardened further by the adoption of a peculiar method which used the venality of papal offices as the machinery for floating a papal debt. Having in the early fifteenth century used the sale of offices as a means of obtaining a windfall income, the popes of the late fifteenth and early sixteenth centuries instituted whole 'colleges' of new offices, most of them with purely ficti/ tious duties, but some still with certain limited obligations. These 'Cavalieri di San Pietro', 'Presidenti di Ripa', 'Archivisti', 'Scudieri' and so on, were in effect shareholders in the papal debt. The purchase price of their office was their invested capital; the salary of their office was their interest, at an average rate of 11 per cent.[1] Not only these new and in a sense supernumerary office/ holders were concerned in the system of papal loans; the older offices such as clerks of the Chamber and scriptors in Chancery continued to be sold on the same basis. In 1521 over 2,000 offices were venal, representing an invested capital of about two and a half million gold florins, and an annual interest of about 300,000 gold florins.[2] An inextricable confusion had grown up, in no way remarkable in the *ancien régime*, but fatal for papal hopes of a reformation *in capite*, between the payment of the public debt of the papacy and the ordinary remuneration of its officials. It is not at all surprising that when Leo X at the Lateran Council was expected to carry out a root/and/branch reform of the Roman Curia, he instead merely issued an ordinance which had the effect of confirming and in some cases increasing the taxes re/ ceived by the papal bureaucracy.[3]

There is, however, a further important factor in papal finances of the Renaissance period, to which attention was drawn thirty years ago in an important article by Clemens Bauer.[4] The

[1] Von Hofmann, *Forschungen*, i, 281–9; C. Bauer, 'Die Epochen der Papst/ finanz', *Historische Zeitschrift*, Bd. 138 (1928), 485–9, drawing heavily on von Hofmann.

[2] Von Hofmann, *Forschungen*, i, 288–9.

[3] Von Hofmann, *Forschungen*, i, 274–5; H. Jedin, *Geschichte des Konzils von Trient*, i (1951), 105.

[4] 'Die Epochen der Papstfinanz', quoted above.

revenues of the Papal State, which in the Avignonese period were only a minor factor in papal calculations[1]—indeed the temporal power was sometimes more of a liability than asset—in the early fifteenth century began to play a far more important part, both relatively and absolutely, in the composition of papal income. The income of Gregory XI (1370–8) varied between 200,000 and 300,000 gold cameral florins annually of which not more than a quarter came from the Papal State.[2] That of Martin V (1417–31) was in 1426–7 about 170,000 gold cameral florins, of which 80,000 florins, or rather less than half, came from the Papal State.[3] Thus the effect of the Great Schism had been drastically to reduce the papal revenues drawn from the Church at large—although less drastically than the commission of cardinals which I have referred to above claimed. But the papal grip on its lands in Italy had so increased as partially to redress the deficiency. The commission of cardinals was right in saying that revenues were only a third of their amount before the Schism, if it referred only to 'spiritual' revenues. If the temporal revenues are added, the fall in revenue was at most no more than half.

For the period between Martin V and Sixtus IV we are dependent on the *Introitus et Exitus* series, which as I have already indicated gives only a partial indication of the state of papal revenues. Thus in 1426–7, a year in which I have reckoned the real total of papal income to be about 170,000 florins, the income actually shown in the *Introitus et Exitus* is only 114,385 florins.[4] Having been thus cautioned, we may gather an impression of papal penury under Eugenius IV, due both to the Council of Basel

---

[1] Some indications of their amount are given by K. H. Schäfer, *Deutsche Ritter und Edelknechte in Italien während des 14. Jahrhunderts*, i (1911), 16–44. A note of 1367-8 in the Avignonese registers estimates the annual surplus in the Papal States in time of peace to be 86,000 florins excluding Rome (Schäfer, pp. 41–2). But this is almost certainly too high.

[2] K. H. Schäfer, *Die Ausgaben der apostolischen Kammer unter den Päpsten Urban V. und Gregor XI. (1362–78)* (*Vatikanische Quellen*, Bd. vi, 1937), *passim*; A. Theiner, *Codex Diplomaticus Dominii Temporalis S. Sedis*, ii (1862), no. 561, p. 556.

[3] P. Partner, *The Papal State under Martin V* (1957), pp. 193–4.

[4] Ibid.

and the revolutions of the Papal State. In 1436 (January–December) the total income recorded in the *Introitus et Exitus* is only 59,160 gold cameral florins.[1] Under Pius II the papal monarchy had been powerfully reasserted both in the Church at large and the Papal State, and income correspondingly rose. The total recorded in the *Introitus et Exitus* for September 1461–August 1462, at a time when particular efforts were being made to finance the Crusade, is 471,694 cameral florins.[2]

But the last two figures I have given above are undifferentiated totals, which can only be split up and analysed by long labour in the Vatican Archives. For the pontificate of Sixtus IV we have two documents, already well known to scholars, which are in effect 'budgets' of the Roman Church, drawn up in the Apostolic Chamber.[3] The more detailed of the two, that of 1480–1, is the more remarkable, since it is evidently a part of a scheme for the reorganization of the central papal financial bureau, the Apostolic Chamber, and the 'budget' is followed by an 'Ordo Camere' drawn up in the form of a draft bull. The second document is a far more summary affair, and may well, as Gottlob suggests, be a rough list of papal revenues for the use of the Florentine bankers then acting as *depositarii* for the Apostolic Chamber.[4]

In spite of its brave attempt to be systematic, the document of 1480–1 displays much of the wayful haphazardness of medieval accountancy. It begins with a list of revenues which it describes as *entrate ordinarie della Camera apostolica secundo il comune uso*, which may perhaps be interpreted 'as they are usually reckoned in the Apostolic Chamber'. There follows a list of net revenues reckoned from the various departments of the Papal State, the last entry being *lo spirituale cioè communi di papa et annate*, which

[1] Calculated from Vatican Archives, Introitus et Exitus, vol. 400.

[2] Calculated from the figures in Gottlob, *Aus der Camera apostolica*, pp. 260–1.

[3] The budget of 1480–1 printed by C. Bauer, 'Studi per la storia delle finanze papali durante il pontificato di Sisto IV', *Archivio della R. Società Romana di Storia Patria*, 1 (1927), 319–400. The other by Gottlob, *Aus der Camera apostolica*, pp. 253–5.

[4] For the depositary see Gottlob, *Aus der Camera apostolica*, pp. 109–12, 159–66, and *The Papal State under Martin V*, p. 137.

is reckoned at *circa* 42,000 ducats. The total of these revenues *secundo il comune uso*, including the *spirituale*, is 160,000 ducats. There follows a list headed *Spese ordinarie del Papa*, giving the ordinary annual expenses of the papal household, about 29,500 ducats excluding the cost of mercenaries. Another list, *Spese della Thesauraria di Roma che si pagano de la Dogana dela grassa*, totalling 9,505 ducats, then has at its foot, without any other supporting figures, *Tucte le entrate ordinarie con spirituale et tutto . . . ducati 160,000*. Then *Uscita ordinaria in tutto . . . ducati 150,580*. How the accountant reaches this last figure he does not here reveal, though the second document makes it clear that the discrepancy of 110,000 ducats in 'ordinary' expenditure is made up of the pensions to cardinals and the cost of the mercenary army.

This, however, is only the preliminary to the main part of the 'budget', which is an itemized list of the revenue and expenses of the various parts of the Papal State, recounted in some instances (e.g. the salt monopoly of Rome and the District) in the utmost detail, in others only summarily. These lists are certainly made up from the accounts of the various provincial treasurers, although I question that Bauer is right when he says that they are 'averaged' from actual receipts.[1] I would suggest that they represent, simply, what is due to the Apostolic Chamber from the subjects, and what it has to pay to its officials. It is in other words an anticipatory budget—although 'anticipatory' is not a very happy word to apply to medieval calculations, since barring political changes the income of the State was reckoned to be the same from one year to another. We may not, therefore, safely assume that the Chamber and its officials actually received the sums said to be due to them —nor that they spent the sums said to be due from them.

At the end of the list of revenue and expenses comes a final entry, headed *Summario di questo libro de tucte le entrate*. There follows a summary, more or less accurate, of the totals of the various heads of income just dealt with at length. Up to a point this *summario* corrects the figures given earlier in the document

[1] 'Studi per la storia delle finanze papali', pp. 323-4.

secundo il comune uso, although some of the entries *secundo il comune uso* are not repeated, notably the 'spiritual' revenues. On the whole, with the exception of the sums reckoned to be received from the customs dues of Rome, the *summario* includes only what can be exactly calculated, and not what has to be estimated roughly.

The second document supplements on some important points the budget just described. In particular, it describes several impor-tant sources of 'extraordinary' income: the moneys from taxes on the registry and issue of bulls (*piombo e registro*), which as earlier in the century are valued at about 36,000 florins; the *composi-tioni* which were shortly afterwards administered by the Datary (here 12,000 florins); the moneys from the sale of venal offices, which are here valued at 15,000 florins. Indulgences and other taxes handled by apostolic collectors are put at 10,000 florins. A postscript, moreover, adds that if the pope is in need of money he can gain up to a further 60,000 florins by taxing vacant bene-fices more strictly and by distributing matrimonial and other dispensations with a more liberal hand. Thus in addition to the 40,000–60,000 ducats which the pope drew on the average from annates and common services, his 'spiritual' income could also count on 73,000 florins from the Registry, Collectorates and Datary. If the screws were tightened, we are led to believe that all these sums could be increased considerably. At all events, a con-servative estimate of the 'spiritual' income, including the proceeds of the sale of offices, would seem to be about 120,000 florins. If I have reckoned rightly the 'spiritual' income of Martin V in 1426–7 at about 90,000 florins, excluding the Registry and at a time when there was virtually no income from the venal offices,[1] then the 'spiritual' income of the popes under Martin V and under Sixtus IV may be reckoned as more or less the same. Its com-position, however, is in process of changing. Indulgences, dis-pensations, and the venal offices are all rapidly expanding in scope.

[1] *The Papal State under Martin V*, pp. 193–4. For the venal offices see von Hofmann, *Forschungen*, i, 162–70.

The income from the temporal power appears to be made up approximately as follows:[1] salt monopoly of Rome, the March of Ancona and Romagna, 31,500 ducats. Revenues from transhumance (*dogana dei pascoli*), 10,000 ducats. The papal alum mines at Tolfa, 50,000 ducats.[2] Indirect taxes from Rome, 36,000 ducats. The Patrimony of St. Peter in Tuscia, 3,500 ducats net. Perugia, 5,000 ducats net. The March of Ancona, 10,000 ducats net. Ascoli, 3,500 ducats net. Romagna, 1,600 ducats net. Licences for the export of grain, 16,000 ducats. Wine tax of Bologna, 4,000 ducats. *Census* for apostolic vicariates (wrongly termed 'feudal' *census* by Bauer), 10,000 ducats. The total of these figures is 181,000 ducats, which is probably not yet a net figure— e.g. 9,000–10,000 ducats were required to meet the expenses of the administration of Rome. It has also to be remembered—a point not sufficiently stressed by Bauer in his analysis of these figures—that this total is the sum due from the taxpayers and may not be the sum actually paid.

We may perhaps take 170,000 ducats as a conservative figure for the net profit made on the Papal State by the Apostolic Chamber, and 120,000 ducats as an average figure for the product of the 'spiritual' taxes and the venal offices, giving a total income for Sixtus IV of about 290,000 ducats. Against this the pope had to meet expenses of some 30,000–40,000 ducats for the ordinary running of the Apostolic Palace, including the cost of Church ceremonies, guards, and ceremonial presents. His main liability was his mercenary army, which under Sixtus IV was reckoned to cost about 100,000 ducats a year (a figure not far off the average military expenditure of Martin V in the second decade of the century). He paid his cardinals eight to ten thousand ducats a year in pensions—a modest figure when it is considered that in the preceding century the cardinals had made good a right to

---

[1] Following Bauer, 'Studi per storia delle finanze papali', pp. 340–3. My totals differ slightly from his, since I have as far as possible given the net rather than the gross yield of the various treasuries.

[2] The revenues from this source went into a special fund for the Crusade; see Gottlob, *Aus der Camera apostolica*, pp. 245 f., 278 f.

half the proceeds of the whole Papal State.[1] The remainder went on buildings and works of art, on diplomatic expenses, on alms. It will not be forgotten that Sixtus IV is responsible for a large part of the structure of the Vatican Palace as we know it today. And finally the Apostolic See from the time of Calixtus III and Pius II onwards was devoting large sums to the war against the Turks. The failure to mention the alum mines in either of these budgets of Sixtus IV may well be because the profits of these mines were still devoted under a special account to the Crusade, as they were under Pius II. If this is so, the income at the pope's disposal decreases by 50,000 florins, and his working margin is thus accurately described by the 'Entrate della chiesa Romana' as about 90,000 florins.

It is of some interest that the *Introitus et Exitus* for the first year of Sixtus IV, from August 1471 to July 1472, records his income as some 218,068 florins.[2] If both the income from the alum mines and a fairly substantial sum to account for that diverted by the pope to his secret treasury are taken to be omitted from this total, then our estimate of the total income as about 290,000 florins seems to gain some support from the actual accounts.

Julius II has the reputation, rightly, of a great consolidator of the temporal and financial power of the papacy. One of his most effective financial measures was the revaluing of the depreciated silver coinage of the papacy, in which many of the spiritual taxes were assessed, and the issue of the new coins later known as *giulii*, a device which in effect raised these taxes in the proportion of $10:13\frac{1}{2}$.[3] The entries in the *Introitus et Exitus* for December 1506 to November 1507 total about 130,567

---

[1] Cf. *The Papal State under Martin V*, pp. 138-40.

[2] Calculated from Gottlob, *Aus der Camera apostolica*, p. 262.

[3] E. Martinori, *Annali della Zecca di Roma* (1918), pp. 45-6, 73-4; von Hofmann, *Forschungen*, i, 287-8; A. Schulte, *Die Fugger in Rom* (1904), i, 10. Cf. E. Albèri, *Relazioni degli Ambasciatori Veneti al Senato*, 2nd ser., iii (1846), 33-4. 'Dove soleano pagare il censo carlini dieci al ducato (perchè la Chiesa era ingannata, che vale carlini tredici e mezzo al ducato) vuole che paghino quello che corre il carlino; e ha fatto una nuova stampa che vale dieci al ducato; e son buoni, di argento; dal che ammigliora da dieci a tredici e mezzo la entrata del papato. . . .'

ducats,[1] but for the reasons already put forward this cannot be taken as a very reliable guide to Julius II's real income. The report of the Venetian ambassador that the pope's ordinary income in 1510 was said to be 200,000 ducats, and extraordinary 150,000 ducats, is too general to be taken very seriously.[2]

For the pontificate of Leo X there is little material on the financial balance in print, save the reports of the Venetian ambassadors. And these can be extremely misleading. Marino Giorgi, ambassador in 1517, reported a total papal income of 420,000 ducats (though the figures he gives add up in fact to 440,000).[3] But he is certainly misinformed: he gives the yield of the indirect taxes (excluding the salt monopoly) of Rome as 100,000 ducats when it was not more than 60,000; his statement that the pope may have 60,000 ducats from each of the provinces of Romagna, the March of Ancona and Spoleto is evidently absurd if it is confronted with the figures current at earlier and later dates. On the other hand he omits entirely certain of the most important revenues such as those from the sale of offices. On balance, Giorgi's report carries little or no conviction. Two letters from the Venetian ambassador Gradenigo at the time of Leo X's death in 1521 report the total expenditure of Leo's pontificate variously as 4,900,000 and 5,050,000 ducats, which would give Leo an annual expenditure of some 580,000 or 590,000 ducats, though leaving him considerably in debt.[4] I know of no data which confirm or contradict this story.

From the pontificate of Clement VII we have a document which gives us a detailed and interesting picture of papal finances at a stage when the evolution from late medieval to Renaissance practice was virtually complete. Preserved in the Vatican archives next door to the 'budget' of Sixtus IV is a similar document of 1525, in which *si farà brevemente nota di tutte l'intrate della Sede Apostolica membro per membro.*[5]

---

[1] Calculated from Gottlob, *Aus der Camera apostolica*, pp. 264–5.

[2] E. Albèri, *Relazioni degli Ambasciatori Veneti*, 2nd ser., iii, 33.

[3] Ibid., pp. 53–4. [4] M. Sanuto, *Diario*, xxxii, 230, 262.

[5] Vatican Archives, Arm. 37, vol. 27, fos. 591–632. Some sections of this

In the forty-five years which separate this budget from that of Sixtus IV the financial system of the papacy has been radically changed by the expansion of the system of venal offices. As has already been remarked, the total capital invested in these offices was in the region of two and a half million gold florins; the total interest about 300,000 gold florins. Stimulated by the system of venal offices, the incomes of most of the papal officials had more or less doubled between 1500 and 1514.[1] But the taxes which they drew from supplicants in the Roman Court still did not suffice to pay these officials, particularly the new 'colleges' of offices which had been created as financial speculations. The pope was forced to assign for the payment of these and of other offices very large sums, both from the Papal State and from the spiritual revenues; of the last, most of the income from annates and common services, in particular, was assigned for the payment of various officials. Of the revenues shown in this budget about 96,000 florins are shown as assigned from the temporal revenues for the payment of officials and 40,000 from the spiritual revenues.[2] Thus rather under half the interest on what may be described as the funded debt of the papacy was paid from the assigned revenues of the pope, and the rest from the taxes of those who frequented the Roman Court.

To come to the detailed examination of this budget, the 'Spiritual' revenues will be examined first. These are in every respect higher than under Sixtus IV. The annates and common services, which under Sixtus were variously assessed at 40,000 ducats and 60,000 (I have taken the lower figure in my total above), are under Clement estimated at 50,000 ducats. The *servitia minuta* I omit, since they are not included in the Sixtus IV budgets, and in both pontificates were assigned to the payment of

document are printed in the Appendix below. I am grateful to Mons. H. Hoberg, Vice-Prefect of the Archives, for his kindness in checking a doubtful point in the microfilm.

[1] Von Hofmann, *Forschungen*, i, 284.

[2] Calculated after the budget of 1525. Von Hofmann, *Forschungen*, i, 289, puts the amount assigned from the Papal State at 110,000 ducats.

various officials.[1] The Datary, which in the earlier period is reckoned at 40,000 ducats (compositions, venal offices, indulgences) is here reckoned to have reached 144,000 ducats in the time of Leo X.[2] To this has to be added the *decime degli offici*, a tax imposed only occasionally on officials of the Roman Court at the early period, but here shown as if permanent, and reckoned at 18,000 ducats. The 'spiritual' revenues therefore total about 212,000 ducats, as against 120,000 in 1480.

The comparison of the temporal revenues is of equal interest. The most striking difference between the two budgets is the revenue anticipated from the city and district of Rome. Under Sixtus IV the three great indirect taxes of Rome, the *dohana di Ripa*, *dohana di merce*, and the *dohana della grascia* are estimated, together with the income from the taxes imposed at the gates of Rome, to yield an income of about 36,000 ducats.[3] Under Clement VII the same taxes are estimated at about 60,000 ducats, and to this must be added the loans issued on the proceeds of the *dohana di Ripa*, the *dua per cento di Ripa*, which are valued at 6,500 ducats. The income from the salt monopoly of Rome and the Roman District is calculated in 1480 at 27,500 ducats;[4] in 1525 at 30,456. The March of Ancona evidently did not share this rising commercial prosperity of Rome; save for Ancona it was an agricultural province, and Ancona was at this period hard put even to maintain its contribution to the Apostolic Chamber.[5] The total income from the March, including the salt monopoly and the district of Ascoli, is shown in the early budget as about 28,000 ducats and in 1525 at 31,300 ducats.[6] Umbria and the Patrimony of St. Peter in Tuscia are also more or less static; the earlier

---

[1] Cf. von Hofmann, *Forschungen*, i, 280, and Goeller, 'Inventar des Finanzarchivs der Renaisaancepäpste', *Miscellanea Ehrle*, v, 243–4.

[2] This does not seem too high; cf. von Hofmann, *Forschungen*, i, 98–9.

[3] Bauer, 'Studi per la storia delle finanze papali', p. 341.

[4] Ibid. For the 1525 figures, see the extracts printed in the Appendix below.

[5] R. Roia, 'L'amministrazione finanziaria del comune di Ancona nel secolo XV', *Atti e memorie della R. Deputazione di Storia Patria per le Marche*, 4th ser., i (1924), 142–6, 210–14.

[6] Bauer, loc. cit.

estimates, including Perugia, the Patrimony, Rieti, Città di Castello, and the transhumance dues handled by the *dogana dei pascoli* of the Patrimony, are reckoned at between 20,000 and 27,000 ducats;[1] the 1525 estimates for the same revenues total 26,900 ducats. Romagna is represented in the earlier period only by the 4,000 ducats from the wine tax of Bologna which the commune, quasi-autonomous under the Bentivoglio family, was bound to pay, besides about 1,600 ducats from the province of Romagna.[2] In 1525, with both Bologna and the independent *signori* of the province all subdued, the province of Romagna is estimated to yield about 8,700 ducats. The virtual extinction of the *signori* by Alexander VI and Julius II, however, meant that only Urbino, Ferrara and Senigaglia remained among the apostolic vicariates owing *census* to the Holy See; the total of 10,000 ducats due under this head in 1480 therefore goes down to 1,700 ducats in 1525. This was a gain and not a loss to the Papacy, for the irregularly paid *census* of these unruly Renaissance tyrants was a small asset compared to the amounts extracted by papal governors from the lands *immediate subjectae*.[3] Modena and Piacenza, which were not acquired by the Holy See until the second decade of the sixteenth century, are shown as yielding a profit of about 26,000 ducats.[4] The new province of Maremma, non-existent in 1480 and carved out from the old province of Marittima and the coastal area (previously part of the Patrimony of St. Peter in Tuscia) up to Civitavecchia north of Rome, in 1525, was expected to yield rather more than 3,500 ducats. Campagna, which previously made a loss, is in 1525 expected to provide 500 ducats, and Benevento, the papal enclave in the

---

[1] Ibid. I have lumped these revenues together in order to compare them with the revenues of 1525, which were farmed under a single contract by a group of bankers, notably Pietro del Bene and the Genovese firm of Sauli.

[2] Bauer, 'Studi per la storia delle finanze papali', pp. 343, 349, 390, 392.

[3] Cf. *The Papal State under Martin V*, p. 390.

[4] Modena had been governed by the historian, Francesco Guicciardini. For the financial aspects of his administration there and in the Romagna, see A. Oţetea, *François Guichardin* (1926), pp. 123-33; *Carteggio di Francesco Guicciardini*, v (ed. P. G. Ricci, 1954), 89, 133.

Kingdom of Naples, which formerly no more than covered its expenses, is said to provide 1,600 ducats. The alum mines appear in the sixteenth century to be in decline; having rendered 50,000 ducats under Sixtus IV and yet more under his predecessors, in 1525 they are farmed for only 18,750 ducats.[1]

Some of the entries on the budget of 1525 do not seem to correspond very closely with political realities. Reggio, which is shown with revenue of 4,500 ducats, was not at this time in the possession of the Holy See. Nor, in the then unsettled condition of Italy, does the item of 7,000 ducats *census* for the Kingdom of Naples seem likely to correspond with anything in the account books.[2] Disregarding these somewhat speculative entries, and including one or two odd items such as the *nole* and the proceeds of certain detached towns such as Narni and Rieti, the total revenue from the temporal power shown in the 1525 budget appears to be in the neighbourhood of 220,000 ducats, made up of 98,000 ducats from Rome and the District, 18,750 ducats from the alum mines, and 103,500 ducats from the rest of the Papal State. The comparable figures from 1480 are: Rome and the District, 64,000 ducats; alum mines, 50,000 ducats; rest of Papal State, 67,000 ducats—total, 181,000 ducats. Turning to the totals of spiritual and temporal income, the figure for Sixtus IV in 1480-1 has already been given as about 290,000 ducats. The total income of Clement VII in 1525 appears to have been in the neighbourhood of 432,000 ducats, made up of 220,000 ducats from the temporal power and 212,000 ducats from the spiritual power.[3] It has to be noted that over 140,000 ducats, or 32 per cent of the revenue of Clement VII, were earmarked for payment of interest on the papal debt, under the form of salaries for officials.

[1] Cf. Bauer, 'Studi per la storia delle finanze papali', pp. 332, 340; Gottlob, *Aus der Camera apostolica*, pp. 278 f.

[2] For Reggio see Guicciardini, *Storia d'Italia*, iv (1929), 199-200; Pastor, *History of the Popes*, ix, 277 f. It is noticeable that the *census* of the Kingdom of Naples is left blank in the budget of Sixtus IV (Bauer, 'Studi per la storia delle finanze papali', p. 389).

[3] My total appears to agree with that of Bauer, 'Die Epochen der Papstfinanz', *Historische Zeitschrift*, Bd. 138 (1928), 477.

This interest payment, however, is exactly offset by the income of 144,000 ducats from the Datary—although this, in so far as half of it is drawn from the sale of offices, consists of new borrowing rather than of true income.

It may be objected to these 'budgets' that they are, as has already been said above, anticipatory, and that they may be far from corresponding with the real state of papal receipts. This is a powerful argument, and one which is not to be disregarded, particularly in so far as it concerns the revenues of the Papal State. If earlier fifteenth-century experience is any indication, the papal officials found the utmost difficulty in collecting from the provincials more than a fraction of the amounts due from them. If Martin V in the third decade of the century found difficulty in collecting more than a third of the *tallia militum* or subsidy due from his subjects,[1] it is hard to believe that by the ninth decade Sixtus IV was without difficulty exacting every penny, although it may be freely allowed that the Papal State made great strides forward in efficiency and centralization during this period. Difficult though it may be to believe, the official in the Chamber who made out the budget of 1480–1 seems to be making this claim when he writes that through 'negligence and disorders' 350 florins of the *census* due from the March of Ancona and 100 florins of the *affictus* remain unpaid, and that he enters this as a debit.[2] It is noteworthy that far into the sixteenth century a President of Romagna could write that 30,000 *scudi* of arrears of taxes remain to be collected there.[3]

On the other hand, it is possible to ascertain that some of the estimates in these 'budgets' are not far wide of the mark. For example, the estimate of the gross income of the Patrimony of St.

[1] *The Papal State under Martin V*, p. 116.

[2] Bauer, 'Studi per la storia delle finanze papali', p. 389. 'Censi de la Marcha per negligentia et disordini sonno mancati circa Duc. 350 di quello glio fatti debitori.' Similarly for the *afficti*.

[3] *Opere di Monsignor Giovanni Guidiccioni* (ed. C. Minutoli, 1867), ii, no. 191, p. 365. 'Qui v'è da riscuotere per la Camera per più di XXX mila scudi, e dove io doverei esser sollecitato per l'esazione, come per altra ho scritto, ho da sollecitare altri.'

Peter in Tuscia in the budget of 1480-1, when set beside the figures of the actual revenue in the account books, is seen to be rather low. Since the expenditure is also underestimated, how, ever, the figure of 3,500 ducats net profit under this head given in the *entrate ordinarie* . . . *secundo il comune uso* is more or less accurate, though still perhaps rather low.[1] The proceeds of the salt mono, poly of the March of Ancona are known to be correctly estimated at 10,500 florins in the 1480-1 budget, since the monopoly was farmed to a Florentine banking firm in 1485 for exactly that sum.[2] The estimated profit of 5,000-6,000 ducats a year on the city and district of Perugia appears to be constant; it is found in the budgets of Sixtus IV, in the account books of provincial treasurers for 1516-20, and in the budget of 1525.[3]

Other points at which it seems likely that the 'budgets' of Sixtus IV and Clement VII are tolerably accurate are the in, direct taxes of Rome, whose amount could easily be estimated at an average figure from the account books, and all those revenues which were put out to farm. In the case of the 1525 budget the greater part of the temporal revenues seem to be farmed to bankers —not always, one suspects, at a price very advantageous to the papacy. Thus the three *dogane* of Rome were farmed to the Roman firm of Della Valle, the salt monopoly of Rome and the District to another Roman firm, that of Bernardo Bracci, the treasury of Perugia and the *dogana dei pascoli* to Pietro del Bene and the Sauli,

[1] See Bauer, 'Studi per storia delle finanze papali', pp. 342, 349; Gottlob, *Aus der Camera apostolica*, p. 254. The account books of the treasurers of the province are analysed by A. Anzilotti, 'Cenni sulle finanze del Patrimonio di S. Pietro in Tuscia nel secolo XV', *Archivio della R. Società Romana di Storia Patria*, xlii (1919), 349-99, especially at p. 364. The figure of 9,000 ducats for the *dogana dei pascoli* of the Patrimony given in the 1480-1 budget (Bauer, p. 349) is if anything low (see Anzilotti, pp. 373-4; Bauer, p. 341). The estimate of 16,000 ducats in the budget published by Gottlob is too high (*Aus der Camera apostolica*, p. 253).

[2] Gottlob, *Aus der Camera apostolica*, p. 243, 4n.

[3] Bauer, 'Studi per la storia delle finanze papali', pp. 343, 349; Gottlob, *Aus der Camera apostolica*, p. 254; L. Fumi, *Inventario e Spoglio dei registri della Tesoreria Apostolica di Perugia e Umbria* (1901), p. 141; Appendix below. At an earlier date the profits on Perugia seem to have been higher; see *The Papal State under Martin V*, pp. 171-2.

the alum mines of Tolfa to the Chigi of Siena, the treasury of the March of Ancona to Luigi Gaddi, that of Romagna to Giacomo Salviati.

The revenues of the papacy which were most open to variation and which are the most difficult to calculate accurately are the spiritual ones. The most variable of these are the most important— those of the Datary. As the 1525 budget remarks in a characteristic but hardly translatable phrase, these revenues amount to more or less 'according to the exigencies of the moment' (*sono più et meno secondo che si fa facendo*). The most essential factor was the spirit in which the pope and the chief officials of the Roman Court cared to interpret the system. If the pope wished to make wholesale promotions to the College of Cardinals, for example, he could thus ensure that many important offices in the Roman Court would have to be vacated under the rules governing the incompatibility of offices, and these offices would thus return to the Datary for resale.[1] Or if he cared to *alarghare la mano* in conceding matrimonial and other dispensations he could again greatly increase the revenues of the Datary under this head. Leo X, more than any other pope of the period, squeezed the system for every ducat that it was worth, and it is not surprising that later officials of the Roman Court looked back to his pontificate and to that of Clement VII as those of the golden age of officialdom.[2] The annates and common services equally yielded essentially variable income which depended to some extent upon the discretion of the pope.

As has already been suggested, the reports of the Venetian ambassadors provide a check on the reliability of the papal 'budgets' which is only of a limited value. On the other hand, Gradenigo's report on his embassy of 1523, in spite of its being written seven years after the event, is extraordinarily accurate as to the capital invested in the venal offices and the salaries drawn from them,[3] and may perhaps be founded on better information

[1] Von Hofmann, *Forschungen*, i, 175–7.

[2] 'Si res curiae redirent ad illa felicia tempora Leonis X vel Clementis VII . . .' (von Hofmann, *Forschungen*, i, 285, n. 3).

[3] Von Hofmann, *Forschungen*, i, 288–9.

than that of Giorgi. Gradenigo estimated the revenue from the temporal power at 300,000 ducats, the 'spiritual' (i.e. annates, common services, other taxes) at 100,000 ducats, and the 'compositions' (i.e. the Datary) at 100,000 or more. The same total of 500,000 ducats is offered by Marco Foscari in 1526.[1] These are round figures which obviously do not lend themselves to minute analysis, and they seem to be somewhat inflated, but they suggest that the statistics of the budget of 1525 are on the whole conservative ones.

All these reservations having been made, some general conclusions may perhaps be drawn from the figures provided by these 'budgets'. They confirm on the whole the picture drawn by Bauer of a gradual recovery by the papacy from the penury which afflicted it after the period of the Councils. This recovery was based on two factors, on the large and regular income drawn by the popes from a pacified Papal State, and on the increased exploitation through the Datary of compositions and dispensations. Supported by this increasing and more regular income, the pope was able to obtain long-term credit at a reasonable rate through the medium of the sale of offices, through which he was able to borrow money (also through the Datary) at the rate of about 70,000 ducats a year. The payments on the interest of this debt were large, and cost the pope not less than 140,000 ducats annually. But at least the papacy was committed to paying only a part of the interest on the capital which it borrowed; the remainder was paid by those who had to do business with the Roman Court, in the form of the taxes which they paid to its officials.

The chronology of these developments is not yet completely clear, but it is probable that as early as Pius II the Papal State was returning a large and regular income to its owners. By the time of Sixtus IV, although the papacy still had to wait for Cesare Borgia to suppress some of the last families of turbulent *signori*, the Papal State was evidently yielding a return equal to about 63 per cent of the total of papal revenues. The pontificate of Sixtus and those following it saw the rapid development of long-term credit

[1] E. Albèri, *Relazioni degli Ambasciatori Veneti*, 2nd ser., iii, 130, 139.

based on the sale of offices, a system which reached its full development under Leo X. The Papal State continued to be most important in that the payment of interest of the new 'colleges' of offices was largely guaranteed by assignments on temporal revenues. As a proportion of papal income, the temporal revenues probably declined slightly at this period; under Clement VII they represent only a little over half the total. But absolutely they increased, and in so far as they guaranteed the payment on the debt they were the hinge on which the whole financial system turned.

In 1526, the year after the compilation of our 'budget', Clement VII set up the *Monte della Fede*, which marks an important step towards the separation of the public debt of the papacy from the remuneration of its officials.[1] The 'colleges' of offices at last began to be publicly recognized for what they were—simple State loans. The importance of this for the future reform of the papacy can at once be seen; so long as the holders of venal offices had to gain at least a part of their salary from taxes levied in the course of an actual performance of that office, the burden of taxes on those who had business with the Roman Court could never be diminished, since attempts at 'reform' would compromise the return on the investments made by those who had purchased office. The recognition of large classes of office-holders as simple stockholders in the papal debt was essential before papal loans could be clearly distinguished from papal administration, and hence before papal administration could be effectively reformed.

[1] Von Hofmann, *Forschungen*, i, 174 f.

APPENDIX

Vatican Archives, Arm. 37, vol. 27

Fo. 591 a. MDXXV. In questo libro si farà brevemente nota di tutte l'intrate della Sede Apostolica membro per membro, et a l'incontro etiam di ciascun membro si notaráno li esiti, et carichi che sono sopra tali membri. Et anchora si farà nota di tutti li offitii specie per specie, et alla valuta d'essi, et d'onde ciascun habbia li suoi emolumenti; et etiam quali di tali offitii si apparten⸗ gano a dare de la santità del Papa; et quali dal Rmo. Camerlingo; et quali dal Rmo. Vicecancelliere; et quali dal Rmo. Maggior Penitentiere, et quali da ad altre persone.

Fo. 594 a. MDXXV. *Depositario.* Nota di quanto riceue ogn' anno il Depositario della Santità di Papa Clemente VII.

Per il censo del Regno di Napoli ogn' anno per San Pietro d. $\frac{M}{7}$ di camera	d. 7 000
Per il censo di Urbino ogn' anno d. milletrecento di camera	1 300
Per le decime delli offitii d. diciotto mila l'anno	18 000
Per li dieci per cento del' annate ragionasi d. cinquemila l'anno	5 000
Per il censo di Sinigaglia d. cento l'anno	100
Per il censo di Ferrara d. cento l'anno	100
Per il censo di Radicofani che si riservete da Senesi d. xi lib. 4	11 lib. 4
Per il censo di Tiboli d. dugento l'anno	200
	d. 31 711

Fo. 595 a. MDXXV. *Dohanieri delle Tre Dohane di Roma.* Nota di quanto pagano ogn' anno di fitto li Dohanieri delle tre Dohane di Roma, cioè la Dohana delle mercantie, la Dohana di Ripa, et la Dohana delle grascie, lequali al presente tiene Bartholomeo della Valle et compagni et finisce la condotta a dì ultimo di giugno 1526.

Pagano ogn'anno detti dohanieri di tutte le sopradette dohane d.
cinquant' otto mila seicento di camera, cioè   58 600
Nota che nelle dette tre Dohane ui è compresa la Dohanna di
Ripetta di S. Rocco, laquale tiene da detti dohanieri Jacomo
Cambii.

    Fo. 596 a. MDXXV. *Salaria di Roma*. Nota di quanto si
vende ogn' anno la Salaria di Roma.

La detta Salara di Roma al presente è allogata a Bernardo Bracci et
compagni di Roma per ducati trentamila settecento venticinque di
baiocchi 72 novi per ducato, che vengano a essere baiocchi 96
vecchi: che in tutto vagliano duc. trentamila quattrocento
cinquantasei ducati di camera l'anno   30 456

    Fo. 597 a. MDXXV. *Dohana delle Pecore del Patrimonio et
Thesaureria di Perugia*. Appresso nota di quanto rende l'anno la
Dohana delle Pecore del Patrimonio insieme con la Thesaureria
di Perugia.

La detta Dohana del Patrimonio è di presente allogata a Pietro
del Bene et compagni et alli Sauli, et altri Portioneri di detta
Dohana et Thesaureria, per ventiseimila novecento d. di camera
l'anno, et di più le Tasse et minuti quali appartengano alla
Camera Apostolica   26 900
Et per le tasse et minuti si ragiona ogn'anno   d. ......
Nota che li sopradetti dohanieri hano anticipato col disborso di
ventisette mila di d. di camera, li quali s'hanno da ritenere in nove
anni, cioè ogn' anno d. trentamila d'oro di camera, et ritenendo
detti ducati trentamila l'anno mancarebbe loro a questo conto
d'assignamento d. mille quattrocento cinquantanove lib. 13 den.
4 di camera.

    Fo. 598 a. MDXXV. *Luminiera della Tolpha*. La lumiera della
Tolpha l'hanno tenuta, et anchora tengano li heredi di Agostino
Ghisi, della quale pagano l'anno duc. venticinquemila di carlini,
delli quali se n'ha a diffalcare quello che si paga per tener serrati
l'altre lumiere, che sono duc. settemila di carlini in circa, et li
detti Ghisi, essendo il contratto l'hanno a tenere sin' a dì primo di
giugno MDXXV, ma secondo la scritta dice per dodici anni, che
comincian' a dì 14 di maggio, dove ve è differenza 17 dì, nel

qual tempo si trova li Ghisi haver fabricato cantara 4 516 di allumi, et li detti d. venticinquemila di carlini si valutano a d. d'oro di camera diciottomila settecento cinquanta.   d. 18 750

Fo. 599 a. MDXXV. *Thesaureria di Perugia.* Nota di quanto rende l'anno la Thesaureria di Perugia.

La Thesaureria di Perugia l'hanno condotta li Sauli delli dohanieri della Dohana delle pecore del Patrimonio per duc. 5 300, come a l'incontro si dice, et ne rispondeno alli detti dohanieri   d. 5 300

Nota di più membri compresi in detta Thesaureria.

Censo di Città di Castello, paga l'anno d.   100

Dohana di Spoleto, paga l'anno d.   2 800

Salara di Todi, benche la tiene il Rmo. Armellino per l'intrate d'Asisi.

Entrate di Fuligno, d.   630

Fo. 600 a. MDXXV. *Thesauraria della Marca, et Ascoli, et Salara della Marca et Ducato.* Appresso nota dell' entrata delle Thesaurarie et Salare. Le sopradette Thesaurarie et Salare le ha condotte da la Camera Apostolica Luigi Gaddi et compagni; qual condotta dura fin a mezzo settembre 1526, per pagare l'anno come appresso, cioè per la Thesauraria della Marca ogn' anno d. diciasette mila d'oro di camera a Julii dieci per ducato   17 000

Et per la Thesauraria d. mille cinquecento l'anno   1 500

Et per la Salara della Marca et Ducato d. novemila cinquecento di camera l'anno   9 500

Et per l'intrata della Marca di che detti conduttori tengano conto per la camera, si può ragionare ogn' anno d. mille di camera   1 000

Et per la diminutione delle rocche circa d. ottocento l'anno   800

Et per li malefitii che si possano ragionare ogn' anno d. mille cinquecento   1 500

Nota che si trahe del sussidio d'Ascoli d. ottocento d'oro l'anno in circa, il quale è impegnato a Gio. battista da Siena Avvocato Concistoriale per d. 41 000 [?] in circa, et lui si vale di detto sussidio.

Fo. 604 a. MDXXV. *Appresso nota delle dette Thesaurerie et Salaria.* Di tutte l'entrate di Romagna, le quale al presente M. Jacomo Salviati tiene, et dura la condotta sua sino a dì . . . che fu per anni . . . se ne cava ogn' anno d. seimila d'oro di camera che tante ne paga il detto M. Jacomo 6 000

Et più le paghe delli minuti che importano l'anno circa d. duemila settecento 2 700

Et di più se n'ha guadagno li tre quarti di tutto l'avarro che si fa di detta Thesaureria et Salaria, detratto prima di tratta la somma di avarro detto, li detti d. seimila diccamera et del restante, et tre quarti appartengan' alla camera, et il quarto al M. Jacomo, che possano li detti tre quarti montare l'anno d. . . . . .

Sono anchora di più le tre quarti dell' utile della salaria del stato di Ferrara, Mantoa et Milano dandosi il sale, che non sendo guerra o altri impedimenti si può ragionare l'anno circa ventimila d. di camera, li quali di presente si ragionano nulla.

Fo. 606 a. MDXXV. *Annate et Comuni della Chiesa.* Entrate dell' annate et comuni.

L'Annate et Comuni si ragiona che rendino ogn' anno cinquanta mila d. d'oro di camera, ma facendosi diligentia arriverebbano a più di d. sessantamila l'anno, et se n'è visto l'essempio nelli tre percento che tiene Luigi Gaddi delle dette Annate quale rendano d. duomila l'anno: che a questo conto venderebbono dette annate d. sessantaseimila seicento senza le dua terzi, ma si ragiona a buon conto l'anno d. 50 000

Fo. 622 a. MDXXV. *Datario et vacantie d'offitii.* L'entrate del Datario le quale sono le compositioni et vacantie d'offitii, sono più et meno secondo che che si fa facendo, et secondo le compositioni che si fanno, et la qualità d'esse, et si trova che alcun' anno al tempo di Leone, le dette entrate arrivavano alla somma di d. dodici mila il mese d'oro di camera. d. . . . . .

E. H. Gombrich

THE EARLY MEDICI AS PATRONS OF ART: A SURVEY OF PRIMARY SOURCES

Aliud est laudatio, aliud historia. The historian of the Italian Renais-sance does well to remember this distinction which Leonardo Bruni put forward in his defence when a Milanese humanist had criticized his panegyric for having exaggerated the beauty and grandeur of Florence.[1] Exaggeration, *amplificatio*, was a legitimate rhetorical trope.[2] For obvious reasons patronage was a parti-cularly suitable object for these rhetorical exercises. Even our own letters of thanks and 'Collinses' are rarely as accurate as police protocols. These changing forms of praise and flattery are in them-selves an interesting subject of study;[3] but they will not be the concern of this essay. Its aim is *historia* rather than *laudatio*—not, be it said at once, in order to 'debunk' a glorious legend, but rather to see the past, as we want to see it, in human and not in mythical terms.

Nowhere is this need felt more urgently than in the story of the early Medici. We seem to know them so well through countless portrayals, and yet their humanity so easily eludes us. The con-ventional phrases of *laudatio* which were heaped on them ever since their descendants rose to eminence among the princely families

---

[1] Th. Klette, *Beiträge zur Geschichte und Litteratur der italienischen Gelehrten-renaissance*, ii (Greifswald, 1889), 32, after Bruni, Epist. ed. Mehus, lib. vii, ep. iv.

[2] Ernst Robert Curtius, *European Literature and the Latin Middle Ages* (London, 1953).

[3] Cf. my 'Renaissance and Golden Age', *Relazioni presentate al X Congresso Internazionale di Scienze Storiche a Roma*, vii (1955), 304-5, of which I hope to pub-lish an *amplificatio* elsewhere.

of Europe fail to hold their image; and so do the clichés of deni-
gration. We must grope our way back, every time, to the primary
sources, and try to see them as human beings, acting under the
pressure of events, sometimes resisting the image created by their
previous actions and sometimes succumbing to it. Only then,
also, can we see them as patrons.

The Oxford English Dictionary defines a patron as 'one who offers
his influential support to advance the interests of a person, cause,
art, etc. . . . also, in tradesman's language, a regular customer'.
In the image of the Medici which they themselves created and
which was reinforced by nostalgia and propaganda all these
meanings fuse into a glorious vision of beneficent bounty. No
wonder; for patronage was indeed one of the chief instruments of
Medici policy during the century when they had no legal title of
authority. The calendars of their correspondence[1] show that they
were always expected to 'offer their influential support to advance
the interests of a person' and that they can rarely have refused to
intervene on behalf of anybody who might be won over to their
camp. Nobody felt too humble to ask for such intervention.
When Benozzo Gozzoli's apprentice got into trouble for pur-
loining three old bedcloths from a monastery the painter turned
to Lorenzo, who made it all come right.[2] In return these people
might be expected to vote for Medici interests in the innumerable
committees of the guild and city government. We have a letter
from the son of Cennini the goldsmith humbly apologizing to
Lorenzo because for once the vote in the *arte della lana* went against
his patron's wish.[3] Some of his fellow-consuls who were Lorenzo's
supporters were out of town and though he had implored the
meeting not to turn *patronum artis Laurentium* into an enemy he
had failed. *Patronum artis*, of course, means the patron of the guild.
For the writer thought in terms of people and communal institutions. The idea of Lorenzo offering his support to the cause of

---

[1] Marcello del Piazzo, *Protocolli del Carteggio di Lorenzo il Magnifico* (Florence,
1956).   [2] Giovanni Gaye, *Carteggio inedito d'Artisti*, i (Florence, 1839), 209.
[3] Letters from Pietro Cennini to Lorenzo, Archivio Mediceo avanti il Principato, Filza xxxiii, 461 and 766, of September 1476.

'art' as such, which so appealed to later generations, would very probably have left him cold. Indeed, it is doubtful if he could easily have expressed it in his language. The support of studies, of learning, of the Muses was easily understood and the Medici were continually praised for their *largesse* in these causes. But the point is precisely that the Nine Sisters were not then thought of as ex/ tending their tutelage to builders, sculptors and painters.[1] The emergence of a deliberate patronage of 'art', such as Vasari cele/ brates, is impossible without the idea of 'art'. It is this shift of emphasis which has yet to be investigated and which may here be exemplified in the three types of patronage offered by Cosimo, Piero and Lorenzo de' Medici. The material for this interpreta/ tion is familiar. It has been collected by such pioneers as Roscoe, Gaye,[2] Reumont[3] and Eugène Muentz.[4] Moreover, it was recently surveyed in an exemplary fashion by Martin Wacker/ nagel in his book on the *ambiente* of Florentine *Quattrocentro* art.[5] In many places this essay merely follows up and expands his references to see how far they lead towards an interpretation.

When the Medici first appear in their role as patrons their activity still fits completely into the age/old traditions of com/ munal religious life. Towards the end of 1418 the prior and chapter of the church of San Lorenzo applied to the *signoria* for permission to pull down some houses since they desired to enlarge the church.[6] The plan was apparently the prior's and the money was to come from the wealthier members of the parish. Eight of them were to take over the building of one chapel each which would then, of course, have been assigned to them for their family burials and the masses to be read for their dead. It is in this

---

[1] P. O. Kristeller, 'The Modern System of the Arts', *Journal of the History of Ideas*, xii (October 1951), xiii (January 1952).

[2] Op. cit.   [3] Alfred von Reumont, *Lorenzo de' Medici* (Leipzig, 1883).

[4] E. Muentz, *I precursori e propugnatori del Rinascimento* (Florence, 1902).

[5] Martin Wackernagel, *Der Lebensraum des Künstlers in der florentinischen Renais/ sance* (Leipzig, 1938), a book missing from S. Comerino's eminently useful *Bibliografia Medicea* (Florence, 1940).

[6] D. Moreni, *Memorie Storiche dell Ambrosiana Basilica di S. Lorenzo di Firenze* (Florence, 1817); C. v. Fabriczy, *Filippo Brunelleschi* (Stuttgart, 1892).

connection that we hear that Giovanni Bicci de' Medici, the richest man in the quarter, undertook not only to build a chapel but also the sacristy. It was a momentous decision for the history of art, for the design of this part of the building was commissioned from Brunelleschi. At the time of Giovanni's death the sacristy was already vaulted. His son Lorenzo, so it seems, then carried on the support of the scheme in honour of his own patron saint.

Cosimo, Giovanni's elder son, first appears as a patron in a similar collective enterprise. That grand communal scheme, the erection of statues to the patron saints of the Florentine guilds, had in 1419 reached a point where the wealthy guild of the bankers felt it necessary to act.[1] They applied for the niche originally assigned to the bakers, who were short of funds, and having obtained it appointed a small committee of exconsuli who should commission a statue of the bankers' patron, St. Matthew the publican. One of the members of this committee of four was Cosimo de' Medici, who thus had his share in assigning the work to Ghiberti. Once more the money was raised collectively and it is interesting to see that Cosimo was careful to show through the amounts he contributed that he was both aware of his superior wealth and of the need not to flaunt it. Where others contributed two florins he gave four; on another list where others gave up to sixteen he contributed twenty florins.

Accident has preserved for us the record of another pious foundation of the Medici brothers in these early years. Ghiberti mentions in his tax returns of 1427 that he has been commissioned by Cosimo and Lorenzo to make a shrine for the martyrs Hyacinthus, Nemesius and Protus.[2] It is one of the few Medici commissions which is not marked in any way by their emblem or coats of arms, though Vasari tells of an inscription.

Perhaps it was at the same time that Cosimo performed the duties of the local squire in his native Mugello, and saw to the

[1] A. Doren, 'Das Aktenbuch für Ghibertis MatthaeusStatue', *Italienische Forschungen*, i (Berlin, 1904).

[2] R. Krautheimer, *Lorenzo Ghiberti* (Princeton, 1956), Docs. 138 and 151.

restoration of the Franciscan church San Francesco al Bosco, a rather traditional design which is attractive precisely because of its rural simplicity.[1] But it was only after Cosimo's return from exile that his pious donations assumed larger proportions.

The most lively and convincing account of this development can be read in Vespasiano's beautiful memoir of his beloved patron.[2] Vespasiano still knew Cosimo, and though his recollection was certainly coloured by gratitude towards a 'regular customer' his account should still rank as a primary source if it is used with caution. Such caution seems particularly necessary when he describes an event which happened when he was only thirteen years old, as in the following passage which is always quoted by Cosimo's biographers:

'When Cosimo had attended to the temporal affairs of his city, in which matters he was bound to burden his conscience a good deal, as do most of those who govern states and desire to advance beyond others, he realized that he had to turn his thoughts to things devout if God was to forgive him and maintain him in the possession of those temporal goods; for he knew full well that otherwise they could not last. In this connection it appeared to him that he had some money, I do not know from what source, which he had not come by quite cleanly. Desirous of lifting this weight from his shoulders, he conferred with his Holiness Pope Eugene IV who told him . . . to spend ten thousand florins on building.'

It is thus that Vespasiano introduces the story of the foundation, or rather rebuilding, of the monastery of San Marco. It would certainly be in keeping with tradition to expiate a sin in such a way. But Vespasiano's account may still be a mere reconstruction. Particularly his reference to those who 'desire to advance beyond others' may be his addition. There was only one statesman Vespasiano was more fond of than Cosimo and that was Palla Strozzi,

---

[1] Ottavio Morisani, *Michelozzo architetto* (Einaudi, 1951).

[2] Vespasiano de' Bisticci, *Vite di Uomini Illustri*, ed. P. d'Ancona and E. Aeschlimann (Milan, 1951); there is an English translation under the title *The Vespasiano Memoirs* (London, 1926), by W. George and E. Waters.

the earlier patron of learning whom Cosimo had ousted and exiled. No doubt Vespasiano would have liked to feel that Cosimo was troubled in his mind about this act of political revenge. Cosimo's opponents may altogether have liked to read into his pious foundations some guilty feelings for particular crimes. We cannot rule out this motif, but it was hardly the over⁄ riding one. For a pious man, such as Cosimo proved himself, the besetting sin may not have been any particular crime but rather his mode of life. His very riches cried out against him. It was not possible to be a banker without breaking the injunction against usury, whatever technical means of evasion were em⁄ ployed.[1] We know from the correspondence of Francesco Datini, recently brought to life by Iris Origo,[2] how strong were the religious and social antagonisms aroused by the banking business. The only way of escaping the stigma of usury was to seek to 'return it all to the poor', as Domenico di Cambio puts it in a letter to the merchant of Prato.[3]

There is evidence that this is precisely what Cosimo tried to do. In an unpublished letter of condolence to his son Piero he is quoted as frequently saying in jest, 'Only have patience with me, my Lord, and I shall return it all to you.'[4] It must have been a phrase he had heard all too often when his debtors came to ask for a period of grace. That he felt himself God's debtor we also know from Vespasiano, and perhaps in a surprisingly literal sense. This would explain the emphasis on the exact amounts spent on his various foundations which we find in Vespasiano and which the Medici tried to keep before the public mind. Lorenzo de' Medici, as is well known, writes in his *memorial* to his sons:[5]

'I find we have spent a large sum of money from 1434 up to 1471, as appears from an account book covering that period. It

[1] R. de Roover, *The Medici Bank* (Oxford, 1948).

[2] Iris Origo, *The Merchant of Prato* (London, 1957).

[3] Origo, op. cit., p. 149.

[4] In a letter attributed to 'Franciscus cognomento padovanus', preserved in the *zibaldone* of B. Fontius in the Riccardiana, *cod.* 907, fo. 141 f., 'eleganter qui tum deo jocaretur dicere solebat, patientiam domine habe in me et omnia reddam tibi'.

[5] W. Roscoe, *Life of Lorenzo de' Medici*, Appendix XII.

shows an incredible sum, for it amounts to 663,755 florins spent on buildings, charities and taxes, not counting other expenses, nor would I complain about this, for though many a man would like to have even part of that sum in his purse I think it gave great lustre to the state and this money seems to be well spent and I am very satisfied.'

The sum mentioned covers mostly Cosimo's lifetime. Could it be that the account book was concerned with the settling of debts to the Supreme Creditor? That it has nothing direct to do with the patronage of art is clear from the way buildings are lumped to/ gether with charities and even taxes—anything, that is, which did not benefit the owners directly.

It is difficult to be clear about figures of this kind. Vespasiano seems more precise, but he too must have taken his round figures from some *ex parte* statement. Adding up what Cosimo is said to have spent on pious foundations we arrive at 193,000 florins. The family fortune, according to one reckoning, was something over 200,000 florins,[1] and Vespasiano actually states that Cosimo regretted not having started on this activity earlier. He also makes Cosimo chide the builders of San Lorenzo for having managed to spend less than those of the Badia. Even Cosimo's palace is represented by Vespasiano as part of his effort to spend, for all these moneys remained within the economy of the city.

These economic and moral arguments only emphasize the pressures under which Cosimo had to act. We are lucky to have a text which specifically sets out to answer Cosimo's enemies, who were not so soon appeased by pious donations. The last recipient of Cosimo's bounty, Timoteo Maffei of Verona, abbot of the Badia of Fiesole, wrote a little Latin dialogue 'Against the Detractors of Cosimo de Medici's Magnificence'.[2]

The detractor takes his stand on Aristotelian ethics: Magnifi/ cence such as Cosimo's is an excess of liberality and every excess is vicious.

The argument is easily disposed of. In his monasteries

---

[1] Curt S. Gutkind, *Cosimo de' Medici* (Oxford, 1938), p. 196.
[2] Printed in G. Lami, *Deliciae Eruditorum*, xii (Florence, 1743), 150–68.

and churches Cosimo modelled his magnificence on Divine excellence. In his palace he thought of what was due to a city such as Florence, indeed he would have appeared lacking in gratitude to his native city if he had been less sumptuous. The detractor now comes out with a stock complaint, which we also know from other anti-Medicean sources[1]: The Medicean coats of arms which are displayed on all Cosimo's ecclesiastical foundations smack more of thirst for glory than of divine worship. Had not Timoteo himself frequently preached against such worldly aspirations? The charge is admitted with qualifications, but Timoteo takes recourse to the distinctions of moral theology: there are only four conditions under which love of glory becomes a mortal sin, and Cosimo is guilty of none of them. He loves to do good in secret. But let it be granted that he affixes his device to his buildings so that those born after him may remember him in their prayers and that those who see his buildings are inspired to emulate them. What is wrong with such motives? Was not Caesar inflamed to great deeds by paintings of Alexander's exploits? Were not Scipio and Quintus Fabius inspired by the images of their ancestors? Why should not men who now see the churches dedicated to God, the monasteries of Christ's servants, the painted and sculpted images not also strive to make posterity pray for them? Are we not enjoined not to hide our light under a bushel? Let his detractors at length cease!

But the opponent has another bolt *in petto* and it is meant to wound:

'What you have just pronounced at such length in Cosimo's praise will only be in the way of his fame with posterity.' According to the philosophers art means the theoretical knowledge of reasons. Magnificence, however, is (by etymological definition) merely 'the making of large things'. 'Hence posterity will count a magnificent man among the manual labourers, that is among the menial craftsmen.' Timoteo pays a compliment to his adversary for the subtlety of this argument. But he can counter it. You

[1] G. Savonarola, *Prediche Italiane*, ed. R. Palmarocchi (Florence, 1930–35), III, i, p. 391.

must look to the moral motive, for it is virtue which prompts Cosimo to build. Moreover a handy Ciceronian quotation goes to prove that magnificence is a mental disposition. There are many rich men but they love their riches too much to spend them. Cosimo only desires riches to be able to give them away. But the moral argument does not go down too well with the detractor. Magnificence must be a strange kind of virtue since it can only be practised by the rich. Timoteo cannot admit this; it is only the exercise of magnificence which is a gift of fortune; the virtue is inherent in the soul and may be possessed by the poor. The very weakness of this concluding argument which is followed by a conventional eulogy brings home to us the pre-cariousness of Cosimo's moral position in a world of Christian standards which he thoroughly shared. If even his own spiritual advisor could not do better, what could he tell himself in the solitude of his study?

But in a way the dialogue is as interesting for the arguments it omits, as it is for those it uses. There is no mention of art or artists. On the contrary. It is Cosimo himself who is seen as the 'maker' of his buildings—with little thanks for his labours. The coats of arms, the Medici *palle* are his own signature, as it were, through which he wants to be remembered by posterity (Plate 2). There may be more in this argument than we are inclined to con-cede. It is hardly fanciful to feel something of Cosimo's spirit in the buildings he founded, something of his reticence and lucidity, his seriousness and his restraint. To the fifteenth century this would have been obvious. The work of art is the donor's. On Filippo Lippi's 'Coronation of the Virgin' in the Uffizi, we see an angel pointing to a kneeling monk with the words *iste perfecit opus*. It used to be thought that we must here have the self-portrait of the painter, but it is now accepted that the donor must be meant. Of course the situation was slowly changing in Cosimo's own lifetime. Filippo Villani, Alberti and others were busy, as we know, propagating the 'liberal' status of painting. But the art-historian's perspective in these matters is easily dis-torted by his knowledge of a few selected texts which are quoted and requoted. Compared with the mass of writings produced during the early Renaissance, references to the arts are surprisingly scarce. One may search the correspondence of many a humanist without finding a single allusion to any of the artists whom he must have constantly met on the *piazza* and who loom so large in our picture of the period. I know only one humanist writer who includes the names of two artists among Cosimo's beneficiaries, Antonio Benivieni who writes in his *Encomium* that Cosimo 'bestowed both honours and countless rewards on Donatello and Desiderio, two highly renowned sculptors'.[1]

Even Vespasiano, who, after all, belonged to the same class as many artists, rarely finds occasion to refer to an architect, sculptor or painter by name. Niccolò Niccoli is mentioned by him as an expert on the arts and a great friend of Brunelleschi, Donatello, Luca della Robbia and Ghiberti. Cosimo's universality of interests is praised by Vespasiano in similar terms: 'When he had dealings with painters or sculptors he knew a good deal about it and possessed in his home something from the hand of the outstanding masters. He was a great expert on sculpture and much favoured the sculptors and all the worthy artists. He was a great friend to Donatello and to all the painters and sculptors, and since in his time the art of sculpture suffered some lack of employment, Cosimo, to prevent this happening to Donatello, commissioned him to make certain pulpits of bronze for San Lorenzo and made him make certain doors which are in the Sacristy, and gave orders to his bank to allow him a certain sum of money every week, enough for him and his four apprentices, and in this way he kept him. Since Donatello did not dress as Cosimo would have liked him to, Cosimo gave him a red cloak with a hood, and a gown under the cloak, and dressed him all afresh. One morning of a feast day he sent it all to him to make him wear it. He did, once or twice, and then he put it aside and did not want to wear it any more, for it seemed too dandified to him. Cosimo used the same liberality to anybody who possessed some *virtù*, because he loved such people. To turn to architecture: he

[1] *Antonii Benivienii ΕΓΚΩΜΙΟΝ Cosmi*, ed. Renato Piattoli, 1949, p. 56.

was most experienced in it, as can be seen from many buildings he had built, because nothing was built or made without his opinion and judgement being asked; and several who had to build something went to him for his opinion.'

To the art-historian who looks at the *Quattrocento* through the eyes of Vasari this passage raises some puzzles. Why does Vespasiano omit to mention the architect whom we have come to know as Cosimo's right-hand man, Michelozzo, who was said to have accompanied his master into exile and to whose palace design he gave preference over that of Brunelleschi because it was less ostentatious?[1] In his detailed account of Cosimo's building operations Vespasiano speaks a good deal about contractors, fraudulent ones and over-confident ones. But no name of an architect occurs. Nor is Vespasiano alone in this omission. Filarete[2] is equally silent, and so are the various humanist poets in whose panegyrics the foundations of Cosimo are listed.[3]

Apparently nobody questioned the fact that the credit for these buildings, even for their invention, had to go to Cosimo. But there may be an additional reason which is suggested by a study of the documents: Cosimo's intervention in these matters, his contribution to pious foundations, was a much more improvised and piecemeal affair at first than Macchiavelli's or Vasari's accounts make one suspect.

Conflicting as are the accounts of the building history of the monastery of San Marco, they add up to the picture of a gradual extension and renovation of the monastery which had once belonged to the Selvestrini and was then transferred to the Dominican Observants whom Cosimo favoured.[1] This first of the post-exile enterprises grew under Cosimo's hands, as it were, till its growth was abruptly halted through the resistance of

---

[1] Vasari Milanesi, ii. For Vasari's dependence on Vespasiano cf. A. Siebenhüner and L. H. Heidenreich, 'Die Klosterkirche von San Francesco al Bosco', *Mitteilungen des kunsthistorischen Instituts in Florenz*, v (1937–40), 183.

[2] Antonio Averlino Filarete, *Tractat über die Baukunst*, ed. W. von Oettingen (Vienna, 1890).

[3] E.g. Ugolino Verino, B. Fontio, and C. Landino.

the families who owned ancient rights to the chapels of the church and refused to surrender them.[2] This thwarting of Cosimo's more ambitious plans is mentioned by both Filarete and Vespasiano. The inscription of 1442, therefore, may well mark the end of the renovations, though some parts may have been added later. It was in that year, by the way, that Michelozzo reported to the *catasto* that he had been and still was without any employment or income from his trade.[3] Tax declarations are notoriously pessi‑ mistic about incomes, but if Michelozzo had been known at that time to be engaged on a Medicean enterprise as famous as San Marco the official would have laughed in his face.

Cosimo certainly was not the man to rouse antagonism by forcing the owners of rights in San Marco to give up their burial places and the masses to be read there for their dead. But he may have had an additional reason for shifting the centre of his patron‑ age elsewhere. His brother Lorenzo had died in 1440, and the need to care for the rebuilding of the main church of his parish may have been impressed on him. We have the minutes of the meeting of the chapter of San Lorenzo of 1441 in which this intervention is recorded.[4] Reading it in its context it is possible to detect a note of apology. Many members of the chapter might have preferred the original collective arrangement; but it had broken down, and nothing had been done to further the building of the church which had been pulled down in vain more than twenty years before. Cosimo, in his turn, knew that he held a strong hand, and imposed his conditions accordingly. One may hear an echo of his difficulties in San Marco in his stipulations: ' . . . provided the choir and nave of the church, as far as the original main altar, were assigned to him and his sons, together with all the structures so far erected, he would pledge himself to complete that section of the building within six years out of the

---

[1] Morisani, op. cit., p. 90. Walter and Elisabeth Paatz, *Die Kirchen von Florenz*, III, Frankfurt‑am‑Main, 1952, pp. 8 ff.

[2] Vasari Milanesi, ii, 440‑1.

[3] R. G. Mather, 'New Documents on Michelozzo', *The Art Bulletin*, xxiv (1942).

[4] Moreni, op. cit., ii, 346‑7.

fortunes that God had granted him, at his own expense and with his own coats of arms and devices; it being understood that no other coats of arms or devices or tombs should be placed in the aforesaid choir and nave, except those of Cosimo and of members of the Chapter.'

There is no more striking illustration of the difference between the legend created by pragmatic historians and the slow and complex course of real events than a fresco in the Palazzo Vecchio in which the court painter of Duke Cosimo I, Giorgio Vasari, extolled the memory of his patron's collateral ancestor[1] (Plate 5). We see Cosimo, with a magnificent gesture of power, pointing to the building of San Lorenzo, while in front of him kneel two submissive figures presenting the model of the finished church. They are meant to portray Brunelleschi in collaboration with Ghiberti, who is here added for good measure, presumably because Vasari remembered the joint enterprise on the Florentine Cathedral. It is not only the document quoted which belies this dramatic account of a ready plan, speedily executed on Cosimo's command. Cosimo, as we have seen, was too cautious to pledge himself to build the whole church. Moreover such an offer might really have looked like an act of vainglory on the part of a private citizen. Perhaps it was to allay this opposition that Cosimo began with the restoration of the priests' dwellings, if we can trust Vespasiano's account. There would always be some who would want to gain glory by building the church, his biographer makes him say, but they would not see to the utilitarian structures.

To us, of course, as to Vasari, San Lorenzo is the creation of Brunelleschi's mind. But the documents indicate that Cosimo's piecemeal methods considerably restricted the power of the architect. Brunelleschi's anonymous biographer, as is well known, blames a carpenterbuilder for having failed to carry out Brunelleschi's design;[2] but did he really leave a design or a model when he died in 1446? There is a curious document which speaks

[1] Illustrated in C. Gutkind, *Cosimo de' Medici* (Florence, 1940), p. 272.

[2] A. Manetti (attributed to), *Vita di Filippo di Ser Brunelleschi*, ed. E. Toesca (Florence, 1927). Fabriczy, op. cit.

against such an assumption. It tells of jealousies and brawls among the carpenters of Florence who were or wanted to be concerned with the completion of San Lorenzo.[1] One of them, Giovanni di Domenico, complained to Cosimo's son Giovanni because the men of his competitor Antonio Manetti had beaten him up in the street. By the standards of professional conduct he may well have deserved it. He had happened to be present when Cosimo inspected and criticized Manetti's model for the cupola over the crossing. Cosimo wondered whether the choir would get enough light and whether the cupola was not 'two millions of weights too heavy'. Needless to say Domenico agreed with all Cosimo said and ultimately produced a model himself which he evidently claimed to be 'in the manner of Filippo, which is light, strong, well-lit and proportioned'. When warned to mind his own business, he produced the rather flimsy plea that he owed his livelihood to Cosimo and therefore was bound to proffer him advice. He was on his way to Cosimo when his rival's revenge overtook him.

The interpretation of the story hinges on the expression *nel modo di Filippo*. If Brunelleschi's intentions had been known, Domenico would probably have said so. All he claims for his cupola is that it follows Brunelleschi's method which was, no doubt, the method applied on the cathedral. Like his competitor Manetti, Domenico had been working for the opera del Duomo.

Whatever our interpretation, the document confirms Vespasiano's account of Cosimo's practical experience in architectural matters. It also shows that fifteen years after his intervention the problems of the vaulting of San Lorenzo were still undecided. It is perhaps fruitless to speculate about the reasons, but one possibility springs to mind. According to a tradition which is older than Vasari—though we do not know how old—Cosimo had originally commissioned Brunelleschi to design his new palace, but had rejected the model as being too showy.[2] We have seen

[1] Gaye, *Carteggio*, i, 167 ff.
[2] *Il Libro di Antonio Billi*, ed. C. Frey (Berlin, 1892), who attributed the second project to Filarete.

how necessary it was for Cosimo to proceed with caution in any show of magnificence, but for Brunelleschi the rejection may have been a heavy blow. It must have happened early in the forties[1] and in consequence Brunelleschi may well have withdrawn *his* patronage from Cosimo. Was that an additional reason for starting with the priests' houses, if Vespasiano is here correctly informed?

Another utilitarian structure was also erected by Cosimo in the forties: the dormitory of the Novices of Santa Croce.[2] Again the documents are strangely ambiguous. Gaye prints a curious injunction of 1448 forbidding the monks to tamper with the existing building:[3]

'Since it is known that a large, noble and ample dormitory has been built by the commune of Florence in the friars' monastery of S. Croce with rooms and other facilities, since there are also other buildings there, and since the aforesaid friars carry out fresh works every day as they please, piercing walls and breaking doors between two rooms, making and widening windows . . . which detract from the beauty, strength and amplitude of the building.'

Was this a move to preserve Cosimo's plan or to prevent his builder from carrying on? Whatever it was it underlines the difficulties of the architectural historian who will never know how far such arbitrary changes were or could be checked.

This study, of course, is not concerned with these problems of architectural history. It merely aims at throwing into relief the conditions under which Cosimo's architectural patronage operated. This was not a matter of simply commissioning Brunelleschi or Michelozzo to design a church here or a palace there, not even one of merely paying out large sums to contractors. Private patronage on such a scale still had to create its instrument and organization. Vasari makes Michelozzo build Careggi and

---

[1] A. Warburg, 'Der Baubeginn des Palazzo Medici', *Gesammelte Schriften* (Leipzig, 1932).

[2] Venturi, *Storia dell Arte Italiana*, viii (Milan, 1923), 273.

[3] Op. cit., i, 558.

other villas for Cosimo, but these were surely country houses in which improvements were made as occasion arose. The case of the city palace is different, but even here our information is sadly incomplete. What we know as the Palazzo Medici Riccardi can ınly have housed Cosimo for the last four or five years of his life. Where was his palace before and what did it look like?

These may be idle questions; but strangely enough we have a detailed and circumstantial description of Cosimo's palace which nowhere tallies with the building we know. It occurs in a curious panegyrical poem by Giovanni Avogrado[1] who is not, alas, a very reliable witness. According to his execrable elegiacs the building was erected from white marble and soft bitumen

> But the façade is not of marble; what the soft bitumen
> leaves free has stones of three bright colours.
> The top is taken up by shining alabaster,
> the right-hand side by porphyry,
> the left is of the stone which our ancestors called
>   serpentine in the vulgar tongue.[2]

There is so much fantasy in Avogrado's description that one might dismiss it all as mere oratorical exercise, all the more since he lived in distant Vercelli. The only trouble is that awkward words such as 'serpentine' are not usually inserted in humanist pane-gyrics without some pressing need. The red, white and dark green colour scheme fits in well with Florentine traditions. Had Avo-grado seen Cosimo's earlier palace? Was there once a polychrome façade on the present one? Or did he dream it all up?

The question becomes more insistent when we turn to Avo-grado's description of the Badia of Fiesole, Cosimo's last founda-tion.

---

[1] Alberti Advogradii Vercellensis, *De Religione et Magnificentia . . . Cosmi Medicis*, Libri ii. Lami, *Deliciae Eruditorum*, xii (Florence, 1742), 117–49. Lami's version, by the way, is hopelessly corrupt in places, as is Cod. Plut., liv, 10, of the Laurenziana which was his source. I hope, one day, to return to the poem in the light of the correct text offered by Laur. Plut., xxxiv, 46.

[2] Ed. cit., p. 142.

The documents tell us all about its progress from the first bills of 1456 to those of 1460 which indicate that the monastery was being roofed and furnished.[1] In 1462 there is an entry about a coverlet of French wool 'for Cosimo's room' which shows that a retreat was held in readiness for him in the Badia, as tradition also reports of San Marco. In this case there is no doubt that the utilitarian structures preceded the renovation of the church—and since Vespasiano was connected with the equipment of the Badia's library he may have mixed up the two foundations when he reported Cosimo's remark about San Lorenzo.

Filarete, who had met Timoteo da Verona, the prior whose defence of Cosimo's 'Magnificence' was discussed above, is eager to confirm Cosimo's practical bent:[2]

'He told me that the Church has still to be restored, and as far as he gave me to understand it will be very beautiful. In brief, he told me, whenever a distinguished visitor comes to see the place he is first shown those parts which are usually kept out of sight, such as the stables, the poultry run, the laundry, the kitchen, and other workshops.'

Filarete is particularly impressed by the ingenious arrangement of the fish-pond which is surrounded by fruit trees so that the fruit falling into the water feeds the fish—one of the many instances in Filarete's *Trattato* where one wonders about his I.Q.

But if this story is to be taken with a grain of salt, what are we to say of Avogrado's description in which again Timoteo da Verona is addressed? 'You, Timoteo, were the first cause that this pile was erected; your words moved him to overturn mountains.' For in the poet's *amplificatio* the gentle hills of Fiesole turn into 'savage mountains and rocky wilderness'.

But though the prior gave Cosimo the idea it is the patron, again, who is seen as the artist, this time, of course, in a laudatory sense, but all the more explicitly:

'Cosimo, you have followed the example of the skilled [*doctus*] painter who desired eternity for his name. The years of his youth

---

[1] Published by Fabriczy, op. cit., pp. 586 ff.
[2] Op. cit., pp. 676-7.

he spent on learning, and his skill increased with his age. But when he grew old and felt that time was running short, he exclaimed: "Should I not rather create an image drawn from my brain or mind which would secure a long memory to my name?" No sooner said than done. The old man created something worthy of eternal fame. You too while you were young erected youthful buildings.' . . .[1]

Cosimo now 'wants speedy and skilled masters who should erect the church and the house in his manner [*more suo*]. Such a skilled master notes it all down on his papers; he marks the house, here will be the porphyry gates, let there be a wide portico here, and here the first step of a marble stairway. He traces the cloisters, to be so many steps long; in the centre there will be a tree, but it must be a cypress. He wants the cloisters to be vaulted and supported by twin columns, the one to be coloured and the companion of snow-white marble. "Let there be the tailor's workshop here, and there the chapter, here the ward for the sick. Turn round; here I want a cookhouse worthy of a duke." . . .'[2]

The architectural fantasy which follows is hardly of sufficient historical value to deserve analysis in the present context. It only helps to show that geographical distance, like distance in time, furthers *amplificatio* when the theme is as inviting as 'magnificence'. But it will have been observed that the architect is *ille quidem doctus* who merely notes down Cosimo's instructions. No architect's name occurs in the many documents of the Badia; tradition ascribed the plan to Brunelleschi who had been dead ten years when operations began. Handbooks now speak of an 'anonymous follower of Brunelleschi', but may not the style of that simple structure really be called 'in the manner of Cosimo'? Admittedly the church was only brought to a rapid completion after Cosimo's death under Piero, whose name is recorded in its humanist inscription. And yet most of the building breathes the spirit of the man who was deeply concerned, to the end, that his riches should not stand in the way of his salvation, and who stipulated that he wanted to be buried in a wooden coffin (Plate 1).

[1] pp. 130 f.   [2] Op. cit., p. 132.

It is particularly against the foil of his son's own commissions that this character of Cosimo's buildings becomes discernible. From the outset there seems to have been a clear division of labour between Cosimo and his two sons in matters of patronage. The royal art of architecture was Cosimo's preserve, and so, perhaps, was contact with a master of bronze foundry if he was of Donatello's fame and excellence. Painters stood lower in the estimates of the time and Cosimo seems to have left negotiations with painters and decorators to Piero and Giovanni.

Already in 1438, when Piero was only twenty-two years old, it was to him that Domenico Veneziano addressed his well-known letter asking for the commission of the altar painting of San Marco.[1] Perhaps he did not dare to write to Cosimo directly, for even his approach to the young man is extremely humble: 'In my low condition, it is not for me to address your Excellency [*gentiliezza*].' But he knows that both Fra Angelico and Fra Filippo are busy and so he would like to undertake the work, having heard that Cosimo wants something magnificent. He did not get the commission, of course, for Fra Angelico did find the time to paint the first real *sacra conversazione* for the high altar of his monastery.[2] It has been suggested on good evidence that Cosimo and his brother Lorenzo disposed of the previous altar painting by giving it to the Dominicans of Cortona, who thanked them profusely.[3]

A year later Piero was addressed by Filippo Lippi and we learn that Piero had not accepted a panel he had painted.[4] It is a real tear-jerker in the best tradition of begging letters:

'I am one of the poorest monks there are in Florence, that is me, and God has left me with six nieces on my hands, all sick and useless. . . . If you could only send me from your household a little grain and wine which you might sell to me, it would be a great joy and you might debit my account for it. I get tears in my eyes when I think that if I die I can leave it to these poor kids. . . .'

[1] Gaye, op. cit., i, 136.
[2] Ibid., i.
[3] Ibid., i, 140.
[4] Ibid., p. 141.

No wonder, perhaps, that, despite Browning, Cosimo felt he had no time to deal with such artists.

If these two letters happen to tell us of commissions the Medici did not give, we are compensated by a third written to Piero two years later, in 1441, which gives us a first glimpse of his taste. It is written by Matteo de' Pasti, from Venice, and deals with a commission to paint the *Trionfi* by Petrarch, which were destined to become so popular in decorative art[1] (Plate 6):

'I want to tell you that since I arrived in Venice I have learnt something which would be particularly suitable for the work you commissioned me to do, a technique of using powdered gold like any other colour; and I have already begun to paint the triumphs in this way so that they will look different from any-thing you have seen before. The highlights on the foliage are all in gold, and I have embroidered the costume of the little lady in a thousand ways. Now please send me the instructions for the other triumph so that I can go ahead. . . . I have got the instruc-tions for the Triumph of Fame but I do not know if you want the sitting woman in a simple dress or in a cloak as I would like her to be. The rest I know: there are to be four elephants pulling her chariot; but please tell me if you want only young men and ladies in her train or also famous old men.'

De Pasti clearly knew how to appeal to Piero, with his tale of powdered gold and his qualms about including old men in his picture.

We find the same preoccupation with the pleasing and the magnificent in a letter which the Medici agent Fruoxino addressed to Piero's brother Giovanni from Bruges in 1448.[2] Like the preceding document it was a text much beloved of Warburg, who frequently alluded to its content. The agent had obviously been charged with finding sumptuous hangings for the Medici. He had looked round at the Antwerp fair but had found nothing suitable. The only set of tapestries that was very well worked was somewhat too large for the room for which it was required. More-over, it represented the story of Samson which contained a great

[1] *Il Buonarroti*, serie ii, vol. iv (Rome, 1869).   [2] Gaye, op. cit., i, 158.

quantity of dead bodies, which was not what one would like in a room. Another set, with the story of Narcissus, would have been right in the measurements, but he would only have bought it 'if it had been of somewhat richer workmanship'.

For the same year of 1448 we can at last point to a surviving monument which testifies to the same love of splendour: the marble tabernacle over the miraculous crucifix in San Miniato al Monte (Plate 3).[1] The documents show that there was the familiar tug-of-war over the Medici arms: in June 1447 the Guild of the Calimala reports that a 'great citizen' (citadino grande) has offered to build such a tabernacle with great splendour and cost and that permission would be granted provided no other coats of arms were shown except those of the guild. A year later the great citizen had his way. Piero was granted the express permission to add his own coats of arms to those of the guild. It may be characteristic that he did not choose the offensive palle but rather his private impresa, the three feathers and the diamond ring with the device semper. This type of private heraldry was in itself in tune with the taste for chivalrous display which Piero may well have acquired in his contacts with his Burgundian customers.

It was probably in the same year, or soon after, that he commissioned another tabernacle over a miraculous image, this time in SS. Annunciata (Plate 4).[1] Its sumptuous structure, which was no doubt originally gilt, carries the truly astounding inscription Costò fior. 4 mila el marmo solo; the marble alone cost 4,000 florins.[2] This is worthy of remark by those who still believe that this type of announcement was invented by American tycoons. If the general assumption is right, that the two tabernacles were designed for the Medici by Michelozzo, who was also Cosimo's right-hand man, it becomes even clearer how far, in works of these kinds, the patron rather than the artist expressed himself.

There is one more famous instance which allows us to gauge the influence of Piero's taste on a work of art he commissioned: that best-remembered of all monuments to Medicean taste, Gozzoli's frescoes in the Medici chapel. There are three letters by

[1] Morisani, op. cit., p. 94. [2] Wackernagel, op. cit., p. 245.

the artist to Piero from the year 1459.[1] Their tone is very different from the earlier letters quoted. The painter addresses Piero as *Amico mio singholarissimo*, my greatest friend. But the theme is strangely similar to the letter of De Pasti's, who worried about including old men, and the letter of Fruoxino, who had his qualms about dead bodies:

'Yesterday I had a letter from your Magnificence through Ruberto Martegli from which I understand that you think that the serafims I made are out of place. I have only made one in a corner among certain clouds; one sees nothing but the tips of his wings, and he is so well hidden and so covered by clouds that he does not make for deformity at all but rather for beauty. . . . I have made another on the other side of the altar but also hidden in a similar way. Ruberto Martegli has seen them and said that there is no reason to make a fuss about them. Nevertheless, I'll do as you command; two little cloudlets will take them away. . . .'

Once more the letters also report on the quantities of gold and ultramarine needed by the artist, which he hopes to get at a favourable price if only Piero advances him money in time.

We need only compare the famous cavalcade of the three Magi with Gozzoli's earlier works to see how far the influence of the patron extended. One wonders what old Cosimo may have thought of this work of Fra Angelico's favourite pupil. Not that it is lacking in piety. A true appreciation of this aspect of the work has become difficult thanks to a number of unsupported legends which have come to overlay its original meaning in the minds of most visitors to Florence. A French guide-book of the late nineteenth century[2] spread the story that the journey of the Magi represented the arrival of the Emperor and Patriarch of Byzantium in Florence for the Council of Union in 1439 and that the youngest of the three kings was a portrait of young Lorenzo il Magnifico. Always eager to give life and substance to the shadowy events of the past, tourists and even historians have seized on this interpretation without reflecting on its improbability. At the

---

[1] Gaye, op. cit., i, 191-4.
[2] J. Marcotti, *Guide Souvenir de Florence* (Florence, 1888).

time when the chapel was painted the Council of Union was twenty years away. It had of course ended in failure and strictly speaking both the Patriarch and the Emperor, having failed to get ratification for their submission to the pope, were most un/ suitable personages to be represented as saints. To single out one ten/year/old boy, young Lorenzo, as the only member of the family thus portrayed would hardly seem more tactful. Of course there are portraits in Gozzoli's frescoes, but they are where they belong, in the retinue of the eastern kings, where the group of the household devoutly follows the saints, as befits the donors and their friends.

There would be little harm in these wrong identifications if they had not diverted attention so much from both the religious and the historical significance of the chapel. In religious terms it represents a splendid *adeste fideles*: it is holy night and the star is visible on the ceiling. The Magi have started on their various journeys from three/quarters of the world and are converging on Bethlehem, just as we see them on a famous page of the *Très riches heures du Duc de Berry* (Plate 10). We know of mystery plays in Italian cities in which the three kings also made their approach from three sides.[1] The confraternity of the Magi was traditionally favoured by the Medici and there is no reason to think that the sacred episode was ever considered a mere pretext for the por/ trayal of secular people and events.

Historically speaking this misreading has blurred the strong connections between Gozzoli's fresco and one of the most famous works of art of pre/Medicean Florence, Gentile da Fabriano's altarpiece for S. Trinità (Plate 13). There is a strange irony in the fact that the decoration of the Medici chapel thus harks back to a work commissioned by their greatest rival, Palla Strozzi. A com/ parison shows that Gozzoli has taken over whole groups (Plate 14). Moreover, a closer inspection of Gentile's three kings, tradi/ tionally representing the three ages of man, reveals that many of the alleged traits of portraiture including the headgears and crowns[2] (Plates 11, 12) are prefigured in the earlier work.

---

[1] Alessandro d'Ancona, *Origini del Teatro Italiano* (Turin, 1891), I, p. 277.
[2] I am indebted for this observation to Mrs. Stella Pearce/Newton.

It is quite in keeping with what we know of the taste of the rich Florentines after the middle of the century that Piero should have referred Gozzoli to a masterpiece of the late international Gothic style. His generation sought contact with the aristocratic style of living which they knew from their customers in Burgundy and France, and it is for this mode of life that Piero came to enlist the aid of art and artists.

We have a pen portrait of Piero in Filarete's treatise which brings out this atmosphere with particular vividness. Filarete knew that Piero was smitten with arthritis and, so he tells us, he inquired from Nicodemi, the Medicean ambassador in Milan, what such a sick man could do all day, the implication being that all the noble pastimes, such as hunting or war, are barred to him.

'He tells me that Piero takes great pleasure in whiling away his time by having himself carried to his studio . . . there he would look at his books as if they were a pile of gold . . . let us not talk about his readings. One day he may simply want for his pleasure to let his eyes pass along these volumes to while away the time and give recreation to the eye. The next day, then, according to what I am told, he takes out some of the effigies and images of all the Emperors and Worthies of the past, some made of gold, some of silver, some of bronze, of precious stones or of marble and other materials, which are wonderful to behold. Their worth is such that they give the greatest enjoyment and pleasure to the eye. . . .'[1]

It is not often that we can enter, at least in imagination, into the pleasures and joys of a distant past. But what Filarete says of Piero's books can still be translated into visual terms. Many of his volumes which are clearly marked as having been written and illuminated for him, his Cicero, his Plutarch, his Josephus (Plate 9), his Pliny (Plate 7) and his Aristotle (Plate 8), are still in the Laurenziana[2] to 'give recreation to the eye' of those who seek them out. Most of his other treasures, of course, have vanished, but we can follow Filarete for a little when he describes how:

[1] Op. cit., pp. 666 f.
[2] Paolo d'Ancona, *La Miniatura Fiorentina* (Florence, 1914).

'The next day he would look at his jewels and precious stones of which he has a marvellous quantity of great value, some engraved in various ways, some not. He takes great pleasure and delight in looking at those and in discussing their various powers and excellences. The next day, maybe, he inspects his vases of gold and silver and other precious material and praises their noble worth and the skill of the masters who wrought them. All in all when it is a matter of acquiring worthy or strange objects he does not look at the price . . . I am told he has such a wealth and variety of things that if he wanted to look at each of them in turn it would take him a whole month and he could then begin afresh and they would again give him pleasure since a whole month had now past since he saw them last.'[1]

There is a touch of d'Annunzio in this wallowing in gold and precious stones which cannot be free from *amplificatio*. Yet it is hardly an accident that in this passion for gems and coins Piero had a predecessor in the north who is explicitly mentioned by Filarete, the great Duc de Berry, one of the first men of taste to turn the princely treasure into a real collection of precious objects.

In our present context the famous collections of the Medici are of relevance only as rivals to their patronage of art.[2] It is too easily assumed sometimes that the two activities are one. But contemporary and past history knows of many cases in which artists complained about collectors who spent all their money on precious antiques and had nothing to spare for the living. The valuations attached to precious tableware and stones in the inventory of the Medici collection must indeed make one pause. The scribe or notary who drew up this inventory may not have been a great expert, but he must have known the correct order of magnitude. He valued the engraved gems of the Medici collection at between 400 and 1,000 florins each, the Tazza Farnese (Plate 15) even at 10,000 fl. Now the average painting by a master of the rank of Filippino Lippi, Botticelli or Pollaiuolo would range between 50 and 100 florins, and even a huge fresco cycle such as Ghirlandajo's

[1] Op. cit., pp. 668–9.
[2] E. Muentz, *Les Collections des Médicis*, Paris, 1888.

'Story of St. John' in Santa Maria Novella only cost about 1,000 florins.[1]

It is particularly interesting to reflect on these figures when considering the patronage of art of the most famous of the Medici, who is also the most enigmatic, Lorenzo il Magnifico.

Novelists and biographers have made us familiar with the typical rhythm of generations in a powerful family: the old man who made the family fortune or secured it, shrewd, reticent and devout, the son who accepts wealth as a matter of course and knows how to enjoy the fruits, a lover of cultured ease but still a man of the world; and his son in turn, burdened with the heritage of fame and responsibility, dissatisfied with mere wealth, striving restlessly for higher things, a gifted dilettante, perhaps the most interesting of the three characters but also the most elusive.

Elusive Lorenzo certainly was. It was not for nothing that Machiavelli, in his famous character sketch, described him as harbouring two persons—what we today would call a split personality. The contradictions of this fascinating mind have presented a perpetual challenge to his biographers, whether they resisted his charm or succumbed to it. The student of his patronage of art is confronted with the same perplexities. The very name of Lorenzo the Magnificent has come to stand for posterity as the embodiment of princely magnificence; indeed it has all but eclipsed the fame of his ancestors. It comes as a shock of surprise to realize how few works of art there are in existence which can be proved to have been commissioned by Lorenzo.

Historical accident may have played a part here. Lorenzo's principal schemes were apparently concentrated outside Florence and were thus more vulnerable to destruction. Vasari tells us of the splendours of the monastery of San Gallo which was razed to the ground during the siege of Florence. Nothing remains of Lorenzo's country house near Arezzo, the Spedaletto, where Filippino Lippi, Ghirlandajo and Botticelli are recorded to have worked.[2] His

[1] Wackernagel, op. cit., pp. 346 f.

[2] According to the *protocolli* published by Piazza, Lorenzo spent a few weeks in the Spedaletto in September 1487, in July 1489, and again in September 1491.

1. Badia of Fiesole, Interior of the Church

2. Badia of Fiesole, Loggia with the Medici Arms

3. The tabernacle of San Miniato al Monte

4. The tabernacle of SS. Annunciata in Florence

5. Vasari, Cosimo de' Medici receiving the model for San Lorenzo.
Florence, Palazzo Vecchio

6. The Triumph of Fame, from a round chest,
c. 1450. Florence, Uffizi

7. Pliny, Natural History (Florence, Bibl. Laur., Plut. 82, 3)

8. Aristotle, *De Interpretatione*   9. Josephus, *Bellum Iudaicum*
(Florence, Bibl. Laur., Plut. 71, 18 and 66, 8)

10. The Journey of the Magi, from the *Très Riches Heures du Duc de Berry*. Chantilly, Musée Condé

11–12. Benozzo Gozzoli, Details from The Journey of the Magi. Florence, Palazzo Medici-Riccardi

13. Gentile da Fabriano, The Adoration of the Magi.
Florence, Uffizi

14. Benozzo Gozzoli, Detail from The Journey of the Magi.
Florence, Palazzo Medici-Riccardi

15. The 'Tazza Farnese'. Naples, Museo Nazionale

16. Bertoldo di Giovanni, Battle. Florence, Museo Nazionale

**17. Alexander the Great before the Priest of Jerusalem
(Malermi Bible, 1493)**

**18. Michelangelo, Alexander the Great before the Priest of Jerusalem.
Detail from the Sistine Ceiling**

19. The Death of Nicanor (Malermi Bible, 1493)

20. Michelangelo, The Death of Nicanor.
Detail from the Sistine Ceiling.

21. The Chastisement of Heliodorus
(Malermi Bible, 1493)

22. Michelangelo, The Chastisement of Heliodorus.
Detail from the Sistine Ceiling.

23. Alexander the Great before the Priest of Jerusalem
(Malermi Bible, 1490)

24. Alessandro Cesati, Alexander the Great
before the Priest of Jerusalem.
Medal of Paul III.

25. The Death of Nicanor (Malermi Bible, 1490)

26. Michelangelo, The Death of Nicanor
(Damaged version of plate 20)

27. Michelangelo, The Cleansing of the Temple.
Detail from the Sistine Ceiling.

28. Cunego, Copy of the Lost Medallion
from the Sistine Ceiling

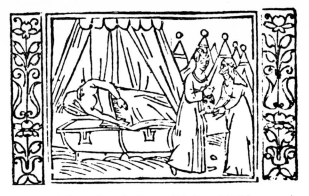

29. Judith and Holofernes (Malermi Bible, 1493)

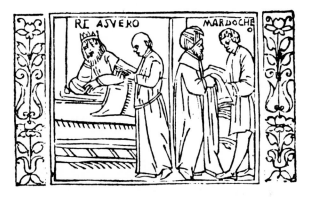

30. Ahasuerus and Mordecai (Malermi Bible, 1493)

31. The Drunkenness of Noah (Malermi Bible, 1493)

32. The astrological and geographical world presented to the future
Henry VII. Paris, BN, ms latin 6276 (*infra*, p. 451)

Original size $5\frac{1}{2}'' \times 6''$

33. In the Temple of Venus Phyzizoa. Woodcut from the
Hypnerotomachia Polifili

34. Three nymphs ('Muses'). Copy of a drawing by Cyriac of
Ancona from a MS in the possession of Professor Bernard Ashmole

35. A monument in Polyandrion. Woodcut from
the *Hypnerotomachia Polifili*

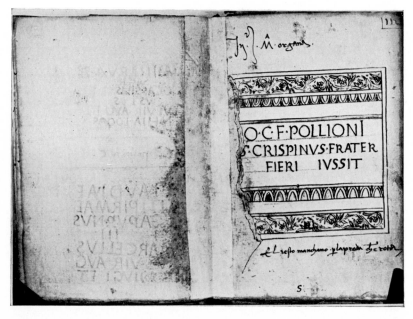

36. Veronese inscription from a manuscript copied by Felice Feliciano
from a lost original by Cyriac of Ancona (Faenza, Bibl. Com. MS 7)

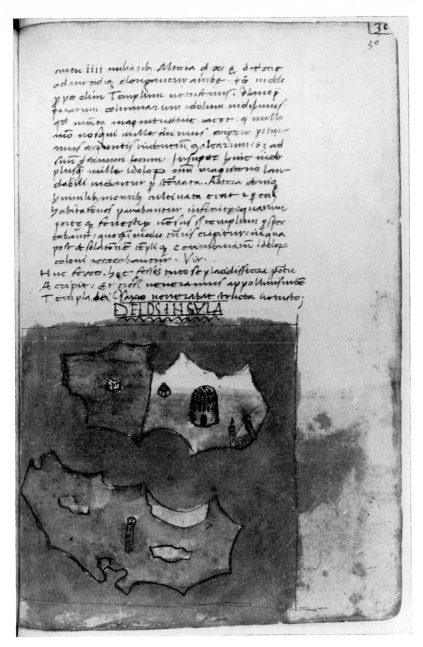

DELOS INSVLA

37. The island of Delos from a manuscript of Cristoforo Buondelmonte's *Liber Insularum* (Oxford, Bodl. Lib. MS Canon. Misc. 280)

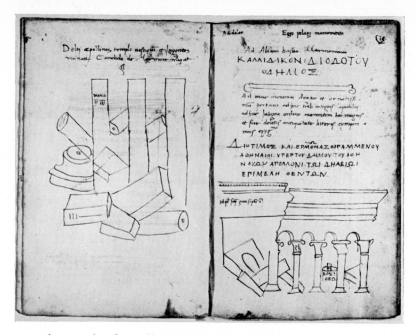

38. The temple of Apollo in Delos. Copy of a drawing by Cyriac of Ancona (MS Vat. Lat. 5252)

39. The theatre at Delos. Copy of a drawing by Cyriac of Ancona (MS Vat. Lat. 5252)

40. The Ruins of Polyandrion. Woodcut from the *Hypnerotomachia Polifili*

favourite country retreat, Poggio a Cajano, was completed and transformed by his successors, and Filippino Lippi's enigmatic fresco in the entrance porch has faded beyond recognition. Per-haps our picture of Lorenzo would have been different if all these works had been preserved; but the historian has to work with such documents as have survived, and these speak a strangely ambiguous language.

The church of the Badia, begun by Cosimo and consecrated under Piero, stood uncompleted, with its medieval façade. It is still in that shape in which Piero left it, for an impassioned appeal by the abbot calling on Lorenzo to do his duty as a patron re-mained unheeded. For all its superficial praise there is a tone of exasperated disapproval in this document which contrasts the vanity of worldly luxury with the eternal benefits Cosimo and Piero acquired by their donations.

'We easily believe and trust that you have long desired the same . . . but we have seen that the times and circumstances stood against your promise. But now when the greatest prosperity favours you . . . set to work and complete our building under a beneficent star and with the aid of our benefactor Jesus Christ.'[1]

The reference to adversities is important. Everybody knew that it was idle to compare the young Lorenzo, struggling at times to preserve his power and mere solvency, with a Cosimo who only worried how to get rid of his surplus cash. It seems in fact that two years after Piero's death Lorenzo decided to close the Account with God which his father and grandfather had kept, for the sum he mentions only covers the period till 1471.

There must have been times when Lorenzo found his family's reputation for unlimited liberality a burden. Yet his position rested on this very fame.

'That enterprise of writing Greek books and the favours you bestow on the learned brings you so much fame and universal good will as no man has enjoyed for many many years',[2] wrote Angelo Poliziano from Venice in 1491. But purely in money terms Greek books were cheap and humanists satisfied with

[1] Roscoe, op. cit., Appendix LXXVI. [2] Ibid., Appendix LI.

small tips. It was different with major works of art, especially with buildings and works of bronze sculpture.

After the exile of the Medici, Verrocchio's brother submitted to the Florentine authorities a list of works which the sculptor had made for the Medici family, implying that he had never been paid and claiming restitution from the confiscated fortunes.[1] The list comprises the tomb of Cosimo and Piero in San Lorenzo, two works for Careggi (probably the 'Boy with the Dolphin' and the 'Relief of the Resurrection'), various works for the *Giostra*, a portrait of Lucrezia Donati and, most surprising of all, the bronze David which Lorenzo and Giuliano had actually resold to the *signoria* in 1475 for 150 florins. Of course it may very well be that the sculptor's brother just tried his luck with the authorities, relying on the fact that no records for payments of this kind were likely to be shown in the Medici ledgers, but at least he must have thought his tale a plausible one.

In whatever way we interpret the document, it seems to indicate that it was not shortage of money alone which accounts for the paucity of documented commissions by Lorenzo. Fastidious men make difficult patrons and Lorenzo had come to think of himself as an arbiter of taste and was so regarded by others.[2]

When the *operai* of S. Jacopo in Pistoia could not make up their minds whether to assign the Forteguerri tomb to Verrocchio or to Piero del Pollaiuolo, they sent the two models to Lorenzo 'since you have a full understanding of such and all other things'.[3] His arbitration was sought in the dispute over the sacristy of S. Spirito,[4] and when the commune assigned an altar panel to Ghirlandajo it was stipulated in 1483 that it should be done 'according to the standards, manner and form as it will seem to and please . . . Lorenzo'.[5]

---

[1] The document is reprinted in M. Cruttwell, *Verrocchio* (London, 1904), pp. 242 f.

[2] For the following examples cf. Wackernagel, op. cit., p. 268, Alfred von Reumont, *Lorenzo de' Medici* (Leipzig, 1883), pp. 136 ff.

[3] Gaye, op. cit., i, 256 f.

[4] Ibid., ii, 450.   [5] Vas. Mil., iii, 270 n.

It was to him that foreign patrons turned for advice and recommendations. He sent Filippino Lippi to Rome,[1] and probably Antonio Pollaiuolo to Milan.[2] He was proud to have recommended Giuliano da Majano to the Duke of Calabria and made it his business to look for a successor after Giuliano had died.[3]

He certainly showed an interest, unique in a layman of the day, in the great architectural achievements of his age. In 1481 he asked for the plans of the Palazzo Ducale in Urbino,[4] in 1485 he requested designs of Alberti's San Sebastiano in Mantua.[5] He was reluctant to lend the Duke of Ferrara Alberti's treatise on architecture since this was a book in which he frequently read.[6]

This interest in architecture, we have seen, he inherited from his grandfather Cosimo. But by now it has taken a more theo-retical turn. There is a subtle but important difference between the terms in which Vespasiano had praised Cosimo's expertise and those of Filippo Redditi in his eulogy of Lorenzo dedicated to the younger Piero:

'How greatly he excels in architecture! In both private and public buildings we all make use of his inventions and his harmonies. For he has adorned and perfected the theory of archi-tecture with the highest reasons of geometry, so that he takes no mean place among the illustrious geometricians of our age; geometry being surely worthy of a prince since our minds and intellects are moved and affected by its power.'[7]

Valori enlarges on this praise and tells of 'many' who built 'many majestic structures' according to Lorenzo's advice. In particular he singles out the Palazzo Strozzi built by Filippo Strozzi who consulted Lorenzo about its proportions (de modulo).[8]

[1] Ibid., iii, 469.
[2] L. Ettlinger, 'Pollaiuolo's Tomb of Pope Sixtus IV', *Journal of the Warburg and Courtauld Institutes*, xvi (1953), 249, 258.
[3] Gaye, op. cit., i, 300.   [4] Ibid., i, 274.   [5] Ibid., i.
[6] E. Armstrong, *Lorenzo de' Medici*, London, 1896, p. 393.
[7] Lami, ed. cit., xii, 198.
[8] Roscoe, op. cit., ch. ix.

It was perhaps to counter this claim that Filippo's son circulated his own version of how his father had managed to have his proud palace built under the nose of the Medici by exploiting Lorenzo's weakness, if weakness it was. Filippo Strozzi, we read,[1] was more desirous of fame than fortune, and being fond of building hoped to leave as a memorial to his name a magnificent palace. But there was one difficulty: 'He who ruled' might envy him this fame. But Filippo was a Florentine and knew how to handle those in power. Instead of concealing his project he talked it over with one craftsman after another, always objecting to their ambitious designs that he wanted utility, not pomp. He was told 'that "he who ruled" desired the city to be adorned and exalted in every way, for just as the good and the bad depended on him so the beautiful and ugly should also be attributed to him'. In other words, Lorenzo wanted control of the building. The bait had worked. He wanted to see the plans and advised an imposing rustic façade. Filippo feigned objections. Such a show would not befit a private citizen. He had rather intended to have many shops and stalls for subletting on the ground floor to earn some extra money. He allowed himself reluctantly to be dissuaded from such a mean practice and agreed to build the very palace he had always hoped to build.

There was not much love lost between the Medici and the Strozzi and the story need not be quite fair. But there is one piece of evidence for the high opinion which Lorenzo had of his own architectural knowledge which cannot be gainsaid: he submitted his own design for the façade of the Florentine Cathedral in 1491. The resulting situation cannot have been without its humorous aspects.[2] There were twenty-nine entries for the competition, bearing such names as Filippino Lippi, Verrocchio, Perugino, Botticelli and Ghirlandajo. But once more their great diplomatic tradition did not let down the Florentines. They chose a perfect gambit and asked Lorenzo himself to decide which design was the best. Lorenzo in his turn was not so easily outmanœuvred. He praised them all, and advised the matter to be adjourned,

[1] Gaye, op. cit., i, 354 ff.   [2] Reumont, op. cit., p. 146.

hoping, no doubt, that the hint would be taken. It looked like a stalemate, and we know that the cathedral had to remain without a façade for another three hundred and fifty years.

Whatever may be the true explanation of this episode, Lorenzo does not emerge from it as the type of patron we got to know in Cosimo and even Piero. We have come to suspect that such moneys as he had to spend on art went into the buying of precious antique gems. Lorenzo certainly knew their value in social life; when Giovanni, the future Leo X, went to Rome as the youngest cardinal Lorenzo wrote to him: 'A man of your kind should use silk and jewellery with discretion. Rather have some exquisite antique and beautiful books. [*Qualche gentilezza di cose antiche.*]'[1]

Such passion could not but influence Lorenzo's attitude towards the artists of his time. Like so many collectors he looked with a certain nostalgia towards the past. He went out of his way to honour the memory of artists, he erected the monuments for Giotto and for Filippo Lippi.[2] But he may have seen his role as a patron not as that of a 'regular customer' but—perhaps for the first time in history—as one who offers his influential support to advance the interest not of individual artists but what he considered the interests of art as such. It has been suggested, for instance, that he deliberately thought to revive the traditional mosaic technique which was to be applied in the Florentine Cathedral.[3] His patronage of the difficult art of cutting precious stones is even more tangible: in 1477 Pietro di Neri Razzati was exempted from taxation on condition that he taught this lost craft to the youth of the town.[4]

This scanty evidence gains substance and meaning through the work of the one artist whom we know to have been in close touch with Lorenzo, Bertoldo di Giovanni. It was Wilhelm von Bode who first suggested that the *œuvre* of this master of small bronzes

[1] Roscoe, op. cit., Appendix LXVI.
[2] Wackernagel, op. cit., p. 268.
[3] W. Haftmann, 'Ein Mosaik der Ghirlandajo-Werkstatt aus dem Besitz des Lorenzo Magnifico', *Mitteilungen des kunsthist. Institutes in Florenz*, vi (1940-1).
[4] E. Kris, *Meister und Meisterwerke der Steinschneidekunst* (Vienna, 1929).

reflected what he called Lorenzo's 'artistic policy'.[1] Bertoldo lived in the Medici palace, perhaps as a kind of valet de chambre; we have a letter from him which is crammed with unintelligible allusions to cookery (or is it to the fear of poisoning?); he formed part of Lorenzo's retinue on a trip to the baths and when he was ill Lorenzo wrote for the doctor.[2]

It may be hard for us to realize the novelty of Bertoldo's *œuvre*. As far as we know he did not work on traditional commissions for churches or monuments. His art is concentrated on collectors' pieces; indeed, in a certain sense it may be called the birth of art for art's sake. Among his works listed as part of the Medici collection the most startling, from an historical point of view, is the famous bronze relief of a battle which repeats and completes a Roman relief from Pisa (Plate 16). As far as we know it has no subject, it does not illustrate a religious or moral tale. It is just 'a' battle *all' antica*, an evocation of ancient art. If Lorenzo was bent on reviving this concept of art which he had absorbed from his readings of classical authors and his contemplation of Greek and Roman works he would indeed have little use for the masters of his time who were steeped in the traditions of the guilds and the church. His patronage had to differ from that of Cosimo or Piero, who accepted the artistic world in which they lived.

Tradition, of course, connects Bertoldo and Lorenzo with precisely such an enterprise; that school for artists which Lorenzo is said to have founded in his gardens. Alas, these famous gardens have proved as elusive as their owner. We do not know where they were or what they contained. No contemporary record mentions the school of which Vasari was to make so much.[3] What is more, the circumstantial account of Michelangelo's transfer to that school in Vasari's first edition was challenged by the aged master who told Condivi merely of having been taken to the Medici

---

[1] W. von Bode, *Bertoldo und Lorenzo dei Medici* (Freiburg, 1925).

[2] Piazza, op. cit., p. 480.

[3] A. Chastel, 'Vasari et la Légende Medicéenne', *Studi Vasariani* (Florence, 1952), a paper which, as the author kindly acknowledges, partly arose out of a conversation in which I had voiced my suspicions of Vasari's account.

gardens by Granacci. Bertoldo is not mentioned, instead we are told most plausibly that 'the Magnificent Lorenzo was having some marble worked and dressed in that place to ornament the most noble library that he and his ancestors had gathered together . . . now these marbles being worked . . . Michelangelo begged a piece from the masters and borrowed chisels from them.'[1] Condivi's account continues with the famous story of how Lorenzo found Michelangelo copying an antique Faun. It was too good a story for Vasari to be missed, who worked it splendidly into his second edition, making Lorenzo inspect the school and noticing the promising pupil.

Once more reality may have been less tidy, less planned and less dramatic than the legend that lives on. But however hard it may be for the historian to grope his way through the *amplificatio* of rhetoric exaggerations there is one solid fact which proves that the seeds of a new kind and conception of art were in fact planted in Lorenzo's garden. It was Michelangelo who first challenged antiquity on her own ground; his unrealized visions of a new race of marble, his contempt for the art of painting and his rebellion against the servitude of ecclesiastical commissions reflect a new attitude which he may well have absorbed in Lorenzo's aura. If that interpretation could be substantiated *historia* might prove even more interesting than conventional *laudatio*.

[1] A. Condivi, *Vita di Michelangiolo* (ed. Maraini) (Florence, 1927).

Edgar Wind

MACCABEAN HISTORIES
IN THE SISTINE CEILING

A Note on Michelangelo's Use of the Malermi Bible

Among the ten bronze medallions which decorate the cornice of
the Sistine Ceiling, the image above the Cumaean Sibyl represents a solemn act of royal submission: a priest receives the homage
of a kneeling king, behind whom one sees a soldier and a horse
(Pl. 18). The subject, at the suggestion of Ernst Steinmann, has
generally been called 'David before Nathan',[1] but this title cannot
be right. In the first place, David did not come to Nathan mar-
tially attended, nor did Nathan receive him in pontifical splendour.
On the contrary, it was Nathan who was sent by the Lord to
David (2 Samuel xii, 1), and to judge by the awful message he
delivered, one would not assume that he spoke to him before
many witnesses; the text does not mention any. Furthermore,
Nathan was a prophet, but not a priest. The Bible clearly and
repeatedly distinguishes between 'Zadok the priest and Nathan
the prophet' (1 Kings i, 34, 38, 44, etc.), a distinction not likely
to be overlooked in a papal chapel.

[1] E. Steinmann, *Die Sixtinische Kapelle*, ii (1905), 261-72, the only serious study
of the medallions. Steinmann, whose results have been accepted by Thode, Tolnay,
and many others, relied too much on Vasari's statement that the subjects are 'taken
from the Books of Kings', in which the Books of Samuel were traditionally included (*Vite*, ed. Milanesi, vii, 180). As so often with Vasari, the statement is half-
true: it applies to five of the ten medallions (see below, pp. 319 ff.). Steinmann
noticed that the *Sacrifice of Isaac*, in the medallion above the Libyan Sibyl, could
not be reconciled with Vasari's description. Nevertheless, he followed Vasari
for the rest of the series and drew all his titles from Samuel and Kings.

The scene can be identified with the help of the *Biblia vulgare* of Niccolò Malermi, first published with illustrations in 1490, and reprinted in 1493 with new illustrations.[1] For Italian readers of Michelangelo's generation it was the most handy Bible in the vernacular. In the edition of 1493, a woodcut illustrating the first book of Maccabees shows the same configuration as Michelangelo's tondo: a king is kneeling before a priest, with other figures in attendance; and again a horse appears in the background (Pl. 17). The text describes how Alexander the Great, on approaching the City of Jerusalem, was so overawed by the apparition of the high-priest, whom he beheld splendidly attired 'in pontifical robes', that he descended from his horse and knelt down before him, to the amazement of his retinue.

It would be in vain to look for this episode in any Bible but Malermi's: for it was an interpolation by the translator. In the original, and also in the Vulgate, the first Book of Maccabees refers to the conquests of Alexander the Great only in general terms, and does not mention his reverence for the priest of Jeru-salem. Malermi had read that story in Petrus Comestor's *Historia Scholastica*,[2] where it is borrowed from Josephus,[3] and Malermi took the liberty, as he explains in the Preface, of inserting it into the first chapter of Maccabees, for the purpose of edifying the nations:

'And as mention is made, at the beginning of the first book of Maccabees, of Alexander, son of Philip, king of Macedonia, we shall, *a consolatione dele genti*, give a more extensive account than is contained in that passage, but without presuming to introduce anything which is not already reported by authentic historical authors. . . . By referring to the Master of the Histories [i.e. Petrus Comestor] for the matter succinctly and shortly des-cribed in the canon, we shall expand the latter by a small, more fully documented addition, but without contradicting the literal sense, or departing from the letter itself.'

---

[1] *Gesamtkatalog der Wiegendrucke*, nos. 4317 and 4319. Six unillustrated editions had already appeared between 1471 and 1487; ibid., nos. 4311-16.

[2] *Pat. Lat.*, clxxxxviii, 1496 f.   [3] *Antiquitates Iudaicae*, XI, viii, 5.

To account for Malermi's freedom in expanding the Bible, it would be a mistake to argue that the Books of Maccabees are apocryphal. While that is the Jewish and also the Protestant opinion, the Catholic tradition includes them within the canon.[1] Malermi's interest in Alexander the Great induced him to inter⁄fere with a canonical text. Although his translation was eventu⁄ally placed on the Index, before 1567 it went through more than thirty editions.[2] Michelangelo, who would naturally consult an Italian rather than a Latin Bible, seems to have used the edition of 1493, since it is in that version that the picture of Alexander kneeling before the high⁄priest so clearly foreshadows his own medallion.

In the illustrations to the first edition (1490) the scene was depicted more poetically (Pl. 23). The king, to show his sub⁄mission to the priest, has taken off his crown and placed it on the ground. His horse is held by a page, with a contingent of cavalry behind him. In the background the door of the temple is open, and the king is seen here a second time, kneeling on the steps. In the edition of 1493 these poetical digressions were omitted; the scene was reduced to a compact composition which, perhaps because of its greater sparseness, inspired Michelangelo's design.

The same subject was adopted later by Pope Paul III for a medal, executed by Alessandro Cesati, with the inscription: OMNES REGES SERVIENT EI (Pl. 24).[3] In his brief discussion of Cesati's works Vasari singles out this particular medal for high praise because, as he is proud to record, Michelangelo had examined and admired it in his presence:

'And who wants to be astounded by his miraculous achieve⁄ments, should look at a medal he made for Pope Paul III . . . on which appears Alexander the Great adoring the High Priest of Jerusalem at whose feet he has thrown himself, figures stupendously

[1] See *Douay Bible*, ed. W. H. McClellan, S.J. (1941), p. 911, citing the Councils of Florence and Trent.

[2] Cf. Padre Vaccari in *Enciclopedia Italiana*, s.v. 'Bibbia'.

[3] The inscription derives from Psalms lxxi, 11 (Vulgate): *et adorabunt eum omnes reges terrae, omnes gentes servient ei.*

executed . . .; and when Michelangelo Buonarroti examined them in the presence of Giorgio Vasari, he said that the hour of death had come for art because it could not be surpassed.'[1]

Sir George Hill, who found the medal mediocre, was baffled by Michelangelo's extravagant praise of it.[2] The grandiloquent report may indeed be nothing but a fine legend spun around the fact that this particular medal is related to one of Michelangelo's designs. A parallel instance is the so-called *cachet de Michelange* by Piermaria da Pescia,[3] an intaglio which Michelangelo is said to have owned and cherished, although the only evidence for his connection with the piece is that a group from the Sistine Ceiling recurs on it.

*　　*　　*

Once it is known that Michelangelo used the Malermi Bible, the subjects of two other medallions, which have offered some difficulties to interpreters of the Sistine Ceiling, can be safely identified. Opposite the peaceful image of Alexander the Great, Michelangelo painted a medallion with a dramatic battle-scene (Pl. 20). The distinguishing feature of the battle is that it takes place under the fearful sign of a severed head and a pair of hands which are suspended from a pole. Steinmann thought (and again his view has been widely accepted) that the picture represents the slaughter of the seventy sons of Ahab, whose heads were collected in baskets (2 Kings x, 7). He suggested that Michelangelo had meant to allude to that scene by exhibiting one head on a pole, the medallion not offering enough room for the others. Borinski sarcastically objected: *für vier mindestens hatte es gereicht*,[4] but his own explanation, that the battle represents the defeat of the Assyrians after the return of Judith, when the people of Bethulia hung the head of Holofernes on the wall (Judith xiv,

---

[1] *Vite di Valerio Vicentino . . . ed altri* (ed. Milanesi), v, 385 f.

[2] *Medals of the Renaissance* (1920), p. 94.

[3] E. Babelon, *Le Cabinet des Antiques à la Bibliothèque Nationale* (1887), pp. 87–90, no. 2337.

[4] *Die Rätsel Michelangelos* (1908), p. 243.

11), is contradicted by a minor detail. A head alone might be Holofernes', but not a head with two hands.

To cut off the head and hands of an enemy was a familiar practice among the Romans. It was done, for example, to Cicero.[1] In the Bible it is an unusual form of punishment, reserved for culprits of a particular kind, and then applied to the head and one hand only, as shown by the famous instance of Nicanor, who had raised his hand in a blasphemous oath against the temple of Jerusalem:

'So the thirteenth day of the month Adar the hosts [of Nicanor and Judas Maccabeus] joined battle: but Nicanor's host was discomfited, and he himself was first slain in the battle. . . . Afterwards they . . . smote off Nicanor's head, and his right hand, which he stretched out so proudly, and brought them away, and hanged them up toward Jerusalem' (1 Maccabees vii, 43–7).

Although the text leaves no doubt that only one hand of Nicanor was cut off—the right hand which he had raised in blasphemy— the Malermi Bible of 1490 illustrates his defeat by showing how both hands were severed at the wrist (Pl. 25). As if to make up for the inadvertent pleonasm, the edition of 1493, in showing Nicanor's head hanging from the citadel, omits the hands altogether, so that it might as well have been the head of Holofernes (Pl. 19). Yet no one seeing this particular image can doubt that it was the model for Michelangelo's design, so markedly similar is the contrivance of suspending the head from a long pole that projects from the wall of the beleagured city (Pl. 20). That Michelangelo over-corrected the image by adding two hands instead of one may be more than a thoughtless transference from the earlier illustration. As the medallions were designed by him in a pseudo-antique style, reminiscent of Roman triumphal reliefs, he may well have favoured a version which recalled a Roman style of punishment.[2]

* * *

[1] Plutarch, *Cicero*, 48.
[2] Our Pl. 20 is taken from an old photograph which shows the picture in a better

A third Maccabean history appears, I believe, in the medallion falsely named *The Death of Uriah* (Pl. 22). This title, again chosen by Steinmann, would lead one to suspect 'the hottest battle', in which Uriah fell fighting (2 Samuel xi, 15). Instead, the man stretched out on the ground is without weapons or armour; he is beaten by two men on foot while a rider rushes in from behind. It should be noticed that the horse's forefeet appear just above the prostrate figure. To the left, a man kneeling in prayer is placed in such a way that he faces the approaching rider. 'For there appeared unto them an horse with a terrible rider upon him . . . and he ran fiercely, and smote at Heliodorus with his forefeet. . . . Moreover two other young men appeared before him, notable in strength . . . who stood by him on either side, and scourged him continually, and gave him many sore stripes. And Heliodorus fell suddenly unto the ground, and was compassed with great darkness' (2 Maccabees iii, 25–7). In the woodcut accompanying this passage in the Malermi Bible, the forefeet of the horse are 'smiting' in the direction of the prostrate Heliodorus while he is also beaten by two men on foot; and in the background two men are kneeling in prayer (Pl. 21). Like Raphael in the Stanza d'Eliodoro, Michelangelo concentrated the act of kneeling in the single figure of Onias, at whose prayer the miraculous rider appeared (Pl. 22). That this famous subject has passed unrecognized is perhaps because Michelangelo rendered the supernatural apparition in a laconic style, compressing into a tondo of five figures the great scene of divine chastisement which Raphael was to stage with such theatrical splendour in the Stanza d'Eliodoro. Michelangelo relied on a frontal foreshortening of the ut

state than it is today (Pl. 26). The damage must have occurred more than fifty years ago since it appears already in Steinmann's illustration (1905). It follows that no trust can be placed in the common assumption that Michelangelo left several of the medallions in a sketchy state. All the medallions which look sketchy are damaged. In the *Death of Absalom*, for example, the figure of Joab has vanished except for one leg which has accidentally survived together with part of the horse. Surely it would be absurd to assume that Michelangelo had sketched the leg without the figure.

317

most daring to convey the impression of an angelic rider on a fantastic horse.[1]

* * *

The fact that both Raphael and Michelangelo painted Macca‚ bean subjects for Julius II points to a predilection of the pope for these martial histories which he seems to have associated with his own campaigns. The religious warfare of Judas Maccabeus supplied indeed a splendid precedent from Holy Script for the military enterprises of Julius II; and the invocation of the Macca‚ bees by this particular pope was sanctioned by a remarkable con‚ cordance in the liturgical calendar: the day of St. Peter in Prison, for Julius a day of personal devotion ever since he became cardinal of San Pietro in Vincoli, coincides with the com‚ memoration of the Maccabean martyrs.[2] Their relics are pre‚ served in the crypt of San Pietro in Vincoli, directly below the chains of St. Peter.

There can be no doubt that this liturgical connection is reflected in the programme of the Stanza d'Eliodoro, where the Maccabean miracle is juxtaposed to the miracle of St. Peter in prison. And it is not unlikely that Maccabean scenes of deliverance were planned also for the Julius Tomb, since the revised contracts of 1513 and 1516 still envisage bronze reliefs with 'histories' in addition to the famous *prigioni*.[3] Hence the question might well be

---

[1] Mr. F. Lugt very kindly quoted my interpretation in 'Man and Angel', *Gazette des Beaux Arts*, xxv (1944), 343 f. C. de Tolnay (*Michelangelo*, ii (1945), 254) raised two objections. First, if the scene represented Heliodorus, it ought to take place within the Temple and show the treasure which Heliodorus tried to seize. But the same objection would apply to the picture in the Malermi Bible (Pl. 21) which certainly does represent the Chastisement of Heliodorus as shown by the text. Secondly, the two men on foot ought to strike Heliodorus 'from either side'. Actually they conform to that requirement very meticulously. While appearing 'before him', as the text prescribes, one man strikes Heliodorus with the right arm, the other with the left.

[2] See R. Lippe, *Missale Romanum Mediolani 1474: A Collation with other Editions printed before 1570*, ii (1907), 218 f.; cf. i, 359 f.

[3] *Lettere ... ricordi ... contratti artistici di Michelangelo Buonarroti*, ed. Milanesi (1875), p. 637 ('tre storie o di marmo o di bronzo'), p. 646 (five histories 'di bronzo').

worth considering whether the three bronze medallions which represent Maccabean scenes in the Sistine Ceiling might not preserve a trace of bronze reliefs originally designed for the Julius Tomb. However, such reflections about their original use would contribute little towards understanding the significance they actually do assume in the Sistine Ceiling, where they belong to a series of ten medallions. Since five of the other medallions represent scenes from the books of Samuel and Kings, and one represents a scene from Genesis, the unity of the series is obviously not, as Vasari supposed and Steinmann believed, a unity of narration. Drawn from three different parts of the Bible, they do not tell a consecutive story. What, then, is their connection, if any?

*   *   *

In the earliest-known sketch for the Sistine Ceiling, when Michelangelo still thought of painting the Twelve Apostles in the places later assigned to Prophets and Sibyls,[1] he designed the vault in such a way that a medallion would have appeared above each of the twelve seated figures.[2] It was only at a later stage, when he replaced the Apostles by Prophets and Sibyls and filled the centre of the vault with scenes from the Old Testament, that the number of medallions was reduced to ten, leaving a plain cornice above the prophet at either end. What the medallions were meant to represent originally we cannot tell,[3] but once reduced to ten and joined to the scenes from Genesis, they can be shown, I believe, to represent the Ten Commandments.

---

[1] Ibid., p. 426, no. 383.

[2] A good reconstruction in Wölfflin, 'Ein Entwurf Michelangelo's zur Sixtin-ischen Decke', *Jahrbuch der preussischen Kunstsammlungen*, xiii (1892), 178-82. On Michelangelo's sketch in the British Museum (1859-6—25-567) see Berenson, *The Drawings of the Florentine Painters*, no. 1483; J. Wilde, *Italian Drawings in the British Museum: Michelangelo and his Studio* (1953), no. 71.

[3] Although the medallions in the earlier design would have been slightly smaller than they are at present, their size, in relation to the seated figures below them, is much too large for purely ornamental knobs. Furthermore, knobs could not be flanked by the winged herms which are seen in the drawing.

The cursory list of titles which follows may perhaps suffice, with a few notes and references added, to state the case, if not to prove it. Six of the subjects listed are those discovered by Steinmann. He was as largely right as anyone can be who places an implicit faith in the accuracy of Vasari. The corrections I have introduced concern only four medallions out of ten—the three Maccabean scenes hitherto unrecognized, and the mysterious blank medallion above the Persica, of which the topic can, I believe, be inferred, and with it the reason for its disappearance. I am listing the medallions in the sequence in which they appear on the Ceiling, beginning with the pair near the entrance:

	(South)					
Entrance	1	3	5	7	9	Altar[1]
(East)	2	4	6	8	10	(West)
	(North)					

1. Joram thrown on to the vineyard of Naboth (1 Kings xxi; 2 Kings ix, 24–6): *Thou shalt not covet.*

2. Abner murdered under the gate (2 Samuel iii, 27): *Thou shall not kill.*

3. The destruction of the idol (2 Kings x, 25–7): *Thou shalt not make unto thee any graven image* (Pl. 27).

4. Heliodorus chastised for seizing the temple treasure (2 Maccabees iii, 25–7): *Thou shalt not steal.*

5. Nicanor punished for his blasphemous oath (1 Maccabees vii, 43–7): *Thou shalt not take the name of the Lord thy God in vain.*

6. Alexander kneeling before the priest (PseudoMaccabees 1, i): *Remember the Sabbath day, to keep it holy* (a commandment generalized by Savonarola as follows: *Ricordati di sanctificare il giorno del sabbato: per loquale s'intende ogni festa. . . . L'huomo debbe dimonstrarsi subiecto a dio per qualche segno exteriore. . . . L'huomo . . . si dimostra essere servidore di Dio e subdito*).

7. The blank medallion: *Thou shalt not commit adultery.* In

---

[1] Owing to 'papal privilege', the altar of the Sistine Chapel is on the west wall. The pope officiates from behind the altar, facing the congregation. He therefore faces east.

Cunego's copy of the Ceiling this medallion still shows a pair of lovers (Pl. 28). There is every reason to assume that this objectionable scene was removed at a time when it was no longer understood as an illustration of one of the Ten Commandments.[1]

8. The death of Absalom (2 Samuel xviii, 9–15): *Honour thy father and thy mother.*

9. Elijah in the chariot of fire (2 Kings ii, 11): *Thou shalt not bear false witness* (cf. MS Eton 177, fo. 6 b, where this commandment is illustrated by the chariot of Elijah).[2] It was customary to identify Elijah and Enoch with the 'two witnesses' of Revelation xi, 3, because on the Day of Judgement, as announced in Malachi iv, 5 and Jude 10–16, they are to testify against those who 'speak evil of those things which they know not . . . , having men's persons in admiration because of advantage'.

10. Abraham's sacrifice (Genesis xxii, 12: 'For now I know that thou fearest God'): *Thou shalt have no other gods before me* (cf. Pico della Mirandola, *Heptaplus* VII, i: *Abraham . . . primus qui cultum unius Dei adversus idola et gentes hominibus persuaderet.* The passage occurs in a discussion of the *Fiat Lux*—the very scene from Genesis to which Michelangelo joined this medallion. In the scheme of the Ceiling both scenes are coordinated with the prophecy of the Libyan sibyl: *Ecce veniet dies et illuminabit condensa tenebrarum*).

Assuming that these are the Ten Commandments, why are they so peculiarly arranged? If we number them in their biblical order, their distribution looks piecemeal and unintelligible:

---

[1] Steinmann referred to a tondo drawing of the Brazen Serpent (Uffizi 18721ᶠ) as a discarded sketch for one of the medallions, and supposed that Michelangelo had abandoned it when he decided to paint the Brazen Serpent as a corner spandrel (*Die Sixtinische Kapelle*, ii, 597, no. 24). But apart from the mistake of assuming that Michelangelo's programme permitted that kind of transference, the argument collapses for two reasons: The drawing is not by Michelangelo (cf. Berenson, no. 1654 A); and it does not represent the Brazen Serpent but the Conversion of St. Paul, a subject unconnected with the programme of the Sistine Ceiling.

[2] Montague James, *A Descriptive Catalogue of the Manuscripts in the Library of Eton College* (1895), 102: 'Non loqueris falsum testimonium.' I am indebted to Mr. Andrew Ritchie for having drawn my attention to this illustration.

6	8	4	5	1
10	2	3	7	9

Equally confusing is the method of demonstration. Some of the pictures illustrate the obedience to a commandment (Alexander kneeling before the priest of Jerusalem), others the violation of the commandment (Joab killing Abner), others the indictment for the violation (Elijah in the Fiery Chariot), still others the punish, ment for the violation (the Death of Joram, the Death of Ab, salom). Is there a plan behind these anomalies?

To anyone accustomed to use biblical quotations in the strict sense prescribed by the Council of Trent or the Protestant reformers, it is difficult to imagine the poetic freedom which had been granted to Renaissance preachers. St. Antonine of Florence, a character not noted for intellectual levity, changed the sequence of the Ten Commandments for the sake of the rhythm when he translated them into Latin hexameters. As long as each command, ment carried the full weight of its lesson, he presumably felt that it was not sinful to rearrange, rephrase, and amplify them to suit the context in which they were quoted. The order in which they appear in the Sistine Ceiling relates each image to the ad, joining Prophet or Sibyl and also to the adjoining scene from Genesis,[1] with the result that all of these images become part of one coherent prophetic system. The vineyard of Naboth, for example, besides illustrating the commandment *Thou shalt not covet,* resumes the motif of the vineyard of Noah, in which the drunken patriarch is mocked; and both images are meant to be connected with the vineyard prophecy of Joel (i, 5–12) as ex, pounded in Acts ii, 13–16: 'Others mocking said, These men are full of new wine. But Peter . . . said unto them . . . hearken to my words: For these are not drunken, as ye suppose. . . . But this is that which was spoken by the prophet Joel.'[2]

[1] Cf. Ascanio Condivi, *Life of Michelangelo*, tr. Holroyd (1911), p. 39.

[2] Cf. E. Wind, 'The Ark of Noah: A Study in the Symbolism of Michelangelo', *Measure*, i (1950), 411–21; also, for questions of method, 'Typology in the Sistine Ceiling: A Critical Statement', *The Art Bulletin*, xxxiii (1951), 41–7.

Again, 'Alexander kneeling before the priest of Jerusalem' is not the most obvious illustration of the third commandment, even though 'honouring the sabbath' was understood in the Renaissance as 'honouring the Church'. The example was chosen because of its relevance to the adjoining panel representing the Creation of Eve which, read as a prophetic image and associated with the Cumaean sibyl, foreshadows the birth of the Church (the second Eve). While Alexander's submission to the priest signifies the Church Triumphant, the Church Militant is repre-sented on the opposite side by the battle of Judas Maccabeus against the blasphemous Nicanor. The heroic figure on horseback in the centre of this medallion (Pl. 20) is undoubtedly intended for Judas Maccabeus himself.

In choosing Alexander the Great and Judas Maccabeus as the heroes of the two central medallions in the Ceiling, Michelangelo surely meant to resume the contrast between *Ecclesia Gentilium* and *Ecclesia Iudaeorum* which is expressed by the Sibyls and Prophets themselves. And it appears, in fact, that each medallion, as it is placed over a prophet or a sibyl, refers to the propensities of that particular church, the former pagans being admonished against polytheism, lust and idolatry, the former Jews against swearing, envy and pride. A zealous church and an indulgent church, each with its vices and singular graces, emerge as exponents of the divine harmony between vengeance and love, which they exhibit even in their failings.

The rearrangement of the Ten Commandments according to this 'mystical' scheme is not without its 'moral' logic. Pride, the most overbearing of vices (Absalom), appears opposite to Lust, the most indulgent (adulterous pair); Sacrilege, which defiles the holy (Heliodorus), opposite to Idolatry, which honours the profane (Baal). Because the antithetical grouping is bound up with the programme and architecture of the Ceiling, it is probably unique in the iconographic history of the Ten Command-ments.

Equally remarkable is a theological idiosyncrasy. In his divi-sion of the Ten Commandments, Michelangelo followed the

323

classification of Origen. As this is an important theological point, it deserves to be examined a little more closely.

*   *   *

Augustine and Aquinas disagreed with Origen on the division of the Ten Commandments.[1] They argued against him that *Thou shalt have no other gods before me* and *Thou shalt not make unto thee any graven image* belong together as part of one commandment referring to the nature of God. Origen, on the contrary, claimed that they are two different commandments because the first is directed against polytheism, the second against idolatry—two errors which, while frequently combined, are demonstrably not identical. (Certain phases of Neoplatonism, for example, are polytheistic without being idolatrous, and it is easy enough to imagine an idolater who believes his fetish to be unique.) Conversely, Augustine and Aquinas declined to accept the fusion of the two last commandments proposed by Origen. They felt that to covet a neighbour's wife is so different a sin from coveting his house or his garden that these should not be classed under the same heading. Origen, on the contrary, argued that by comprising the neighbour's wife together with his house and his other possessions, covetousness stood out as a peculiar vice regardless of its object, and noticeably different in its operation from downright adultery or theft—for which two other commandments were already provided.

While Protestant logic has generally inclined to side with Origen in this dispute, the Catholic Church has in the end abided by the judgement of Augustine and Aquinas. In the years when the Sistine Ceiling was painted (1508–12), the issue was not yet strained by the Protestant schism. A revival of Origen was advocated by a group of Catholic humanists who favoured a return to ancient Christianity, leading back from the Scholastics to the early Fathers, and from the Latin Fathers to the Greek.

---

[1] See Thomas Aquinas, *Summa Theologica*, II, i, Q. 100, Art. 4, where the debate is summarized.

The movement was supported by Julius II. As on so many other issues, he resumed a policy begun by his uncle, Sixtus IV, to whom the first edition of Origen's *Contra Celsum* was dedicated in 1481. An ingredient of Origenism must hence be admitted among the characteristics of Rovere theology.[1] The breadth of the movement may be judged by the names of a few who took part in it: Platina, Palmieri, Marsilio Ficino, Pico della Mirandola, Aldus Manutius, Egidio da Viterbo, Sante Pagnini, Jean Vitrier, Symphorien Champier, Jacques Merlin, Erasmus. Depending on their particular bent of mind, they venerated Origen either as the founder of biblical philology, or as a master of biblical allegory, or as the relentless proponent of a fusion of Christianity and Hebraism with Plato.[2] In the words of Porphyry quoted by Eusebius: 'While his manner of life was Christian . . . in his opinions . . . he played the Greek. . . . For he was always consorting with Plato, and was conversant with the writings of . . . the distinguished men among the Pythagoreans . . ., from whom he learnt the figurative interpretation, as employed in the Greek mysteries, and applied it to the Jewish writings.'[3] The programme of the Sistine Ceiling is entirely conceived in this figurative spirit, and demonstrable traces of Origen's theology extend far beyond the Ten Commandments.[4]

Michelangelo himself did not read Origen, nor did he read his Renaissance commentators, but it is certain that he conversed with some of them; and it is at this point that the Malermi Bible assumes a singularly important rôle. While critics of Origen have always complained of his failure to distinguish between

[1] Wind, 'The Revival of Origen', *Studies in Art and Literature for Belle da Costa Greene* (1954), pp. 419 f.

[2] For a masterly statement of the divergent components which entered into Origen's exegetical method, see the concise paper of J. Daniélou, 'Origène comme exégète de la Bible', *Studia Patristica*, i (1957), 280–90.

[3] Eusebius, *Ecclesiastical History*, VI, xix, 4–8.

[4] Cf. Wind, 'Sante Pagnini and Michelangelo', *Gazette des Beaux Arts* (1944), pp. 218–32, with particular reference to the Genealogy of Christ in the lunettes of the Sistine Chapel. For Michelangelo's figure of the *Deliciosus* ('Eleazar'), see Pierio Valeriano, *Hieroglyphica* (1575), fo. 265, who quotes the full text from Origen.

canonical and apocryphal evidence, his Renaissance followers regarded that failure as part of Origen's genius: he delighted them by enriching the canon, and encouraged their own skill in syncretizing. Some of the imaginative wealth of the Sistine Ceiling derives from the indiscriminate practice of seeking concordances beyond the canon, of placing Sibylline prophecies on one level with biblical, of revising or amplifying the biblical stories in the light of apocryphal revelations. The insertion of Josephus into the text of the Maccabees is a minor example of that liberality. Hence the theologians who invented the programme of the Sistine Ceiling did not take exception to the Malermi Bible; on the contrary, it is probably they who placed it in Michelangelo's hand.

With what sympathy he entered into the thoughts of his instructors is shown by the claim he made, some sixteen years later, to have invented the programme of the Ceiling by himself,[1] but that is manifestly impossible. The Origenist portions he could not have conceived, nor would he have been competent to judge their admissibility into a papal chapel, particularly as some of Origen's views were condemned by the Fifth Ecumenical Council. But given the points of doctrine he was asked to illustrate, we can well picture him thumbing the Malermi Bible, as he did the popular tracts of Savonarola,[2] refreshing his memory of certain episodes, or proposing alternatives for illustration which he would debate with the exacting doctors. It shows the depth and copiousness of Renaissance theology that a sensible dialogue could thus be carried on, one party expounding the mysteries of Origen, another answering with quotations from Savonarola or Malermi. In the end it was by the force of Michelangelo's imagination that the popular and the recondite matter were fused in his figures: they have remained to this day among the most tangible religious images ever conceived, and also among the most remote and esoteric.

In order to understand Michelangelo's method of invention, it is of inestimable value to know that he consulted the Malermi Bible. Besides the three medallions discussed as Maccabean, four

---

[1] *Lettere* (ed. cit.), no. 383.　　　　[2] Condivi, op. cit., p. 74.

other medallions show unmistakable traces of the edition of 1493;[1] and the evidence is not confined to the medallions. Certain odd reminiscences of the woodcuts have slipped into the great histories of Noah, Judith and Esther, where they produce, by virtue of the grandeur to which they have been raised, a surprisingly stark and aggressive effect. The eccentric placing of Judith and her maid, for the purpose of allowing a full view of the dead Holofernes lying in his tent (Pl. 29); the interposition of a dividing wall between the scenes of Mordecai and Ahasuerus (Pl. 30); the prominent display of a jug and bowl in the foreground of the *Drunkenness of Noah* (Pl. 31)—these brusque devices of Michelangelo appear in the Malermi Bible as primitive makeshifts. Since the woodcuts, particularly in the edition of 1493, approach the *gauche* style of *imagerie populaire*, it is of considerable interest that they should have appealed to Michelangelo so strongly that he thought fit to translate some of their discords into his own heroic idiom.

[1] See in particular *The Death of Absalom*, *The Death of Joram*, and *The Death of Abner*. The medallion showing the destruction of an idol (Pl. 27) should be compared with the illustration of 1 Maccabees ii. Michelangelo may have meant to represent that scene rather than the destruction of Baal, although it is difficult to distinguish one biblical act of iconoclasm from another. As a curiosity it may be noted that Mr. Berenson, looking at this medallion, thought of 'Caesar's address to his army at Rimini' (op. cit., no. 1545).

Sir Maurice Bowra

SONGS OF DANCE AND
CARNIVAL

In the latter part of the fifteenth century the highest honours in
Italian poetry fall to the writers of chivalrous epic, and though at
intervals story-tellers like Boiardo were driven by the urgency of
their passions or fancies into irresistible song, it was incidental,
if not accidental, to their main achievement. Many poets seem to
have found it difficult to escape from the manner so masterfully
imposed by Petrarch or to find any new thing to say or new way
to say it. Though among the people song continued its lively
career, in cultivated circles it seemed for the most part to have come
to a dead end. But at Florence circumstances and personalities
combined to foster not indeed a new movement in lyrical poetry,
but a revival of old forms with a new curiosity and a new intention. Though both Lorenzo de' Medici (1449–93) and Angelo
Poliziano (1454–94) may have felt that their gifts were best displayed in the stately measures of *rime* and *stanze*, they also experi-
mented with something different which is no less characteristic
of their age and throws a revealing light on their tastes and talents.
Their *canzoni a ballo* and *canti carnascialeschi* are far removed from
the vast, crowded panoramas of chivalrous romance, but pursue
in their narrow limits a distinctive way of life. These two men, in
whom a passion for the Greek and Latin classics might have
been expected to stifle an appreciation of vulgar, vernacular
poetry, found in it a new source of strength, and with a notable
dexterity turned its forms to their own ends.

The *canzone a ballo*, as Lorenzo and Poliziano wrote it, is an
extension in a special direction of the *ballata*, which is itself an
ancient, indigenous, and popular form in Mediterranean lands.

In Provence the *balada* was not much taken up by the practitioners of courtly song, but it had a respectable position, and enough examples of it survive to show that it could be both popular and polished. Such songs as:

> Coindeta sui, si cum n'ai greu cossire,
> Per mon marit, quar ne·l voil ne·l desire,[1]
>
> (*Lovely am I, and yet is grief my lot;*
> *My husband I desire not, and love not,*)

or

> Mort m'an li semblan que ma dona·m fai
> E li seu bel oil amores e gai,[2]
>
> (*My lady's glances take my life away,*
> *And her fine eyes, so amorous and gay,*)

are certainly accomplished, but they are derived from a humble dance-song which had already a long history when they were written. Behind the Provençal *balada* and the Italian *ballata* lies an ancient form, in which a theme is first stated at the beginning and then stated again at intervals while variations are made on it. It was something of this kind which a Moorish poet called Mocádem, from Cabra near Cordova, is more likely to have discovered than invented about A.D. 900, when he composed the form called *zéjel* (*zekhel*) and brought into it words from the Romance language of his day.[3] The form survived and in due course caught the notice of cultivated poets in Latin countries. The *ballata* is the Italian version of it.

In the *ballata* the theme is stated at the beginning; then variations on it are given in the succeeding stanzas, after each of which it reappears. The reason for this lies in the circumstances of performance, on which we are well informed by a Latin poem of Giovanni del Virgilio, who describes what took place at Bologna on St. John the Baptist's Day.[4] Men and women were drawn up

---

[1] A. Berry, *Florilège des Troubadours*, p. 6. [2] Idem, p. 10.
[3] G. Brenan, *The Literature of the Spanish People*, pp. 26 ff.
[4] G. Bertoni, *Il Duecento*, pp. 206-7.

in separate ranks, and then joined together in a dance. The soloist, whose task was to speak in the general character of the lover, sang a *recantus* or refrain, in which he struck the dominating note of the occasion and summoned Cupid to hear the entreaties of the participants. The refrain was repeated by the whole company; then the soloist sang the first stanza, which was of unfulfilled love, and after it the company repeated the refrain. This happened at least twice more, and while the stanzas developed the theme, the refrain remained constant, and with its final appearance the song and the dance came to an end. This is the essential *ballata*, a combination of words and music and dance, performed in the open air at a popular festival and well suited to the amorous associations of Midsummer Day.

The *ballata* seems to have meant nothing to the poets of the *magna curia* of Frederick II, perhaps because it was too popular to suit their exalted ideas of courtly song, but in northern Italy it caught the fancy of poets before Lorenzo and Poliziano and especially of the masters of the *dolce stil nuovo*. Here was a song traditionally associated with love, cast in a neat and wellbalanced shape, capable of transformation into something refined and sweet and gay. Guido Cavalcanti, Cino da Pistoia, and Lapo Gianni all made use of it, and Dante himself wrote at least six *ballate* and displays a delightfully happy touch in *Per una ghirlandetta*. Though any of these songs could have been performed in the traditional way, it is doubtful whether they were or whether they were intended to be. They are personal poems, for which a popular form has been chosen for its unaffected grace, rather as the first Minnesingers, like Der von Kurenberg and Dietmar von Aist, wrote lovesongs in the old measure of the *trûtliet*, or the early Portuguese poets, who culminated in King Diniz, made brilliant variations on the ancient *cantiga d'amor*. Gifted Italians loosed the *ballata* from its old moorings to move as a work of art in its own right. In doing this they took some liberties with it and tended to vary the standard form. The refrain, which was indispensable to the full and proper performance, was not always repeated completely, but it was often thought enough to repeat its beginning or its end or merely to make the close of each stanza rhyme with the closing word of the refrain. None the less the *ballata* kept some of its essential characteristics as a song which reflected the spirit of a lively occasion and was well suited to any poet who liked to state a theme and then develop it in a graceful and orderly manner.

While the *ballata* was trimmed and polished in this way, it continued to have at the same time a popular vogue in its old shape and to be concerned with love less as an urgent personal necessity than as a natural and sociable pastime. Even so it was not confined to uncultivated songsters or a low level of society. It was popular in the sense that all classes enjoyed it and took part in it. Boccaccio reflects contemporary conditions, when in the *Decameron*, on the tenth day, the king tells Fiammetta to sing a song while the company dances, and her song, *S'amor venisse senza gelosia*, is a *ballata*. Franco Sacchetti (1314–1409), who was born of an old Florentine family at Ragusa and came to Florence in childhood, wrote *ballate* on the traditional model, which keep much of their native vigour and must have been performed much as Giovanni del Virgilio describes. From Sacchetti and his kind, no less than from less sophisticated performers, Lorenzo and Poliziano learned about *ballate* before turning them into *canzoni a ballo*. This popular art was much less restrained and less refined than that of Cavalcanti and his friends. It smacked of the soil and the streets, of bucolic pranks and primitive banter, of pungent ribaldry and unashamed appetites. No doubt Lorenzo and Poliziano were drawn to it just because it was a popular art; for they themselves came from the people and were bred on its songs. Their special achievement was to exploit both kinds of *ballata*, and though they kept them reasonably distinct, they gave to both a fine style and a deliberate elegance. With them the *ballata* resumed its function as a real song intended to be sung to the accompaniment of music and dancing.

This means that the *canzone a ballo*, despite its small scale and limited opportunities, has a certain dramatic element. In its brief compass it acts an episode and is, both in its origin and its development, a secular counterpart to the religious *laude*, which is constructed on a like scheme and uses a refrain for a like purpose. If *laudi* dramatized scenes from Holy Writ, *canzoni a ballo* dramatized scenes from the no less familiar gospel of love-making. Though the one was sacred and the other profane, both tended to use a simple metre with a lively lilt, especially the line of seven (or eight) syllables. This was regarded by Dante as not alien to the 'tragic style', but, perhaps with the Sicilian poets in mind, he felt that *si ad eorum sensum subtiliter intrare velimus, non sine quodam elegie umbraculo processisse videbitur* (*Vulg. Eloq.*, II, xii, 6). It is just this elegiac quality which makes the line suitable for love-poetry, and that is why the masters of the *canzone a ballo*, fully aware of what they were doing, followed tradition in their attachment to it. Despite its dramatic qualities it remains a song. Just as popular *ballate* were composed for the festivals of the seasons, so these songs were composed, as Poliziano says, to be *carmina festis excipienda choris* (*Nutricia*, 764–5). Their performance was a festal rite, which had both its own rules and its own liberties. In some sense they offered an escape from reality into a world of make-believe, but only by clothing familiar things with a fantastic air, and they admitted almost any mood from ideal devotion to reckless gaiety or gentle pathos or sardonic satire. Just as the narrative-poems of Pulci or Boiardo or Ariosto cover an astonishingly varied range of senti-ment, so the *canzoni a ballo* are, in their own small way, a lyrical counterpart to them and delight in a remarkable scope of tone and temper.

The transformation of the *canti a ballo* into the *canti carnascialeschi* was the personal achievement of Lorenzo. In dedicating his *Tutti i Trionfi, Carri, Canti Carnascialeschi* to Francesco de' Medici in 1559 Anton Francesco Grazzini, known as 'Il Lasca', explains that originally at Florence on the carnival of May Day masked men used to accost women and sing a traditional song to them, but Lorenzo changed this by extending the wearing of masks to the wearing of fancy costumes and by substituting a variety of songs for the single old song. That he gave serious attention to the change is clear from his insistence that special music should be composed for each occasion by *un certo Arrigo Tedesco*, that is Heinrich Isaac, who was master of music at the chapel of San Giovanni. Lorenzo's songs confirm this report. Each is composed for a new occasion, and the classes into which Il Lasca divides them stand for differences in their manner of performance. In addition to the ordinary songs of dance and carnival there are the *trionfi*, in which mythological figures take the chief part, and the *carri*, in which men and women, dressed as chosen classes of crafts-men and the like, appear on cars with their appropriate attributes. The simple old song was dignified by a processional element, and more was made of its possibilities as a masquerade. It must have kept some of the old formality, but it was more gay and more stylish. Beneath the costumes and the make-believe it kept the old spirit which insisted that the spring is the time for frank declara-tions of love and for the consideration of issues which arise from it.

We cannot determine how much Lorenzo and Poliziano learned from each other in the composition of *canti a ballo*, but it is clear that they shared a common interest and common aims. They were united by their love of poetry and their belief that it could gain fresh strength from the adaptation of popular forms. But their close association does not hide considerable divergences of temperament and manner between them. Each flung himself fully into these songs and revealed much about himself in them, and each fashioned for them his own style and technique. Lorenzo, the hard-headed statesman and adroit man of affairs, writes with all the robust vigour that we should expect from his eager appetites and disdain of timorous inhibitions; Poliziano, the learned scholar and the arbiter of taste, picks his way daintily as he distils his experience into delicate shapes and omits any-thing which is not strictly relevant to his main point. Lorenzo succeeds through the impetus of his attack and the irresistible candour of his revelations; Poliziano chooses his words with careful discrimination and is truly classical in the balance and ease and clarity which he gives to them. The two poets comple-ment each other and show what different effects could be secured from a single, rather limited range of themes.

The most prominent, most admired, and most testing theme of this poetry is love. Ever since courtly song burst on the Mediter-ranean scene at the end of the eleventh century this had been the case, and the common choice was canonized by Dante when he proclaimed love to be the highest of all themes. Lorenzo and Poliziano accepted this without question, no doubt because it appealed to their personal inclinations, could hardly be avoided in a courtly society, and agreed with the practice of popular song. Their conception of love was not indeed as exalted as that of Dante or even of Sordello. They took a more human and less idealistic view of it, but they were no less aware of its claims and fascinations. For them the essence of courtly love is that the lover sets all his hopes on the *gentilezza* of his lady, and this binds him to her in a devotion which absorbs his whole being. This is indeed the spirit of the first Provençal troubadours, of the *magna curia*, of the great Minnesingers, but Lorenzo and Poliziano give it rather a different emphasis. Unlike Arnaut Daniel or Bernart de Ventadour, they are not greatly interested in the cult of love as a moral discipline, in which the lady evokes in her lover all the finest qualities and makes an ideal knight of him. They may take this for granted, but they do not say much about it. Their special concern is with a radiant, life-giving joy, which they find in love and which transforms experience and sets an exhilarating and enthralling enchantment on their every action. Each of them inter-preted this in his own way and set the impress of his own tempera-ment on it, but it remains the centre of their poetical theory and their translation of it into practice.

When Lorenzo writes a *canzone a ballo* about love, he throws his whole being into it. The dance becomes a central rite in love-making. He catches its exuberant ardour and makes his words swing in lively response to it. His mood is not relaxation or even pleasure, but a passionate concentration on the enthralling pre-sence or prospect of love. The dance is a ceremony to which only initiates, only those who are really and truly in love, should be admitted:

Chi non è innamorato
Esca di questo ballo. (13, 1–2)[1]

(Let him who is no lover
Forthwith forsake our dances.)

The rite calls for a special frame of mind, for emotions directed to
a single end and entirely occupied with it, for a devotion in which
jealousy has no place and modesty must be displayed not in the
false restraint of cowardice but in the true expansiveness of
generous intentions. The high sentiments, which in isolation
might be a little arid and abstract, are transcended and transformed
in joy, and there is none of that defiant disregard of other men
which earlier poets like Bertran de Born and Arnaut Daniel pay
as an indispensable tribute to the unique supremacy of their love.
Each point is made firmly and finely, with emphasis and assurance. Lorenzo is certain that it is right for men to love in this way
and wishes the movement of the dance to stir their lurking, shy
desires into confidence and action. He himself displays this confidence with all the fervour of his abounding appetites and sets a
lead for others to follow.

The joy which Lorenzo seeks through love is all-absorbing and
leaves no room for anything else. Because it promises such rewards,
the lover is ready to undergo setbacks and delays, knowing that
in the end his joy will be all the richer for them. So Lorenzo tells
of the magical moment when he finds himself in the presence of a
woman whom he suddenly knows that he loves. He, who has
lost his heart and not known what has happened to it, discovers
that it is she who holds it, and to this his response is overwhelming
gratitude:

Ringraziato sie tu, Amore,
Ch'io l'ho pure al fin trovato. (11, 3–4)

(To thee, O Love, let thanks be given;
For I have found my heart at last.)

The fancy that the poet's heart has been lost and that, to his

---

[1] References to Lorenzo are from Lorenzo de' Medici, *Scritti Scelti*, ed. E. Bigi.

unbounded delight, he finds the thief, is in itself charming enough, but it gains in aptness and humanity from the surroundings in which the discovery takes place. The background of the dance, with its gallant company and its eager excitement, emphasizes the unique exultation of the lover and provides the process of which his sudden revelation is the climax.

The theme of gratitude for being in love must have been one which Lorenzo discussed with Poliziano; for Poliziano also makes use of it:

> Io ti ringrazio, Amore,
> D'ogni pena e tormento,
> E son contento omai d'ogni dolore. (7, 1-3)[1]

> (*For each pain that torments me*
> *Thanks to thee, Love, I offer;*
> *Now all I suffer in my grief contents me.*)

The main idea is the same, but Poliziano goes his own way with it. While Lorenzo presents sensations and emotions crowding in a crowded scene, Poliziano is wafted by his love to some ideal, almost Platonic paradise. His sufferings have earned him a place in it, and his chief delight is that he can look into the bright eyes of his beloved and know that she is gay, beautiful, and true. While love impels Lorenzo to see the immediate, present scene bathed in a fascinating light, and to find all that he desires in it, Poliziano's imagination flies to another world, where nothing matters but the beauty of his beloved. Lorenzo is busy with questions and hopes and anticipations, but Poliziano's whole being is absorbed in something akin to vision, in which there is no place for anything but celestial joy.

If love provides such moments of flawless felicity, it has also its failures and defeats, without which its victories would be less prized than they are. In the poetry of courtly love the well-worn theme of frustration wears a different look because it is pitched at a lofty level of sentiment and associated with a whole company of abstract notions which concern the worth and the end of life. The

---

[1] References are to Poliziano, *Rime*, ed. P. Mastri.

sense of deprivation, of undeserved rejection, of hoping against hope, is much more than an occasion for uncontrolled emotions; it makes its victim doubt the validity of much which he has hitherto assumed without question, and feel that he has been fooled and betrayed. He, who has believed love to be an incarnation of *gentilezza* and *cortesia*, now sees what deceit and hardness of heart can lurk in it. Though Lorenzo passed rapidly from one passion to another, there is no need to think that he was not sincerely engaged in all. His strong hold on reality saves him from exaggerating his sorrows, and his self-command and self-knowledge give power to his complaints. He attains an impressive dignity when he abandons the seven-syllable line, so well suited to enthralled delight, for the eleven-syllable, whose aptness for grave themes was approved by Dante—*cum tragice poetari conamur, endecasillabum propter quandam excellentiam in contextu vincendi privilegium promeretur* (*Vulg. Eloq.*, II, xii, 3). All that the dance means to Lorenzo when he is happy forsakes him in his distress, and he writes with a frank and urgent seriousness:

> Io non credevo al tuo falso sembiante,
> E ben ti conoscevo in altre cose:
> Ma de' begli occhi lo splendor prestante
> E le fattezze sì belle e vezzose,
> Fecion che l'alma mia speranza pose
> In tue promesse; e morte n'acquistai. (7, 15–29)

> (*I never did believe in your false face,*
> *I knew you well in every other thing,*
> *But your fine eyes shone with so bright a grace,*
> *Your features were so sweet and cozening,*
> *That to your promises my hopes would cling;*
> *My soul believed them; and for this I die.*)

Though the lines were written for a *canzone a ballo*, we accept them as a personal revelation. Lorenzo faces his failure by analysing his state and allows himself no excuse. His sincerity cannot be denied, and he convinces us that he means every word, that the lines have been wrung out of him by his frank recognition of his plight. This is the way in which a man, whose intellect is as strong as his passions, may take his failure, and there is nothing factitious or stagy about it.

Poliziano also knows the bitterness of defeat and sees it as a denial of the best prizes which life has to offer, but he treats it in a different spirit with a different art. He masters his emotions and turns them into song, and that is why he keeps the seven-syllable line, which Lorenzo rejects for such a theme, and through it reveals his unimpaired confidence in himself and his cause. He asserts his own right to live and to love, to be himself and not to be treated as the helpless victim of a heartless rejection. His love has not quite turned to hatred, but it refuses to be despised without saying something hard in return. He sets out the situation in deft, everyday words, and short, stabbing phrases, and at each stage proclaims the force of his resistance:

Ecco l'ossa, ecco la carne,
Ecco il core, ecco la vita:
O crudel, che vuo' tu farne?
Ecco l'anima smarrita.
Perché innovi mia ferita,
E del sangue mio se' ingorda?
Questa bella aspida sorda
Chi verrà che me la incanti? (9, 29–36)

(*Here's the flesh, and here the bone,*
Here's the life, and here the heart:
What's your purpose, cruel one?
Here death rends my soul apart.
Why renew my wound and smart?
Can my blood your frenzy slake?
Ah, that deaf and lovely snake,
What a spell she sets on me!)

Poliziano's terse, dramatic language sharpens his point and makes it deadly. He has none of Lorenzo's gravity or restraint. If his lady shows no *gentilezza* to him, he shows little to her. With a keen eye for a striking effect, he concentrates on a single mood

338

and makes all he can of its possibilities. He is kept to his task by
his acute recognition of his mistress as she really is and of his own
feelings about her. It is this distillation of his emotions which
keeps his poem at the level of song. The two poets illustrate the
different ways in which emotions can be treated in poetry. Lorenzo
is still in the grip of them, and their conflict, sincerely and strongly
recorded, gives depth and richness to his words; Poliziano has
reduced them to a unity which absorbs his whole being and
enables him to assert himself and triumph over his disaster by the
vigour of his defence.

This difference in poetical manner arose from a difference in
temperament, and was accentuated by it. Lorenzo had in him a
vein of melancholy, which was not present on the same scale or
in the same quality in Poliziano. It is of a kind that comes often
to men of robust appetites and bounding vitality, who in the
intervals of effort and indulgence are assailed by nagging misgivings that time passes and they are missing their chances.
Lorenzo felt this, not indeed as the black annihilation which
made Greek poets declare that it is best not to be born, nor with
an Elizabethan sweetness which makes despair itself a pleasure.
For him it was a conviction reached by active experience and
matured by intimate meditation. He saw it not merely as his own
private doom but as a curse which dogs the young and beautiful.
In his verse he looks about him at beautiful women who behave
as if they were unaware of the future and its menaces, and he
addresses them not, as Horace would, with ugly forecasts of
decaying beauty, but with compassionate understanding:

> Donna, vano è il pensier che mai non crede
> Che venga il tempo della sua vecchiezza,
> E che la giovinezza
> Abbi sempre a star ferma in una tempre.
>
> Vola l'etate e fugge;
> Presto di nostra vita manca il fiore:
> E però dé' pensar il gentil core
> Ch'ogni cosa ne porta il tempo e strugge.

Dunque dé' gentil donna aver merzede
E non di sua bellezza essere altèra:
Perché folle è chi spera
Viver in giovinezza e bella sempre. (2)

(Lady, vain is the thought that dare not say
That with the years old age will surely come,
And youth has no sure home
In which to bide for ever in one stay.

Time's on the wing and flies;
Soon from our life the blossom must depart:
This thought must therefore stir the gentle heart,
That everything is snatched by time and dies.

Let gentle ladies give their thanks for this,
And in their beauty not be arrogant;
Foolish are they who want
Always to live in youth and loveliness.)

No doubt Lorenzo implies the lesson that, since this is so, we should enjoy ourselves while we can, but he does not say so, and his mind is occupied by this tyrannical, melancholy foreboding. In this mood he reveals something deeply and firmly rooted in his nature, and that is why the slow, solemn movement of the lines is admirably suited to his theme. Elsewhere indeed he has an answer to this trouble, but here is concerned with the trouble itself, and his poem has its own grave and compassionate strength.

Poliziano was no less aware of the brevity of youth, but faced it in a less troubled, less brooding spirit. To convey the delights of youth as he saw them he shaped an effective imagery in which a garden in springtime stands for youth and its opportunities. He sets out the theme with his usual attention to what is strictly relevant:

I' mi trovai, fanciulle, un bel mattino
Di mezzo maggio in un verde giardino. (3, 1–2)

(On one fine morn, maidens, I found my way
To a green garden in the month of May.)

The garden comes from medieval romance and allegory, and in front of it lie the magical gardens of Ariosto and Tasso, but Poliziano presents it so simply that we do not think of its literary associations and accept it without ado as a fit image for the beauty of youth and the glory of love. He develops its implications neatly and prettily. In it there are flowers of every kind and colour, and he begins by picking violets and lilies, only to see that the roses have a sweeter scent, and he fills his bosom with them. The rose thus gets a more distinctive character than usual and becomes the image of mature love, which displaces earlier, less radiant affections. Then Poliziano advances to his conclusions:

> Quando la rosa ogni sua foglia spande,
> Quando è più bella, quando è più gradita,
> Allora è buona a mettere in ghirlande,
> Prima che sua bellezza sia fuggita:
> Sicché, fanciulle, mentre è più fiorita,
> Cogliam la bella rosa del giardino. (3, 27–32)

> (*For when the rose bursts from her tender sheath,*
> *When she is sweetest and her grace is spread,*
> *Then is the time to bind her in your wreath*
> *Before her glowing loveliness has fled;*
> *So, maidens, while she lifts her petalled head,*
> *Gather the garden's glorious rose that day.*)

Unlike Lorenzo, Poliziano does not mention old age or decay, but concentrates on the sunlit moment of youth and love. He does not even mention himself. His appeal is universal, and all the more persuasive because it is based not on fear but on the unique opportunity of the present. He is concerned not to argue a case, nor even to unburden his own thoughts, but simply to catch a mood and to present it without any attraction but its own essential appeal.

In developing the courtly and romantic possibilities of the *canzone a ballo* Lorenzo and Poliziano followed an aristocratic tradition which believed in restraint and decorum and impeccable sentiments. Parallel to this was another tradition with a very different temper. Since *ballate* were sung at seasonal festivals, they had a strong popular element of satire, gibes, and lubricious jocosity. Once they were performed by a 'king' and a 'queen', of whom the first was the lover, the second the beloved. The illusion was maintained by gala costumes, a crown of flowers on the 'queen's' head and a certain simple formality in the whole occasion. But the 'king' soon lost what small dignity he had and became the jealous and hot-tempered husband, who tried in vain to keep the devotion of his wife the 'queen'. Such songs favoured a primitive licence and were a useful way of mocking unloved husbands. An early example comes from Poitou:

> A l'entrada del tens clar, *eya*
> Per joia recomençar, *eya*
> E per jelos irritar, *eya*
> Vol la regina mostrar
>   Qu'el' es si amoroza.[1]

> (*In the days of cloudless skies*, eya
> *That desire for joy may rise*, eya
> *And give pain to jealous eyes*, eya
> *Then the queen to all men cries*
>   *That in love she's fallen.*)

The 'king' has become a figure of fun, who is derided and driven out of the dance as one unfit for love. It is this spirit of ribald and illicit love-making which lives again in some of the *canzoni a ballo* of Lorenzo and Poliziano.

It is idle to pretend that in these songs either poet shows his talents at their best. The question is rather why they wrote them at all, and what they made of them. With Lorenzo the motive may well have been partly political, since by such means he was able to show that he understood the Florentines and shared some of their less reputable tastes. No doubt Poliziano followed his example because they worked together, but also because he had his seamy side which found satisfaction in this kind of poetry. Yet both men may have felt a deeper need than these. Just as Provençal poets, like Guillaume of Aquitaine, felt at times a need

[1] Berry, op. cit., p. 18.

342

to abandon the strains and stresses of selfless love for something crude and earthy, so perhaps the two Florentines needed some violent corrective to chivalrous devotion, which kept them in a strait-jacket and allowed almost no deviation from its exacting rules. It must have been a relief to turn things upside down and to make fun of the love which they must otherwise treat so seriously. This does not mean that we should attach much importance to these poems, which are only a by-product of their authors' activity. But in them both poets evolved a neat, colloquial style, which can say appalling things in a quiet, modest way. They have an element of low comedy and make something dramatic from such well-worn themes as wives who decry their husbands, or young women who fleece young men, or daughters who put into practice their mothers' all too worldly advice. Yet for the most part these songs fall flat because they lack the true Aristophanic ebullience. Their trouble is not so much that they have aged with time as that they are calculated rather than instinctive and snigger rather than laugh. None the less among them are a few pieces which show their authors in a new light and have a real claim to originality.

Poliziano is most successful when he keeps his humour in a quiet key and turns it into some small and engaging comedy. He wishes, for instance, to tell his audience of ladies that he suffers from something of which he cannot speak, and though we cannot guess what it is, we can admire the parable which sets out his situation:

Donne mie, voi non sapete
Ch'i'ho il mal ch'avea quel prete.

Fu un prete (questa è vera)
Ch'avea morto il porcellino.
Ben sapete che una sera
Gliel rubò un contadino,
Ch'era quivi suo vicino
(Altri dice suo compare):
Poi s'andò a confessare
E contò del porco al prete.

343

Il messer se ne voleva
Pure andare alla ragione:
Ma pensò che non poteva
Ché l'avea in confessione.
Dicea poi tra le persone:
—Oimè, ch'i'ho un male,
Ch'io noi posso dire avale—
Et anch'io ho il mal del prete. (17)

(Once a priest—'tis really so—
Killed a little pig to eat,
But at dusk, I'd have you know,
It was stolen by a cheat
Who lived in a nearby street;
—Others say he knew him well—
Of the pig he went to tell
In confession to the priest.

For this theft the good priest wanted
To resort to legal session,
But from doing it was daunted
Since he heard it in confession.
To his friends he made admission:
'Woe, by what a grief I'm hit;
I can never speak of it!'
I too suffer like the priest.

The skill of this poem lies partly in its tone, with its conversational ease and asides and comments, in which the situation is
first set out with a flat and factual verisimilitude, and then made
to reveal its inherent absurdity. The theme, reminiscent of
Boccaccio, is economically and neatly handled. Priests were a
legitimate subject for fun of this kind, and Poliziano laughs at
himself when he compares his position with that of the frustrated
confessor.

Priests are one thing, but the rites and ceremonies of the Church
are another, and it is surprising to find Lorenzo using them as
imagery for the cult of love. Something may be due to an ancient

kinship between *canzoni a ballo* and ecclesiastical *laudi*. The original mime, from which both arose, must have been crude and primitive, and it is understandable that the secular arm should borrow themes from the sacred, but we would hardly expect this to be done so audaciously as Lorenzo does it. In one poem of his we almost feel that we are in the presence of some disciple of Baudelaire, who deliberately perverts the language of religion to the purposes of profane love. Lorenzo begins by stating his topic:

> Donne e fanciulle, io mi fo coscienza
> D'ogni mio fallo, e vo' far penitenza. (15, 1–2)

> (*Ladies and maids, myself I pass my sentence*
> *On all my faults, and for them make repentance.*)

One of the most solemn rites of the Christian religion is turned to an unashamedly secular end. For Lorenzo then proceeds to enumerate his faults in love and models his manner closely on that of the confessional as he speaks of his *peccati* and reaches his conclusion in the language of contrition:

> Dico 'mia colpa', ed ho molto dolore
> Di viltà, negligenzia, e d'ogni errore:
> Ricordi o non ricordi, innanzi Amore
> Generalmente io mi fo coscienza. (15, 27–30)

> (*I say the fault is mine; my grief is great*
> *For vileness and neglect and error's state;*
> *Remembering or not, with Love I wait,*
> *And for my every fault I make repentance.*)

The manner is that of Lorenzo's own *laudi*, and behind it lies a long tradition of religious poetry which uses just this metre and this language and whose early exponents would indeed have been startled to see them put to such a purpose.

Yet after all there is nothing very surprising in a man of the *Quattrocento* using the language of Christian devotion for illicit love. It is the logical conclusion of the process which began in Provence when the idealized mistress was regarded as the source of all virtue and worshipped with self-abasing devotion. Christian mythology provided symbols for most conditions and occasions and was so inextricably mingled with men's habits of thought that they would not always stop to ask whether it was appropriate or permissible. If it could be applied to one kind of love, it was easy and not entirely unreasonable to apply it to another, especially if this evoked its own reverence and imposed its own obligations. Lorenzo approaches his faults in love with what looks like real contrition and we must take him at his word. His poem is certainly not a blasphemous parody. Its significance is rather that he feels his faults as a lover to resemble his faults as a Christian and to call for the same kind of treatment. The cult of love, as he knew it, exacted humility and self-effacement and imposed a special state of mind. This was in fact at war with some fundamental tenets of the Christian ethic, but it was not so obviously at war with much of Christian feeling. In this spirit Lorenzo feels that he must make confession of his faults, and hopes that he will be forgiven for them.

Though the *canzone a ballo* encouraged its exponents to explore the purlieus and even the slums of contemporary sentiment, it also called for something gayer and brighter which appealed to the Florentine love of visible show and splendour. That no doubt is why Lorenzo elaborated the *canzone a ballo* into the *canto carnascialesche*. It had always had an element of masquerade, and when he accentuated this, he gave it new opportunities and extended its range. The vivid costumes caught the eye and became inspiriting incentives to love-making. Songs of carnival may begin by pretending that they are concerned with some condition or calling, but it is soon clear that their chief concern is with love. Beggars have been reduced by it to their present state; pilgrims have taken to solitude because failure in love has made human society unendurable; muleteers are interested solely in their female patrons. The songs of carnival were the progeny of the songs of dance and added a new spice by making their occasions look more promising and more adventurous.

The most resplendent of the songs of carnival were the *trionfi*, composed to present not trades or callings or classes, but popular fables or classical myths, which embodied some theme of love. Lorenzo's *Canzone delle Cicale* consists of a *contrasto* or debate between girls and 'cicadas', who no doubt because of their un-ceasing noise stand for the tittle-tattlers and gossip-mongers who spy upon lovers and make their life a misery. The theme goes back to the beginnings of Provençal song, where the *lausengiers* are stock characters, who, from meanness and malice, work against lovers. Lorenzo makes something fresh of them by allow-ing them to state their own case. The girls attack them, and the *cicale* put up a good defence by arguing that it is their nature to behave as they do, but at least they give the girls a chance, when they tell them that their best policy is simply not to be found out. This gives a more laughable and less contemptible role to the shabby figure of the sneak. The choice offered to the girls is not between love and virtue, but between indiscretion and discretion. Even so they cannot submit. They refuse to be secretive, since it is against their characters and their principles. So they defy their critics and do not care what price they have to pay:

> Or che val nostra bellezza,
> Se si perde per parole?
> Viva amore e gentilezza!
> Muoia invidia e a chi ben duole!
> Dica pur chi mal dir vuole,
> Noi faremo e voi direte. (3, 27–32)
>
> (*What's the worth of all our beauty,*
> *If words spoken can destroy it?*
> *Long live love and gentle duty!*
> *Death to hate, if good annoy it!*
> *Let them slander who enjoy it;*
> *We shall act, and you will chatter.*)

The girls are not frightened by the *cicale*, but act in the best tradi-tions of *gentilezza*, which, being dedicated to the service of love, refuses to betray its ideals.

If this poem dramatizes a social aspect of love-making, another poem reveals its need for some kind of philosophy to counter

Christian disapproval. In this Lorenzo presents as his characters the seven planets, and appeals to the taste for astrology which has obsessed many minds ever since it came from the East to Greece soon after 200 B.C. Lorenzo's planets begin, in the best classical manner, by proclaiming their power, for good and for ill, over human beings, animals, plants, and even stones. In the second stanza the range of their dominion is deftly and rapidly suggested, and Lorenzo enumerates some main types of human beings as astrologers classified them. So far he follows tradition. But at this point the poet of love asserts himself, and he turns his special attention to Venus, who is for him by far the most important of the planets and receives a notable tribute in the three remaining stanzas. Young men and women are summoned to forget their melancholy thoughts and follow her. The other planets are not even named but lumped together as the source of troubles and trials. It is wiser to follow Venus while we can. Part of the charm of the poem is that the weapons of astrology are turned against itself. Instead of a mechanistic system beyond human control we are presented with a field of choice in which the wise will certainly make the right decision. Venus becomes, if not a divine, at least a superhuman and supernatural power, and her cult receives the kind of authority that generations have given to the stars and their influences.

Poliziano did not, so far as we know, write songs of carnival in the strict sense, but in the *Favola di Orfeo*, which he composed for dramatic performance in 1479, when he was the guest of the Gonzagas at Mantua, he included a song which is very like a *trionfo*. It is the song of the Maenads with which the *Favola* ends, and it resembles a *trionfo* in its form, its reckless spirit, and its dramatic action. That Poliziano should end an unusually painful and tragic story with an uproarious song is indeed remarkable. Perhaps he felt that his episodes were so painful that they deserved a cheerful ending; perhaps after all he did not care very much for the poignant story and was determined to introduce something that he really liked. Whatever his motives, Poliziano gives a surprising turn to the story of Orpheus, which is abandoned and

348

forgotten in a lively song on the powers of Bacchus. No Greek or
Roman Maenads are dominated to this degree by wine. The
Bacchants of Euripides have indeed their exultant and reckless
songs, but their first concern is with the worship of their god.
Poliziano, with his usual instinct for selection, goes for a single
theme and makes the most of it.

The song reveals its excited character at the start:

> Ciascun segua, o Bacco, te:
> Bacco, Bacco, oè, oè!
>
> (*Bacchus, all must follow thee!*
> *Bacchus, Bacchus! Hey! Obey!*)

As they sing the Maenads become progressively more drunken.
The song is indeed a drinking-song, and during it the wine is
passed round and the cups are filled. But it differs from most
drinking-songs in being both exuberant and elegant. Too many
of such songs are either shapeless and frothy or pompous and self-
justifying. Poliziano writes an essential and ideal drinking-song—
just what such a song ought to be, if it is also to be authentic
poetry. At the end of it the Maenads are on the brink of collapse:

> Ognun gridi: Bacco! Bacco!
> E pur cacci del vin giù:
> Poi col sôno farem fiacco.
> Bevi tu, e tu, e tu.
> Io non posso ballar più.
> Ognun gridi: oè, oè!
> Ciascun segua, o Bacco, te:
> Bacco, Bacco, oè, oè!
>
> (*Calling, calling 'Bacchus! Bacchus!'*
> *Fill the cups with wine anew,*
> *Till we fall and sleep attack us,*
> *Drinking you, and you, and you!*
> *Everyone cry out 'Obey!'*
> *Bacchus, all must follow thee:*
> *Bacchus, Bacchus! Hey! Obey!*

Poliziano embodies the Dionysiac spirit in its most elemental, most intelligible form. The art of the *trionfo*, transferred to the stage and given a new freedom of action and expression, enables him to transmute a common experience into brilliant art.

Poliziano gained in strength by detaching himself from the immediate scene and letting his imagination play in an inde-pendent world of poetry. He needed this distance to set his facul-ties to work, and when he had found it, he achieved an unusual distinction of style and manner. Always a lover of the vivid, precise word, he was able to make the best use of it when he was not disturbed by personal considerations and immediate needs. His masterpiece is perhaps the song which he composed for May Day, when the jousters entered the lists and, before competing, crowned their ladies with garlands. It is a song of spring and love and akin to a *canzone a ballo* in its spirit and its art. It concentrates on the inner meaning and the essential character of a resplendent occasion. Behind it lie many songs of spring, and with these it has something in common when it summons to love as an awaken-ing of earth and all its creatures. But it also reflects a chivalrous festival, when gallants exert their manhood for the ladies whom they adore. In Poliziano's skilful art the two occasions become one, and the season of spring is inextricably that of glittering gallantry. Love is displayed through masculine feats of prowess, and all moves from a single centre. The song begins with a pro-clamation and a challenge:

> Ben venga Maggio,
> E'l gonfalon selvaggio!
>
> (*Gladly let May come on,*
> *And her wild gonfalon.*)

Each stanza catches something new in the stirring of life in hearts and thews, in nature and in man. Poliziano convinces us that in the ceremonies of May Day the flowers and birds are not a back-ground but part of the whole delighted ritual. The poem is true to its age in its high-pitched passions and its proud endeavours, its sense of supernatural powers present and at work, its formal elegance and its bursting, unflagging gaiety. In it Poliziano achieves his own kind of pure poetry, in which he makes everything contribute to an enthralling joy. This is his most special gift, and in its exercise he shows how, from his firm idea of what poetry is, he is able to distil some of its essential qualities and to see that every word contains them in as undiluted a purity as possible.

If this song shows Poliziano's powers at their fullest and best, Lorenzo's may be seen in the *trionfo* of Bacchus and Ariadne. In it he is most himself because he is inspired by powerful emotions and uses all his dramatic skill to give a lively and concrete form to them. The figures of Bacchus and Ariadne might have been used for an occasion of unclouded delight, but Lorenzo uses them to shape his own anxieties about the fleeting character of youth and the uncertainty of tomorrow. The unforgettable theme sets the tone at the start:

> Quant' è bella giovinezza,
> Che si fugge tuttavia!
> Chi vuol esser lieto, sia:
> Di doman non c'è certezza. (1, 1–4)

> (*Fair is youth and void of sorrow:*
> *But it hourly fades away—*
> *Youths and maids, enjoy today:*
> *Nought ye know about tomorrow.*)
>
> (J. A. SYMONDS)

In the pageant that follows the allegorical figures are chosen with a keen eye for their relevance to the main theme. Bacchus and Ariadne may typify love at an almost celestial level, but even with them we suspect a faint hint that their love soon comes to an end. The Nymphs and Satyrs, creatures of nature and animal appetites, stand almost in antithesis to the leading figures and present love as something easy and irresponsible and not very serious. Then Lorenzo unexpectedly introduces Silenus and Midas, and with them presents contrasting ideas. While Silenus is an example of self-indulgent age, which still remains able to keep the happiness of youth, Midas wastes his years in a pursuit which does him no good and brings him no pleasure. As we look on these figures, we understand what it means to love in the present:

> Ciascun apra ben gli orecchi:
> Di doman nessun si paschi;
> Oggi sian, giovani e vecchi,
> Lieti ognun, femmine e maschi;
> Ogni tristo pensier caschi:
> Facciam festa tuttavia.
> Chi vuol esser lieto, sia:
> Di doman non c'è certezza. (1, 45–52)

> (*Listen well to what we're saying;*
> *Of tomorrow have no care!*
> *Young and old together playing,*
> *Boys and girls be blithe as air!*
> *Every sorry thought forswear!*
> *Keep perpetual holiday—*
> *Youths and maids, enjoy today;*
> *Nought ye know about tomorrow.*)   (J. A. SYMONDS)

This is close to the spirit in which the Greeks spent their happiest moments. Well aware of the limitations of mortality, they none the less believed that at certain times they partook of a celestial felicity and almost resembled the gods, that just because such moments are rare and life is fleeting, they must be all the more enjoyed while they last. Lorenzo is concerned with this, but his concentration on the moment is a little more deliberate and more conscious than that of the Greeks. His gaiety is achieved almost by an effort of will, by shutting his eyes to what lies before him, by flinging all his zest for pleasure into the immediate occasion. The poem gains from a hint of melancholy in the background, and shows Lorenzo as he really was when he turned his full atten⁄tion to the delights that meant so much to him.

The songs of dance and carnival form but a small part of the complete works of Lorenzo and Poliziano, and they are not the most important part of them. Yet the best among these songs show their authors at their finest, and even the more mediocre have some interest for the historian of manners. They display that union of the medieval and the classical which was characteristic of the *Quattrocento* and accounts for much that is most attractive in it. The *ballata* and its progeny are indeed medieval not merely in their origin but in their special kind of formality. Greek choral odes have an elaborate and impressive formality, which is similarly due to the demands of accompaniment in music and dancing, but they are far freer to develop their themes. The *ballata* is limited to almost a single theme, and its task is to make variations on it rather than to move boldly into uncharted regions. On the other hand these pieces have a quality which is not to be found in the masters of medieval song and is certainly derived from classical examples. They have a new brevity and concentration, a gift for going straight to the point without preliminaries and asides, a feeling for the precise worth of words, a love of clear outline and striking effects. The medieval form is used to embody a classical temper, and the result is something new in Europe.

Just because love is an indispensable theme and has its own ritual and ceremonies, it creates in its adepts a dual system of thinking for which there is no parallel in Greece or Rome. Neither Lorenzo nor Poliziano shows in his poetry a unified personality. They accept eagerly the challenges of experience, and respond with all the ardour of their natures, but we do not feel with them, as we feel with Greek and Roman poets, that all moves from a single centre. Their inconsistencies may have been increased by the impact of the new learning on a traditional Christian outlook, but they were already inherent in the insoluble contradictions of courtly love. On the other hand their classical training gives a new depth to established notions of this love by stressing that, since all things are transitory, they must for this very reason be sought and enjoyed. This cleared and tidied the poets' minds and made them think more purposively what their tastes and desires meant. Though in many ways they are the loyal heirs of a medieval tradition and maintain it with a sincere attachment, they bring to it a more inquiring and more searching spirit, a more discriminating and more intellectual art.

John Sparrow

LATIN VERSE OF THE HIGH
RENAISSANCE

Je me défie beaucoup des vers latins modernes.

VOLTAIRE

There are several reasons why the Latin verse of the Renaissance is so rarely read. First of all, there is so much of it. Of the published poetry of classical Rome not a great deal has been preserved;[1] and a large proportion of that modest corpus consists of master/ pieces—its very quality, no doubt, helped to preserve it. But the vast production of the Renaissance, good, bad and indifferent, has been largely saved for us by the printing press; and, even if we look only at what was written in Italy[2] in the last thirty years of the fifteenth and the first thirty years of the sixteenth centuries, the volume that confronts us is daunting enough.

[1] The *Corpus Poetarum Latinorum* contains the works of only a score or so of poets, and even if we add to it the contents of Baehrens' *Poetae Latini Minores*, the total falls far short, in bulk, of the *Carmina Illustrium Poetarum Italorum*.

[2] I speak of 'Italy' as though it were itself a unitary whole, and could be con/ sidered separately from the rest of Europe. For my purposes, perhaps both assump/ tions may be justified. There were 'centres' of the production of Latin poetry in this period at Rome, Naples, Florence, Ferrara, Mantua, Venice—to name no other places; but there was continual interchange; poets travelled freely from one city to another, and I cannot myself detect any recognizable 'schools' of verse. And Italy was so far the leader and teacher of the rest of Europe in this field that what was essentially, and became eventually, a European literature was still an Italian pre/ serve: foreigners flocked to Rome for instruction, and learned from Italians resident in their own countries (cf. D. Murarasu, *La Poésie néo/latine en France, 1500–49*, Paris, 1928), but no other nation had yet created a Latin literature of its own.

A few figures will suggest the scale upon which Latin verse was manufactured in Italy at this time. Of those who frequented the literary gatherings of Johann Goritz, more than eighty poets are named by Francesco Arsilli in the lines *De Poetis Urbanis* which he appended to *Coryciana* (Rome, 1524).[1] Léger du Chesne collected his *Flores Epigrammatum* (Paris, 1555, 1560) from nearly a hundred poets, almost all of them contemporary, or nearly contemporary, Italians. Twenty years later, Giovanni Matteo Toscano included about the same number in his *Carmina Illustrium Poetarum Italorum* (Paris, 1576, 1577), and twice as many—a round two hundred—are represented in Gruter's *Delitiae C C Italorum Poetarum, huius superiorisque aevi illustrium* (Frank/furt, 1608), a collection which, though it contains only a selection from the works of each author, runs to nearly three thousand pages. Finally, the number of poets is swelled to more than four hundred in the great collection of *Carmina Illustrium Poetarum Italorum* published in eleven volumes, containing over five thousand pages, in Florence (1719–28).

Through this vast continent the reader must make his way practically unaided.[2] Burckhardt, almost a hundred years ago, compressed his report upon it into a score of shrewd, suggestive, penetrating pages; his vision took in both distance and detail, and he had an unerring eye for the significant. In 1877 John Addington Symonds, in *The Revival of Learning*, recorded at

---

[1] I take the figure from the extended version of the poem printed by Tiraboschi at the end of the third Book of his *Storia della Letteratura Italiana*.

[2] Sixteenth-century critics provide little more than catalogues of names, with scraps of biographical information and naïve critical comment; such are the con/tents of Toscano's *Peplus Italiae* (1578) and Lelio Gregorio Giraldi's *De Poetis nostrorum temporum* (1551). Giovanni Pierio Valeriano's *De litteratorum infelicitate* (written in about 1534) and Paolo Giovio's *Elogia Doctorum Virorum* (1546) con/tain amusing biographical particulars, and Iacopo Gaddi's *De Scriptoribus non Ecclesiasticis* (1648) is worth referring to, as is Book VI of J. C. Scaliger's *Poetice* (1561). Hallam reviewed this department of poetry in his *Introduction to the Literature of Europe* (1837–9), but the best account of the Italian contributors to it is still that contained in the two chapters on Latin poetry in the fifteenth and sixteenth centuries contained in Tiraboschi's *Storia della Letteratura Italiana*.

length the impressions of an aesthete who was also a scholar; fifty years later Georg Ellinger, with native thoroughness, com‚ piled a sort of literary gazetteer of the territory;[1] and more recently M. Paul van Tieghem, in a brief and close‚packed survey, has covered the whole field of Renaissance Latin literature.[2] But no one has attempted to do for this great body of verse what Manitius and more recently Mr. F. J. E. Raby have done for the Latin verse of the Middle Ages—to trace its history and analyse its component strains, to estimate its worth as poetry and to place it in a proper relation to the world out of which it grew.

The taste of the intervening centuries, however, has done a little sifting;[3] something like a canon of 'major' poets has been established: Politian, Pontano, Sannazaro, Bembo, Navagero, Vida, Fracastoro, M. A. Flaminio—these are the names that have been set against Lucretius, Horace, Catullus, Virgil, Proper‚ tius, Tibullus, and Ovid;[4] and scholars have recently made

[1] *Italien und der deutsche Humanismus in der neulateinischen Lyrik* (Berlin, 1929).

[2] *La Littérature latine de la Renaissance* (Paris, 1944).

[3] *Carmina quinque illustrium poetarum* (Venice, 1548; reprinted Florence 1549, 1552) contained Bembo, Navagero, Castiglione, Cotta, and M. A. Flaminio. Pope's anthology, *Selecta Poemata Italorum* (1740; founded upon the anonymously edited Ἀνθολογία *seu Selecta quaedam Poemata Italorum*, 1684) contains poems from the works of these five poets and the others mentioned in the text above, and also from the following: 'Janus Etruscus', the Strozzi, F. M. Molza, Ariosto, Augurello, P. Crinito, Niccolò d'Arco, the Amaltei, Buchanan, P. G. Vaxis, Fascitelli, Parlistaneo, and Sadoleto. In 1753 there appeared at Bergamo another *Carmina quinque illustrium poetarum*, containing Bembo, Navagero, Castiglione, della Casa and Politian. These (with Flaminio and Sadoleto substituted for the last pair) were, according to Gravina (*Della Ragione Poetica*, I, xl), *i cinque poeti illustri che per lo più nelle stampe vanno congiunti*. A well‚chosen collection, with the same title as Pope's, but limited to the sixteenth century, was published at Oxford, without the editor's name, in 1808.

I know of no modern anthology of Renaissance Latin verse except E. Costa's *Antologia della lirica latina in Italia nei Secoli XV e XVI* (Città di Castello, 1888), which is confined to lyrical verse and is now, at any rate in England, almost unprocurable; this contains a long Introduction and selections from thirty poets. Miss Florence Gragg's excellent *Latin Writings of the Italian Humanists* (Scribner's, 1927), which consists largely of prose extracts, is also unprocurable in this country.

[4] Cf. Trissino, enumerating in Book XXIV of *Italia Liberata* the most cele‚ brated of his contemporaries:

some of them available, like classical authors, in up-to-date editions.[1]

But even when everything has been done to make these texts available and attractive to read, the poets of ancient Rome have still an immense advantage over them: they are, after all, the Old Masters. Landor puts this well in his essay *Quamobrem Poetae Latini recentiores minus legantur: Unde igitur fieri existimemus*, he asks, *neminem, post literas renatas, Latinis usum, cum veteribus comparari posse? Brevi dicam quid sentio. Etiamsi minus hi elegantes essent, minus ingenio valerent . . . tamen ab optimo quoque et aequissimo judice plus favoris et gratiae conciliarent, quia in mentem teneram insederint, et primis animi et suavissimis affectibus insinuaverint sese, ac nexu quodam indis-solubili inseruerint.*

Today, a sensitive reader, even if 'the classics' have not made their impression, as they did for Landor's contemporaries, upon his youthful mind, can hardly help being affected by their prestige; their works are so closely woven into literature and history, into the aesthetic consciousness of the world, that even the most dispassionate of critics needs a rare power of detachment if he is to approach them without preconceptions in their favour. It is hard to embark in an equally receptive frame of mind upon the *De rerum natura* of Lucretius and (say) the *Urania* of Pontano, the *Ars Poetica* of Horace and the *Ars Poetica* of Vida, the *Eclogues* of Virgil and the *Eclogues* of Sannazaro; in every case the classical poet has half won the battle for our appreciation before we begin to read him.

E'l ottimo Pontano, e'l Sannazaro,
E'l Sadoleto, col Flaminio: e'l Bembo,
E'l Fracastoro, e'l Navagero, e'l Cotta.

[1] It seems probable that Latin scholarship on both sides of the Atlantic, when it has done all that can be done for classical texts, will turn its attention to Renais-sance poets. Mustard and Pepper prepared the way in America thirty or forty years ago, the former with his series of editions of Latin pastorals, the latter with his work (with Padelford) on Scaliger's *Poetice*. Among many other such works that have recently appeared in Europe I may mention *Areosti Carmina*, ed. A. Bolaffi (Rome, 1938); *Pontani Carmina*, ed. J. Oeschger (Bari, 1948); *Marulli Carmina*, ed. A. Perosa (Zürich, 1951); and *The Poems of Erasmus*, ed. C. Reedijk (Leiden, 1956).

Even if we clear our minds of such preconceptions, there remains another impediment: the classical poets are not only the Old Masters, they are also the Real Thing: their poetry was written in a living language and sprang directly from their life; the Renaissance poets (we are told) wrote artificial verse in a dead language, and such verse must be, in the phrase of Professor C. S. Lewis, 'stillborn'.[1]

Such criticisms imply too simple an idea of the concept 'artificial' and a wrong estimate of the part played by the Latin language in the life of the time. For most educated men in Renaissance Italy, Latin was a natural means of expression; they had learned at school to use it for the purposes of everyday;[2] they read it and wrote it as easily as they read and wrote their native tongue; for them it was not merely the language of discourse and diplomacy and of polite or learned correspondence, it could be even the language of joke and dream.[3] Most of the Latin poets of the age were men of the world—courtiers and ambassadors like Castiglione and Navagero, physicians like Fracastoro, country gentlemen like Niccolò d'Arco, and soldiers of fortune like

---

[1] *English Literature in the Sixteenth Century excluding Drama* (Oxford, 1954), p. 21.

[2] The point is well put by E. P. Goldschmidt, *The Printed Book of the Renaissance* (1950), pp. 8–9: 'In the fifteenth or early sixteenth century, Latin was not yet a dead learned language, it was *the* language in which people read and wrote, although they did not generally speak it. It is an important point, much too often overlooked by historians in all branches of the discipline, that *all* education in those times was Latin education. Boys were not 'taught Latin', they were taught *in* Latin, they were not allowed to utter a single vernacular word while at school. When they were taught to read, they were taught to read Latin; if they were taught to write, they were taught in Latin to write Latin.'

[3] Pontano's six Books on Conversation (*De Sermone*, 1499)—not to mention his Dialogues (excellently edited by C. Previtera, Florence, 1943) and those of his contemporaries (though we are not to suppose that these are faithful records of actual conversations)—show how spontaneously Latin could be used among educated men. For dreaming in Latin, cf. Vida *De Arte Poetica*, ii, 440–5. An interesting example is to be found in the *Poemata Varia* of Giano Anisio (Naples, 1531), p. 8, where Anisio prints an unmetrical Latin epitaph on Pontano, explaining that he composed it in a dream and that when he woke he tried with the help of friends to improve it by turning it into verse, but without success.

Marullo. To such men, no less than to scholars and men of letters like Politian and Pontano, Latin, as a language to write, if not to talk, must have come as easily as 'la lingua moderna'. Nor was it used only by the educated; most of the Grub Street produc⁄ tions stuck up on the statue of Pasquillus were in Latin, and even women could be fluent in the 'dead' tongue. One of Casti⁄ glione's elegies opens with lines—worth quoting for their own sake —in which he gives a picture of Elisabetta Gonzaga singing Virgil to the lyre:

'Dulces exuviae, dum fata Deusque sinebant'
    dum canit, et querulum pollice tangit ebur,
formosa e caelo deducit Elisa Tonantem,
    et trahit immites ad pia verba feras . . .
Atque aliquis tali captus dulcedine sentit
    elabi ex imo pectore sensim animam;
flebile nescio quid tacite in praecordia serpit
    cogit et invitos illacrimare oculos[1]

—and *cortesanae honestae* would embellish their letters with Latin of pure classical idiom.[2]

Perhaps the most striking proof of the degree to which Latin was a living language is to be found in the feats of the *improvisa⁄ tori* who frequented the Vatican under Leo X—feats to which the Pope would himself contribute by capping their verses off hand. Of many recorded examples only one or two need be given here.

---

[1] The *Dulces exuviae* passage from *Aen.* IV was apparently a favourite with com⁄ posers. Two settings—by Josquin Desprez (1450-1521) and Adrian Willaert (1480⁄90-1562)—are reprinted by Möseler in *Fünf Vergil⁄Motetten* (Wolfenbüttel, 1956). They show, incidentally, that the composers made no attempt to reproduce in their setting the syllabic or the quantitative structure of the text. Cf. a passage from the *De Numero Oratorio* of Iovita Rapicius (ed. Aldina, 1554, p. 7), where he says that 'rhythmici . . . qui vulgo musici, et cantores nominantur, syllabarum quantitatem et syllabicos pedes negligunt, ac breves pro longis, et rursus longos pro brevibus cantando efferunt; et temporum suo quodam modo dimensorum ordine et proportione contenti, utcunque ratio cantici postulat, vel procurrunt, vel subsistunt; atque hunc rhythmum suum aerem [*sc.* 'aria'] vocant'.

[2] See E. Rodocanachi, *Le Pontificat de Clément VII* (Hachette, 1933), p. 125.

Paolo Giovio, for instance, thus describes Andrea Marone declaiming his extemporary Latin verses: *Is enim cum summa eruditorum admiratione ex tempore ad quam iusseris quaestionem, Latinos versus variis modis et numeris fundere consuevit. . . . Fidibus et cantu Musas evocat, et . . . tanta vi in torrentis morem citatus fertur, ut fortuita et subitariis tractibus ducta, multum ante provisa et meditata carmina videantur.* That these were indeed no cold, meditated performances was plain from the poet's outward aspect as he sang: *Canenti defixi exardent oculi, sudores manant, frontis venae contumescunt, et quod mirum est, eruditae aures tanquam alienae et intentae, omnem impetum profluentium numerorum exactissima ratione moderantur.*

Panfilo Sassi, another frequenter of Goritz's gatherings, possessed the same facility: *Quod peculiare hoc aevo arbitror,* says Giovanni Taberio,[1] *incredibili dictat velocitate.* At a recent dinner-party, continues Taberio, when dessert was put upon the table, *ecce tibi Pamphilus ad lyram. . . . Materiam nosti. Brixiam suo, id est schedico, cantu laudabat omniferam. Hic tu imprimis patriae laudis studiosus iam statim cohortabaris ut carmen emitteret. Ille qui non hoc facit ostentatione, sed vel animi relaxatione vel amicorum obsequio, paulisper haesit, annuenti tamen similis.* Next day, *amicis idem efflagitantibus,* he yielded: *opus multiforme in varia disiectum membra collegit, inclytoque Maecenati suo dedicatum impressoribus tradidit.*[2]

It is wrong, then, to suppose that the Renaissance Latinists

---

[1] Dedicating Sassi's poems (Brescia, 1499) to 'Helias Capreolus'.

[2] Giraldi testifies to the power of extemporary composition possessed by these two poets (*De Poetis nostrorum temporum* (1551), p. 42): 'Maronem extemporalis facultas commendat adeo ut superioribus his mensibus . . . in Cosmiano Leonis X convivio caeteros, qui multi aderant, poetas proposita materia, quam referrent ex tempore, obmutescere quasi elingues fecerit. . . . Pamphilus etiam Sassius Mutinensis extemporalis poeta, qui ut interloquendum celerrime verba volvit, ita in faciendis versibus promptissimus. . . .'

Valeriano (*De Litteratorum Infelicitate* (1620), p. 66) speaks of Marone's 'felicissimam pangendis carminibus extemporalitatem', adding 'Nil absurdum et inane, nil hiulcum emodulari quotiescumque amicorum rogatu invitaretur. Id quod tribus praecipue versuum generibus indifferenter factitare consuerat, sive elegum, sive Phalaecium, seu Saphicum Hendecasyllabum deposceres, nihil contatus, quod proposuisses argumentum, horum quovis carminis numero continebat.'

had to struggle, like schoolboys or students, with an alien tongue. One comes rarely upon solecisms and awkwardnesses which are there because the writer was not master of his medium, or could not adapt it to contemporary needs; more often one marvels at the ease with which these poets respond to every occasion and embroider every theme. Sometimes their mastery enables them to be diffuse—'the chief fault of his verses', says Symonds of Politian, 'is their fluency', and no one who has attempted to read the thousands of hexameters in which Joannes Baptista Mantuanus rambles through the story of the Virgin Birth will cast doubt upon the fluency of that indefatigable Carmelite—sometimes it enables them to be obscure, as with Lancino Corte, a powerful, difficult, and unpleasant poet, whose control over his Latin is so complete that he positively twists it into knots. If writing Latin did not come naturally to such men, at least it was their second nature.[1]

Indeed, for the writing of poetry, Latin was at least as natural a medium as the vernacular. It was still the only language in which a writer could feel sure that he would be understood throughout Italy, let alone in foreign countries, and the only language of which he could feel sure (though time was to prove this certainty ill-founded) that it would outlast the changing fashions of speech, so that if he wrote in it he would be understood for ever. The 'volgare illustre', the common literary language for all Italians, sedulously pursued by Dante through the length and breadth of

---

[1] Half a century earlier, Antonio Baratella surpassed even Mantuanus in prolixity. I take the following from Bernardino Scardeone's *De Antiquitate Urbis Patavii* (Basel, 1560, p. 237): 'Infinita paene carmina lusit. . . . Poemata quae composuit ut in unum conferam, haec sunt: *Polifodia* constat versibus 1500; *Lavandula* 3181; *Rustica* 2144; *Echaton* 4538; *Polidemonareis* 556; *Elegia* 3982; *Foschara* 1500; *Calliopea* 300; *Musonea* 1145; *Baratella* 2489; *Antonia* 4866; *Laureia* 5287; *Centena* 2463; *Rovea* 3972; *Apollinea* . . . sine numero; *Balliopes* 2800; *Campi petrea* 3100; *Antenoreis* 2050; *Gorgostus* 3711; *Camella* 3825; *Monosodia* vero et *Cribatura* et *Disodia* numeris carent; *Polidoreis* 2481; *Sylvia* 1736; *Protesilaris* 3264; *Metrologia* 2377; Fragmenta vulgarium rerum 2330; *Phleginis* 3360. Libelli ergo 25, versus autem 74060.' Fuller particulars of Baratella's works will be found in A. Segarizzi's *Antonio Baratella e i suoi Corrispondenti* (Venice, 1916).

the peninsula, was still an unrealized ideal; not only the struggle between 'il Latino' and 'il volgare', but the struggle between the literary 'Toscana' and the living dialects which disputed its claim to be accepted as the 'lingua comune', was still unresolved; and it was not until the end of the sixteenth century that the spoken tongue achieved supremacy in the field of literature.[1] Meanwhile, most men of letters—Politian, Bembo, Sannazaro, Ariosto, Castiglione, Navagero, della Casa, Molza, Berardino Rota, to name no others—wrote poetry both in Italian and in Latin, and in each medium no doubt with equal ease. 'It was well for Italian poetry', says Burckhardt, 'to have had both means of expressing itself. In both something great and characteristic was achieved. . . . Perhaps the same may be said of prose. . . . Italian prose was written best of all by those to whom it cost an inward effort not to write in Latin.'

Both languages, literary Italian as well as classical Latin, were (but in different degrees) artificial—neither corresponded exactly with any spoken tongue. The poet who wrote in either certainly precluded himself from writing poetry which had the popular, colloquial appeal of (say) the *Nencia da Barberino*, or the Satires of Burchiello, or the *Opere Burlesche* of Berni.[2] But those who wrote in Latin present a peculiar problem. For though Latin came naturally to them, it was not their native tongue, and though it was a 'living' language, it was not, as was even the literary 'volgare', made of the same stuff as the spoken vernacular; the two vocabularies did not overlap, as literary and spoken French or English overlap each other, and as did the spoken and literary Latin of classical times. Could a language which was, even in

---

[1] I summarize as best I can a very complicated matter; see the article in the present volume by Professor Grayson, and the articles by V. Cian and B. Migliorini referred to by him.

[2] 'O Berni divino', says the editor of the Giuntine edition (1548), 'non ci vendi lucciole per lanterne; ma con parole non stitiche, o forestiere, ma usate, e naturali, con versi non gonfiati, o scuri, ma sentenziosi, con rime non stiracchiate, o aspre, ma dolci, e pure, ci fai conoscere . . . la bonta della Gelatina . . . la dolcezza dell' Anguille, e i segreti, e la profondita di mille altre cose belle, e buone, che nell' opere tue . . . si truovano sparse, e seminate.'

this degree, 'artificial' be an adequate instrument for a poet whose aim it was to give full expression to his deepest feelings?[1]

I leave this question to be answered in the light of the examples quoted later in this essay. Before we pass to those examples, how-ever, another critical question presents itself. How far did these poets handicap themselves by their craving to imitate their classical precursors? The humanists, according to Professor Lewis,[2] wasted their energy 'on a copying of the ancients so close as to approach to forgery or conjuring'; they were mere imitators; their 'poetry' was not genuine poetry at all: 'Only rarely does real poetry force its way through the doubled and trebled artifice of the masquerade.' This is the popular view: how far does it correspond with fact?

Of course it is true that in their passion to revive antiquity, to re-create to the last detail in their surroundings the society of classical Rome, and to become themselves reincarnations of its citizens, the Italian humanists not only latinized their names, their thoughts, their feelings and (on occasion) their dress and their behaviour; they also classicized their verse. There is no need to retell at length the familiar stories of cardinals who would not read the Vulgate for fear of spoiling their style; of poets who passed off their poems, and even their plays, as 'genuine antiques'; or of Navagero, who loathed Martial so much that every year he burned a copy of his works, and so passionately worshipped Virgil that he once destroyed his own poems when he was told that they betrayed a similarity to Statius.[3] Famiano Strada (who, writing a century later, is the authority for this last story) has painted an amusing picture of an imaginary contest between some of the leading poets of the age—Giampaolo Parisio, Bembo,

---

[1] Professor F. T. Prince, in *The Italian Element in Milton's Verse* (Oxford, 1954), p. x, has some interesting observations on the problems of poetry in a language which is not 'a medium in which the poet lives'.

[2] Op. cit., pp. 20–2.

[3] 'Cum Sylvas aliquot ab se conscriptas legisset, ut solebat, in concilio poetarum audissetque Statiano characteri similes videri, iratus sibi, quod a Martiale fugiens alio declinasset a Virgilio, cum primum se recepit domum, protinus in Sylvas coniecit ignem.' Famiano Strada, S.J., *Prolusiones* (Rome, 1617), II, v.

Castiglione, Ercole Strozzi, Pontano, Navagero (besides Camillo Querno, the grotesque 'Archipoeta')—in which, under the presidency of Sadoleto, each impersonates his favourite poet and declaims at length in his style.[1] The story, told with a wealth of picturesque and amusing detail, is an elaborate historical fiction, but its literary basis is a true one: the poetry of many of the Renaissance humanists seems often to be nothing but an echo or a shadow of their classical originals.

But anyone who thinks that by imitating the form of existing models a writer disables himself from sincerely expressing his own feelings, or from expressing them with artistic originality, can know little of the ways in which the impulse to create fulfils itself in poetry and in prose. And those who dismiss the Latin poetry of the Renaissance *a priori* as artificial and insincere because it is imitative betray a particular ignorance of what imitation of the classics meant, both in art and in life, to the humanists of the time. I cannot enter here into the controversies which circled for over a century round the doctrine of imitation;[2] it must suffice to point out that that doctrine, as preached by Bembo, its foremost champion, was concerned not with matter but with style: *nihil est enim aliud totum hoc de quo agimus imitari, nisi alieni styli similitudinem transferre in tua scripta.* His aim was simply to purify language, to make it more fully articulate, and so to recover for his contem, poraries an adequate medium (both in Italian and in Latin) for literary expression.[3] And Bembo insists that, having chosen your

---

[1] *Prolusiones*, II, v–vi. The poets imitated are (respectively) Lucan, Lucretius, Claudian, Ovid, Statius, and Virgil; Querno's effort is original. The *pastiche* of Claudian allotted to Castiglione became famous throughout Europe as 'Strada's Nightingale'.

[2] For Politian's exchange of letters on the subject with Paolo Cortese see his *Epistolae*, VIII, xvi, xvii; for Gianfrancesco Pico's exchange with Bembo, see *Le Epistole 'De Imitatione' di Giovan,Francesco Pico della Mirandola e di Pietro Bembo* (ed. G. Santangelo, Florence, 1954).

[3] The *locus classicus* for this is (or should be) the Life of Bembo by his friend Giovanni della Casa (*Ioannis Casae Latina Monimenta* (Florence, 1564), pp. 54–5); see also J. Sambucus, *De Imitatione a Cicerone petenda* (Antwerp, 1563). Bembo is chiefly concerned with prose, in which Cicero (he says) should always

model, it is not enough that you should copy him; you must excel him: *Hoc in genere toto . . . ea esse lex potest: primum, ut qui sit optimus, eum nos imitandum proponamus; deinde, sic imitemur, ut assequi contendamus; nostra demum contentio omnis id respiciat, ut quem assequuti fuerimus, etiam praetereamus.* So far was imitation from being, even in the view of Bembo, the arch/imitator, a mere matter of uninventive copying.

If our ears are troubled, as we read the verses of Bembo's con/temporaries and followers, by persistent echoes of familiar classical lines and phrases, that is due less to their obedience to his doctrine of imitation than to their indulgence in another practice which he also recommended but carefully distinguished from it, the practice of borrowing.

'Je prends mon bien où je le trouve': what we call 'plagiarism' was deemed legitimate by the writers of the Renaissance, as it had been in old Rome and as it was later by Molière. It was per/missible, it was even admirable, to incorporate into your poems *sententias, aut similitudines, comparationesque aut alias scribendi figuras atque lumina* from classical writers or indeed from your own con/temporaries. But here again, says Bembo, you must not be content merely to borrow, you must improve the material in the process, so as to make of it something original and truly your own: *non sane, quia sumere etiam multa recte nequeamus . . . sed propterea quod praeclarius est illa omnia invenire nos, et quasi parere, quam ab aliis inventa mutuari*—again, he stresses the importance of originality, in the very breath with which he commends the practice of borrowing.

Indeed, there is an Art of Stealing, and to it Vida devotes an instructive passage (iii, 210–66) in his *Ars Poetica.* Ordinarily, he says, one should disguise one's thefts by digesting them and re/wording them so that they become unrecognizable; but there is

be your model, for he is flexible enough to suit all requirements; in poetry, your model should be Virgil, or whoever is the acknowledged master in your chosen *genre.* Bembo was, of course, no mere Latinizer; in his lines *Ad Sempronium, a quo fuerat reprehensus, quod materna lingua scripserit,* he protests that it is important that his contemporaries should know how to write well in their mother/tongue.

a more excellent way, and that is to display the classic phrase or line boldly and without concealment, but to place it in a new context and a new light so as to give it a new meaning:

> Saepe palam quidam rapiunt, cupiuntque videri
> omnibus intrepidi, ac furto laetantur in ipso
> deprensi . . . cum dictis, nihil ordine verso,
> longe alios iisdem sensus mira arte dedere,
> exueruntque animos verborum impune priores.

A supreme—or extreme—instance of this sort of borrowing is to be found at a moment of climax in the *De Partu Virginis* of Sannazaro. The legend of the ox and the ass kneeling in adoration before the Holy Child at Bethlehem is familiar to us, in its English extension, from a well-known poem of Thomas Hardy:

> Christmas Eve, and twelve of the clock.
> 'Now they are all on their knees' . . .

Into this picture Sannazaro introduces two familiar and remote Virgilian phrases—as remote, almost, from each other as each is remote from the sacred context into which he incorporates them:

> Protinus agnoscens dominum *procumbit humi bos*
> cernuus, et mora nulla, simul procumbit asellus,
> submittens caput et trepidanti poplite adorat.
> *Fortunati ambo!*[1]

To some modern readers this consecration of alien, pagan, material, this feat of literary transubstantiation, may seem grotesque, or even gross. But can such critics be sure that by complaining of the poet's insensitiveness they are not demonstrating their own?

Tours de force like this abound in the poetry of the time; they were no doubt received by Sannazaro's earliest readers with delight, as examples of the miraculous art of literary transmutation; the

---

[1] *Fortunati ambo*—used by Virgil (*Aen.*, ix, 446) of Nisus and Euryalus—is doubly a borrowing, for Mantuanus had applied the words 'Fortunata ambo' to the *iumenta* in the corresponding context in his *Parthenice*, and Sannazaro (who borrows elsewhere from the *Parthenice*) must have been aware of this.

greater the incongruity in such a case the greater the miracle and the consequent enjoyment. Used with subtlety, the device can add, as it were, a dimension to poetry, and please a sort of sixth sense in the percipient reader. When it is used indiscriminately, as it is by the second-rate performers, it leads to the manufacture of empty echoes; and it finds its *reductio ad absurdum* in such productions as the centos of the Capilupi and the *Christias Virgilii Evangelisantis* of Alexander Ross.

If many of the poems in the *Delitiae Italorum Poetarum* abound in empty verbal echoes and second-hand images, that is not to be put down to the discredit of Bembo and Vida and their precepts of borrowing and imitation; it is because most of the contributors to that collection were not poets and were writing frankly 'occasional' verses. How many, we may ask, of the 'poets' of any age really deserve that name? How much of the contents of the Elizabethan song-books or of Dodsley's *Collection*—to take the most easily comparable examples from our own literature— can claim to be anything but verse? Such verse consists inevitably of echoes. But where a true poet is writing, however closely he follows his classical original, one is not troubled by the thought of 'imitation'; indeed, one is often conscious of a paradox: the more thoroughly he has imbued himself with the classical spirit, the more naturally does he express himself in the alien idiom; if he has achieved the end of imitation in his own person, he will become a Latin poet without imitating any other writer and without ceasing to be himself.

In the pages that follow I attempt, not indeed to give a representative selection from the vast and varied field of Renaissance Latin verse, but to exhibit some of the hybrid blossoms that emerge from the crossing of so many strains—ancient and modern, pagan and Christian, classical and vernacular—and to show what varied use the best poets of the time made of their inheritance of classical forms and imagery, and how little the practices of borrowing and imitation affected the originality of their work.

.   .   .

No better example can be found of personal emotion expressed in a purely classical form than the famous elegy in which Politian condoles with Sigismondo della Stufa on the death of his bride Albiera degli Albizzi. Here are its opening lines:

Et merito: quis enim tantum perferre dolorem?
　　aut quis jam miseris temperet a lachrymis?
sed tamen heu frustra crudelia sidera damnas
　　Sismunde, et frustra numina surda vocas!
Proh dolor! ah quantos rapta pro conjuge fletus
　　ingeminas! quanto perluis imbre genas! . . .
Ac tecum, infaustus vates, consortia luctus
　　en repeto, et querulam pectine plango lyram.
Nec, Sismunde, tuos gemitus aegrumque dolorem
　　arceo: sunt lachrymis funera digna piis;
majus habes vulnus secreto in pectore, quam quo
　　te deceat madidas non habuisse genas. . . .

The sentiment that animates these lines is a commonplace to be found in many forms and many languages;[1] the especial beauty of Politian's verses derives from the peculiarly Latin way in which it is expressed; the last two couplets, with their subtly emotional negatives—tender, in 'nec arceo', constrained with the constraint of strangled grief in 'maius . . . quam quo . . . non'—are clearly the work of someone who not only wrote, but actually felt, in Latin.

The poem reaches its climax where Albiera addresses Sigis‐ mondo from her death‐bed:

Pars animae, Sismunde, meae, si conjugis in te
　　quicquam juris habent ultima verba tuae,
parce, precor, lachrymis: vixi, cursumque peregi,
　　jam procul a vobis me mea fata vocant.

---

[1] We hear it in Molière's sonnet to Le Vayer on the death of his son:

Aux larmes, Le Vayer, laisse tes yeux ouverts,
　Ton deuil est raisonnable, encor qu'il soit extrême,
Et lorsque pour toujours on perd ce que tu perds,
　La sagesse, crois‐moi, peut pleurer elle‐même.

Immatura quidem morior, sed pura sub umbras
    discedam et nullis sordida de maculis.
Discedam virgo facibus nec victa maritis;
    cessi conjugii nil nisi nomen habens:
est mihi dulce mori, vitamque impendere famae.
    Edita mortali conditione fui:
at nisi nunc morerer fueram moritura subinde;
    est mihi dulce etiam, te superante, mori.
Nil mihi jam poterant anni conferre seniles,
    vita brevis longi temporis instar habet.
Mi dederat teneri leges natura pudoris,
    mi dederat mores cum probitate pios.
Nil mutari in me cuperes, nisi tristia fata:
    humanae vici conditionis opus.

The poetry and the passion of that are not inferior to the poetry
and passion of Propertius' Elegy on Cornelia; Politian could
hardly have written it if he had not been familiar with that elegy,
but what he has given us is a poem of his own, not a mere copy
of Propertian verses.

More elaborately classical in its imagery is the elegy written by
Basilio Zanchi for Andrea Navagero:

Tumulus Andreae Naugerii

Naugeri, tibi Nereides statuere sepulchrum
    aequoris Adriaci qua levis unda silet,
qua solitae in numerum, numeros dum pectine ducis,
    concinere, et virides ducere saepe choros;
et Doris tumulo conchas, et lucida texit
    coralia, et placidis marmora lambit aquis.
Ipse etiam circum affusis pater Adria lymphis
    ingemit, et moestum littora murmur habent.
Parva loquor; tete amisso dolet Itala virtus,
    moeret et infractis Faunus arundinibus.

This *cimetière marin* is painted with extreme artifice—observe
the rise and fall of the ripple at the close of the first pentameter,

the suggestive repetition of *numerum, numeros* in the next line; the onomatopoeic alliteration of *moestum . . . murmur*, the change of key which comes with the concluding couplet—and the imagery is conventional from beginning to end; yet this classical imagery provides a perfect vehicle for the emotion with which the poem is suffused.

It was not only in set pieces, formal elegies written for a patron or in memory of a friend, that classical images came naturally to the poets' lips; equally classical, for instance, are the verses written in anticipation of his own death by Francesco Maria Molza. Molza was a man of dissolute life: *et liberius justo vixit*, we are told, *et rem familiarem adeo neglexit, ut a patre exhaeredari meruerit, et mulierum amoribus nimium indulgendo, in extremum vitae discrimen non semel adductus est.* In Paolo Giovio's compendious phrase, *Venerem quam Minervam impensius colebat*; and he finally died of the disease celebrated by Fracastoro. Seeing his end approach, he addressed to his friends a series of elegiacs—*Ad Sodales graviter aegrotus*— so 'classical' that they might well be taken for the work of Tibullus:

> Ultima jam properant, video, mea fata, sodales,
>   meque aevi metas jam tetigisse monent.
> Si foret hic certis morbus sanabilis herbis,
>   sensissem medicae jam miser artis opem;
> si lacrimis, vestrum quis me non luxit? et ultro
>   languentem toties non miseratus abit?
> Obstruxere aures nostris contraria votis
>   numina, et haec ventos irrita ferre jubent.
> Vos mihi, quos olim colui, dum fata sinebant,
>   ultima jam cineri dona parate meo.

The tomb they are to prepare is, of course, to be of an Arcadian simplicity, and it is to bear only the brief legend:

> His jacet ante annos crudeli tabe peremptus
>   Molsa; ter injecto pulvere, pastor, abi.

Shepherdesses, he hopes, will come to dance beside his grave—

Scilicet huc, diti pecoris comitata magistro,
  conveniet festo pulchra puella die,
quae molles ductet choreas, et veste recincta
  ad certos norit membra movere modos—

and shepherds will vie with each other in singing of his 'faciles
mores' and (more surprisingly) the blamelessness of his life—in
proof of which he refers to his rejection of Lutheran heresy and his
devotion to the cause of Ippolito de' Medici, who will make him
welcome, he hopes, in the Elysian Fields. Then he takes a final
farewell of his friends:

Interea dulces coetus valeatis amici;
  jam vocat in nigros mors tenebrosa lacus;
increpitatque moras Lethaeae portitor undae,
  et remi auditus per loca senta fragor.
Dii tamen in melius vertant haec omina, si quem
  humanis precibus non pudet esse locum.

What gods was he really invoking? As he wrote these lines, with
the prospect of death before him, what vision of the after-world
was present to his mind? It is answer enough, perhaps, to say that
Charon must have been as natural an image for the expression of
his forebodings as he can ever have been for Virgil or for Horace
or for Ovid.

A more considerable figure than Molza, considerable both
for the volume and quality of his work in poetry and prose and
for the respect with which he was treated by his contemporaries,
was Giovanni Pontano, or, as he preferred to be called, Joannes
Jovianus Pontanus. Pontano reminds one in some ways of Dr.
Johnson: *Musas per omnes numeros exercuit*, says Giovio, *tanta
habilis ingenii fecunditate, ut neque poetis, neque oratoribus, qui tum
maxime florerent, dignum secundae famae locum relinqueret*; and he was
Johnsonian in personality as well as in literary achievement:
*Erat austero supercilio, et toto oris habitu subagrestis: sed stylo et sermone
perurbanus, quum saepissime vel in seriis multo cum sale iocaretur.
Habitus tamen est in omni censura quamquam absolute pius, supra aequum*

mordax . . . sicuti ex variis Dialogis . . . intemperanter ostendit. Sannazaro, Marullo, Manilio Rallo, Altilio, Gravina—were all of them among the company who, in the words of Giraldi, *a Pontano . . . profluxere tum in poetica, tum in arte dicendi celebres. Unde*, he adds, *Pontani Academia nunc vulgo ut Troianus equus dicitur.* Pontano's own poetical works included a number of Eclogues, two Books of *Amores*, three Books *De Amore Conjugali*, an astronomical poem, *Urania*, of five Books, two Books of hendecasyllables and one of memorial poems, or *Tumuli*. This large collection of verse reflects, directly and spontaneously, every aspect of Pontano's life—his loves, his friendships, his domestic affections, his literary and intellectual interests, his political allegiances—yet it is always entirely classical in form,[1] and almost always purely classical in feeling and in the way it treats its subject.

I pass by the bulk of Pontano's finest work, to call attention to a few of the passages where, from time to time, through the classic and conventional music of his verse, there sounds a romantic note, a note which at times reminds one of Ausonius. Sometimes we detect it in a simile—

> Quale per aestatem, sub sole rigentibus herbis,
> blanditur lapsis aura recens foliis,
> quale per arentes hortos in vere tepenti
> nox mulcet teneras rore madente rosas—

sometimes in a flight of fancy:

> Evolat e gremio terrae levis halitus, illum
> in rorem vertit noctis amica quies:
> e facie tenerae lenis fluit aura puellae,
> vertit eam in mentis dulce levamen Amor—

or in a line of mere description—

> mira fides; periere rosae, cecidere hyacinthi.

---

[1] The elegiac couplet predominates, and he avoids almost entirely the lyric metres.

Is that the felicity of art or of chance? In the first half of the line, light, pink petals seem to disengage; a thick stem snaps off short in *cecidere*, and with *hyacinthi* the cluster of blossoms falls to earth. Art or chance, the felicity here lies altogether in the choice and arrange-ment of words; sometimes the romantic fancy goes deeper and shapes the idea out of which the poem grows, as in the epitaph upon a slave-girl's baby, where the tomb itself is made to speak:

> Hanc mater mihi commendat post funera, et inquit:
>   'Ipsa tibi hanc peperi, nata futura tua est.'
> Hanc alui in tenebris; nutrix nox; ubera suxit
>   noctis, et infanti lac fuit ipse sopor—[1]

or in the fable of the two palm trees, in which Pontano strangely anticipates the vegetable love of Heine's *Fichtenbaum*:

DE PALMA BRUNDUSINA ET HYDRUNTINA

> Brundusii latis longe viret ardua terris
>   arbor Idumaeis usque petita locis;
> altera Hydruntinis in saltibus aemula palma;
>   illa virum referens, haec muliebre decus.
> Non uno crevere solo, distantibus agris;
>   nulla loci facies nec socialis amor.
> Permansit sine prole diu, sine fructibus arbor
>   utraque frondosis et sine fruge comis;
> at, postquam patulos fuderunt brachia ramos
>   coepere et coelo liberiore frui,
> frondosique apices se conspexere, virique
>   illa sui vultus, coniugis ille suae,
> hausere et blandum venis sitientibus ignem,
>   optatos fetus sponte tulere sua,
> ornarunt ramos gemmis (mirabile dictu),
>   implevere suos melle liquente favos.

---

[1] The complex alliteration in the last line is matched in Langhorne's picture of a destitute mother suckling her child: 'The big drops mingling with the milk he drew.'

> Mirum, si ex oculis et Amor sua spicula iactat
> et Venus accensas spargit ab ore faces?
> Mirum, si Eridanus, si vel regnator aquarum
> rore suo nostras temperat usque faces?[1]

The form of that is entirely conventional, but how unexpected the fancy and the feeling!

Pontano made a bolder experiment in the modernizing of his verse in the remarkable series of twelve *Naeniae* (cf. the Italian *ninne-nanne*), cradle-songs which he wrote when his son Lucius was still in the nursery; here is one of them:

AD VAGITUM SEDANDUM: NUTRIX CANIT

> Ne vagi, ne, blande puer, ne, parvule, vagi;
> blanda rogat blandum Lucia Luciolum.
> Ne vagi, ne lacrimulis corrumpe misellis
> turgidulosque oculos turgidulasque genas.
> Ecce tibi balbo ore sonat, blaeso ore susurrat
> Eugenia et dulces garrit in aure iocos;
> ecce tibi mollem inflectens Aurelia vocem
> fabellas bellas, carmina bella canit.
> Ne vagi, mellite puer; tibi Luscula ludit,
> gestit et ad cunas blanda catella tuas;
> Curtiolus tibi subsultans en se erigit, en se
> iactitat, en teneri cruscula lambit heri.
> An lingis, lascive, genas? Ah, curtule Curti,
> ipsa tibi irascar, curtule Curtiole.
> Tune genas, tune ora? Meus puer, improbe Curti,
> Luciolus meus est, improbe Curtiole.
> Curtiole, anne audes? Ah risit Lucius, ah se
> iecit in amplexus Lucius ipse meos.
> En pectus, formose, tuum; mihi dulcia iunge
> oscula et in solito molle quiesce sinu.[2]

---

[1] Pontano has a weakness for repetition, which is often (as, surely, in the last two couplets of this poem) an artistic blemish.

[2] Pontano's *Naeniae* found an imitator a century later in Gasparo Murtola, and were reprinted with Murtola's *Naeniae* at Viterbo in 1617.

Pontano was a poet whose work, as we have seen, reflected every aspect of his life. Marco Girolamo Vida was a writer of a very different kind: almost all his poems are long, studied, literary performances—his three Books *De Arte Poetica*, his treatises (in hexameters) on the keeping of silkworms and on the Game of Chess, and his *Christias*, an epic, as frigid as the interior of S. Maria della Salute, recounting in six Books the life of Christ. In all these he obeys the rules which he himself enjoins upon the budding poet: he eschews originality and he imitates Virgil. Yet even Vida, the High Priest of Virgilian imitation, can make the hexameter a medium for poetry which is in the last degree personal. In *Parentum Manibus* he expresses his sorrow at the death of his aged parents, the news of which reached him in Rome, when he was at the peak of his career.

Like Victor Hugo in the first anguish of bereavement, he went into the country to be alone and to be quiet; and he there composed a poem which recalls *A Villequier*, not only in its opening lines:

> Hic tamen umbrosum nactus nemus, hic loca sola
> ne mea quis carpsit nimium lamenta severus,
> et nimium teneros fletus irriserit asper,
> mecum indulgebo luctu sub Tusculo alto,
> et lacrimis oculos explebo et pectora planctu.

Vida describes the worldly success which he owes to his parents' self-denial, and says that he values it not for its own sake but for the pleasure they would have taken in it:

> Vos unos agitabam animo, vestraque fruebar
> laetitia exultans et gaudia vestra fovebam,
> mecum animo versans, quam vobis illa futura
> laeta dies qua me vestris amplexibus urgens
> irruerem improvisus ad oscula, vix bene utrique
> agnitus, insolitis titulis et honoribus auctus
> scilicet, et longo tandem post tempore visus,
> dum tenuit me Roma, humili vos sede Cremona.
> Una erat haec merces tantorum digna laborum.

Then, in lines containing touches of almost unbearable realism, he describes the care with which he would have nursed them in their second childhood:

> Nil unquam, nisi quae vestris placitura fuissent
> auribus, effari potuissem; saepe ego ficto
> tristia celassem mentitus gaudia vultu,
> ne vos afficeret, siquid me carperet intus.
> Quicquid amarum, in me latuisset, quicquid acerbum:
> ad vos arte pia transissent dulcia tantum.
> Taedia me vestrae cepissent nulla senectae,
> nec quae multa solent vitia, atque incommoda in illa
> esse aetate, meos poterant avertere sensus.
> Quum spueret vestrum alteruter gravis, exque crearet
> plurimus et rauca conspergeret omnia tussi,
> nulla horrescentis vultu asper signa dedissem,
> cuncta ferens; vos aetatis namque ante tulistis
> plura immunda meae, quum cultus nescius infans
> foedarem toties in cunis humida strata.
> Si qua autem vobis cassa atque incondita verba
> exciderent, quando rerum illa est immemor aetas,
> riderem mecum; omnia pro puerilibus essent
> lusibus illa mihi, ceu vos risistis et ipsi
> ad teneros lusus nati, imperfectaque verba,
> quum primas vix inciperem rudis edere voces.
> Et quando mihi relligio sobolem abnuit, ambo
> cara fuissetis mihi pignora, dulcis uterque
> ceu puer, in nostra qui parvus luderet aula:
> cuncta, utcumque forent, mihi dulcia vestra fuissent.

He praises their loving care for him:

> Non me adeo fugit quantis, pater optime, curis
> anxius, aut quanto indulgebas sponte labori,
> ut mihi res tenues per tot discrimina rerum
> eriperes tantis bellorum fluctibus, ut nil
> detractum, licet irent tempora dura, periret.

Tu quoque, sancta parens, variis exercita curis
pro gnato quas non aras, quae non sacra adibas
templa? quibus non tunc onerabas aethera votis,
caro cuncta timens capiti, bona cuncta precata?
Ut mihi ad ingenuas nitenti desuper artes
auxilium foret et favor omnipotentis Olympi,
et fors usque comes crescenti innexa veniret,
virtuti, quae nos ad opes efferret avitas.
Praecipue mihi ne maculae ob contagia turpes
aut animi pestes commerciave ulla nocerent,
sed mihi mens puro foret usque in corpore pura,
ductaque ad extremum inculpata adolesceret aetas,
omnibus ornatum dum vis excellere rebus.

And he concludes with a paean of gratitude and love:

Quae vobis meritis pro tantis mutua contra
persolvam infelix? quae vobis digna rependam?
quum mihi sint et opes, animus quoque et ampla voluntas,
idque unum affectarem—ast, o mortalia nunquam
gaudia plena satis! numquam secura voluptas!
Aut aliquid cumulo semper deest, aut revocat se
fors infida repente, oculosque avertit amicos.
Fallaces hominum spes! Heu nostra irrita vota!
Nil firmum satis, aut stabili munimine tutum:
Omnia in humanis rebus dubia; omnia nutant.
Vos mihi, laeta forent quum caetera, fata tulerunt,
queis sine dulce mihi nihil est nec amabile quicquam.
Accipite has saltem lacrimas, haec carmina moesta,
quae longum nati absentis testentur amorem.
Salvete aeternum cari, atque valete, parentes.
Vida Gelelme, vale! vale, Oscasala Leona!
Sit precor o vobis requies aeterna sepultis,
sit lux, quae vestris aeternum affulgeat umbris.

There are faint echoes of Virgil in the phrasing of this, but its
eloquence and movement are entirely un-Virgilian, and its
periods are shaped solely by the force of the writer's feelings.

377

Side by side with Vida's elegy may be set another poem of filial love, Niccolò d'Arco's *Naenia de Morte Matris*.

Niccolò d'Arco has left us a distinct impression of himself: he looks out from the frontispiece of his Poems,[1] richly dressed, with challenging eyes, merry lips, and a full forked beard, a genial, even a jovial, country squire; and his poems make that impression still more vivid. Born in 1479, he was a page at the Court of Maximilian I and won applause for his valour under arms; but he retired early to his estate at the head of the Lago di Garda, to pass his days reading philosophy, writing poetry, and exchanging visits and letters with his acquaintances among the nobles and men of letters of North Italy, of whom Fracastoro, Marcantonio Flaminio and Paolo Giovio were evidently his especial friends. All this we can gather from his poems—occasional pieces, most of them, describing his rural surroundings and occupations; conversational epistles; memorial verses. He did not take himself very seriously, either as a person or as an author, and his poems were not published until the year in which he died, and then without his knowledge.[2]

Catullus and Horace were his chief models, and he does not often venture far away from them, but there is nothing derivative about the youthful lines—he must have been about twenty-three years old when he wrote them—in which he recalls, after twenty years, the circumstances of his mother's death. They are not, perhaps, very elegant, but they are vivid and pathetic: through the eyes and ears of the child, still at its wet-nurse's breast, we see the crowd of relations and dependants gathered round the death-chamber, and hear the solemn accents of the priest from within:

---

[1] Edited by Zacharias Betti (Verona, 1762). This edition reprints most but not all of the contents of the original edition (see *infra*, n. 2) and prints for the first time a large number of poems, from a MS in the library of Giulio, Marchese Saibante. No complete edition of Niccolò d'Arco's poems has yet appeared.

[2] *Nicolai Archii Comitis Numeri* (Mantua, 1546). This book has always been of extreme rarity; see pp. x–xi of Volpi's Preface to his edition (Padua, 1739) of the Poems of Fracastoro, Fumano, and Niccolò d'Arco: 'raram illam et unicam . . . Editionem Mantuanam . . . paucis cognitam'; of his own copy, Volpi says: 'nos quidem tanti facimus, quanti quivis Codex summi cujusvis pretii a doctis viris fit'.

Illa tempestate meae nutricis alebar
complexu in molli, me tertia viderat aestas
vix bene firmantem gressum, et blaeso ore loquentem,
cum te pallida Mors tenebris involvit opacis,
injecitque manum viridi sub flore juventae.
Vidi ego cum tristi procederet ordine pompa,
horrenda extremum caneret cum voce sacerdos,
ingentis turbae gemitus; nam turba gemebat
subjecti populi, et fatum damnabat avarum,
justitia et placida vivens quam pace fovebas.

The child felt, without knowing, what the scene portended:

Attonitus visu immani agnovisse videbar
ipse nefas, querulis implens vagitibus auras
nutricis gremio; tunc illa nocte papillas
(sedula namque olim mihi retulit omnia nutrix)
non ego libavi, digitis non ubera pressi.
Seu natura, aliud seu quid divinitus esset,
tantum praesago suspiria corde trahebam,
haerebamque genis pendens nutricis amatae;
quae mihi linteolo madidos dum tergit ocellos,
singultusque ciet, trepidantem ad pectora pressit,
et, Taceas, mellite puer, puer optime, dixit;[1]
mater enim spirat; mors illi saeva pepercit:
rus abiit, dixitque mihi, Cito laeta redibo.

Then follows the funeral, the unrestrained grief of the children
and their father, and his own unsatisfied longing for the mother
who came no more to play with him:

Praecipue infelix ego te per tecta vocabam
ut poteram, balba interrumpens verba loquela.

---

[1] Is this an echo of Pontano's *Naenia V*, 'Scite puer, mellite puer, nate unice,
dormi'? Or are they independent echoes of the Italian nursery? Pontano's *Naeniae*
were first published (piratically) at Venice in 1498; Niccolò's poem (not published
until 1546) must have been written two or three years later.

Nam mihi fingebas lusus, et grata canebas
ad cunas, blandum invitabas voce soporem;
tu flores intertexens, et mixta corollis
lilia, puniceaque rosa, rubroque hyacintho
ornabas caput, et fulgentia tempora sertis;
nectebasque meo ramosa coralia collo.
Nonnunquam flenti arridens blandiris alumno;
ubere nonnunquam exserto perfundis ocellos.
Te modo fingis anum, simulata et imagine terres,
dum cohibes flentem falsae formidine formae.
Heu matris sortem et nati infelicis acerbam!
Tunc mihi te rapuit fatum, cum solvere justa,
nec matris fugientem animam excipere ore liceret,
oscula nec pia ferre genis, nec more parentum
claudere languentes oculos, aut dicere amato
extremum ore vale, meritosque intendere honores
manibus.

Nothing quite like this is to be found in the poetry of ancient Rome—but how vividly it recalls, in feeling and in detail, Cowper's lines on the same subject![1] The two descriptions are close to each other because both of them are close to life.

Two shorter pieces of Niccolò d'Arco deserve quotation; both are love-poems. And here a word about the Latin love-poem of the period may not be out of place. I cannot agree with the high estimate that others have put upon its worth. *La più mirabile vivezza e profondità di sentimento*, says Costa,[2] *la troviamo nelle liriche d'argomento amoroso. Cantando d'amore, que' poeti attinsero le ispirazioni, quasi tutti, esclusivamente dalla vita; il sentimento e il pensiero è ne' carmi*

[1] I heard the bell toll'd on thy burial day,
  I saw the hearse, that bore thee slow away,
  And turning from my nurs'ry window, drew
  A long, long sigh, and wept a last adieu!
  . . . Thy maidens, griev'd themselves at my concern,
  Oft gave me promise of thy quick return. . . .
              (*On the receipt of my Mother's Picture out of Norfolk*)

[2] *Antologia della lirica latina*, p. xvii.

d'amore vivo e vero, e le forme stesse hanno una semplicità e una novità non consueta.

I should say rather that when they write about love these poets tend to become shallow, imitative, monotonous. Pigna, Cotta, Crotto, Angeriano, della Casa, the Amaltei, the Strozzi—all of them repeat *ad nauseam* the sentiments of Petrarch in the manner of Catullus or Propertius. The objects of their adoration— Hyella and Neaera, Caelia and Glycere, Stella and Lycoris, and the rest—are indistinguishable, and hardly ever come to life.[1] Their love-lyrics are catalogues of beauties, gardens of sensuous delights. Joannes Secundus found the recipe for this kind of writing, and, garnished with all the dressings of classical mytho- logy, it took the taste of a century over the whole of Europe.

In such poetry one looks in vain for depth of emotion; relief from the prevailing prettiness is to be found only on the same sen- suous level, when the poet describes 'lust in action' or the revulsion that follows it; their love-poetry, one might almost say, is best when it is least pleasant. Niccolo d'Arco provides us with one or two such moments:

ODE AD LYCISCUM

Ne tu ne amplius (obsecro)
ne tu, care Lycisce, excrucies tui
    corpus dulcis amiculi!
Ah, quid saevus agis? nonne vides uti
    virus nescio quod meo
dirum continuo stillet ab inguine?
    paulatimque meo effluat
vitalis calor et pectore spiritus?
    Poenarum satis et super
exhausto dedimus sanguine; iam malos
    cantus amoveas, meam

[1] The best conspectus that I know of the Latin love-poetry of the period is *Veneres Blyenburgicae sive Amorum Hortus*, a stout octavo of more than 950 pages, published at Dordraecht in 1600. The editor, D. Blyenburg, has assembled selec- tions from about 150 poets of the fifteenth and sixteenth centuries. It is probably unfair to judge them thus in the mass, but the total effect is intolerably cloying.

factam in perniciem subtrahe imaginem.
Has artes potius tuas
vertas in fugitivum et tenerum Lycem, aut
rivalem in furias age
carpentem nitidae basia Persiae.

How close a relation that poem bears to its author's experience one can but guess;[1] its ending is entirely Horatian, but the broken, panting lines with which it opens are a vivid expression of the agonized experience that they describe.

Niccolò has also left two unusual introspective pieces, addressed, somewhat oddly, to his own eyes and feet. The second of these is successful enough to deserve quotation:

PEDIBUS SUIS

Amabo, quo me, lassuli pedes, fertis,
vix sustinentes semimortuum corpus?
An ad cruentum limen, ad fores illas
ubi hanc miselli paene liquimus vitam?
Quid, ah, quid ultro convolatis ad mortem?
Quid sponte in acres ponitis manum flammas?
Ni vos (sed olim viderit sator Divum)
tot eiulatus, lacrimasque pertaesi,
utcumque tantis quaeritis malis finem.

---

[1] The poem raises also a question which recurs frequently in this literature, for the poet is evidently describing in it, not altogether unsympathetically, a kind of amatory relationship which elsewhere he strongly and even coarsely condemns. Many contemporary poets are similarly equivocal in their treatment of the subject. What did they really feel? Is it all simply a literary 'topic', an imaginative reproduction of Catullus or of Martial—another example of 'romanizing'? If the social historians are right (and the evidence seems to be compelling), the literature which seems almost indiscriminately to accept and to reprobate these practices reflects a like paradox in the life of the time. 'Dignitaries of the Church', in the words of Symonds (*The Revival of Learning* (1877), p. 406), 'thought it no shame to parade their preference for Giton', and a vice which was punished, as Bonfadio discovered to his cost, with the extremest penalties was, according to Molmenti (*Venice*, pt. ii, vol. ii, p. 238, where he refers to a series of laws against it passed in Venice between 1455 and 1598), 'especially rampant among the clergy and men of letters. . . . Rome' (he adds) 'was its chief hot-bed, but Venice was not exempt.'

The limping scazons suggest, with their heavy concluding spondees, the almost automatic motion with which the tired feet drag the reluctant body to its familiar haunt; and the sequence of flat, long, line-stopped questions conveys more effectively than any display of rhetoric the repeated assaults of self-reproach.

The mood of revulsion is still more vividly expressed in the following forcible lines by Lancino Corte, a poet who in many respects—he is harsh, difficult, ingenious, ugly, coarse—reminds one of Donne, though he has not Donne's poetic power:

AD IULIAM

Frustra blanditias, Iulia, Iulia,
frustra et nequitias congeris; amplius
nec lusu moveor; me illecebrae et nihil
stringunt; nilque libido opprimit. Occidi
possem vivere quo liber; ago deis
virtuti, studio, tempori et ultimas
grates. Sum meus; et sum quia homo tamen
te interdum repeto, sive aliam; est opus;
ut cogitque mala ac sola necessitas
naturae stimulat. Dii, nimium diu
est natura potens; sed sit ut arbitra
vis est nunc eadem qua futuo et caco.[1]

Whatever one may think of that, one must admit its force and directness; even Professor Lewis might agree that the poet has effectively broken through what he calls 'the doubled and trebled artifice of the masquerade'.

The religious poetry of the age presents a different, but perhaps analogous, problem: why should there be so little of it? Hymns, classical both in form and diction, are common enough; the saints are invoked (in company often with an incongruous contingent from Olympus) in Horatian odes or Virgilian hexameters;

---

[1] Some of Corte's obscurities may be due to the fact that his poetry was published posthumously (in 1521) and at some points it is clear that the text is faulty. In the penultimate line of *Ad Iuliam*, I take *sit ut arbitra* to depend on *vis*, and *natura* to be the subject of *sit*: 'The force that puts her [*natura*] in control of me. . . .'

and there is no dearth of religious narrative poems, from the *Parthenice* of Mantuanus to the *De Partu Virginis* of Sannazaro. But we look equally in vain for the simple piety of the Middle Ages and for the ecstatic fervour of the Jesuit poetry of a century later; nor was the religious lyric for these writers what it became for later poets from Herbert to Hopkins, a record of the interior dialogue of the soul.[1] The explanation most often given by the critics—that the poets who wrote in Latin were humanists, and humanists were pagans—is unsatisfying, for it is a familiar paradox of the Renaissance mind that 'paganism' was not in the least degree incompatible with complete religious orthodoxy.

However that may be, almost all the religious verse of the period (I pass over the metrical renderings of the psalms and biblical paraphrases with which, from time to time, humanists kept their pens in training) belonged to one or other of two very formal kinds, the hymn and the epic. In setting Ferreri to revise the Hymnal,[2] Leo X was classicizing the poetry of the Church; in encouraging Vida to write the *Christias* he was sanctifying the pagan epic; in the one case, classical forms were to be imposed upon religious matter; in the other, religious matter was to be poured into a classical mould. Neither kind of poetry provided a suitable vehicle for the expression of a personal emotion.

It is not surprising, therefore, that the greatest achievement of the Renaissance in the field of religious verse should be a poem which was a triumph of formal art: the *De Partu Virginis* of Sannazaro. Sannazaro's masterpiece did not win unqualified praise from his contemporaries: *rem sacram*, said Erasmus, *nec dormitanter nec inamoene tractavit. Sed meo quidem suffragio plus laudis erat laturus, si materiam sacram tractasset aliquanto sacratius.* Posterity

---

[1] There are exceptions: I wish I had space to exhibit them. In particular I would draw attention to the religious poems of Giovanni Carga (which are fervent, pious meditations, mostly in iambic verse) and to a series of poems on old age and the approach of death by Tarquinio Frangipani, Adamo Fumano, Giuseppe Parli-staneo, G. M. Toscano, Crinito, Carga himself, and 'incertus auctor'. These will be found in the *Delitiae Italorum Poetarum*: their relationship with each other awaits investigation.

[2] See below, p. 401, n. 2.

has been more forthright: *meruit*, says Landor, *uno epigrammate ut condonetur ei quae effutiit de ostreorum pastoribus et partu Virginis*.[1]

Sannazaro, according to Paolo Giovio, was equally at home in Latin and Italian: *scripsit, tamquam ambidexter, Etrusca simul atque Latina carmina, pari lepore saleque, arridentibus utrimque Musis*. But he was, in the phrase of Giraldi, *statarius poeta*: his verses did not flow, and so devoted was he to the labour of the file that Pontano, whose pupil he was, applied to him what Apelles said of Proto-genes: *eum manum de tabula tollere nescire*. He spent nearly twenty years on polishing the 1,500 lines of the *De Partu*, and the final version, published in 1526, was the last of many drafts.[2]

The *De Partu* presents an easy target for the critic to whom piety and 'paganism', the Christian and the classical world, are sharply divided, and irreconcilable, spheres of imagination and feeling. For the humanists, no such division existed; and a reader of the *De Partu* who feels it to be blasphemous that the shepherds at Bethlehem should rehearse, with trivial amendments, the fourth Eclogue of Virgil, or finds it grotesque that the river-god Jordan should recount to a gathering of Naiads a prophecy by Proteus of the Feeding of the Five Thousand, might with profit consider whether *Lycidas* is really destitute of feeling or the *Ode on the Morning of Christ's Nativity* of piety, and ask himself why he is not equally shocked by similar anachronisms and incongruities in the religious painting of the time.

It is by his treatment of the main theme of his poem, however, and not by its machinery, that Sannazaro should be judged. No

---

[1] The reference is to his famous six-line epigram on Venice, for which the Republic made him a present of 600 scudi, and to his Piscatory Eclogues—imita-tions of Virgil in everything except the novelty of their setting. Landor might have mentioned Sannazaro's Elegies, in which he shows real poetic feeling and a love of natural beauty. A collection of Sannazaro's poems, other than the *De Partu*, was 'edited' by G. Castello (Milan, 1938). This is a careless reprint, with a translation and scanty notes; several poems are omitted on grounds of propriety. An excellent and scholarly edition of the *De Partu* was published at Naples in 1948, ed. A. Altamura.

[2] The stages through which the poem passed are explained in the introduction to Altamura's edition.

subject could be more forbidding; the tasks that Milton set himself in his two sacred epics offered no comparable difficulty.
Sannazaro's theme is tremendous, sacred, intimate: a poet might
well despair of treating without indecency the two great mystical
moments which must form the twofold climax of his story—the
Conception and the Delivery. It is a measure of his triumph that
at these points his poem rises to the heights of its subject: the
recounted miracle is matched by a miracle of art.

The first Book opens with an account of the Annunciation.
When Gabriel has told his story and reassured her misgivings,
the Virgin accepts 'the intolerable honour' with proud submission:

> 'Iam iam vince, fides' (*she exclaims*) 'vince,
>   obsequiosa voluntas:
> en adsum, accipio venerans tua iussa tuumque
> dulce sacrum, pater omnipotens'—

and then the miracle occurs:

> Tantum effata, repente nova micuisse penates
> luce videt, nitor ecce domum complerat: ibi illa,
> ardentum haud patiens radiorum ignisque corusci,
> extimuit magis. At venter (mirabile dictu!
> non ignota cano) sine vi, sine labe pudoris,
> arcano intumuit verbo: vigor actus ab alto
> irradians, vigor omnipotens, vigor omnia complens
> descendit, Deus ille, Deus, totosque per artus
> dat sese, miscetque utero: quo tacta, repente
> viscera contremuere; silet natura, pavetque
> adtonitae similis, confusaque turbine rerum
> insolito occultas conatur quaerere causas.

To turn, after reading that, to Mantuanus' treatment of the theme
is to turn from an Annunciation by Titian to the rustic efforts of
a Bassano:

> Tum divina gravem subitis conceptibus alvum
> extulit, atque sinus soboles extendit onustos:

sicut in adductos penetrat cum lubrica folles
aura; cavernosum surgens tumor exit in orbem.
Mirata est crevisse uterum natura: suumque
esse negavit opus, trepidas ut virginis aures
aliger afflavit coelesti nuncius ore.

Sannazaro's account of the Birth forms the climax of his second
Book. Night has fallen on the stable in Bethlehem—

iamque in cineres consederat ignis
ultimus, et sera perfusus membra quiete
scruposo senior caput adclinaverat antro[1]—

when the Heavenly choir is heard, and Mary, realizing that the
hour has come, rises confidently to her feet:

Iam laeta laborum,
iam non tacta metu, saecli regina futuri
stabat adhuc, nihil ipsa suo cum corde caducum,
nil mortale putans: illam natusque paterque
quique prius quam sol caelo, quam luna niteret,
spiritus obscuras ibat super igneus undas,
stant circum et magnis permulcent pectora curis.
Praeterea redeunt animo quaecumque verendus
dixerat interpres: acti sine pondere menses,
servatusque pudor; clausa cum protinus alvo
(o noctem superis laetam et mortalibus aegris!)
sicut erat, foliis stipulaque innixa rigenti,
divinum, spectante polo, spectantibus astris,
edit onus. Qualis rorem cum vere tepenti
per tacitum matutinus desudat Eous,
et passim teretes lucent per gramina guttae;
terra madet, madet adspersa sub veste viator
horridus et, pluviae vim non sensisse cadentis
admirans, gelidas udo pede proterit herbas.

---

[1] This touch seems to be borrowed from Mantuanus: iam languidus ignis/
in cineres ibat . . . aegra cum coniuge fessus/procumbit senior, tepidoque ob-
ductus amictu/stertit.

Again, one has only to glance at Mantuanus' version[1] if one wishes to appreciate the deftness of Sannazaro's art: the suspense, the expectation, prolonged by a series of beautifully modulated parentheses, and then—almost before we are aware the thing has happened—the simile, to divert our attention and explain away our astonishment. The allegory of the dew is familiar enough from medieval literature—

> He came all so still
> There his mother was,
> As dew in April
> That falleth on the grass—

but what a pleasure it is to see the old image *treated*, put to work in the service of art!

It is by these passages rather than by its occasional beauties[2] that the *De Partu* should be judged. But, though his finest effects, so far from being merely decorative, occur at the key points in the structure of the poem and are instinct with deep emotion, it is as an artist rather than as a poet that we naturally think of San-nazaro—an artist, in that his primary concern was with the thing he was making and not with the expression of his own emotions, and an artist in the narrower sense, in that he used the Latin language as a painter uses his paints. If we are looking for a writer to whom that language came with absolute naturalness, and who used it in poetry with greatest effect when, without thought of an audience, he was uttering his inmost feelings, we may turn to one

---

[1] This is how he hurries past the difficult moment:

> Occiderant ignes et caligaverat antrum
> quum subito matris clausa puer editus alvo
> extulit umbrosam coelesti lumine noctem.
> Advenere chori superum, etc.

[2] For instance, the lovely simile in Book I (adapted from Heliodorus' *Aethiopica*) in which the Virgin is likened to a girl gathering shells on the sea-shore; or the lines in which he describes the sad silence of the underworld:

> qua tacite labuntur aquae mutaeque volucres
> ducunt per steriles aeterna silentia ramos.

who, strangely enough, was not an Italian by birth and whose native tongue we must presume to have been Greek.

Mystery surrounds the figure and the fortunes of Michele Marullo, and most of what is known about him has to be gathered from his own self-conscious, self-revealing poems. His father's family came, it seems, from Achaia, but he regarded himself as 'Constantinopolitanus'; he was born in the year in which Byzantium fell, and his parents brought him to Italy as a child. From boyhood he was a displaced person: he tells of his sufferings on the banks of the Danube, in Thrace, near the Black Sea, and on the Dalmatian coast; and, grateful though he was for his home from home in Italy, he remained a Greek at heart and his longing for his native land never left him.

Returning from his Balkan wanderings, Marullo frequented Pontano's Academy in Naples in the 1480's; we find him at Rome in 1489, and then in Florence in the last years of Lorenzo de' Medici; there he made the acquaintance of Giovanni Pico, there he fell out with Politian, and there, shortly before his death, he married Alessandra Scala, a lady whose learning seems to have been at least as impressive as her beauty. He died in 1500, drowned by a mishap in the river Caecina, a copy of Lucretius in his pocket.

Marullo was a member, it seems, of the mysterious association of Strathioti, wandering mercenaries, driven from Greece by the armed power of the Byzantine Church, and united by a common love for their lost country and a common antipathy to the Church, if not to Christianity itself.[1] He spent much of his life under arms, and towards the end of it saw service under Charles VIII in his expedition against Naples. Never, in camp or in exile, did Marullo's love of poetry desert him; but he was not a prolific writer: all that he published in his lifetime was four Books of *Epigrammata* and a collection of *Hymni Naturales*, and at his death he left only a score or so of unpublished poems and the beginning of a projected lengthy hexameter poem, *Institutiones Principales*.

[1] See C. N. Sathas, *Documents inédits relatifs à l'histoire de la Grèce au moyen âge*, vol. vii (Paris, 1888), 'Documenta Strathiotes illustrantia'.

Marullo's *Epigrammata* are made up largely of the familiar ingredients—verses to friends and patrons in Catullan hendeca-syllables or elegiac couplets, love-poems, and memorial verses, besides epigrams in the strict sense. Many of his poems are addressed to one 'Neaera', whom he loved, it seems, hopelessly for years, and continued to love after she had died. Marullo's love-poetry, though it often echoes Catullus,[1] has always an authentic ring; it is serious and (almost ostentatiously) unsensual:

> Non ego (*he says*) virgineum venio temerare cubile,
> nec formosa magis quam mihi casta places.

Such protestations by poets are not to be taken at their face-value, but Marullo evidently means what he says, and the two poems in which his passion is most movingly expressed are not love-poems in the ordinary sense, but were written after Neaera's death. In one (*Epigr.* IV, xxi) he describes the fears for her safety that still haunt his dreams; in the other (*Epigr.* IV, xi) he tells us how even after the lapse of years he cannot escape from the recollection of her beauty:

> nequicquam mihi me subripio miser:
> nam quaecunque oculis patent,
> illic continuo vultus et aurei
> occursat capitis decor,
> et quae nec fugere est lumina nec pati.

'Quae nec fugere est lumina nec pati'—that is characteristic: where others would have described the beauty of Neaera's eyes, Marullo, always something of a psychologist, tells us simply of their effect upon him.

The best of Marullo's poems are those in which the exile gives utterance to his longing for his native land. In these, and in the *Hymni Naturales*—strange poems which excited the admiration, but also the suspicion, of his contemporaries—he speaks with an individual and a compelling voice. Nothing could less resemble

---

[1] And Petrarch, according to A. Sainati, *La lirica latina del Rinascimento* (Pisa, 1919), pp. 95–100; but I suspect that he overestimates that influence.

the fluent and melodious ingenuities with which Ovid beguiled and bewailed his years of exile. These poems are often harsh to the ear and hard to construe, for their author is not concerned to create a thing of beauty or to please his hearers; he wants to con‚ vey his own sense of loneliness and frustration and (in the Hymns) his feelings about the forces that animate the natural world and control the universe.

It is by their earnestness, their reality, that the exile poems attract and hold us:[1] they are indeed what Croce called them: 'voci dell' anima'.[2] Perhaps the most poignant of them is *Nenia* II, in which Marullo, looking eastwards from the cliffs of the Adriatic coast, protests his envy of the waves and sea‚breezes that come, like him, from the shores of the Bosphorus, but—more fortunate than he—can revisit their home whenever the tide turns or the wind changes:

> Haec certe patriae dulcia littora
> contra saxa iacent, haec pelage impete
> huc propulsa gravi Bosphorici freti
>   plangunt Hesperium latus.

> Ipsae nonne vides mitius aurulae
> ut spirant memores unde videlicet[3]
> tantum innata potest rebus in omnibus
>   natura et patrium solum?

> Quid, tantis spatiis monstriferi aequoris,
> tanto tempore post lassulae, adhuc tamen
> halant nescio quid, quod patrium, et novis
>   mulcet aera odoribus?

[1] One can see why Scaliger said 'Marullus totus durus, morosus, aliorum obtrectator, sui admirator simul, et diffidens. Anxius enim quo dicat modo, haeret negotiosus, omnino invenustus'—even if one does not agree with his judgement.

[2] See his *Michele Marullo Tarcaniota Le elegie per la patria perduta ed altri suoi carmi* (Bari, 1938)—a short but full biography and critique, with a text and translation of selected poems. This and the excellent 'Index Nominum' in Perosa's edition of the *Carmina* are the best available guides to the facts of Marullo's life.

[3] It is tempting to suggest *ut spirant, memores unde volaverint? tantum* (etc.) . . . *solum!*

Felices nimium, vespere quae domo
egressae redeunt mane Aquilonibus
versis, nec peregre perpetuo exigunt
    aetatem exilio gravem.

Happier still, he says, are the winds that have never had to leave
their home:

Felices sed enim multo etiam magis,
si tantum patriae fluminibus suae
et primi solita littoris algula
    contentae lateant domi,

nec longinqua velint flumina visere
et terrae varios et pelagi sinus—

and he pictures them asking their wandering sisters for news of
him in his exile:

Quae multum referant deinde rogantibus
    vergentem usque sororibus

ad noctem—quis enim suavia nesciat
auditu et vacuis apposita auribus,
quae diversa locis alter et hic refert
    mille exhausta laboribus?

Inter quae memorant mutua dum invicem
quaeruntque, admonitae forsitan et mei,
narrant nunc Boreae sedibus intimis
    visum, qua vagus alluit

Rhodos Mesta suos, nunc Byce lintea
dantem plena, modo littora Dacica
scrutantem. . . .

His misfortunes wore him down, as he tells us in another *Nenia*:

    paries velut
aere exesus et imbribus
    inclinatus abit quo semel incipit

> praeceps, sic miseri altera
> in fata ex aliis mittimur—heu dolorem
> indignum!—neque iam quies
> aut spes effugii urgentibus est deis—

but they did not subdue his spirit:

> Sed quis est ita perditus,
> unus qui patriae et civibus optimis
> dedignetur idem pati
> communemque deum non ferat aequiter?

He sounds a less despondent note in his farewell to Florence; even Scaliger[1]—a harsh critic of Marullo generally and of this Hymn in particular—admits that its first six lines are 'belluli'. The poet and his man 'Hyllus' are setting out at daybreak and, while the horses are being harnessed, they raise their voices in a hymn to the setting moon. Marullo first addresses the hills and rivers, the city, the friends and patrons he is leaving:

> Colles Etrusci, vosque non ultra meas
> sensura voces flumina,
> totiensque dicta iam mihi Florentia,
> adeste supremum, rogo,
> dum pauca vobis, grata sed grati, ultimo
> mandata discessu damus,
> testati amica civium commertia
> et Medicis hospitium mei.
> O fida quondam tot cohors sodalium,
> duri levamen exili,
> ego ne, relictis, heu miser, vobis, queam
> exilia perpeti altera?
> Sed fati acerba vis ferenda fortiter!
> duc, Hylle, mannos ocius,
> dum mane primus subrubet oriens novo;
> amo ego viatorem impigrum.

---

[1] *Poetice*, VI, iv, *ad init.*

Interea amicis hinc et hinc sermonibus
  viae levanda incommoda:
vel tu virorum fortium aut laudes Deum
  incipe; canentem subsequar.

Then Hyllus invokes the moon-goddess, and Marullo answers him:

Hyllus

Miles Gradivum cantat, upilio Palen,
  udus Lyaeum vinitor,
Cererem perustus messor aestivo die,
  mercator undarum patrem,
nos tot per alta nemora, per sylvas vagi,
  nemorum potentem Deliam.

Marullus

Enses Gradivus sufficit, pascua Pales,
  libera Lyaeus pocula,
pingues aristas flava gentibus Ceres,
  opes pater tridentifer,
hunc lucis haustum Delia et sanctum iubar,
  Lucina dicta matribus.

Hyllus

Levisomna pubes, navitae, umbras temnite,
  temnite, viatores vagi;
At vos sub ima fugite—si sapitis—vada,
  vis, helluones, humida,
dum noctis atrum Delia horrorem excutit
  et plena replet omnia.

Marullus

Carpite cupita gaudia et fructus breves
  lacrimarum, amantes, carpite,
nec tu laborem differ, agricola impiger,
  sylvaeque lignator sciens,
dum fratris almo Delia amplexu silet
  tenebrisque densat omnia.

After exchanging three or four more stanzas, they set out upon their way:

> Sed haec triformi sat deae: nunc iter, age,
> coeptum sequamur ocius,
> vias precati prosperas tamen prius
> laetam viarum Deliam.

This charming night-piece—what could be more romantic than 'fructus breves Lacrimarum, amantes, carpite'?—leads us to consider the *Hymni Naturales* and the creed that they reveal—or fail to reveal. Nowhere in Marullo's poems[1] is there a word to suggest any concern with the Christian religion, let alone any belief in its truth. In the sixteenth century he was suspected to have been an enemy of the Faith; the paganism of his Hymns, his membership of the Strathioti, and his admiration for Lucretius no doubt lent colour to the charge.

The *Hymni Naturales* have puzzled later readers as they did Marullo's contemporaries.[2] Scaliger thought them impious, but his criticisms are naïve: *Quae vero cecinit Amori*, he says of the Hymn to Love, *ad Dei Spiritum sanctum nisi dirigantur, tota impia sunt; si dirigantur, ridicula. . . . Facit patrem ab eo [Amore] vulnerari. Nefanda profecto Atheologia! Non movetur a Spiritu Pater, sed ipsum producit.* Erasmus was milder: *Marulli*, he observed, *pauca legi tolerabilia, si minus haberent paganitatis.* Beatus Rhenanus thought that in his Hymns he far excelled the poets of ancient Rome, but regretted that he should have written *velut ethnicum*.

The obvious defence was made by Guglielmo Cripio, in his dedication of the 1561 edition of the *Epigrammata et Hymni*.[3] People, says Cripio, who call Marullo an infidel because he puts into his poems things that are not compatible with Christianity, only betray their ignorance of the real aim of poetry,

---

[1] If we except a reference in a poem (*Ep. IV*, 32) addressed to Charles VIII and one slight piece in which he dedicates his discarded armour to St. George.

[3] See especially P. L. Ciceri in *Giornale Storico della letteratura italiana*, lxiv (1914), 289–357.

[2] Quoted by Croce, op. cit., p. 114.

which is not edification, but enjoyment—*Non veritas a Poetis, sed oblectatio exigitur: quam qui consequitur, probe suo munere perfunctus est.* Besides, no one could be so foolish as to suppose that Marullo really believed in the pagan deities: *Quasi vero Marullus ita insanus aut mentis expers fuerit, ut aut Iovem umquam fuisse aut Martem crediderit!*

Of course Marullo did not believe in the existence of the pagan gods, nor can Scaliger really have supposed that he did so; and of course a poet is not upon affidavit in his poetry. Yet Cripio's defence misses fire, for Marullo was not one of those poets who write simply to give pleasure, and no one can read his Hymns without feeling that in them he is somehow trying to express his beliefs, or at least his feelings, about the natural and the super- natural order; they are not pastiches, fanciful recreations of classical myths by one who, like Hérédia or Keats, was strongly attracted to the beauty of antiquity; they are hymns in feeling as well as in form. It was, no doubt, because they were recognized as religious poems that they were suspect to his contemporaries: in a way, Scaliger was nearer the mark in his criticism than Cripio in his defence.

But if the Hymns express Marullo's religious feelings, what was it that he worshipped? What did he believe in? Did he really, indeed, believe in anything? At times he comes near to confessing a complete scepticism:

> Et dubitem sancti in terris nihil esse fateri?

at times he hints at an agnostic hope:

> Sol pater, et si quis misero deus aethere in alto est
> praeterea, nec cuncta carent mea pondere vota . . .

Sometimes the being he invokes is a god or goddess—Pallas or Pan or Bacchus—sometimes it is an abstraction or a force or phenomenon of nature—Eternity, the Heavens, the stars, the Earth. He will adorn a mythical figure with irreconcilable attributes drawn from the most recondite learning, and a moment later lose himself in an *O altitudo!* of Platonic or neo-Platonic metaphysical speculation,[1] only to end on what sounds like a note of simple pagan worship.

So he opens his Hymn to Pallas by calling upon *suprema maximi proles Iovis* and investing her with spear and aegis and all her traditional attributes; then he invokes her as the principle of Wisdom at work in human affairs—

> Prima inquietis gentibus certas domos
> stabilemque dederis patriam,
> prima arce, prima moenibus ditaveris,
> prima optimis tot artibus.
> Tu sancta prima iura, tu legem invenis,
> commenta vim dignam malis,
> tu prima mentes compari nectis iugo,
> tu propria tribuis pignora,
> tu celsa raptos tollis ad templa aetheris,
> tu patriam antiquam doces
> coelumque patrem maximum rerum omnium
> curis caducis subiicis—

and after this exalted flight he ends by bringing the goddess before us once more as a visible person—

> Salve, beati lucidum germen patris,
> vere Phaneta splendide,
> eadem virago, mas eadem, eadem furor,
> sapientiaque eadem et quies,
> animisque nostris ades et atra nubila
> discute tua immensa face.

Pallas indeed, with her torch (never displayed with more terrify‑ ing splendour than in those last four words), but—*eadem furor, sapientiaque eadem et quies*—she has ceased to be the goddess of the classical dictionaries and is transformed into a mystical figure born, no doubt, of the poet's neo‑Platonic reading.

---

[1] Pico, Giraldi tells us, helped him in the composition of his Hymns. An exactly similar conflation of elements occurs in Giano Anisio, *Varia Poemata* (Naples, 1531), f. 70. *Ad Iovem.*

The Hymn to Love follows the same pattern: first, an invocation of the conventional 'volucer Cupido' who wounds gods and
mortals alike with his archery; then an address to the power of
love that turned chaos into order in the Creation and still sustains
the Universe; finally, a renewed appeal to a deity, addressed indeed
as 'puer', but hardly to be identified with the Cupid of the opening
stanza:

> O quies magnae reparatioque
> grata naturae columenque rerum,
> O adoratum mihi rite primis
> numen ab annis:

> huc ades tandem, puer o beate,
> dexter, et caecos miseratus aegri
> pectoris motus, agedum, profanis
> exime curis.

O quies magnae reparatioque Grata naturae: love shares with Wisdom
the stillness at the centre of the whirlpool—a conception hard to
recognize in the figure of Cupid with his bow and arrows.

It was Scaliger's complaint that, though Marullo was capable
of a fine and fervid opening, his Hymns dragged as they proceeded and petered out at the finish: *Hoc enim viri illius ingenio
maximo atque praeclarissimo vitium fuit peculiare ut magnifico spiritu
scribere aggressus, elangueseret in orationis tractu: fervor ille egregios
primos illos impetus, iudicium deinceps destitueret, aut voluntas.*

I should rather have said that the most eloquent and poetical
passages in his Hymns are their perorations. The Hymn to
Jupiter, for example, after a hundred lines of semi-philosophical
reflection, ends with a passage of exalted poetry:

> Exutos olim terrenae pondera molis
> rursus in antiquam patriam das posse reverti,
> unde hominum curas tot despectemus inanes
> incertasque vices rerum metuendaque fata
> et quanta mortale genus nox occupet umbra.
> Salve, sancte parens, vere pater optime rerum,

vere opifex, terraeque mala compage gravatos
dum data vincla nefas dirumpere carceris atri,
eripe tot pelagi iactatos tristibus undis,
tot caecis pressos tenebris, pater; exue vota
impia; nil vanum, nil admiremur inane,
antiquae memores patriae; et quem corporis aegri
non licet, ingenii quaeramus lumine puro.

Characteristically, the concluding note is one not of discovery
but—*quaeramus*—of search, a search of which the object (faintly
personified in the pronoun *quem*) remains for the reader, if not for
the poet, a mystery.

The last of Marullo's Hymns is addressed to Earth. In its
opening he identifies 'Terra' with the Magna Mater; then he
enlarges on man's debt to the soil from which he springs; and
he concludes with a touching appeal to that Mother Earth in
whose bosom we must all alike seek repose at the last:

Verum quid iuvat eximie iam vocibus uti,
si pia tam foedis sceleramus nomina factis
turbamusque malis inter nos quaeque rapinis,
partiri communem ausi per vulnera matrem?
Hinc versum fas atque nefas scelerataque bella
invasere, tenet furor exitialis habendi
luxuriesque, nec imperii spe turbidi inanis
cessamus placidam gentis turbare quietem,
immemores eadem in terra mox esse cubandum
omnibus, assueta ducibus confundere egenos
affectuque pari natos quoscunque fovere
materno exceptos gremio per saecula longa.
At tu, magna parens, quando omnis adempta quietis
spes aliter, iam tandem adsis et nos quoque humatis
adiice, tot duros genitrix miserata labores.

Quando omnis adempta quietis Spes aliter—even in his **Hymni
Naturales** the despair of the exile makes itself heard. And no⁄
where in them does it sound more clearly than at the close of the

Hymn in which he invokes the stars. Everything upon earth, he says, animate and inanimate, is subject to the stellar influence; but the stars themselves are ruled by the unalterable decrees of fate. Men pursue their various aims, as though they were masters of their own destiny—

> At ipsa coelo lucida sydera
> affixa cursus deproperant suos,
>   secura privati laboris,
>   dum stet opus solida catena
>
> naturae et aeterni imperium Iovis
> fixum per omnes lege dies data,
>   gaudentque nil prorsus relinqui
>   alterius moderandum habenis.

Then, with the directness that marks everything he wrote, he looks up at the serenity of the constellations and recalls, but without complaint, his own unhappiness:

> Gaudete, Noctis progenies sacra,
> stellae beatae: nos procul a domo
>   quae fata nascenti dedistis
>   interea miseri feremus.

It is, as always, the exile that is speaking; he speaks in classical alcaics, but the poetry is his own, and in his voice there is no hint of an echo either of Horace or of Ovid.

The poems I have quoted from Politian, Vida, Marullo and the rest will have given some idea of the variety of the Latin poetry of the Italian Renaissance. Written in a 'literary' language, and by men who, most of them, aimed at a more or less strict reproduction of classical style, it can yet be poetry, deeply felt, individual, original, alive. Indeed, it is to this very opposition between distinctively modern strains of thought and feeling and the traditional images and forms in which they find expression that much of their work owes its peculiar power to move us. For the form, as opposed to the content, remained obstinately traditional.

It was a true sense of the proper virtue of the Latin language that led these poets to reject accentual and rhyming measures and revert to the traditional forms; they drew strength from the limita/ tions thus imposed upon them. Nowhere is the wisdom of their classicism made plainer than in the field of metre; and it is made plainest in the rare cases where, like their medieval predecessors, Renaissance poets abandoned, with unfortunate effects, classical metres and stanza/forms in favour of attempts at rhyme and rhythm.

The humanist lecturers expounded the classical metres and of course enjoined a strict adherence to them; few of their hearers can have needed such injunctions, or have felt tempted to disobey them.[1] Even for their religious poems, where reversion to medieval forms might have been pardoned, they stuck to classical models.[2] None the less, there were those who ventured on metrical experi/ ments; some, no doubt, simply for love of what was new, others

[1] 'Rhythmus est: cum more vulgarium poetarum in similes mixtim desinat syllabas', says Quintianus Stoa, in his *Ars Brevissima* (1511); and 'Leoninum cum media carminis pars in eundem sonum ultimam secum trahit syllabam . . . hoc usi sunt barbari poetae, quos pudet nostris inserere papiris.'

[2] Politian composed a couple of hymns in accentual iambic dimeters, and there are occasional assonances in the hymns of Flaminio. In the Breviary itself the old accentual measures survived. Instigated by Leo X, and with the approval of Clement VII, Zaccharia Ferreri published in 1524 his *Hymni Novi Ecclesiastici* 'iuxta veram metri et Latinitatis normam'. This collection of hymns, strictly classical in diction and in quantitative metres, was intended to replace the existing Breviary hymns (in which, according to Ferreri, the barbarities of diction and metre must have provoked to laughter not only those priests 'qui bona latinitate praediti sunt' but even the angels themselves); but it was never, so far as I know, reprinted, and its contents were disregarded in Quignon's revision of the Breviary. A century later, Urban VIII's Jesuit revisers were much more tender with the medieval originals, and practically confined themselves to correcting errors of quantity in the hymns written in classical metres, though they allowed themselves somewhat greater liberties with hymns 'qui nominis obscurioris habuerunt Authores, neque Superiorum elegantiae et dignitati sunt pares, et in quibus mensura carminis et latini sermonis integritas desiderari potest'. A clear statement of the admirable principles they adopted is contained in the address *Ad sacram Rituum Congregationem* prefixed to the first edition of their version (Rome, Typis Vaticanis, 1629).

because they enjoyed exercising their own ingenuity,[1] and a few who found that they could not naturally or adequately express their thoughts and feelings within the framework of the con-ventional lyric metres, or were irked by the limits of the mechanical elegiac couplet, where almost inevitably, as Croce puts it, *si vede alternare nell' esametro la frase nata e nel pentametro la frase fatta.* But their efforts were experiments, not a survival of, or a reversion to, the rhymed and accentual measures of the Middle Ages.

There was one metrical innovation that seems to have answered a felt poetic need: the introduction of a refrain into lyrical measures. Once, in a poem by Panfilo Sassi, we find the device worked into an orthodox Sapphic ode; indeed, the whole poem is built round the refrain, and the resulting pattern is curious enough, and perhaps pretty enough, to justify quotation:

LOCA AMANTI IAMPRIDEM IUCUNDA

Fons sacer, rivo vitreo per herbas
qui fluens murmur virides amicum
concinis somno; mea lux, meum cor,
    qua manet ora?

Arbor, excelsis super astra ramis
quae caput tollis, Satyros amoena

---

[1] Most ambitious, if least successful, of these early experimenters was Bene-detto Lampridio, a protégé of Leo X, who disregarded the advice of Horace and sought fame as the Latin Pindar. His odes (published in 1540, the year of his death) consist of lengthy strophes, each line of which 'scans' quantitatively. But these elaborate and arbitrary structures give no pleasure to the ear, and only a sharp-eyed and persevering reader will recognize the correspondence between strophe and antistrophe. Lampridio's contemporaries judged his performances a failure, and did not imitate them.

    Lancino Corte experimented boldly with rhyme, inventing and exploiting a sort of sonnet-form of his own; but though he was very ingenious, his efforts in this line are nothing but curiosities, and they too proved to be a still-birth. Of about 2,100 poems in his twenty Books of *Epigrammata* (1521) more than 170 are in rhyme, and of these just over 100 are in one or other of his sonnet-forms. Corte experimented also in other directions: his *Repotia* consists of 1,200 (unrhymed) hendecasyllabic lines.

protegens umbra; mea lux, meum cor,
    qua manet ora?

Mons iugis pulcher, nemus et beatum,
quod tegunt laurus, coryli, cupressus,
fagus et myrti; mea lux, meum cor,
    qua manet ora?

Prata quae fertis thyma, quae marathra,
lilium, thymbram, violas, anethum,
quae rosas, mentam; mea lux, meum cor,
    qua manet ora?

Aura, quae dulci resonas susurro,
arborum frondes quatiens virentes
cum furit Titan; mea lux, meum cor,
    qua manet ora?

Fons niger, latis viduata ramis
arbor, obscuri iuga montis, herba
arida, et pratum, coryli, cupressi,
    aura, valete!

Vos Venus spernit, tener et Cupido;
nox tegit densis tenebris opaca,
sedibus postquam mea lux, meum cor,
    non manet istis.

One can see the poet singing this to his own accompaniment on the lyre; one can hear the change of key in the last two stanzas. And what he is singing is surely, in everything but language, an Italian *canzone*.

Sassi used a sort of refrain also in a series of lyrics[1] lamenting the troubled state of Italy in the last years of the century: *Deflet calamitates Italiae*; *In Italiae Principes*; *Lamentatio Italiae*. The first and last stanzas of the first of these poems will give some idea of their form and feeling:

---

[1] Printed in *Agislariorum vetustissimae gentis origo et de eisdem epigrammaton liber* (Brescia, 1502); never, so far as I know, reprinted.

O scelus, scelus! domina gentium
Italia, et genetrix potentum
regum, barbarici fulminis impetu
ustis visceribus, pectore saucio,
tristatur gemens, suspirat gemens. . . .

O pudor, pudor! miser et improbe!
O furor, O furor! horride, amens!
Vos pellunt sceleris robore flammeo
vires—desidiae, pignus, amor, decus!
Nos cogit dolor, nos stringit dolor.

Here again one can surely hear the voice of the *improvisatore* and the accompaniment of his lyre.

Sassi's lament seems to echo, perhaps consciously, a poem composed a year or two earlier by Politian himself—the *Monodia* which he wrote in 1492 on the death of Lorenzo de' Medici:

Quis dabit capiti meo
aquam? quis oculis meis
fontem lacrimarum dabit?
ut nocte fleam,
ut luce fleam.
Sic turtur viduus solet,
sic cycnus moriens solet,
sic luscinia conqueri.
Heu miser, miser!
O dolor, dolor!
Laurus impete fulminis
illa illa jacet subito,
laurus omnium celebris
Musarum choris,
Nympharum choris.
Sub cujus patula coma
et Phoebi lyra blandius
et vox dulcius insonat;
nunc muta omnia,
nunc surda omnia.

Quis dabit capiti meo
aquam? quis oculis meis
fontem lacrimarum dabit?
ut nocte fleam,
ut luce fleam.
Sic turtur viduus solet,
sic cycnus moriens solet,
sic luscinia conqueri.
Heu miser, miser!
O dolor, dolor!

The more one thinks about this poem—the last tribute by the greatest scholar to the greatest ruler of the day—the more remark-able it seems.[1] Nothing like it had been written—at least by Poli-tian—before. The opening words are taken from the Vulgate: 'Quis dabit capiti meo aquam et oculis meis fontem lacrimarum?' (Jer., ix, 1). It is unclassical in form and feeling, and it is—surely? —an artistic failure. But, set to music,[2] it evidently took the ear of the time, and when, two years later, Politian himself died and Bembo in turn came forward as an elegist, it was this *Monodia* that he singled out for mention; and with considerable poetic licence (but in entirely conventional elegiacs) he represented Politian as dying while in the act of reciting it at Lorenzo's funeral:

[1] The extremely puzzling problem of its metre has not been solved. It can hardly be accounted for (despite U. E. Paoli, 'La Trenodia del Poliziano "In Laurentium Medicum"', *Studi italiani di filologica classica*, n.s., xvi (1939), 165 ff.) by supposing that Politian took Greek tragic choruses for his model. Nor is there any reason to think that 'in the midst' of composing it 'he was intercepted by the hand of death' —a hypothesis by which Roscoe (*Life of Lorenzo de' Medici*, Ch. X) seeks to explain away the very different accounts of the circumstances of his death that were current among Politian's contemporaries.

I am grateful to Professor Eduard Fraenkel for guidance which has saved me from error in investigating the metre of the poem, and for the suggestion, which I have adopted, of *impete* for *impetu* in l. 11.

[2] By Heinrich Isaac, 'Arrigo Tedesco'; his setting is printed, from MS, in H. Isaac, *Weltliche Werke*, ed. Johannes Wolf (*Denkmäller der Tonkunst in Österreich*, xiv Jahrgang, Erster Teil) (Vienna, 1907), pp. 45-8.

POLITIANI TUMULUS

Duceret extincto cum Mors Laurente triumphum
    laetaque pullatis inveheretur equis,
respicit insano ferientem pollice chordas
    viscera singultu concutiente virum.
Mirata est, tenuitque iugum. Furit ipse, pioque
    Laurentem cunctos flagitat ore deos;
miscebat precibus lachrymas, lachrymisque dolorem;
    verba ministrabat liberiora dolor.
Risit, et antiquae non immemor illa querelae,
    Orphei Tartareae cum patuere viae,
'Hic etiam infernas tentat rescindere leges,
    fertque suas', dixit, 'in mea iura manus'.
Protinus et flentem percussit dura poetam,
    rupit et in medio pectora docta sono.
Heu sic tu raptus, sic te mala fata tulerunt,
    arbiter Ausoniae, Politiane, lyrae.

It is clear from this that Politian's *verba liberiora* created a deep impression. They were certainly imitated by admirers who evidently did not understand their metrical basis. I have quoted from the dirges of Sassi; here is the opening of Quintianus Stoa's *Monodia* on Anne, wife of Louis XII (d. 1514):

> Quo communis abit quies?
> Certe concidit. Ah, potens
> Mors! Fatum, ah, nimium ferox!
> abivit Anna,
> proh dolor, dolor!
> recessit Anna. . . .

Here Stoa is lamenting the death of the younger Beroaldo (1518):

> Huc, huc Pieridum chorus,
> huc, huc cum Charitum choro
> Cypris cincta Cupidine;
> Philippus obiit,

ah, Fatum, Fatum,
Beroaldus obiit. . . .[1]

And here is an undated (and untitled) elegiac fragment of
Andrea Dazzi:[2]

Agite tristes oculis
maestas fundite lacrimas,
ut mater unico super
vidua filio.
Perennis eat
fluor per genas;
non cessent gemitus die
non ululatus tenebris.

Quis dabit, quis, meo pares
dolori lachrymas?
Miser, vae, miser!
Dolor, heu, dolor!
Lapis ille, ille fulgidus,
tot erutus laboribus,

---

[1] This *Monodia* is said to have been 'recitata, extempore' in *Poemata aliquot insignia*
(Basel, 1544). These and other similar dirges of Stoa will be found in vol. ii of the
Delitiae Italorum Poetarum. His long elegy *In obitum Annae, Reginae Gallorum*
contains an interesting survey of elegiac forms:

> Tristia collachryment cunctis Epigrammata muris
>   fixa, gemat ruptis moesta Elegia comis.
> Multa fleat querulo gemebunda Monodia cantu
>   adcinat et raucum quaelibet Oda melos.
> Silva Lycambaeos secum aspera ducat iambos
>   et fleat immistis dactylus Alcaicis.
> Si quis Pindaricum ferat illachrymabile plectrum
>   det tamen infaustae consona verba chely.
> Sapphica flebilibus sint carmina rauca trochaeis,
>   clamitet ad tumulum carminis omne genus.

[2] Printed on p. 113 of *Andreae Dactii Florentini Poemata* (Florence, 1549). I have
supplied punctuation. I think I detect in the poem attempts at dactylic accentual
scansion. Dazzi (1475–1548) taught Greek and Latin in Florence, where he was a
friend of Politian and Crinitus.

> tot agitatus casibus,
> quae nec Mors abstulit
> nec ira Iovis,
> aquis premitur. . . .

I suspect that these lines were written on the death (by drowning, in 1500) of Marullo,[1] and that in the last line but two we should read *quem nec Mars* for *quae nec Mors*.

A century later, these echoes had not entirely died away: among the *Meletae Pomeridianae* of Francesco Roggeri (Milan, 1627) I find (p. 156) a *Naenia ad sepulchrum Virginis* which con-tains the refrains 'Ne nocte fleam, Ne luce fleam' and 'O miser, miser, O dolor, dolor'; and the lyrics of Vincenzo Guiniggi, S.J. (Venice, 1654), include (p. 198) a long *Monodia* 'Nascenti Iesu' consisting of glyconics with interspersed refrains, among them 'Ah furor, furor, O dolor, dolor!' and 'Et lacte pluit, Et melle fluit'. But at the time we are concerned with such metrical experiments as this were few and far between; and it was not until nearly a century after Politian's death that poets generally indulged in the 'mixed ode', the dithyramb, and the extravagant freedom of *carmina lapidaria*.[2] Nor was purely accentual verse revived (so far as I can discover) until the Jesuit drama of the seventeenth century.[3]

Anyone who reads these later efforts at novelty will understand how wise the poets of the High Renaissance were to eschew such superficial originality and to let freedom assert itself in the matter and not in the form of their verses.

·   ·   ·

[1] For whom Dazzi (*Poemata*, p. 88) composed the following epitaph:

> Evasit toties hostilia tela Marullus
> ut Cecinae tumidis obrueretur aquis.

[2] No doubt they availed themselves of the elaborate analyses of Greek metres contained in Scaliger's *Poetice* (1561), as Professor Leicester Bradner suggests in his interesting account of such efforts in England in the late sixteenth and the seventeenth centuries; see his *Musae Anglicanae* (New York, 1940), pp. 104–10.

[3] See *Libellus de Novis Metris et Lyrica Poesi*, by 'Dionysius Ronsfertus' (Parma, 1614)—a source of information as yet, I think, untapped by scholars.

Looking back on this vast field of poetry, I must confess that I cannot detect in it, within the period under review, any 'schools' of Latin verse, any local influences, or any literary 'trends' or stages of 'development'. A few general observations, indeed, suggest themselves: one may say, for instance, that the Quattro-cento can show little Latin verse worth reading until, in the last three decades of the century, the lectures of the humanist teachers and the availability of printed texts began to have their effect upon literary production; and it would seem that, while Rome was always a real metropolis for men of letters from every quarter, an increasing number of poets, with the turn of the century, came from the north—Venice, Mantua, Cremona, and Ferrara, for example—and fewer from Florence and from Naples. By the end of the 1540's, one might add, the stream of Latin poetical produc-tion which had its source in Politian and Pontano and was in full flood in Rome under Leo X, had subsided in Italy and diffused itself over Europe; and in the second half of the century, with the Counter-Reformation and the Jesuit schools, the reader of Latin poetry finds himself in a different world. More such generalizations, and more significant ones, might occur to someone better acquainted with the lives of the writers and the world they lived in; for myself, I can see only an innumerable host of versifiers, and among them not a few who were truly poets, responding each in accordance with his individual temperament to an irresistible and well-nigh universal impulse: *Sur des pensers nouveaux faisons des vers antiques.*

C. Grayson

LORENZO, MACHIAVELLI
AND THE ITALIAN LANGUAGE

No other subject was probably more exhaustively, and certainly
not more exhaustingly, talked and written about in the late
fifteenth and sixteenth centuries than that of the Italian language;
and in this mass of literature the names of Lorenzo de' Medici and
Machiavelli occupy a significant place, if not so decisive a position
as that of Pietro Bembo.[1] Since the two great Florentines reflect
different moments in the development of the most critical phase
of the linguistic and literary controversy between the two centuries,
the discussion and historical situation of their views will enable
us in this essay to illustrate the principal trends and motives of the
process which virtually determined the linguistic unity of Italy.
To this process the works of Lorenzo may be regarded as the preface, preceding by some thirty years the climax reached in the
first two decades of the sixteenth century, precisely, that is, at the
time when Machiavelli entered the lists with his vigorous defence
of the Florentine language. The coincidence of this climax with
the upheavals consequent on the foreign invasions of Italy invites
reflection upon the paradox of political disunity and linguistic
unity, and also upon the possible relation between the two
crises.

---

[1] The best and most lucid account of this complex debate, of which the present
essay aims to illuminate only certain aspects and figures, is B. Migliorini's 'La
questione della lingua', in *Questioni e correnti di storia letteraria*, ed. A. Momigliano
(Milan, 1949), pp. 1–75, with a good select bibliography. For the sixteenth century
in particular, see also B. T. Sozzi, *Aspetti e momenti della questione linguistica* (Padua,
1955). Only the most relevant and essential references to other studies are made in
the following notes.

In order to appreciate the situation of Lorenzo in this matter, it is necessary to recall briefly the position of the vernacular in the fifteenth century;[1] especially that of the Florentine vernacular, which had two major claims to pre-eminence: it was believed (rightly or wrongly) to have a native superiority to all other languages of Italy;[2] and it was adorned by the three great writers of verse and prose, Dante, Petrarch and Boccaccio. Simultaneously, however, with this consecration of the vernacular, and from the time of Dante himself, there had begun that humanist revival which was to restore both the knowledge of classical antiquity and the purity of its eloquence, and in so doing look disdainfully on the 'barbarousness' of the Middle Ages. As this revival progressed, men of letters turned away from the vernacular, regarding it as inferior and fit only for those writings which it was not desired to commit to posterity. The most critical period of such depression of the vernacular lies between 1400 and 1440. It is not surprising, therefore, that at that time the language of Dante's *Comedy* should have been called in question, that his important treatise on vernacular eloquence was forgotten, that the inheritance of the Latin Petrarch was more prized by humanists than his *Rime*. It would be mistaken, however, to believe that the *secolo senza poesia*, as Croce called the age between Boccaccio and Lorenzo, was without poetry or prose in the vernacular; for there was a great production, particularly in verse in imitation of Dante and Petrarch. It is important to stress its quality as well as its quantity, the popular unrefined nature of its language, and outside Tuscany, the formation on the basis of the Tuscan tradition of hybrid vernaculars, especially in the politically important

[1] Cf. V. Cian, 'Contro il volgare', in *Miscellanea Rajna* (Milan, 1911), pp. 251-97; B. Migliorini, 'Latino e volgare nel Quattrocento', in *Lettere Italiane*, vi (1954), 321-35, and 'Panorama dell' Italiano Quattrocentesco', in *La Rassegna della Lett. Ital.*, lix (1955), 193-231.

[2] An important testimony is that of Bruni in his *Laudatio Urbis Florentinae* (cf. *Della Laud. Urbis Flor. di L. Bruni. Notizia di G. Kirner* (Livorno, 1889), pp. 26-27). For discussion and dating of this work (1402-3) see H. Baron, *Humanistic and Political Literature in Florence and Venice at the beginning of the Quattrocento* (Cambridge, Mass., 1955), ch. iv.

and culturally developing state of Lombardy.[1] Yet in spite of political centrifugal forces (and above all the threat of Milanese domination), and in spite of the opposition from learned quarters of Latin, it is true to say that the foundations of a unified language in poetry were already unconsciously laid by the end of the fourteenth and the early fifteenth centuries; and that on the basis of the Tuscan tradition. In the less specialized field of prose (and not only literary prose) the example of Boccaccio and his more popular Tuscan followers like Sacchetti carried much less weight against Latin on the one hand and provincial dialects on the other; and in this sector resistance to the hegemony of Tuscan persisted not only into the sixteenth, but into the nineteenth century.[2] It is, however, important to note that the vernacular began in the early years of the fifteenth century to oust Latin in official documents of courts and chancelleries.[3]

It is undoubtedly true that the antagonism to the vernacular of the early fifteenth century has been exaggerated on the basis of a few vociferous critics of the time. Yet without some degree of antagonism, the defence of the vernacular taken up by various writers from about 1435 onwards is inexplicable.[4] The terms of this defence are the revindication of the capabilities and potentialities of the vernacular to express the most serious and important thought; not exactly as yet on terms of parity with Latin, but by no means so confined to the marginal role of poetic expression and popular entertainment in romances and *novelle*. Broadly speaking, this separation of Latin and the vernacular

[1] Cf. E. Levi, *Francesco di Vannozzo e la lirica nelle corti lombarde durante la seconda metà del XIV secolo* (Florence, 1908), especially pp. 425 ff.

[2] The different fortunes of the traditions of prose and verse are well brought out and illustrated by P. O. Kristeller, 'L'origine e lo sviluppo della prosa volgare italiana', in *Cultura Neolatina*, x (1950), 137–56.

[3] Cf. M. Vitale, *La lingua volgare della Cancelleria Visconteo-Sforzesca* (Milan, 1953). In Lombardy the vernacular is used from 1426 onwards.

[4] Cf. Kristeller, op. cit., and H. Baron, *The Crisis of the Early Italian Renaissance* (Princeton, 1955), i, 297–312, and ii, 422–9 and 578–91, in mild polemic with earlier views on the 'conflict' between humanism and the vernacular (cf. also *Ital. Studies*, xii (1957), 48 n.).

on two parallel but distinct planes is the fundamental character‑ istic of the linguistic and literary situation of the first part of the fifteenth century. The fusion of the two, whereby the vernacular, assumed by humanists for the expression of more significant subjects, learns from, and models itself on Latin, is the dominant feature of the latter half of the century.

It is not surprising that this conscious desire to rehabilitate the vernacular with literary dignity should appear first in Florence, and in humanists like Bruni, who (though late in his career) wrote the lives of Petrarch and Dante, and made the pregnant assertion that all languages were in a sense equal.[1] Yet it was a Florentine who appears to have had little or no concern with the achievements of the fourteenth‑century giants, and spent the greater part of his life outside Florence, who more than Bruni championed the cause of *la nostra oggi toscana*: L. B. Alberti. The eloquent plea of the Proem to the third Book of his *Famiglia* ridicules the idea earlier attributed to Bruni, that Rome had two languages, Latin and the vernacular, and maintaining that it is preferable *giovare a molti che piacere a pochi*, declares that if Latin has achieved eminence through its many learned writers, *simile certo sarà la nostra, s'e' docti la vorranno molto con suo studio e vigilie essere elimata e polita.*[2] This assertion of the usefulness of *questa oggi nostra quale usiamo lingua*, and its future capabilities, is devoid in Alberti of any local patriotism or historical justification by tradition. The *toscana* is not contrasted or compared with any‑ thing but Latin, while the tangible demonstrations of its abilities in Dante, Petrarch and Boccaccio are completely ignored. Nor is this a casual omission. His own writings show no direct

---

[1] In his *Vita di Dante*, he wrote: ' . . . lo scrivere in istile litterato o vulgare non ha a fare al fatto, né altra differenza è se non scrivere in greco o in latino. Ciascuna lingua ha sua perfezione, e suo suono, e suo parlare limato e scientifico' (cf. G. L. Passerini, *Le vite di Dante scritte da Giovanni e Fr. Villani*, etc. . . . (Florence, 1917), p. 223). See Baron, loc. cit., for a reappraisal of Bruni's position in the matter of the vernacular.

[2] The quotation is from *I primi tre libri della Famiglia*, ed. Pellegrini, revised by R. Spongano (Florence, 1946), pp. 228 ff. Note also Spongano's excellent introduction on 'La prosa letteraria del Quattrocento'.

dependence on that tradition as a literary or linguistic model. He left others to show their somewhat crude attachment to it in the clamorous and significant, but poetically unfruitful *Certame coronario*, which he organized together with Piero di Cosimo de' Medici in October 1441.[1] In his own prose he modelled himself, both in syntax and vocabulary, very largely on Latin; while his more vigorous verse was linked with the popular tradition and with realist and burlesque poets like Burchiello.

The next step forward, which was to add the celebration of the past Tuscan tradition and the glorification of the inherent qualities of the language of Tuscany, belongs to the younger generation of Landino and Lorenzo, with whom Alberti was linked in friendship—a generation that also shows more awareness of the expansion and influence of that language in the rest of the peninsula. For, since the fourteenth century, the diffusion of Tuscan literature, and to a lesser degree the dispersal of Tuscans, especially Florentines, all over Italy in commercial pursuits (and also regrettably in exile) had undoubtedly had a progressively increasing effect on the non-literary as well as the literary idiom of other regions. This becomes more and more evident after the middle of the fifteenth century, when the political influence and cultural patronage of the Medicis gather momentum; and it then begins to appear more markedly and more deliberately in the field of prose, i.e. in the language of written usage, as distinct from the marginal and essentially literary language of poetry.[2] For sheer weight of prestige and quantity as well as quality of literary production of all kinds, Tuscan had virtually no possible challenger, and it is extremely rare to hear any voice raised in favour of the language of any other region or against the threat of Tuscan

---

[1] Cf. A. Altamura, *Il Certame Coronario* (Naples, 1952).

[2] This penetration of Tuscan into non-literary documents is well illustrated by the collection of *Testi non Toscani del Quattrocento*, ed. B. Migliorini and G. Folena (Modena, 1953), with a brief but highly informative introduction by Folena. For literary influence, cf. G. Fatini, 'Il volgare preariosteo a Ferrara', in Supp. 25 of *Giorn. Stor. della Lett. Ital.* (1934), and A. Altamura, 'Appunti sulla diffusione della lingua nel Napoletano', in *Convivium* (1949), pp. 288-303.

domination.[1] It must be emphasized that these observations relate to the written language, and not to modifications in spoken dialects. This penetration of Tuscan was accompanied and in part assisted by the parallel influence on written vernacular prose, of Latin, which even before the practice of Alberti and the theory evolved from it by Landino, had lent its support in varying ways to learned and semi-learned writings in different regions.[2] The closer correspondence of Tuscan forms with Latin undoubtedly contributed to give them greater prestige and currency.

Landino formulates quite clearly the necessity for the assimilation into the vernacular of the merits of Latin (*è necessario essere Latino chi vuole essere buono Toscano*), the marriage of humanistic eloquence and the natural capabilities of the Tuscan language. This enrichment of the vernacular by Latin he found in the tradition of the past, from Dante through Petrarch and Boccaccio down to his friend Alberti, while the superior adaptability of the *fiorentino idioma* he saw demonstrated in her writers, and most of all in Dante, on whose *Comedy* he wrote a famous commentary. He even goes so far as to declare Florentine, *lingua comune a tutta Italia et a molte externe nazioni assai familiare*. Though not to be taken too literally, this assertion is clear testimony to what has been said above about the diffusion and penetration of the Tuscan tradition in the rest of Italy. A recent writer on Landino goes so far as to see at this time (i.e. of Lorenzo de' Medici) *da parte degli scrittori toscani una vera offensiva in tutta Italia per la diffusione del volgare toscano sul piano nazionale*, and to suggest the possibility of a political motive.[3] Certainly there is in those years a firm consciousness of the past, present and future mission of the Tuscan language, and this not so much in opposition to Latin, as drawing from it

[1] A voice in favour of Ferrarese is cited by Fatini, op. cit., p. 16: '. . . . ferrarese idioma. Il quale, secondo il mio parere, non ha manco elegantia che alcuno altro italiano parlare. . . .' For the reaction to Tuscan hegemony, see later in this essay.

[2] Cf. A. Vallone, 'L'influsso del latino sulla prosa del '400', in *Giornale Ital. di Filologia*, vi (1953), 221–32; also Spongano, intro. cit.

[3] M. Santoro, 'Cristoforo Landino e il Volgare', in *Giorn. Stor. della Lett. Ital.* cxxxi (1954), 501–47; the statement quoted is on p. 543. For the passages cited above from Landino, see ibid., pp. 509 and 521–2.

the essential means of achieving its own advancement and proper dignity. It is more pertinent now to turn this inquiry to Lorenzo himself, and to those other members of his circle who, like Landino, supported and practised the Tuscan idiom.

Among the many works in Tuscan (both original and trans/lations from Latin) dedicated to or commissioned by 'foreign' princes which might be included in the 'offensive', an important place must be given to the famous collection of Tuscan poetry known as the *Raccolta Aragonese*, which Lorenzo sent in 1476 to Federigo d'Aragona. This anthology was accompanied by an epistle in the name of Lorenzo, most probably penned by Poliziano,[1] which opens with typically humanistic praise of the glory and immortality of the ancients—an immortality guaranteed by poetry, which in its turn has been preserved through the magnanimity and generosity of great rulers, as, for example, Pisistratus who collected together the fragments of Homer. But that was in the great days of the illustrious past, whose virtues are now not only inimitable but scarcely credible, such has been the decline in the intervening centuries, with the consequent loss and neglect of much of that ancient inheritance. And here he laments *la dolorosa perdita di tanti e sì mirabili greci e latini scrittori*, and in the same breath of *molti venerabili poeti, li quali il diserto campo della toscana lingua cominciorono a cultivare in guisa tale, che in questi nostri secoli tutta di fioretti e d'erba è rivestita*. It is a measure of the esteem which the vernacular tradition had by this time achieved that it should here be coupled with the renaissance of classical antiquity. Like Pisistratus with Homer, Frederick has called back into being this heritage of vernacular poetry, by expressing his wish at a meeting with Lorenzo in Pisa in the preceding year to have such a collection of Tuscan verse. So that this *raccolta* comes to be symbolical of a vernacular poetic renaissance, and an historical document of some importance, in that it records by example the taste and interest in the past fortune of the language

---

[1] For this epistle and the *Comento* discussed later, I have used the ed. of Lorenzo's *Opere*, ed. A. Simioni (Bari, 1913), vol. i. For the attribution to Poliziano, see M. Santoro, 'Poliziano o il Magnifico?', in *Giorn. Ital. di Filol.*, i (1948).

which Landino also expresses. The epistle goes on to defend Tuscan, and to praise its capabilities, demonstrated in this collection of verse, to express all manner of subjects and moods: *Né sia però nessuno che questa toscana lingua come poco ornata e copiosa disprezzi. Imperocché si bene e giustamente le sue ricchezze ed ornamenti saranno estimati, non povera questa lingua, non rozza, ma abundante e pulitissima sarà reputata.*[1] The letter then proceeds to trace an interesting sketch of the *dirozzamento* of the language from Guittone d'Arezzo, Cavalcanti, Dante, Cino, Petrarch, down to the present time; for the collection includes contemporaries and closes with poems of Lorenzo himself, which the epistle with false modesty suggests are unworthy to appear among *sì maravigliosi scritti di vecchi poeti*, whose virtues perhaps by contrast they may serve to throw into greater relief.

If this epistle deals more explicitly with poetry than with language (though the two are inseparable), and if some of its merit is probably to be attributed to Poliziano rather than to Lorenzo, we may find in the latter's *Comento sopra alcuni de' suoi sonetti* a clearer and more substantial statement of his views on language. Like Dante in his *Convivio*, Lorenzo undertakes a defence of his actiom, *avendo scritto in lingua volgare, secondo il giudicio di qualcuno, non capace o degna di alcuna eccellente materia e subietto.*[2] The objection of its inferiority *per essere più comune* (in which we may note an allusion to the linguistic unity of Italy) is removed by a philosophical argument, which reflects the contemporary Neoplatonic background; and then Lorenzo passes to the more realistic problem of what contributes to the dignity and perfection of any language, considering this to fall under four heads. First, its own natural capacities for expressing thought and feeling. Second, its own sweetness and harmony, which he recognizes, however, to depend to a certain degree on the variability of human taste. Third, the fact that in a particular language, subtle and significant arguments and thoughts of great usefulness to mankind have been treated; though, he acutely observes, *quando questo avviene, è necessario confessare che più presto sia degno il*

[1] Ed. cit., p. 5.   [2] Ibid., pp. 18 ff.

subietto che la lingua, perché il subietto è fine e la lingua mezzo. Fourth, the fortunes of worldly events which cause one language to become extended from its native city or province to a wider territory; which, rather than on the merits of the language itself, depends on *felicità e prosperità di fortuna.* This is what happened to Latin, but it does not constitute its true superiority as a language, since its acceptance did not rest in the will of those who received it. Of these four virtues, then, only the first two genuinely constitute the intrinsic merits of a language; and that Tuscan possesses these, he goes on to show by illustration of the great writers, finding that Dante, Petrarch and Boccaccio have proved the capacity of this vernacular to express all manner of thought and feeling. In them, and in his favourite Guido Cavalcanti, he sees not only great range of expression, but the marriage of *gravità* and *dolcezza*, and more than sufficient indication of the innate qualities of sweetness and harmony of the Tuscan language. *E però concluderemo più tosto essere mancati alla lingua uomini che la esercitino che la lingua agli uomini e alla materia.* Here he echoes Alberti's view, developing it historically and affectionately, and looking to the future for the fuller realization of these potentialities of the Tuscan language, which he now regards as being in its adolescence: *E potrebbe facilmente nella gioventù ed adulta età sua venire ancora in maggiore perfezione; e tanto più aggiugnendosi qualche prospero successo ed augumento al fiorentino imperio, come si debbe non solamente sperare, ma con tutto l'ingegno e forze per li buoni cittadini aiutare.* Here, if anywhere, is the hint of a political motive in the extension of the Tuscan language, which finds its general explanation in the fourth consideration listed above, and its particular justification in the singular and central position which an expanding Florence under Lorenzo came to occupy in the political equilibrium of Italy.

It would be incorrect, however, to exaggerate the contribution of this position to the diffusion of the Tuscan language, at the expense of other forces already at work, or just beginning to have their effect. First, the accumulated influence in the rest of Italy of the Tuscan literary tradition, whereby in centres of growing cultural importance like Ferrara and Naples a Petrarchan *canzoniere* and the beginnings of a Tuscanized prose are evident in a Boiardo and a Masuccio da Salerno;[1] and behind this, the general spread of Tuscan influence by other means already noted. Second, the example of the new impulse given to refined poetry in Tuscany, not only by Lorenzo himself, but also by others, and chief among them the humanist Poliziano, in whom the assimilation of the virtues of classical poetry and its perfection of form is supremely apparent. Third, the invention of printing, which from 1470 onwards undoubtedly exercises a decisive influence in the greater spread of vernacular writings of all types, and to a large extent precipitates the need for a commonly understood language and regular orthographical practice.[2] That these forces, and others we shall presently discuss, were of greater weight than any Florentine political influence, seems borne out by the later coincidence of the determined appropriation of Tuscan by non-Tuscans, with the decline of the political and cultural pre-eminence of Florence.[3]

Apart from this political consideration, which is not major to Lorenzo's argument, his observations on the Tuscan language clearly reflect the position in the closing decades of the fifteenth century (seen from a Florentine viewpoint), when the vernacular shakes off the last vestiges of inferiority, becomes fully aware of its past (which could not be other than largely Tuscan), and looks confidently to the future. Only may we note in him a certain absence of that attachment to Latin, which is fundamental to the approach of Landino. Two further points remain to be emphasized with regard to Lorenzo, which are closely related. In his closing remarks in defence of the *volgare*, he writes that he cannot be reproached for having written in his native tongue, *massime perché la ebrea e la greca e la latina erano nel tempo loro tutte*

---

[1] For Boiardo, cf. Fatini, op. cit.; for Masuccio, see G. Petrocchi, *M. Guardati e la narrativa napoletana del '400* (Florence, 1953).

[2] For these problems in the sixteenth century, cf. B. Migliorini, 'Note sulla grafia italiana nel Rinascimento', in *Studi di Filol. Ital.*, xiii (1955), 259-96.

[3] This point, which our essay attempts to develop and illustrate, was brought out clearly in the stimulating inaugural lecture of C. Dionisotti, printed in *Ital. Studies*, vi (1951), under the title, 'Geografia e storia della Lett. Italiana'. See especially pp. 83 ff.

lingue materne e naturali, ma parlate o scritte più accuratamente e con qualche regola o ragione da quelli che ne sono in onore e in prezzo, che generalmente dal vulgo e turba popolare. This is not the first implied recognition of the possibility of similar refinement and regulariza⁄ tion of the vernacular, but it acquires greater importance in rela⁄ tion to the first grammar of Tuscan, possibly written in those years and by some scholars attributed to Lorenzo.[1] Arising out of this recognition of regularity, and implied in the words quoted, is the distinction between popular and more literary and refined usage. It may be said that the grammar referred to above falls between the two. And it may be added that in his own poetical works Lorenzo equally practised the two almost without discrimination —which is a clear indication of the as yet non⁄humanistic approach to vernacular literature, of the absence, that is, of any definite aesthetic criterion with which to distinguish between the idiom of contemporary usage and the refinement of a language of art. It is this linguistic and literary eclecticism which constitutes the variety and vigour of the Florentine tradition of the age of Lorenzo, and distinguishes it, generally speaking, from that of the *Cinquecento*.

At this stage of developments persisting to Lorenzo's death, nothing could appear more pacific and laudable than the revival of the Tuscan language and its even more intensive influence on other cultural centres of Italy. Twenty years later, Machiavelli is found fighting a rearguard action in defence of Florentine, which some dare to call Tuscan, and others, worse still, Italian; crying thief against a movement designed to rob Florence of her cherished possessions. To understand his indignation and his spirited argu⁄ ments, we must attempt to bridge the interval, and to explain how, why and in what sense the rest of Italy chose to appro⁄ priate the language of Florence.

---

[1] Cf. C. Trabalza, *Storia della grammatica italiana* (Milan, 1908), ch. 1 and Appendix. Alberti is a stronger candidate for the authorship of this grammar (see Trabalza in *Miscellanea Torraca* (Naples, 1912); but cf. my 'Appunti sulla lingua di L.B.A.', in *Lingua Nostra*, xvi (1955), especially p. 109, and G. Fumagalli, 'Leonardo e Poliziano', in *Il Poliziano e il suo tempo* (Florence, 1957), pp. 131-60, and especially pp. 139 ff.).

As Florence sent out her last rays of splendour under Lorenzo and passed into eclipse and political isolation with Savonarola, the courts of Mantova, Ferrara, Urbino, Milan, Naples and Rome, and the republic of Venice attained still more political and cultural importance. In each of them there flourished humanist and vernacular poets and writers, who assimilated in varying degrees and forms the Tuscan literary tradition and its language, without being especially conscious or feeling guilty of appro′ priating a purely local patrimony, and without submitting to the authority of local linguistic usage. For all that the resultant writings may be contaminated with their authors' own regional linguistic peculiarities (e.g., the *canzoniere* of Boiardo, or the *Arcadia* of Sannazaro), there was a basic general practice of the Tuscan language of literature, for which Florentine birth or residence was not an essential qualification.[1] It is the accumulated practice of such language, which becomes more and more fre′ quent and intensive in the last decade of the century, together with the rapid expansion of court societies, that fosters the idea of the existence of a universal idiom of literature not necessarily now centred in Florence, but representative of all the regions of Italy. Unless we appreciate this separation, which could never have taken place in Florence itself, between the live speech of the city and its illustrious literary and linguistic tradition now become the patrimony of all, the insistent claims of the non′Tuscans and the defence of the Florentines (among them Machiavelli) cannot be understood.

It is difficult to believe that the drastic political changes of the period did not also have their effect on this problem. Though Italian is not used then for the first time to designate the language of the peninsula,[2] and although it is not then used in theoretical

---

[1] On the general situation and on Sannazaro in particular, see G. Folena, *La crisi linguistica del Quattrocento e l' 'Arcadia' del S.* (Florence, 1952).

[2] Some examples are cited by Migliorini, 'Panorama' cit., p. 200; cf. also the important review by P. Rajna to G. Belardinelli's book on *La Quest. della lingua* (Rome, 1904), in *Bull. della Società Dantesca*, n.s., xiii (1906), 81-100, especially pp. 88 ff.

writings on the subject in any specific political context, there is abroad at that time a new sense of Italian unity, if only in misery and under the pressure of foreign occupation.[1] One clear effect, however, would seem to be in the central function of Rome. If we are to believe Bembo's account of Calmeta's theory of the *lingua cortigiana* formulated about 1507, and expounded in a work *Della volgare poesia*, now no longer extant, he set up as the model of excellence the language of the court of Rome, a kind of *koiné* born from the mixture of various languages used in this inter- regional and international centre: *non la spagnuola, la francese o la milanese o la napoletana da sé sola, o alcun' altra, ma quelle che del mescolamento di tutte queste è nata, e ora è tra le genti della corte quasi parimente a ciascuna comune.*[2] Castelvetro's version of this theory is very different: Calmeta was speaking of a language of poetry, which should start primarily from Florentine, Dante and Petrarch, and then receive refinement in the court of Rome, where it would shed certain impurities and assume new elements from the other languages of Italy: whence its denomination of *corti- giana*.[3] Though the detail is important for a correct evaluation of the concept of the *lingua cortigiana*, the general point is quite clear from both these accounts, viz., the idea of a universal and noble languages, probably largely based on Tuscan, but drawing widely on the other languages of Italy as represented in the refined usage

---

[1] See V. Cian, 'La coscienza politica nazionale nel Rinascimento', in *Scritti Minori* (Turin, 1936), ii, 143-73, with many illustrations for the first half of the sixteenth century.

[2] P. Bembo, *Prose della Volgar Lingua*, ed. C. Dionisotti (Turin, 1931), pp. 22-5, and introduction, pp. xx-xxii.

[3] L. Castelvetro, *Giunte alle 'Prose'*, in Bembo, *Opere* (Venice, 1729), i, 34-41. For discussion of the conflicting accounts of Calmeta's theory, see V. Cian, *Un decennio della vita di M. P. Bembo* (Turin, 1885), pp. 51 ff. The most balanced and complete account of the subject is P. Rajna, 'La lingua cortigiana', in *Miscel- lanea. . . . G. Ascoli* (Turin, 1901), pp. 295-314, with the important additions by S. Debenedetti in *Zeitschrift für Rom. Philol.*, xxviii (1904), 56-93. For a fuller bibliography and new light on Calmeta's position see now the intro. to my ed. of his *Prose e lettere edite e inedite* (Bologna, 1959), pp. xxxvi-xxxviii and xlvi ff.

of a particular centre, the court of Rome, become in these years of more vital political and cultural eminence.

If this importance attributed to Rome as a kind of crucible of the languages of Italy did not have prolonged fortune, and belonged more specifically to the society of the *Orti Colocciani*,[1] the idea of a universal vernacular representing and assimilating elements from the various regional languages of Italy was much to the fore in the first thirty years of the sixteenth century. Its chief exponents were Trissino and Castiglione.[2] The former had the great fortune to present in evidence a work by no less a writer than the greatest Florentine of all time, Dante Alighieri. Despite some suggestive correspondence of general idea, it is probable that Calmeta and other supporters of the *lingua cortigiana* had no knowledge of the *De Vulgari Eloquentia* at least in the early years of the century.[3] Dante's quest in that work for a *volgare illustre*, a superior Italian idiom of literary expression, and an ideal in which all the dialects of Italy mirror themselves, could not have found a more welcoming audience for its reappearance than that of the linguistic debaters of the early sixteenth century; especially as his arguments not only deliberately excluded Florentine claims, along with those of the other regional speeches of Italy, but pointed in the definition of the ideal language to the intellectual circles of the *aula* and the *curia*. If these did not exist in Italy when Dante was writing, and if social and political circumstances in the sixteenth century were not those envisaged by Dante, nothing could have been more natural than that these arguments, appropriately interpreted, should furnish material to the partisans of an Italian language, and of a *courtly* language, not identifiable with any particular

[1] Cf. Debenedetti's art. cit. in preceding note.

[2] It is unfortunately not possible within the limits of this essay to discuss the forceful and personal ideas of Castiglione on this subject, expressed in his *Cortegiano*, Bk. I, and in the dedicatory letter to Don Michel de Silva; and I must be content to refer to V. Cian, *La lingua di B. Castiglione* (Florence, 1942), from which I quote: 'l'idea d'una unità linguistica italiana doveva tanto più riuscirgli allettante e cara, quasi d'un simbolo e d'uno strumento dell' unità politica nazionale' (p. 15).

[3] This is discussed by Rajna in the review cit. *sup.* in *Bull. della Soc. Dantesca*, pp. 96–100.

region of Italy. And this was heavy ammunition indeed, coming from the most authoritative Florentine himself.[1]

A MS of Dante's treatise was possibly known in Florence as early as 1506, but Trissino did not publish an edition (and that in an Italian translation) until 1529, when he also published his major defence of an Italian language in his *Castellano*. There can be no doubt, however, that he had developed these ideas much earlier, and expounded them with the help of Dante's work; and on one notable occasion in 1513 had sustained this 'heretical' view before the Florentines in the society of the *Orti Oricellari*.[2] It is easy now to point to the weakness and even the fatuity of some of Tris-sino's arguments (as of others of the tedious series of dialogues on this question throughout the rest of the century); it is the conviction and tenacity of purpose of non-Tuscans like him (and it is note-worthy that they are almost without exception northern and not southern Italians) which strike the student of this problem, and persuade him that, if there was anything like an offensive from Tuscany on the rest of Italy in Lorenzo's time, there is in the first thirty years of the sixteenth century a determined offensive by the rest of Italy on Tuscany. The purpose of this, as represented by Trissino, was to prove that Dante, Petrarch and Boccaccio did not write in Florentine, but in *una lingua eletta, illustre e cortegiana*; in short, in Italian.[3] In other words, if the tradition of those giants had persuaded the generation of Lorenzo in Florence of the superiority and adaptability of their own language (which meant

---

[1] For the interpretation of Dante's treatise, and its part in the linguistic discussions, see the Introduction to A. Marigo's ed. (Florence, 1938); also M. Barbi, *Della fortuna di Dante nel secolo XVI* (Pisa, 1890), pp. 95-100. The impact of the *De Vulg. Eloqu.* is also, of course, discussed in many of the articles and books already cited above.

[2] Cf. P. Rajna's intro. to his ed. of the *De Vulg. Eloqu.* (Florence, 1896), pp. xlix ff. The treatise was put out in 1529 (Vicenza) in a translation attributed to a certain Gio. Doria. If this did not hide Trissino's part, it contributed to in-creasing a prevalent doubt as to Dante's authorship. Trissino's discussions in Florence are attested by Gelli (cf. Barbi, op. cit., p. 96; also the art. by P. Rajna cit. *infra*, p. 425, n. 2).

[3] G.-G. Trissino, *Il Castellano: della lingua Toscana* (Milan, 1864), p. 37.

the language that they spoke, too), that same tradition was now to prove a very different thesis, viz., the existence of a superior com﹍ mon idiom, belonging to no locality, and available to all writers irrespective of their provenance. Trissino's strongest arguments, besides Dante's treatise, were the eclecticism of the vocabulary of the *Comedy*, the demonstration of a common stock of words between the various regions of Italy, and certain variations of pronunciation which he saw between current Florentine and what he envisaged and practised as a courtly, Italian language.[1] Such contentions show great awareness of the linguistic unity of Italy, if little true linguistic perspicacity; and it is not the inten﹍ tion here to elaborate or evaluate them further. Our business now is with Machiavelli, who replies to Trissino with a great deal more linguistic perspicacity and a good measure of local patriotism.

Machiavelli's *Dialogo intorno alla lingua* was most probably written in 1514, long before Trissino's published work on the subject, but quite evidently aimed at him and his verbal exposi﹍ tion of his views in Florence in 1513, and showing a first﹍hand knowledge of the *De Vulgari Eloquentia*.[2] From the very outset of this brilliant document, Machiavelli shows himself cut to the quick by the appropriation of the Florentine writers even as Tuscan, let alone as Italian, and particularly by the testimony of Dante against Florence, which he regards as provoked by the bitterness of exile (and consequently disgraceful), or in any case lacking authenticity. But it is not only the linguistic treachery of Dante that Machiavelli deplores; it is his whole attitude to﹍ wards Florence, and his fundamentally different political outlook. Did he not put Brutus in the mouth of Lucifer?[3] This republican *campanilismo* of Machiavelli sharpens the edge of his trenchant

[1] Trissino distinguished these differences, in his proposals for orthographical reforms, in his *Epistola a Papa Clemente VII delle lettere nuovamente aggiunte nella lingua italiana* (1524); cf. Migliorini in *Lingua Nostra*, xi (1950).

[2] Cf. P. Rajna, 'La data del *Dialogo int. alla lingua* di N. Machiavelli', in *Rendi﹍ conti Accad. dei Lincei* (Cl. Sc. Mor.), ser. V, ii (1893), 203–22. The quotations that follow in the text are taken from the ed. of the *Dialogo* in Machiavelli's *Opere*, ed. A. Panella, i (Milan, 1938), 713–27.

[3] Ed. cit., p. 717. Cf. *Discorsi*, I, x.

linguistic arguments, which eschew any vague semi-philo-sophical theories about genus and species, and descend, as he does elsewhere, to the *verità effettuale delle cose*. He sets the great writers for a moment on one side, separates Italy into five regions: Lombardy, Romagna, Tuscany, Rome, Naples, and recognizes that there is a certain similarity of speech on which some base *questa lingua comune italiana*, particularly in the verb (*catena e il nervo della lingua*), but not in pronunciation. This approach to the problem through morphology and phonology is one of the most novel features of the dialogue. But if his was more likely in principle to achieve sounder results than that of Trissino, in practice the two views were irreconcilable for a different reason. Trissino's concern, in spite of his philological interests, is with a selective and eclectic language of art, something consequently hardly definable, whereas Machiavelli is concerned with the basic natural idiom from which art is excluded, or at least on which it cannot improve. This is clear from his desire to control the language of Dante's *Comedy* on *qualche scrittura mera fiorentina o lombarda o d'altra provincia d'Italia, dove non sia arte ma tutta natura*: and he eventually chooses Pulci's *Morgante*! We should not, therefore, expect Machiavelli's argument to move on the plane of ideal or artistic unity, but upon that of practical human intercourse. This permits him to see that *le lingue non possono essere semplici, ma conviene che sieno miste con l'altre lingue*, by virtue of the relations between people of different provinces, and the transmission of new ideas and trades which bring with them new words. Consequently the clear identity of the various speeches of the regions of Italy, as regards vocabulary, is a matter of degree. But such exchange of vocabulary does not alter the fundamental character of the language, for new words are assimilated into the Florentine system of phonology and morphology, and so become Florentine. Only after a long period of time may such influx of outside elements cease to enrich a language, and instead bastardize and deform it—which is not at all yet the case with Florentine. In this way, Machiavelli disposes of the argument of a common language based on similarity of vocabulary: . . . *quella lingua si chiama d'una patria, la quale convertisce i vocaboli ch'ella ha accattati da altri nell' uso suo, ed è sì potente che i vocaboli accattati non la disordinano, ma ella disordina loro; perché quello ch'ella reca da altri, lo tira a sé in modo che par suo.* This is the capacity of Florentine *par excellence.*

Whatever the misinterpretation and misrepresentation of Dante's views and practice may be in this dialogue,[1] they do not invalidate this fundamental recognition that adventitious elements of vocabulary are nothing compared to *i casi, i tempi e i modi e le desinenze fiorentine,* which he finds abundantly in Dante's usage in the *Comedy.* For even if these also exist in other regions of Italy, they differ in pronunciation, changing consonant values, dropping final vowels, and the like. Furthermore, he postulates that whatever virtues exist in the *parlare curiale* of centres like Milan and Naples, derive from imitation of Tuscan, and this he demonstrates by pointing to writers of different regions who have followed Dante. It is they who have taken his language, he says, apostrophizing the poet: *e così apparirà che la lingua in che essi oggi scrivano, è la vostra, e, per consequenza, vostra; e la vostra non è comune con la loro.* In other words, Machiavelli saw here with a clarity uncommon to that age the progressive diffusion and influence of the Tuscan language outlined in the earlier part of this essay. And naturally, being a Florentine, he could not accept the separation of that language from its live origins, so much favoured by the non-Tuscans. He points to the shortcomings of their attempts to imitate his language: *vedrai in mille luoghi essere da loro male e perversamente usata, perché gli è impossibile che l'arte possa più che la natura*— the last phrase of which clearly indicates again the basic difference of approach between himself and men like Trissino. His special example is the genre of comedy (particularly suited to his 'natural' approach), where he finds an uneasy and ineffectual hybridism of local and Florentine speech in the Ferrarese Ariosto that disproves the existence of a common idiom: *donde nasce che uno che non sia toscano non farà mai questa parte bene.*

---

[1] E.g., the complete inability to understand Dante's concept of the 'volgare illustre', and the assumption of the identity of the language of the *Comedy* with these theories of the *De Vulg. Eloqu.*

His conclusion is that many things cannot be well and properly expressed, *senza intendere le cose proprie e particulari di quella lingua che è più in prezzo; e volendoli proprii, conviene andare alla fonte donde quella lingua ha auto origine.* This is, of course, Florentine, in which all the best writers since Dante have written, and which has shown itself to be the most adapted to use in both prose and verse. And he argues that the poetic tradition passed from Provence to Sicily, and thence to Italy, and within Italy to Tuscany, *e di tutta Toscana, in Firenze, non per altro che per esser la lingua più atta; perché non per commodità di sito, né per ingegno, né per alcuna altra particulare occasione meritò Firenze esser la prima, e procreare questi scrittori, se non per la lingua commoda a prendere simile disciplina; il che non era nell' altre città.* Here again is the argument of the natural superiority of the Florentine language, prevalent at least since Dante's time (in the minds of the Florentines, of course), and enunciated, though not so forcefully, by Lorenzo. From that language and from those who have written in it, Italy has taken her example, and must continue to do so: *alla quale in ogni defetto, come a vero fonte e fondamento loro, è necessario che ricorrino.* No other common language exists, whether Italian or courtly, that does not have its origin in and need to repair to Florentine.

In his final words, Machiavelli expresses himself satisfied that he has convinced Dante by his arguments, but he is not sure that he will have done the same for those who refuse to recognize the benefits conferred on them by Florence, and who *vogliono accomunare con essa lei nella lingua Milano, Vinegia e Romagna, e tutte le bestemmie di Lombardia.* It is extremely doubtful, even had his *Dialogo* then been published (it had to wait until 1730), whether he would have convinced his contemporaries, unless they were fellowFlorentines or Tuscans like Martelli and Tolomei.[1] For the current, at least at the time, was against him, and against his realistic and 'natural' approach to the problem. His attitude to Florence anticipates that of a later age, in particular that of the

---

[1] Martelli wrote a spirited reply to Trissino's *Epistola* (see p. 425, n. 1), published in 1524, taking up a position similar to Machiavelli's. Tolomei, a Sienese, propounded in his *Cesano* (1527-8) the thesis of the 'lingua Toscana'.

nineteenth century, when the question arises again in changed cultural and political circumstances, and when a Manzoni will feel the necessity to *lavare i suoi cenci in Arno*, and to formulate the view that Florence is as much the linguistic capital of Italy as Paris of France.[1] In his own day, Machiavelli as much under-estimated the non-Tuscans' ambitions (not to mention Dante's) to achieve a refined and non-provincial literary idiom, as they underestimated the real Florentine basis of their linguistic ideal. Both sides were looking from different standpoints at the same authors, Dante, Petrarch and Boccaccio, and both were regarding that same linguistic tradition as a common inheritance. The difference, however, was not one merely of the name to be given to that inheritance, but a fundamental contrast between a view of language and a view of art, between a linguistic and an aesthetic approach, between quantity and quality.[2]

In his search to establish a quality of language (one might term it an aristocracy, as opposed to Machiavelli's democracy), Trissino confused the issue with many weak arguments of quantity; and Machiavelli's *Dialogo* is a sufficient answer to these. Bembo, how-ever, did not make Trissino's mistake. His *Prose della volgar lingua*, probably begun in the early days of the century and pub-lished in 1525, stand outside and above these problems of the identity of the language to be used, and resolve the question of the Florentine literary-linguistic tradition and the demands of the present, solely on the plane of art. On this plane he is able to assert categorically the distinction between the language of poetry (and, to a lesser extent, of prose) and the language of ordinary usage, which leads him to say: *e viemmi talora in openione di credere, che l'essere a questi tempi nato fiorentino, a ben volere fiorentino scrivere,*

---

[1] A. Manzoni, 'Sulla Lingua Italiana. Lettera al Carena', in *Opere*, ed. Barbi and Ghisalberti, ii (Milan, 1943), 753-4. On Manzoni's position, for which this is an inadequate reference, see Migliorini, 'La questione della lingua', cit. on p. 410, n. 1.

[2] These differences are acutely discussed by M. Sansone, 'Aspetti della questione della lingua in Italia nel sec. XVI', in *La Rassegna della Lett. Ital.*, lix (1955), 361-88, with special reference to Bembo, Trissino and Machiavelli.

non sia di molto vantaggio. He can do this, not by denying the Florentinity of the literary tradition (like Trissino), nor by denying to Florentine its natural qualities of sweetness and harmony dis-cussed by Lorenzo, and bluntly asserted by Machiavelli, but by seeing clearly and also historically in the literature of the past, the essentially qualitative distinction between art and speech. It is not the purpose of this essay to elaborate Bembo's theory, and to show its dependence on the humanist canon of imitation.[1] Suffice it to say that he is able, with Alberti, Landino and Lorenzo behind him, finally to situate Latin as a language of the past, and the vernacular as the language of the future.[2] But unlike them, and unlike Trissino, he does not confuse his excellent vernacular with Latin, or elements of regional provenance, or even con-temporary Florentine. His purism is that of the literary usage of the great writers of the *Trecento,* with only very guarded openings on to the progressive developments of the vernacular. It was this attachment to the past excellence of the Tuscan literary language of the fourteenth century, from which later emerged the myth of the *buon secolo della lingua,* that constituted the basis of the *Voca-bolario degli Accademici della Crusca*; though this did not come about without some *rapprochement* to the usage of Florence.

For all Bembo's superior vision and domination of the question from the literary point of view, his arguments were often mis-interpreted, misrepresented and adapted during the sixteenth century (not to mention later); and that largely because of the persistence of other approaches to the subject like those of Machia-velli and Trissino. Salviati and his Florentine colleagues of the Crusca inherit much from their predecessor, Machiavelli's point of view.[3] It seems insufficient to regard these debates as vain or purely literary discussions, or even as *fermenta cognitionis* breaking

---

[1] Besides the intro. to the ed. of Dionisotti cit. *sup.,* see M. Sansone, 'Lettura delle *Prose . . .*', in *Studi di storia letteraria* (Bari, 1950), pp. 5–54, and G. Sant-angelo, *Il Bembo critico e il principio d'imitazione* (Florence, 1950).

[2] For the persistence into the sixteenth century of the claims of Latin, see Cian, 'Contro il volgare', cit. *sup.*

[3] For Salviati, see Sozzi, op. cit., pp. 103–73.

the ground for the developments of aesthetics or more modern philosophies of language.[1] The feeling and seriousness with which they were undertaken suggest they were at the time quite other than vain, and from some points of view excite greater interest than the equanimity of the admittedly superior, and seemingly aloof, Pietro Bembo. The echoes of strong regional animosity (particularly the traditional one of Lombardy and Florence), the desire to prove at all costs that there exists a common Italian language, the deliberate, if not wholly effective, attempts to write in such a language, and to resist subservience to Tuscan, to break the monopoly of Florentine as the unique fount of linguistic and literary widsom, the ferment, in other words, of 'deprovincialization' of expression with no specific centre, or with the one open to all influences, Rome; all this reflects a society in crisis, and not only in a linguistic and literary crisis. It is not intended to suggest that the political events of 1494–1530 alone produced that crisis, which, as we have tried to show, was prepared for long before. But it seems pertinent to ask whether they did not help to precipitate and in some respects condition it: first by disturbing the balance of states, and bringing more into prominence centres and powers other than Florence; and second, by stimulating, if only temporarily, some sense of Italian unity in the face of foreign invaders. Machiavelli paradoxically reflects both this sense in politics, and a powerful provincialism in language. The tension is less apparent in his contemporaries, but their concern for linguistic unity, if only in literature, appears indirectly to reflect the conditions of political change.[2]

Although along the lines of Bembo's theories, as modified by the Florentine Academy, that unity came to be firmly established from the end of the sixteenth century, its inherent weakness of

---

[1] Th. LabandeJeanroy set out to show in her book, *La Question de la Langue en Italie* . . . (Paris, 1925), that the debates were futile and not worth attention. B. Croce sees the controversies in the light of his own philosophy in *Poeti e scrittori del pieno e del tardo Rinascimento*, ii (Bari, 1945), 74–84.

[2] This seems the case with Castiglione, more than any other writer, if his attitudes on politics and language are related as Cian sees them (cf. p. 423, n. 2 above).

representing restricted and often antiquated usage could not survive the philosophical and scientific advances of the seventeenth and eighteenth centuries, and the Romantic revolution of the nineteenth. It was necessary to find a new instrument of expression to replace the old, which, like Italy's divided political situation, had become fossilized and dated. This was not a problem to be resolved overnight by individual writers or theorists, like Manzoni. A new truly national language that should correspond to a unified Italy could not be discovered by appealing any longer to Floren‑ tine usage, which had, as Ascoli pointed out, been surpassed by the partial growth of an Italian language in certain respects different from that of the locality from which originally it had its birth.[1] The conditions and communications of the twentieth century have completed in this direction a process of natural if slow development towards a common idiom, whose roots go back to the age discussed in this essay. Though it may now be said that the *questione della lingua* is closed, the spirit of Machiavelli may yet occasionally be heard speaking through the mouth of the modern Florentine.[2]

[1] Cf. A. Schiaffini, 'Le origini dell' italiano letterario e la soluzione manzoniana del problema della lingua dopo G. I. Ascoli', in *Italia dialettale*, v (1929), 129‑71; and B. Terracini, 'L'aureo Trecento e lo spirito della lingua italiana', in *Giorn. Stor. della Lett. Ital.*, cxxxiv (1957), 1‑36.

[2] The question may be said to survive only in certain aspects of pronunciation. Cf. e.g. Ornella Fracastoro Martini, *La lingua e la radio* (Florence, 1951).

C. A. J. Armstrong

AN ITALIAN ASTROLOGER
AT THE COURT OF HENRY VII

With superb self-confidence the Italians of the Renaissance made
a career for themselves abroad by endowing the countries of their
adoption with styles of literature and art previously unrepresented.
Polydor Vergil supplied England with a critical national history,
which no Englishman had been capable of doing up to then.[1]
Although the artists came off better than the historians, for
neither Torrigiano in England nor Primaticcio in France seem
to have been quite so tormented by native rivals as Polydor
Vergil or Paolo Aemilio, the migratory Italians worked for the
most part in an atmosphere of jealousy and the value of their
performance has often been overlooked right up to recent times.

One of these enterprising intellectuals from Italy, we should
hesitate to call him an adventurer, succeeded if only for a few
years in setting up under the patronage of Henry VII a regular
astrological forecasting business. A common ambition among
astrologers was to combine the specialized service of princes with
the production of cheap annual prognostications for the widest
possible market. Paul of Middelburg and more than one generation of the de Laet family realized this ambition in a twofold
exploitation of their professional skill.[2]

Judging by his literary remains the most successful astrologer
in England in Henry VII's reign was Master William Parron to
give him the anglicized name under which he is referred to in

---

[1] *The Anglica Historia*, ed. D. Hay, Camden Soc., lxxiv, 1950.

[2] D. J. Struik, 'Paulus van Middelburg, 1445–1533'. *Mededeelingen van het Neder-
landsch historisch Instituut te Rome*, v (1925), 79–118.

the accounts of the King's Chamber for 1499.[1] Gulielmus Parronus Placentinus he called himself in his own Latin works. It may be assumed that he or his family originated at Piacenza since he calls the territory of the Duchy of Milan *patria mea*, and he declares that in the year of the overthrow of Ludovico Sforza he wrote for the duke a *libellus* containing a warning based on his horoscope.[2] As he was writing in 1499 about a severe illness in his fortieth year which he only survived by prescribing for himself a diet of lemons and lettuces, Parron was born no later than 1460.[3] His academic qualifications he described as *artium et medicine doctor*[4] and as regards his profession and practice *phisicus* and *prefessor in astrologia*.[5]

On the Continent predictions may have been printed as early as 1469;[6] but certainly by the last decade of the fifteenth century the quantity of annual astrological almanacks that issued from the presses was enormous. From his Italian background Parron would be familiar with the long-standing custom of an official astrologer preparing an annual prognostication for the benefit both of rulers and citizens alike. This was the practice which, through the agency of the press, he strove to introduce into England. Of printing he held a high opinion, and quoted it to Henry VII as one of the great new inventions of the day.[7]

Parron's later reports of his former dealings with William Ashley and Edward Frank presuppose that he was working in England soon after 1487; but his verifiable publishing activity in this country extends from 1498 to 1503. Writing in 1499 he recalled how he had produced an almanack three years before

[1] *Excerpta Historica*, ed. S. Bentley, p. 121.

[2] *Anni MD Pronosticon*, sig. a, vi^r and b, ii^v.

[3] Bodleian, MS Selden Supra 77, fo. 47v.

[4] *Anni MDII Pronosticon*.

[5] MS Selden Supra 77, fo. 4.

[6] Symon de Pharès, *Recueil des plus célèbres astrologues*, ed. E. Wickersheimer, p. 263. D. Kurze, 'Prophecy and History', *Journal of the Warburg and Courtauld Institutes*, xxi (1958), pp. 62–85.

[7] 'Sunt etiam quotidie nove artes prout nunc inventa fuit ista nobilissima ac celestis ars imprimendi libros', MS Selden Supra 77, fo. 51r.

which would indicate 1496 or 1497;[1] but the earliest-surviving almanack that can be attributed to him is a fragmentary printed prognostication in English for the year 1498.[2] In the autumn of 1499, Parron was boasting to Henry VII that the readers of his prognostication for the current year had been forewarned of the abnormally heavy rains[3] which, as we know from other sources, afflicted England in 1499.[4] His printed Latin almanacks dedi-cated to Henry VII for the years 1500, 1502, 1503 have survived if only in a fragmentary condition. These will be referred to later; but it is worth observing that all the surviving almanacks of Parron come from the press of Richard Pynson, with the exception of the English fragment for 1498 printed by Wynkyn de Worde.[5]

This fragment certainly belongs to 1498 for its mention of members of the royal family indicates Henry VII's reign, and the Cornish rebellion spoken of in the text as having occurred in the previous year is unmistakably the rebellion of 1497. The ascrip-tion of the work to Parron is more circuitous. The 1498 fragment refers its reader to the author's medico-astrological work in Latin for the current and the preceding year, that is to 1498 and 1497: 'as for the pockes and the cure of theym, who lust to rede, lete theym see the latyn boke of this yere and the last and there he shall fynde that shal contente his mynde'. Now, in Parron's Latin almanack for 1500, he excuses himself from writing about the treatment of syphilis, because he had written so fully on the matter three years previously, in other words in 1497 or 1498.[6] The question is not without interest, for it presupposes that Parron put out a Latin besides a vernacular almanack at least for 1498, of which there seems to be no surviving trace.

[1] Ibid., fo. 14v.

[2] Bodleian, Douce, fragments e, ii. E. F. Bosanquet, *English Printed Almanacks and Prognostications . . . to 1600*, Bibliographical Soc. (1917), p. 79.

[3] MS Selden Supra 77, fo. 48r.

[4] *Six Town Chronicles*, ed. R. Flenley, p. 174.

[5] Bosanquet, op. cit., pp. 79 f.

[6] 'De variolis vero novis et de istis malignis membrorum doloribus et apostema-tibus ad ossa usque, his tribus elapsis annis ita copiose scripsi, quod nihil nunc scribo', *Anni MD Pronosticon*, sig. a, iv^v.

For an intellectually well-equipped Italian, late fifteenth-century England was an astrologer's market. In Merlin's island prophecies were as rife as ever, indeed the Wars of the Roses had stimulated cryptic, mostly seditious, predictions. Native English prognostication tended, however, to be heraldic and symbolist, while being deficient in that classical literary and scientific background which played so important a part in Italian astrology. The patronage of the crown would be indispensable for any astrologer, native or foreign, who proposed to issue prognostications, which by means of the press were going to reach a large public, for Tudor governments had inherited from their medieval predecessors a mistrust of the prognostication. During the session of Henry VII's first parliament, it was believed—perhaps erroneously—that 'all maner of profycyes is mayd felony'; and in 1499, while Parron was being rewarded as a court astrologer, the bailiff of Winchester was rewarded for seizing the works of an unauthorized prophet.[1]

The connection between the occult and treason loomed unmistakably in the indictment of Thomas Astwode, charged with delivering to Warbeck on 2 August 1499 'a certain book of prognostication comforting him by the said book to execute more swiftly his purpose', which was to escape from the king's custody.[2] To dispel the cloud of conspiracy that bore like an incubus upon the English crown two human sacrifices were enacted in 1499 at Tyburn and Tower Hill.

The first victim was the so-called 'White Rose' executed on 23 November, after he had confessed to being Parkin Warbeck of Tournai, who impersonated the son of an English king. The second was a Plantagenet with a better hereditary right to the crown than Henry VII, Edward Earl of Warwick, executed on 28 November 1499, who was condemned in Westminster Hall 'without any processe of the lawe'.[3] This is no place to

---

[1] *Plumpton Correspondence*, ed. T. Stapleton, Camden Soc. (1839), p. 50; *Excerpta Historica*, p. 123; M. H. Dodds, 'Political Prophecies in the reign of Henry VIII', *Modern Language Review*, xi (1916), 276–84.

[2] *53rd Report of the Deputy Keeper of the Public Records* (1892), App. ii, p. 34.

[3] *Great Chronicle of London*, ed. A. H. Thomas, pp. 291–2, 446.

examine the reasons which decided Henry VII to remove within a week both the spurious and the genuine pretender; but for Parron the season posed acute problems of self-adaptation, if he wished to *godere i benefici del tempo* as a royal and public astrologer.

In order to justify his science and himself he completed writing the *De astrorum vi fatali* on 15 October 1499 and presented it to the king probably as a Christmas and New Year's gift for 1499–1500. At the same time he was engaged on his almanack of prognostications for the year 1500, the *Anni MD Pronosticon*, so that Pynson could print it over the date 24 December 1499 for sale to the public.[1]

The two works were inevitably closely interrelated. The *De astrorum vi fatali* survives in Bodleian MS Selden Supra 77, which most likely was the presentation copy. It is an academic and personal apologia to the king, which incidentally assumes considerable familiarity on the part of Henry VII with the state of the question. Not unnaturally it contained scholarly and private material quite out of place in a printed prognostication such as the *Anni MD Pronosticon*; but the basic argument underlying alike the manuscript opuscule presented to the king and the almanack addressed to all who could read Latin was the ineluctable influence of the stars. Taken as they ought to be, that is together, the pair reveal Parron's double ambition as a courtier and as an authorized astrologer to the king's subjects.

The *De astrorum vi fatali* is dated 15 October[2] without any year. It cannot be earlier than 15 October 1498 because Louis XII, who ascended the throne of France in April 1498, is named among the ruling monarchs.[3] The references in the *Anni MD Pronosticon* leave no doubt that the *De astrorum vi fatali* was finished on 15 October 1499. In dedicating his almanack for 1500 to the king, Parron directly invokes what he had just written *prout alias pluries scripsi et nunc in libello de hominum vi fatali nuper tue maiestati dedicato largiter ostendi*[4] which he again refers to as

---

[1] Bosanquet, op. cit., p. 80, and *Short Title Catalogue*, ed. A. W. Pollard and G. R. Redgrave, no. 19325.

[2] MS Selden Supra 77, fo. 55r. [3] Ibid., fo. 11v. [4] Sig. a, 1r.

a certain book *quem nuper paucos ante dies composui*.[1] In the first extract the allusion is unmistakably to the *De astrorum vi fatali*, of which the full title was *De astrorum succincte vi fatali hominum et particulariter cuiusdam nati ac adversus detestantes astrologiam iudicialem*.[2] In the *Anni MD Pronosticon* by a printer's oversight the operative word *astrorum* was just dropped. Pynson did not take great trouble in printing these cheap prognostications; and the unique copy of the almanack for 1503, which he printed for Parron, has at the end of the colophon a note—scribbled perhaps by Parron—*a Richardo Pynson incorrecte impressa ut patet per correctionem pennae*.[3]

The small change of classical scholarship was never out of place in fashionable literature, so that Parron circulated occasional quotations from Juvenal[4] and the theory of the transition of empires from one race to another in antiquity.[5] Although unlike the next generation he shrank from applying the theory to contemporary power-politics.[6]

For an astrologer with a propensity to determinism, he laid unusual emphasis on innovation and change wrought by the power of the stars *qua propter saepe innovantur et ordinantur nove leges et nove consuetudines*.[7] Among his own literary ghosts he referred to a work denying the value of experience, which he wrote before he himself had had time to become experienced;[8] and, despite repeated invocations of the authority of the school-men, Albertus Magnus, Aquinas and Scotus,[9] his apology for his science was ultimately that of an experimentalist. Perhaps like the late-Tudor astrologer, John Dee, he kept a case-book,[10] but Parron for good reasons only named his clients accused of treason.

But a few years previously the notable astrologer Symon de Pharès had been severely vexed by the ecclesiastical courts in

[1] Sig. a, vi[v].   [2] MS Selden Supra 77, fo. 4r.

[3] See *infra*, p. 451, n. 4.

[4] Fo. 10v. Juvenal, vii, 200; xvi, 4–5.   [5] Fo. 51v.

[6] L. da Porto, *Lettere storiche*, ed. E. Bressan (Florence, 1857), p. 66.

[7] Fo. 51v.   [8] Fo. 41v.   [9] Fos. 46r, 49r.

[10] *Diary of Dr. John Dee*, ed. J. O. Halliwell, Camden Soc. (1842.)

France despite the patronage of King Charles VIII.[1] Nevertheless, Parron, who made it his principal task to demonstrate that
judicial astrology was corroborated by scripture and who indig-
nantly repudiated charges of irreligion,[2] could never have written
in such confident tones had he sensed the least danger of being
exposed to ecclesiastical censures. Far from courting the favour of
the clergy, he dismissed their opinions about a matter which he
felt to pertain to secular politics.[3]

He defended in the first place judicial astrology, not only as a
practitioner, who foretold individual destinies, but because judicial
was more fiercely attacked than natural astrology. As a producer
of annual almanacks Parron could not be indifferent to natural
astrology, but to defend judicial astrology was also to defend the
natural form, which the opponents of astrology as a whole had
distinguished from the judicial and were indeed prepared to
tolerate as being unobjectionable on theological grounds and
susceptible of rational investigation.

For centuries controversy had raged around astrology, although
the arguments used on both sides scarcely varied. Parron, for
instance, employs—without acknowledgement—the contention
of Albumasar that at all events erroneous prognostications of
astrologers are less disastrous than the mistakes of physicians.[4]
The bitterness of the controversy rose and fell from age to age.
Astrology was never more popular than in the early sixteenth
century. The printing press had extended its appeal; and then
public attention had been drawn by the competition of business-
men and by the strife of princes to the utilitarian and notorious
aspects of judicial astrology. Meanwhile, Renaissance learning,
which intensified the study and to some extent raised the dignity
of astrologers, also stimulated that criticism which questioned the
very principles on which astrology was grounded.

The most destructive critic of astrology both on account of the
cogency of his polemic and because of his personal distinction
was, in Parron's generation, Giovanni Pico della Mirandola,

[1] Symon de Pharès, op. cit., pp. viii–ix.   [2] Fo. 32v.
[3] Fo. 20r.   [4] Fo. 49v.

for he combined close reasoning—too close by the limp standards of some neo-classical men of letters—with an aristocrat's sense of fun that played havoc with pedantic charlatanry. In singling out Mirandola as the adversary whose arguments he chose to refute, Parron picked on an assailant of astrology who had brought against it factual examples as well as theories. Pico's *Disputationes adversus astrologiam divinatricem* were unfinished at the time of his death, 17 November 1494, and were printed at Bologna in July 1495 or more probably 1496.[1] They remained therefore in 1499 something of a novelty; but Pico's reputation was probably even then well established in England, though this reputation apparently depended more on his devotional than his speculative studies. In French translation the exposition by Pico of the Fifteenth Psalm and his 'Twelve Rules' were presented to Henry VII about this time.[2] There is no need to dwell on the subsequent influence of Pico on Colet; but by 1506 Thomas More remodelled the spiritual exercises and the life of Pico in an English form for the benefit of Joyce Leigh, a minoress of Aldgate.[3]

In the *Disputationes*[4] Pico had adduced numerous examples drawn from contemporary Italian society to show how rarely the predictions of astrologers were realized in practice; and even if Parron had not been by nature a pragmatist—as I believe he was —his rejoinder to Pico would have compelled him also to imitate Pico and invoke practical examples to control theories. The quarrel between those who put their faith in the empirical weather forecasts of countrymen and those who believed the pseudo-scientific prognostications of astrologers, provided a well-worn subject of mirth in contemporary court literature. Molinet retold with pleasure how a king of France, who had been promised a

---

[1] E. Garin, *Giovanni Pico della Mirandola*, Pubblicazioni della università di Firenze, Facoltà di lettere, 3, v (1937), 50, and *Disputationes*, ed. E. Garin, 2 vols. (Florence, 1952), Edizione nazionale dei classici del pensiero italiano ii and iii.

[2] British Museum, MSS Royal, 16, E. xxiv, 16, E. xxv; cf. also 16, E. xiv.

[3] *English Works of Sir Thomas More*, ed. W. E. Campbell and A. W. Reed, i, 345; R. W. Chambers, *Thomas More*, pp. 92–4.

[4] Ed. E. Garin, i, 162–4.

fine day by his astrologer, set out for the hunt, but was warned by a miller driving a donkey that a storm was at hand because of the horse/flies tormenting the poor animal. When the king still trusting the man of letters persisted in the chase, he was drenched to the skin, and returned vowing: *puisque les asnes sont plus sages que les hommes en la mutacion du temps, je n'ay plus que faire de maistre pronostiqueur. Je veulx que dès maintenant il soit licentiet, mais le monnier et l'asne demourront à mes gaiges.*[1] Parron who no doubt shared the contempt which most Renaissance scholars felt for rustics was exasperated by the preference which Pico gave to countrymen over astrologers as weather prophets.[2]

He did, however, deliver two shrewd counter/blows at Pico. In the first place, although he paid lip/service to his adversary's reputation by calling him *elegantissimus ille*, he went on to suggest that Pico, having been overcome by a desire to write, but lacking a subject worthy of his genius, had been deflected to the facile task of attacking certain dubious astrologers.[3] As regards Pico's rustic weather sages, he maintained that when they beheld changes in the clouds and in the behaviour of birds, they were really ob/serving alterations in the weather that had already taken place, and therefore they were not predicting at all in the proper sense.[4] Parron, of course, had in mind the long/range meteorological forecasting over a period of not less than a year of which his generation of prognosticators were looking for the secret.[5]

Politics remained more treacherous than the weather; and Parron presented the king with a transparent justification of Henry's treatment of the Earl of Warwick, whom he had taken into custody almost immediately after the battle of Bosworth. Should Warwick recover his liberty, the rekindling of civil strife

[1] N. Dupire, *Jean Molinet* (1932), pp. 100–1, quoting from Molinet's *Roman de la rose moralisé*, which according to his view would be exactly contemporary with the *De astrorum vi fatali*.

[2] *Disputationes*, ed. Garin, i, 360. MS Selden Supra 77, fo. 43r.

[3] Fo. 42.

[4] Fo. 43r.

[5] G. Hellmann, *Die Wettervorhersage im ausgehenden Mittelalter*, ii (Berlin, 1917), 224–30.

was the most foreseeable consequence; and with an eye to the plausible and not unreasonable, Parron propounded the obvious argument in favour of Tudor policy. 'Unless he acts through evil intention, one prince may without sin keep prisoner another prince or a lord on whose account he fears an insurrection within his own territory.'[1]

Warwick was executed on 28 November 1499, and Parron, who concluded his offering to the king on 15 October, had with' out mentioning Warwick by name as good as advocated this judicial murder to Henry VII. 'It is expedient that one man should die for the people and the whole nation perish not,[2] for an insurrection cannot occur in any state without the death of a great part of the people and the destruction of many great families with their property.'[3] Significantly, it was at this point that he introduced his grievance against ecclesiastics intervening in secular politics: *Quod minime considerunt ecclesiastici qui de huiusmodi rebus se intromittunt.*[4]

In 1499 an intelligent prognosticator might have foreseen the approaching end of the Earl of Warwick, but no one could easily foresee who would be involved in the same doom, and relative obscurity was no safeguard against being made a public example of under the Tudors. Parron had grounds for uneasiness, for as a practising astrologer he had been consulted by at least one Yorkist conspirator, so that not the least important purpose of the *De astrorum vi fatali* and of the *Anni MD Pronosticon* was to shield their author from any suspicion of disloyalty.

While discussing in a determinist sense the inescapable power of the stars, the *De astrorum vi fatali* recalled those traitors whom

---

[1] 'Cum quamvis magnus princeps detinet alium principem vel dominum propter quod timet insurreccionem in suo dominio per ipsum, et tunc, ille actus, nisi aliter sit mala voluntas, est sine peccato', MS Selden Supra 77, fo. 20.

[2] John xii, 50.

[3] 'Quia ut concluditur de morte nostri salvatoris cum Iudei dixerunt melius est quod unus homo moriatur quam ut totus populus pereat. Non potest namque fieri insurreccio in aliquo dominio quin magna pars bonarum familiarum et bonorum eorum destruatur', ibid., fo. 20v.

[4] Ibid.

he had warned after their release from prison to keep out of mis-
chief, because he could tell 'by the true science of cheiromancy'
that they would come to a bad end *mala morte*. Needless to say
Parron implies an unlucky rather than an untheological end. In
the same way a continuator of the Croyland Chronicle dis-
claimed any particular knowledge as to how the Duke of Clarence
had died in 1478, but *utinam finis mali*.[1] Speaking of those whom
he had warned, he instanced one Edward Frank 'who was taken
prisoner in the "Lincoln battle" and imprisoned in the Tower,
but on receiving a pardon of his life was at liberty for about three
years until he fell again to treason and lost his head. He remembered too late the advice I gave him.'[2]

In the next chapter devoted to those born under lucky stars
he refers to those who, humanly speaking, could never come to
a bad end, 'one of whom was William Ashley born in Calais.
After I had ascertained that he would not come to a bad end, he
was imprisoned three times on charges including treason and
three times badly wounded. A little before he was assaulted at
Bruges and left for dead in the street; but he is still alive, and,
without prejudice to divine omnipotence, he will certainly die
in his bed.'[3]

This is hardly the sort of career of which could be said *bene
vixit, bene latuit*, but William Ashley is none the less hard to
identify. He is, probably, the William Ashley (Asshelaye) of
Calais, 'gentleman, alias scholar, alias commoner, alias yeoman,
the son of John, deceased late of Calais, a baker',[4] who received

---

[1] Fulman, *Rerum Anglicarum*, i (1684), 562.

[2] 'Quorum unus fuit Edwardus Franch captus in bello linconiensi et in turri
incarceratus, qui post habitam gratiam de vita sua in libertate per tres annos vel
circa stetit. Tandem venit ad actum publicum ubi amisit caput suum, qui tunc
bene fuit memor de iudicio meo in ipsum', fos. 16–17.

[3] 'Quorum unus est Gulielmus Aschele natus in Calisia, qui postquam cognovi
eum non mala morte moriturum, fuit ter incarceratus et pro lesionis sacre maiestatis
crimine et ter vulneratus fortiter, et nuper Brugiis paulo ante in via fuit prostratus
et vulneratus ac dimissus pro mortuo, et tamen vivit et infallibiliter non derogando
potencie divine, morietur in lecto', fo. 17v.

[4] *Cal. Pat. Rolls, 1476–85*, p. 328.

a general pardon 9 November 1482. Considering that Parron talks about Ashley's treasonable activity, and yet cheerfully tells Henry VII that Ashley will die peacefully in his bed, it can only be supposed that he had wholly recovered the favour of Henry VII. More than likely Parron's Ashley is the prominent London grocer, William Ashley, who at the end of Henry VII's reign and at the beginning of that of Henry VIII was active with the Merchant Adventurers in trading to the Low Countries.[1] This trading connection with Flanders might account for the incident at Bruges to which Parron refers. If the grocer Ashley and Parron's Ashley are the same, astrology was for once justified, since the grocer died apparently from natural causes, and his will was proved in 1515.[2]

In the case of the other, the unfortunate person, quoted by Parron no difficulty of identification arises. Edward Frank came of a Yorkshire family[3] and occupied under Richard III the shrievalty of Oxon. and Berks. The family of Frank is a good example of the advancement which King Richard conferred on the northern gentry, for, besides Edward, Geoffrey, Randolph and Thomas Frank were granted minor offices by that king.[4] Edward, starting in the service of Lord Fitzhugh of Ravens⁄worth (Yorks.), passed on, through the marriage of Anne Fitz⁄hugh to Francis Lord (later Viscount) Lovel, to the enjoyment of local office around Oxford, the sphere of Lovel influence.

Edward Frank was implicated in a petty insurrection which Henry Lord Fitzhugh started in July 1470, and he was then described in a pardon, granted to the rebels in September 1470, as of Ravensworth, gentleman.[5] From at least 1482 onwards he

---

[1] *Acts of Court of the Mercers' Company, 1453–1527*, ed. L. Lyell (1936), pp. 346, 349, 353, 370, 386.

[2] *Prerogative Court of Canterbury*, F, 7, Holder.

[3] *Victoria County History, North Riding* (Yorks), 1, 197; *Yorkshire Archaeological and Topographical Journal*, i (1870), 62; ii (1871–2), 289; *Itinerary of John Leland*, ed. T. Hearne (1745), v, 12, viii, 13.

[4] Geoffrey, receiver of Middleham, and Sheriff Hutton, British Museum, MS Harleian, 433, fos. 117v, 201v. Randolph, ibid., fo. 99, Thomas escheator of Yorks, *Cal. Pat. Rolls, 1476–85*, p. 533.   [5] *Cal. Pat. Rolls, 1467–77*, p. 215.

was acting in transactions for Francis Lovel, the son-in-law of Lord Fitzhugh,[1] and his opportunity arrived when under Richard III royal favour was bestowed on Lovel. Having been a commissioner and a justice of the peace for Oxon. in 1483, he rose to be sheriff of the county in November 1484.[2] He remained in the confidence of Viscount Lovel, and when in the summer of 1485 mounting French intervention on behalf of the Tudor pretender threatened the survival of Richard III's monarchy, so that partisans of the king such as Lovel took precautions to shelter their fortune in case of a dynastic revolution, Edward Frank was named one of the feoffees in respect of certain estates granted by Francis for the use of his wife Anne Lovel.[3]

Viscount Lovel fought for Richard III at Bosworth, but escaping from the battle he hid himself so successfully that even his wife could not ascertain his whereabouts. She accordingly sent Edward Frank to the north to make inquiries for him. By the end of February 1486 Frank had returned to London, having according to his own story failed to find him.[4] Perhaps he preferred to keep silence about Lovel, who was already plotting against Henry VII, whom he planned to seize later in the spring when the king visited York. This plot miscarried, because the rebellion of Humphrey Stafford, with which it was designed to synchronize, was pinched in the bud.[5] Edward Frank was deeply involved in this network of treason, for in July 1486 he was said to be hiding in the wilder parts of the north country, and he was excluded by name from an offer of royal pardon to rebels.[6]

Edward Frank met Viscount Lovel as soon as the latter landed on 4 June 1487 with an army from Ireland and the Pretender,

[1] *Cal. Close Rolls, 1476-85*, nos. 945, 1397.

[2] *Cal. Pat. Rolls, 1476-85*, pp. 371, 400, 554, 569. *Lists and Indexes, Public Record Office*, ix (1898), 108.

[3] *Catalogue of Ancient Deeds in the Public Record Office*, iii, no. A. 4790.

[4] *Paston Letters*, ed. J. Gairdner, vi (1904), 91-2.

[5] C. H. Williams, 'Rebellion of Humphrey Stafford', *English Historical Review*, xliii (1928), 181-3.

[6] *Cal. Pat. Rolls, 1485-94*, pp. 132, 133.

who styled himself Edward V[1] but who is known to history as Lambert Simnel. He accompanied this Yorkist expedition until it ended disastrously at the stubbornly contested battle of Stoke-on-Trent, 16 June 1487.[2] This is the 'Lincoln battle' of Parron's reference. Stoke is, of course, just outside Lincolnshire; but seeing that after the battle Henry went with his captives to Lincoln, the name is not only in itself tolerably good but possibly corresponds with the idiomatic usage of the time.[3] After the battle Lovel disappeared, this time for ever, and Edward Frank was attainted in the parliament of November 1487.[4] He was put into the Tower immediately and was quickly released if Parron was anywhere near correct in saying that he recovered his liberty for about three years, for Frank was executed not much later than the end of March 1490.

As a former sheriff of Oxon. and Berks., Frank must have been acquainted with John Sant, Abbot of Abingdon already in 1468,[5] who was the architect of the fatal plot into which Frank now entered. Since 1485 Margaret of York, the Dowager Duchess of Burgundy, had acted as the central figure in all the intrigues against Henry VII, and even before the battle of Stoke the Abbot of Abingdon had sent a private emissary to her. Sant was more than usually travelled for a Benedictine of the fifteenth century, and had been befriended by Margaret in 1474 on his way to Italy[6] whither he had gone in an embassy of Edward IV to Rome and Naples.[7]

It was no accident, therefore, that brought together in December 1489 Frank and an agent of Sant in London, where they

---

[1] *York Civic Records*, ed. A. Raine, Yorkshire Archaeological Soc., Record Series, ciii (1940), ii, 20-1.

[2] *Rotuli Parliamentorum*, vi, 397-8.

[3] *Anglica Historia of Polydore Vergil*, ed. D. Hay, p. 26.

[4] *Rot. Parl.*, vi, 397-8.

[5] A. B. Emden, *A Biographical Register of the University of Oxford to 1500*, iii (1959), 1641.

[6] Malines, Archives communales, lettres missives, no. 247.

[7] Federico da Montefeltre, *Lettere di stato e d'arte*, ed. P. Alatri (Rome, 1949), *passim*.

plotted the release of the Earl of Warwick from prison. Save for the fact that they were imperfectly informed about the exact place of Warwick's confinement, their plans might not have miscarried; but the conspirators sought for Warwick at the wrong spot, so that they were detected and seized. No small tribute to the practical usefulness of King Henry's secretiveness. Edward Frank was again attainted in parliament, session of January–February 1490, but this time he did not receive a pardon, and he suffered at Tower Hill about mid-Lent 1490.[1] Sant later received a pardon[2] and another Benedictine, Miles Saley, who was implicated in the affair lived to become Bishop of Llandaff in 1500; but in 1499 the condemnation of the Earl of Warwick could but arouse anxiety in Parron over his former relations with Frank.

In the days immediately after the battle of Bosworth Italian men of letters at the English court found an easy way of flattering Henry by denouncing Richard III. Thus Giovanni Gigli applauding the marriage of Henry VII with Elizabeth of York, and Pietro Carmeliano commemorating the birth of their son Arthur decried Richard as the murderer of his own nephews.[3] Poor Carmeliano had to live down the compliments he had paid to King Richard in a former work dedicated to Sir Robert Brackenbury, then constable of the Tower.[4]

Parron did not add to the legend of the monster Richard III, although he contributed to the creation of another Tudor myth, by reminding Henry VII how Edward IV had seen in him while he was only Earl of Richmond a successor on the throne of England.[5] The story of Edward's gloomy premonition that the Tudor would replace the Yorkist dynasty appears in the work—finished after 1499—of the Frenchman Bernard Andreas of Toulouse[6] and received its final elaboration at the hands of

---

[1] *Rot. Parl.*, vi, 436–7, *Leland Collectanea*, ed. T. Hearne, iv (1770), 257.

[2] *Cal. Pat. Rolls, 1485–94*, p. 381.

[3] *Memorials of Henry VII*, ed. J. Gairdner, Rolls Series (1858), pp. lvii, lix.

[4] D. Mancinus, *De occupatione regni Anglie per Riccardum tercium*, ed. C. A. J Armstrong, p. 17, n.

[5] MS Selden Supra 77, fo. 15r.   [6] *Memorials of King Henry VII*, p. 23.

Polydor Vergil.[1] In point of fact Edward IV with characteristic laziness made one half-hearted attempt to extradite from Brittany the future Henry VII, but when this proved unsuccessful Edward did little more about it.[2]

By 1499 there was little to be gained by calling Richard III a murderer of his nephews, though it was necessary to profess a belief that the sons of Edward IV, Edward V and his brother Richard, were dead. In the De astrorum vi fatali the death of the sons of Edward IV was therefore adduced as an extreme example of unkind destiny. 'What but the fate of the stars presiding at their nativity could have destroyed such innocents.'[3] Parron then appealed to the evidence of an almanack for the year 1473, in which Richard the younger son of Edward IV was born. According to this source a white rose was seen to fall into the Thames accompanied by apocalyptic phenomena.[4]

'De Innocentibus' was the heading given to this chapter of the De astrorum vi fatali;[5] and just about this time the second chronicler, who continued The Great Chronicle of London, wrote in the margin of his manuscript Innocentes and Mors Innocentium against the passages referring to the end of Edward V and his brother.[6]

The closest that Henry came to formally accusing Richard of their murder was in the words 'shedding of infants' blood' chosen for one of the charges in the act of attainder brought against Richard and his adherents in Henry's first parliament 1485–6.[7] Such an abnormal formula would scarcely have been introduced

---

[1] Edn. by A. Thysius (Leiden, 1651), p. 679.

[2] B. A. Pocquet Du Haut-Jussé, François II duc de Bretagne et l'Angleterre (1929), pp. 218–20.

[3] 'Que quidem lex destruxit innocentissimos filios regis Eduardi nisi fata astrorum suarum nativitatum', fo. 18r.

[4] 'Visio . . . de alba rosa et sole et luna pallidis et de duabus sagittis tonitrui ignis flammantis cadentibus in medium Tamisie. Hoc inveni scriptum in almanach anni sue geniture et tempus eciam sue nativitatis', fo. 18v, cf. also Chronicle . . . by John Warkworth, ed. J. O. Halliwell, Camden Soc. (1839), p. 24.

[5] Fo. 17v.

[6] Great Chronicle, ed. A. H. Thomas, pp. xxii, 234, 236.

[7] Rot. Parl., vi, 276ᵃ.

into the act unless it was intended to be understood as referring to Edward V and his brother. It is significant of altered circum, stances since 1485, that when in 1499 Warbeck was executed, his confession that he was not the younger son of Edward IV was widely publicized by being proclaimed and printed;[1] but the outcry against Richard as the murderer of the genuine sons of Edward IV was not renewed.

Clearly the king thought that no propaganda was as good as silence, for he had at his disposal many survivors from the days of 1483, ranging from dubious witnesses like Thomas Howard and Sir James Tyrell to a theologian John Argentine, who was also physician of the king's son.[2] Before becoming physician to Arthur, Prince of Wales, Argentine had served in the same capacity Edward, eldest son of Edward IV.[3] For some time I have been convinced that Argentine was the same person as *Argentinus medicus* on whose authority Domenico Mancini reported in 1483 that Edward V felt his own death to be impending.[4] *Argentinus medicus* in Mancini's text has nothing to do with *argentinensis* the adjectival form of the Latin place-name for Stras, bourg, but means 'Argentine the doctor' in the same way as Mancini refers to Lord Hastings, the king's chamberlain, as *Astinco cubicularius*.[5]

It was not strange, then, if Parron in 1499 unlike Gigli and Carmeliano in 1486 refrained from attacking Richard by name; but in maintaining that Edward IV's sons had been dead for over fourteen years Parron was doubtless following a line approved at court. He was nothing if not determined to please. Had he not reserved for Henry VII the most promising stars? The 1484 conjunction of Saturn and Jupiter, out of regard for which

[1] *Great Chronicle of London*, pp. 284, 445.

[2] The materials for the career of Argentine are listed by Dennis E. Rhodes, 'Provost Argentine of King's and his Books', *Trans. Cambridge Bibliographical Soc.*, ii (1956), 205–12.

[3] Tanner, *Bibliotheca* (1748), p. 48; Bodleian, MS Rawlinson, B. 274, fo. 10, and B. 276, p. 11.

[4] D. Mancinus, op. cit., p. 112.

[5] Ibid., p. 86.

Melanchton wanted to alter the accepted date of Luther's birth,[1] was deemed by Parron to foreshadow the Battle of Bosworth.[2] Although he criticized a fellow-astrologer, Paul of Middelburg, for making the pope and emperor, who were Paul's patrons, superior to the influence of the stars[3] Parron could not himself avoid the accusation of flattering.

This accusation he parried by contending in the *Anni MD Pronosticon* that he had aroused jealousy because in talking and writing he had insisted that Edward V and his brother had been dead for over fourteen years, in other words since before Henry VII's accession.[4] Facetiously he advised his critics to purge themselves of their delusions by swallowing the confession of Warbeck, who admitted to having impersonated the brother of Edward V; and he went on to compare the credulity of his detractors with that of the Cornish, who expected Arthur to return, or of the Flemings who thought that Charles the Bold was still alive.[5]

The audacity of comparing Arthur with the rumours of Charles the Bold's survival shows that a critical spirit could master Parron's discretion, for the belief that Charles survived the Battle of Nancy, 1477, had been confined to his feminine admirers or to merchants prepared to bet on long odds.[6] The Arthurian cult, on the other hand, was flourishing at the Tudor court; and in 1498 Arthur, Prince of Wales, had been welcomed in a pageant at Coventry by the figure of a revived King Arthur.[7] At least the reference to Cornwall satisfied the requirements of prudence and of historical accuracy, for since their rebellion of 1497, the Cornishmen could be abused with impunity, and moreover already in the twelfth

[1] A. Warburg, *Gesammelte Schriften*, ii (Leipzig, 1932), 497-505.

[2] MS Selden Supra 77, fo. 15v.

[3] *Anni MD Pronosticon*, sig. a, vi^v.

[4] 'Ex nigra ab infirmis bili adulator vocatur fui, cum scripseram et dicebam quod filii regis Edwardi iam per annos quatuordecim preterritos sub pena capitis mei non essent vivi', sig. b, i^r.

[5] Ibid.

[6] References in *Les actz et dictz de Jean Molinet*, ed. N. Dupire, Soc. des anciens textes français, iii (1939), 966, 1004.

[7] T. D. Kendrick, *British Antiquity* (1950), pp. 34-8.

century the belief in Arthur's return to earth was established in the neighbourhood of Bodmin.[1]

In the *Anni MD Pronosticon*, Parron announced his intention of bringing out yearly an almanack dedicated to the king.[2] His prognostication almanack for 1501 does not appear to have survived, but for 1502 there are surviving fragments of a printed one, dedicated to the king,[3] and another for 1503 has recently been brought to light.[4] In conjunction with the production of almanacks, he continued his career as a courtier and presented to Henry VII and Elizabeth of York a horoscope of their second son Henry combined with their own.

This small treatise, *Liber de optimo fato Henrici Eboraci ducis et optimorum ipsius parentum*, was a panegyric in astrological guise to console the Tudor dynasty suffering under the blow of Prince Arthur's death. It survives in two presentation manuscripts, one in London, the other in Paris.[5] The latter contains two items lacking in the former, a dedication to Prince Henry,[6] and an explanation of the full-page miniature, which in both manuscripts precedes the text. According to this explanation three stages were displayed in the accompanying miniature. 'First, a picture of the sky at the creation of the world with the signs and planets in their houses and positions following the opinion of prophets, astrologers and theologians. Second, various scenes painted to indicate the significance for the earth below of the twelve houses depicted in the sky. Third, a map of the world complete and correct with the four winds.' (Pl. 32.)[7]

Although their iconography is identical, a comparison of the

[1] Migne, *Patrologia Latina*, clvi, 983.

[2] Sig. b, i[r].

[3] Bosanquet, op. cit., p. 80.

[4] Described under item 147, catalogue 6, 1946, issued by A. Rosenthal Ltd., 5 Turl Street, Oxford, acquired by Mr. A. Ehrman to whom together with Messrs. Rosenthal my thanks are due for affording me facilities to examine it.

[5] British Museum, MS Royal 12 B, vi; Paris, Bibliothèque nationale, MS latin 6276.

[6] MS latin 6276, fo. 1v.

[7] Ibid., fo. 3r.

miniatures in the London and Paris manuscripts reveals some discrepancies. The London manuscript does not refer to the creation, since the signs of the Zodiac are seen from a different angle to those in the Paris example and the planets are in different positions. In each a world map occupies the centre of the design; but the London example has two extra place-names, Greenland and a mysterious 'MHYP' somewhere beyond Russia. There is no vestige of an American continent in either. Both manuscripts have the same embellishment, which besides the astrological miniature consists of an illuminated initial and many borders of badly grown fruit and flowers. The work is done by an atelier that produced uninspired renderings of the cosmopolitan Flemish style of book decoration. The ornament is more lavish than that previously used in the *De astrorum vi fatali*, but the taste is similar.

The *Liber de optimo fato* stood in the same relationship to Parron's prognostication for 1503, printed 24 December 1502, as the *De astrorum vi fatali* to his prognostication for 1500, also dated on Christmas Eve. In both cases the manuscript treatise was a personal gift to the king timed to coincide with the appearance of the author's public prognostication for the coming year. The *Liber de optimo fato* was composed after 2 April 1502, the date of Arthur's death, for which it attempts an astrological explanation, and it was finished before 11 February 1503, for it contains an unfortunate prediction that Elizabeth, Queen of Henry VII, would live to be eighty at least,[1] but in fact she died aged exactly thirty-seven on 11 February 1503. The indications are that the work was completed for Christmas 1502, when it would have been quite in order to address Prince Henry as Prince of Wales for he had been regarded as such ever since Arthur's death. The Bill enacted in the parliament of 1504 cannot be held to have created Henry Prince of Wales, for its text studiously avoided any reference to a creation in his favour and merely stated that it 'pleased Allmyghty Gode to calle the king's sone Henry duke of York to be nowe . . . prince of Wales'. In other words he had

[1] Ibid., fo. 28r.

automatically succeeded to that title since his brother's death. The act of 1504 only saved for Henry the revenues conferred on him when Duke of York.[1]

In certain respects the *Liber de optimo fato* betrays signs of haste; and in one place Parron complains of writing against time.[2] Perhaps he drew hurriedly on a prognostication, which he had written when Henry was only second in order of succession, and then combined it with new material appropriate to the heir apparent. In the first part of the *Liber de optimo fato* there is frequent emphasis on the religious qualities of Prince Henry's future career, with such remarks as *indubitanter devotus erit et bonus ecclesiasticus*;[3] but in the latter end the emphasis is laid exclusively upon the success of his future reign, in particular upon the felicity of Henry's married life and the large number of sons who would survive him.[4]

The death of the queen, Elizabeth of York, may have driven Parron from the Tudor court and kingdom, since it is hard to find anything later produced by him in England. In the *De astrorum vi fatali* he had emphasized the trustworthiness of astrology to Henry VII, who readily took offence if he suspected that he had been deceived by writers who dedicated their works to him. Erasmus, who knew all the people concerned, remembered how, when Bernard Andreas, tutor to Prince Arthur, warned Henry VII that the translation of Proclus which Linacre presented to him was not the first translation of Proclus, the king looked on Linacre as an impostor.[5] Sir Thomas More's dislike for astrologers is apparent from his Latin epigrams, but More's *Ruful lamentacion . . . of the deth of quene Elizabeth* puts into the mouth of the dead queen a rejection of astrology that possibly repeats a sentiment sufficiently prevalent at court to have cost Parron his position.

---

[1] Rot. Parl., vi, 522ᵇ.

[2] MS. latin 6276, fo. 8v.

[3] Ibid., fo. 7v.

[4] Ibid., fos. 46, 47.

[5] *Opus Epistolarum Des. Erasmi*, ed. P. S. Allen and H. W. Garrod, no. 2422, lines 67-75.

Yet was I late promised otherwyse,
This yere to live in welth and delice,
Lo where to commeth thy blandishyng promyse,
O false astrolagy devynatrice,
Of goddes secretes makyng thy selfe so wyse?
How true is for this yere thy prophecy?
The yere yet lasteth, and lo nowe here I ly.[1]

If, as I suspect, Parron returned to the Continent, it was probably also because in the long run he found the climate of opinion un-favourable to the further development of his business of publishing annual prognostications. The patronage which Henry VII extended to foreigners exacerbated local hatred. 'The king has the greatest desire to employ foreigners, but can not do so for the envy of the English is diabolical', wrote the Spanish resident in 1498;[2] and as the reign progressed foreigners came to be identified with the most unpopular side of Tudor rule. Giovanni Battista Grimaldi of Genoa, known as Grumbold to the Londoners, was working hand-in-glove with the king's hated minister Empson, on whose fall in 1509 'Grumbold' was fortunate to escape with nothing worse than becoming the target of 'shamefull rymys'.[3]

Parron's time in England coincided with the apogee of xeno-phobia in London, where from the great anti-alien riots of 1456 until 'Evil May Day' in 1517 animosity against foreigners was always ready to break out in violence. No wonder that in July 1517 Erasmus made this his principal excuse for not coming back to England.[4]

[1] *English Works of Sir Thomas More*, ed. W. E. Campbell and A. W. Reed' i, i, 336.
[2] *Cal. of State Papers, Spanish*, 1, 178.
[3] *Great Chronicle*, pp. 337, 343–4, 345, 352–65, 441, 453, 454.
[4] *Opus Epistolarum*, ed. P. S. Allen, no. 597, line 51.

Charles Mitchell

ARCHAEOLOGY AND ROMANCE
IN RENAISSANCE ITALY

If we want to appreciate the aims and methods of antiquarian scholarship at its best in the later Renaissance we could hardly choose a more reliable guide than the learned and witty sixteenth-century bishop Antonio Agustin. When Paulus Manutius called him an *arca universae antiquitatis*—a 'repository of all antiquarian knowledge'—he fairly summed up his contemporary reputation among qualified judges.[1]

Agustin was a Spaniard of noble blood, born at Saragossa in 1517 and bred to the law. After taking his doctorate in Civil Law at Salamanca in 1534 he migrated, as promising Spanish students often did, to Italy to continue his studies at the Collegio di Spagna in Bologna—still a grave retreat of learning where Agustin's name is remembered with pride. There in 1541 he graduated as *doctor utriusque iuris*. During his later student days in Bologna he heard the lectures of Alciati, who was then revolutionizing the schools by applying humanistic methods to the interpretation of legal texts in opposition to the scholastic, unhistorical system of the Bartolists. To Agustin, already an accomplished and fastidious classical scholar, the new approach was most congenial, and very soon—despite his Bartolist training and his initial scepticism about Alciati to whom he never took personally—he was an even more thorough-going exponent of the humanistic method himself. The first-fruits of his conversion was to publish the results of his brilliant collation of the Florentine codex of the Digest in 1543 at the age of twenty-six.

[1] P. Manutius, *Epistolae* (Venice, 1588), p. 72; F. de Zulueta, *Don Antonio Agustin* (Glasgow, 1939) (with bibliography), is a convenient study.

In 1544 he was appointed one of the Auditors of the Rota, the papal tribunal, and spent the next decade continuously in Rome. They were years of discovery and delight on which he always looked back with regret. It was then that he laid the foundations of his immense and flexible antiquarian learning. Any time he could spare from his legal duties he devoted to investigating and discussing antiquities; his house became the meeting-place of a remarkable group of antiquaries, his contemporaries or juniors— men like Gentile Delfini, Ottavio Pantegato, Basilio Zanchi, Pirro Ligorio and Onufrio Panvinio. He was the leader among them. In the later fifties he was much occupied on diplomatic missions, and he took an active and skilful part in the delibera- tions of the Council of Trent. These were the years of his editions of Varro's *De lingua latina* (1557) and Festus (1559), and of his close and growing association with Carlo Sigonio and the young Fulvio Orsini,[1] the Farnese librarian; with the latter he was to collaborate in great books on Roman prosopography and law, the *Familiae Romanae* (1577) and the *De legibus et senatusconsultis* (1583). Meanwhile, having been consecrated Bishop of Alife near Naples and translated to the Spanish see of Lerida, he returned to his native land in 1564 and remained there till his death in 1586. From 1576 he was Archbishop of Tarragona. His Spanish years of maturity were an Indian summer. He ruled his province with firmness and urbanity; he had leisure for corre- spondence and publication; he brought out works on Canon Law to match his earlier researches in Civil; and his relish for anti- quities did not abate. 'He lived jocundly in Tarragona [his funeral eulogist tells us] because of the vestiges of Roman antiquity that filled the city, the theatre, the circus, the *tituli*, coins and inscrip- tions, so that all the walls seemed to talk Latin.' As his volumi- nous correspondence shows, he enjoyed a unique reputation as an archaeological expert, consulted by hosts of scholars in Italy and Spain; his superb library and collection of coins were at every colleague's disposal.

His favourite fields were numismatics and epigraphy, and he

[1] See P. de Nolhac, *La bibliothèque de Fulvio Orsini* (1887).

presented his views and reflections on both in his posthumously published *Dialogues on Medals, Inscriptions and other Antiquities*,[1] one of the most engaging and lively things in all Renaissance antiquarian literature. What attracts us from the start is Agustin's scepticism and the self-deprecating air of critical detachment that tempered his enthusiasm. 'The nerve and sinews of wisdom', he said, quoting from Cicero's brother a line of Epicharmus, 'is never to believe rashly.' The dialogues opened with a confession that his ignorance was greater than his knowledge. His aim was a critical knowledge of antiquity; and he was convinced that coins, inscriptions and other inscribed or figured remains were more trustworthy witness than literary texts, because they were actual surviving fragments of the past whereas ancient literature had come down corrupted by later hands. This idea he emphasized again and again: 'I would rather see the original than the copy' —that was his constant principle. As we should expect he had a keen nose for fakes: his eleventh dialogue on false medals and inscriptions is in fact the earliest reasoned discussion of the subject we have. 'How do you detect them?' his interlocutor asked. By flair, he replied in effect, 'like money-changers who can tell false coin at a glance'. Yet he was not simply a connoisseur relying on instinct. When he analyses a fake we are struck by the modernity of his method. He discussed, for example, the once famous stone on the Rubicon forbidding Roman troops to cross the river in arms, as Caesar did when the die was cast. The younger Aldus, a careful antiquary, was taken in by it; he made a journey to inspect the stone itself, and believed it genuine. True, admitted Agustin, the stone is ancient, and so is the inscription on one side; but the Rubicon text on the other side is a modern forgery. In other words, concluded the questioner, you call your opponents liars and enemies. Agustin's mind went back to his happy evenings in Rome. In Rome, he answered, educated people argue these matters together gently and dispassionately, without losing their tempers as they do here in Spain. Whereupon he set forth

[1] Spanish edition (Tarragona, 1587); I have used the Italian translation by D. O. Sada (Rome, 1592).

his considered arguments against the genuineness of the inscription: the state of the stone, its orthography at variance with that
of the Florentine codex of the Digest, and the forger's evident
ignorance of Roman constitutional usage. Mommsen himself
had no other or sharper critical weapons.

These being Agustin's views on the value of authentic evidence,
it may come as a surprise to learn that he had quite a relish for
certain kinds of fakes—fakes that were calculated to deceive and
even got accepted in the antiquarian books. He admired, for
instance, the fake coins of the Paduan Cavino. They were so
perfectly counterfeited, he said, that they were the greatest pleasure
to look at; if it were not for a few trifling errors in lettering and
imagery one could not ask for better. He commended the fakes of
Panvinio, who lifted passages from classic authors, put them into
epigraphic form and then pretended that they came from books
of inscriptions, so that later compilers incorporated them in
theirs. 'O for three hundred of such quality!' said his friend, who
a moment before had been puzzled by Agustin's argument that
an inscription could be both false and good. 'Twenty are quite
enough for me,' was the dry comment, 'and to tell you the truth,
I'd rather have the original texts.' Most unexpected, perhaps, is
Agustin's respect for his friend Pirro Ligorio,[1] the blackest name
in the calendar of Renaissance forgers. 'Forgery on paper and
on stone now begins its dirty work', was Christian Hülsen's
puritanic judgement on him.[2] Agustin was not shocked at all,
though he would have known as well as Hülsen that Ligorio's
sketch-books were riddled with made-up monuments. Failing
evidence from coins, he even quoted drawings by Ligorio of
Roman circuses as things worth looking at. He considered
Ligorio a 'great antiquary', that is to say, a man who could
convincingly restore antiquity; and without taking him too
seriously, he applauded the skill of a painter who never properly

[1] E. Mandowsky, 'Some Observations on Pyrrho Ligorio's Drawings' in *Rendiconti della Pontificia Accademia Romana di Archeologia*, xxvii (1952–4), 335–58, gives
a critical and sympathetic account of Ligorio's methods.

[2] *Römische Mitteilungen*, xvi (1901), 130.

learnt Latin and could so adroitly crib and utilize the learning of others.

Agustin was of course quite consistent; and once we recognize the difference between the task of the sixteenth-century antiquary and that of the modern classical archaeologist,[1] it is easy to see why the historical fakes that appalled Hülsen left Agustin's withers unwrung. Hülsen and his fellow-editors of the Corpus of Latin Inscriptions had obligations to writers of ancient history, and sternly segregated the *falsae* to keep the wells of truth pure. Agustin had no such scruples, simply because there was no ancient history to be written: the authority of the ancient authors still stood, 'holding the field', as Salutati put it, 'with standards planted and unmoved'. The sixteenth-century antiquary was a humanist in a new medium. His first task was to correct, elucidate and supple-ment the classical texts where they were deficient. He could restore something like the spelling of the words Cicero or Caesar had in mind when they dictated their works (restoring monuments spoilt by age and neglect was evidently in the same category); he could also systematically illustrate the various departments, the *anti-quitates*, of ancient Greek and Roman life. All this Agustin patiently explained to his companions; and he especially noted the excellent antiquarian work done by his friend Fulvio Orsini on the names of Roman families, and by Panvinio, the editor of the consular *fasti*. But at the same time, the antiquary, like the literary humanist, was an original composer. He invented inscrip-tions to show his taste, and he could fake them too to exhibit his skill and his ability to rival the ancients.[2] The more like the genuine article his products were, the greater credit they were to his scholarship. Agustin evaluated them by the same standards as he applied when judging and dating original monuments—by their elegance.

But when Agustin looked back on the efforts of pre-sixteenth-century fabricators, he found very much less to please him.

[1] Pointed out by A. Momigliano, 'Ancient History and the Antiquarian' in *Journal of the Warburg and Courtauld Institutes*, xiii (1950), 285-315.

[2] Cf. Vasari's story of Michelangelo's sleeping Cupid.

Pontano and Pomponio Leto, he allowed, invented with great learning and considerable grace 'for their time'. He even admitted that Annius of Viterbo, the notorious faker of historical texts, was an ingenious artist in his way, though he deeply regretted that the forgeries of Annius and others had so corrupted the modern chronicles of Spain; he did not like to see the Spaniards fooled by the Italians. Most early fictions, however, he considered simply ridiculous and beneath contempt. His interlocutor asked him about one he had read of in the bishop's palace at Viterbo. 'Always a suspect provenance,' said Agustin, 'what is it?' And his friend quoted a favourite inscription among fifteenth-century collectors, the memorial of Collatinus Tarquin to his wife Lucretia. 'Don't go on; Lucrece did not deserve such a wretched epitaph.' His friend started to recite another riddling rhymed piece about one Hersilius and Marulla, who was at once his mother, sister and wife. Agustin again implored him to stop; it gave him a headache to listen to. Yet he was quick to catch the lady's name and conjecture that the author was the poet Marullo, just as on similar grounds he attributed another bogus inscription beginning *Ego Gallus Favonius Iucundus* to the antiquary and architect Fra Giocondo. Another popular one they discussed was a gnomic sibylline text on an arch, made up of P's, S's, V's and F's, supposed to have been interpreted by Bede.[1] Agustin dis-missed it as a 'pastime for children', plainly, without a moment's study, a fake.

Now the book to which Agustin referred his friends for many of these frivolities was a serious antiquarian work, the *Inscriptiones Sacrosanctae Vetustatis* of Petrus Apianus, the first world-corpus of classical inscriptions to appear in print, published at Ingol-stadt in 1534, the year Agustin graduated at Salamanca. Apianus perfectly represented the half-medieval type of antiquarian learn-ing swept aside by the critical methods of Agustin's Roman circle

---

[1] C. Hülsen, 'Die Inschriftensammlung des Erfurter Humanisten Nicolaus Marschalk', *Jahrb. d. königl. Akad. zu Erfurt*, n.f. xxxviii (1912), 180 ff.; H. Silvestre, *Les manuscrits de Bède à la bibliothèque royale de Bruxelles* (Leopoldville, 1959).

in the fifties. Though it claimed to discriminate, it was a quite uncritical jumble of genuine and false inscriptions without any order except a rough geographical one. The book had no index, and looks like a picture-book, many of the inscriptions being set in impressive lapidary capitals and framed in made-up monu-mental woodcuts. The compiler did not go to inspect the stones, but simply strung together what he received. Agustin could not be bothered to go through the items in it one by one; he had marked the *falsae* with a cross in his copy, and invited his friends to inspect it at their leisure.

Nor did he say much about the sources, except to mention Leto and Cyriac of Ancona, both of whom are named in the preface, and a book called the *Hypnerotomachia Polifili*. Cyriac of Ancona was the key-name. Apianus was not, after all, a very original work. It was a gathering up, through late copies and German conflations, of the main fifteenth-century epigraphic manuscript tradition which went back through Michele Ferrarini, Felice Feliciano, and others to Cyriac himself.[1] In fact, Apianus opened his display like a trumpet-blast with one of Cyriac's sauciest and most characteristic fictions: an epitaph he said he had found at Gades—beyond the Pillars of Hercules—on the tomb of a mad Carthaginian called Heliodorus, who had had himself buried there for the fun of seeing if anybody madder than he should ever penetrate so far west to visit him. 'This inscription which they praise', said Agustin, 'is one of the very worst.' His friends wondered how such things ever got into a respectable antiquarian work at all. Agustin replied that if one believed all one saw in print, one might as well believe Lucian's *True History* or the romancing fables of Roland and Amadis of Gaul. And indeed the third source of Apianus which he singled out *was* a romance—

---

[1] On these see G. B. de Rossi, *Inscriptiones Christianae Urbis Romae*, ii; E. Ziebarth, 'Cyriacus von Ancona als Begründer der Inschriftenforschung' in *Neue Jahrbücher*, ix (1902), 214–26, and idem, 'Die Nachfolger des Cyriacus von Ancona', ibid., xi (1903), 480–93. F. Saxl, 'The Classical Inscription in Renaissance Art and Politics' in *Journ. of the Warb. and Court. Inst.*, iv (1940–1), 18–46, studies Renais-sance epigraphy from a humanistic standpoint.

'Polifilo's Strife of Love in a Dream', an archaeological rhapsody, full of medieval love/allegory and imaginary inscriptions, pub/ lished by Aldus in Venice in 1499 and in France (where it had a wide influence on architecture and esoteric thought)[1] in a first French translation in 1546. 'Poor fellow, whoever he was,' was all Agustin could say, 'to waste his time translating such a dread/ ful book.' 'What language is it written in, please,' asked his tireless questioner, 'Greek, Latin or Italian?' 'In all three, yet in none.' 'But how can that be?' 'Because it appears the author wanted to write down his dreams and imbecilities in Italian, but he mixed it up with so many Greek and Latin words, and so wilfully studied obscurity and the confusion of the tongues, that you can say he did not really write in any of them.'

Again Agustin was thoroughly consistent. By any Ciceronian standards of elegance the language, scholarship and fictions of Cyriac and the *Polifilo* were obviously absurd—to be dismissed without shrift; and doubtless this was the right caustic reply at the time for Agustin to give his enquirers. But still their question remains unanswered, and today we cannot brush it so cavalierly aside. For it is clear, from this distance, that Agustin did his predecessors rather the same injustice, in defence of sound learning, as Hülsen and the editors of the Corpus did theirs—judging them by the wrong standards. What fixed the gulf between Agustin and the older antiquaries was not so much their ignorance and lack of taste as the fact that they had quite different objectives. Apianus and his early sixteenth/century readers knew that the *Polifilo* was a romance, and to anybody familiar with Cyriac's reputation for hilarious travel to the ends of the earth the case of 'elective affinity' at Gades was too good to be true. And yet, as scholars, they embraced such things with relish. How was it possible? Here, reluctantly, we must say farewell to Agustin's congenial guidance and try instead, as sympathetically as we can, to appreciate the ideals and criteria of the earlier Renaissance epigraphists on their own terms. We shall see that from their

[1] See A. Blunt, 'The H.P. in Seventeenth/century France' in *Journ. of the Warb. Inst.*, i (1937), 117-37.

point of view—to take the extreme case—the *Polifilo*, the 'frenzied raptures of a pedant', as the late E. P. Goldschmidt called it,[1] was not eccentric at all but a work of the choicest learning. Linked as it was in language and matter to the central Cyriacesque tradition, and refusing to touch the common earth firmly at any point, this fantastic romance was in many respects the perfect flower and consummation of fifteenth-century antiquarian scholarship.]

The *Hypnerotomachia Polifili*[2] never quite emerges out of a dream world. Polifilo, the hero, signed it at the end, 'Treviso, May Day 1467'. His beloved, Polia, speaks of herself in the second book, a kind of inner plot in the form of an epilogue. The first book, containing the main story told by Polifilo in the first person, closes with the lovers finally united in the gardens of Adonis, toying and playing while nymphs make music around them. The nymphs asked Polia to tell the tale of her love, and so—weaving a chaplet of roses for Polifilo as she speaks—she began. Her name was that of the chaste Roman who killed herself when Tarquin's son dishonoured her—Lucrezia. She belonged to the noble Lelio family, living in Treviso. One day in the year 1462, as she was drying her hair on the balcony of their palace, Polifilo spied her and lost his heart. Soon afterwards the plague came to Treviso and Polia caught it. She vowed that if she recovered she would dedicate herself to Diana. And so it happened. Polia recovered and entered Diana's service. Polifilo sent her love-letters which she scorned; he visited her in Diana's church, was repulsed and fell dead to the ground. Polia fled terrified, but—warned by a vision of Cupid lashing two naked maidens harnessed to his flaming car (we can see it all in the pictures) and a dream of herself torn in pieces by monsters, and by her nurse's tales of the

---

[1] *The Printed Book of the Renaissance* (Cambridge, 1950), p. 51.

[2] A. Khomentovskaia, *Bibliofilia*, xxxvii (1936), 154-5, lists a selection of the literature on the *H.P.* I have used the facsimile edition, London (Methuen) 1904. There is a useful synopsis of the story with a speculative Jungian commentary by Linda Fierz-David, *The Dream of Polifilo* (New York (Bollingen Series, XXV) 1950).

punishment that comes to girls who resist love—she returned in the morning to the temple, and hugged and cried over her lover's corpse. Whereupon his soul returned, and they embraced rapturously, only to be surprised and driven out by Diana's priestesses. However, Venus came to their aid, and the lovers met at last in her temple. There before Venus's lady-bishop Polia confessed her cruelty, and Polifilo told how in his swoon of death in Diana's church he had been transported to heaven where Venus had shown him Polia's image pierced by Cupid's dart. The high priestess then blessed and joined them, uniting Polifilo and Polia for ever in faithful love. Thus the complicated plot wound back to its finale. Polia finished her story and put her chaplet on Polifilo's head, kissing him with honeyed, dovelike lips. The nymphs shouted, danced and sang, and then departed, leaving them alone to enjoy their bliss: too short—for the dawn came and Polia dissolved from Polifilo's arms. A nightingale sang, and he awoke to the misery of regret.

Out of this dreamy mist historic shapes half-appear. There was a Lelio, the Bishop in Treviso at this time, and the plague came there in 1464. Already in 1512 it was noticed that the chapter initials of the book made an acrostic: 'Fra Francesco Colonna was Polia's lover'; and the same note, in a lost copy of the book, said that the author was this same Colonna, a friar who loved a lady Hippolita ardently in Treviso, while an additional note (as it seems) of 1521 said he was still living at SS. Giovanni e Paolo in Venice. This was an historic Fra Francesco Colonna, born in 1433, who spent many years of his life in a Dominican house in Treviso and his later life, till his death in 1527, mostly at SS. Giovanni e Paolo. Was he the author?—a learned antiquary who left no other mark on literature, who kept clear of the publication and yet identified himself so precisely in a soon-decyphered acrostic. And what was his relation to Leonardo Crasso of Verona,[1] who paid for the publication in 1499 and, as we shall see, revealed a singularly intimate knowledge of the author's

[1] See G. Biadego, 'Intorno al sogno di Polifilo' in *Atti del Reale Instituto Veneto*, lx (1900–1).

intentions in his preface? Crasso was qualified in arts as well as law and acquainted with architecture, one of Polifilo's dominant interests in the book. Could he have had a hand in the writing? And there is a mystery about the date of composition. The whole thing has the air of a work of the eighties or early nineties, and certain pictures, integral to the text, appear to be taken from antiques not otherwise recorded before 1475.[1] May Day 1467 could be part of the dream too.

Polifilo's story in the first book, the elaborate outer shell of romance corresponding to the inner shell of Polia's autobio-graphy, is all dream. He falls asleep and is lost in a dark wood; he comes at length to the temple of the sun, a vast stepped pyramid with an obelisk on top (the Mausoleum of Halicarnassus). After losing himself in its dark vaults, he visits the kingdom of Queen Eleutherylida who has him conducted on to the gates of Queen Telosia. Later on in his dream he meets a nymph, not knowing her to be Polia, and they witness the triumphs of Jove's mistresses. Then they come to the temple of Venus Phyzizoa. Polia declares herself, their love is hallowed by mystic sacrifices, and Polifilo visits the forlorn graves of dead lovers in Polyandrion. So they cross in Cupid's boat to the island of Cythera, where Venus by her fountain manifests herself, and Cupid transfixes the lovers with his dart. Then the nymphs at last lead them to the gardens of Adonis.

What kind of story is this? Its plot, of course, owes much to medieval romance. There are echoes in it of the *Roman de la Rose*, we are often reminded of Dante's pilgrimage, and the skeleton of the earlier part was fairly certainly borrowed from Boccaccio's *Amorosa Visione*.[2] Boccaccio's poet fell asleep in a desert plain and came to a great castle, as Polifilo came to the sun-temple. Boccac-cio's dreamer had a choice of doors, one narrow, the other wide and leading to love; so Polifilo chose the middle gate of Queen Telosia, labelled in Arabic, Hebrew, Greek and Latin 'the

[1] C. Hülsen, *Le Illustrazioni della 'H.P.' e le antichità di Roma* (Florence, 1910).
[2] D. Gnoli, *Il Sogno di Polifilo* (Florence, 1900).

Mother of Love', and entered in. Boccaccio's wanderer saw pictures of Jove's loves and afterwards, to teach him of the vanity of human wishes, the pictures of ill-fortune, just as Polifilo beheld first the triumphs and later the tombs. Parallels with the *Amorosa Visione* and other Boccaccian romances can easily be multiplied.

But what a different setting it is from that of the fourteenth-century tales, different in landscape and sentiment. From a world of Gothic gardens of love and fancy-dress mythology we pass into a world of classical and even pre-classical antiquity: a world of enigmatic hieroglyphs and awesome creeper-grown ruins, of fallen columns and broken friezes, exquisitely cut cameos and huge gleaming temples of strange measured proportions, where at any moment Danae drawn by white unicorns might come clattering past in her triumphal car, or the next meadow discover a troop of girls pelting a rustic ithyphallic Priapus with flowers and sacrificing a garlanded heifer in his honour. It was the world discovered, explored and recorded in all its sharp pristine shapes by the early Renaissance archaeologists.

The language, too, is hybrid and 'antiquarian'—an intoxicated *gergo* weaving across nearly five hundred close pages like the intricate never-ending design of a Gothic tapestry. Here are specimens of it. After being purged by the sacred ceremonies of Venus Phyzizoa, the lovers came to the ruins of Polyandrion, and sat down to enjoy the scenery round about:

'il serenissimo celo, il salutare & mitissimo aire, il delectevole sito, la deliciosa patria, le ornate virdure, gli piacevoli, & temprati colli ornati di opaci nemoruli, il clemente tempo & aure pure, & il venusto & amoeno loco, dignificato dagli fiumi defluenti per la nemorosa convalle irrigui, apresso gli curvi colli, alla dextra & leva parte mollemente discurrenti al proximo mare precipitabondi, agro saluberrimo & di gramine periucundo, referto di multiplici arbori canoro di concento di avicule. . . .'

Soon they went on to explore a subterranean vault under the temple, dedicated to Pluto, and wondered with pity and sorrow at a mosaic depicting the *absorbentissima voragine* in which lovers too cold or too hot in love suffered torments of fire and ice:

' . . . cum tale dispositione mirai questo odioso, spaventevole & evitando Barathro, Che dove gli lachi se rincontravano, cioe il frigorifico, cum lardentissimo, per la contrarietate fare dovevano cum aeterna controversia uno terribile tonare, perche poscia obvii se immergevano ambi dui in abrupto precipitio effusi in scuro vasto & profundissimo meato & immenso abysso'. . . .

Then they passed on to examine the graves one by one. Or an excited passage: the final ecstasies when Polia embraced at last the *solida colonna et colume della mia vita* and her lover's speech all but burst its banks in a froth of diminutives and superlatives:

'Et inulnati amplexabonda gli lactei & immaculati bracchii circa il mio iugulo, suavemante mordicula cum la coraliata buccula basiantime strinse. Et io propero la turgidula lingua ioculante Zacharissimamente succidula consaviantila ad extremo interito. Et io immorigero in extrema dulcitudine delapso, cum melitissimo morsuinculo osculantila, piu lacessita me strophiosa- mente strinse . . .' till with the end of the dream she melted away '& cum veloce fuga se tolse dicendo. Polifilo caro mio amante. Vale.'

Again no doubt Boccaccio made a large contribution. Polifilo's sentences often run like his, while other flotsam—old common- places like *loci amoeni* and *opaca nemora*, words ending in *-undu* (Polifilo's obsession) reminding us of Aulus Gellius, Apuleius and Beroaldo,[1] echoes of late Latin and the style of the *vagantes* —swells the stream. But once more the author, with his head full of antiquarian writing, Horapollo's hieroglyphs and pagan religion, meant to transport us into an antique world. Polifilo told Polia in his letter of dedication that he had begun to write in another style, but had changed it at her behest; and Crasso explained the reason in his preface. The theme of the book was Ancient Wisdom (though Crasso did not use the phrase), the 'hidden things of Nature', drawn from the 'inmost sanctuary of philosophy and the founts of the Muses', not for vulgar under- standings. Polia, if we wish to be prosaic, was the personification

---

[1] Gnoli discusses the sources of the language of the *H.P.*, see also B. Croce, 'La "H.P."' in *Quaderni della 'Critica'*, xvii–xviii (1950), 46–54.

of this *prisca theologia*. And so, Crasso said, the author had de-vised a 'new manner of speech', a compound of Greek, Latin, Tuscan and vernacular, which would permit the very learned to penetrate the inner sense without entirely putting off the ignorant. Polifilo's hermetic language was a sort of paradigm of the *sacrae litterae* of the ancient sages, who (as Pico argued in a famous letter to Ermolao Barbaro) had spoken in many tongues, Greek, Arabic, Hebrew. All these occur in the book with many hieroglyphs, the nearest symbols to ineffable truth.[1]

So in his dream Polifilo has an ambiguous character. Still the traditional wanderer of medieval love-romance, rewarded at last after a long and often baffled search for his beloved, he has somehow become a learned Renaissance archaeologist as well, moved to fervid wonder by the memorials of antiquity. He en-countered monuments of marvellous beauty in desolate places (*in campestri loco ab accessu hominum remoto* was a favourite location for a fifteenth-century epigraphic fiction); he described in enraptured phrases the appearance of pyramids; he measured the vast ruins of classic temples; he deciphered the *vetustissime et sacre scripture* of Egyptian hieroglyphs; traced and interpreted the images on antique porphyry reliefs. He could not express with what *hilaritu-dine* he so *acuratissimanente* read and admired the epitaphs inscribed on the tombs in Polyandrion. And this 'hilariousness'—an odd emotion in a graveyard—betrays at once the identity of the hilarious traveller in whose steps he trod.

Cyriac of Ancona[2] was the archetype of the peripatetic early Renaissance antiquary. He started life as a clerk in a shipping firm, working at his desk in Ancona or on shipboard. But soon

---

[1] J. Giehlow, 'Die Hieroglyphenkunde des Humanismus' in *Jahrbuch der Kunstsammlungen des Allerhöchsten Kaiserhauses*, xxxii (Vienna, 1915), is funda-mental; a recent study with literature is D. P. Walker, 'The *Prisca Theologia* in France' in *Journ. of the Warb. and Court. Inst.*, xvii (1954), 204–59.

[2] See de Rossi and Ziebarth, opp. cit.; Scalamonti's life printed by G. Colucci, *Antichità Picene*, xv (1792); L. Mehus, *Kyriaci Anconitani Itinerarium* (Florence, 1742).

the irresistible desire to see the world overmastered him, and he became a commercial traveller, a very glorified commercial traveller, with the eastern Mediterranean as his area of operation. For more than forty years this busy, inquistive, foot-loose, garrulous merchant journeyed *hilariter* through all the classic lands, Italy, Dalmatia, Greece and the islands, to Crete, Cyprus, all over Asia Minor, only interrupting his peregrinations for impatient and never very long stays at home in Ancona, where his energetic talents soon marked him out for civic office, or for business and diplomatic conferences in Rome, Florence and elsewhere. He got to know every corner of the Levant from Cairo to Bosphorus. He was familiar with many courts. His knowledge of Greek and Turkish affairs, at a time when the eastern empire was collapsing, won him a unique reputation as an unofficial political consultant. As he travelled his eye missed nothing—a pyramid, a boar-hunt, a sequestered cavern, an elephant, a giraffe, a snaky crocodile; and these he would describe sometimes with a drawing, in self-advertising extravagant letters to friends, or to the great and learned in Italy, Filippo Visconti or Leonello d'Este, Cosimo de' Medici, his old friend and patron Eugenius IV, Pietro Donato, Bishop of Padua, Leonardo Bruni, or his fellow-mercurial Filelfo. Thus, for example, he described his visit to a cave near Zara in Dalmatia (the author of the *Polifilo* probably had something like it in mind when he pictured the *profundissimo meato & immenso abysso* of the *barathro* in Polyandrion) to his friend Andreolo Giustiniani, Governor of Chios:[1]

'Et primum fatelem illam draconigenam Esculapii serpentis longevi speluncam videre cupientes, cum in medio delete veternis-sime civitatis solio ad antri fauces veneremus, accensas taedas manibus ferentes per revolutas graduum insinuatasque vivo sub ingenti saxo cavernas ad imam baratri profunditatem descendentes venimus, ubi alta sub testudine saxi mirificum quippe nature opus aquam dulcem nitidamque in fundo comperimus. . . .'

When he was about thirty Cyriac's insatiable curiosity suddenly

[1] Florence, Bibl. Naz. MS Targ. 49, fo. 25v (printed in G. Targioni Tozzetti, *Relazioni d'alcuni viaggi*, v (Florence, 1773), 413).

crystallized into the master-passion of his life: to discover antiquities. Thereafter, wherever his business took him, he would be
off like a whippet to sniff them out; clambering over ruins in
remote parts of Asia Minor, exploring the Greek islands, eager to
record every monument he saw, to measure it, draw it, copy out
its inscriptions into his notebooks in Latin or Greek (both tongues
he learnt late, becoming fluent but not academically perfect in
each). And from these journals, of which only a few precious
fragments remain, he was always extracting choice items to whet
the appetite of correspondents at home. The most fastidious
collectors anxious to acquire his wares, the most quarrelsome,
envious humanists, had to take this inspired autodidact seriously,
who was opening their dazzled eyes to the art of classic Greece.

It all started, Cyriac said, with the inscriptions and images on
Trajan's arch in his native Ancona. This monument, copied out
again and again at the head of excerpts from his papers, became
for him—like Cardinal Newman's Trinity snapdragons—an
emblem of his perpetual dedication: to the quest of antiquities
over the whole world. What was his aim? He said it was to 'wake
the dead'. He wanted by his 'potent and divine art to revive the
glorious things which were alive to the living in antiquity but had
become buried and defunct through the lapse of ages and persistent injury at the hands of the half-dead; to bring them from
the dark tomb to light, to live once more among living men'; and
this not simply for the sake of reviving 'dead titles', but in order
to reveal to his contemporaries their 'own names'.[1] In antiquity
they would discover their true selves.

Behind Cyriac's restless activity, all his lizard-like darting in
every direction, we can descry a larger purpose. In 1423 he climbed
a ladder in Fano to transcribe the inscription on the arch of
Augustus. Then he assembled the citizens and harangued them
on their 'half-buried glories', their *semisepulta gloria*. We recall
Cola di Rienzo's sermon a century before to the citizens of Rome
on the Capitol on the text of the *lex regia*. Again in 1432 Eugenius
IV sent Cyriac with an embassy to greet the Emperor Sigismund

[1] Mehus, pp. 54-5.

470

in Siena. During his interview Cyriac argued for a crusade against the Turks, and gave the emperor a gold coin of Trajan 'as an example, for imitation, of a good prince'. Next year he was in the pope's train when Sigismund came to Rome to be crowned; he sat as an expert at the discussions on the union of the Greek and Roman Churches, and afterwards showed Sigismund round the ruins of Rome. We remember Petrarch's similar dealings with the Emperor Charles IV. It was the old imperial nostalgia, one of the great themes of Italian history. The relics of antiquity, for Cyriac as for Petrarch, were living voices crying across the waste for the torn fabric of the empire to be reknit—now to enfold the Greeks as well as the sons of Troy. Later on Cyriac attended Bessarion at the council for church union at Florence in 1439. There he must have met among the Greek delegation the philo‑ sopher Gemisthos Pletho, whose ideas fascinated everyone at the council. We do not know exactly what proposals Pletho had for a new world‑order and a new pagan religion; his great book the *Laws* is now a hardly intelligible fragment, almost obliterated for heresy by an orthodox Patriarch. But Cyriac did not forget him: in 1448 we find him working alongside Pletho in Mistra.[1] What did they discuss? The times were desperate, and the sands of Christendom, as the Turk advanced, seemed to be running out. Cyriac's mind, drunk with visions of pagan Greece, would per‑ haps have been open to non‑Christian schemes (as Pius II's was later) for saving the empire. At any rate we know this.[2] The last agony of Christian Byzantium saw Cyriac in 1452 inspecting antiquities in the neighbourhood, and it is recorded that before the walls of Byzantium he was reading to Mahomet II himself the authorities on empire and its translation—the Greek and Roman historians, chronicles of popes and emperors, and the

---

[1] See A. Diller, 'Pletho and Plutarch' in *Scriptorium*, viii (1954), 123 ff.

[2] E. Jacobs, 'Cyriacus von Ancona und Mehemmed II' in *Byzantinische Zeit‑ schrift*, xxx (1929–30), 197–202. For Cyriac and the Turks see J. Dabrowski, 'L'année 1444' in *Bulletin International de l'Académie Polonaise des Sciences et des Lettres* (Classe d'Histoire et de Philosophie), no. supplémentaire 6, 1951 (Cracow, 1952), pp. 8–18.

history of the Franks. And when the city fell, to endure one of the cruellest sacks in history, Cyriac rode with the Turk into New Rome, and there, among other things, investigated the equestrian statue of Justinian.[1] Did Cyriac perhaps conceive of the statue as another *caballus Constantini*, the very symbol of empire, like the one before the Lateran in Old Rome—just as Charlemagne, at an earlier phase in the drama, set up the equestrian statue of Theodoric before *his* Lateran in Aachen?

This does not mean, however, that Cyriac's archaeology was like Cola's simply a function of his politics. If his zest for antiquity had not found that sanction, it would certainly have found another. The irrepressible fantasy of his antiquarianism manifested itself in everything he did. We see it in his handwriting, curly, imaginative, utterly individual, varying between a bold formal aplomb and an almost pathological raggedness. We see it in his drawings, which added a touch of extra wide-eyed vitality to the figures he copied from the stones. We see it in his illumination, letters of burnished gold, brick red, olive green, saffron yellow and chalky blue, the colours he saw on antique buildings and sculpture in Greece.[2] We see it in his fantastic language, nourished by Dante and Boccaccio and late-Latin writers, sprinkled with Greek and transmuted into something quite his own. And we see it, above all, in the bizarre fervour of his cult of his 'SS. Genio' Mercury. There is a volume of geographical texts in Oxford[3] copied from manuscripts that once belonged to Cyriac himself, including a copy of his autograph transcript of the *Liber Insularum* of Cristoforo Buondelmonte, who visited the Cyclades twenty-five years before Cyriac did and

[1] See now P. Williams Lehmann, 'Theodosius or Justinian?' *Art Bulletin*, xli (1959), 39 ff.

[2] Examples of Cyriac's hand reproduced by D. Fava in *Miscellanea Federici* (1945); autograph drawings by R. Sabbadini in *Miscellanea Ceriani* (1910); the illumination I have in mind is an autograph codex in Florence, Bibl. Laurenziana MS Plut. 90 inf. 55.

[3] Bodl. MS Canon. Misc. 280. I hope to discuss Cyriac's connection with this codex in detail elsewhere. Meanwhile I owe best thanks to Dr. Richard Hunt for advice on its collation.

brought home to Florence the text of Horapollo. On one page Buondelmonte described the attributes of Mercury. Cyriac duly noted 'Mercurius' in the margin of his transcript, and at the end drew a picture of Mercury with a distich of his own—one of the *falsae*—to accompany it. Years ago Fritz Saxl[1] found the model for this drawing in an archaic relief: the correspondence of type was exact. From his wintry medieval disguise Hermes sprang forth in his true Greek character. But if Cyriac's image of Mercury was pure classic, his worship of Mercury was goliardic. *Pater alme Mercuri*,[2] he prayed as he embarked for Ephesus:

'Glory of Arts, Mind, Intelligence and Speech, best Lord of Ways and Journeys, who of Thy most holy power hast long blessed the mind and heart of Thy servant Cyriac: as aforetime Thou hast made safe, straight and easy our most jocund travels by land and sea through Latium, Illyria, Greece, Asia and Egypt; so, bright Genius, vouchsafe this happy day, sacred to Thy name, as we now on the Kalends of March depart from Phocaea to visit Ephesus and to investigate the ancient remains of the most noble temple of Thy quiver-bearing sister, Diana of the Ephesians, to favour, succour and direct our voyage, make it safe, and grant us happy auguries.'

On the eve of other voyages—so often begun on a Wednesday, Mercury's and Cyriac's day, that there must have been magic in it—he would vary the petition, but keep the liturgical formula. And after the landfall, when he had ridden out the bitter storms, he wrote with golden pen a poetical prayer of thanksgiving to Mercury, thanks as myriad as the stars you see in the sky on a mild night, or as the April flowers and lovely nymphs in the fields of Thrace.[3]

It may seem, perhaps, a far cry from these orisons, however seriously they came from a colleague of Pletho (who also indited prayers to the heathen gods), to the solemn prayers and liturgies that

---

[1] E. Panofsky and F. Saxl, 'Classical Mythology in Medieval Art' in *Metropolitan Museum Studies*, iv (1933).

[2] A. Olivieri, *Comment. Cyriaci Ancon. Nova Fragmenta* (Pesaro, 1763), p. 68.

[3] G. Colucci, *Ant. Picene*, xv.

played such a prominent part in the *Polifilo*: Polia's confession, abso׳
lution and betrothal before Venus's priestess, and the corresponding
elaborate sequence of rites in the temple of Venus Phyzizoa,
culminating in a sacrificial nuptial Love׳Mass with a mitred
Lady׳Bishop pontificating, who fed the lovers with the mystic
fruit of a miraculous rose׳bush.[1] The courtly Religion of Love,
it is true, reached the author of the *Polifilo* in a broad tradition,
from Ovid through the *Council of Remiremont* in the twelfth
century, Andrew the Chaplain in the thirteenth and Boccaccio
in the fourteenth.[2] But was it so far a cry, after all? The antiquarian
lore in which every page of the *Polifilo* was steeped was saturated
with Cyriacesque matter and Cyriacesque sentiment. Surely
Cyriac, in the circumstances, again intervened. And it is signifi׳
cant that the nymphs, holding hands in a row, who encircle the
sacred Cistern in Venus Phyzizoa's temple, derived quite clearly
from Cyriac's drawing of the Muses, as he named them, on a
relief he saw in Samothrace, now in the Louvre (Pls. 33 and 34).

Such were Cyriac's personal style, the goliardic streak in his
make׳up, and the way his fancy festooned the whole business of
antiquarian study with a luxuriant literary ornamentation, which
we can now begin to see trailing over into the *Polifilo*, there to
become entwined with foliage from other romance and classic
stems. But that is not all the story. Others took up the tradition in
between, and further decorated and modified it, notably Felice
Feliciano of Verona.[3] Felice was a born eccentric, a Renaissance
vagabond: a brilliant professional scribe whose pages outshine
Cyriac's with a harlequin rainbow of coloured inks, a printer
and draughtsman, familiar of artists, dabbler in alchemy, a cleric
in minor orders possibly with heretical Joachimite leanings. Like

[1] See F. Saxl, 'Pagan Sacrifice in the Italian Renaissance' in *Journ. of the Warb.
Inst.*, ii (1939), 359–63.

[2] See C. S. Lewis, *The Allegory of Love* (Oxford, 1936), pp. 32–43.

[3] L. Pratilli's uncritical 'Felice Feliciano alla luce dei suoi codici' in *Atti del
Reale Istituto Veneto*, xcix (1939–40), 33–105, is the most recent general account
of Felice.

Cyriac he bubbled in original prose and verse, Italian and Latin, and was a voluminous letter-writer. Like Cyriac he loved far-fetched images and superlatives; he never called a spade a spade if he could put a more recondite mythological synonym to it; occasionally he showed off a bit of Greek. The elements of his style are sometimes quite close to the *Polifilo*'s, and a serious attempt has been made to attribute the book to him.[1] If Felice had stood alone and not in Cyriac's line, if his attested work suggested that he was at all capable of the *Polifilo*'s sustained rhetoric, and if he had not written a little romance of his own— the *Justa Victoria*, delightfully printed by Hans Mardersteig in 1943—in a style that scarcely squares with that of the *Polifilo*, the theory would be attractive. As it is, it remains a valid indication that both Felice's language and that of the *Polifilo* came of the same Cyriacesque stock.

Not least, Felice was an ardent antiquary—his sobriquet was *Felix Antiquarius*—who hitched his wagon to Cyriac's star. It is not known that they ever met; Felice was only twenty-two when Cyriac died in about 1455. But he left ample proofs of his devotion, among them an elegant transcript of Francesco Scalamonti's life of Cyriac, now in the Capitular library in Treviso with inscriptions collected by himself added to a select body of Cyriac's finds, which he wrote for his friend Samuele da Tradate, a Gonzaga courtier. He also wrote out an important number of *syllogai* of inscriptions, largely for himself or his friend Giovanni Marcanova, a Paduan doctor who had started collecting independently, but later welcomed Felice's collaboration as scribe, epigrapher and general bibliographical expert. The finest of Marcanova's *syllogai*, most of it in Felice's hand, is now in Modena.[2] These *syllogai*, moreover, constituted Felice's *scriptorium*, the chief

[1] A. Khomentovskaia, 'F.F. da Verona comme l'auteur de l' "H.P." ' in *Bibliofilia*, xxxvii (1935), 154–74 and 200–12, and ibid., xxxviii (1936), 20–48 and 92–102. Croce (op. cit.) quotes the *Justa Victoria* against the attribution.

[2] Bibl. Estense MS xi, G.2 (some illustrations published by C. Hülsen, *La Roma Antica di Ciriaco d'Ancona* (Rome, 1907)). I believe Dr. Augusto Campana first observed Felice's hand in this codex. I am very grateful to him for telling me of the Faenza MS (see Plate 2).

collecting and disseminating centre of Cyriac's epigraphic material in the third quarter of the fifteenth century. And they in turn provided the basis for important subsequent collections, especially those of Michele Ferrarini, a Carmelite of Reggio. Whoever designed the illustrations of the tombs in Polyandrion for the *Polifilo* (and despite small discrepancies between text and pictures, he must have worked closely with the author, who had the graphic models in his head when he wrote and probably gave them to the artist to use) evidently knew Felice's and Ferrarini's epigraphic drawings, or versions of them. Though he never appears to have taken monuments direct from them, their style shines through his[1] (Pls. 35 and 36).

As an epigrapher Felice sealed himself unmistakably of Cyriac's tribe by the way he developed his own style from the master's—in script, layout and the exuberance of his field-reports. This is a typical example of the sort of letter to which Cyriac usually attached inscriptions found on a trip (though in this he happened not to); it is addressed again to Giustiniani:[2]

'Ad Kal. Aprilium faustum genialemque nostrum atlantia-deum diem una viris cum prestantissimis Francisco Drapperio Paride Visconteque Iustinianis, cum vestro e portu Cetea quidem et oneraria navi, Uberto Grimaldo Ienuensi viro nobili prefecto, Aurora iam albescente concederemus, secundis aspirantibus Euris eodem ipso felicissimo die plenis et equatis transiecto equore velis Phoceam expetitam venimus, novum in Ionia alumineum-que Phocee veternissime civitatis Emporium, omnes et incolumes, optimo iuvante Iove et Genio illo sanctissimo lubricante Mer-curio, nec non nympharum nereydum nostrarum preclaris-simarum (ʔagmine, ʔcaterva) favitante et equore modulante ...' and so on for two pages. Hence Felice very artfully composed —as the manuscripts show—his sunny account of a late-summer

---

[1] Hülsen rightly rejects Gnoli's theory that the illustrations derive from Fra Giocondo, preferring Felice or Ferrarini. His comparison of the altar of the Palmyrene sun-god in the Museo Capitolino with the *Polifilo* woodcut taken from it well illustrates the way the artist varied on his models.

[2] MS Targ. 49, fo. 11v—printed part by Targioni Tozzetti, v, 436.

jaunt in 1464 round the southern shores of Lake Garda with Mantegna, the painter, Samuele da Tradate and Marcanova to collect antiquities:[1]

MEMORATU DIGNA

'A.d. Kl. Oct. MCCCCLXIIII. Una cum Andrea Mantegna Patavo amico incomparabili et Samuele de Tradate et me Feliciano Veronense existente solandi animi gratia ex agro tuschulano per Benacum ad viridarios paradiseos ut ortos in amoenissimum Musarum diversorium venimus. Eos non modo roseis et purpureis floribus amoenos et redolentes comperimus verum etiam citreisque et limoneis frondosis undique ramis umbrosis quin etiam eiusdem insulas per prata et fontibus exuberantissime defluentes et palmiferis laureis altis annosis et carpoferis arboribus exornatas inspeximus. Ubi plura antiquitatis vestigia vidimus et primo ad insulam fratrum in pillo marmoreo litteris ornatissimis. . . .'

The next day's exploration he headed—'JUBILATIO':

'Sub imperio faceti viri Samuellis de Tradate. Consulibus viris primariis Andrea Mantegna Patavino et Ioanne Antenoreo. Procurante me Felice Feliciano una cum florentissima caterva sequente per opacas Lauros Thusculana in villa ad viridaria caelestia solatia capiente, myrto provinca hedera ac diversarum frondium coronata, Samuellem ipsum comitante et aedem antiquam beati Dominici ingressi comperimus digmissiam Marci Antonini Pii Germanici Sarmatici imperatoris memoriam. . . .'

So they pursued their quest, crossing the lake in their laurelwreathed boat towards Maderno, while their 'emperor' Samuele,

---

[1] Critical text by Ziebarth, *Nachfolger*, pp. 492–3. The 'Jubilatio' formula seems to be echoed in Taddeo Solazio's late fifteenthcentury *sylloge* of Brescian inscriptions on p. 107 of the MS in Lonato, printed by P. Guerrini, *Le cronache bresciane inedite dei secoli XV–XIX*, ii (Brescia, 1927), 137; also by Bernardo Bembo in a marginal note on a trip to Nemi in 1489 in his MS of Alberti's *De re aedificatoria*, Eton College MS 128, printed in James's catalogue at pp. 58–9 and by C. Grayson in *Miscellanea Santini* (Palermo, 1955), p. 6 of offprint. H. Thode was reminded of the 'Jubilatio' by Fortunato Martinengo's trip on Lake Garda in 1552 (Thode, *Somnii Explanatio, Traumbilder vom Gardasee in S. Vigilio* (Berlin, 1909)).

crowned with myrtle and ivy, twanged his lute *citharizante et iubilante*; till at length they came to—

'the temple of the blessed Peter in Sermione, entered in, and offered mighty praises with the deepest devotion to the High Thunderer and his glorious Mother, especially because he had illuminated their hearts to make up the party, opened their minds to seek and search out such noble places, granted them so many fine and pleasant sights and such speedy discovery of quite a few antiquities, given them such a happy flowery day, and accorded them a smooth passage and a safe anchorage in their desired harbour.'

It is a charming set-piece; but though Cyriac's formal inspiration is undeniable, the spirit is different. These jubilant antiquaries, enjoying their jolly excursion round the local lake, were not cast in Cyriac's heroic mould; and their devout thanksgivings to the *Summus Tonans* at St. Peter's, Sermione, contrast strangely with Cyriac's more perilous devotion to the heathen Mercury. The poison of 'gentile' antiquity is becoming diluted into a safer *gentilezza*, and the mentality of research is changing. Cyriac might summon a bevy of nymphs and nereids from the deep to attend him, but he did not run to fancy-dress: his eye was fixed on new discoveries ahead. Felice and his companions, following in a fashion which Cyriac (a rare achievement in any field) personally created, had in a sense reached their goal; their learning, as they acted (or pretended to act) *à l'antique*, already anticipated their objective; they were looking, not so much for novel finds, as for fresh reflections and confirmations of an antiquity that shone in their imaginations. Antiquity was becoming an ideal of life, rather than an object of inquiry. On a less urbane level, they begin to remind us of refined Florentines like Niccolo Niccoli, as Vespasiano portrayed him, sitting at home 'like an ancient' with his precious vases, his gems, coins and fine codices around him, or of Piero de' Medici cultivating an 'antique' civility among his collections, looking out on to his courtyard to contemplate an ancestral Roman *atrium*.

.   .   .

This shift of interest from antiquity on the site to antiquity in the mind, from a world of fact to a world of imagination, comes out clearly in the manuscripts. Cyriac's drawings were usually very faithful records of the objects he saw; his measurements of buildings were careful and practical. It has proved possible to reconstruct the appearance of the great temple at Cyzicus, buried since Cyriac visited it, largely from his survey.[1] The drawings of ancient Rome in Marcanova's codices,[2] on the other hand, show a Rome altered and transfigured by his imagina/ tive conception of it. The buildings are brought to life with all sorts of learned excrescences and Rome is peopled with lively figures, driving through a triumphal arch or executing a criminal on the Capitol. No architect could build the arch from Mar/ canova's pictures; it is not even clear whether any particular arch was intended at all.

The epigraphical codices tell the same story. Cyriac's lost notebooks, which can partially be restored from extracts and copies, naturally contained 'fakes', facetious, pathetic, naughty, historical. If he came across a red marble stone in Verona men/ tioning the elder Pliny, who was born there, of course he put it in, doubtless recognizing it expertly as fifteenth/century handi/ work—as Mommsen did when he found it, four centuries later, covered with creepers in an old garden near Verona.[3] If such important historical documents did not exist, then they needed supplying as testimonies to known truth. Likewise all the early *syllogai* contain Lucretia's epitaph, a forbidding tomb inscribed OSSA NERONIS, and an *Epitaphium Caesaris*, for was not Lucretia the model of chastity, and Nero an example of luxury, and was not Caesar murdered? This was simply the normal medieval idea of historical evidence, as students of 'forged' monastic charters[4]

[1] T. Reinach, *Bulletin de Correspondence hellénique* (1889), and B. Ashmole, *Journ. of the Warb. and Court. Inst.*, xix (1956), 179–91.

[2] Reproduced by Hülsen; another set in the MS in Princeton Univ. Library, N.J.   [3] C.I.L. v, 365*.

[4] See V. H. Galbraith, 'Monastic Foundation Charters' in *Cambridge Historical Journal*, iv (1932), 205–22, 296–8.

and of Christian relic-cult are aware. The scepticism of Guibert of Nogent who argued in the twelfth century that either St. John the Baptist had two heads, or that of the heads in Constantinople and Saint-Jean d'Angely one was supposititious,[1] was a rare attitude, even in the Renaissance. The earliest epigrapher to distinguish fakes in his *syllogai* was Fra Giocondo, late in the fifteenth century, who occasionally noted in the margin, 'this, I think, is false'. Again Cyriac's gallant, half-serious joke about Heliodorus, or a pathetic piece of self-revelation like Felice Feliciano's epitaph on himself (which was accepted as genuine evidence of early Christian piety into the eighteenth century)[2] was perfectly in place in a Renaissance *sylloge*. Feeling like Petrarch placed in time between 'two peoples—the ancients and the unborn—looking both behind and ahead', a fifteenth-century antiquary wanted to leave to posterity memorials of himself as expressive as those he had received from the past. But when Cyriac came to record inscriptions he saw, he did not invent: on the whole his versions (which once had a bad reputation on account of corrupt copies) are astoundingly faithful, even by modern standards, to the originals.

Felice's manuscripts,[3] on the other hand, are shot through and through with the beams of his imagination. Basically, since that was his training, he was a good medieval copyist, and stuck to his exemplars. He was particularly careful—since a relic must have its local habitation—to preserve notes of location. But at the same time he had no hesitation about brightening up the colour or design of a monument if it was weak or unimpressive in the version before him, or if he judged that the codex in hand (Marcanova's *sylloge* in Modena is the outstanding example) called for more sumptuous treatment. Sometimes he would go further and invent quite fresh monumental frames for the texts he was copying; nor did he mind giving the same monument varying treatment

---

[1] *De pignoribus sanctorum*, quoted by C. H. Haskins, *The Renaissance of the Twelfth Century* (Cambridge, Mass., 1933), p. 235.

[2] Text and history of it in Khomentovskaia, *Bibliofilia*, xxxviii (1936), 96–102.

[3] I hope to demonstrate these conclusions by analysis of the MSS elsewhere.

in different manuscripts, either or both looking unlike the original stone which might easily be accessible to him, even in his own city of Verona—with the curious result that in Ferrarini's *syllogai*, compiled from various Felician exemplars, we sometimes come across two inconsistent drawings of the same monument in a single manuscript. But Felice's principles of 'falsification' were not meaningless, though we must always allow for occasional unpredictable flirts of fancy. His changes were always in the direction of making the antique look more antique still. He wanted to bring it up to the pitch of the brilliant colours and sharp-edged outlines of the antique world as it lived in his imagination. So long as his drawings achieved that quality, antiquity bodied forth bright, tangible and *à l'antique*, they were valid documents, with life-enhancing antique virtue in them.

From Felice and Ferrarini, now, it is only a 'step or two of dubious twilight' into the wholly imaginative, wholly fictitious world of the *Polifilo*. To read the pages and go through the pictures where Polifilo visited Polyandrion is like dipping into Cyriac's news-letters—we remember the *barathro*—or turning the leaves of one of the later fifteenth-century *syllogai*. Pausing to contemplate the tombs one by one, Polifilo described each in the by now technical terms of Cyriacesque manuscript headings and locations. The accompanying woodcuts, too, exactly follow the style of the drawings in the pre-Fra Giocondo *syllogai*—monuments standing up in large outline, showing breaks in the stones, dolphins or birds in the pediments, and inscriptions in classic lapidary style (including the typically Cyriacesque Greek capital Y). And as Polifilo muses before these memorials of dead lovers, we seem to recapture the emotions that stirred the breasts of fifteenth-century antiquaries as they pondered over their collections. One tomb enraptured Polifilo by the marvel of its antique workmanship, another saddened him by its story; he sighed as he turned from the grave of two lovers cut off in the act of love, the next moment he was 'overjoyed with incredible solace at such a variety of antiquities'. Thus they wandered, Felice and Ferrarini and Polifilo, among the graves of the *spiriti gentili* of the ancient world, touching here one relic, there another, like pilgrims at a shrine; finding an image of their 'true selves'—the longings, ecstasies and anguish of love and death—in the memorials of 'sacrosanct' pagan antiquity: distant, once perfect, and now alive again to hand and eye in forms discovered first by Cyriac of Ancona.

Before he visited Delos in 1445 all Cyriac knew of its appear-ance was the map drawn in 1422 by Buondelmonte in his *Liber Insularum* (Pl. 37). Buondelmonte's drawing was hardly more than a schematic medieval *stadtplan*, showing a domed edifice rather like the baptistery in Florence, a twin-towered bastion by the shore, and two minor buildings inland. Who could see that this was once the holiest shrine of the Delian Apollo? Then Cyriac saw its ruins with his own eyes, surveyed, measured and drew them. He drew[1] the remains of the great temple with its white marble columns standing or fallen among jutting angular blocks of masonry beside a fallen capital (Pl. 38). He inspected the near-by ruins of a semi-circular theatre beside the shore, noting its height and breadth and the size of the stones (Pl. 39). So Polifilo and Polia came to the ruins of Polyandrion. Polifilo described the mole by the seashore and the huge ruined temple, overgrown with samphire and dank vegetation, a confused heap of collapsed white marble blocks and fallen columns without bases or capitals. And the artist drew it for the book with all its jutty angular masonry (Pl. 40): the 'first Renaissance picture of ruins',[2] roman-tic, imaginary ruins in the shape of Cyriac's authentic, sunlit vision of ancient Greece.

'False dreams, all false, mad heart, were yours.' It is true. Polia was dead when the *Hypnerotomachia* came out; 'the withered flower

[1] Copy of Cyriac's journal of the Cyclades, Vatican MS Vat. Lat. 5252; another copy by Schedel in Munich.

[2] J. Burckhardt, *Civilization of the Renaissance in Italy*, pt. III, ch. 1; and see Rose Macaulay, *Pleasure of Ruins* (1953), pp. 15–16. Hülsen detects other borrow-ings in the ruins woodcut.

can never bloom again', she told Polifilo, speaking from her own epitaph on the last page:

HEV POLIPHILE DESINE
FLOS SIC EXSICCATUS
NUNQVAM REVIVISCIT
VALE

But before the morning dispersed his dream, the old Dominican in SS. Giovanni e Paolo with his Trevisan memories did have all his bliss in an antique world not entirely of his imagining. And which shall we say better fitted the facts?—the cold awakening or the scholar's heaven perpetuated in Aldus's silvery pages:

ubi non prevenit rem desiderium;
nec desiderio minus est premium.

BIOGRAPHICAL NOTE

Cecilia Mary Ady, M.A., D.Litt., came up to St. Hugh's Hall, now St. Hugh's College, Oxford, in 1900 as a scholar and was Tutor in Modern History there from 1909 to 1923. Differences of opinion between herself and the then Principal, Miss Jourdain, led to her leaving her tutorship in 1923; throughout them she behaved with dignity and restraint, firmly refusing to be made into the leader of an opposition against a woman who for many years had been a friend and confidante. From 1924 to 1929 she was tutor to the Society of Home Students, returning to her own college in 1929 as Research Fellow, and on her retirement in 1951, she was elected to an Honorary Fellowship. In the counsels of the college she was steadfast, forthright and fair-minded. Her many contacts with senior members, former pupils, schools, learned societies and other universities kept her aware of general problems of education at all stages. She was deeply devoted to the college, and by her learning and by the force of her personality brought it great prestige. In the college's 'Conversation Piece', by Henry Lamb, she is given a look which is half crusader, half man-of-affairs.

Academically, her career as a historian of Renaissance Italy was single-minded without being narrow or repetitive. She was the daughter of Julia Cartwright, an amateur historian and connoisseur whose lives of Castiglione, Isabella d'Este and Beatrice d'Este still receive serious attention. So dominating a personality might well have daunted an only child, but in the words of the author of an article, 'A Talented Mother and Daughter' (published in an illustrated paper in 1907), who had paid a visit to the Cartwright home at Ockham: 'Mrs. Ady is not the only author to be met with at the pretty country rectory. Her daughter, Miss Cecily Ady, who is still very young—in fact, still a girl—bids fair to win as great, if not a greater reputation than that enjoyed by her mother.' And underneath a photograph of Cecilia with a very

484

tall bicycle, the author continued: 'Like mother, like daughter, for Miss Ady composes quickly, writes charmingly, converses brilliantly and works incessantly.'

In 1907 appeared her first book, *Milan under the Sforza,* which she was encouraged to write by her tutor, Edward Armstrong, general editor of the series 'The States of Italy', in which it appeared. It was followed in 1913 by *Pius II*—and she finished an article on Pius II in the last days before her death. Both these books remain in demand and have not been replaced by anything comparably useful in English. In 1937 came her most solid book, *The Bentivoglio of Bologna,* and in 1955 she wrote perhaps one of the most satisfying works yet to appear in Dr. Rowse's 'Teach Yourself History' series, her *Lorenzo dei Medici and Renaissance Italy.* These full-scale works were interspersed with lesser ones. In 1917 she contributed a section to *Italy, Medieval and Modern*; in 1930 C. W. Previté-Orton, who had hoped himself to do the chapter on 'Florence and North Italy, 1414–1492' in Volume VIII of the *Cambridge Medieval History,* found his other tasks too burdensome and invited Miss Ady to take it on. This was followed up only in 1957 by her chapter in the first volume of the *New Cambridge Modern History,* 'The Invasions of Italy'.

Her influence on Italian studies, however, was not limited to books and articles.[1] She read papers at conferences of Italian studies both here in Oxford and abroad—with her paper on *Humanism and Tyranny* she was England's only representative at the Congresso Internazionale di Studi Umanistici at Rome in 1949—and in 1942 she delivered the annual Italian lecture of the British Academy on the theme *Manners and Morals of the Quattrocento.* And her influence went further again in reviews; for a lengthy period it was likely that the serious student of Renaissance Italy would receive his first impression of English and foreign books on the subject from Dr. Ady's moderate but definite evaluation of them. She was, too, vice-chairman of the Society for Italian studies for a time.

[1] A bibliography of her writings on Italian subjects will be found in *Italian Studies* (1959.)

From her reviews one can see something of her own approach
to historical writing. Complicated events should not be made to
appear falsely simple; the historian should explain and re-create
and never, in any circumstance, use the past to display his
own learning; conscious reaction against her mother's sometimes
unprofessional standards did not tempt her into austerity; more
than once she complained that an author lacked lightness of
touch. Typical of her approach is this comment on a work by an
Oxford colleague, which she praised for being 'based on energetic study of the available sources, and steeped in the spirit of
the times'.

Her *Lorenzo* was dedicated 'To the pupils who for many years
have stimulated my interest in studies in the Italian Renaissance'.
All these pupils will remember this encouraging, almost over-
indulgent, readiness to see a fresh point of view and to revise, in
the light of a chance guess in the brashest of essays, ideas she had
derived from an unfaltering pursuit of her chosen studies. They
will remember, too, an unvarying kindliness, shrewdness and
good judgement. She clearly enjoyed teaching and took immense
trouble with under-graduates and post-graduates. She genuinely
liked the young and was at ease with them, as she was with the
audiences of her university and extra-mural lectures; it was an
art for which she had a natural gift and a markedly effective style:
orderly, humorous and pungent.

Throughout her life she was a devoted churchwoman. One of
the earliest members of the House of Laity in the Church
Assembly, she was a member of the Central Council of Women's
Work, which published the booklet she wrote, *The Rôle of
Women in the Church* (1948), describing some of the many opportunities now open to them whether in the professional order of
deaconesses or in the educational and parochial fields. Her historical knowledge she used abundantly in two works, *The
Apostolic Ministry, Essays on the History and Doctrine of Episcopacy*,
ed. K. E. Kirk (bishop of Oxford), in which she wrote the section
from the Restoration to the Present Day; and in her book, *The
English Church and how it works* (1940). These reveal her as a

moderate Anglo-Catholic, believing in the spiritual independence of the Church of England, but with marked respect for English local custom, and they display the fusion of trenchancy, wisdom and generosity so characteristic not only of her writing, but of her life. She died on March 27th, 1958.

INDEX

If this index had been exhaustive it would have been so unwieldy as to try the patience of any but the most specialist reader: it is, therefore, arbitrary and selective. Place names are given (as a rule) in familiar English form, and persons also where this seemed advisable. Common sense has been preferred to logic, in conformity with Dr. Ady's well-known views on index-making.

Scala, Alessandro, 389
Bartolomeo, 74, 163
Scalamonti, Francesco, 475
Scaliger, Julius Caesar, 64, 93, 355 n. 2,
    391, 393, 398, 408
Scardeone, Bernardino, 361
Scholarship (*see also* Archaeology,
    Classics), 53, 61, 64, 75, 88, 93,
    463
  compatible with Christianity (q.v.),
    64
Scholasticism, 20, 21, 85, 88, 90, 324,
    455
Scotland, *see under* Universities
Scotti, family of Vigoleno, 186, 187, 192
  Count Bartolomeo Scotto, 185, 186,
    187, 188, 190, 191, 192, 208 n. 3
  Count Cristoforo, 187, 188, 189, 191
  Count Giovanni, 188
  Count Matteo, 209
  Count Piero, 187, 188, 189, 191
Scotus, Duns, 91, 438
Sculpture (*see also under* Verrocchio,
    etc.), 288, 306, 311
Sellyng, William, 79
Sermione (Sirmione), 478
Settignano, 26
Sforza, Dukes of Milan, family of, 15,
    45, 51, 193, 194, 204, 209, 215
  Caterina, 218–19, 220–1, 248
  Chiara, 200
  Francesco, 194, 231
  Galeazzo Maria, 200, 208
  Giangaleazzo, 208
  Ludovico (Lodovico il Moro), 51,
    184 ff., 216
  Sforza Secondo, Count of Borgo-
    novo, 191, 192, 195, 196, 197, 201
  Lodovico Sforza di Fogliano, Mar-
    quis, 186
  Giovanni Sforza of Pesaro, 220, 221,
    254

Sicily, 49–50, 51, 53, 102
Siena, 99, 272, 471
  merchants of, 25
Sigismund, Emperor, 186, 470, 471
Sigonio, Carlo, 456
Simnel, Lambert, 446
Sixtus IV, Pope (Francesco della
    Rovere), 251, 252, 259, 260, 262,
    263, 264, 266, 267, 269, 270, 271,
    273, 325
Slavs, 48, 55
Soderini, Piero, 180, 183
  Tommaso, 137 n. 4, 141
Solderini, Paulantonio, 135
Songs (*see also* Music, Poetry), 328 ff.,
    354 ff.
  ballate, 328 ff.
  canti di ballo, 17, 46, 328 ff.
  cantigar d'amor, 330
  canzoni, 57, 328 ff., 403
  cradle-songs (*Naeniae*), 374, 378, 379
  trionfi, 333, 346, 347, 348, 350, 351
  drinking songs, 349–50
  licentious, 341–3
  medieval, 353
  the Minnesingers, 330, 334
Spoleto, 265
Stafford, Humphrey, rebellion of, 445
Stanga, Gaspare, 190, 191
  Marchesino, 191
Statius, 363, 364
Stoa, Quintianus, 406, 407 n. 1
Strada, Famiano, 363
Strassburg, 85
Strozzi, family of, 46, 163, 308, 381
  Ercole, 364
  Filippo, 307–8
  Palla, 283–4, 301
Stufa, Sigismondo della, 368
Supernatural (*see also* Astrology,
    Legend), 39–40
  Miracles, 39, 102